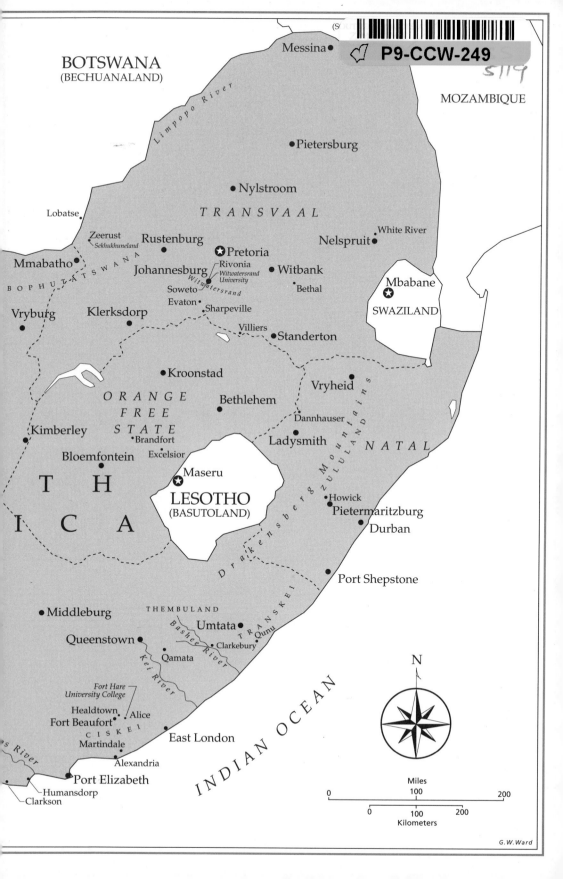

BOTSWANA
(BECHUANALAND)

MOZAMBIQUE

Messina

P9-CCW-249

Limpopo River

Pietersburg

Nylstroom

T R A N S V A A L

Lobatse

Zeerust
Sekhukhuneland

Rustenburg

Nelspruit

White River

Mmabatho

Pretoria

Rivonia
Witwatersrand University

Johannesburg

Witbank

B O P H U T H A T S W A N A

Soweto

Witwatersrand

Bethal

Mbabane

Vryburg

Klerksdorp

Evaton

Sharpeville

Villiers

Standerton

SWAZILAND

Kroonstad

Vryheid

O R A N G E
F R E E
S T A T E

Bethlehem

Dannhauser

Drakensberg & Zululand Mountains

N A T A L

Kimberley

Brandfort

Ladysmith

T   H

Bloemfontein

Excelsior

Maseru

I   C   A

LESOTHO
(BASUTOLAND)

Howick

Pietermaritzburg

Durban

Port Shepstone

Middleburg

T H E M B U L A N D

Umtata

T R A N S K E I

Bashee River

Qunu

Queenstown

Clarkebury

Qamata

Kei River

Fort Hare
University College

Healdtown

Alice

Fort Beaufort

C I S K E I

East London

Martindale

River

Alexandria

Port Elizabeth

Humansdorp

Clarkson

I N D I A N   O C E A N

N

Miles
0   100   200

0   100   200
Kilometers

G. W. Ward

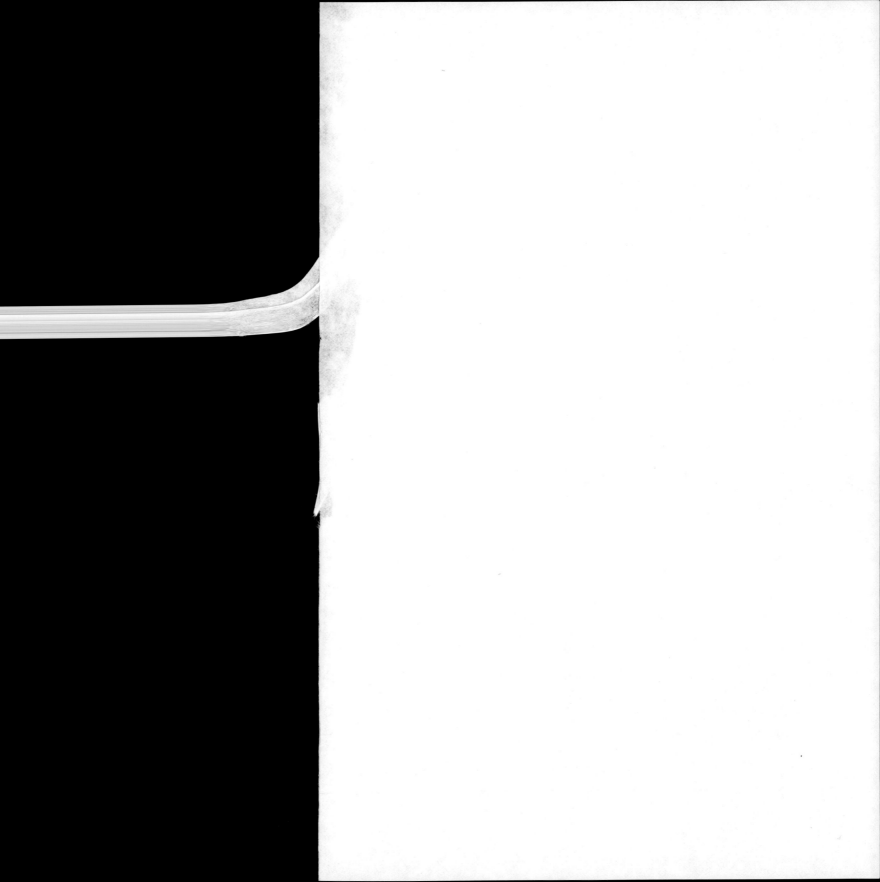

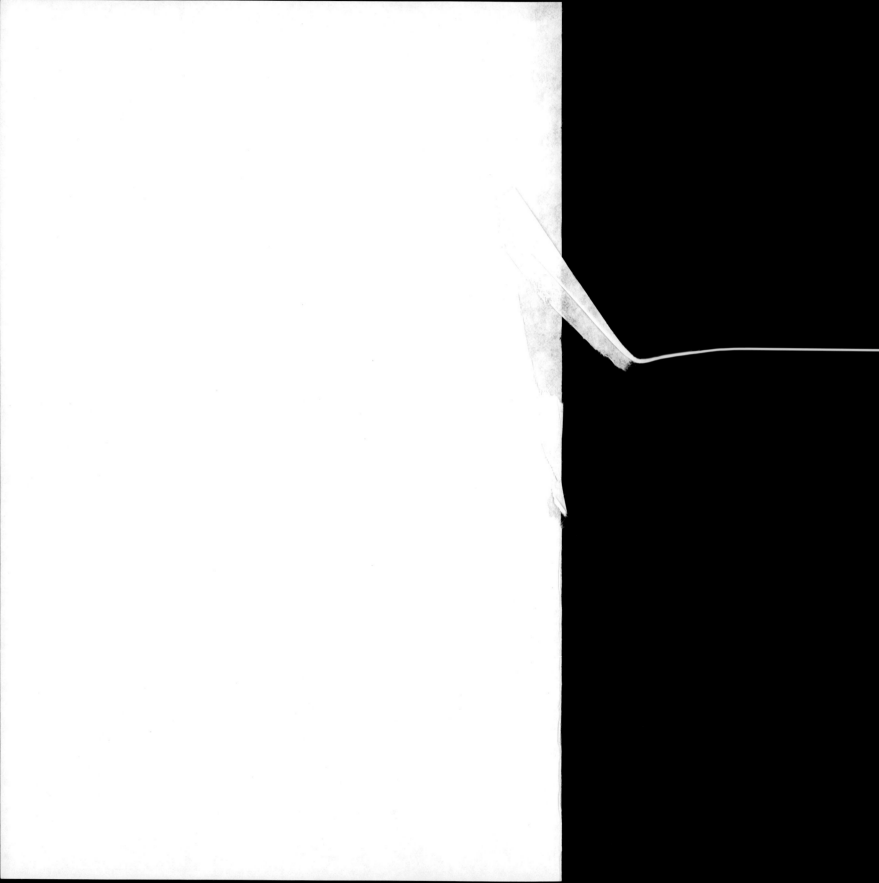

LONG WALK
TO FREEDOM

———

LONG WALK TO FREEDOM

The Autobiography of

NELSON MANDELA

Little, Brown and Company

Boston New York Toronto London

First Edition

ISBN 0-316-54585-6
Library of Congress Catalogue Card Number 94-79980

10 9 8 7 6 5 4 3 2 1

HAD

*Published simultaneously in Canada
by Little, Brown & Company (Canada) Limited*

Printed in the United States of America

I dedicate this book to my six children, Madiba and Makaziwe (my first daughter), who are now deceased, and to Makgatho, Makaziwe, Zenani, and Zindzi, whose support and love I treasure; to my twenty-one grandchildren and three great-grandchildren who give me great pleasure; and to all my comrades, friends, and fellow South Africans whom I serve and whose courage, determination, and patriotism remain my source of inspiration.

CONTENTS

Acknowledgments

As readers will discover, this book has a long history. I began writing it clandestinely in 1974 during my imprisonment on Robben Island. Without the tireless labor of my old comrades Walter Sisulu and Ahmed Kathrada for reviving my memories, it is doubtful the manuscript would have been completed. The copy of the manuscript which I kept with me was discovered by the authorities and confiscated. However, in addition to their unique calligraphic skills, my co-prisoners Mac Maharaj and Isu Chiba had ensured that the original manuscript safely reached its destination. I resumed work on it after my release from prison in 1990.

Since my release, my schedule has been crowded with numerous duties and responsibilities, which have left me little free time for writing. Fortunately, I have had the assistance of dedicated colleagues, friends, and professionals who have helped me complete my work at last, and to whom I would like to express my appreciation.

I am deeply grateful to Richard Stengel who collaborated with me in the creation of this book, providing invaluable assistance in editing and revising the first parts and in the writing of the latter parts. I recall with fondness our early morning walks in the Transkei and the many hours of interviews at Shell House in Johannesburg and my home in Houghton. A special tribute is owed to Mary Pfaff who assisted Richard in his work. I have also benefited from the advice and support of Fatima Meer, Peter Magubane, Nadine Gordimer, and Ezekiel Mphahlele.

I want to thank especially my comrade Ahmed Kathrada for the long hours spent revising, correcting, and giving accuracy to the story. Many thanks to my ANC office staff, who patiently dealt with the logistics of the making of this book, but in particular to Barbara Masekela for her efficient coordination. Likewise, Iqbal Meer has devoted many hours to watching over the business aspects of the book. I am grateful to my editor, William Phillips of Little, Brown, who has guided this project from early 1990 on, and edited the text, and to his colleagues Jordan Pavlin, Steve Schneider, Mike Mattil, and Donna Peterson. I would also like to thank Professor Gail Gerhart for her factual review of the manuscript.

Part One

A COUNTRY CHILDHOOD

1

APART FROM LIFE, a strong constitution, and an abiding connection to the Thembu royal house, the only thing my father bestowed upon me at birth was a name, Rolihlahla. In Xhosa, Rolihlahla literally means "pulling the branch of a tree," but its colloquial meaning more accurately would be "troublemaker." I do not believe that names are destiny or that my father somehow divined my future, but in later years, friends and relatives would ascribe to my birth name the many storms I have both caused and weathered. My more familiar English or Christian name was not given to me until my first day of school. But I am getting ahead of myself.

I was born on the eighteenth of July, 1918, at Mvezo, a tiny village on the banks of the Mbashe River in the district of Umtata, the capital of the Transkei. The year of my birth marked the end of the Great War; the outbreak of an influenza epidemic that killed millions throughout the world; and the visit of a delegation of the African National Congress to the Versailles peace conference to voice the grievances of the African people of South Africa. Mvezo, however, was a place apart, a tiny precinct removed from the world of great events, where life was lived much as it had been for hundreds of years.

The Transkei is eight hundred miles east of Cape Town, five hundred fifty miles south of Johannesburg, and lies between the Kei River and the Natal border, between the rugged Drakensberg mountains to the north and the blue waters of the Indian Ocean to the east. It is a beautiful country of rolling hills, fertile valleys, and a thousand rivers and streams, which keep the landscape green even in winter. The Transkei used to be one of the largest territorial divisions within South Africa, covering an area the size of Switzerland, with a population of about three and a half million Xhosas and a tiny minority of Basothos and whites. It is home to the Thembu people, who are part of the Xhosa nation, of which I am a member.

My father, Gadla Henry Mphakanyiswa, was a chief by both blood and custom. He was confirmed as chief of Mvezo by the king of the Thembu tribe, but under British rule, his selection had to be ratified by the government, which in Mvezo took the form of the local magistrate. As a government-appointed chief, he was eligible for a stipend as well as a portion of the fees the government levied on the community for vaccination of livestock and communal grazing land. Although the role of chief was a venerable and esteemed one, it had, even seventy-five years ago, become debased by the control of an unsympathetic white government.

The Thembu tribe reaches back for twenty generations to King Zwide. According to tradition, the Thembu people lived in the foothills of the Drakensberg mountains and migrated toward the coast in the sixteenth century, where they were incorporated into the Xhosa nation. The Xhosa are part of the Nguni people who have lived, hunted, and fished in the rich and temperate southeastern region of South Africa, between the great interior plateau to the north and the Indian Ocean to the south, since at least the eleventh century. The Nguni can be divided into a northern group — the Zulu and the Swazi people — and a southern group, which is made up of amaBaca, amaBomyana, amaGcaleka, amaMfengu, amaMpodomis, amaMpondo, abeSotho, and abeThembu, and together they comprise the Xhosa nation.

The Xhosa are a proud and patrilineal people with an expressive and euphonious language and an abiding belief in the importance of laws, education, and courtesy. Xhosa society was a balanced and harmonious social order in which every individual knew his or her place. Each Xhosa belongs to a clan that traces its descent back to a specific forefather. I am a member of the Madiba clan, named after a Thembu chief who ruled in the Transkei in the eighteenth century. I am often addressed as Madiba, my clan name, a term of respect.

Ngubengcuka, one of the greatest monarchs, who united the Thembu tribe, died in 1832. As was the custom, he had wives from the principal royal houses: the Great House, from which the heir is selected, the Right Hand House, and the Ixhiba, a minor house that is referred to by some as the Left Hand House. It was the task of the sons of the Ixhiba or Left Hand House to settle royal disputes. Mthikrakra, the eldest son of the Great House, succeeded Ngubengcuka and amongst his sons were Ngangelizwe and Matanzima. Sabata, who ruled the Thembu from 1954, was the grandson of Ngangelizwe and a senior to Kalzer Daliwonga, better known as K. D. Matanzima, the former chief minister of the Transkei — my nephew, by law and custom — who was a descendant of Matanzima. The eldest son of the Ixhiba house was Simakade, whose younger brother was Mandela, my grandfather.

Although over the decades there have been many stories that I was in the line of succession to the Thembu throne, the simple genealogy I have just outlined exposes those tales as a myth. Although I was a member of the royal household, I was not among the privileged few who were trained for rule. Instead, as a descendant of the Ixhiba house, I was groomed, like my father before me, to counsel the rulers of the tribe.

My father was a tall, dark-skinned man with a straight and stately posture, which I like to think I inherited. He had a tuft of white hair just above his forehead, and as a boy, I would take white ash and rub it into my hair in imitation of him. My father had a stern manner and did not spare the rod when disciplining his children. He could be exceedingly stubborn, another trait that may unfortunately have been passed down from father to son.

My father has sometimes been referred to as the prime minister of Thembuland during the reigns of Dalindyebo, the father of Sabata, who ruled in the early 1900s, and that of his son, Jongintaba, who succeeded him. That is a misnomer in that no such title existed, but the role he played was not so different from what the designation implies. As a respected and valued counselor to both kings, he accompanied them on their travels and was usually to be found by their sides during important meetings with government officials. He was an acknowledged custodian of Xhosa history, and it was partially for that reason that he was valued as an adviser. My own interest in history had early roots and was encouraged by my father. Although my father could neither read nor write, he was reputed to be an excellent orator who captivated his audiences by entertaining them as well as teaching them.

In later years, I discovered that my father was not only an adviser to kings but a kingmaker. After the untimely death of Jongilizwe in the 1920s, his son Sabata, the infant of the Great Wife, was too young to ascend to the throne. A dispute arose as to which of Dalindyebo's three most senior sons from other mothers — Jongintaba, Dabulamanzi, and Melithafa — should be selected to succeed him. My father was consulted and recommended Jongintaba on the grounds that he was the best educated. Jongintaba, he argued, would not only be a fine custodian of the crown but an excellent mentor to the young prince. My father, and a few other influential chiefs, had the great respect for education that is often present in those who are uneducated. The recommendation was controversial, for Jongintaba's mother was from a lesser house, but my father's choice was ultimately accepted by both the Thembus and the British government. In time, Jongintaba would return the favor in a way that my father could not then imagine.

All told, my father had four wives, the third of whom, my mother, Nosekeni Fanny, the daughter of Nkedama from the amaMpemvu clan of the Xhosa, belonged to the Right Hand House. Each of these wives — the Great Wife, the Right Hand wife (my mother), the Left Hand wife, and the wife of the Iqadi or support house — had her own kraal. A kraal was a homestead and usually included a simple fenced-in enclosure for animals, fields for growing crops, and one or more thatched huts. The kraals of my father's wives were separated by many miles and he commuted among them. In these travels, my father sired thirteen children in all, four boys and nine girls. I am the eldest child of the Right Hand House, and the youngest of my father's four sons. I have three sisters, Baliwe, who was the oldest girl, Notancu, and Makhutswana. Although the eldest of my father's sons was Mlahlwa, my father's heir as chief was Daligqili, the son of the Great House, who died in the early 1930s. All of his sons, with the exception of myself, are now deceased, and each was my senior not only in age but in status.

When I was not much more than a newborn child, my father was involved in a dispute that deprived him of his chieftainship at Mvezo and revealed a strain in his character I believe he passed on to his son. I maintain that nurture, rather than nature, is the primary molder of personality, but my father possessed a proud rebelliousness, a stubborn sense of fairness, that I recognize in myself. As a chief — or headman, as it was often known among the whites — my father was compelled to account for his stewardship not only to the Thembu king but to the local magistrate. One day one of my father's subjects lodged a complaint against him involving an ox that had strayed from its owner. The magistrate accordingly sent a message ordering my father to appear before him. When my father received the summons, he sent back the following reply: *"Andizi, ndisaqula"* (I will not come, I am still girding for battle). One did not defy magistrates in those days. Such behavior would be regarded as the height of insolence — and in this case it was.

My father's response bespoke his belief that the magistrate had no legitimate power over him. When it came to tribal matters, he was guided not by the laws of the king of England, but by Thembu custom. This defiance was not a fit of pique, but a matter of principle. He was asserting his traditional prerogative as a chief and was challenging the authority of the magistrate.

When the magistrate received my father's response, he promptly charged him with insubordination. There was no inquiry or investigation; that was reserved for white civil servants. The magistrate simply deposed my father, thus ending the Mandela family chieftainship.

I was unaware of these events at the time, but I was not unaffected. My father, who was a wealthy nobleman by the standards of his time, lost both his fortune and his title. He was deprived of most of his herd and land, and the revenue that came with them. Because of our straitened circumstances, my mother moved to Qunu, a slightly larger village north of Mvezo, where she would have the support of friends and relations. We lived in a less grand style in Qunu, but it was in that village near Umtata that I spent the happiest years of my boyhood and whence I trace my earliest memories.

2

THE VILLAGE OF QUNU was situated in a narrow, grassy valley crisscrossed by clear streams, and overlooked by green hills. It consisted of no more than a few hundred people who lived in huts, which were beehive-shaped structures of mud walls, with a wooden pole in the center holding up a peaked, grass roof. The floor was made of crushed ant-heap, the hard dome of excavated earth above an ant colony, and was kept smooth by smearing it regularly with fresh cow dung. The smoke from the hearth escaped through the roof, and the only opening was a low doorway one had to stoop to walk through. The huts were generally grouped together in a residential area that was some distance away from the maize fields. There were no roads, only paths through the grass worn away by bare-footed boys and women. The women and children of the village wore blankets dyed in ocher; only the few Christians in the village wore Western-style clothing. Cattle, sheep, goats, and horses grazed together in common pastures. The land around Qunu was mostly treeless except for a cluster of poplars on a hill overlooking the village. The land itself was owned by the state. With very few exceptions, Africans at the time did not enjoy private title to land in South Africa but were tenants paying rent annually to the government. In the area, there were two small primary schools, a general store, and a dipping tank to rid the cattle of ticks and diseases.

Maize (what we called mealies and people in the West call corn), sorghum, beans, and pumpkins formed the largest portion of our diet, not because of any inherent preference for these foods, but because the people could not afford anything richer. The wealthier families in our village supplemented their diets with tea, coffee, and sugar, but for most people in Qunu these were exotic luxuries far beyond their means. The water used for farming, cooking, and washing had to be fetched in buckets from streams and springs. This was women's work, and indeed, Qunu was a village of women and children: most of the men spent the greater part of the year working on remote farms or in the mines along the Reef, the great ridge of gold-bearing rock and shale that forms the southern boundary of Johannesburg. They returned perhaps twice a year, mainly to plow their fields. The hoeing, weeding, and harvesting were left to the women and children. Few if any of the people in the village knew how to read or write, and the concept of education was still a foreign one to many.

My mother presided over three huts at Qunu which, as I remember, were always filled with the babies and children of my relations. In fact, I hardly recall any occasion as a child when I was alone. In African culture, the sons and daughters of one's aunts or uncles are considered brothers and sisters, not cousins. We do not make the same distinctions among relations practiced by whites. We have no half brothers or half sisters. My mother's sister is my mother; my uncle's son is my brother; my brother's child is my son, my daughter.

Of my mother's three huts, one was used for cooking, one for sleeping, and one for storage. In the hut in which we slept, there was no furniture in the Western sense. We slept on mats and sat on the ground. I did not discover pillows until I went to Mqhekezweni. My mother cooked food in a three-legged iron pot over an open fire in the center of the hut or outside. Everything we ate we grew and made ourselves. My mother planted and harvested her own mealies. Mealies were harvested from the field when they were hard and dry. They were stored in sacks or pits dug in the ground. When preparing the mealies, the women used different methods. They could ground the kernels between two stones to make bread, or boil the mealies first, producing *umphothulo* (mealie flour eaten with sour milk) or *umngqusho* (samp, sometimes plain or mixed with beans). Unlike mealies, which were sometimes in short supply, milk from our cows and goats was always plentiful.

From an early age, I spent most of my free time in the veld playing and fighting with the other boys of the village. A boy who remained at home tied to his mother's apron strings was regarded as a sissy. At night, I shared my food and blanket with these same boys. I was no more than five when I became a herd-boy, looking after sheep and calves in the fields. I discovered the almost mystical attachment that the Xhosa have for cattle, not only as a source of food and wealth, but as a blessing from God and a source of happiness. It was in the fields that I learned how to knock birds out of the sky with a slingshot, to gather wild honey and fruits and edible roots, to drink warm, sweet milk straight from the udder of a cow, to swim in the clear, cold streams, and to catch fish with twine and sharpened bits of wire. I learned to stick-fight — essential knowledge to any rural African boy — and became adept at its various techniques, parrying blows, feinting in one direction and striking in another, breaking away from an opponent with quick footwork. From these days I date my love of the veld, of open spaces, the simple beauties of nature, the clean line of the horizon.

As boys, we were mostly left to our own devices. We played with toys we made ourselves. We molded animals and birds out of clay. We made ox-drawn sleighs out of tree branches. Nature was our playground. The hills above Qunu were dotted with large smooth rocks which we transformed into our own roller coaster. We sat on flat stones and slid down the face of the large rocks. We did this until our backsides were so sore we could hardly sit down. I learned to ride by sitting atop weaned calves — after being thrown to the ground several times, one got the hang of it.

I learned my lesson one day from an unruly donkey. We had been taking turns climbing up and down its back and when my chance came I jumped on and the donkey bolted into a nearby thornbush. It bent its head, trying to unseat me, which it did, but not before the thorns had pricked and scratched my face, embarrassing me in front of my friends. Like the people of the East, Africans have a highly developed sense of dignity, or what the Chinese call "face." I had lost face among my friends. Even though it was a donkey that unseated me, I learned that to humiliate another person is to make him suffer an unnecessarily cruel fate. Even as a boy, I defeated my opponents without dishonoring them.

Usually the boys played among themselves, but we sometimes allowed our sisters to join us. Boys and girls would play games like *ndize* (hide-and-seek) and *icekwa* (touch-and-run). But the game I most enjoyed playing with the girls was what we called *khetha*, or choose-the-one-you-like. This was not so much an organized game, but a spur-of-the-moment sport that took place when we accosted a group of girls our own age and demanded that each select the boy she loved. Our rules dictated that the girl's choice be respected and once she had chosen her favorite, she was free to continue on her journey escorted by the lucky boy she loved. But the girls were nimble-witted — far cleverer than we doltish lads — and would often confer among themselves and choose one boy, usually the plainest fellow, and then tease him all the way home.

The most popular game for boys was *thinti*, and like most boys' games it was a youthful approximation of war. Two sticks, used as targets, would be driven firmly into the ground in an upright position about one hundred feet apart. The goal of the game was for each team to hurl sticks at the opposing target and knock it down. We each defended our own target and attempted to prevent the other side from retrieving the sticks that had been thrown over. As we grew older, we organized matches against boys from neighboring villages, and those who distinguished themselves in these fraternal battles were greatly admired, as generals who achieve great victories in war are justly celebrated.

After games such as these, I would return to my mother's kraal where she was preparing supper. Whereas my father once told stories of historic battles and heroic Xhosa warriors, my mother would enchant us with

Xhosa legends and fables that had come down from numberless generations. These tales stimulated my childish imagination, and usually contained some moral lesson. I recall one story my mother told us about a traveler who was approached by an old woman with terrible cataracts on her eyes. The woman asked the traveler for help, and the man averted his eyes. Then another man came along and was approached by the old woman. She asked him to clean her eyes, and even though he found the task unpleasant, he did as she asked. Then, miraculously, the scales fell from the old woman's eyes and she became young and beautiful. The man married her and became wealthy and prosperous. It is a simple tale, but its message is an enduring one: virtue and generosity will be rewarded in ways that one cannot know.

Like all Xhosa children, I acquired knowledge mainly through observation. We were meant to learn through imitation and emulation, not through questions. When I first visited the homes of whites, I was often dumbfounded by the number and nature of questions that children asked of their parents — and their parents' unfailing willingness to answer them. In my household, questions were considered a nuisance; adults imparted information as they considered necessary.

My life, and that of most Xhosas at the time, was shaped by custom, ritual, and taboo. This was the alpha and omega of our existence, and went unquestioned. Men followed the path laid out for them by their fathers; women led the same lives as their mothers had before them. Without being told, I soon assimilated the elaborate rules that governed the relations between men and women. I discovered that a man may not enter a house where a woman has recently given birth, and that a newly married woman would not enter the kraal of her new home without elaborate ceremony. I also learned that to neglect one's ancestors would bring ill-fortune and failure in life. If you dishonored your ancestors in some fashion, the only way to atone for that lapse was to consult with a traditional healer or tribal elder, who communicated with the ancestors and conveyed profound apologies. All of these beliefs seemed perfectly natural to me.

I came across few whites as a boy at Qunu. The local magistrate, of course, was white, as was the nearest shopkeeper. Occasionally white travelers or policemen passed through our area. These whites appeared as grand as gods to me, and I was aware that they were to be treated with a mixture of fear and respect. But their role in my life was a distant one, and I thought little if at all about the white man in general or relations between my own people and these curious and remote figures.

The only rivalry between different clans or tribes in our small world at Qunu was that between the Xhosas and the amaMfengu, a small number of whom lived in our village. AmaMfengu arrived on the eastern Cape after fleeing from Shaka Zulu's armies in a period known as the iMfecane, the great wave of battles and migrations between 1820 and 1840 set in motion by the rise of Shaka and the Zulu state, during which the Zulu warrior sought to conquer and then unite all the tribes under military rule. AmaMfengu, who were not originally Xhosa-speakers, were refugees from the iMfecane and were forced to do jobs that no other African would do. They worked on white farms and in white businesses, something that was looked down upon by the more established Xhosa tribes. But amaMfengu were an industrious people, and because of their contact with Europeans, they were often more educated and "Western" than other Africans.

When I was a boy, amaMfengu were the most advanced section of the community and furnished our clergymen, policemen, teachers, clerks, and interpreters. They were also amongst the first to become Christians, to build better houses, and to use scientific methods of agriculture, and they were wealthier than their Xhosa compatriots. They confirmed the missionaries' axiom, that to be Christian was to be civilized, and to be civilized was to be Christian. There still existed some hostility toward amaMfengu, but in retrospect, I would attribute this more to jealousy than tribal animosity. This local form of tribalism that I observed as a boy was relatively harmless. At that stage, I did not witness nor even suspect the violent tribal rivalries that would subsequently be promoted by the white rulers of South Africa.

My father did not subscribe to local prejudice toward amaMfengu and befriended two amaMfengu brothers, George and Ben Mbekela. The brothers were an exception in Qunu: they were educated and Christian. George, the older of the two, was a retired teacher and Ben was a police sergeant. Despite the proselytizing of the Mbekela brothers, my father remained aloof from Christianity and instead reserved his own faith for the great spirit of the Xhosas, Qamata, the God of his fathers. My father was an unofficial priest and presided over ritual slaughtering of goats and calves and officiated at local traditional rites concerning planting, harvest, birth, marriage, initiation ceremonies, and funerals. He did not need to be ordained, for the traditional religion of the Xhosas is characterized by a cosmic wholeness, so that there is little distinction between the sacred and the secular, between the natural and the supernatural.

While the faith of the Mbekela brothers did not rub off on my father, it did inspire my mother, who became a Christian. In fact, Fanny was literally her Christian name, for she had been given it in church. It was due to the influence of the Mbekela brothers that I myself was baptized into the Methodist, or Wesleyan Church as it was then known, and sent to school. The brothers would often see me playing or minding sheep and come over to talk to me. One day, George Mbekela paid a visit to my mother. "Your son is a clever young fellow," he said. "He should go to school." My mother remained silent. No one in my family had ever attended school and my mother was unprepared for Mbekela's suggestion. But she did relay it to my father, who despite — or perhaps because of — his own lack of education immediately decided that his youngest son should go to school.

The schoolhouse consisted of a single room, with a Western-style roof, on the other side of the hill from Qunu. I was seven years old, and on the day before I was to begin, my father took me aside and told me that I must be dressed properly for school. Until that time, I, like all the other boys in Qunu, had worn only a blanket, which was wrapped around one shoulder and pinned at the waist. My father took a pair of his trousers and cut them at the knee. He told me to put them on, which I did, and they were roughly the correct length, although the waist was far too large. My father then took a piece of string and cinched the trousers at the waist. I must have been a comical sight, but I have never owned a suit I was prouder to wear than my father's cut-off pants.

On the first day of school, my teacher, Miss Mdingane, gave each of us an English name and said that from thenceforth that was the name we would answer to in school. This was the custom among Africans in those days and was undoubtedly due to the British bias of our education. The education I received was a British education, in which British ideas, British culture, British institutions, were automatically assumed to be superior. There was no such thing as African culture.

Africans of my generation — and even today — generally have both an English and an African name. Whites were either unable or unwilling to pronounce an African name, and considered it uncivilized to have one. That day, Miss Mdingane told me that my new name was Nelson. Why she bestowed this particular name upon me I have no idea. Perhaps it had something to do with the great British sea captain Lord Nelson, but that would be only a guess.

3

ONE NIGHT, when I was nine years old, I was aware of a commotion in the household. My father, who took turns visiting his wives and usually came to us for perhaps one week a month, had arrived. But it was not at his accustomed time, for he was not scheduled to be with us for another few days. I found him in my mother's hut, lying on his back on the floor, in the midst of what seemed like an endless fit of coughing. Even to my young eyes, it was clear that my father was not long for this world. He was ill with some type of lung disease, but it was not diagnosed, as my father had never visited a doctor. He remained in the hut for several days without moving or speaking, and then one night he took a turn for the worse. My mother and my father's youngest wife, Nodayimani, who had come to stay with us, were looking after him, and late that night he called for Nodayimani. "Bring me my tobacco," he told her. My mother and Nodayimani conferred, and decided that it was unwise that he have tobacco in his current state. But he persisted in calling for it, and eventually Nodayimani filled his pipe, lit it, and then handed it to him. My father smoked and became calm. He continued smoking for perhaps an hour, and then, his pipe still lit, he died.

I do not remember experiencing great grief so much as feeling cut adrift. Although my mother was the center of my existence, I defined myself through my father. My father's passing changed my whole life in a way that I did not suspect at the time. After a brief period of mourning, my mother informed me that I would be leaving Qunu. I did not ask her why, or where I was going.

I packed the few things that I possessed, and early one morning we set out on a journey westward to my new residence. I mourned less for my father than for the world I was leaving behind. Qunu was all that I knew, and I loved it in the unconditional way that a child loves his first home. Before we disappeared behind the hills, I turned and looked for what I imagined was the last time at my village. I could see the simple huts and the people going about their chores; the stream where I had splashed and played with the other boys; the maize fields and green pastures where the herds and flocks were lazily grazing. I imagined my friends out hunting for small birds, drinking the sweet milk from the cow's udder, cavorting in the pond at the end of the stream. Above all else, my eyes rested on the three simple huts where I had enjoyed my mother's love and protection. It was these three huts that I associated with all my happiness, with life itself, and I rued the fact that I had not kissed each of them before I left. I could not imagine that the future I was walking toward could compare in any way to the past that I was leaving behind.

We traveled by foot and in silence until the sun was sinking slowly toward the horizon. But the silence of the heart between mother and child is not a lonely one. My mother and I never talked very much, but we did not need to. I never doubted her love or questioned her support. It was an exhausting journey, along rocky dirt roads, up and down hills, past numerous villages, but we did not pause. Late in the afternoon, at the bottom of a shallow valley surrounded by trees, we came upon a village at the center of which was a large and gracious home that so far exceeded anything that I had ever seen that all I could do was marvel at it. The buildings consisted of two *iingxande* (rectangular houses) and seven stately rondavels (superior huts), all washed in white lime, dazzling even in the light of the setting sun. There was a large front garden and a maize field bordered by rounded peach trees. An even more spacious garden spread out in back, which boasted apple trees, a vegetable garden, a strip of flowers, and a patch of wattles. Nearby was a white stucco church.

In the shade of two gum trees that graced the doorway of the front of the main house sat a group of about twenty tribal elders. Encircling the property, contentedly grazing on the rich land, was a herd of at least fifty cattle and perhaps five hundred sheep. Everything was beautifully tended, and it was a vision of wealth and order beyond my imagination. This was the Great Place, Mqhekezweni, the provisional capital of Thembuland, the royal residence of Chief Jongintaba Dalindyebo, acting regent of the Thembu people.

As I contemplated all this grandeur, an enormous motorcar rumbled through the western gate and the men sitting in the shade immediately arose. They doffed their hats and then jumped to their feet shouting, *"Bayete a-a-a, Jongintaba!"* (Hail, Jongintaba!), the traditional salute of the Xhosas for their chief. Out of the motorcar (I learned later that this majestic vehicle was a Ford V8) stepped a short, thickset man wearing a smart suit. I could see that he had the confidence and bearing of a man who was used to the exercise of authority. His name suited him, for Jongintaba literally means "One who looks at the mountain," and he was a man with a sturdy presence toward whom all eyes gazed. He had a dark complexion and an intelligent face, and he casually shook hands with each of the men beneath the tree, men who as I later discovered comprised the highest Thembu court of justice. This was the regent who was to become my guardian and benefactor for the next decade.

In that moment of beholding Jongintaba and his court I felt like a sapling pulled root and branch from the earth and flung into the center of a stream whose strong current I could not resist. I felt a sense of awe mixed with bewilderment. Until then I had had no thoughts of anything but my own pleasures, no higher ambition than to eat well and become a champion stick-fighter. I had no thought of money, or class, or fame, or power. Suddenly a new world opened before me. Children from poor homes often find themselves beguiled by a host of new temptations when suddenly confronted by great wealth. I was no exception. I felt many of my established beliefs and loyalties begin to ebb away. The slender foundation built by my parents began to shake. In that instant, I saw that life might hold more for me than being a champion stick-fighter.

*   *   *

I learned later that, in the wake of my father's death, Jongintaba had offered to become my guardian. He would treat me as he treated his other children, and I would have the same advantages as they. My mother had no choice; one did not turn down such an overture from the regent. She was satisfied that although she would miss me, I would have a more advantageous upbringing in the regent's care than in her own. The regent had not forgotten that it was due to my father's intervention that he had become acting paramount chief.

My mother remained in Mqhekezweni for a day or two before returning to Qunu. Our parting was without fuss. She offered no sermons, no words of wisdom, no kisses. I suspect she did not want me to feel bereft at her departure and so was matter-of-fact. I knew that my father had wanted me to be educated and prepared for a wide world, and I could not do that in Qunu. Her tender look was all the affection and support I needed, and as she departed she turned to me and said, *"Uqinisufokotho, Kwedini!"* (Brace yourself, my boy!) Children are often the least sentimental of creatures, especially if they are absorbed in some new pleasure. Even as my dear mother and first friend was leaving, my head was swimming with the delights of my new home. How could I not be braced up? I was already wearing the handsome new outfit purchased for me by my guardian.

I was quickly caught up in the daily life of Mqhekezweni. A child adapts rapidly, or not at all — and I had taken to the Great Place as though I had been raised there. To me, it was a magical kingdom; everything was delightful; the chores that were tedious in Qunu became an adventure in Mqhekezweni. When I was not in school, I was a plowboy, a wagon guide, a shepherd. I rode horses and shot birds with slingshots and found boys to joust with, and some nights I danced the evening away to the beautiful singing and clapping of Thembu maidens. Although I missed Qunu and my mother, I was completely absorbed in my new world.

I attended a one-room school next door to the palace and studied English, Xhosa, history, and geography. We read *Chambers English Reader* and did our lessons on black slates. Our teachers, Mr. Fadana, and later, Mr. Giqwa, took a special interest in me. I did well in school not so much through cleverness as through doggedness. My own self-discipline was reinforced by my aunt Phathiwe, who lived in the Great Place and scrutinized my homework every night.

Mqhekezweni was a mission station of the Methodist Church and far more up-to-date and Westernized than Qunu. People dressed in modern clothes. The men wore suits and the women affected the severe Protestant style of the missionaries: thick long skirts and high-necked blouses, with

a blanket draped over the shoulder and a scarf wound elegantly around
the head.

If the world of Mqhekezweni revolved around the regent, my smaller
world revolved around his two children. Justice, the elder, was his only
son and heir to the Great Place, and Nomafu was the regent's daughter.
I lived with them and was treated exactly as they were. We ate the same
food, wore the same clothes, performed the same chores. We were later
joined by Nxeko, the older brother to Sabata, the heir to the throne. The
four of us formed a royal quartet. The regent and his wife No-England
brought me up as if I were their own child. They worried about me,
guided me, and punished me, all in a spirit of loving fairness. Jongintaba
was stern, but I never doubted his love. They called me by the pet name
of Tatomkhulu, which means "Grandpa," because they said when I was
very serious, I looked like an old man.
  Justice was four years older than I and became my first hero after my
father. I looked up to him in every way. He was already at Clarkebury, a
boarding school about sixty miles distant. Tall, handsome, and muscular,
he was a fine sportsman, excelling in track and field, cricket, rugby, and
soccer. Cheerful and outgoing, he was a natural performer who enchanted
audiences with his singing and transfixed them with his ballroom dancing.
He had a bevy of female admirers — but also a coterie of critics, who
considered him a dandy and a playboy. Justice and I became the best of
friends, though we were opposites in many ways: he was extroverted, I
was introverted; he was lighthearted, I was serious. Things came easily
to him; I had to drill myself. To me, he was everything a young man
should be and everything I longed to be. Though treated alike, our des-
tinies were different: Justice would inherit one of the most powerful
chieftainships of the Thembu tribe, while I would inherit whatever the
regent, in his generosity, decided to give me.
  Every day I was in and out of the regent's house doing errands. Of
the chores I did for the regent, the one I enjoyed most was pressing his
suits, a job in which I took great pride. He owned half-a-dozen Western
suits, and I spent many an hour carefully making the crease in his trousers.
His palace, as it were, consisted of two large Western-style houses with
tin roofs. In those days, very few Africans had Western houses and they
were considered a mark of great wealth. Six rondavels stood in a semicircle
around the main house. They had wooden floorboards, something I had
never seen before. The regent and the queen slept in the right-hand
rondavel, the queen's sister in the center one, and the left-hand hut served
as a pantry. Under the floor of the queen's sister's hut was a beehive, and
we would sometimes take up a floorboard or two and feast on its honey.

Shortly after I moved to Mqhekezweni, the regent and his wife moved to the *uxande* (middle house), which automatically became the Great House. There were three small rondavels near it: one for the regent's mother, one for visitors, and one shared by Justice and myself.

The two principles that governed my life at Mqhekezweni were chieftaincy and the Church. These two doctrines existed in uneasy harmony, although I did not then see them as antagonistic. For me, Christianity was not so much a system of beliefs as it was the powerful creed of a single man: Reverend Matyolo. For me, his powerful presence embodied all that was alluring in Christianity. He was as popular and beloved as the regent, and the fact that he was the regent's superior in spiritual matters made a strong impression on me. But the Church was as concerned with this world as the next: I saw that virtually all of the achievements of Africans seemed to have come about through the missionary work of the Church. The mission schools trained the clerks, the interpreters, and the policemen, who at the time represented the height of African aspirations.

Reverend Matyolo was a stout man in his mid-fifties, with a deep and potent voice that lent itself to both preaching and singing. When he preached at the simple church at the western end of Mqhekezweni, the hall was always brimming with people. The hall rang with the hosannas of the faithful, while the women knelt at his feet to beg for salvation. The first tale I heard about him when I arrived at the Great Place was that the reverend had chased away a dangerous ghost with only a Bible and a lantern as weapons. I saw neither implausibility nor contradiction in this story. The Methodism preached by Reverend Matyolo was of the fire-and-brimstone variety, seasoned with a bit of African animism. The Lord was wise and omnipotent, but He was also a vengeful God who let no bad deed go unpunished.

At Qunu, the only time I had ever attended church was on the day that I was baptized. Religion was a ritual that I indulged in for my mother's sake and to which I attached no meaning. But at Mqhekezweni, religion was a part of the fabric of life and I attended church each Sunday along with the regent and his wife. The regent took his religion very seriously. In fact the only time that I was ever given a hiding by him was when I dodged a Sunday service to take part in a fight against boys from another village, a transgression I never committed again.

That was not the only rebuke I received on account of my trespasses against the reverend. One afternoon, I crept into Reverend Matyolo's garden and stole some maize, which I roasted and ate right there. A young girl saw me eating the corn in the garden and immediately reported my presence to the priest. The news quickly made the rounds and reached the regent's wife. That evening, she waited until prayer time — which was a daily ritual in the house — and confronted me with my misdeed, reproaching me for taking the bread from a poor servant of God and disgracing the family. She said the devil would certainly take me to task for my sin. I felt an unpleasant mixture of fear and shame — fear that I would get some cosmic comeuppance and shame that I had abused the trust of my adopted family.

Because of the universal respect the regent enjoyed — from both black and white — and the seemingly untempered power that he wielded, I saw chieftaincy as being the very center around which life revolved. The power and influence of chieftaincy pervaded every aspect of our lives in Mqhekezweni and was the preeminent means through which one could achieve influence and status.

My later notions of leadership were profoundly influenced by observing the regent and his court. I watched and learned from the tribal meetings that were regularly held at the Great Place. These were not scheduled, but were called as needed, and were held to discuss national matters such as a drought, the culling of cattle, policies ordered by the magistrate, or new laws decreed by the government. All Thembus were free to come — and a great many did, on horseback or by foot.

On these occasions, the regent was surrounded by his *amaphakathi,* a group of councilors of high rank who functioned as the regent's parliament and judiciary. They were wise men who retained the knowledge of tribal history and custom in their heads and whose opinions carried great weight.

Letters advising these chiefs and headmen of a meeting were dispatched from the regent, and soon the Great Place became alive with important visitors and travelers from all over Thembuland. The guests would gather in the courtyard in front of the regent's house and he would open the meeting by thanking everyone for coming and explaining why he had summoned them. From that point on, he would not utter another word until the meeting was nearing its end.

Everyone who wanted to speak did so. It was democracy in its purest form. There may have been a hierarchy of importance among the speakers, but everyone was heard, chief and subject, warrior and medicine man, shopkeeper and farmer, landowner and laborer. People spoke without interruption and the meetings lasted for many hours. The foundation of self-government was that all men were free to voice their opinions and equal in their value as citizens. (Women, I am afraid, were deemed second-class citizens.)

A great banquet was served during the day, and I often gave myself a bellyache by eating too much while listening to speaker after speaker. I noticed how some speakers rambled and never seemed to get to the point. I grasped how others came to the matter at hand directly, and who made a set of arguments succinctly and cogently. I observed how some speakers used emotion and dramatic language, and tried to move the audience with such techniques, while other speakers were sober and even, and shunned emotion.

At first, I was astonished by the vehemence — and candor — with which people criticized the regent. He was not above criticism — in fact, he was often the principal target of it. But no matter how flagrant the charge, the regent simply listened, not defending himself, showing no emotion at all.

The meetings would continue until some kind of consensus was reached. They ended in unanimity or not at all. Unanimity, however, might be an agreement to disagree, to wait for a more propitious time to propose a solution. Democracy meant all men were to be heard, and a decision was taken together as a people. Majority rule was a foreign notion. A minority was not to be crushed by a majority.

Only at the end of the meeting, as the sun was setting, would the regent speak. His purpose was to sum up what had been said and form some consensus among the diverse opinions. But no conclusion was forced on people who disagreed. If no agreement could be reached, another meeting would be held. At the very end of the council, a praise-singer or poet would deliver a panegyric to the ancient kings, and a mixture of compliments to and satire on the present chiefs, and the audience, led by the regent, would roar with laughter.

As a leader, I have always followed the principles I first saw demonstrated by the regent at the Great Place. I have always endeavored to listen to what each and every person in a discussion had to say before venturing my own opinion. Oftentimes, my own opinion will simply represent a consensus of what I heard in the discussion. I always remember the regent's axiom: a leader, he said, is like a shepherd. He stays behind the flock, letting the most nimble go out ahead, whereupon the others follow, not realizing that all along they are being directed from behind.

It was at Mqhekezweni that I developed my interest in African history. Until then I had heard only of Xhosa heroes, but at the Great Place I learned of other African heroes like Sekhukhune, king of the Bapedi, and the Basotho king, Moshoeshoe, and Dingane, king of the Zulus, and others such as Bambatha, Hintsa and Makana, Montshiwa and Kgama. I learned of these men from the chiefs and headmen who came to the Great Place to settle disputes and try cases. Though not lawyers, these men presented cases and then adjudicated them. Some days, they would finish early and sit around telling stories. I hovered silently and listened. They spoke in an idiom that I'd never heard before. Their speech was formal and lofty, their manner slow and unhurried, and the traditional clicks of our language were long and dramatic.

At first, they shooed me away and told me I was too young to listen. Later they would beckon me to fetch fire or water for them, or to tell the women they wanted tea, and in those early months I was too busy running errands to follow their conversation. But, eventually, they permitted me to stay, and I discovered the great African patriots who fought against Western domination. My imagination was fired by the glory of these African warriors.

The most ancient of the chiefs who regaled the gathered elders with ancient tales was Zwelibhangile Joyi, a son from the Great House of King Ngubengcuka. Chief Joyi was so old that his wrinkled skin hung on him like a loose-fitting coat. His stories unfolded slowly and were often punctuated by a great wheezing cough, which would force him to stop for minutes at a time. Chief Joyi was the great authority on the history of the Thembus in large part because he had lived through so much of it.

But as grizzled as Chief Joyi often seemed, the decades fell off him when he spoke of the young *impis,* or warriors, in the army of King Ngangelizwe fighting the British. In pantomime, Chief Joyi would fling his spear and creep along the veld as he narrated the victories and defeats. He spoke of Ngangelizwe's heroism, generosity, and humility.

Not all of Chief Joyi's stories revolved around the Thembus. When he first spoke of non-Xhosa warriors, I wondered why. I was like a boy who worships a local soccer hero and is not interested in a national soccer star with whom he has no connection. Only later was I moved by the broad sweep of African history, and the deeds of all African heroes regardless of tribe.

Chief Joyi railed against the white man, who he believed had deliberately sundered the Xhosa tribe, dividing brother from brother. The white man had told the Thembus that their true chief was the great white queen across the ocean and that they were her subjects. But the white queen brought nothing but misery and perfidy to the black people, and if she was a chief she was an evil chief. Chief Joyi's war stories and his indictment of the British made me feel angry and cheated, as though I had already been robbed of my own birthright.

Chief Joyi said that the African people lived in relative peace until the coming of the *abelungu,* the white people, who arrived from across the sea with fire-breathing weapons. Once, he said, the Thembu, the Mpondo, the Xhosa, and the Zulu were all children of one father, and lived as brothers. The white man shattered the *abantu,* the fellowship, of the various tribes. The white man was hungry and greedy for land, and the black man shared the land with him as they shared the air and water; land was not for man to possess. But the white man took the land as you might seize another man's horse.

I did not yet know that the real history of our country was not to be found in standard British textbooks, which claimed South Africa began with the landing of Jan Van Riebeeck at the Cape of Good Hope in 1652. It was from Chief Joyi that I began to discover that the history of the Bantu-speaking peoples began far to the north, in a country of lakes and green plains and valleys, and that slowly over the millennia we made our way down to the very tip of this great continent. However, I later discovered that Chief Joyi's account of African history, particularly after 1652, was not always so accurate.

In Mqhekezweni, I felt not unlike the proverbial country boy who comes to the big city. Mqhekezweni was far more sophisticated than Qunu, whose residents were regarded as backward by the people of Mqhekezweni. The regent was loath to have me visit Qunu, thinking I would regress and fall into bad company back in my old village. When I did visit, I sensed that my mother had been briefed by the regent, for she would question me closely as to whom I was playing with. On many occasions, however, the regent would arrange for my mother and sisters to be brought to the Great Place.

When I first arrived in Mqhekezweni I was regarded by some of my peers as a yokel who was hopelessly unequipped to exist in the rarefied atmosphere of the Great Place. As young men will, I did my best to appear suave and sophisticated. In church one day, I had noticed a lovely young woman who was one of the daughters of the Reverend Matyolo. Her name was Winnie, and I asked her out and she accepted. She was keen on me, but her eldest sister, nomaMpondo, regarded me as hopelessly backward. She told her sister that I was a barbarian who was not good enough for the daughter of Reverend Matyolo. To prove to her younger sister how uncivilized I was, she invited me to the rectory for lunch. I was still used to eating at home, where we did not use knife and fork. At the family table, this mischievous older sister handed me a plate that contained a single chicken wing. But the wing, instead of being soft and tender, was a bit tough, so the meat did not fall easily off the bone.

I watched the others using their knives and forks with ease and slowly picked up mine. I observed the others for a few moments, and then attempted to carve my little wing. At first I just moved it around the plate, hoping that the flesh would fall from the bone. Then I tried in vain to pin the thing down, and cut it, but it eluded me, and in my frustration I was clanking my knife on the plate. I tried this repeatedly and then noticed that the older sister was smiling at me and looking knowingly at the younger sister as if to say, "I told you so." I struggled and struggled and became wet with perspiration, but I did not want to admit defeat and pick the infernal thing up with my hands. I did not eat much chicken that day at luncheon.

Afterward the older sister told the younger, "You will waste your whole life if you fall in love with such a backward boy," but I am happy to say the young lady did not listen — she loved me, as backward as I was. Eventually, of course, we went different ways and drifted apart. She attended a different school, and qualified as a teacher. We corresponded for a few years and then I lost track of her, but by that time I had considerably improved my table etiquette.

4

WHEN I WAS SIXTEEN, the regent decided that it was time that I became a man. In Xhosa tradition, this is achieved through one means only: circumcision. In my tradition, an uncircumcised male cannot be heir to his father's wealth, cannot marry or officiate in tribal rituals. An uncircumcised Xhosa man is a contradiction in terms, for he is not considered a man at all, but a boy. For the Xhosa people, circumcision represents the formal incorporation of males into society. It is not just a surgical procedure, but a lengthy and elaborate ritual in preparation for manhood. As a Xhosa, I count my years as a man from the date of my circumcision.

The traditional ceremony of the circumcision school was arranged principally for Justice — the rest of us, twenty-six in all — were there mainly to keep him company. Early in the new year, we journeyed to two grass huts in a secluded valley on the banks of the Mbashe River, known as Tyhalarha, the traditional place of circumcision for Thembu kings. The huts were seclusion lodges, where we were to live isolated from society. It was a sacred time; I felt happy and fulfilled taking part in my people's customs and ready to make the transition from boyhood to manhood.

We had moved to Tyhalarha by the river a few days before the actual circumcision ceremony. These last few days of boyhood were spent with the other initiates, and I found the camaraderie enjoyable. The lodge was near the home of Banabakhe Blayi, the wealthiest and most popular boy at the circumcision school. He was an engaging fellow, a champion stick-fighter and a glamour boy, whose many girlfriends kept us all supplied with delicacies. Although he could neither read nor write, he was one of the most intelligent among us. He regaled us with stories of his trips to Johannesburg, a place none of us had ever been before. He so thrilled us with tales of the mines that he almost persuaded me that to be a miner was more alluring than to be a monarch. Miners had a mystique; to be a miner meant to be strong and daring, the ideal of manhood. Much later, I realized that it was the exaggerated tales of boys like Banabakhe that caused so many young men to run away to work in the mines of Johannesburg, where they often lost their health and their lives. In those days, working in the mines was almost as much of a rite of passage as circumcision school, a myth that helped the mine-owners more than it helped my people.

A custom of circumcision school is that one must perform a daring exploit before the ceremony. In days of old, this might have involved a cattle raid or even a battle, but in our time the deeds were more mischievous than martial. Two nights before we moved to Tyhalarha, we decided to steal a pig. In Mqhekezweni there was a tribesman with an ornery old pig. To avoid making noise and alarming him, we arranged for the pig to do our work for us. We took handfuls of sediment from homemade African beer, which has a strong scent much favored by pigs, and placed it upwind of the pig. The pig was so aroused by the scent that he came out of the kraal, following a trail we had laid, gradually made his way to us, wheezing and snorting and eating the sediment. When he got near us, we captured the poor pig, slaughtered it, and then built a fire and ate roast pork underneath the stars. No piece of pork has ever tasted as good before or since.

The night before the circumcision, there was a ceremony near our huts with singing and dancing. Women came from the nearby villages, and we danced to their singing and clapping. As the music became faster and louder, our dance turned more frenzied and we forgot for a moment what lay ahead.

At dawn, when the stars were still in the sky, we began our preparations. We were escorted to the river to bathe in its cold waters, a ritual that signified our purification before the ceremony. The ceremony was at midday, and we were commanded to stand in a row in a clearing some distance from the river where a crowd of parents and relatives, including the regent, as well as a handful of chiefs and counselors, had gathered. We were clad only in our blankets, and as the ceremony began, with drums pounding, we were ordered to sit on a blanket on the ground with our legs spread out in front of us. I was tense and anxious, uncertain of how I would react when the critical moment came. Flinching or crying out was a sign of weakness and stigmatized one's manhood. I was determined not to disgrace myself, the group, or my guardian. Circumcision is a trial of bravery and stoicism; no anesthetic is used; a man must suffer in silence.

To the right, out of the corner of my eye, I could see a thin, elderly man emerge from a tent and kneel in front of the first boy. There was excitement in the crowd, and I shuddered slightly knowing that the ritual was about to begin. The old man was a famous *ingcibi,* a circumcision expert, from Gcalekaland, who would use his assegai to change us from boys to men with a single blow.

Suddenly, I heard the first boy cry out, *"Ndiyindoda!"* (I am a man!), which we were trained to say in the moment of circumcision. Seconds later, I heard Justice's strangled voice pronounce the same phrase. There were now two boys before the *ingcibi* reached me, and my mind must have gone blank because before I knew it, the old man was kneeling in front of me. I looked directly into his eyes. He was pale, and though the day was cold, his face was shining with perspiration. His hands moved so fast they seemed to be controlled by an otherworldly force. Without a word, he took my foreskin, pulled it forward, and then, in a single motion, brought down his assegai. I felt as if fire was shooting through my veins; the pain was so intense that I buried my chin into my chest. Many seconds seemed to pass before I remembered the cry, and then I recovered and called out, *"Ndiyindoda!"*

I looked down and saw a perfect cut, clean and round like a ring. But I felt ashamed because the other boys seemed much stronger and braver than I had been; they had called out more promptly than I had. I was distressed that I had been disabled, however briefly, by the pain, and I did my best to hide my agony. A boy may cry; a man conceals his pain.

I had now taken the essential step in the life of every Xhosa man. Now, I might marry, set up my own home, and plow my own field. I could now be admitted to the councils of the community; my words would be taken seriously. At the ceremony, I was given my circumcision name, Dalibunga, meaning "Founder of the Bungha," the traditional ruling body of the Transkei. To Xhosa traditionalists, this name is more acceptable than either of my two previous given names, Rolihlahla or Nelson, and I was proud to hear my new name pronounced: Dalibunga.

Immediately after the blow had been delivered, an assistant who follows the circumcision master takes the foreskin that is on the ground and ties it to a corner of your blanket. Our wounds were then dressed with a healing plant, the leaves of which were thorny on the outside but smooth on the inside, which absorbed the blood and other secretions.

At the conclusion of the ceremony, we returned to our huts, where a fire was burning with wet wood that cast off clouds of smoke, which was thought to promote healing. We were ordered to lie on our backs in the smoky huts, with one leg flat, and one leg bent. We were now *abakhwetha,* initiates into the world of manhood. We were looked after by an *ama-khankatha,* or guardian, who explained the rules we must follow if we were to enter manhood properly. The first chore of the *amakhankatha* was to paint our naked and shaved bodies from head to foot in white ocher, turning us into ghosts. The white chalk symbolized our purity, and I still recall how stiff the dried clay felt on my body.

That first night, at midnight, an attendant, or *ikhankatha,* crept around the hut, gently waking each of us. We were then instructed to leave the hut and go tramping through the night to bury our foreskins. The tra-ditional reason for this practice was so that our foreskins would be hidden before wizards could use them for evil purposes, but, symbolically, we were also burying our youth. I did not want to leave the warm hut and wander through the bush in the darkness, but I walked into the trees and, after a few minutes, untied my foreskin and buried it in the earth. I felt as though I had now discarded the last remnant of my childhood.

We lived in our two huts — thirteen in each — while our wounds healed. When outside the huts, we were covered in blankets, for we were not allowed to be seen by women. It was a period of quietude, a kind of spiritual preparation for the trials of manhood that lay ahead. On the day of our reemergence, we went down to the river early in the morning to wash away the white ocher in the waters of the Mbashe. Once we were clean and dry, we were coated in red ocher. The tradition was that one should sleep with a woman, who later may become one's wife, and she rubs off the pigment with her body. In my case, however, the ocher was removed with a mixture of fat and lard.

At the end of our seclusion, the lodges and all their contents were burned, destroying our last links to childhood, and a great ceremony was held to welcome us as men to society. Our families, friends, and local chiefs gathered for speeches, songs, and gift-giving. I was given two heifers and four sheep, and felt far richer than I ever had before. I who had never owned anything suddenly possessed property. It was a heady feeling, even though my gifts were paltry next to those of Justice, who inherited an entire herd. I was not jealous of Justice's gifts. He was the son of a king; I was merely destined to be a counselor to a king. I felt strong and proud that day. I remember walking differently on that day, straighter, taller, firmer. I was hopeful, and thinking that I might someday have wealth, property, and status.

The main speaker of the day was Chief Meligqili, the son of Dalindyebo, and after listening to him, my gaily colored dreams suddenly darkened. He began conventionally, remarking on how fine it was that we were continuing a tradition that had been going on for as long as anyone could remember. Then he turned to us and his tone suddenly changed. "There sit our sons," he said, "young, healthy, and handsome, the flower of the Xhosa tribe, the pride of our nation. We have just circumcised them in a ritual that promises them manhood, but I am here to tell you that it is an empty, illusory promise, a promise than can never be fulfilled. For we Xhosas, and all black South Africans, are a conquered people. We are slaves in our own country. We are tenants on our own soil. We have no strength, no power, no control over our own destiny in the land of our birth. They will go to cities where they will live in shacks and drink cheap alcohol all because we have no land to give them where they could prosper and multiply. They will cough their lungs out deep in the bowels of the white man's mines, destroying their health, never seeing the sun, so that the white man can live a life of unequaled prosperity. Among these young men are chiefs who will never rule because we have no power to govern ourselves; soldiers who will never fight for we have no weapons to fight with; scholars who will never teach because we have no place for them to study. The abilities, the intelligence, the promise of these young men will be squandered in their attempt to eke out a living doing the simplest, most mindless chores for the white man. These gifts today are naught, for we cannot give them the greatest gift of all, which is freedom and independence. I well know that Qamata is all-seeing and never sleeps, but I have a suspicion that Qamata may in fact be dozing. If this is the case, the sooner I die the better because then I can meet him and shake him awake and tell him that the children of Ngubengcuka, the flower of the Xhosa nation, are dying."

The audience had become more and more quiet as Chief Meligqili spoke and, I think, more and more angry. No one wanted to hear the words that he spoke that day. I know that I myself did not want to hear them. I was cross rather than aroused by the chief's remarks, dismissing his words as the abusive comments of an ignorant man who was unable to appreciate the value of the education and benefits that the white man had brought to our country. At the time, I looked on the white man not as an oppressor but as a benefactor, and I thought the chief was enormously ungrateful. This upstart chief was ruining my day, spoiling the proud feeling with wrongheaded remarks.

But without exactly understanding why, his words soon began to work in me. He had planted a seed, and though I let that seed lie dormant for a long season, it eventually began to grow. Later, I realized that the ignorant man that day was not the chief but myself.

After the ceremony, I walked back to the river and watched it meander on its way to where, many miles distant, it emptied into the Indian Ocean.

I had never crossed that river, and I knew little or nothing of the world beyond it, a world that beckoned me that day. It was almost sunset and I hurried on to where our seclusion lodges had been. Though it was forbidden to look back while the lodges were burning, I could not resist. When I reached the area, all that remained were two pyramids of ashes by a large mimosa tree. In these ash heaps lay a lost and delightful world, the world of my childhood, the world of sweet and irresponsible days at Qunu and Mqhekezweni. Now I was a man, and I would never again play *thinti,* or steal maize, or drink milk from a cow's udder. I was already in mourning for my own youth. Looking back, I know that I was not a man that day and would not truly become one for many years.

5

UNLIKE MOST OF THE OTHERS with whom I had been at circumcision school, I was not destined to work in the gold mines on the Reef. The regent had often told me, "It is not for you to spend your life mining the white man's gold, never knowing how to write your name." My destiny was to become a counselor to Sabata, and for that I had to be educated. I returned to Mqhekezweni after the ceremony, but not for very long, for I was about to cross the Mbashe River for the first time on my way to Clarkebury Boarding Institute in the district of Engcobo.

I was again leaving home, but I was eager to see how I would fare in the wider world. The regent himself drove me to Engcobo in his majestic Ford V8. Before leaving, he had organized a celebration for my having passed Standard V and been admitted to Clarkebury. A sheep was slaughtered and there was dancing and singing — it was the first celebration that I had ever had in my own honor, and I greatly enjoyed it. The regent gave me my first pair of boots, a sign of manhood, and that night I polished them anew, even though they were already shiny.

Founded in 1825, Clarkebury Institute was located on the site of one of the oldest Wesleyan missions in the Transkei. At the time, Clarkebury was the highest institution of learning for Africans in Thembuland. The regent himself had attended Clarkebury, and Justice had followed him there. It was both a secondary school and a teacher training college, but it also offered courses in more practical disciplines, such as carpentry, tailoring, and tinsmithing.

During the trip, the regent advised me on my behavior and my future. He urged me to behave in a way that brought only respect to Sabata and to himself, and I assured him that I would. He then briefed me on the

Reverend C. Harris, the governor of the school. Reverend Harris, he explained, was unique: he was a white Thembu, a white man who in his heart loved and understood the Thembu people. The regent said when Sabata was older, he would entrust the future king to Reverend Harris, who would train him as both a Christian and a traditional ruler. He said that I must learn from Reverend Harris because I was destined to guide the leader that Reverend Harris was to mold.

At Mqhekezweni I had met many white traders and government officials, including magistrates and police officers. These were men of high standing and the regent received them courteously, but not obsequiously; he treated them on equal terms, as they did him. At times, I even saw him upbraid them, though this was extremely rare. I had very little experience in dealing directly with whites. The regent never told me how to behave, and I observed him and followed his example. In talking about Reverend Harris, however, the regent, for the first time, gave me a lecture on how I was to conduct myself. He said I must afford the reverend the same respect and obedience that I gave to him.

Clarkebury was far grander even than Mqhekezweni. The school itself consisted of a cluster of two dozen or so graceful, colonial-style buildings, which included individual homes as well as dormitories, the library, and various instructional halls. It was the first place I'd lived that was Western, not African, and I felt I was entering a new world whose rules were not yet clear to me.

We were taken in to Reverend Harris's study, where the regent introduced me and I stood to shake his hand, the first time I had ever shaken hands with a white man. Reverend Harris was warm and friendly, and treated the regent with great deference. The regent explained that I was being groomed to be a counselor to the king and that he hoped the reverend would take a special interest in me. The reverend nodded, adding that Clarkebury students were required to do manual labor after school hours, and he would arrange for me to work in his garden.

At the end of the interview, the regent bade me good-bye and handed me a pound note for pocket money, the largest amount of money I had ever possessed. I bade him farewell and promised that I would not disappoint him.

Clarkebury was a Thembu college, founded on land given by the great Thembu king Ngubengcuka; as a descendant of Ngubengcuka, I presumed that I would be accorded the same deference at Clarkebury that I had come to expect in Mqhekezweni. But I was painfully mistaken, for I was treated no differently than everyone else. No one knew or even cared that I was a descendant of the illustrious Ngubengcuka. The boarding master received me without a blowing of trumpets and my fellow students did not bow and scrape before me. At Clarkebury, plenty of the boys had distinguished lineages, and I was no longer unique. This was an important lesson, for I suspect I was a bit stuck up in those days. I quickly realized that I had to make my way on the basis of my ability, not my heritage. Most of my classmates could outrun me on the playing field and outthink me in the classroom, and I had a good deal of catching up to do.

Classes commenced the following morning, and along with my fellow students I climbed the steps to the first floor where the classrooms were located. The room itself had a beautifully polished wooden floor. On this first day of classes I was clad in my new boots. I had never worn boots before of any kind, and that first day, I walked like a newly shod horse. I made a terrible racket walking up the steps and almost slipped several times. As I clomped into the classroom, my boots crashing on that shiny wooden floor, I noticed two female students in the first row were watching my lame performance with great amusement. The prettier of the two leaned over to her friend and said loud enough for all to hear: "The country boy is not used to wearing shoes," at which her friend laughed. I was blind with fury and embarrassment.

Her name was Mathona and she was a bit of a smart aleck. That day I vowed never to talk to her. But as my mortification wore off (and I became more adept at walking with boots) I also got to know her, and she was to become my greatest friend at Clarkebury. She was my first true female friend, a woman I met on equal terms with whom I could confide and share secrets. In many ways, she was the model for all my subsequent friendships with women, for with women I found I could let my hair down and confess to weaknesses and fears I would never reveal to another man.

I soon adapted myself to the life at Clarkebury. I participated in sports and games as often as I could, but my performances were no more than mediocre. I played for the love of sport, not the glory, for I received none. We played lawn tennis with homemade wooden rackets and soccer with bare feet on a field of dust.

For the first time, I was taught by teachers who had themselves been properly educated. Several of them held university degrees, which was extremely rare. One day, I was studying with Mathona, and I confided to her my fear that I might not pass my exams in English and history at the end of the year. She told me not to worry because our teacher, Gertrude Ntlabathi, was the first African woman to obtain a B.A. "She is too clever to let us fail," Mathona said. I had not yet learned to feign knowledge that I did not possess, and as I had only a vague idea what a B.A. was, I questioned Mathona. "Oh, yes, of course," she answered. "A B.A. is a very long and difficult book." I did not doubt her.

Another African teacher with a bachelor of arts degree was Ben Mahlasela. We admired him not only because of his academic achievement, but because he was not intimidated by Reverend Harris. Even the white faculty behaved in a servile manner to Reverend Harris, but Mr. Mahlasela would walk into the reverend's office without fear, and sometimes would even fail to remove his hat! He met the reverend on equal terms, disagreeing with him where others simply assented. Though I respected Reverend Harris, I admired the fact that Mr. Mahlasela would not be cowed by him. In those days, a black man with a B.A. was expected to scrape before a white man with a grade-school education. No matter how high a black man advanced, he was still considered inferior to the lowest white man.

Reverend Harris ran Clarkebury with an iron hand and an abiding sense of fairness. Clarkebury functioned more like a military school than a teacher training college. The slightest infractions were swiftly punished. In assemblies, Reverend Harris always wore a forbidding expression and was not given to levity of any kind. When he walked into a room, members of the staff, including white principals of the training and secondary schools, together with the black principal of the industrial school, rose to their feet.

Among students, he was feared more than loved. But in the garden, I saw a different Reverend Harris. Working in Reverend Harris's garden had a double benefit: it planted in me a lifelong love of gardening and growing vegetables, and it helped me get to know the reverend and his family — the first white family with whom I had ever been on intimate terms. In that way, I saw that Reverend Harris had a public face and a private manner that were quite different from one another.

Behind the reverend's mask of severity was a gentle, broad-minded individual who believed fervently in the importance of educating young African men. Often, I found him lost in thought in his garden. I did not disturb him and rarely talked to him, but as an example of a man unselfishly devoted to a good cause, Reverend Harris was an important model for me.

His wife was as talkative as he was taciturn. She was a lovely woman and she would often come into the garden to chat with me. I cannot for the life of me remember what we talked about, but I can still taste the delicious warm scones that she brought out to me in the afternoons.

*   *   *

After my slow and undistinguished start, I managed to get the hang of things, and accelerated my program, completing the junior certificate in two years instead of the usual three. I developed the reputation of having a fine memory, but in fact, I was simply a diligent worker. When I left Clarkebury, I lost track of Mathona. She was a day scholar, and her parents did not have the means to send her for further education. She was an extraordinarily clever and gifted person, whose potential was limited because of her family's meager resources. This was an all too typical South African story. It was not lack of ability that limited my people, but lack of opportunity.

My time at Clarkebury broadened my horizons, yet I would not say that I was an entirely open-minded, unprejudiced young man when I left. I had met students from all over the Transkei, as well as a few from Johannesburg and Basutoland, as Lesotho was then known, some of whom were sophisticated and cosmopolitan in ways that made me feel provincial. Though I emulated them, I never thought it possible for a boy from the countryside to rival them in their worldliness. Yet I did not envy them. Even as I left Clarkebury, I was still, at heart, a Thembu, and I was proud to think and act like one. My roots were my destiny, and I believed that I would become a counselor to the Thembu king, as my guardian wanted. My horizons did not extend beyond Thembuland and I believed that to be a Thembu was the most enviable thing in the world.

6

IN 1937, when I was nineteen, I joined Justice at Healdtown, the Wesleyan College in Fort Beaufort, about one hundred seventy-five miles southwest of Umtata. In the nineteenth century, Fort Beaufort was one of a number of British outposts during the so-called Frontier Wars, in which a steady encroachment of white settlers systematically dispossessed the various Xhosa tribes of their land. Over a century of conflict, many Xhosa warriors achieved fame for their bravery, men like Makhanda, Sandile, and Maqoma, the last two of whom were imprisoned on Robben Island by the British authorities, where they died. By the time of my arrival at Healdtown, there were few signs of the battles of the previous century, except the main one: Fort Beaufort was a white town where once only the Xhosa lived and farmed.

Located at the end of a winding road overlooking a verdant valley, Healdtown was far more beautiful and impressive than Clarkebury. It was, at the time, the largest African school below the equator, with more than a thousand students, both male and female. Its graceful ivy-covered colonial buildings and tree-shaded courtyards gave it the feeling of a privileged academic oasis, which is precisely what it was. Like Clarke-bury, Healdtown was a mission school of the Methodist Church, and provided a Christian and liberal arts education based on an English model.

The principal of Healdtown was Dr. Arthur Wellington, a stout and stuffy Englishman who boasted of his connection to the Duke of Wellington. At the outset of assemblies, Dr. Wellington would walk onstage and say, in his deep bass voice, "I am the descendant of the great Duke of Wellington, aristocrat, statesman, and general, who crushed the Frenchman Napoleon at Waterloo and thereby saved civilization for Europe — and for you, the natives." At this, we would all enthusiastically applaud, each of us profoundly grateful that a descendant of the great Duke of Wellington would take the trouble to educate natives such as ourselves. The educated Englishman was our model; what we aspired to be were "black Englishmen," as we were sometimes derisively called. We were taught — and believed — that the best ideas were English ideas, the best government was English government, and the best men were Englishmen.

Healdtown life was rigorous. First bell was at 6 A.M. We were in the dining hall by 6:40 for a breakfast of dry bread and hot sugar water, watched over by a somber portrait of George VI, the king of England. Those who could afford butter on their bread bought it and stored it in the kitchen. I ate dry toast. At 8 we assembled in the courtyard outside of our dormitory for "observation," standing at attention as the girls arrived from separate dormitories. We remained in class until 12:45, and then had a lunch of samp, sour milk and beans, seldom meat. We then studied until 5 P.M., followed by an hour's break for exercise and dinner, and then study hall from 7 until 9. Lights were out at 9:30.

Healdtown attracted students from all over the country, as well as from the protectorates of Basutoland, Swaziland, and Bechuanaland. Though it was a mostly Xhosa institution, there were also students from different tribes. After school and on weekends, students from the same tribe kept together. Even the members of various Xhosa tribes would gravitate together, such as amaMpondo with amaMpondo, and so on. I adhered to this same pattern, but it was at Healdtown that I made my first Sotho-speaking friend, Zachariah Molete. I remember feeling quite bold at having a friend who was not a Xhosa.

Our zoology teacher, Frank Lebentlele, was also Sotho-speaking and was very popular among the students. Personable and approachable, Frank was not much older than we and mixed freely with students. He even played on the college's first soccer team, where he was a star performer.

But what most amazed us about him was his marriage to a Xhosa girl from Umtata. Marriages between tribes were then extremely unusual. Until then, I had never known of anyone who married outside his tribe. We had been taught that such unions were taboo. But seeing Frank and his wife began to undermine my parochialism and loosen the hold of the tribalism that still imprisoned me. I began to sense my identity as an African, not just a Thembu or even a Xhosa.

Our dormitory had forty beds in it, twenty on either side of a central passageway. The housemaster was the delightful Reverend S. S. Mokitimi, who later became the first African president of the Methodist Church of South Africa. Reverend Mokitimi, who was also Sotho-speaking, was much admired among students as a modern and enlightened fellow who understood our complaints.

Reverend Mokitimi impressed us for another reason: he stood up to Dr. Wellington. One evening, a quarrel broke out between two prefects on the main thoroughfare of the college. Prefects were responsible for preventing disputes, not provoking them. Reverend Mokitimi was called in to make peace. Dr. Wellington, returning from town, suddenly appeared in the midst of this commotion, and his arrival shook us considerably. It was as if a god had descended to solve some humble problem.

Dr. Wellington pulled himself to a great height and demanded to know what was going on. Reverend Mokitimi, the top of whose head did not even reach Dr. Wellington's shoulders, said very respectfully, "Dr. Wellington, everything is under control and I will report to you tomorrow." Undeterred, Dr. Wellington said with some irritation, "No, I want to know what is the matter right now." Reverend Mokitimi stood his ground: "Dr. Wellington, I am the housemaster and I have told you that I will report to you tomorrow, and that is what I will do." We were stunned. We had never seen anyone, much less a black man, stand up to Dr. Wellington, and we waited for an explosion. But Dr. Wellington simply said, "Very well," and left. I realized then that Dr. Wellington was less than a god and Reverend Mokitimi more than a lackey, and that a black man did not have to defer automatically to a white, however senior he was.

Reverend Mokitimi sought to introduce reforms to the college. We all supported his efforts to improve the diet and the treatment of students, including his suggestion that students be responsible for disciplining themselves. But one change worried us, especially students from the countryside. This was Reverend Mokitimi's innovation of having male and female students dine together in hall at Sunday lunch. I was very much against this for the simple reason that I was still inept with knife and fork, and I did not want to embarrass myself in front of these sharp-eyed girls. But Reverend Mokitimi went ahead and organized the meals and every Sunday, I left the hall hungry and depressed.

I did, however, enjoy myself on the playing fields. The quality of sports at Healdtown was far superior to Clarkebury. In my first year, I was not skilled enough to make any of the teams. But during my second year, my friend Locke Ndzamela, Healdtown's champion hurdler, encouraged me to take up a new sport: long-distance running. I was tall and lanky, which Locke said was the ideal build for a long-distance runner. With a few hints from him, I began training. I enjoyed the discipline and solitariness of long-distance running, which allowed me to escape from the hurly-burly of school life. At the same time, I also took up a sport that I seemed less suited for, and that was boxing. I trained in a desultory way, and only years later, when I had put on a few more pounds, did I begin to box in earnest.

During my second year at Healdtown, I was appointed a prefect by Reverend Mokitimi and Dr. Wellington. Prefects have different responsibilities, and the newest prefects have the least desirable chores. In the beginning, I supervised a group of students who worked as window cleaners during our manual work time in the afternoon, and led them to different buildings each day.

I soon graduated to the next level of responsibility, which was night duty. I have never had a problem in staying up through the night, but during one such night I was put in a moral quandary that has remained in my memory. We did not have toilets in the dormitory, but there was an outhouse about one hundred feet behind the residence. On rainy evenings, when a student woke up in the middle of the night, no one wanted to trudge through the grass and mud to the outhouse. Instead, students would stand on the veranda and urinate into the bushes. This practice, however, was strictly against regulations and one job of the prefect was to take down the names of students who indulged in it.

One night, I was on duty when it was pouring rain, and I caught quite a few students — perhaps fifteen or so — relieving themselves from the veranda. Toward dawn, I saw a chap come out, look both ways, and stand at one end of the veranda to urinate. I made my way over to him and announced that he had been caught, whereupon he turned around and I realized that he was a prefect. I was in a predicament. In law and philosophy, one asks, *"Quis custodiet ipsos custodes?"* (Who will guard the guardians themselves?) If the prefect does not obey the rules, how can the students be expected to obey? In effect, the prefect was above the law because he *was* the law, and one prefect was not supposed to report another. But I did not think it fair to avoid reporting the prefect and mark down the fifteen others, so I simply tore up my list and charged no one.

In my final year at Healdtown, an event occurred that for me was like a comet streaking across the night sky. Toward the end of the year, we were informed that the great Xhosa poet Krune Mqhayi was going to visit the school. Mqhayi was actually an *imbongi,* a praise-singer, a kind of oral historian who marks contemporary events and history with poetry that is of special meaning to his people.

The day of his visit was declared a holiday by the school authorities. On the appointed morning, the entire school, including staff members both black and white, gathered in the dining hall, which was where we held school assemblies. There was a stage at one end of the hall and on it a door that led to Dr. Wellington's house. The door itself was nothing special, but we thought of it as Dr. Wellington's door, for no one ever walked through it except Dr. Wellington himself.

Suddenly, the door opened and out walked not Dr. Wellington, but a black man dressed in a leopard-skin kaross and matching hat, who was carrying a spear in either hand. Dr. Wellington followed a moment later, but the sight of a black man in tribal dress coming through that door was electrifying. It is hard to explain the impact it had on us. It seemed to turn the universe upside down. As Mqhayi sat on the stage next to Dr. Wellington, we were barely able to contain our excitement.

But when Mqhayi rose to speak, I confess to being disappointed. I had formed a picture of him in my mind, and in my youthful imagination, I expected a Xhosa hero like Mqhayi to be tall, fierce, and intelligent-looking. But he was not terribly distinguished and, except for his clothing, seemed entirely ordinary. When he spoke in Xhosa, he did so slowly and haltingly, frequently pausing to search for the right word and then stumbling over it when he found it.

At one point, he raised his assegai into the air for emphasis and accidentally hit the curtain wire above him, which made a sharp noise and caused the curtain to sway. The poet looked at the point of his spear and then the curtain wire and, deep in thought, walked back and forth across the stage. After a minute, he stopped walking, faced us, and, newly energized, exclaimed that this incident — the assegai striking the wire — symbolized the clash between the culture of Africa and that of Europe. His voice rose and he said, "The assegai stands for what is glorious and true in African history; it is a symbol of the African as warrior and the African as artist. This metal wire," he said, pointing above, "is an example of Western manufacturing, which is skillful but cold, clever but soulless.

"What I am talking about," he continued, "is not a piece of bone touching a piece of metal, or even the overlapping of one culture and another; what I am talking to you about is the brutal clash between what is indigenous and good, and what is foreign and bad. We cannot allow these foreigners who do not care for our culture to take over our nation. I predict that one day, the forces of African society will achieve a momentous victory over the interloper. For too long, we have succumbed to the false gods of the white man. But we will emerge and cast off these foreign notions."

I could hardly believe my ears. His boldness in speaking of such delicate matters in the presence of Dr. Wellington and other whites seemed utterly astonishing to us. Yet at the same time, it aroused and motivated us, and began to alter my perception of men like Dr. Wellington, whom I had automatically considered my benefactor.

Mqhayi then began to recite his well-known poem in which he apportions the stars in the heavens to the various nations of the world. I had never before heard it. Roving the stage and gesturing with his assegai toward the sky, he said that to the people of Europe — the French, the Germans, the English — "I give you the Milky Way, the largest constellation, for you are a strange people, full of greed and envy, who quarrel over plenty." He allocated certain stars to the Asian nations, and to North and South America. He then discussed Africa and separated the continent into different nations, giving specific constellations to different tribes. He had been dancing about the stage, waving his spear, modulating his voice, and now suddenly he became still, and lowered his voice.

"Now, come you, O House of Xhosa," he said, and slowly began to lower himself so that he was on one knee. "I give unto you the most important and transcendent star, the Morning Star, for you are a proud and powerful people. It is the star for counting the years — the years of manhood." When he spoke this last word, he dropped his head to his chest. We rose to our feet, clapping and cheering. I did not want ever to stop applauding. I felt such intense pride at that point, not as an African, but as a Xhosa; I felt like one of the chosen people.

I was galvanized, but also confused by Mqhayi's performance. He had moved from a more nationalistic, all-encompassing theme of African unity to a more parochial one addressed to the Xhosa people, of whom he was one. As my time at Healdtown was coming to an end, I had many new and sometimes conflicting ideas floating in my head. I was beginning to see that Africans of all tribes had much in common, yet here was the great Mqhayi praising the Xhosa above all; I saw that an African might stand his ground with a white man, yet I was still eagerly seeking benefits from whites, which often required subservience. In a sense, Mqhayi's shift in focus was a mirror of my own mind because I went back and forth between pride in myself as a Xhosa and a feeling of kinship with other Africans. But as I left Healdtown at the end of the year, I saw myself as a Xhosa first and an African second.

7

UNTIL 1960, the University College of Fort Hare, in the municipality of Alice, about twenty miles due east from Healdtown, was the only residential center of higher education for blacks in South Africa. Fort Hare was more than that: it was a beacon for African scholars from all over Southern Central and Eastern Africa. For young black South Africans like myself, it was Oxford and Cambridge, Harvard and Yale, all rolled into one.

The regent was anxious for me to attend Fort Hare and I was gratified to be accepted there. Before I went up to the university, the regent bought me my first suit. Double-breasted and gray, the suit made me feel grown-up and sophisticated; I was twenty-one years old and could not imagine anyone at Fort Hare smarter than I.

I felt that I was being groomed for success in the world. I was pleased that the regent would now have a member of his clan with a university degree. Justice had remained at Healdtown to pursue his junior certificate. He enjoyed playing more than studying, and was an indifferent scholar.

Fort Hare had been founded in 1916 by Scottish missionaries on the site of what was the largest nineteenth-century frontier fort in the eastern Cape. Built on a rocky platform and moated by the winding arc of the Tyume River, Fort Hare was perfectly situated to enable the British to fight the gallant Xhosa warrior Sandile, the last Rharhabe king, who was defeated by the British in one of the final frontier battles in the 1800s.

Fort Hare had only one hundred fifty students, and I already knew a dozen or so of them from Clarkebury and Healdtown. One of them, whom I was meeting for the first time, was K. D. Matanzima. Though K.D. was my nephew according to tribal hierarchy, I was younger and far less senior to him. Tall and slender and extremely confident, K.D. was a third-year student and he took me under his wing. I looked up to him as I had to Justice.

We were both Methodists, and I was assigned to his hostel, known as Wesley House, a pleasant two-story building on the edge of the campus. Under his tutelage, I attended church services with him at nearby Loveday, took up soccer (in which he excelled), and generally followed his advice. The regent did not believe in sending money to his children at school and I would have had empty pockets had not K.D. shared his allowance with me. Like the regent, he saw my future role as counselor to Sabata, and he encouraged me to study law.

Fort Hare, like Clarkebury and Healdtown, was a missionary college. We were exhorted to obey God, respect the political authorities, and be grateful for the educational opportunities afforded to us by the church and the government. These schools have often been criticized for being colonialist in their attitudes and practices. Yet, even with such attitudes, I believe their benefits outweighed their disadvantages. The missionaries built and ran schools when the government was unwilling or unable to do so. The learning environment of the missionary schools, while often morally rigid, was far more open than the racist principles underlying government schools.

Fort Hare was both home and incubator of some of the greatest African scholars the continent has ever known. Professor Z. K. Matthews was the very model of the African intellectual. A child of a miner, Z.K. had been influenced by Booker Washington's autobiography, *Up from Slavery,* which preached success through hard work and moderation. He taught social anthropology and law and bluntly spoke out against the government's social policies.

Fort Hare and Professor D. D. T. Jabavu are virtually synonymous. He was the first member of the staff when the university opened in 1916. Professor Jabavu had been awarded a baccalaureate in English at the University of London, which seemed an impossibly rare feat. Professor Jabavu taught Xhosa, as well as Latin, history, and anthropology. He was an encyclopedia when it came to Xhosa genealogy and told me facts about my father that I had never known. He was also a persuasive spokesman for African rights, becoming the founding president of the All-African Convention in 1936, which opposed legislation in Parliament designed to end the common voters' roll in the Cape.

I recall once traveling from Fort Hare to Umtata by train, riding in the African compartment, which were the only seats open to blacks. The white train conductor came to check our tickets. When he saw that I had gotten on at Alice, he said, "Are you from Jabavu's school?" I nodded yes, whereupon the conductor cheerfully punched my ticket and mumbled something about Jabavu being a fine man.

In my first year, I studied English, anthropology, politics, native administration, and Roman Dutch law. Native administration dealt with the laws relating to Africans and was advisable for anyone who wanted to work in the Native Affairs Department. Although K.D. was counseling me to study law, I had my heart set on being an interpreter or a clerk in the Native Affairs Department. At that time, a career as a civil servant was a glittering prize for an African, the highest that a black man could aspire to. In the rural areas, an interpreter in the magistrate's office was considered second only in importance to the magistrate himself. When, in my second year, Fort Hare introduced an interpreting course taught by a distinguished retired court interpreter, Tyamzashe, I was one of the first students to sign up.

Fort Hare could be a rather elitist place and was not without the hazing common to many institutions of higher learning. Upperclassmen treated their juniors with haughtiness and disdain. When I first arrived on campus, I spotted Gamaliel Vabaza across the central courtyard. He was several years older and I had been with him at Clarkebury. I greeted him warmly, but his response was exceedingly cool and superior, and he made a disparaging remark about the fact that I would be staying in the freshman dormitory. Vabaza then informed me that he was on the House Committee of my dormitory even though, as a senior, he no longer shared the dormitory. I found this odd and undemocratic, but it was the accepted practice.

One night, not long after that, a group of us discussed the fact that no residents or freshmen were represented on the House Committee. We decided that we should depart from tradition and elect a House Committee made up of these two groups. We caucused among ourselves and lobbied all the residents of the house, and within weeks elected our own House Committee, defeating the upperclassmen. I myself was one of the organizers and was elected to this newly constituted committee.

But the upperclassmen were not so easily subdued. They held a meeting at which one of them, Rex Tatane, an eloquent English-speaker, said, "This behavior on the part of freshers is unacceptable. How can we seniors be overthrown by a backward fellow from the countryside like Mandela, a fellow who cannot even speak English properly!" Then he proceeded to mimic the way I spoke, giving me what he perceived to be a Gcaleka accent, at which his own claque laughed heartily. Tatane's sneering speech made us all more resolute. We freshers now constituted the official House Committee and we assigned the seniors the most unpleasant chores, which was a humiliation for them.

The warden of the college, Reverend A. J. Cook, learned of this dispute and called us into his office. We felt we had right on our side and were not prepared to yield. Tatane appealed to the warden to overrule us, and in the midst of his speech, broke down and wept. The warden asked us to modify our stand, but we would not bend. Like most bullies, Tatane had a brittle but fragile exterior. We informed the warden that if he overruled us we would all resign from the House Committee, depriving the committee itself of any integrity or authority. In the end, the warden decided not to intervene. We had remained firm, and we had won. This was one of my first battles with authority, and I felt the sense of power that comes from having right and justice on one's side. I would not be so lucky in the future in my fight against the authorities at the college.

My education at Fort Hare was as much outside as inside the classroom. I was a more active sportsman than I had been at Healdtown. This was due to two factors: I had grown taller and stronger, but more important, Fort Hare was so much smaller than Healdtown, I had less competition. I was able to compete in both soccer and cross-country running. Running taught me valuable lessons. In cross-country competition, training counted more than intrinsic ability, and I could compensate for a lack of natural aptitude with diligence and discipline. I applied this in everything I did. Even as a student, I saw many young men who had great natural ability, but who did not have the self-discipline and patience to build on their endowment.

I also joined the drama society and acted in a play about Abraham Lincoln that was adapted by my classmate Lincoln Mkentane. Mkentane came from a distinguished Transkeian family, and was another fellow whom I looked up to. This was literally true, as he was the only student at Fort Hare taller than I was. Mkentane portrayed his namesake, while I played John Wilkes Booth, Lincoln's assassin. Mkentane's depiction of Lincoln was stately and formal, and his recitation of one of the greatest of all speeches, the Gettysburg Address, won a standing ovation. My part was the smaller one, though I was the engine of the play's moral, which was that men who take great risks often suffer great consequences.

I became a member of the Students Christian Association and taught Bible classes on Sundays in neighboring villages. One of my comrades on these expeditions was a serious young science scholar whom I had met on the soccer field. He came from Pondoland, in the Transkei, and his name was Oliver Tambo. From the start, I saw that Oliver's intelligence was diamond-edged; he was a keen debater and did not accept the platitudes that so many of us automatically subscribed to. Oliver lived in Beda Hall, the Anglican hostel, and though I did not have much contact with him at Fort Hare, it was easy to see that he was destined for great things.

On Sundays, a group of us would sometimes walk into Alice, to have a meal at one of the restaurants in town. The restaurant was run by whites, and in those days it was inconceivable for a black man to walk in the front door, much less take a meal in the dining hall. Instead, we would pool our resources, go round to the kitchen, and order what we wanted.

I not only learned about physics at Fort Hare, but another precise physical science: ballroom dancing. To a crackly old phonograph in the dining hall, we spent hours practicing fox-trots and waltzes, each of us taking turns leading and following. Our idol was Victor Sylvester, the world champion of ballroom dancing, and our tutor was a fellow student, Smallie Siwundla, who seemed a younger version of the master.

In a neighboring village, there was an African dance-hall known as Ntselamanzi, which catered to the cream of local black society and was off-limits to undergraduates. But one night, desperate to practice our steps with the gentler sex, we put on our suits, stole out of our dormitory, and made it to the dance-hall. It was a sumptuous place, and we felt very daring. I noticed a lovely young woman across the floor and politely asked her to dance. A moment later, she was in my arms. We moved well together and I imagined what a striking figure I was cutting on the floor. After a few minutes, I asked her her name. "Mrs. Bokwe," she said softly. I almost dropped her right there and scampered off the floor. I glanced across the floor and saw Dr. Roseberry Bokwe, one of the most respected African leaders and scholars of the time, chatting with his brother-in-law and my professor, Z. K. Matthews. I apologized to Mrs. Bokwe and then sheepishly escorted her to the side under the curious eyes of Dr. Bokwe and Professor Matthews. I wanted to sink beneath the floorboards. I had violated any number of university regulations. But Professor Matthews, who was in charge of discipline at Fort Hare, never said a word to me. He was willing to tolerate what he considered high spirits as long as it was balanced by hard work. I don't think I ever studied more diligently than in the weeks after our evening at Ntselamanzi.

Fort Hare was characterized by a level of sophistication, both intellectual and social, that was new and strange to me. By Western standards, Fort Hare's worldliness may not seem like much, but to a country boy like myself, it was a revelation. I wore pajamas for the first time, finding them uncomfortable in the beginning, but gradually growing used to them. I had never used a toothbrush and toothpaste before; at home, we used ash to whiten our teeth and toothpicks to clean them. The water-flush toilets and hot-water showers were also a novelty to me. I used toilet soap for the first time, not the blue detergent that I had washed with for so many years at home.

Perhaps as a result of all this unfamiliarity, I yearned for some of the simple pleasures that I had known as a boy. I was not alone in this feeling and I joined a group of young men who engaged in secret evening expeditions to the university's farmland, where we built a fire and roasted mealies. We would then sit around, eating the ears of corn and telling tall tales. We did not do this because we were hungry, but out of a need to recapture what was most homelike to us. We boasted about our conquests, our athletic prowess, and how much money we were going to make once we had graduated. Although I felt myself to be a sophisticated young fellow, I was still a country boy who missed country pleasures.

While Fort Hare was a sanctuary removed from the world, we were keenly interested in the progress of World War II. Like my classmates, I was an ardent supporter of Great Britain, and I was enormously excited to learn that the speaker at the university's graduation ceremony at the end of my first year would be England's great advocate in South Africa, the former prime minister Jan Smuts. It was a great honor for Fort Hare to play host to a man acclaimed as a world statesman. Smuts, then deputy prime minister, was campaigning around the country for South Africa to declare war on Germany while the prime minister, J. B. Hertzog, advocated neutrality. I was extremely curious to see a world leader like Smuts from up close.

While Hertzog had, three years earlier, led the drive to remove the last African voters from the common voters roll in the Cape, I found Smuts a sympathetic figure. I cared more that he had helped found the League of Nations, promoting freedom around the world, than the fact that he had repressed freedom at home.

Smuts spoke about the importance of supporting Great Britain against the Germans and the idea that England stood for the same Western values that we, as South Africans, stood for. I remember thinking that his accent in English was almost as poor as mine! Along with my fellow classmates, I heartily applauded him, cheering Smuts's call to do battle for the freedom of Europe, forgetting that we did not have that freedom here in our own land.

Smuts was preaching to the converted at Fort Hare. Each evening, the warden of Wesley House used to review the military situation in Europe, and late at night, we would huddle around an old radio and listen to BBC broadcasts of Winston Churchill's stirring speeches. But even though we supported Smuts's position, his visit provoked much discussion. During one session, a contemporary of mine, Nyathi Khongisa, who was considered an extremely clever fellow, condemned Smuts as a racist. He said that we might consider ourselves "black Englishmen," but the English had oppressed us at the same time they tried to "civilize" us. Whatever the mutual antagonism between Boer and British, he said, the two white groups would unite to confront the black threat. Khongisa's views stunned us and seemed dangerously radical. A fellow student whispered to me

that Nyathi was a member of the African National Congress, an orga-
nization that I had vaguely heard of but knew very little about. Following
South Africa's declaration of war against Germany, Hertzog resigned and
Smuts became prime minister.

During my second year at Fort Hare, I invited my friend Paul Mahabane
to spend the winter holidays with me in the Transkei. Paul was from
Bloemfontein and was well known on campus because his father, the
Reverend Zaccheus Mahabane, had twice been president-general of the
African National Congress. His connection to this organization, about
which I still knew very little, gave him the reputation of a rebel.

One day, during the holiday, Paul and I went to Umtata, the capital
of the Transkei, which then consisted of a few paved streets and some
government buildings. We were standing outside the post office when
the local magistrate, a white man in his sixties, approached Paul and asked
him to go inside to buy him some postage stamps. It was quite common
for any white person to call on any black person to perform a chore. The
magistrate attempted to hand Paul some change, but Paul would not take
it. The magistrate was offended. "Do you know who I am?" he said, his
face turning red with irritation. "It is not necessary to know who you
are," Mahabane said. "I know what you are." The magistrate asked him
exactly what he meant by that. "I mean that you are a rogue!" Paul said
heatedly. The magistrate boiled over and exclaimed, "You'll pay dearly for
this!" and then walked away.

I was extremely uncomfortable with Paul's behavior. While I respected
his courage, I also found it disturbing. The magistrate knew precisely
who I was and I know that if he had asked me rather than Paul, I would
have simply performed the errand and forgotten about it. But I admired
Paul for what he had done, even though I was not yet ready to do the
same thing myself. I was beginning to realize that a black man did not
have to accept the dozens of petty indignities directed at him each day.

After my holiday, I returned to school early in the new year feeling
strong and renewed. I concentrated on my studies, pointing toward examinations in October. In a year's time, I imagined that I would have a
B.A., just like clever Gertrude Ntlabathi. A university degree, I believed,
was a passport not only to community leadership but to financial success.
We had been told over and over again by the principal, Dr. Alexander
Kerr, and Professors Jabavu and Matthews how, as graduates of Fort Hare,
we were the African elite. I believed that the world would be at my feet.

As a B.A., I would finally be able to restore to my mother the wealth
and prestige that she had lost after my father's death. I would build her
a proper home in Qunu, with a garden and modern furniture and fittings.

I would support her and my sisters so that they could afford the things that they had so long been denied. This was my dream and it seemed within reach.

During that year, I was nominated to stand for the Student Representative Council, which was the highest student organization at Fort Hare. I did not know at the time that the events surrounding a student election would create difficulties that would change the course of my life. The SRC elections were held in the final term of the year, while we were in the midst of examination preparations. According to the Fort Hare constitution, the entire student body elected the six members of the SRC. Shortly before the election, a meeting of all students was held to discuss problems and voice our grievances. The students unanimously felt that the diet at Fort Hare was unsatisfactory and that the powers of the SRC needed to be increased so that it would be more than a rubber stamp for the administration. I agreed with both motions, and when a majority of students voted to boycott the elections unless the authorities accepted our demands, I voted with them.

Shortly after this meeting, the scheduled voting took place. The lion's share of students boycotted the election, but twenty-five students, about one-sixth of the student body, showed up and elected six representatives, one of whom was myself. That same day, the six elected in absentia met to discuss these events. We unanimously decided to tender our resignations on the grounds that we supported the boycott and did not enjoy the support of the majority of the students. We then drafted a letter, which we handed to Dr. Kerr.

But Dr. Kerr was clever. He accepted our resignations and then announced that new elections were to be held the next day in the dining hall at suppertime. This would ensure that all the students would be present and that there would be no excuse that the SRC did not have the support of the entire student body. That evening the election was held, as the principal ordered, but only the same twenty-five voted, returning the same six SRC members. It would seem we were back where we started.

Only this time when the six of us met to consider our position, the voting was very different. My five colleagues held to the technical view that we had been elected at a meeting in which all students were present and therefore we could no longer argue that we did not represent the student body. The five believed we should now accept office. I countered that nothing in fact had changed; while all the students had been there, a majority of them had not voted, and it would be morally incorrect to say that we enjoyed their confidence. Since our initial goal was to boycott the election, an action that had the confidence of the student body, our duty was still to abide by that resolution, and not be deterred by some trickery on the part of the principal. Unable to persuade my colleagues, I resigned for the second time, the only one of the six to do so.

The following day I was called in to see the principal. Dr. Kerr, a graduate of Edinburgh University, was virtually the founder of Fort Hare and was a greatly respected man. He calmly reviewed the events of the past few days and then asked me to reconsider my decision to resign. I told him I could not. He told me to sleep on it and give him my final decision the following day. He did warn me, however, that he could not allow his students to act irresponsibly, and he said that if I insisted on resigning, he would be compelled to expel me from Fort Hare.

I was shaken by what he had said and I spent a restless night. I had never had to make such a consequential decision before. That evening, I consulted with my friend and mentor, K.D., who felt that as a matter of principle I was correct to resign, and should not capitulate. I think at the time I feared K.D. even more than I did Dr. Kerr. I thanked K.D. and returned to my room.

Even though I thought what I was doing was morally right, I was still uncertain as to whether it was the correct course. Was I sabotaging my academic career over an abstract moral principle that mattered very little? I found it difficult to swallow the idea that I would sacrifice what I regarded as my obligation to the students for my own selfish interests. I had taken a stand, and I did not want to appear to be a fraud in the eyes of my fellow students. At the same time, I did not want to throw away my career at Fort Hare.

I was in a state of indecision when I reached Dr. Kerr's office the next morning. It was only when he asked me if I had reached a decision, that I actually made up my mind. I told him that I had and that I could not in good conscience serve on the SRC. Dr. Kerr seemed a bit taken aback by my response. He thought for a moment or two before speaking. "Very well," he said. "It is your decision, of course. But I have also given the matter some thought, and I propose to you the following: you may return to Fort Hare next year provided you join the SRC. You have all summer to consider it, Mr. Mandela."

I was, in a way, as surprised by my response as Dr. Kerr. I knew it was foolhardy for me to leave Fort Hare, but at the moment I needed to compromise, I simply could not do so. Something inside me would not let me. While I appreciated Dr. Kerr's position and his willingness to give me another chance, I resented his absolute power over my fate. I should have had every right to resign from the SRC if I wished. This injustice rankled, and at that moment I saw Dr. Kerr less as a benefactor than as a not-altogether-benign dictator. When I left Fort Hare at the end of the year, I was in an unpleasant state of limbo.

8

USUALLY, when I returned to Mqhekezweni I did so with a sense of ease and completion. But not so this time. After passing my exams and returning home, I told the regent what had transpired. He was furious, and could not comprehend the reasons for my actions. He thought it utterly senseless. Without even hearing my full explanation, he bluntly informed me that I would obey the principal's instructions and return to Fort Hare in the fall. His tone invited no discussion. It would have been pointless as well as disrespectful for me to debate my benefactor. I resolved to let the matter rest for a while.

Justice had also returned to Mqhekezweni and we were mightily glad to see one another. No matter how long Justice and I were apart, the brotherly bonds that united us were instantly renewed. Justice had left school the year before and was living in Cape Town.

Within a few days, I resumed my old life at home. I looked after matters for the regent, including his herd and his relations with other chiefs. I did not dwell on the situation at Fort Hare, but life has a way of forcing decisions on those who vacillate. It was an entirely different matter unrelated to my studies that forced my hand.

A few weeks after my homecoming, the regent summoned Justice and me to a meeting. "My children," he said in a very somber tone, "I fear that I am not much longer for this world, and before I journey to the land of the ancestors, it is my duty to see my two sons properly married. I have, accordingly, arranged unions for both of you."

This announcement took us both by surprise, and Justice and I looked at each other with a mixture of shock and helplessness. The two girls came from very good families, the regent said. Justice was to marry the daughter of Khalipa, a prominent Thembu nobleman, and Rolihlahla, as the regent always called me, was to marry the daughter of the local Thembu priest. The marriages, he said, were to take place immediately. *Lobola,* the brideprice or dowry, is normally paid in the form of cattle by the groom's father, and would be paid by the community in Justice's case and in my own by the regent himself.

Justice and I said little. It was not our place to question the regent, and as far as he was concerned, the matter was settled. The regent brooked no discussion: the bride had already been selected and *lobola* paid. It was final.

Justice and I walked out of our interview with our heads down, dazed and dejected. The regent was acting in accordance with Thembu law and custom, and his own motives could not be maligned: he wanted us to be settled during his lifetime. We had always known that the regent had the right to arrange marriages for us, but now it was no longer an abstract possibility. The brides were not fantasies, but flesh-and-blood women whom we actually knew.

With all due respect to the young woman's family, I would be dishonest if I said that the girl the regent had selected for me was my dream bride. Her family was prominent and respected and she was attractive in a rather dignified way, but this young lady, I am afraid, had long been in love with Justice. The regent would not have known this, as parents rarely know the romantic side of their children's lives. My intended partner was undoubtedly no more eager to be burdened with me than I was with her.

At that time, I was more advanced socially than politically. While I would not have considered fighting the political system of the white man, I was quite prepared to rebel against the social system of my own people. Ironically, it was the regent himself who was indirectly to blame for this, for it was the education he had afforded me that had caused me to reject such traditional customs. I had attended college and university with women for years, and had had a small handful of love affairs. I was a romantic, and I was not prepared to have anyone, even the regent, select a bride for me.

I made an appointment with the queen, the regent's wife, and put my case to her. I could not tell her that I did not want the regent to arrange a bride for me under any circumstances, as she would naturally have been unsympathetic. Instead, I devised an alternative plan, and told her that I preferred to marry a girl who was a relative of the queen's, whom I found desirable as a prospective partner. This young lady was in fact very attractive, but I had no idea as to what she thought of me. I said I would marry her as soon as I completed my studies. This was half a ruse, but it was a better alternative than the regent's plan. The queen took my side in the matter, but the regent could not be dissuaded. He had made his decision and he was not going to alter it.

I felt as though he had left me no choice. I could not go through with this marriage, which I considered unfair and ill-advised. At the same time, I believed that I could no longer remain under the regent's guidance if I rejected his plan for me. Justice agreed, and the two of us decided that the only option remaining was to run away, and the only place to run to was Johannesburg.

In retrospect, I realize that we did not exhaust all the options available to us. I could have attempted to discuss the matter with the regent through intermediaries and perhaps come to some settlement within the framework of our tribe and family. I could have appealed to the regent's cousin, Chief Zilindlovu, one of the most enlightened and influential chiefs at the court of Mqhekezweni. But I was young and impatient, and did not see any virtue in waiting. Escape seemed the only course.

We kept our plot secret while we worked out its details. First, we needed an opportunity. The regent believed Justice and I brought out the worst in each other, or at least Justice's penchant for adventures and high-jinks influenced my more conservative disposition. As a result, he took pains to keep us separate as much as possible. When the regent was traveling, he generally asked one of us to accompany him so that we would not be alone together in his absence. More often than not, he took Justice with him, as he liked me to remain in Mqhekezweni to look after his affairs. But we learned that the regent was preparing to leave for a full week to attend a session of the Bungha, the Transkeian legislative assembly, without either of us, and we decided this was the ideal time to steal away. We resolved that we would depart for Johannesburg shortly after the regent left for the Bungha.

I had few clothes and we managed to get whatever we had in a single suitcase. The regent left early on Monday, and by late morning we were ready to go. But just as we were preparing to leave, the regent unexpectedly returned. We saw his car drive in and we ran into the garden and hid among the mealie stalks. The regent came into the house and his first question was "Where are those boys?" Someone replied, "Oh, they are around." But the regent was suspicious, and was not content with that explanation. He had returned, he said, because he had forgotten to take his Epsom salts. He looked around a bit, and then seemed satisfied. I realized that he must have had some kind of premonition because he could easily buy Epsom salts in town. When his car disappeared behind the hills, we were on our way.

We had almost no money between us, but that morning, we went to see a local trader and made a deal to sell him two of the regent's prize oxen. The trader assumed that we were selling the animals at the regent's behest, and we did not correct him. He paid us a very good price, and with that money we hired a car to take us to the local train station where we would catch a train to Johannesburg.

All seemed to be going smoothly, but unbeknown to us, the regent had driven to the local train station and instructed the manager that if two boys fitting our description came to buy tickets for Johannesburg, the manager must turn them away because we were not to leave the

Transkei. We arrived at the station only to find that the manager would not sell us tickets. We asked him why and he said, "Your father has been here and says you are trying to run away." We were stunned by this, and dashed back to our hired car and told him to drive to the next station. It was nearly fifty miles away, and it took us more than an hour to get there.

We managed to get on a train there but it only went as far as Queenstown. In the 1940s, traveling for an African was a complicated process. All Africans over the age of sixteen were compelled to carry "Native passes" issued by the Native Affairs Department and were required to show that pass to any white policeman, civil servant, or employer. Failure to do so could mean arrest, trial, a jail sentence or fine. The pass stated where the bearer lived, who his chief was, and whether he had paid the annual poll tax, which was a tax levied only on Africans. Later, the pass took the form of a booklet or "reference book," as it was known, containing detailed information that had to be signed by one's employer every month.

Justice and I had our passes in order, but for an African to leave his magisterial district and enter that of another for the purpose of working or living, he needed traveling documents, a permit, and a letter from his employer or, as in our case, his guardian — none of which we had. Even at the best of times, when one had all these documents, a police officer might harass you because one was missing a signature or had an incorrect date. Not having any of them was extremely risky. Our plan was to disembark in Queenstown, make our way to the house of a relative, and then make arrangements for the necessary documents. This was also an ill-considered plan, but we came in for a bit of luck because at the house in Queenstown we accidentally met Chief Mpondombini, a brother of the regent's, who was fond of Justice and myself.

Chief Mpondombini greeted us warmly and we explained that we needed the requisite travel documents from the local magistrate. We lied about why we required them, claiming that we were on an errand for the regent. Chief Mpondombini was a retired interpreter from the Native Affairs Department and knew the chief magistrate well. He had no reason to doubt our story and not only escorted us to the magistrate, but vouched for us and explained our predicament. After listening to the chief, the magistrate rapidly made out the necessary traveling documents and affixed the official stamp. Justice and I looked at each other and smiled in complicity. But just as the magistrate was handing over the documents to us, he recalled something and said that, as a matter of courtesy, he ought to inform the chief magistrate of Umtata, in whose jurisdiction we fell. This made us uneasy, but we stayed seated in his office. The magistrate cranked the telephone and reached his colleague in Umtata. As luck would have it, the regent was just then paying a call on the chief magistrate of Umtata and was in his very office.

As our magistrate was explaining our situation to the chief magistrate of Umtata, the latter gentleman said something like, "Oh, their father just happens to be right here," and then put the regent on the telephone. When the magistrate informed the regent what we were requesting, the regent exploded. "Arrest those boys!" he shouted, loud enough that we could hear his voice through the receiver. "Arrest them and bring them back here immediately!" The chief magistrate put down the phone. He regarded us angrily. "You boys are thieves and liars," he told us. "You have presumed upon my good offices and then deceived me. Now, I am going to have you arrested."

I immediately rose to our defense. From my studies at Fort Hare, I had a little knowledge of law and I put it to use. I said that we had told him lies, that was true. But we had committed no offense and violated no laws, and we could not be arrested simply on the recommendation of a chief, even if he happened to be our father. The magistrate backed off and did not arrest us, but told us to leave his office and never to darken his door again.

Chief Mpondombini was also annoyed, and left us to our own devices. Justice remembered that he had a friend in Queenstown named Sidney Nxu who was working in the office of a white attorney. We went to see this fellow, explained our situation, and he told us that the mother of the attorney he worked for was driving into Johannesburg and he would see if she would offer us a lift. He told us that his mother would give us a ride if we paid a fee of fifteen pounds sterling. This was a vast sum, far more than the cost of a train ticket. The fee virtually depleted our savings, but we had no choice. We decided to risk getting our passes stamped and the correct travel documents once we were in Johannesburg.

We left early the following morning. In those days, it was customary for blacks to ride in the back seat of the car if a white was driving. The two of us sat in that fashion, with Justice directly behind the woman. Justice was a friendly, exuberant person and immediately began chatting to me. This made the old woman extremely uncomfortable. She had obviously never been in the company of a black who had no inhibitions around whites. After only a few miles, she told Justice that she wanted him to switch seats with me, so that she could keep an eye on him, and for the rest of the journey she watched him like a hawk. But after a while, Justice's charm worked on her and she would occasionally laugh at something he said.

*   *   *

At about ten o'clock that evening, we saw before us, glinting in the distance, a maze of lights that seemed to stretch in all directions. Electricity, to me, had always been a novelty and a luxury, and here was a vast landscape of electricity, a city of light. I was terribly excited to see the city I had been hearing about since I was a child. Johannesburg had always been depicted as a city of dreams, a place where one could transform oneself from a poor peasant to a wealthy sophisticate, a city of danger and of opportunity. I remembered the stories that Banabakhe had told us at circumcision school, of buildings so tall you could not see the tops, of crowds of people speaking languages you had never heard of, of sleek motorcars and beautiful women and dashing gangsters. It was eGoli, the city of gold, where I would soon be making my home.

On the outskirts of the city the traffic became denser. I had never seen so many cars on the road at one time — even in Umtata, there were never more than a handful of cars and here there were thousands. We drove around the city, rather than through it, but I could see the silhouette of the tall, blocky buildings, even darker against the dark night sky. I looked at great billboards by the side of the road, advertising cigarettes and candy and beer. It all seemed tremendously glamorous.

Soon we were in an area of stately mansions, even the smallest of which was bigger than the regent's palace, with grand front lawns and tall iron gates. This was the suburb where the old lady's daughter lived, and we pulled into the long driveway of one of these beautiful homes. Justice and I were dispatched to the servants' wing, where we were to spend the night. We thanked the old lady, and then crawled off to sleep on the floor. But the prospect of Johannesburg was so exciting to me that I felt like I slept on a beautiful feather bed that night. The possibilities seemed infinite. I had reached the end of what seemed like a long journey, but was actually the very beginning of a much longer and more trying journey that would test me in ways that I could not then have imagined.

Part Two

JOHANNESBURG

9

IT WAS DAWN when we reached the offices of Crown Mines, which were located on the plateau of a great hill overlooking the still dark metropolis. Johannesburg was a city built up around the discovery of gold on the Witwatersrand in 1886, and Crown Mines was the largest gold mine in the city of gold. I expected to see a grand building like the government offices in Umtata, but the Crown Mine offices were rusted tin shanties on the face of the mine.

There is nothing magical about a gold mine. Barren and pockmarked, all dirt and no trees, fenced in all sides, a gold mine resembles a war-torn battlefield. The noise was harsh and ubiquitous: the rasp of shaft-lifts, the jangling power drills, the distant rumble of dynamite, the barked orders. Everywhere I looked I saw black men in dusty overalls looking tired and bent. They lived on the grounds in bleak, single-sex barracks that contained hundreds of concrete bunks separated from each other by only a few inches.

Gold-mining on the Witwatersrand was costly because the ore was low grade and deep under the earth. Only the presence of cheap labor in the form of thousands of Africans working long hours for little pay with no rights made gold-mining profitable for the mining houses — white-owned companies that became wealthy beyond the dreams of Croesus on the backs of the African people. I had never seen such enterprise before, such great machines, such methodical organization, and such backbreaking work. It was my first sight of South African capitalism at work, and I knew I was in for a new kind of education.

We went straight to the chief *induna*, or headman. His name was Piliso, a tough old fellow who had seen life at its most pitiless. Piliso knew about Justice, as the regent had sent a letter months before making arrangements for him to receive a clerical job, the most coveted and respected job in the mine compound. I, however, was unknown to him. Justice explained that I was his brother.

"I was expecting only Justice," Piliso responded. "Your father's letter mentions nothing about a brother." He looked me over rather skeptically. But Justice pleaded with him, saying it had simply been an oversight, and that the regent had already posted a letter about me. Piliso's crusty exterior hid a sympathetic side, and he took me on as a mine policeman, saying that if I worked out, he would give me a clerical post in three months' time.

The regent's word carried weight at Crown Mines. This was true of all chiefs in South Africa. Mining officials were eager to recruit labor in the countryside, and the chiefs had authority over the men they needed. They wanted the chiefs to encourage their subjects to come to the Reef. The chiefs were treated with great deference; the mining houses provided special lodgings for them whenever they came to visit. One letter from the regent was enough to secure a man a good job, and Justice and I were treated with extra care because of our connection. We were to be given free rations, sleeping quarters, and a small salary. We did not stay in the barracks that first night. For our first few days, Piliso, out of courtesy to the regent, invited Justice and me to stay with him.

Many of the miners, especially those from Thembuland, treated Justice as a chief and greeted him with gifts of cash, the custom when a chief visited a mine. Most of these men were in the same hostel; miners were normally housed according to tribe. The mining companies preferred such segregation because it prevented different ethnic groups from uniting around a common grievance and reinforced the power of the chiefs. The separation often resulted in factional fights between different ethnic groups and clans, which the companies did not effectively discourage.

Justice shared some of his booty with me and gave me a few extra pounds as a bonus. For those first few days, my pockets jingling with newfound riches, I felt like a millionaire. I was beginning to think I was a child of fortune, that luck was shining on me, and that if I had not wasted precious time studying at college I could have been a wealthy man by then. Once again, I did not see that fate was busy setting snares around me.

I started work immediately as a night watchman. I was given a uniform, a new pair of boots, a helmet, a flashlight, a whistle, and a knobkerrie, which is a long wooden stick with a heavy ball of wood at one end. The job was a simple one: I waited at the compound's entrance next to the sign that read, "BEWARE: NATIVES CROSSING HERE," and checked the credentials of all those entering and leaving. For the first few nights, I patrolled the grounds of the compound without incident. I did challenge a rather drunken miner late one evening, but he meekly showed his pass and retired to his hostel.

Flushed with our success, Justice and I boasted of our cleverness to a friend of ours whom we knew from home, who was also working at the mines. We explained how we had run away and tricked the regent in the bargain. Although we swore this fellow to secrecy, he went straightaway to the *induna* and revealed our secret. A day later, Piliso called us in and the first question he asked Justice was: Where is the permission from the regent for your brother? Justice said that he had already explained that the regent had posted it. Piliso was not mollified by this, and we sensed that something was wrong. He then reached inside his desk and produced a telegram. "I have had a communication from the regent," he said in a serious tone of voice, and handed it to us. It contained a single sentence: "SEND BOYS HOME AT ONCE."

Piliso then vented his anger on us, accusing us of lying to him. He said we had presumed on his hospitality and the good name of the regent. He told us that he was taking up a collection among the miners to put us on a train back to the Transkei. Justice protested against going home, saying that we simply wanted to work at the mine, and that we could make decisions for ourselves. But Piliso turned a deaf ear. We felt ashamed and humiliated, but we left his office determined not to return to the Transkei.

We rapidly hatched another plan. We went to see Dr. A. B. Xuma, an old friend of the regent's who was the president-general of the African National Congress. Dr. Xuma was from the Transkei, and was an extremely well-respected physician.

Dr. Xuma was pleased to see us, and politely questioned us about family matters in Mqhekezweni. We told him a series of half-truths about why we were in Johannesburg, and that we greatly desired jobs in the mines. Dr. Xuma said he would be glad to assist us, and immediately telephoned a Mr. Wellbeloved at the Chamber of Mines, a powerful organization representing the mining houses and exerting monopoly control over the hiring of mine labor. Dr. Xuma told Mr. Wellbeloved what splendid fellows we were and how he should find places for us. We thanked Dr. Xuma and went off to see Mr. Wellbeloved.

Mr. Wellbeloved was a white man whose office was grander than any I had ever seen; his desk seemed as wide as a football field. We met him in the company of a mine boss named Festile, and we told him the same fabrications that we had told Dr. Xuma. Mr. Wellbeloved was impressed with my not-entirely-truthful explanation that I had come to Johannesburg to continue my studies at the University of the Witwatersrand. "Well, boys," he said, "I will put you in touch with the manager of Crown Mines, a Mr. Piliso, and I will tell him to give you jobs as clerks." He said he had worked with Mr. Piliso for thirty years and in all that time, Piliso had never lied to him. Justice and I squirmed at this but said nothing. Despite some misgivings, we naively felt we had the upper hand with Mr. Piliso now that we had his boss, Mr. Wellbeloved, on our side.

We returned to the Crown Mine offices, where the white compound manager was considerate to us because of the letter we presented from Mr. Wellbeloved. Just then, Mr. Piliso passed by the office, saw us, and then stormed in. "You boys! You've come back!" he said with irritation. "What are you doing here?"

Justice was calm. "We've been sent by Mr. Wellbeloved," he replied, his tone bordering on defiance. Mr. Piliso considered this for a moment. "Did you tell him that you ran away from your father?" Piliso then countered. Justice was silent.

"You'll never be employed in any mine that I run!" he yelled. "Now, get out of my sight!" Justice waved Wellbeloved's letter. "I don't give a damn about a letter!" Piliso said. I looked to the white manager, hoping that he might overrule Piliso, but he was as still as a statue and seemed as intimidated as we were. We had no rejoinder for Piliso, and we sheepishly walked out of the office, feeling even more humbled than we had on the first occasion.

Our fortunes were now reversed. We were without jobs, without prospects, and without a place to stay. Justice knew various people in Johannesburg, and he went into town to investigate a place for us to stay. In the meantime, I was to fetch our suitcase, which was still at Piliso's, and then meet Justice at George Goch, a small township in southern Johannesburg, later that day.

I prevailed upon a fellow named Bikitsha, whom I knew from home, to help me carry the suitcase to the front gate. A watchman at the gate stopped us both and said he needed to search the bag. Bikitsha protested, asserting there was no contraband in the suitcase. The watchman replied that a search was routine, and he looked through the bag in a cursory way, not even disturbing the clothing. As the watchman was closing it, Bikitsha, who was a cocky fellow, said, "Why do you make trouble? I told you there was nothing there." These words irked the watchman, who then decided to search the case with a fine-toothed comb. I became increasingly nervous as he opened every compartment and probed every pocket. He then reached all the way to the bottom of the case and found the very thing I prayed he would not: a loaded revolver wrapped inside some of my clothing.

He turned to my friend and said, "You are under arrest." He then blew his whistle, which brought a team of guards over to us. My friend looked at me with a mixture of consternation and confusion as they led him away to the local police station. I followed them at a distance, considering my options. The gun, an old revolver, had been my father's and he had left it to me when he died. I had never used it, but as a precaution, I had brought it with me to the city.

I could not let my friend take the blame in my stead. Not long after he had entered the police station, I went inside and asked to see the officer in charge. I was taken to him and spoke as directly and forthrightly as I could: "Sir, that is my gun that was found in my friend's suitcase. I inherited it from my father in the Transkei and I brought it here because I was afraid of gangsters." I explained that I was a student from Fort Hare, and that I was only in Johannesburg temporarily. The officer in charge softened a bit as I spoke, and said that he would release my friend straightaway. He said he would have to charge me for possession of the gun, though he would not arrest me, and that I should appear in court first thing on Monday morning to answer the charge. I was grateful, and told him that I would certainly appear in court on Monday. I did go to court that Monday and received only a nominal fine.

In the meantime, I had arranged to stay with one of my cousins, Garlick Mbekeni, in George Goch Township. Garlick was a hawker who sold clothing, and had a small boxlike house. He was a friendly, solicitous man, and after I had been there a short while, I told him that my real aspiration was to be a lawyer. He commended me for my ambition and said he would think about what I had said.

A few days later, Garlick told me that he was taking me to see "one of our best people in Johannesburg." We rode the train to the office of an estate agent on Market Street, a dense and rollicking thoroughfare with trams groaning with passengers, sidewalk vendors on every street, and a sense that wealth and riches were just around the next corner.

Johannesburg in those days was a combination frontier town and modern city. Butchers cut meat on the street next to office buildings. Tents were pitched beside bustling shops and women hung out their washing next door to high-rise buildings. Industry was energized due to the war effort. In 1939, South Africa, a member of the British Commonwealth, had declared war on Nazi Germany. The country was supplying men and goods to the war effort. Demand for labor was high, and Johannesburg became a magnet for Africans from the countryside seeking work. Between 1941, when I arrived, and 1946, the number of Africans in the city would double. Every morning, the township felt larger than it had the day before. Men found jobs in factories and housing in the "non-European townships" of Newclare, Martindale, George Goch, Alexandra, Sophiatown, and the Western Native Township, a prisonlike compound of a few thousand matchbox houses on treeless ground.

Garlick and I sat in the estate agent's waiting room while a pretty African receptionist announced our presence to her boss in the inner office. After she relayed the message, her nimble fingers danced across the keyboard as she typed a letter. I had never in my life seen an African typist before, much less a female one. In the few public and business offices that I had visited in Umtata and Fort Hare, the typists had always been white and male. I was particularly impressed with this young woman because those white male typists had only used two slow-moving fingers to peck out their letters.

She soon ushered us into the inner office, where I was introduced to a man who looked to be in his late twenties, with an intelligent and kindly face, light in complexion, and dressed in a double-breasted suit. Despite his youth, he seemed to me an experienced man of the world. He was from the Transkei, but spoke English with a rapid urban fluency. To judge from his well-populated waiting room and his desk piled high with papers, he was a busy and successful man. But he did not rush us and seemed genuinely interested in our errand. His name was Walter Sisulu.

Sisulu ran a real estate office that specialized in properties for Africans. In the 1940s, there were still quite a few areas where freehold properties could be purchased by Africans, small holdings located in such places as Alexandra and Sophiatown. In some of these areas, Africans had owned their own homes for several generations. The rest of the African areas were municipal townships containing matchbox houses for which the residents paid rent to the Johannesburg City Council.

Sisulu's name was becoming prominent as both a businessman and a local leader. He was already a force in the community. He paid close attention as I explained about my difficulties at Fort Hare, my ambition to be a lawyer, and how I intended to register at the University of South Africa to finish my degree by correspondence course. I neglected to tell him the circumstances of my arrival in Johannesburg. When I had finished, he leaned back in his chair and pondered what I had said. Then, he looked me over one more time, and said that there was a white lawyer with whom he worked named Lazar Sidelsky, who he believed to be a decent and progressive fellow. Sidelsky, he said, was interested in African education. He would talk to Sidelsky about taking me on as an articled clerk.

In those days, I believed that proficiency in English and success in business were the direct result of high academic achievements and I assumed as a matter of course that Sisulu was a university graduate. I was greatly surprised to learn from my cousin after I left the office that Walter Sisulu had never gone past Standard VI. It was another lesson from Fort Hare that I had to unlearn in Johannesburg. I had been taught that to have a B.A. meant to be a leader, and to be a leader one needed a B.A. But in Johannesburg I found that many of the most outstanding leaders had never been to university at all. Even though I had done all the courses in English that were required for a B.A., my English was neither as fluent nor as eloquent as many of the men I met in Johannesburg who had not even received a school degree.

*   *   *

After a brief time staying with my cousin, I arranged to move in with Reverend J. Mabutho of the Anglican Church at his home on Eighth Avenue in Alexandra Township. Reverend Mabutho was a fellow Thembu, a friend of my family's, and a generous, God-fearing man. His wife, whom we called Gogo, was warm, affectionate, and a splendid cook who was liberal with her helpings. As a Thembu who knew my family, Reverend Mabutho felt responsible for me. "Our ancestors have taught us to share," he once told me.

But I had not learned from my experience at Crown Mines, for I did not tell Reverend Mabutho about the circumstances of my leaving the Transkei. My omission had unhappy consequences. A few days after I had moved in with the Mabuthos, I was having tea with them when a visitor arrived. Unfortunately, their friend was Mr. Festile, the *induna* at the Chamber of Mines who had been present when Justice and I met with Mr. Wellbeloved. Mr. Festile and I greeted each other in a way that suggested we knew one another, and though nothing was said of our previous meeting, the next day Reverend Mabutho took me aside and made it clear that I could no longer remain under their roof.

I cursed myself for not having told the whole truth. I had become so used to my deceptions that I lied even when I did not have to. I am sure that Reverend Mabutho would not have minded, but when he learned of my circumstances from Festile, he felt deceived. In my brief stay in Johannesburg, I had left a trail of mistruths, and in each case, the falsehood had come back to haunt me. At the time, I felt that I had no alternative. I was frightened and inexperienced, and I knew that I had not gotten off on the right foot in my new life. In this instance, Reverend Mabutho took pity on me and found me accommodation with his next-door neighbors, the Xhoma family.

Mr. Xhoma was one of an elite handful of African landowners in Alexandra. His house — 46, Seventh Avenue — was small, particularly as he had six children, but it was pleasant, with a veranda and a tiny garden. In order to make ends meet, Mr. Xhoma, like so many other residents of Alexandra, rented rooms to boarders. He had built a tin-roofed room at the back of his property, no more than a shack, with a dirt floor, no heat, no electricity, no running water. But it was a place of my own and I was happy to have it.

In the meantime, on Walter's recommendation, Lazar Sidelsky had agreed to take me on as a clerk while I completed my B.A. degree. The firm of Witkin, Sidelsky and Eidelman was one of the largest law firms in the city and handled business from blacks as well as whites. In addition to studying law and passing certain exams, in order to qualify as an attorney in South Africa one had to undergo several years of apprenticeship to a practicing lawyer, which is known as serving articles. But in order for me to become articled, I first had to complete my B.A. degree. To that end, I was studying at night with UNISA, short for the University of South Africa, a respected educational institution that offered credits and degrees by correspondence.

In addition to trying conventional law cases, Witkin, Sidelsky and Eidelman oversaw real estate transactions for African customers. Walter brought the firm clients who needed a mortgage. The firm would handle their loan applications, and then take a commission, which it would split with the real estate agent. In fact, the law firm would take the lion's share of the money, leaving only a pittance for the African real estate agent. Blacks were given the crumbs from the table, and had no option but to accept them.

Even so, the law firm was far more liberal than most. It was a Jewish firm, and in my experience, I have found Jews to be more broad-minded than most whites on issues of race and politics, perhaps because they themselves have historically been victims of prejudice. The fact that Lazar Sidelsky, one of the firm's partners, would take on a young African as an articled clerk — something almost unheard of in those days — was evidence of that liberalism.

Mr. Sidelsky, whom I came to respect greatly and who treated me with enormous kindness, was a graduate of the University of the Witwatersrand and was in his mid-thirties when I joined the firm. He was involved in African education, donating money and time to African schools. A slender, courtly man, with a pencil mustache, he took a genuine interest in my welfare and future, preaching the value and importance of education — for me individually and for Africans in general. Only mass education, he used to say, would free my people, arguing that an educated man could not be oppressed because he could think for himself. He told me over and over again that becoming a successful attorney and thereby a model of achievement for my people was the most worthwhile path I could follow.

I met most of the firm's staff on my first day in the office, including the one other African employee, Gaur Radebe, with whom I shared an office. Ten years my senior, Gaur was a clerk, interpreter, and messenger. He was a short, stocky, muscular man, fluent in English, Sotha, and Zulu, expressing himself in all of them with precision, humor, and confidence. He had strong opinions and even stronger arguments to back them up and was a well-known figure in black Johannesburg.

That first morning at the firm, a pleasant young white secretary, Miss Lieberman, took me aside and said, "Nelson, we have no color bar here at the law firm." She explained that at midmorning, the tea-man arrived in the front parlor with tea on a tray and a number of cups. "In honor of your arrival, we have purchased two new cups for you and Gaur," she said. "The secretaries take cups of tea to the principals, but you and Gaur will take your own tea, just as we do. I will call you when the tea comes, and then you can take your tea in the new cups." She added that I should convey this message to Gaur. I was grateful for her ministrations, but I knew that the "two new cups" she was so careful to mention were evidence of the color bar that she said did not exist. The secretaries might share tea with two Africans, but not the cups with which to drink it.

When I told Gaur what Miss Lieberman had said, I noticed his expression change as he listened, just as you can see a mischievous idea enter the head of a child. "Nelson," he said, "at teatime, don't worry about anything. Just do as I do." At eleven o'clock, Miss Lieberman informed us that tea had arrived. In front of the secretaries and some of the other members of the firm, Gaur went over to the tea tray and ostentatiously ignored the two new cups, selecting instead one of the old ones, and proceeded to put in generous portions of sugar, milk, and then tea. He stirred his cup slowly, and then stood there drinking it in a very self-satisfied way. The secretaries stared at Gaur and then Gaur nodded to me, as if to say, "It is your turn, Nelson."

For a moment, I was in a quandary. I neither wanted to offend the secretaries nor alienate my new colleague, so I settled on what seemed to me the most prudent course of action: I declined to have any tea at all. I said I was not thirsty. I was then just twenty-three years old and just finding my feet as a man, as a resident of Johannesburg, and as an employee of a white firm, and I saw the middle path as the best and most reasonable one. Thereafter, at teatime, I would go to the small kitchen in the office and take my tea there in solitude.

The secretaries were not always so thoughtful. Some time later, when I was more experienced at the firm, I was dictating some information to a white secretary when a white client whom she knew came into the office. She was embarrassed, and to demonstrate that she was not taking dictation from an African, she took a sixpence from her purse and said stiffly, "Nelson, please go out and get me some hair shampoo from the chemist." I left the room and got her shampoo.

In the beginning, my work at the firm was quite rudimentary. I was a combination of a clerk and messenger. I would find, arrange, and file documents and serve or deliver papers around Johannesburg. Later, I would draw up contracts for some of the firm's African clients. Yet, no matter how small the chore, Mr. Sidelsky would explain to me what it was for and why I was doing it. He was a patient and generous teacher, and sought to impart not only the details of the law but the philosophy behind it. His view of the law was broad rather than narrow, for he believed that it was a tool that could be used to change society.

While Mr. Sidelsky imparted his views of the law, he warned me against politics. Politics, he said, brings out the worst in men. It was the source of trouble and corruption, and should be avoided at all costs. He painted a frightening picture of what would happen to me if I drifted into politics, and counseled me to avoid the company of men he regarded as troublemakers and rabble-rousers, specifically, Gaur Radebe and Walter Sisulu. While Mr. Sidelsky respected their abilities, he abhorred their politics.

Gaur was indeed a "troublemaker," in the best sense of that term, and was an influential man in the African community in ways that Mr. Sidelsky did not know or suspect. He was a member of the Advisory Board in the Western Native Township, an elected body of four local people who dealt with the authorities on matters relating to the townships. While it had little power, the board had great prestige among the people. Gaur was also, as I soon discovered, a prominent member of both the ANC and the Communist Party.

Gaur was his own man. He did not treat our employers with exaggerated courtesy, and often chided them for their treatment of Africans. "You people stole our land from us," he would say, "and enslaved us. Now you are making us pay through the nose to get the worst pieces of it back." One day, after I returned from doing an errand and entered Mr. Sidelsky's office, Gaur turned to him and said, "Look, you sit there like a lord whilst my chief runs around doing errands for you. The situation should be reversed, and one day it will, and we will dump all of you into the sea." Gaur then left the room, and Mr. Sidelsky just shook his head ruefully.

Gaur was an example of a man without a B.A. who seemed infinitely better educated than the fellows who left Fort Hare with glittering degrees. Not only was he more knowledgeable, he was bolder and more confident. Although I intended to finish my degree and enter law school, I learned from Gaur that a degree was not in itself a guarantee of leadership and that it meant nothing unless one went out into the community to prove oneself.

I was not the only articled clerk at Witkin, Sidelsky and Eidelman. A fellow about my age named Nat Bregman started work shortly before I had. Nat was bright, pleasant, and thoughtful. He seemed entirely color-blind and became my first white friend. He was a deft mimic and could do fine imitations of the voices of Jan Smuts, Franklin Roosevelt, and Winston Churchill. I often sought his counsel on matters of law and office procedure, and he was unfailingly helpful.

One day, at lunchtime, we were sitting in the office and Nat took out a packet of sandwiches. He removed one sandwich and said, "Nelson, take hold of the other side of the sandwich." I was not sure why he asked me to do this, but as I was hungry, I decided to oblige. "Now, pull," he said. I did so, and the sandwich split roughly in two. "Now, eat," he said. As I was chewing, Nat said, "Nelson, what we have just done symbolizes the philosophy of the Communist Party: to share everything we have." He told me he was a member of the party and explained the rudiments of what the party stood for. I knew that Gaur was a member of the party, but he had never proselytized for it. I listened to Nat that day, and on many subsequent occasions when he preached the virtues of communism and tried to persuade me to join the party. I heard him out, asked questions, but did not join. I was not inclined to join any political organization, and the advice of Mr. Sidelsky was still ringing in my ears. I was also quite religious, and the party's antipathy to religion put me off. But I appreciated half that sandwich.

I enjoyed Nat's company and we often went places together, including a number of lectures and CP meetings. I went primarily out of intellectual curiosity. I was just becoming aware of the history of racial oppression in my own country, and saw the struggle in South Africa as purely racial. But the party saw South Africa's problems through the lens of the class struggle. To them, it was a matter of the Haves oppressing the Have-nots. This was intriguing to me, but did not seem particularly relevant to present-day South Africa. It may have been applicable to Germany or England or Russia, but it did not seem appropriate for the country that I knew. Even so, I listened and learned.

Nat invited me to a number of parties where there was a mixture of whites, Africans, Indians, and Coloureds. The get-togethers were arranged by the party, and most of the guests were party members. I remember being anxious the first time I went, mainly because I did not think I had the proper attire. At Fort Hare, we were taught to wear a tie and jacket to a social function of any kind. Though my wardrobe was severely limited, I managed to find a tie to wear to the party.

I discovered a lively and gregarious group of people who did not seem to pay attention to color at all. It was one of the first mixed gatherings I had ever attended, and I was far more of an observer than a participant. I felt extremely shy, wary of committing a faux pas, and unequipped to participate in the high-flown and rapid-fire conversations. My thoughts seemed undeveloped by comparison to the sophisticated dialogue around me.

At one point in the evening, I was introduced to Michael Harmel, who I was told had a master's degree in English from Rhodes University. I was impressed with his degree, but when I met him, I thought to myself, "This chap has an M.A. and he is not even wearing a tie!" I just could not reconcile this discrepancy. Later, Michael and I became friends, and I came to admire him greatly, in no small measure because he rejected so many of the rather foolish conventions I once embraced. He was not only a brilliant writer, but was so committed to communism that he lived in a manner no different from an African.

10

LIFE IN ALEXANDRA was exhilarating and precarious. Its atmosphere was alive, its spirit adventurous, its people resourceful. Although the township did boast some handsome buildings, it could fairly be described as a slum, living testimony to the neglect of the authorities. The roads were unpaved and dirty, and filled with hungry, undernourished children scampering around half-naked. The air was thick with the smoke from coal fires in tin braziers and stoves. A single water tap served several houses. Pools of stinking, stagnant water full of maggots collected by the side of the road. Alexandra was known as "Dark City" for its complete absence of electricity. Walking home at night was perilous, for there were no lights, the silence pierced by yells, laughter, and occasional gunfire. So different from the darkness of the Transkei, which seemed to envelop one in a welcome embrace.

The township was desperately overcrowded; every square foot was occupied either by a ramshackle house or a tin-roofed shack. As so often happens in desperately poor places, the worst elements came to the fore. Life was cheap; the gun and the knife ruled at night. Gangsters — known as *tsotsis* — carrying flick-knives or switchblades were plentiful and prominent; in those days they emulated American movie stars and wore fedoras and double-breasted suits and wide, colorful ties. Police raids were a regular feature of life. The police routinely arrested masses of people for pass violations, possession of liquor, and failure to pay the poll tax. On almost every corner there were shebeens, illegal saloons that were shacks where home-brewed beer was served.

In spite of the hellish aspects of life in Alexandra, the township was also a kind of heaven. As one of the few areas of the country where Africans could acquire freehold property and run their own affairs, where people did not have to kowtow to the tyranny of white municipal authorities, Alexandra was an urban Promised Land, evidence that a section of our people had broken their ties with the rural areas and become permanent city dwellers. The government, in order to keep Africans in the countryside or working in the mines, maintained that Africans were by nature a rural people, ill suited for city life. Alexandra, despite its problems and flaws, gave the lie to that argument. Its population, drawn from all African language groups, was well adapted to city life and politically conscious. Urban life tended to abrade tribal and ethnic distinctions, and instead of being Xhosas, or Sothos, or Zulus, or Shangaans, we were Alexandrians. This created a sense of solidarity, which caused great concern among the white authorities. The government had always utilized divide-and-rule tactics when dealing with Africans and depended on the strength of ethnic divisions among the people. But in places like Alexandra, these differences were being erased.

Alexandra occupies a treasured place in my heart. It was the first place I ever lived away from home. Even though I was later to live in Orlando, a small section of Soweto, for a far longer period than I did in Alexandra, I always regarded Alexandra Township as a home where I had no specific house, and Orlando as a place where I had a house but no home.

In that first year, I learned more about poverty than I did in all my childhood days in Qunu. I never seemed to have money and I managed to survive on the meagerest of resources. The law firm paid me a salary of two pounds per week, having generously waived the premium the articled clerks normally paid the firm. Out of that two pounds, I paid thirteen shillings and fourpence a month for my room at the Xhomas'. The cheapest means of transport to and from Alexandra was the "Native" bus — for Africans only — which at one pound tenpence a month made a considerable dent in my income. I was also paying fees to the University of South Africa in order to complete my degree by correspondence. I spent another pound or so on food. Part of my salary was spent on an even more vital item — candles — for without them I could not study. I could not afford a kerosene lamp; candles allowed me to read late into the night.

I was inevitably short more than a few pence each month. Many days I walked the six miles to town in the morning and the six back in the evening in order to save bus fare. I often went days without more than a mouthful of food, and without a change of clothing. Mr. Sidelsky, who was my height, once gave me an old suit of his and, assisted by considerable stitching and patching, I wore that suit every day for almost five years. In the end, there were more patches than suit.

One afternoon, I was returning to Alexandra by bus and took a seat next to another fellow about my age. He was one of those young men who affected a style of dress that mimicked the well-tailored gangsters in

American movies. I realized that my suit was just touching the hem of his jacket. He noticed it also and very carefully moved away so that my jacket would not sully his. It was a tiny gesture, comical in retrospect, but painful at the time.

There is little favorable to be said about poverty, but it was often an incubator of true friendship. Many people will appear to befriend you when you are wealthy, but precious few will do the same when you are poor. If wealth is a magnet, poverty is a kind of repellent. Yet, poverty often brings out the true generosity in others. One morning, I decided to walk to town to save money and spotted a young lady who had been with me at Fort Hare. Her name was Phyllis Maseko and she was walking toward me on the same side of the street. I was embarrassed by my threadbare clothing and crossed to the other side hoping she would not recognize me. But I heard her call out, "Nelson . . . Nelson!" I stopped and crossed over, pretending that I had not noticed her until that moment. She was pleased to see me, but I could tell that she observed how shabby I looked. "Nelson," she said, "here is my address, 234 Orlando East. Come and visit me." I resolved not to humiliate myself again, but one day I was in need of a proper meal and dropped by. She fed me without alluding to my poverty, and from then on I continued to visit her.

My landlord, Mr. Xhoma, was not wealthy, but he was a kind of philanthropist. Every Sunday, for all of the time I lived on his property, he and his wife gave me lunch, and those steaming plates of pork and vegetables were often my only hot meal of the week. No matter where I was or what I was doing, I would never fail to be at the Xhomas' on Sunday. For the rest of the week, I would sustain myself on bread, and sometimes the secretaries at the firm would bring me some food.

I was very backward in those days and the combination of poverty and provincialism made for some amusing incidents. One day, not long after I had moved in with the Xhomas, I was on my way home from Johannesburg and very hungry. I had a bit of money that I had saved and decided to splurge on some fresh meat, something I had not had in a long time. I did not see a proper butcher around, so I went into a delicatessen, a type of shop I had never encountered until I went to Johannesburg. Through the glass, I saw a large and appetizing piece of meat and asked the man behind the counter to carve off a piece. He wrapped it up, and I put it under my arm and headed home, dreaming of the dinner that awaited me.

When I returned to my room in Alexandra, I called to one of the young daughters in the main house. She was only seven, but a clever girl. I said to her, "Would you take this piece of meat to one of your older sisters and ask her to cook it for me?" I could see her trying to suppress a smile.

but she was too respectful of her elders to laugh. With some irritation, I asked her whether something was wrong. Very softly, she said, "This meat is cooked." I asked her what she was talking about. She explained that I had bought a piece of smoked ham, and that it was meant to be eaten just as it was. This was entirely new to me, and rather than confess complete ignorance, I told her that I knew it was smoked ham but that I wanted it warmed up. She knew I was bluffing, but ran off anyway. The meat was very tasty.

In Alexandra I rekindled a friendship with the lively, ever-cheerful Ellen Nkabinde, whom I had known from Healdtown, and who was then teaching at one of the township schools. In fact, Ellen and I fell in love. I had known her only slightly at Healdtown, and it was not until I saw her again in Alexandra that our relationship blossomed. What little spare time I had in those months I spent with Ellen. Courtship was difficult; we were always surrounded by people, and there were few places to go. The only place we could be alone was outside under the sun or the stars. So, Ellen and I wandered together in the veld and hills surrounding the township. Mostly, we would just walk, and when we both had the time, we might have a picnic.

Ellen was a Swazi, and though tribalism was fading in the township, a close friend of mine condemned our relationship on purely tribal grounds. I categorically rejected this. But our different backgrounds posed certain problems. Mrs. Mabutho, the reverend's wife, did not care for Ellen, largely because she was a Swazi. One day, while I was at the Mabuthos', Mrs. Mabutho answered a knock at the door. It was Ellen, who was looking for me, and Mrs. Mabutho told her I was not inside. Only later did Mrs. Mabutho say to me, "Oh, Nelson, some girl was here looking for you." Mrs. Mabutho then said to me, "Is that girl a Shangaan?" Although the Shangaans are a proud and noble tribe, at the time, Shangaan was considered a derogatory term. I took offense at this and I said, "No, she is not a Shangaan, she is a Swazi." Mrs. Mabutho felt strongly that I should take out only Xhosa girls.

Such advice did not deter me. I loved and respected Ellen, and felt not a little bit noble in discarding the counsel of those who disapproved. The relationship was to me a novelty, and I felt daring in having a friendship with a woman who was not a Xhosa. I was young and a bit lost in the city, and Ellen played the role not only of romantic partner, but of a mother, supporting me, giving me confidence, and endowing me with strength and hope. But within a few months Ellen moved away, and sadly, we lost touch with one another.

The Xhoma family had five daughters, each of them lovely, but the loveliest of all was named Didi. Didi was about my age and spent most of the week working as a domestic worker in a white suburb of Johannesburg. When I first moved to the house, I saw her only seldom and fleetingly. But later, when I made her acquaintance properly, I also fell in love with her. But Didi barely took any notice of me, and what she did notice was the fact that I owned only one patched-up suit and a single shirt, and that I did not present a figure much different from a tramp.

Every weekend Didi returned to Alexandra. She was brought home by a young man who I assumed was her boyfriend, a flashy, well-to-do fellow who had a car, something that was most unusual. He wore expensive, double-breasted American suits and wide-brimmed hats, and paid a great deal of attention to his appearance. He must have been a gangster of some sort, but I cannot be sure. He would stand outside in the yard and put his hands in his waistcoat and look altogether superior. He greeted me politely, but I could see that he did not regard me as much competition.

I yearned to tell Didi I loved her, but I was afraid that my advances would be unwanted. I was hardly a Don Juan. Awkward and hesitant around girls, I did not know or understand the romantic games that others seemed to play effortlessly. On weekends, Didi's mother would sometimes ask her to bring out a plate of food to me. Didi would arrive on my doorstep with the plate and I could tell that she simply wanted to perform her errand as quickly as possible, but I would do my best to delay her. I would query her opinion on things, ask her all sorts of questions. "Now, what standard did you attain in school?" I would say. Standard five, she replied. "Why did you leave?" I asked. She was bored, she replied. "Ah, well, you must go back to school," I said. "You are about the same age as I am," I continued, "and there is nothing wrong with returning to school at this age. Otherwise you will regret it when you are old. You must think seriously about your future. It is nice for you now because you are young and beautiful and have many admirers, but you need to have an independent profession."

I realize that these are not the most romantic words that have ever been uttered by a young man to a young woman with whom he was in love, but I did not know what else to talk to her about. She listened seriously, but I could tell that she was not interested in me, that in fact she felt a bit superior to me.

I wanted to propose to her but I was unwilling to do so unless I was certain she would say yes. Although I loved her, I did not want to give her the satisfaction of rejecting me. I kept up my pursuit of her, but I was timid and hesitant. In love, unlike politics, caution is not usually a virtue. I was neither confident enough to think that I might succeed nor secure enough to bear the sense of failure if I did not.

I stayed at that house for about a year, and in the end, I uttered nothing about my feelings. Didi did not show any less interest in her boyfriend or any more interest in me. I bade my good-bye with expressions of gratitude for her friendliness and the hospitality of the family. I did not see Didi again for many years. One day, much later, when I was practicing law in Johannesburg, a young woman and her mother walked into my office. The woman had had a child, and her boyfriend did not want to marry her; she was seeking to institute an action against him. That young woman was Didi, only now she looked haggard and wore a faded dress. I was distressed to see her, and thought how things might have turned out differently. In the end, she did not bring a suit against her boyfriend, and I never saw her again.

Despite my romantic deficiencies, I gradually adjusted to township life, and began to develop a sense of inner strength, a belief that I could do well outside the world in which I had grown up. I slowly discovered I did not have to depend on my royal connections or the support of family in order to advance, and I forged relationships with people who did not know or care about my link to the Thembu royal house. I had my own home, humble though it was, and I was developing the confidence and self-reliance necessary to stand on my own two feet.

At the end of 1941, I received word that the regent was visiting Johannesburg and wanted to see me. I was nervous, but knew that I was obligated to see him, and indeed wanted to do so. He was staying at the WNLA compound, the headquarters of the Witwatersrand Native Labor Association, the recruiting agency for mineworkers along the Reef.

The regent seemed greatly changed, or perhaps it was I who had changed. He never once mentioned the fact that I had run away, Fort Hare, or the arranged marriage that was not to be. He was courteous and solicitous, questioning me in a fatherly way about my studies and future plans. He recognized that my life was starting in earnest and would take a different course from the one he had envisaged and planned for. He did not try to dissuade me from my course, and I was grateful for this implicit acknowledgment that I was no longer his charge.

My meeting with the regent had a double effect. I had rehabilitated myself and at the same time restored my own regard for him and the Thembu royal house. I had become indifferent to my old connections, an attitude I had adopted in part to justify my flight and somehow alleviate the pain of my separation from a world I loved and valued. It was reassuring to be back in the regent's warm embrace.

While the regent seemed satisfied with me, he was vexed with Justice, who he said must return to Mqhekezweni. Justice had formed a liaison with a young woman, and I knew he had no intention of going home.

After the regent departed, Bangindawo, one of his headmen, instituted proceedings against Justice, and I agreed to help Justice when he was called before the native commissioner. At the hearing, I pointed out that Justice was an adult, and was not obligated to return to Mqhekezweni merely because his father ordered it. When Bangindawo spoke, he did not reply to my argument but played on my own loyalties. He addressed me as Madiba, my clan name, something that was well calculated to remind me of my Thembu heritage. "Madiba," he said, "the regent has cared for you, educated you, and treated you like his own son. Now you want to keep his true son from him. This is contrary to the wishes of the man who has been your faithful guardian, and contrary to the path that has been laid out for Justice."

Bangindawo's speech hit me hard. Justice did have a different destiny from that of myself. He was the son of a chief, and a future chief in his own right. After the hearing, I told Justice that I had changed my mind, and that I thought he should return. Justice was mystified by my reaction and refused to listen to me. He resolved to stay and must have informed his girlfriend of my advice, for she never thereafter spoke to me.

At the beginning of 1942, in order to save money and be closer to downtown Johannesburg, I moved from the room at the back of the Xhomas' to the WNLA compound. I was assisted by Mr. Festile, the *induna* at the Chamber of Mines, who was once again playing a fateful role in my life. On his own initiative he had decided to offer me free accommodation in the mining compound.

The WNLA compound was a multiethnic, polyglot community of modern, urban South Africa. There were Sothos, Tswanas, Vendas, Zulus, Pedis, Shangaans, Namibians, Mozambicans, Swazis, and Xhosas. Few spoke English, and the lingua franca was an amalgam of many tongues known as Fanagalo. There, I saw not only flare-ups of ethnic animosity, but the comity that was also possible among men of different backgrounds. Yet I was a fish out of water there. Instead of spending my days underground, I was studying or working in a law office where the only physical activity was running errands or putting files in a cabinet.

Because the WNLA was a way station for visiting chiefs, I had the privilege of meeting tribal leaders from all over southern Africa. I recall on one occasion meeting the queen regent of Basutoland, or what is now Lesotho, Mantsebo Moshweshwe. She was accompanied by two chiefs, both of whom knew Sabata's father, Jongilizwe. I asked them about Jongilizwe, and for an hour I seemed to be back in Thembuland as they told colorful tales about his early years.

The queen took special notice of me and at one point addressed me directly, but she spoke in Sesotho, a language in which I knew few words. Sesotho is the language of the Sotho people as well as the Tswana, a large number of whom live in the Transvaal and the Orange Free State. She looked at me with incredulity, and then said in English, "What kind of lawyer and leader will you be who cannot speak the language of your own people?" I had no response. The question embarrassed and sobered me; it made me realize my parochialism and just how unprepared I was for the task of serving my people. I had unconsciously succumbed to the ethnic divisions fostered by the white government and I did not know how to speak to my own kith and kin. Without language, one cannot talk to people and understand them; one cannot share their hopes and aspirations, grasp their history, appreciate their poetry, or savor their songs. I again realized that we were not different people with separate languages; we were one people, with different tongues.

Less than six months after the regent's visit, Justice and I learned of his father's death in the winter of 1942. He had seemed weary when last I saw him, and his death did not come as a great surprise. We read of the regent's death in the newspaper because the telegram that had been sent to Justice had gone astray. We hastened down to the Transkei, arriving the day after the regent's funeral.

Though I was disappointed to miss the regent's burial, I was inwardly glad that I had reconciled with him before his death. But I was not without stabs of guilt. I always knew, even when I was estranged from the regent, that all my friends might desert me, all my plans might founder, all my hopes be dashed, but the regent would never abandon me. Yet I had spurned him, and I wondered whether my desertion might have hastened his death.

The passing of the regent removed from the scene an enlightened and tolerant man who achieved the goal that marks the reign of all great leaders: he kept his people united. Liberals and conservatives, traditionalists and reformers, white-collar officials and blue-collar miners, all remained loyal to him, not because they always agreed with him, but because the regent listened to and respected all different opinions.

I spent nearly a week in Mqhekezweni after the funeral and it was a time of retrospection and rediscovery. There is nothing like returning to a place that remains unchanged to find the ways in which you yourself have altered. The Great Place went on as before, no different from when I had grown up there. But I realized that my own outlook and worldviews had evolved. I was no longer attracted by a career in the civil service, or being an interpreter in the Native Affairs Department. I no longer saw my future bound up with Thembuland and the Transkei. I was even informed that my Xhosa was no longer pure and was now influenced by Zulu, one of the dominant languages in the Reef. My life in Johannesburg, my exposure to men like Gaur Radebe, my experiences at the law firm, had radically altered my beliefs. I looked back on that young man who had left Mqhekezweni as a naive and parochial fellow who had seen very little of the world. I now believed I was seeing things as they were. That too, of course, was an illusion.

I still felt an inner conflict between my head and my heart. My heart told me that I was a Thembu, that I had been raised and sent to school so that I could play a special role in perpetuating the kingship. Had I no obligations to the dead? To my father, who had put me in the care of the regent? To the regent himself, who had cared for me like a father? But my head told me that it was the right of every man to plan his own future as he pleased and choose his role in life. Was I not permitted to make my own choices?

Justice's circumstances were different from my own, and after the regent's death he had important new responsibilities thrust upon him. He was to succeed the regent as chief and had decided to remain in Mqhekezweni and take up his birthright. I had to return to Johannesburg, and I could not even stay to attend his installation. In my language there is a saying: *"Ndiwelimilambo enamagama"* (I have crossed famous rivers). It means that one has traveled a great distance, that one has had wide experience and gained some wisdom from it. I thought of this as I returned to Johannesburg alone. I had, since 1934, crossed many important rivers in my own land: the Mbashe and the Great Kei, on my way to Healdtown; and the Orange and the Vaal, on my way to Johannesburg. But I had many rivers yet to cross.

At the end of 1942 I passed the final examination for my B.A. degree. I had now achieved the rank I once considered so exalted. I was proud to have achieved my B.A., but I also knew that the degree itself was neither a talisman nor a passport to easy success.

At the firm, I had become closer to Gaur, much to Mr. Sidelsky's exasperation. Education, Gaur argued, was essential to our advancement, but he pointed out that no people or nation had ever freed itself through education alone. "Education is all well and good," Gaur said, "but if we are to depend on education, we will wait a thousand years for our freedom. We are poor, we have few teachers and even fewer schools. We do not even have the power to educate ourselves."

Gaur believed in finding solutions rather than in spouting theory. For Africans, he asserted, the engine of change was the African National Congress; its policies were the best way to pursue power in South Africa.

He stressed the ANC's long history of advocating change, noting that the ANC was the oldest national African organization in the country, having been founded in 1912. Its constitution denounced racialism, its presidents had been from different tribal groups, and it preached the goal of Africans as full citizens of South Africa.

Despite Gaur's lack of formal education, he was my superior in virtually every sphere of knowledge. During lunch breaks he would often give impromptu lectures; he loaned me books to read, recommended people for me to talk to, meetings for me to attend. I had taken two courses in modern history at Fort Hare, and while I knew many facts, Gaur was able to explain the causes for particular actions, the reasons that men and nations had acted as they did. I felt as though I was learning history afresh.

What made the deepest impression on me was Gaur's total commitment to the freedom struggle. He lived and breathed the quest for liberation. Gaur sometimes attended several meetings a day where he featured prominently as a speaker. He seemed to think of nothing but revolution.

I went along with Gaur to meetings of both the Township Advisory Board and the ANC. I went as an observer, not a participant, for I do not think I ever spoke. I wanted to understand the issues under discussion, evaluate the arguments, see the caliber of the men involved. The Advisory Board meetings were perfunctory and bureaucratic, but the ANC meetings were lively with debate and discussion about Parliament, the pass laws, rents, bus fares — any subject under the sun that affected Africans.

In August 1943, I marched with Gaur, and ten thousand others, in support of the Alexandra bus boycott, a protest against the raising of fares from fourpence to five. Gaur was one of the leaders and I watched him in action. This campaign had a great effect on me. In a small way, I had departed from my role as an observer and become a participant. I found that to march with one's people was exhilarating and inspiring. But I was also impressed by the boycott's effectiveness: after nine days, during which the buses ran empty, the company returned the fare to fourpence.

Gaur's views were not the only ones I paid attention to at the firm. Hans Muller was a white estate agent who did business with Mr. Sidelsky and would engage me in discussion. He was the prototypical businessman who saw the world through the prism of supply and demand. One day, Mr. Muller pointed out the window. "Look out there, Nelson," he said. "Do you see those men and women scurrying up and down the street? What is it that they are pursuing? What is it they are working for so feverishly? I'll tell you: all of them, without exception, are after wealth and money. Because wealth and money equal happiness. That is what you must struggle for: money, and nothing but money. Once you have enough cash, there is nothing else you will want in life."

William Smith was a Coloured man involved in the African real estate trade who was often around the office. Smith was a veteran of the ICU (the Industrial and Commercial Workers Union), South Africa's first black trade union, founded by Clements Kadalie, but his views had shifted dramatically since those days. "Nelson," he said, "I have been involved in politics for a long time, and I regret every minute of it. I wasted the best years of my life in futile efforts serving vain and selfish men who placed their interests above those of the people they pretended to serve. Politics, in my experience, is nothing but a racket to steal money from the poor."

Mr. Sidelsky did not join these discussions. He seemed to regard discussing politics as almost as much of a waste of time as participating in it. Again and again, he would counsel me to avoid politics. He warned me about Gaur and Walter Sisulu. These men will poison your mind, he said. "Nelson," he asked, "you want to be a lawyer, don't you?" I said yes. "And if you are a lawyer, you want to be a successful lawyer, do you not?" Again, I said yes. "Well, if you get into politics," he said, "your practice will suffer. You will get into trouble with the authorities who are often your allies in your work. You will lose all your clients, you will go bankrupt, you will break up your family, and you will end up in jail. That is what will happen if you go into politics."

I listened to these men and weighed their views carefully. All of the arguments had some merit. I was already leaning toward some type of political involvement, but I did not know what or how, and I lingered on the sidelines, uncertain what to do.

As far as my profession was concerned, it was Gaur who did more than just offer advice. One day in early 1943, when I had been at the firm for less than two years, Gaur took me aside and said, "My boy, as long as I am here at the firm, they will never article you, whether or not you have a degree." I was startled, and told Gaur that it could not be true, as he was not even in training to be a lawyer. "That does not make a difference, Nelson," he continued. "They will say, 'We have Gaur, he can speak law to our people, why do we need someone else? Gaur is already bringing in clients to the firm.' But they will not tell you this to your face; they will just postpone and delay. It is important to the future of our struggle in this country for you to become a lawyer, and so I am going to leave the firm and start my own estate agency. When I am gone, they will have no choice but to article you."

I pleaded with him not to resign, but he was immovable. Within a few days, he gave Mr. Sidelsky his resignation, and Mr. Sidelsky eventually articled me as promised. I cannot say whether Gaur's absence had anything at all to do with it, but his resignation was another example of his generosity.

Early in 1943, after passing my examination through UNISA, I returned to Fort Hare for my graduation. Before leaving for the university, I decided to outfit myself in a proper suit. In order to do so, I had to borrow the money from Walter Sisulu. I had had a new suit when I went up to Fort Hare, purchased for me by the regent, and now I would have a new suit when I went down. I borrowed academic dress from Randall Peteni, a friend and fellow alumnus.

My nephew, K. D. Matanzima, who had graduated several years before, drove my mother and No-England, the regent's widow, to the ceremony. I was gratified to have my mother there, but the fact that No-England came made it seem as though the regent himself had blessed the event.

After the graduation, I spent a few days with Daliwonga (K.D.'s clan name, which is what I called him), at his home in Qamata. Daliwonga had already chosen the path of traditional leadership. He was in the line of succession to become the head of Emigrant Thembuland, which lies in the westernmost part of the Transkei, and while I was staying with him he pressed me to return to Umtata after qualifying as an attorney. "Why do you stay in Johannesburg?" he said. "You are needed more here."

It was a fair point; there were certainly more professional Africans in the Transvaal than in the Transkei. I told Daliwonga that his suggestions were premature. But in my heart, I knew I was moving toward a different commitment. Through my friendship with Gaur and Walter, I was beginning to see that my duty was to my people as a whole, not just a particular section or branch. I felt that all the currents in my life were taking me away from the Transkei and toward what seemed like the center, a place where regional and ethnic loyalties gave way before a common purpose.

The graduation at Fort Hare offered a moment of introspection and reflection. I was struck most forcefully by the discrepancy between my old assumptions and my actual experience. I had discarded my presumptions that graduates automatically became leaders and that my connection to the Thembu royal house guaranteed me respect. Having a successful career and a comfortable salary were no longer my ultimate goals. I found myself being drawn into the world of politics because I was not content with my old beliefs.

In Johannesburg, I moved in circles where common sense and practical experience were more important than high academic qualifications. Even as I was receiving my degree, I realized that hardly anything I had learned at university seemed relevant in my new environment. At the university, teachers had shied away from topics like racial oppression, lack of opportunities for Africans, and the nest of laws and regulations that subjugate the black man. But in my life in Johannesburg, I confronted these things every day. No one had ever suggested to me how to go about removing the evils of racial prejudice, and I had to learn by trial and error.

When I returned to Johannesburg at the beginning of 1943, I enrolled at the University of the Witwatersrand for an LL.B., a bachelor of laws degree, the preparatory academic training for a lawyer. The University of the Witwatersrand, known to all as "Wits," is located in Braamfontein in north-central Johannesburg, and is considered by many to be the premier English-speaking university in South Africa.

While working at the law firm brought me into regular contact with whites for the first time, the university introduced me to a group of whites my own age. At Fort Hare we had occasional contacts with white students from Rhodes University in Grahamstown, but at Wits, I was attending classes with white students. This was as new to them as it was to me, for I was the only African student in the law faculty.

The English-speaking universities of South Africa were great incubators of liberal values. It was a tribute to these institutions that they allowed black students. For the Afrikaans universities, such a thing was unthinkable.

Despite the university's liberal values, I never felt entirely comfortable there. Always to be the only African, except for menial workers, to be regarded at best as a curiosity and at worst as an interloper, is not a congenial experience. My manner was guarded, and I met both generosity and animosity. Although I was to discover a core of sympathetic whites who became friends and later colleagues, most of the whites at Wits were not liberal or color-blind. I recall getting to a lecture a few minutes late one day and taking a seat next to Sarel Tighy, a classmate who later became a member of Parliament for the United Party. Though the lecture had already started and there were only a few empty seats, he ostentatiously collected his things and moved to a seat distant from me. This type of behavior was the rule rather than the exception. No one uttered the word *kaffir;* their hostility was more muted, but I felt it just the same.

Our law professor, Mr. Hahlo, was a strict, cerebral sort, who did not tolerate much independence on the part of his students. He held a curious view of the law when it came to women and Africans: neither group, he said, was meant to be lawyers. His view was that law was a social science and that women and Africans were not disciplined enough to master its intricacies. He once told me that I should not be at Wits but studying for my degree through UNISA. Although I disagreed with his views, I did little to disprove them. My performance as a law student was dismal.

At Wits, I met many people who were to share with me the ups and downs of the liberation struggle, and without whom I would have accomplished very little. Many white students went out of their way to make me feel welcome. During my first term at Wits I met Joe Slovo and his future wife, Ruth First. Then as now, Joe had one of the sharpest, most incisive minds I have ever encountered. He was an ardent Communist, and was known for his high-spirited parties. Ruth had an outgoing personality and was a gifted writer. Both were the children of Jewish immigrants to South Africa. I began lifelong friendships with George Bizos and Bram Fischer. George, the child of Greek immigrants, was a man who combined a sympathetic nature with an incisive mind. Bram Fischer, a part-time lecturer, was the scion of a distinguished Afrikaner family: his grandfather had been prime minister of the Orange River Colony and his father was judge-president of the Orange Free State. Although he could have been a prime minister of South Africa, he became one of the bravest and staunchest friends of the freedom struggle that I have ever known. I befriended Tony O'Dowd, Harold Wolpe, Jules Brawde and his wife, Selma, all of whom were political radicals and members of the Communist Party.

I also formed close friendships with a number of Indian students. Although there had been a handful of Indian students at Fort Hare, they stayed in a separate hostel and I seldom had contact with them. At Wits I met and became friends with Ismail Meer, J. N. Singh, Ahmed Bhoola, and Ramlal Bhoolia. The center of this tight-knit community was Ismail's apartment, flat 13, Kholvad House, four rooms in a residential building in the center of the city. There we studied, talked, and even danced until the early hours in the morning, and it became a kind of headquarters for young freedom fighters. I sometimes slept there when it was too late to catch the last train back to Orlando.

Bright and serious, Ismail Meer was born in Natal, and while at law school at Wits he became a key member of the Transvaal Indian Congress. J. N. Singh was a popular, handsome fellow, who was at ease with all colors and also a member of the Communist Party. One day, Ismail, J.N., and myself were in a rush to get to Kholvad House, and we boarded the tram despite the fact that while Indians were allowed, Africans were not. We had not been on long when the conductor turned to Ismail and J.N. and said in Afrikaans that their "kaffir friend" was not allowed on. Ismail and J.N. exploded at the conductor, telling him that he did not even understand the word *kaffir* and that it was offensive to call me that name. The conductor promptly stopped the tram and hailed a policeman, who arrested us, took us down to the station, and charged us. We were ordered to appear in court the following day. That night, Ismail and J.N. arranged for Bram Fischer to defend us. The next day, the magistrate seemed in awe of Bram's family connections. We were promptly acquitted and I saw firsthand that justice was not at all blind.

Wits opened a new world to me, a world of ideas and political beliefs and debates, a world where people were passionate about politics. I was among white and Indian intellectuals of my own generation, young men who would form the vanguard of the most important political movements of the next few years. I discovered for the first time people of my own age firmly aligned with the liberation struggle, who were prepared, despite their relative privilege, to sacrifice themselves for the cause of the oppressed.

Part Three

———

BIRTH OF A FREEDOM FIGHTER

11

I CANNOT PINPOINT a moment when I became politicized, when I knew that I would spend my life in the liberation struggle. To be an African in South Africa means that one is politicized from the moment of one's birth, whether one acknowledges it or not. An African child is born in an Africans Only hospital, taken home in an Africans Only bus, lives in an Africans Only area, and attends Africans Only schools, if he attends school at all.

When he grows up, he can hold Africans Only jobs, rent a house in Africans Only townships, ride Africans Only trains, and be stopped at any time of the day or night and be ordered to produce a pass, failing which he will be arrested and thrown in jail. His life is circumscribed by racist laws and regulations that cripple his growth, dim his potential, and stunt his life. This was the reality, and one could deal with it in a myriad of ways.

I had no epiphany, no singular revelation, no moment of truth, but a steady accumulation of a thousand slights, a thousand indignities, a thousand unremembered moments, produced in me an anger, a rebelliousness, a desire to fight the system that imprisoned my people. There was no particular day on which I said, From henceforth I will devote myself to the liberation of my people; instead, I simply found myself doing so, and could not do otherwise.

I have mentioned many of the people who influenced me, but more and more, I had come under the wise tutelage of Walter Sisulu. Walter was strong, reasonable, practical, and dedicated. He never lost his head in a crisis; he was often silent when others were shouting. He believed that the ANC was the means to effect change in South Africa, the repository of black hopes and aspirations. Sometimes one can judge an organization by the people who belong to it, and I knew that I would be proud to belong to any organization in which Walter was a member. At the time, there were few alternatives. The ANC was the one organization that welcomed everyone, that saw itself as a great umbrella under which all Africans could find shelter.

Change was in the air in the 1940s. The Atlantic Charter of 1941, signed by Roosevelt and Churchill, reaffirmed faith in the dignity of each human being and propagated a host of democratic principles. Some in the West saw the charter as empty promises, but not those of us in Africa. Inspired by the Atlantic Charter and the fight of the Allies against tyranny and oppression, the ANC created its own charter, called African Claims, which called for full citizenship for all Africans, the right to buy land, and the repeal of all discriminatory legislation. We hoped that the government and ordinary South Africans would see that the principles they were fighting for in Europe were the same ones we were advocating at home.

Walter's house in Orlando was a mecca for activists and ANC members. It was a warm, welcoming place and I was often there either to sample a political discussion or MaSisulu's cooking. One night in 1943 I met Anton Lembede, who held master of arts and bachelor of law degrees, and A. P. Mda. From the moment I heard Lembede speak, I knew I was seeing a magnetic personality who thought in original and often startling ways. He was then one of a handful of African lawyers in all of South Africa and was the legal partner of the venerable Dr. Pixley ka Seme, one of the founders of the ANC.

Lembede said that Africa was a black man's continent, and it was up to Africans to reassert themselves and reclaim what was rightfully theirs. He hated the idea of the black inferiority complex and castigated what he called the worship and idolization of the West and their ideas. The inferiority complex, he affirmed, was the greatest barrier to liberation. He noted that wherever the African had been given the opportunity, he was capable of developing to the same extent as the white man, citing such African heroes as Marcus Garvey, W. E. B. Du Bois, and Haile Selassie. "The color of my skin is beautiful," he said, "like the black soil of Mother Africa." He believed blacks had to improve their own self-image before they could initiate successful mass action. He preached self-reliance and self-determination, and called his philosophy Africanism. We took it for granted that one day he would lead the ANC.

Lembede declared that a new spirit was stirring among the people, that ethnic differences were melting away, that young men and women thought of themselves as Africans first and foremost, not as Xhosas or Ndebeles or Tswanas. Lembede, whose father was an illiterate Zulu peasant from Natal, had trained as a teacher at Adam's College, an American Board of Missions institution. He had taught for years in Orange Free State, learned Afrikaans, and came to see Afrikaner nationalism as a prototype of African nationalism.

As Lembede later wrote in the newspaper *Inkundla ya Bantu,* an African newspaper in Natal:

The history of modern times is the history of nationalism. Nationalism has been tested in the people's struggles and the fires of battle and found to be the only antidote against foreign rule and modern imperialism. It is for that reason that the great imperialistic powers feverishly endeavor with all their might to discourage and eradicate all nationalistic tendencies among their alien subjects; for that purpose huge and enormous sums of money are lavishly expended on propaganda against nationalism which is dismissed as "narrow," "barbarous," "uncultured," "devilish," etc. Some alien subjects become dupes of this sinister propaganda and consequently become tools or instruments of imperialism for which great service they are highly praised by the imperialistic power and showered with such epithets as "cultured," "liberal," "progressive," "broadminded," etc.

Lembede's views struck a chord in me. I, too, had been susceptible to paternalistic British colonialism and the appeal of being perceived by whites as "cultured" and "progressive" and "civilized." I was already on my way to being drawn into the black elite that Britain sought to create in Africa. That is what everyone from the regent to Mr. Sidelsky had wanted for me. But it was an illusion. Like Lembede, I came to see the antidote as militant African nationalism.

Lembede's friend and partner was Peter Mda, better known as A.P. While Lembede tended to imprecision and was inclined to be verbose, Mda was controlled and exact. Lembede could be vague and mystical; Mda was specific and scientific. Mda's practicality was a perfect foil for Lembede's idealism.

Other young men were thinking along the same lines and we would all meet to discuss these ideas. In addition to Lembede and Mda, these men included Walter Sisulu; Oliver Tambo; Dr. Lionel Majombozi; Victor Mbobo, my former teacher at Healdtown; William Nkomo, a medical student who was a member of the CP; Jordan Ngubane, a journalist from Natal who worked for *Inkundla* as well as the *Bantu World,* the largest-selling African newspaper; David Bopape, secretary of the ANC in the Transvaal and member of the Communist Party, and many others. Many felt, perhaps unfairly, that the ANC as a whole had become the preserve of a tired, unmilitant, privileged African elite more concerned with protecting their own rights than those of the masses. The general consensus was that some action must be taken, and Dr. Majombozi proposed forming a Youth League as a way of lighting a fire under the leadership of the ANC.

In 1943, a delegation including Lembede, Mda, Sisulu, Tambo, Nkomo, and myself went to see Dr. Xuma, who was head of the ANC, at his rather grand house in Sophiatown. Dr. Xuma had a surgery at his home in addition to a small farm. Dr. Xuma had performed a great service to the ANC. He had roused it from its slumbering state under Dr. ka Seme, when the organization had shrunk in size and importance. When he assumed the presidency, the ANC had seventeen shillings and sixpence in its treasury, and he had boosted the amount to four thousand pounds. He was admired by traditional leaders, had relationships with cabinet ministers, and exuded a sense of security and confidence. But he also carried himself with an air of superciliousness that did not befit the leader of a mass organization. As devoted as he was to the ANC, his medical practice took precedence. Xuma presided over the era of delegations, deputations, letters, and telegrams. Everything was done in the English manner, the idea being that despite our disagreements we were all gentlemen. He enjoyed the relationships he had formed with the white establishment and did not want to jeopardize them with political action.

At our meeting, we told him that we intended to organize a Youth League and a campaign of action designed to mobilize mass support. We had brought a copy of the draft constitution and manifesto with us. We told Dr. Xuma that the ANC was in danger of becoming marginalized unless it stirred itself and took up new methods. Dr. Xuma felt threatened by our delegation and strongly objected to a Youth League constitution. He thought the league should be a more loosely organized group and act mainly as a recruiting committee for the ANC. In a paternalistic way, Dr. Xuma went on to tell us that Africans as a group were too unorganized and undisciplined to participate in a mass campaign and that such a campaign would be rash and dangerous.

Shortly after the meeting with Dr. Xuma, a provisional committee of the Youth League was formed, under the leadership of William Nkomo. The members of the committee journeyed to the ANC annual conference in Bloemfontein in December of 1943, where they proposed the formation of a Youth League to help recruit new members to the organization. The proposal was accepted.

The actual formation of the Youth League took place on Easter Sunday, 1944, at the Bantu Men's Social Center on Eloff Street. There were about one hundred men there, some coming from as far away as Pretoria. It was a select group, an elite group, a great number of us being Fort Hare graduates; we were far from a mass movement. Lembede gave a lecture on the history of nations, a tour of the horizon from ancient Greece to medieval Europe to the age of colonization. He emphasized the historical achievements of Africa and Africans, and noted how foolish it was for whites to see themselves as a chosen people and an intrinsically superior race.

Jordan Ngubane, A. P. Mda, and William Nkomo all spoke, and emphasized the emerging spirit of African nationalism. Lembede was elected the president, Oliver Tambo, the secretary, and Walter Sisulu became the treasurer. A. P. Mda, Jordan Ngubane, Lionel Majombozi, Congress Mbata, David Bopape, and I were elected to the executive committee. We were later joined by such prominent young men as Godfrey Pitje, a student (later teacher then lawyer); Arthur Letele, Wilson Conco, Diliza Mji, and Nthatho Motlana, all medical doctors; Dan Tloome, a trade unionist; and Joe Matthews, Duma Nokwe, and Robert Sobukwe, all students. Branches were soon established in all the provinces.

The basic policy of the league did not differ from the ANC's first constitution in 1912. But we were reaffirming and underscoring those original concerns, many of which had gone by the wayside. African nationalism was our battle cry, and our creed was the creation of one nation out of many tribes, the overthrow of white supremacy, and the establishment of a truly democratic form of government. Our manifesto stated: "We believe that the national liberation of Africans will be achieved by Africans themselves. . . . The Congress Youth League must be the brainstrust and power-station of the spirit of African nationalism."

The manifesto utterly rejected the notion of trusteeship, the idea that the white government somehow had African interests at heart. We cited the crippling, anti-African legislation of the past forty years, beginning with the 1913 Land Act, which ultimately deprived blacks of 87 percent of the territory in the land of their birth; the Urban Areas Act of 1923, which created teeming African slums, politely called "native locations," in order to supply cheap labor to white industry; the Color Bar Act of 1926, which banned Africans from practicing skilled trades; the Native Administration Act of 1927, which made the British Crown, rather than the paramount chiefs, the supreme chief over all African areas; and finally, in 1936, the Representation of Natives Act, which removed Africans from the Common Voters' Roll in the Cape, thereby shattering any illusion that whites would allow Africans to have control over their own destiny.

We were extremely wary of communism. The document stated, "We may borrow . . . from foreign ideologies, but we reject the wholesale importation of foreign ideologies into Africa." This was an implicit rebuke to the Communist Party, which Lembede and many others, including myself, considered a "foreign" ideology unsuited to the African situation. Lembede felt that the Communist Party was dominated by whites, which undermined African self-confidence and initiative.

A number of committees were formed that day, but the primary purpose of the Youth League was to give direction to the ANC in its quest for political freedom. Although I agreed with this, I was nervous about joining the league and still had doubts about the extent of my political commitment. I was then working full-time and studying part-time, and had little time outside of those two activities. I also possessed a certain insecurity, feeling politically backward compared to Walter, Lembede, and Mda. They were men who knew their minds, and I was, as yet, unformed. I still lacked confidence as a speaker, and was intimidated by the eloquence of so many of those in the league.

Lembede's Africanism was not universally supported because his ideas were characterized by a racial exclusivity that disturbed some of the other Youth Leaguers. Some of the Youth Leaguers felt that a nationalism that would include sympathetic whites was a more desirable course. Others, including myself, countered that if blacks were offered a multiracial form of struggle, they would remain enamored of white culture and prey to a continuing sense of inferiority. At the time, I was firmly opposed to allowing Communists or whites to join the league.

Walter's house was my home away from home. For several months in the early 1940s, it actually was my home when I had no other place to stay. The house was always full, and it seemed there was a perpetual discussion going on about politics. Albertina, Walter's wife, was a wise and wonderful presence, and a strong supporter of Walter's political work. (At their wedding, Anton Lembede said: "Albertina, you have married a married man: Walter married politics long before he met you.")

It was in the lounge of the Sisulus' home that I met Evelyn Mase, my first wife. She was a quiet, pretty girl from the countryside who did not seem overawed by the comings and goings at the Sisulus'. She was then training as a nurse with Albertina and Peter Mda's wife, Rose, at the Johannesburg non-European General Hospital.

Evelyn was from Engcobo, in the Transkei, some distance west of Umtata. Her father, a mineworker, had died when she was an infant, and her mother when she was twelve. After completing grade school, Evelyn was sent to Johannesburg to attend high school. She stayed with her brother, Sam Mase, who was then living at the Sisulus' house. MaSisulu, Walter's mother, was the sister of Evelyn's father's mother. The Sisulus treated Evelyn as if she was a favorite daughter, and she was much loved by them.

I asked Evelyn out very soon after our first meeting. Almost as quickly, we fell in love. Within a few months I had asked her to marry me and she accepted. We were married in a civil ceremony requiring only signatures and a witness at the Native Commissioner's Court in Johannesburg, for we could not afford a traditional wedding or feast. Our most immediate problem was finding a place to live. We first went to stay with her brother in Orlando East and then later with Evelyn's sister at City Deep Mines, where her sister's husband, Msunguli Mgudlwa, worked as a clerk.

12

IN 1946, a number of critical events occurred that shaped my political development and the direction of the struggle. The mineworkers' strike of 1946, in which 70,000 African miners along the Reef went on strike, affected me greatly. At the initiative of J. B. Marks, Dan Tloome, Gaur Radebe, and a number of ANC labor activists, the African Mine Workers Union (AMWU) had been created in the early 1940s. There were as many as 400,000 African miners working on the Reef, most of them making no more than two shillings a day. The union leadership had repeatedly pressed the Chamber of Mines for a minimum wage of ten shillings a day, as well as family housing and two weeks' paid leave. The chamber ignored the union's demands.

In one of the largest such actions in South African history, the miners went on strike for a week and maintained their solidarity. The state's retaliation was ruthless. The leaders were arrested, the compounds surrounded by police, and the AMWU offices ransacked. A march was brutally repulsed by police; twelve miners died. The Natives Representative Council adjourned in protest. I had a number of relations who were mineworkers, and during the week of the strike I visited them, discussed the issues, and expressed my support.

J. B. Marks, a longtime member of the ANC and the Communist Party, was then president of the African Mine Workers Union. Born in the Transvaal, of mixed parentage, Marks was a charismatic figure with a distinctive sense of humor. He was a tall man with a light complexion. During the strike I sometimes went with him from mine to mine, talking to workers and planning strategy. From morning to night, he displayed cool and reasoned leadership, with his humor leavening even the most difficult crisis. I was impressed by the organization of the union and its ability to control its membership, even in the face of such savage opposition.

In the end, the state prevailed: the strike was suppressed and the union crushed. The strike was the beginning of my close relationship with Marks. I visited him often at his house, and we discussed my opposition to communism at great length. Marks was a stalwart member of the party, but he never personalized my objections, and felt that it was natural for a young man to embrace nationalism, but that as I grew older and more experienced, my views would broaden. I had these same discussions with Moses Kotane and Yusuf Dadoo, both of whom believed, like Marks, that communism had to be adapted to the African situation. Other Communist members of the ANC condemned me and the other Youth Leaguers, but Marks, Kotane, and Dadoo never did.

After the strike, fifty-two men, including Kotane, Marks, and many other Communists, were arrested and prosecuted, first for incitement then for sedition. It was a political trial, an effort by the state to show that it was not soft on the Red Menace.

That same year, another event forced me to recast my whole approach to political work. In 1946, the Smuts government passed the Asiatic Land Tenure Act, which curtailed the free movement of Indians, circumscribed the areas where Indians could reside and trade, and severely restricted their right to buy property. In return, they were provided with representation in Parliament by token white surrogates. Dr. Dadoo, president of the Transvaal Indian Congress, castigated the restrictions and dismissed the offer of parliamentary representation as "a spurious offer of a sham franchise." This law — known as the Ghetto Act — was a grave insult to the Indian community and anticipated the Group Areas Act, which would eventually circumscribe the freedom of all South Africans of color.

The Indian community was outraged and launched a concerted, two-year campaign of passive resistance to oppose the measures. Led by Drs. Dadoo and G. M. Naicker, president of the Natal Indian Congress, the Indian community conducted a mass campaign that impressed us with its organization and dedication. Housewives, priests, doctors, lawyers, traders, students, and workers took their place in the front lines of the protest. For two years, people suspended their lives to take up the battle. Mass rallies were held; land reserved for whites was occupied and picketed. No less than two thousand volunteers went to jail, and Drs. Dadoo and Naicker were sentenced to six months' hard labor.

The campaign was confined to the Indian community and the participation of other groups was not encouraged. Even so, Dr. Xuma and other African leaders spoke at several meetings and along with the Youth League gave full moral support to the struggle of the Indian people. The government crippled the rebellion with harsh laws and intimidation, but we in the Youth League and the ANC had witnessed the Indian people register an extraordinary protest against color oppression in a way that Africans and the ANC had not. Ismail Meer and J. N. Singh suspended their studies, said good-bye to their families, and went to prison. Ahmed Kathrada, who was still a high-school student, did the same thing. I often visited the home of Amina Pahad for lunch, and then suddenly, this charming woman put aside her apron and went to jail for her beliefs. If I had once questioned the willingness of the Indian community to protest against oppression, I no longer could.

The Indian campaign became a model for the type of protest that we in the Youth League were calling for. It instilled a spirit of defiance and radicalism among the people, broke the fear of prison, and boosted the popularity and influence of the NIC and TIC. They reminded us that the freedom struggle was not merely a question of making speeches, holding meetings, passing resolutions, and sending deputations, but of meticulous organization, militant mass action, and, above all, the willingness to suffer and sacrifice. The Indian campaign hearkened back to the 1913 passive resistance campaign in which Mahatma Gandhi led a tumultuous procession of Indians crossing illegally from Natal to the Transvaal. That was history; this campaign was taking place before my own eyes.

Early in 1946, Evelyn and I moved to a two-room municipal house of our own in Orlando East and thereafter to a slightly larger house at No. 8115 Orlando West. Orlando West was a dusty, spartan area of boxy municipal houses that would later become part of Greater Soweto, Soweto being an acronym for South-Western Townships. Our house was situated in an area nicknamed Westcliff by its residents after the fancy white suburb to the north.

The rent of our new home was seventeen shillings and sixpence per month. The house itself was identical to hundreds of others built on postage-stamp-size plots on dirt roads. It had the same standard tin roof, the same cement floor, a narrow kitchen, and a bucket toilet in back. Although there were streetlamps outside, we used kerosene lamps inside as the homes were not yet electrified. The bedroom was so small that a double bed took up almost the entire floor space. These houses were built by the municipal authorities for workers who needed to be near town. To relieve the monotony, some people planted small gardens or painted their doors bright colors. It was the very opposite of grand, but it was my first true home of my own and I was mightily proud. A man is not a man until he has a house of his own. I did not know then that it would be the only residence that would be entirely mine for many, many years.

The state had allocated the house to Evelyn and me because we were no longer just two, but three. That year, our first son, Madiba Thembekile, was born. He was given my clan name of Madiba, but was known by the nickname Thembi. He was a solid, happy little boy who most people said resembled his mother more than his father. I had now produced an heir, though I had little as yet to bequeath to him. But I had perpetuated the Mandela name and the Madiba clan, which is one of the basic responsibilities of a Xhosa male.

I finally had a stable base, and I went from being a guest in other people's homes to having guests in my own. My sister Leabie joined us and I took her across the railroad line to enroll her at Orlando High School. In my culture, all the members of one's family have a claim to the hospitality of any other member of the family; the combination of my large extended family and my new house meant a great number of guests.

I enjoyed domesticity, even though I had little time for it. I delighted in playing with Thembi, bathing him and feeding him, and putting him to bed with a little story. In fact, I love playing with children and chatting with them; it has always been one of the things that makes me feel most at peace. I enjoyed relaxing at home, reading quietly, taking in the sweet and savory smells emanating from pots boiling in the kitchen. But I was rarely at home to enjoy these things.

During the latter part of that year, the Reverend Michael Scott came to stay with us. Scott was an Anglican clergyman and a great fighter for African rights. He had been approached by a man named Komo, who was representing a squatter camp outside of Johannesburg that the government was seeking to relocate. Komo wanted Scott to make a protest against the removal. Scott said, "If I am going to help you I must be one of you," and he proceeded to move to the squatter camp and start a congregation there. Scott's shantytown for the homeless was built near a rocky knoll and the residents christened it Tobruk, after the battle in the North Africa campaign of the war. It was a place I sometimes took Thembi on Sunday morning, as he liked to play hide-and-seek among the rocks. After Scott had set up his congregation, he found that Komo was embezzling money from people who were contributing to the fight against the removal. When Scott confronted Komo, Komo drove Scott out of camp and threatened his life.

Scott took refuge with us in Orlando and brought along an African priest named Dlamini, who also had a wife and children. Our house was tiny, and Scott slept in the sitting room, Dlamini and his wife slept in another room, and we put all the children in the kitchen. Reverend Scott was a modest, unassuming man, but Dlamini was a bit hard to take. At mealtimes, he would complain about the food. "Look, here," he would say, "this meat of yours, it's very lean and hard, not properly cooked at all. I'm not used to meals like this." Scott was appalled by this, and admonished Dlamini, but Dlamini took no heed. The next night he might say, "Well, this is a bit better than yesterday, but far from well prepared. Mandela, you know your wife just cannot cook."

Dlamini indirectly caused the situation to be resolved because I was so eager to have him out of the house that I went to the squatter camp myself and explained that Scott was a true friend of theirs, unlike Komo, and that they had to choose between the two. They then organized an election in which Scott triumphed, and he moved back to the squatter camp, taking Father Dlamini with him.

Early in 1947, I completed the requisite period of three years for articles and my time at Witkin, Sidelsky and Eidelman came to an end. I resolved to become a full-time student in order to earn my LL.B. so that I could go out on my own and practice as an attorney. The loss of the eight pounds, ten shillings, and one penny per month that I earned at Sidelsky was devastating. I applied to the Bantu Welfare Trust at the South African Institute of Race Relations in Johannesburg for a loan of £250 sterling to help finance my law studies, which included university fees, textbooks, and a monthly allowance. I was given a loan of £150.

Three months later, I wrote to them again, noting that my wife was about to take maternity leave, and we would lose her salary of seventeen pounds per month, which was absolutely necessary to our survival. I did receive the additional money, for which I was grateful, but the circumstances which warranted it were unfortunate. Our daughter Makaziwe's birth was not difficult, yet she was frail and sickly. From the start, we feared the worst. Many nights, Evelyn and I took turns looking after her. We did not know the name of whatever was consuming this tiny girl and the doctors could not explain the nature of the problem. Evelyn monitored the baby with the combination of a mother's tirelessness and a nurse's professional efficiency. When she was nine months old, Makaziwe passed away. Evelyn was distraught, and the only thing that helped temper my own grief was trying to alleviate hers.

In politics, no matter how much one plans, circumstances often dictate events. In July of 1947, during an informal discussion with Lembede about Youth League business, he complained to me of a sudden pain in his stomach and an accompanying chill. When the pain worsened, we drove him to Coronation Hospital, and that same night, he was dead at the age of thirty-three. Many were deeply affected by his death. Walter Sisulu seemed almost prostrate with grief. His passing was a setback to the movement, for Lembede was a fount of ideas and attracted others to the organization.

Lembede was succeeded by Peter Mda, whose analytical approach, ability to express himself clearly and simply, and tactical experience made him an excellent politician and an outstanding leader of the Youth League. Mda was a lean fellow; he had no excess weight, just as he used no excess words. In his broad-minded tolerance of different views, his own thinking was more mature than that of Lembede. It took Mda's leadership to advance Lembede's cause.

Mda believed the Youth League should function as an internal pressure group, a militant nationalistic wing within the ANC as a whole that would propel the organization into a new era. At the time, the ANC did not have a single full-time employee, and was generally poorly organized, operating in a haphazard way. (Later, Walter became the first and only full-time ANC staff member at an extremely meager salary.)

Mda quickly established a branch of the Youth League at Fort Hare under the guidance of Z. K. Matthews and Godfrey Pitje, a lecturer in anthropology. They recruited outstanding students, bringing in fresh blood and new ideas. Among the most outstanding were Professor Matthews's brilliant son Joe, and Robert Sobukwe, a dazzling orator and incisive thinker.

Mda was more moderate in his nationalism than Lembede, and his thinking was without the racial tinge that characterized Lembede's. He hated white oppression and white domination, not white people themselves. He was also less extreme in his opposition to the Communist Party than Lembede — or myself. I was among the Youth Leaguers who were suspicious of the white left. Even though I had befriended many white Communists, I was wary of white influence in the ANC, and I opposed joint campaigns with the party. I was concerned that the Communists were intent on taking over our movement in the guise of joint action. I believed that it was an undiluted African nationalism, not Marxism or multiracialism, that would liberate us. With a few of my colleagues in the league, I even went so far as breaking up CP meetings by storming the stage, tearing up signs, and capturing the microphone. At the national conference of the ANC in December, the Youth League introduced a motion demanding the expulsion of all members of the Communist Party, but we were soundly defeated. Despite the influence the Indian passive resistance campaign of 1946 had on me, I felt about the Indians the same way I did about the Communists: that they would tend to dominate the ANC, in part because of their superior education, experience, and training.

In 1947, I was elected to the Executive Committee of the Transvaal ANC and served under C. S. Ramohanoe, president of the Transvaal region. This was my first position in the ANC proper, and represented a milestone in my commitment to the organization. Until that time, the sacrifices I had made had not gone much further than being absent from my wife and family during weekends and returning home late in the evening. I had not been directly involved in any major campaign, and I did not yet understand the hazards and unending difficulties of the life of a freedom fighter. I had coasted along without having to pay a price for my commitment. From the time I was elected to the Executive Committee of the Transvaal region, I came to identify myself with the congress as a whole, with its hopes and despairs, its successes and failures; I was now bound heart and soul.

Ramohanoe was another one of those from whom I learned. He was a staunch nationalist and a skillful organizer who was able to balance divergent views and come forward with a suitable compromise. While Ramohanoe was unsympathetic to the Communists, he worked well with them. He believed that the ANC was a national organization that should welcome all those who supported our cause.

In 1947, in the wake of the Indian passive resistance campaign, Drs. Xuma, Dadoo, and Naicker, presidents, respectively, of the ANC, the Transvaal Indian Congress, and the Natal Indian Congress, signed the Doctors' Pact agreeing to join forces against a common enemy. This was a significant step toward the unity of the African and Indian movements. Rather than create a central political body to direct all the various movements, they agreed to cooperate on matters of common interest. Later, they were joined by the APO, the African People's Organization, a Coloured organization.

But such an agreement was at best tentative, for each national group faced problems peculiar to itself. The pass system, for example, barely affected Indians or Coloureds. The Ghetto Act, which had prompted the Indian protests, barely affected Africans. Coloured groups at the time were more concerned about the race classification and job reservation, issues that did not affect Africans and Indians to the same degree.

The Doctors' Pact laid a foundation for the future cooperation of Africans, Indians, and Coloureds, since it respected the independence of each individual group, but acknowledged the achievements that could be realized from acting in concert. The Doctors' Pact precipitated a series of nonracial, antigovernment campaigns around the country, which sought to bring together Africans and Indians in the freedom struggle. The first of these campaigns was the First Transvaal and Orange Free State Peoples Assembly for Votes for All, a campaign for the extension of the franchise to all black South Africans. Dr. Xuma announced ANC participation at a press conference over which I presided. At the time, we believed the campaign would be run by the ANC, but when we learned that the ANC would not be leading the campaign, the Transvaal Executive Committee decided that the ANC should withdraw. My idea at the time was that the ANC should be involved only in campaigns that the ANC itself led. I was more concerned with who got the credit than whether the campaign would be successful.

Even after the withdrawal, Ramohanoe, the president of the Transvaal region of the ANC, issued a press statement calling on Africans in the province to take part in the campaign of Votes for All in clear contravention of the decision of the Transvaal Executive Committee. This was an act of disobedience the committee could not tolerate. At a conference called to resolve this dispute, I was asked to move a no-confidence motion against Ramohanoe for his disobedience. I felt an acute conflict between duty and personal loyalty, between my obligations to my organization and to my friend. I well knew that I would be condemning the action of a man whose integrity and devotion to the struggle I never questioned, a man whose sacrifice in the liberation struggle was far greater than my own. I knew that the action that he had called for was in fact a noble one; he believed that Africans should help their Indian brothers.

But the seriousness of Ramohanoe's disobedience was too strong. While an organization like the ANC is made up of individuals, it is greater than any of its individual parts, and loyalty to the organization takes precedence over loyalty to an individual. I agreed to lead the attack and offered the motion condemning him, which was seconded by Oliver Tambo. This caused an uproar in the house, with verbal battles between those in the region who supported their president and those who were on the side of the executive. The meeting broke up in disorder.

13

AFRICANS could not vote, but that did not mean that we did not care who won elections. The white general election of 1948 matched the ruling United Party, led by General Smuts, then at the height of his international regard, against the revived National Party. While Smuts had enlisted South Africa on the side of the Allies in World War II, the National Party refused to support Great Britain and publicly sympathized with Nazi Germany. The National Party's campaign centered around the *swart gevaar* (the black danger), and they fought the election on the twin slogans of *Die kaffer op sy plek* (The nigger in his place) and *Die koelies uit die land* (The coolies out of the country) — *coolies* being the Afrikaner's derogatory term for Indians.

The Nationalists, led by Dr. Daniel Malan, a former minister of the Dutch Reform Church and a newspaper editor, were a party animated by bitterness — bitterness toward the English, who had treated them as inferiors for decades, and bitterness toward the African, who the Nationalists believed was threatening the prosperity and purity of Afrikaner culture. Africans had no loyalty to General Smuts, but we had even less for the National Party.

Malan's platform was known as apartheid. *Apartheid* was a new term but an old idea. It literally means "apartness" and it represented the codification in one oppressive system of all the laws and regulations that had kept Africans in an inferior position to whites for centuries. What had been more or less de facto was to become relentlessly de jure. The often haphazard segregation of the past three hundred years was to be consolidated into a monolithic system that was diabolical in its detail, inescapable in its reach, and overwhelming in its power. The premise of apartheid was that whites were superior to Africans, Coloureds, and Indians, and the function of it was to entrench white supremacy forever. As the Nationalists put it, *"Die wit man moet altyd baas wees"* (The white man must always remain boss). Their platform rested on the term *baasskap*, literally boss-ship, a freighted word that stood for white supremacy in all its harshness. The policy was supported by the Dutch Reform Church, which furnished apartheid with its religious underpinnings by suggesting that Afrikaners were God's chosen people and that blacks were a subservient species. In the Afrikaner's worldview, apartheid and the church went hand in hand.

The Nationalists' victory was the beginning of the end of the domination of the Afrikaner by the Englishman. English would now take second place to Afrikaans as an official language. The Nationalist slogan encapsulated their mission: *"Eie volk, eie taal, eie land"* — Our own people, our own language, our own land. In the distorted cosmology of the Afrikaner, the Nationalist victory was like the Israelites' journey to the Promised Land. This was the fulfillment of God's promise, and the justification for their view that South Africa should be a white man's country forever.

The victory was a shock. The United Party and General Smuts had beaten the Nazis, and surely they would defeat the National Party. On election day, I attended a meeting in Johannesburg with Oliver Tambo and several others. We barely discussed the question of a Nationalist government because we did not expect one. The meeting went on all night and we emerged at dawn and found a newspaper vendor selling the *Rand Daily Mail:* the Nationalists had triumphed. I was stunned and dismayed, but Oliver took a more considered line. "I like this," he said. "I like this." I could not imagine why. He explained, "Now we will know exactly who our enemies are and where we stand."

Even General Smuts realized the dangers of this harsh ideology, decrying apartheid as "a crazy concept, born of prejudice and fear." From the moment of the Nationalists' election, we knew that our land would henceforth be a place of tension and strife. For the first time in South African history, an exclusively Afrikaner party led the government. "South Africa belongs to us once more," Malan proclaimed in his victory speech.

That same year, the Youth League outlined its policy in a document written by Mda and issued by the league's executive committee. It was a rallying cry to all patriotic youth to overthrow white domination. We rejected the Communist notion that Africans were oppressed primarily as an economic class rather than as a race, adding that we needed to create a powerful national liberation movement under the banner of African nationalism and "led by Africans themselves."

We advocated the redivision of land on an equitable basis; the abolition of color bars prohibiting Africans from doing skilled work; and the need for free and compulsory education. The document also articulated the push-and-pull between two rival theories of African nationalism, between the more extreme, Marcus Garvey–inspired, "Africa for the Africans" nationalism and the Africanism of the Youth League, which recognized that South Africa was a multiracial country.

I was sympathetic to the ultra-revolutionary stream of African nationalism. I was angry at the white man, not at racism. While I was not prepared to hurl the white man into the sea, I would have been perfectly happy if he climbed aboard his steamships and left the continent of his own volition.

The Youth League was marginally more friendly to the Indians and the Coloureds, stating that Indians, like Africans, were oppressed, but that Indians had India, a mother country that they could look to. The Coloureds, too, were oppressed, but unlike the Indians had no mother country except Africa. I was prepared to accept Indians and Coloureds provided they accepted our policies; but their interests were not identical with ours, and I was skeptical of whether or not they could truly embrace our cause.

In short order, Malan began to implement his pernicious program. Within weeks of coming to power, the Nationalist government pardoned Robey Leibbrandt, the wartime traitor who had organized uprisings in support of Nazi Germany. The government announced their intention to curb the trade union movement and do away with the limited franchises of the Indian, Coloured, and African peoples. The Separate Representation of Voters Act eventually robbed the Coloureds of their representation in Parliament. The Prohibition of Mixed Marriages Act was introduced in 1949 and was followed in rapid succession by the Immorality Act, making sexual relations between white and nonwhite illegal. The Population

Registration Act labeled all South Africans by race, making color the single most important arbiter of individuals. Malan introduced the Group Areas Act — which he described as "the very essence of apartheid" — requiring separate urban areas for each racial group. In the past, whites took land by force; now they secured it by legislation.

In response to this new and much more powerful threat from the state, the ANC embarked on an unaccustomed and historic path. In 1949, the ANC launched a landmark effort to turn itself into a truly mass organization. The Youth League drafted a Program of Action, the cornerstone of which was a campaign of mass mobilization.

At the ANC annual conference in Bloemfontein, the organization adopted the league's Program of Action, which called for boycotts, strikes, stay-at-homes, passive resistance, protest demonstrations, and other forms of mass action. This was a radical change: the ANC's policy had always been to keep its activities within the law. We in the Youth League had seen the failure of legal and constitutional means to strike at racial oppression; now the entire organization was set to enter a more activist stage.

These changes did not come without internal upheaval. A few weeks before the conference, Walter Sisulu, Oliver Tambo, A. P. Mda, and I met privately with Dr. Xuma at his home in Sophiatown. We explained that we thought the time had come for mass action along the lines of Gandhi's nonviolent protests in India and the 1946 passive resistance campaign, asserting that the ANC had become too docile in the face of oppression. The ANC's leaders, we said, had to be willing to violate the law and if necessary go to prison for their beliefs as Gandhi had.

Dr. Xuma was adamantly opposed, claiming that such strategies were premature and would merely give the government an excuse to crush the ANC. Such forms of protest, he said, would eventually take place in South Africa, but at the moment such a step would be fatal. He made it clear that he was a doctor with a wide and prosperous practice that he would not jeopardize by going to prison.

We gave Dr. Xuma an ultimatum: we would support him for reelection to the presidency of the ANC provided he supported our proposed Program of Action. If he would not support our program, we would not support him. Dr. Xuma became heated, accusing us of blackmail and laying down conditions on which we would vote for him. He told us that we were young and arrogant, and treating him without respect. We remonstrated with him, but to no avail. He would not go along with our proposal.

He unceremoniously showed us out of his house at 11 P.M., and closed the gate behind him. There were no streetlights in Sophiatown and it was a moonless night. All forms of public transport had long since ceased and we lived miles away in Orlando. Oliver remarked that Xuma could have at the very least offered us some transport. Walter was friendly with a family that lived nearby, and we prevailed upon them to take us in for the night.

At the conference that December, we in the Youth League knew we had the votes to depose Dr. Xuma. As an alternative candidate, we sponsored Dr. J. S. Moroka for the presidency. He was not our first choice. Professor Z. K. Matthews was the man we wanted to lead us, but Z.K. considered us too radical and our plan of action too impractical. He called us naive firebrands, adding that we would mellow with age.

Dr. Moroka was an unlikely choice. He was a member of the All-African Convention (AAC), which was dominated by Trotskyite elements at that time. When he agreed to stand against Dr. Xuma, the Youth League then enrolled him as a member of the ANC. When we first approached him, he consistently referred to the ANC as the African National "Council." He was not very knowledgeable about the ANC nor was he an experienced activist, but he was respectable, and amenable to our program. Like Dr. Xuma, he was a doctor, and one of the wealthiest black men in South Africa. He had studied at Edinburgh and Vienna. His great-grandfather had been a chief in the Orange Free State, and had greeted the Afrikaner *voortrekkers* of the nineteenth century with open arms and gifts of land, and then been betrayed. Dr. Xuma was defeated and Dr. Moroka became president-general of the ANC. Walter Sisulu was elected the new secretary-general, and Oliver Tambo was elected to the National Executive Committee.

The Program of Action approved at the annual conference called for the pursuit of political rights through the use of boycotts, strikes, civil disobedience, and noncooperation. In addition, it called for a national day of work stoppage in protest against the racist and reactionary policies of the government. This was a departure from the days of decorous protest, and many of the old stalwarts of the ANC were to fade away in this new era of greater militancy. Youth League members had now graduated to the senior organization. We had now guided the ANC to a more radical and revolutionary path.

I could only celebrate the Youth League's triumph from a distance, for I was unable to attend the conference myself. I was then working for a new law firm and they did not give me permission to take two days off to attend the conference in Bloemfontein. The firm was a liberal one, but wanted me to concentrate on my work and forget politics. I would have lost my job if I had attended the conference and I could not afford to do that.

*   *   *

The spirit of mass action surged, but I remained skeptical of any action undertaken with the Communists and Indians. The "Defend Free Speech Convention" in March 1950, organized by the Transvaal ANC, the Transvaal Indian Congress, the African People's Organization, and the District Committee of the Communist Party, drew ten thousand people at Johannesburg's Market Square. Dr. Moroka, without consulting the executive, agreed to preside over the convention. The convention was a success, yet I remained wary, as the prime mover behind it was the party.

At the instigation of the Communist Party and the Indian Congress, the convention passed a resolution for a one-day general strike, known as Freedom Day, on May 1, calling for the abolition of the pass laws and all discriminatory legislation. Although I supported these objectives, I believed that the Communists were trying to steal the thunder from the ANC's National Day of Protest. I opposed the May Day strike on the grounds that the ANC had not originated the campaign, believing that we should concentrate on our own campaign.

Ahmed Kathrada was then barely twenty-one and, like all youth, eager to flex his muscles. He was a key member of the Transvaal Indian Youth Congress and had heard I was opposed to the May Day strike. One day, while walking on Commissioner Street, I met Kathrada and he heatedly confronted me, charging that I and the Youth League did not want to work with Indians or Coloureds. In a challenging tone, he said, "You are an African leader and I am an Indian youth. But I am convinced of the support of the African masses for the strike and I challenge you to nominate any African township for a meeting and I guarantee the people will support me." It was a hollow threat, but it angered me all the same. I even complained to a joint meeting of the Executive Committee of the ANC, the South African Indian Congress, and the Communist Party, but Ismail Meer calmed me down, saying, "Nelson, he is young and hotheaded, don't you be the same." I consequently felt a bit sheepish about my actions and I withdrew the complaint. Although I disagreed with Kathrada, I admired his fire, and it was an incident we came to laugh about.

The Freedom Day strike went ahead without official ANC support. In anticipation, the government banned all meetings and gatherings for May 1. More than two-thirds of African workers stayed at home during the one-day strike. That night, Walter and I were in Orlando West on the fringes of a Freedom Day crowd that had gathered despite the government's restrictions. The moon was bright, and as we watched the orderly march of protesters, we could see a group of policemen camped across a stream about five hundred yards away. They must have seen us as well, because all of a sudden, they started firing in our direction. We dove to the ground, and remained there as mounted police galloped into the crowd, smashing people with batons. We took refuge in a nearby nurses' dormitory, where we heard bullets smashing into the wall of the building. Eighteen Africans died and many others were wounded in this indiscriminate and unprovoked attack.

Despite protest and criticism, the Nationalist response was to tighten the screws of repression. A few weeks later, the government introduced the notorious Suppression of Communism Act and the ANC called an emergency conference in Johannesburg. The act outlawed the Communist Party of South Africa and made it a crime, punishable by a maximum of ten years' imprisonment, to be a member of the party or to further the aims of communism. But the bill was drafted in such a broad way that it outlawed all but the mildest protest against the state, deeming it a crime to advocate any doctrine that promoted "political, industrial, social or economic change within the Union by the promotion of disturbance or disorder." Essentially, the bill permitted the government to outlaw any organization and to restrict any individual opposed to its policies.

The ANC, the SAIC, and the APO again met to discuss these new measures, and Dr. Dadoo, among others, said that it would be foolish to allow past differences to thwart a united front against the government. I spoke and echoed his sentiments: clearly, the repression of any one liberation group was repression against all liberation groups. It was at that meeting that Oliver uttered prophetic words: "Today it is the Communist Party. Tomorrow it will be our trade unions, our Indian Congress, our APO, our African National Congress."

Supported by the SAIC and the APO, the ANC resolved to stage a National Day of Protest on June 26, 1950, against the government's murder of eighteen Africans on May 1 and the passage of the Suppression of Communism Act. The proposal was ratified, and in preparation for the Day of Protest, we closed ranks with the SAIC, the APO, and the Communist Party. Here, I believed, was a sufficient threat that compelled us to join hands with our Indian and Communist colleagues.

Earlier that year I had been coopted onto the National Executive Committee of the ANC, taking the place of Dr. Xuma, who had resigned after his failure to be reelected president-general. I was not unmindful of the fact that it had been Dr. Xuma who had tried to help me get my first job when I came to Johannesburg ten years before, when I had no thought of entering politics. Now, as a member of the National Executive Committee, I was playing on the first team with the most senior people in the ANC. I had moved from the role of a gadfly within the organization to one of the powers that I had been rebelling against. It was a heady feeling, and not without mixed emotions. In some ways, it is easier to be a dissident, for then one is without responsibility. As a member of the executive, I had to weigh arguments and make decisions, and expect to be criticized by rebels like myself.

Mass action was perilous in South Africa, where it was a criminal offense for an African to strike, and where the rights of free speech and movement were unmercifully curtailed. By striking, an African worker stood not only to lose his job but his entire livelihood and his right to stay in the area in which he was living. In my experience, a political strike is always riskier than an economic one. A strike based on a political grievance rather than on clear-cut issues like higher wages or shorter hours is a more precarious form of protest and demands particularly efficient organization. The Day of Protest was a political rather than an economic strike.

In preparation for June 26, Walter traveled around the country consulting local leaders. In his absence, I took charge of the bustling ANC office, the hub of a complicated national action. Every day, various leaders looked in to see that matters were going according to plan: Moses Kotane, Dr. Dadoo, Diliza Mji, J. B. Marks, president of the Transvaal ANC, Yusuf Cachalia and his brother Maulvi, Gaur Radebe, secretary of the Council of Action, Michael Harmel, Peter Raboroko, Nthatho Motlana. I was coordinating the actions in different parts of the country, and talking by phone with regional leaders. We had left ourselves little time, and the planning was hastily done.

The Day of Protest was the ANC's first attempt to hold a political strike on a national scale and it was a moderate success. In the cities, the majority of workers stayed home and black businesses did not open. In Bethal, Gert Sibande, who later became president of the Transvaal ANC, led a demonstration of five thousand people, which received headlines in major papers all across the country. The Day of Protest boosted our morale, made us realize our strength, and sent a warning to the Malan government that we would not remain passive in the face of apartheid. June 26 has since become a landmark day in the freedom struggle and within the liberation movement it is observed as Freedom Day.

It was the first time I had taken a significant part in a national campaign, and I felt the exhilaration that springs from the success of a well-planned battle against the enemy and the sense of comradeship that is born of fighting against formidable odds.

The struggle, I was learning, was all-consuming. A man involved in the struggle was a man without a home life. It was in the midst of the Day of Protest that my second son, Makgatho Lewanika, was born. I was with Evelyn at the hospital when he came into the world, but it was only a brief respite from my activities. He was named for Sefako Mapogo

Makgatho, the second president of the ANC, from 1917 until 1924, and Lewanika, a leading chief in Zambia. Makgatho, the son of a Pedi chief, had led volunteers to defy the color bar that did not permit Africans to walk on the sidewalks of Pretoria, and his name for me was an emblem of indominability and courage.

One day, during this same time, my wife informed me that my elder son, Thembi, then five, had asked her, "Where does Daddy live?" I had been returning home late at night, long after he had gone to sleep, and departing early in the morning before he woke. I did not relish being deprived of the company of my children. I missed them a great deal during those days, long before I had any inkling that I would spend decades apart from them.

I was far more certain in those days of what I was against than what I was for. My long-standing opposition to communism was breaking down. Moses Kotane, the general-secretary of the party and a member of the executive of the ANC, often came to my house late at night and we would debate until morning. Clear-thinking and self-taught, Kotane was the son of peasant farmers in the Transvaal. "Nelson," he would say, "what do you have against us? We are all fighting the same enemy. We do not seek to dominate the ANC; we are working within the context of African nationalism." In the end, I had no good response to his arguments.

Because of my friendships with Kotane, Ismail Meer, and Ruth First, and my observation of their own sacrifices, I was finding it more and more difficult to justify my prejudice against the party. Within the ANC, party members J. B. Marks, Edwin Mofutsanyana, Dan Tloome, and David Bopape, among others, were devoted and hardworking, and left nothing to gainsay as freedom fighters. Dr. Dadoo, one of the leaders of the 1946 resistance, was a well-known Marxist whose role as a fighter for human rights had made him a hero to all groups. I could not, and no longer did, question the bona fides of such men and women.

If I could not challenge their dedication, I could still question the philosophical and practical underpinnings of Marxism. But I had little knowledge of Marxism, and in political discussions with my Communist friends I found myself handicapped by my ignorance of Marxist philosophy. I decided to remedy this.

I acquired the complete works of Marx and Engels, Lenin, Stalin, Mao Tse-tung, and others and probed into the philosophy of dialectical and historical materialism. I had little time to study these works properly. While I was stimulated by the *Communist Manifesto*, I was exhausted by *Das Kapital*. But I found myself strongly drawn to the idea of a classless society, which, to my mind, was similar to traditional African culture where life was shared and communal. I subscribed to Marx's basic dictum, which has the simplicity and generosity of the Golden Rule: "From each according to his ability; to each according to his needs."

Dialectical materialism seemed to offer both a searchlight illuminating the dark night of racial oppression and a tool that could be used to end it. It helped me to see the situation other than through the prism of black and white relations, for if our struggle was to succeed, we had to transcend black and white. I was attracted to the scientific underpinnings of dialectical materialism, for I am always inclined to trust what I can verify. Its materialistic analysis of economics rang true to me. The idea that the value of goods was based on the amount of labor that went into them seemed particularly appropriate for South Africa. The ruling class paid African labor a subsistence wage and then added value to the cost of the goods, which they retained for themselves.

Marxism's call to revolutionary action was music to the ears of a freedom fighter. The idea that history progresses through struggle and change occurs in revolutionary jumps was similarly appealing. In my reading of Marxist works, I found a great deal of information that bore on the type of problems that face a practical politician. Marxists gave serious attention to national liberation movements and the Soviet Union in particular supported the national struggles of many colonial peoples. This was another reason why I amended my view of Communists and accepted the ANC position of welcoming Marxists into its ranks.

A friend once asked me how I could reconcile my creed of African nationalism with a belief in dialectical materialism. For me, there was no contradiction. I was first and foremost an African nationalist fighting for our emancipation from minority rule and the right to control our own destiny. But at the same time, South Africa and the African continent were part of the larger world. Our problems, while distinctive and special, were not entirely unique, and a philosophy that placed those problems in an international and historical context of the greater world and the course of history was valuable. I was prepared to use whatever means to speed up the erasure of human prejudice and the end of chauvinistic and violent nationalism. I did not need to become a Communist in order to work with them. I found that African nationalists and African Communists generally had far more uniting them than dividing them. The cynical have always suggested that the Communists were using us. But who is to say that we were not using them?

14

IF WE HAD ANY HOPES or illusions about the National Party before they came into office, we were disabused of them quickly. Their threat to put the kaffir in his place was not an idle one. Apart from the Suppression of Communism Act, two laws passed in 1950 formed the cornerstones of apartheid: the Population and Registration Act and the Group Areas Act. As I have mentioned, the Population and Registration Act authorized the government officially to classify all South Africans according to race. If it had not already been so, race became the sine qua non of South African society. The arbitrary and meaningless tests to decide black from Coloured or Coloured from white often resulted in tragic cases where members of the same family were classified differently, all depending on whether one child had a lighter or darker complexion. Where one was allowed to live and work could rest on such absurd distinctions as the curl of one's hair or the size of one's lips.

The Group Areas Act was the foundation of residential apartheid. Under its regulations, each racial group could own land, occupy premises, and trade only in its own separate area. Indians could henceforth only live in Indian areas, Africans in African, Coloureds in Coloured. If whites wanted the land or houses of the other groups, they could simply declare the land a white area and take them. The Group Areas Act initiated the era of forced removals, when African communities, towns, and villages in newly designated "white" urban areas were violently relocated because the nearby white landowners did not want Africans living near them or simply wanted their land.

At the top of the list for removal was Sophiatown, a vibrant community of more than fifty thousand people, which was one of the oldest black settlements in Johannesburg. Despite its poverty, Sophiatown brimmed with a rich life and was an incubator of so much that was new and valuable in African life and culture. Even before the government's efforts to remove it, Sophiatown held a symbolic importance for Africans disproportionate to its small population.

The following year, the government passed two more laws that directly attacked the rights of the Coloureds and Africans. The Separate Representation of Voters Act aimed to transfer Coloureds to a separate voters' roll in the Cape, thereby diluting the franchise rights that they had enjoyed for more than a century. The Bantu Authorities Act abolished the Natives Representative Council, the one indirect forum of national representation for Africans, and replaced it with a hierarchical system of tribal chiefs appointed by the government. The idea was to restore power to traditional and mainly conservative ethnic leaders in order to perpetuate ethnic differences that were beginning to erode. Both laws epitomized the ethos of the Nationalist government, which pretended to preserve what they were attempting to destroy. Laws stripping people of their rights were inevitably described as laws restoring those rights.

The Coloured people rallied against the Separate Representation of Voters Act, organizing a tremendous demonstration in Cape Town in March of 1951 and a strike in April that kept shops closed and schoolchildren at home. It was in the context of this spirit of activism by Indians, Coloureds, and Africans that Walter Sisulu first broached the idea to a small group of us of a national civil disobedience campaign. He outlined a plan under which selected volunteers from all groups would deliberately invite imprisonment by defying certain laws.

The idea immediately appealed to me, as it did to the others, but I differed with Walter on the question of who should take part. I had recently become national president of the Youth League, and in my new role I urged that the campaign should be exclusively African. The average African, I said, was still cautious about joint action with Indians and Coloureds. While I had made progress in terms of my opposition to communism, I still feared the influence of Indians. In addition, many of our grassroots African supporters saw Indians as exploiters of black labor in their role as shopkeepers and merchants.

Walter vehemently disagreed, suggesting that the Indians, Coloureds, and Africans were inextricably bound together. The issue was taken up at a meeting of the National Executive Committee and my view was voted down, even by those who were considered staunch African nationalists. But I was nevertheless persistent and I raised the matter once more at the national conference in December 1951, where the delegates dismissed my view as emphatically as the National Executive Committee had done. Now that my view had been rejected by the highest levels of the ANC, I fully accepted the agreed-upon position. While my speech advocating a go-it-alone strategy was met with a lukewarm reception, the speech I gave as president of the Youth League after the league pledged its support for the new policy of cooperation was given a resounding ovation.

At the behest of a joint planning council consisting of Dr. Moroka, Walter, J. B. Marks, Yusuf Dadoo, and Yusuf Cachalia, the ANC conference endorsed a resolution calling upon the government to repeal the Suppression of Communism Act, the Group Areas Act, the Separate Representation of Voters Act, the Bantu Authorities Act, the pass laws, and stock limitation laws by February 29, 1952. The law was intended to reduce overgrazing by cattle, but its impact would be to further abridge land for Africans. The council resolved that the ANC would hold demonstrations on April 6, 1952, as a prelude to the launching of the Campaign for the Defiance of Unjust Laws. That same day white South Africans would be celebrating the three hundredth anniversary of Jan Van Riebeeck's arrival at the Cape in 1652. April 6 is the day white South Africans annually commemorate as the founding of their country — and Africans revile as the beginning of three hundred years of enslavement.

The ANC drafted a letter to the prime minister advising him of these resolutions and the deadline for repealing the laws. Because the letter was to go out under the name of Dr. Moroka, and Dr. Moroka had not participated in the writing of it, I was instructed to take him the letter by driving to his home in Thaba 'Nchu, a town near Bloemfontein in the Orange Free State, a very conservative area of the country. I almost did not make it there to see him.

Only a few weeks before, I had taken my driver's test. In those days, a driver's license was an unusual thing for an African, for very few blacks had cars. On the appointed day, I borrowed a car to use for the test. I was a bit cocky, and decided to drive the car there myself. I was running late and was driving faster than I should have been, and as I maneuvered the car along a side street that met a main road, I failed to look both ways and collided with a car coming in another direction. The damage was minimal, but now I would certainly be late. The other driver was a reasonable fellow and we simply agreed to pay our own expenses.

When I reached the testing station, I observed a white woman ahead of me in the middle of her test. She was driving properly and cautiously. When the test was finished, the driving inspector said, "Thank you. Would you please park the car over there," gesturing to a space nearby. She had performed the test well enough to pass, but as the woman drove over to the parking place, she did not negotiate a corner properly and the back wheel jumped the curb. The inspector hurried over and said, "I'm sorry, madam, you've failed the test; please make another appointment." I felt my confidence ebbing. If this fellow tricks a white woman into failing her test, what hope would I have? But I performed well on the test, and when the inspector told me to park the car at the end of the exam, I drove so carefully that I thought he might penalize me for going too slowly.

Once I could legally drive, I became a one-man taxi service. It was one's obligation to give rides to comrades and friends. I was thus deputized to take the letter to Dr. Moroka. This was no hardship to me as

I have always found it enjoyable to gaze out the window while driving. I seemed to have my best ideas while driving through the countryside with the wind whipping through the window.

On my way down to Thaba 'Nchu, I passed through Kroonstad, a conservative Free State town about 120 miles south of Johannesburg. I was driving up a hill and saw two white boys ahead of me on bicycles. My driving was still a bit unsteady, and I came too close to the boys, one of whom suddenly made a turn without signaling, and we collided. He was knocked off his bicycle and was groaning when I got out of the car to help him. He had his arms out signaling for me to pick him up, but just as I was about to do so, a white truck driver yelled for me not to touch the boy. The truck driver scared the child, who then dropped his arms as though he did not want me to pick him up. The boy was not badly hurt, and the truck driver took him to the police station, which was close by.

The local police arrived a short time later, and the white sergeant took one look at me and said, *"Kaffer, jy sal kak vandag!"* (Kaffir, you will shit today!) I was shaken by the accident and the violence of his words, but I told him in no uncertain terms that I would shit when I pleased, not when a policeman told me to. At this, the sergeant took out his notebook to record my particulars. Afrikaans policemen were surprised if a black man could speak English, much less answer back.

After I identified myself, he turned to the car, which he proceeded to ransack. From under the floor mat he pulled out a copy of the left-wing weekly *The Guardian,* which I had hidden immediately after the accident. (I had slipped the letter for Dr. Moroka inside my shirt.) He looked at the title and then held it up in the air like a pirate with his booty: *"Wragtig ons het 'n Kommunis gevang!"* he cried. (My word, we've caught a Communist!) Brandishing the newspaper, he hurried off.

The sergeant returned after about four hours, accompanied by another officer. This sergeant, while also an Afrikaner, was intent on doing his duty correctly. He said he would need to take measurements at the site of the accident for police records. I told the sergeant that it was not proper to take the measurements at night when the accident had occurred in the daylight. I added that I intended to spend the night in Thaba 'Nchu, and that I could not afford to stay in Kroonstad. The sergeant eyed me impatiently and said, "What is your name?"

"Mandela," I said.

"No, the first one," he said. I told him.

"Nelson," the sergeant said, as if he were talking to a boy, "I want to help you resume your journey. But if you are going to be difficult with me I will have no alternative but to be difficult with you and lock you up for the night." That brought me down to earth and I consented to the measurements.

I resumed my journey late that night, and the next morning I was traveling through the district of Excelsior when my car ground to a halt. I had run out of petrol. I walked to a nearby farmhouse and explained in English to an elderly white lady that I would like to buy some petrol. As she was closing the door, she said, "I don't have any petrol for you." I tramped two miles to the next farm and, chastened by my unsuccessful first effort, tried a different approach. I asked to see the farmer, and when he appeared I assumed a humble demeanor. "My *baas* has run out of petrol," I said. (*Baas*, the Afrikaans word for boss or master, signifies subservience.) Friendly and helpful, the farmer was a relation of Prime Minister Strydom. Yet, I believe he would have given me the petrol had I told him the truth and not used the hated word *baas*.

The meeting with Dr. Moroka proved far less eventful than my journey there. He approved of the letter and I made my way back to Johannesburg without incident. The letter to the prime minister noted that the ANC had exhausted every constitutional means at our disposal to achieve our legitimate rights, and that we demanded the repeal of the six "unjust laws" by February 29, 1952, or else we would take extra-constitutional action. Malan's reply, signed by his private secretary, asserted that whites had an inherent right to take measures to preserve their own identity as a separate community, and ended with the threat that if we pursued our actions the government would not hesitate to make full use of its machinery to quell any disturbances.

We regarded Malan's curt dismissal of our demands as a declaration of war. We now had no alternative but to resort to civil disobedience, and we embarked on preparations for mass action in earnest. The recruitment and training of volunteers was one of the essential tasks of the campaign and would in large part be responsible for its success or failure. On April 6, preliminary demonstrations took place in Johannesburg, Pretoria, Port Elizabeth, Durban, and Cape Town. While Dr. Moroka addressed a crowd at Freedom Square in Johannesburg, I spoke to a group of potential volunteers at the Garment Workers Union. I explained to a group of several hundred Africans, Indians, and Coloureds that volunteering was a difficult and even dangerous duty, as the authorities would seek to intimidate, imprison, and perhaps attack the volunteers. No matter what the authorities did, the volunteers could not retaliate, otherwise they would undermine the value of the entire enterprise. They must respond to violence with nonviolence; discipline must be maintained at all cost.

On May 31, the executives of the ANC and the SAIC met in Port Elizabeth and announced that the Defiance Campaign would begin on June 26, the anniversary of the first National Day of Protest. They also created a National Action Committee to direct the campaign and a National Volunteer Board to recruit and train volunteers. I was appointed national volunteer-in-chief of the campaign and chairman of both the Action Committee and the Volunteer Board. My responsibilities were to organize the campaign, coordinate the regional branches, canvass for volunteers, and raise funds.

We also discussed whether the campaign should follow Gandhian principles of nonviolence, or what the Mahatma called *satyagraha,* a nonviolence that seeks to conquer through conversion. Some argued for nonviolence on purely ethical grounds, saying it was morally superior to any other method. This idea was strongly affirmed by Manilal Gandhi, the Mahatma's son and the editor of the newspaper *Indian Opinion,* who was a prominent member of the SAIC. With his gentle demeanor, Gandhi seemed the very personification of nonviolence, and he insisted that the campaign be run along identical lines to that of his father's in India.

Others said that we should approach this issue not from the point of view of principles but of tactics, and that we should employ the method demanded by the conditions. If a particular method or tactic enabled us to defeat the enemy, then it should be used. In this case, the state was far more powerful than we, and any attempts at violence by us would be devastatingly crushed. This made nonviolence a practical necessity rather than an option. This was my view, and I saw nonviolence in the Gandhian model not as an inviolable principle but as a tactic to be used as the situation demanded. The principle was not so important that the strategy should be used even when it was self-defeating, as Gandhi himself believed. I called for nonviolent protest for as long as it was effective. This view prevailed, despite Manilal Gandhi's strong objections.

The joint planning council agreed upon an open-ended program of noncooperation and nonviolence. Two stages of defiance were proposed. In the first stage, a small number of well-trained volunteers would break selected laws in a handful of urban areas. They would enter proscribed areas without permits, use Whites Only facilities such as toilets, Whites Only railway compartments, waiting rooms, and post office entrances. They would deliberately remain in town after curfew. Each batch of defiers would have a leader who would inform the police in advance of the act of disobedience so that the arrests could take place with a minimum of disturbance. The second stage was envisioned as mass defiance, accompanied by strikes and industrial actions across the country.

Prior to the inauguration of the Defiance Campaign, a rally, called the Day of the Volunteers, was held in Durban on June 22. Chief Luthuli, president of the Natal ANC, and Dr. Naicker, president of the Natal Indian Congress, both spoke and committed themselves to the campaign. I had driven down the day before and was the main speaker. About ten thousand people were in attendance, and I told the crowd that the Defiance Campaign would be the most powerful action ever undertaken by the oppressed masses in South Africa. I had never addressed such a great crowd before, and it was an exhilarating experience. One cannot speak to a mass of people as one addresses an audience of two dozen. Yet I have always tried to take the same care to explain matters to great audiences as to small ones. I told the people that they would make history and focus the attention of the world on the racist policies of South Africa. I emphasized that unity among the black people — Africans, Coloureds, and Indians — in South Africa had at last become a reality.

All across the country, those who defied on June 26 did so with courage, enthusiasm, and a sense of history. The campaign began in the early morning hours in Port Elizabeth, where thirty-three defiers, under the leadership of Raymond Mhlaba, entered a railway station through a Whites Only entrance and were arrested. They marched in singing freedom songs, to the accompanying cheers of friends and family. In a call and response, the defiers and the crowd yelled, *"Mayibuye Afrika!"* (Let Africa come back!)

On the morning of the twenty-sixth, I was in the ANC office overseeing the day's demonstrations. The Transvaal batch of volunteers was scheduled to go into action at midday at an African township near Boksburg, east of Johannesburg. Led by Reverend N. B. Tantsi, they were to court arrest by entering the township without permission. Reverend Tantsi was an elderly fellow, a minister in the African Methodist Episcopal Church, and the acting president of the Transvaal ANC.

It was late morning, and I was waiting for Reverend Tantsi to arrive from Pretoria, when he telephoned me at the office. With regret in his voice, he told me that his doctor advised him against defying and going to prison. I assured him that we would provide him with warm clothing and that he would spend only a night in jail, but to no avail. This was a grave disappointment, for Reverend Tantsi was a distinguished figure and had been selected in order to show the authorities that we were not just a group of young rabble-rousers.

In place of Reverend Tantsi, we quickly found someone equally venerable: Nana Sita, the president of the Transvaal Indian Congress, who had served a month in jail for his passive resistance during the 1946 protest campaign. Despite his advanced age and acute arthritis, Sita was a fighter and agreed to lead our defiers.

In the afternoon, as we were preparing to go to Boksburg, I realized that the secretary of the Transvaal branch of the ANC was nowhere to be found. He was meant to accompany Nana Sita to Boksburg. This was another crisis, and I turned to Walter and said, "You must go." This was our first event in the Transvaal, and it was necessary to have prominent figures lead the defiers, otherwise the leaders would appear to be hanging back while the masses took the punishment. Even though Walter was one of the organizers and was scheduled to defy later, he readily agreed. My main concern was that he was wearing a suit, impractical dress for prison, but we managed to find him some old clothes instead.

We then left for Boksburg, where Yusuf Cachalia and I planned to deliver a letter to the Boksburg magistrate, advising him that fifty of our volunteers would enter the African township in his area that day without permits. When we arrived at the magistrate's office, we found a large contingent of pressmen and photographers. As I handed the envelope to the magistrate, the photographers went into action. The magistrate shielded himself from the camera flashes and then invited Yusuf and myself into his chambers to discuss the matter privately. He was a reasonable man, and said his office was always open to us, but that excessive publicity would only worsen matters.

From the magistrate's office, we went straight to the township where the demonstration was taking place, and even from half a mile away we heard the robust singing of our volunteers and the great crowd of supporters who had come to encourage them. At the scene, we found the high metal gates to the township locked and our volunteers waiting patiently outside, demanding entrance. There were fifty-two volunteers in all, both Africans and Indians, and a crowd of several hundred enthusiastic spectators and journalists. Walter was at the head of the defiers; his presence was evidence that we meant business. But the guiding spirit of the demonstrators was Nana Sita, who, despite his arthritis, was moving among the demonstrators in high spirits, clapping them on the back, and bolstering their confidence with his own.

For the first hour there was a standoff. The police were uncharacteristically restrained and their behavior baffled us. Was their restraint a strategy to exhaust the volunteers? Were they waiting for the journalists to depart and then stage a massacre under the cover of darkness? Or were they faced with the dilemma that by arresting us — which is what they would have normally done — they would be doing the very thing we wanted? But even while we were wondering, the situation suddenly changed. The police ordered the gates opened. Immediately the volunteers surged through the gates, thus breaking the law. A police lieutenant blew a whistle and seconds later the police surrounded the volunteers and began arresting them. The campaign was under way. The demonstrators were carted off to the local police station and charged.

That same evening, the leaders of the Action Committee, which included Oliver Tambo, Yusuf Cachalia, and myself, attended a meeting in the city to discuss the day's events and to plan for the week ahead. It was near the area where the second batch of defiers, led by Flag Boshielo, chairman of the central branch of the ANC, were courting arrest. Shortly after eleven o'clock, we found them marching in unison in the street; at eleven, curfew regulations went into effect and Africans needed a permit to be outside.

We emerged from our meeting at midnight. I felt exhausted and was thinking not of defiance but of a hot meal and a night's sleep. At that moment, a policeman approached Yusuf and me. It was obvious that we were going home, not protesting. "No, Mandela," the policeman called out. "You can't escape." He pointed with his nightstick to the police wagon parked nearby and said, "Into the van." I felt like explaining to him that I was in charge of running the campaign on a day-to-day basis and was not scheduled to defy and be arrested until much later, but of course, that would have been ridiculous. I watched as he arrested Yusuf, who burst out laughing at the irony of it all. It was a lovely sight to see him smiling as he was led away by the police.

Moments later, Yusuf and I found ourselves among the more than fifty of our volunteers led by Flag Boshielo who were being taken in trucks to the red-brick police station known as Marshall Square. As the leaders of the Action Committee, we were worried that the others would wonder at our absence and I was concerned about who would be running the campaign. But spirits were high. Even on the way to prison, the vans swayed to the rich voices of the defiers singing *"Nkosi Sikelel' iAfrika"* (God Bless Africa), the hauntingly beautiful African national anthem.

That first night, in the drill yard, one of us was pushed so violently by a white warder that he fell down some steps and broke his ankle. I protested to the warder about his behavior, and he lashed out at me by kicking me in the shin. I demanded that the injured man receive medical attention and we initiated a small but vocal demonstration. We were curtly informed that the injured man could make a request for a doctor the next day if he so wished. We were aware throughout the night of his acute pain.

Until then I had spent bits and pieces of time in prison, but this was my first concentrated experience. Marshall Square was squalid, dark, and dingy, but we were all together and so impassioned and spirited that I barely noticed my surroundings. The camaraderie of our fellow defiers made the two days pass very quickly.

On that first day of the Defiance Campaign, more than 250 volunteers around the country violated various unjust laws and were imprisoned. It was an auspicious beginning. Our troops were orderly, disciplined, and confident.

Over the next five months, 8,500 people took part in the campaign. Doctors, factory workers, lawyers, teachers, students, ministers, defied and went to jail. They sang, "Hey, Malan! Open the jail doors. We want to enter." The campaign spread throughout the Witwatersrand, to Durban, to Port Elizabeth, East London, and Cape Town, and smaller towns in the eastern and western Cape. Resistance was beginning to percolate even in the rural areas. For the most part, the offenses were minor, and the penalties ranged from no more than a few nights in jail to a few weeks, with the option of a fine which rarely exceeded ten pounds. The campaign received an enormous amount of publicity and the membership of the ANC shot up from some 20,000 to 100,000, with the most spectacular increase occurring in the eastern Cape, which contributed half of all new members.

During the six months of the campaign I traveled a great deal throughout the country. I generally went by car, leaving at night or very early in the morning. I toured the Cape, Natal, and the Transvaal, explaining the campaign to small groups, sometimes going from house to house in the townships. Often, my task was to iron out differences in areas that were about to launch actions or had recently done so. In those days, when mass communication for Africans was primitive or nonexistent, politics were parochial. We had to win people over one by one.

On one occasion I drove to the eastern Cape to resolve a dispute involving Alcott Gwentshe, who was running the campaign in East London. Gwentshe had been a successful shopkeeper and had played an important role in organizing East London for the stay-at-home of June 26, two years before. He had briefly gone to jail at the beginning of the Defiance Campaign. He was a strong and able man, but he was an individualist who ignored the advice of the executive and took decisions unilaterally. He was now at odds with his own executive, which was mainly populated with intellectuals.

Gwentshe knew how to exploit certain issues in order to discredit his opponents. He would speak before local members who were workers not intellectuals, and say — in Xhosa, never English, for English was the language of the intellectuals — "Comrades, I think you know that I have suffered for the struggle. I had a good job and then went to jail at the beginning of the Defiance Campaign and I lost that job. Now that I am out of prison, these intellectuals have come along and said, 'Gwentshe, we are better educated than you, we are more capable than you, let us run this campaign.' "

When I investigated the situation I found that Gwentshe had indeed ignored the advice of the executive. But the people were behind him, and he had created a disciplined and well-organized group of volunteers who had defied in an orderly fashion even while Gwentshe was in prison. Although I thought Gwentshe was wrong for disregarding the executive, he was doing a good job and was so firmly entrenched that he could not easily be dislodged. When I saw the members of the executive, I explained that it was impractical to do anything about the situation now, but if they wanted to remedy it, they must defeat him at the next election. It was one of the first times that I saw that it was foolhardy to go against the masses of people. It is no use to take an action to which the masses are opposed, for it will then be impossible to enforce.

The government saw the campaign as a threat to its security and its policy of apartheid. They regarded civil disobedience not as a form of protest but as a crime, and were perturbed by the growing partnership between Africans and Indians. Apartheid was designed to divide racial groups, and we showed that different groups could work together. The prospect of a united front between Africans and Indians, between moderates and radicals, greatly worried them. The Nationalists insisted that the campaign was instigated and led by Communist agitators. The minister of justice announced that he would soon pass legislation to deal with our defiance, a threat he implemented during the 1953 parliamentary session with the passage of the Public Safety Act, which empowered the government to declare martial law and to detain people without trial, and the Criminal Laws Amendment Act, which authorized corporal punishment for defiers.

The government tried a number of underhanded means to interrupt the campaign. Government propagandists repeatedly claimed that the leaders of the campaign were living it up in comfort while the masses were languishing in jail. This allegation was far from the truth, but it achieved a certain currency. The government also infiltrated spies and agents provocateurs into the organization. The ANC welcomed virtually anyone who wanted to join. In spite of the fact that our volunteers were carefully screened before they were selected to defy, the police managed to penetrate not only our local branches but some of the batches of defiers. When I was arrested and sent to Marshall Square, I noticed two fellows among the defiers, one of whom I had never seen before. He wore unusual prison garb: a suit and tie with an overcoat and a silk scarf. What kind of fellow goes to jail dressed like that? His name was Ramaila, and on the third day when we were due to be released, he simply vanished.

The second fellow, whose name was Makhanda, stood out because of his military demeanor. We were out in the courtyard and we were all in high spirits. The defiers would march in front of Yusuf and myself and salute us. Makhanda, who was tall and slender, marched in a soldierly manner and then gave a crisp, graceful salute. A number of the fellows teased him that he must be a policeman to salute so well.

Makhanda had previously worked as a janitor at ANC headquarters. He was very industrious and was popular among the fellows because he would run out and get fish and chips whenever anyone was hungry. But at a later trial we discovered that both Makhanda and Ramaila were police spies. Ramaila testified that he had infiltrated the ranks of the defiers; the trusty Makhanda was actually Detective-Sergeant Motloung.

Africans who worked as spies against their own brothers generally did so for money. Many blacks in South Africa believed that any effort by the black man to challenge the white man was foolhardy and doomed to failure; the white man was too smart and too strong. These spies saw us as a threat not to the white power structure but to black interests, for whites would mistreat all blacks based on the conduct of a few agitators.

Yet, there were many black policemen who secretly aided us. They were decent fellows and found themselves in a moral quandary. They were loyal to their employer and needed to keep their jobs to support their families, but they were sympathetic to our cause. We had an understanding with a handful of African officers who were members of the security police that they would inform us when there was going to be a police raid. These men were patriots who risked their lives to help the struggle.

The government was not our only impediment. Others who might have helped us instead hindered us. At the height of the Defiance Campaign, the United Party sent two of its MPs to urge us to halt the campaign. They said that if we abandoned our campaign in response to a call made by J. G. N. Strauss, the United Party leader, it would help the party defeat the Nationalists in the next election. We rejected this and Strauss proceeded to attack us with the same scorn used by the Nationalists.

We also came under attack from a breakaway ANC group called the National Minded Bloc. Led by Selope Thema, a former member of the National Executive Committee, the group bolted from the ANC when J. B. Marks was elected president of the Transvaal ANC. Thema, who was editor of the newspaper the *Bantu World,* fiercely criticized the campaign in his paper, claiming that Communists had taken over the ANC and that Indians were exploiting the Africans. He asserted that the Communists were more dangerous now that they were working underground, and that Indian economic interests were in conflict with those of Africans. Although he was in a minority in the ANC, his views got a sympathetic hearing among certain radical Youth Leaguers.

In May, during the middle of the Defiance Campaign, J. B. Marks was banned under the 1950 Suppression of Communism Act for "furthering the aims of communism." Banning was a legal order by the government, and generally entailed forced resignation from indicated organizations, and restriction from attending gatherings of any kind. It was a kind of walking imprisonment. To ban a person, the government required no proof, offered no charges; the minister of justice simply declared it so. It was a strategy designed to remove the individual from the struggle, allowing him to live a narrowly defined life outside of politics. To violate or ignore a banning order was to invite imprisonment.

At the Transvaal conference that year in October, my name was proposed to replace the banned J. B. Marks, who had recommended that I succeed him. I was the national president of the Youth League, and the favorite for Marks's position, but my candidacy was opposed by a group from within the Transvaal ANC that called itself "Bafabegiya" (Those Who Die Dancing). The group consisted mainly of ex-Communists turned extreme African nationalists. They sought to cut all links with Indian activists and to move the ANC in the direction of a more confrontational strategy. They were led by MacDonald Maseko, a former Communist who had been chairman of the Orlando Branch of the ANC during the Defiance Campaign, and Seperepere Marupeng, who had been the chief volunteer for the Defiance Campaign in the Witwatersrand. Both Maseko and Marupeng intended to stand for the presidency of the Transvaal.

Marupeng was considered something of a demagogue. He used to wear a military-style khaki suit replete with epaulets and gold buttons, and carried a baton like that made famous by Field Marshal Montgomery. He would stand up in front of meetings, his baton clutched underneath his arm, and say: "I am tired of waiting for freedom. I want freedom now! I will meet Malan at the crossroads and I will show him what I want." Then, banging his baton on the podium, he would cry, "I want freedom now!"

Because of speeches like these, Marupeng became extremely popular during the Defiance Campaign, but popularity is only one factor in an election. He thought that because of his newfound prominence he would win the presidency. Before the election, when it was known that I would be a candidate for the presidency, I approached him and said, "I would like you to stand for election to the executive so that you can serve with me when I am president." He regarded this as a slight, that I was in effect demoting him, and he refused, choosing instead to run for the presidency himself. But he had miscalculated, for I won the election with an overwhelming majority.

On July 30, 1952, at the height of the Defiance Campaign, I was at work at my then law firm of H. M. Basner when the police arrived with a warrant for my arrest. The charge was violation of the Suppression of Communism Act. The state made a series of simultaneous arrests of campaign leaders in Johannesburg, Port Elizabeth, and Kimberley. Earlier in the month, the police had raided homes and offices of ANC and SAIC officials all over the country and confiscated papers and documents. This type of raid was something new and set a pattern for the pervasive and illegal searches that subsequently became a regular feature of the government's behavior.

My arrest and those of the others culminated in a trial in September in Johannesburg of twenty-one accused, including the presidents and general-secretaries of the ANC, the SAIC, the ANC Youth League, and the Transvaal Indian Congress. Among the twenty-one on trial in Johannesburg were Dr. Moroka, Walter Sisulu, and J. B. Marks. A number of Indian leaders were arrested, including Dr. Dadoo, Yusuf Cachalia, and Ahmed Kathrada.

Our appearances in court became the occasion for exuberant political rallies. Massive crowds of demonstrators marched through the streets of Johannesburg and converged on the city's Magistrate's Court. There were white students from the University of the Witwatersrand; old ANC campaigners from Alexandra; Indian schoolchildren from primary and secondary schools; people of all ages and colors. The court had never been deluged with such crowds before. The courtroom itself was packed with people, and shouts of *"Mayibuye Afrika!"* punctuated the proceedings.

The trial should have been an occasion of resolve and solidarity, but was sullied by a breach of faith by Dr. Moroka. Dr. Moroka, the president-general of the ANC and the figurehead of the campaign, shocked us all by employing his own attorney. The plan was for all of us to be tried together. My fellow accused designated me to discuss the matter with Dr. Moroka and attempt to persuade him not to separate himself. The day before the trial, I went to see Dr. Moroka at Village Deep, Johannesburg.

At the outset of our meeting, I suggested alternatives to him, but he was not interested and instead aired a number of grievances. Dr. Moroka felt that he had been excluded from the planning of the campaign. Yet,

Moroka was often quite uninterested in ANC affairs and content to be so. But he said the matter that disturbed him more than any other was that by being defended with the rest of us, he would be associated with men who were Communists. Dr. Moroka shared the government's animosity to communism. I remonstrated with him and said that it was the tradition of the ANC to work with anyone who was against racial oppression. But Dr. Moroka was unmoved.

The greatest jolt came when Dr. Moroka tendered a humiliating plea in mitigation to Judge Rumpff and took the witness stand to renounce the very principles on which the ANC had been founded. Asked whether he thought there should be equality between black and white in South Africa, Dr. Moroka replied that there would never be such a thing. We felt like slumping in despair in our seats. When his own lawyer asked him whether there were some among the defendants who were Communists, Dr. Moroka actually began to point his finger at various people, including Dr. Dadoo and Walter. The judge informed him that that was not necessary.

His performance was a severe blow to the organization and we all immediately realized that Dr. Moroka's days as ANC president were numbered. He had committed the cardinal sin of putting his own interests ahead of the organization and the people. He was unwilling to jeopardize his medical career and fortune for his political beliefs, thereby he had destroyed the image that he had built during three years of courageous work on behalf of the ANC and the Defiance Campaign. I regarded this as a tragedy, for Dr. Moroka's faintheartedness in court took away some of the glow from the campaign. The man who had gone round the country preaching the importance of the campaign had now forsaken it.

On December 2, we were all found guilty of what Judge Rumpff defined as "statutory communism" — as opposed to what he said "is commonly known as communism." According to the statutes of the Suppression of Communism Act, virtually anyone who opposed the government in any way could be defined as — and therefore convicted of — being a "statutory" Communist, even without ever having been a member of the party. The judge, who was fair-minded and reasonable, said that although we had planned acts that ranged from "open noncompliance of laws to something that equals high treason," he accepted that we had consistently advised our members "to follow a peaceful course of action and to avoid violence in any shape or form." We were sentenced to nine months' imprisonment with hard labor, but the sentence was suspended for two years.

We made many mistakes, but the Defiance Campaign marked a new chapter in the struggle. The six laws we singled out were not overturned; but we never had any illusion that they would be. We selected them as the most immediate burden pressing on the lives of the people, and the best way to engage the greatest number of people in the struggle.

Prior to the campaign, the ANC was more talk than action. We had no paid organizers, no staff, and a membership that did little more than pay lip service to our cause. As a result of the campaign, our membership swelled to 100,000. The ANC emerged as a truly mass-based organization with an impressive corps of experienced activists who had braved the police, the courts, and the jails. The stigma usually associated with imprisonment had been removed. This was a significant achievement, for fear of prison is a tremendous hindrance to a liberation struggle. From the Defiance Campaign onward, going to prison became a badge of honor among Africans.

We were extremely proud of the fact that during the six months of the campaign, there was not a single act of violence on our side. The discipline of our resisters was exemplary. During the later part of the campaign, riots broke out in Port Elizabeth and East London in which more than forty people were killed. Though these outbreaks had nothing whatsoever to do with the campaign, the government attempted to link us with them. In this, the government was successful, for the riots poisoned the views of some whites who might otherwise have been sympathetic.

Some within the ANC had unrealistic expectations and were convinced that the campaign could topple the government. We reminded them that the idea of the campaign was to focus attention on our grievances, not eradicate them. They argued that we had the government where we wanted them, and that we should continue the campaign indefinitely. I stepped in and said that this government was too strong and too ruthless to be brought down in such a manner. We could embarrass them, but overthrowing them as a result of the Defiance Campaign was impossible.

As it was, we continued the campaign for too long. We should have listened to Dr. Xuma. The Planning Committee met with Dr. Xuma during the tail end of the campaign and he told us that the campaign would soon lose momentum and it would be wise to call it off before it fizzled out altogether. To halt the campaign while it was still on the offensive would be a shrewd move that would capture the headlines. Dr. Xuma was right: the campaign soon slackened, but in our enthusiasm and even arrogance, we brushed aside his advice. My heart wanted to keep the campaign going but my head told me that it should stop. I argued for closure but went along with the majority. By the end of the year, the campaign foundered.

The campaign never expanded beyond the initial stage of small batches of mostly urban defiers. Mass defiance, especially in the rural areas, was never achieved. The eastern Cape was the only region where we succeeded in reaching the second stage and where a strong resistance movement emerged in the countryside. In general, we did not penetrate the countryside, an historical weakness of the ANC. The campaign was hampered by the fact that we did not have any full-time organizers. I was attempting to organize the campaign and practice as a lawyer at the same time, and that is no way to wage a mass campaign. We were still amateurs.

I nevertheless felt a great sense of accomplishment and satisfaction: I had been engaged in a just cause and had the strength to fight for it and win. The campaign freed me from any lingering sense of doubt or inferiority I might still have felt; it liberated me from the feeling of being overwhelmed by the power and seeming invincibility of the white man and his institutions. But now the white man had felt the power of my punches and I could walk upright like a man, and look everyone in the eye with the dignity that comes from not having succumbed to oppression and fear. I had come of age as a freedom fighter.

Part Four

THE STRUGGLE IS
MY LIFE

15

AT THE ANC annual conference at the end of 1952, there was a changing of the guard. The ANC designated a new, more vigorous president for a new, more activist era: Chief Albert Luthuli. In accordance with the ANC constitution, as provisional president of the Transvaal, I became one of the four deputy presidents. Furthermore, the National Executive Committee appointed me as first deputy president, in addition to my position as president of the Transvaal. Luthuli was one of a handful of ruling chiefs who were active in the ANC and had staunchly resisted the policies of the government.

The son of a Seventh-Day Adventist missionary, Luthuli was born in what was then Southern Rhodesia and educated in Natal. He trained as a teacher at Adam's College near Durban. A fairly tall, heavyset, dark-skinned man with a great broad smile, he combined an air of humility with deep-seated confidence. He was a man of patience and fortitude, who spoke slowly and clearly as though every word was of equal importance.

I had first met him in the late 1940s when he was a member of the Natives Representative Council. In September of 1952, only a few months before the annual conference, Luthuli had been summoned to Pretoria and given an ultimatum: he must either renounce his membership in the ANC and his support of the Defiance Campaign, or he would be dismissed from his position as an elected and government-paid tribal chief. Luthuli was a teacher, a devout Christian, and a proud Zulu chief, but he was even more firmly committed to the struggle against apartheid. Luthuli refused to resign from the ANC and the government dismissed him from his post. In response to his dismissal, he issued a statement of principles called "The Road to Freedom Is via the Cross," in which he reaffirmed his support for nonviolent passive resistance and justified his choice with words that still echo plaintively today: "Who will deny that thirty years of my life have been spent knocking in vain, patiently, moderately and modestly at a closed and barred door?"

I supported Chief Luthuli, but I was unable to attend the national conference. A few days before the conference was to begin, fifty-two leaders around the country were banned from attending any meetings or gatherings for six months. I was among those leaders, and my movements were restricted to the district of Johannesburg for that same period.

My bans extended to meetings of all kinds, not just political ones. I could not, for example, attend my son's birthday party. I was prohibited from talking to more than one person at a time. This was part of a systematic effort by the government to silence, persecute, and immobilize the leaders of those fighting apartheid and was the first of a series of bans on me that continued with brief intervals of freedom until the time I was deprived of all freedom some years hence.

Banning not only confines one physically, it imprisons one's spirit. It induces a kind of psychological claustrophobia that makes one yearn not only for freedom of movement but spiritual escape. Banning was a dangerous game, for one was not shackled or chained behind bars; the bars were laws and regulations that could easily be violated and often were. One could slip away unseen for short periods of time and have the temporary illusion of freedom. The insidious effect of bans was that at a certain point one began to think that the oppressor was not without but within.

Although I was prevented from attending the 1952 annual conference, I was immediately informed as to what had transpired. One of the most significant decisions was one taken in secret and not publicized at the time.

Along with many others, I had become convinced that the government intended to declare the ANC and the SAIC illegal organizations, just as it had done with the Communist Party. It seemed inevitable that the state would attempt to put us out of business as a legal organization as soon as it could. With this in mind, I approached the National Executive Committee with the idea that we must come up with a contingency plan for just such an eventuality. I said it would be an abdication of our responsibility as leaders of the people if we did not do so. They instructed me to draw up a plan that would enable the organization to operate from underground. This strategy came to be known as the Mandela-Plan, or simply, M-Plan.

The idea was to set up organizational machinery that would allow the ANC to make decisions at the highest level, which could then be swiftly transmitted to the organization as a whole without calling a meeting. In other words, it would allow an illegal organization to continue to function and enable leaders who were banned to continue to lead. The M-Plan was designed to allow the organization to recruit new members, respond to local and national problems, and maintain regular contact between the membership and the underground leadership.

I held a number of secret meetings among ANC and SAIC leaders, both banned and not banned, to discuss the parameters of the plan. I worked on it for a number of months and came up with a system that was broad enough to adapt itself to local conditions and not fetter individual initiative, but detailed enough to facilitate order. The smallest unit was the cell, which in urban townships consisted of roughly ten houses on a street. A cell steward would be in charge of each of these units. If a street had more than ten houses, a street steward would take charge and the cell stewards would report to him. A group of streets formed a zone directed by a chief steward, who was in turn responsible to the secretariat of the local branch of the ANC. The secretariat was a subcommittee of the branch executive, which reported to the provincial secretary. My notion was that every cell and street steward should know every person and family in his area, so that he would be trusted by the people and would know whom to trust. The cell steward arranged meetings, organized political classes, and collected dues. He was the linchpin of the plan. Although the strategy was primarily created for more urban areas, it could be adapted to rural ones.

The plan was accepted, and was to be implemented immediately. Word went out to the branches to begin to prepare for this covert restructuring. The plan was accepted at most branches, but some of the more far-flung outposts felt that the plan was an effort by Johannesburg to centralize control over the regions.

As part of the M-Plan, the ANC introduced an elementary course of political lectures for its members throughout the country. These lectures were meant not only to educate but to hold the organization together. The lectures were given in secret by branch leaders. Those members in attendance would in turn give the same lectures to others in their homes and communities. In the beginning, the lectures were not systemized, but within a number of months there was a set curriculum.

There were three courses, "The World We Live In," "How We Are Governed," and "The Need for Change." In the first course, we discussed the different types of political and economic systems around the world as well as in South Africa. It was an overview of the growth of capitalism as well as socialism. We discussed, for example, how blacks in South Africa were oppressed both as a race and an economic class. The lecturers were mostly banned members, and I myself frequently gave lectures in the evening. This arrangement had the virtue of keeping banned individuals active as well as keeping the membership in touch with these leaders.

During this time, the banned leadership would often meet secretly and alone, and then arrange to meet the present leaders. The old and the new leadership meshed very well, and the decision-making process was collective as it had been before. Sometimes it felt as if nothing had changed except that we had to meet in secret.

The M-Plan was conceived with the best intentions, but it was instituted with only modest success and its adoption was never widespread. The most impressive results were once again in the eastern Cape and Port Elizabeth. The spirit of the Defiance Campaign continued in the eastern Cape long after it vanished elsewhere, and ANC members there seized on the M-Plan as a way of continuing to defy the government.

The plan faced many problems: it was not always adequately explained to the membership; there were no paid organizers to help implement or administer it; and there was often dissension within branches that prevented agreement on imposing the plan. Some provincial leaders resisted it because they believed it undermined their power. To some, the government's crackdown did not seem imminent so they did not take the precautions necessary to lessen its effect. When the government's iron fist did descend, they were not prepared.

16

MY LIFE, during the Defiance Campaign, ran on two separate tracks: my work in the struggle and my livelihood as an attorney. I was never a full-time organizer for the ANC; the organization had only one, and that was Thomas Titus Nkobi. The work I did had to be arranged around my schedule as an attorney. In 1951, after I had completed my articles at Witkin, Sidelsky and Eidelman, I went to work for the law firm of Terblanche & Briggish. When I completed my articles, I was not yet a fully-fledged attorney, but I was in a position to draw court pleadings, send out summonses, interview witnesses — all of which an attorney must do before a case goes to court.

After leaving Sidelsky, I had investigated a number of white firms — there were, of course, no African law firms. I was particularly interested in the scale of fees charged by these firms and was outraged to discover that many of the most blue-chip law firms charged Africans even higher fees for criminal and civil cases than they did their far wealthier white clients.

After working for Terblanche & Briggish for about one year, I joined the firm of Helman and Michel. It was a liberal firm and one of the few that charged Africans on a reasonable scale. In addition, the firm prided itself on its devotion to African education, toward which they donated handsomely. Mr. Helman, the firm's senior partner, was involved with African causes long before they became popular or fashionable. The firm's other partner, Rodney Michel, a veteran of World War II, was also extremely liberal. He was a pilot, and years later helped fly ANC people out of South Africa during the worst periods of repression. Michel's only discernible vice was that he was a heavy smoker who puffed on one cigarette after another all day long at the office.

I stayed at Helman and Michel for a number of months while I was studying for my qualification exam, which would establish me as a fully-fledged attorney. I had given up studying for an LL.B. degree at the University of the Witwatersrand after failing my exams several times. I opted to take the qualifying exam so that I could practice and begin to earn enough money to support my family. At the time, my sister was living with us, and my mother had come to visit, and Evelyn's wages as a nurse trainee plus my own paltry income were not enough to keep everyone warm and fed.

When I passed the qualification exam, I went to work as a fully-fledged attorney at the firm of H. M. Basner. Basner had been an African Representative in the Senate, an early member of the Communist Party, and a passionate supporter of African rights. As a lawyer, he was a defender of African leaders and trade unionists. For the months that I worked there, I was often in court representing the firm's many African clients. Mr. Basner was an excellent boss and as long as I got my work done at the firm he encouraged my political work. After the experience I gained there, I felt ready to go off on my own.

In August of 1952, I opened my own law office. What early success I enjoyed I owed to Zubeida Patel, my secretary. I had met her when she had gone to work at H. M. Basner as a replacement for an Afrikaans-speaking secretary, Miss Koch, who had refused to take my dictation. Zubeida was the wife of my friend Cassim Patel, a member of the Indian Congress, and she was without any sense of color bar whatsoever. She had a wide circle of friends, knew many people in the legal world, and when I went out on my own, she agreed to work for me. She brought a great deal of business through the door.

Oliver Tambo was then working for a firm called Kovalsky and Tuch. I often visited him there during his lunch hour, and made a point of sitting in a Whites Only chair in the Whites Only waiting room. Oliver and I were very good friends, and we mainly discussed ANC business during those lunch hours. He had first impressed me at Fort Hare, where I noticed his thoughtful intelligence and sharp debating skills. With his cool, logical style he could demolish an opponent's argument — precisely the sort of intelligence that is useful in a courtroom. Before Fort Hare, he had been a brilliant student at St. Peter's in Johannesburg. His even-tempered objectivity was an antidote to my more emotional reactions to issues. Oliver was deeply religious and had for a long time considered the ministry to be his calling. He was also a neighbor: he came from Bizana in Pondoland, part of the Transkei, and his face bore the distinctive scars of his tribe. It seemed natural for us to practice together and I asked him to join me. A few months later, when Oliver was able to extricate himself from his firm, we opened our own office in downtown Johannesburg.

"Mandela and Tambo" read the brass plate on our office door in Chancellor House, a small building just across the street from the marble statues of justice standing in front of the Magistrate's Court in central Johannesburg. Our building, owned by Indians, was one of the few places where Africans could rent offices in the city. From the beginning, Mandela and Tambo was besieged with clients. We were not the only African lawyers in South Africa, but we were the only firm of African lawyers. For Africans, we were the firm of first choice and last resort. To reach our offices each morning, we had to move through a crowd of people in the hallways, on the stairs, and in our small waiting room.

Africans were desperate for legal help in government buildings: it was a crime to walk through a Whites Only door, a crime to ride a Whites Only bus, a crime to use a Whites Only drinking fountain, a crime to walk on a Whites Only beach, a crime to be on the streets past eleven, a crime not to have a pass book and a crime to have the wrong signature in that book, a crime to be unemployed and a crime to be employed in the wrong place, a crime to live in certain places and a crime to have no place to live.

Every week we interviewed old men from the countryside who told us that generation after generation of their family had worked a scraggly piece of land from which they were now being evicted. Every week we interviewed old women who brewed African beer as a way to supplement their tiny incomes, who now faced jail terms and fines they could not afford to pay. Every week we interviewed people who had lived in the same house for decades only to find that it was now declared a white area and they had to leave without any recompense at all. Every day we heard and saw the thousands of humiliations that ordinary Africans confronted every day of their lives.

Oliver had a prodigious capacity for work. He spent a great deal of time with each client, not so much for professional reasons but because he was a man of limitless compassion and patience. He became involved in his clients' cases and in their lives. He was touched by the plight of the masses as a whole and by each and every individual.

I realized quickly what Mandela and Tambo meant to ordinary Africans. It was a place where they could come and find a sympathetic ear and a competent ally, a place where they would not be either turned away or cheated, a place where they might actually feel proud to be represented by men of their own skin color. This was the reason I had become a lawyer in the first place, and my work often made me feel I had made the right decision.

We often dealt with a half-dozen cases in a morning, and were in and out of court all day long. In some courts we were treated with courtesy; in others we were treated with contempt. But even as we practiced and fought and won cases, we always knew that no matter how well we pursued our careers as attorneys, we could never become a prosecutor, a magistrate, a judge. Although we were dealing with officials whose competence was no greater than our own, their authority was founded on and protected by the color of their skin.

We frequently encountered prejudice in the court itself. White witnesses often refused to answer questions from a black attorney. Instead of citing them for contempt of court, the magistrate would then pose the questions they would not answer from me. I routinely put policemen on the stand and interrogated them; though I would catch them in discrepancies and lies, they never considered me anything but a "kaffir lawyer."

I recall once being asked at the outset of a trial to identify myself. This was customary. I said, "I am Nelson Mandela and I appear for the accused." The magistrate said, "I don't know you. Where is your certificate?" A certificate is the fancy diploma that one frames and hangs on the wall; it is not something that an attorney ever carries with him. It would be like asking a man for his university degree. I requested that the magistrate begin the case, and I would bring in my certificate in due course. But the magistrate refused to hear the case, even going so far as to ask a court officer to evict me.

This was a clear violation of court practice. The matter eventually came before the Supreme Court and my friend George Bizos, an advocate, appeared on my behalf. At the hearing, the presiding judge criticized the conduct of the magistrate and ordered that a different magistrate must hear the case.

Being a lawyer did not guarantee respect out of court either. One day, near our office, I saw an elderly white woman whose motorcar was sandwiched between two cars. I immediately went over and pushed the car, which helped free it. The English-speaking woman turned to me and said, "Thank you, John" — John being the name whites used to address any African whose name they did not know. She then handed me a sixpence coin, which I politely refused. She pushed it toward me, and again I said no thank you. She then exclaimed, "You refuse a sixpence. You must want a shilling, but you shall not have it!" and then threw the coin at me, and drove off.

Within a year, Oliver and I discovered that under the Urban Areas Act we were not permitted to occupy business premises in the city without ministerial consent. Our request was denied, and we received instead a temporary permit, under the Group Areas Act, which soon expired. The authorities refused to renew it, insisting that we move our offices to an African location many miles away and virtually unreachable for our clients. We interpreted this as an effort by the authorities to put us out of business, and occupied our premises illegally, with threats of eviction constantly hanging over our heads.

Working as a lawyer in South Africa meant operating under a debased system of justice, a code of law that did not enshrine equality but its opposite. One of the most pernicious examples of this is the Population Registration Act, which defined that inequality. I once handled the case of a Coloured man who was inadvertently classified as an African. He had fought for South Africa during World War II in North Africa and Italy, but after his return, a white bureaucrat had reclassified him as African. This was the type of case, not at all untypical in South Africa, that offered a moral jigsaw puzzle. I did not support or recognize the principles in the Population Registration Act, but my client needed representation, and he had been classified as something he was not. There were many practical advantages to being classified as Coloured rather than African, such as the fact that Coloured men were not required to carry passes.

On his behalf, I appealed to the Classification Board, which adjudicated cases falling under the Population Registration Act. The board consisted of a magistrate and two other officials, all white. I had formidable documentary evidence to establish my client's case and the prosecutor formally indicated that he would not oppose our appeal. But the magistrate seemed uninterested in both my evidence and the prosecutor's demurral. He stared at my client and gruffly asked him to turn around so that his back faced the bench. After scrutinizing my client's shoulders, which sloped down sharply, he nodded to the other officials and upheld the appeal. In the view of the white authorities those days, sloping shoulders were one stereotype of the Coloured physique. And so it came about that the course of this man's life was decided purely on a magistrate's opinion about the structure of his shoulders.

We tried many cases involving police brutality, though our success rate was quite low. Police assaults were always difficult to prove. The police were clever enough to detain a prisoner long enough for the wounds and bruises to heal, and often it was simply the word of a policeman against our client. The magistrates naturally sided with the police. The coroner's verdict on a death in police custody would often read, "Death due to multiple causes," or some vague explanation that let the police off the hook.

Whenever I had a case outside Johannesburg, I applied to have my bans temporarily lifted, and this was often granted. For example, I traveled to the eastern Transvaal, and defended a client in the town of Carolina. My arrival caused quite a sensation, as many of the people had never before seen an African lawyer. I was received warmly by the magistrate and prosecutor, and the case did not begin for quite a while, as they asked me numerous questions about my career and how I became a lawyer. The court was similarly crowded with curious townspeople.

In a nearby village I appeared for a local medicine man charged with witchcraft. This case also attracted a large crowd — not to see me, but to find out whether the white man's laws could be applied to a *sangoma*. The medicine man exerted tremendous power in the area, and many people both worshipped and feared him. At one point, my client sneezed violently, causing a virtual stampede in the courtroom; most observers believed he was casting a spell. He was found not guilty, but I suspect that the local people attributed this not to my skill as a lawyer, but to the power of the medicine man's herbs.

As an attorney, I could be rather flamboyant in court. I did not act as though I were a black man in a white man's court, but as if everyone else — white and black — was a guest in my court. When trying a case, I often made sweeping gestures and used high-flown language. I was punctilious about all court regulations, but I sometimes used unorthodox tactics with witnesses. I enjoyed cross-examinations, and often played on racial tension. The spectators' gallery was usually crowded, because people from the township attended court as a form of entertainment.

I recall once defending an African woman employed as a domestic worker in town. She was accused of stealing her "madam's" clothes. The clothing that was allegedly stolen was displayed on a table in court. After the "madam" had testified, I began my cross-examination by walking over to the table of evidence. I perused the clothing and then, with the tip of my pencil, I picked up an item of ladies' underwear. I slowly turned to the witness box brandishing the panties and simply asked, "Madam, are these . . . yours?" "No," she replied quickly, too embarrassed to admit that they were hers. Because of this response, and other discrepancies in her evidence, the magistrate dismissed the case.

17

SITUATED FOUR MILES WEST of Johannesburg's center, on the face of a rocky outcrop overlooking the city, was the African township of Sophiatown. Father Trevor Huddleston, one of the township's greatest friends, once compared Sophiatown to an Italian hill town and from a distance the place did indeed have a good deal of charm: the closely packed, red-roofed houses; the smoke curling up into a pink sky; the tall and slender gum trees that hugged the township. Up close one saw the poverty and squalor in which too many of Sophiatown's people lived. The streets were narrow and unpaved, and every lot was filled with dozens of shanties huddled close together.

Sophiatown was part of what was known as the Western Areas townships, along with Martindale and Newclare. The area was originally intended for whites, and a real estate developer actually built a number of houses there for white buyers. But because of a municipal refuse dump in the area, whites chose to live elsewhere. Reluctantly, the developer sold his houses to Africans. Sophiatown was one of the few places in the Transvaal where Africans had been able to buy stands, or plots, prior to the 1923 Urban Areas Act. Many of these old brick and stone houses, with their tin-roofed verandas, still stood in Sophiatown, giving the township an air of Old World graciousness. As industry in Johannesburg grew, Sophiatown became the home of a rapidly expanding African workforce. It was convenient and close to town. Workers lived in shanties that were erected in the back and front yards of older residences. Several families might all be crowded into a single shanty. Up to forty people could share a single water tap. Despite the poverty, Sophiatown had a special character; for Africans, it was the Left Bank in Paris, Greenwich Village in New York, the home of writers, artists, doctors, and lawyers. It was both bohemian and conventional, lively and sedate. It was home to both Dr. Xuma, where he had his practice, and assorted *tsotsis* (gangsters), like the Berliners and the Americans, who adopted the names of American movie stars like John Wayne and Humphrey Bogart. Sophiatown boasted the only swimming pool for African children in Johannesburg.

In Johannesburg, the Western Areas Removal scheme meant the evacuation of Sophiatown, Martindale, and Newclare, with a collective population that was somewhere between 60,000 and 100,000. In 1953, the Nationalist government had purchased a tract of land called Meadowlands, thirteen miles from the city. People were to be resettled there in seven different "ethnic groups." The excuse given by the government was slum clearance, a smokescreen for the government policy that regarded all urban areas as white areas where Africans were temporary residents.

The government was under pressure from its supporters in the surrounding areas of Westdene and Newlands, which were comparatively poor white areas. These working-class whites were envious of some of the fine houses owned by blacks in Sophiatown. The government wanted to control the movements of all Africans, and such control was far more difficult in freehold urban townships, where blacks could own property, and people came and went as they pleased. Though the pass system was still in effect, one did not need a special permit to enter a freehold township as was the case with municipal locations. Africans had lived and owned property in Sophiatown for over fifty years; now the government was callously planning on relocating all Sophiatown's African residents to another black township. So cynical was the government's plan that the removal was to take place even before the houses were built to accommodate the evacuated people. The removal of Sophiatown was the first major test of strength for the ANC and its allies after the Defiance Campaign.

Although the government's removal campaign for Sophiatown had started in 1950, efforts by the ANC to combat it did not begin in earnest until 1953. By the middle of the year, the local branches of the ANC and the TIC and the local Ratepayers Association were mobilizing people to resist. In June of 1953, a public meeting was called by the provincial executive of the ANC and the TIC at Sophiatown's Odin cinema to discuss opposition to the removal. It was a lively, exuberant meeting attended by more than twelve hundred people, none of whom seemed intimidated by the presence of dozens of heavily armed policemen.

Only a few days before the meeting, my banning orders, as well as Walter's, had expired. This meant that we were no longer prevented from attending or speaking at gatherings, and arrangements were quickly made for me to speak at the theater.

Shortly before the meeting was to begin, a police officer saw Walter and me outside the cinema talking with Father Huddleston, one of the leaders of the opposition to the removal. The officer informed the two of us that as banned individuals we had no right to be there, and he then ordered his officers to arrest us. Father Huddleston shouted to the policemen coming toward us, "No, you must arrest me instead, my dears." The officer ordered Father Huddleston to stand aside, but he refused. As the policemen moved Father Huddleston out of the way, I said to the officer, "You must make sure if we are under a ban or not. Be careful, because it would be a wrongful arrest to take us in if our bans have expired. Now, do you think we would be here tonight talking to you if our bans had not expired?"

The police were notorious for keeping very poor records and were often unaware when bans ended. The officer knew this as well as I did. He pondered what I had said, then told his officers to pull back. They stood aside as we entered the hall.

Inside, the police were provocative and contemptuous. Equipped with pistols and rifles, they strutted around the hall pushing people around, making insulting remarks. I was sitting onstage with a number of other leaders, and as the meeting was about to begin, I saw Major Prinsloo come swaggering in through the stage door, accompanied by a number of armed officers. I caught his eye, and I made a gesture as if to say, "Me?" and he shook his head no. He then walked over to the podium, where Yusuf Cachalia had already begun to speak, and ordered the other officers to arrest him, whereupon they took him by the arms and started to drag him off. Outside, the police had already arrested Robert Resha and Ahmed Kathrada.

The crowd began yelling and booing, and I saw that matters could turn extremely ugly if the crowd did not control itself. I jumped to the podium and started singing a well-known protest song, and as soon as I pronounced the first few words the crowd joined in. I feared that the police might have opened fire if the crowd had become too unruly.

The ANC was then holding meetings every Sunday evening in Freedom Square, in the center of Sophiatown, to mobilize opposition to the removal. These were vibrant sessions, punctuated by repeated cries of *"Asihambi!"* (We are not moving!) and the singing of *"Sophiatown likhaya lam asihambi"* (Sophiatown is my home; we are not moving). The meetings were addressed by leading ANC members, standholders, tenants, city councillors, and often by Father Huddleston, who ignored police warnings to confine himself to church affairs.

One Sunday evening, not long after the incident at the Odin, I was scheduled to speak in Freedom Square. The crowd that night was passionate, and their emotion undoubtedly influenced mine. There were a great many young people present, and they were angry and eager for action. As usual, policemen were clustered around the perimeter, armed with both guns and pencils, the latter to take notes as to who was speaking and what the speaker was saying. We tried to make this into a virtue by being as open with the police as possible to show them that in fact we had nothing to hide, not even our distaste for them.

I began by speaking about the increasing repressiveness of the government in the wake of the Defiance Campaign. I said the government was now scared of the might of the African people. As I spoke, I grew more and more indignant. In those days, I was something of a rabble-rousing speaker. I liked to incite an audience, and I was doing so that evening.

As I condemned the government for its ruthlessness and lawlessness, I stepped across the line: I said that the time for passive resistance had ended, that nonviolence was a useless strategy and could never overturn a white minority regime bent on retaining its power at any cost. At the end of the day, I said, violence was the only weapon that would destroy apartheid and we must be prepared, in the near future, to use that weapon.

The crowd was excited; the youth in particular were clapping and cheering. They were ready to act on what I said right then and there. At that point I began to sing a freedom song, the lyrics of which say, "There are the enemies, let us take our weapons and attack them." I sang this song and the crowd joined in, and when the song was finished, I pointed to the police and said, "There, there are our enemies!" The crowd again started cheering and made aggressive gestures in the direction of the police. The police looked nervous, and a number of them pointed back at me as if to say, "Mandela, we will get you for this." I did not mind. In the heat of the moment I did not think of the consequences.

But my words that night did not come out of nowhere. I had been thinking of the future. The government was busily taking measures to prevent anything like the Defiance Campaign from reoccurring. I had begun to analyze the struggle in different terms. The ambition of the ANC was to wage a mass struggle, to engage the workers and peasants of South Africa in a campaign so large and powerful that it might overcome the status quo of white oppression. But the Nationalist government was making any legal expression of dissent or protest impossible. I saw that they would ruthlessly suppress any legitimate protest on the part of the African majority. A police state did not seem far off.

I began to suspect that both legal and extra-constitutional protests would soon be impossible. In India, Gandhi had been dealing with a foreign power that ultimately was more realistic and farsighted. That was not the case with the Afrikaners in South Africa. Nonviolent passive resistance is effective as long as your opposition adheres to the same rules as you do. But if peaceful protest is met with violence, its efficacy is at an end. For me, nonviolence was not a moral principle but a strategy; there is no moral goodness in using an ineffective weapon. But my thoughts on this matter were not yet formed, and I had spoken too soon.

That was certainly the view of the National Executive Committee. When they learned of my speech, I was severely reprimanded for advocating such a radical departure from accepted policy. Although some on the executive sympathized with my remarks, no one could support the intemperate way that I had made them. The executive admonished me, noting that the impulsive policy I had called for was not only premature but dangerous. Such speeches could provoke the enemy to crush the organization entirely while the enemy was strong and we were as yet still weak. I accepted the censure, and thereafter faithfully defended the policy of nonviolence in public. But in my heart, I knew that nonviolence was not the answer.

In those days, I was often in hot water with the executive. In early 1953, Chief Luthuli, Z. K. Matthews, and a handful of other high-ranking

ANC leaders were invited to a meeting with a group of whites who were in the process of forming the Liberal Party. A meeting of the ANC executive took place afterward at which a few of us asked for a report of the earlier meeting with the white liberals. The attendees refused, saying that they had been invited in their private capacity, not as members of the ANC. We continued to pester them, and finally Professor Matthews, who was a lawyer, said that it had been a privileged conversation. In a fit of indignation, I said, "What kind of leaders are you who can discuss matters with a group of white liberals and then not share that information with your colleagues at the ANC? That's the trouble with you, you are scared and overawed of the white man. You value his company more than that of your African comrades."

This outburst provoked the wrath of both Professor Matthews and Chief Luthuli. First, Professor Matthews responded: "Mandela, what do you know about whites? I taught you whatever you know about whites and you are still ignorant. Even now, you are barely out of your student uniform." Luthuli was burning with a cold fire and said, "All right, if you are accusing me of being afraid of the white man then I have no other recourse but to resign. If that is what you say then that is what I intend to do." I did not know whether Luthuli was bluffing or not, but his threat frightened me. I had spoken hastily, without thinking, without a sense of responsibility, and I now greatly regretted it. I immediately withdrew my charge and apologized. I was a young man who attempted to make up for his ignorance with militancy.

At the same time as my speech in Sophiatown, Walter informed me that he had been invited to attend the World Festival of Youth and Students for Peace and Friendship in Bucharest as a guest of honor. The timing of the invitation gave Walter virtually no opportunity to consult with the National Executive Committee. I was keen that he should go and encouraged him to do so, whether or not he conferred with the executive. Walter resolved to go and I helped him arrange for a substitute passport, an affidavit stating his identity and citizenship. (The government would never have issued him a proper passport.) The group, which was headed by Walter Sisulu and Duma Nokwe, traveled on the only airline that would accept such an affidavit: the Israeli airline, El Al.

I was convinced, despite my reprimand from the executive, that the policies of the Nationalists would soon make nonviolence an even more limited and ineffective policy. Walter was privy to my thoughts and before he left, I made a suggestion: he should arrange to visit the People's Republic of China and discuss with them the possibility of supplying us with weapons for an armed struggle. Walter liked the idea and promised to make the attempt.

This action was taken purely on my own and my methods were highly unorthodox. To some extent, they were the actions of a hotheaded revolutionary who had not thought things through and who acted without discipline. They were the actions of a man frustrated with the immorality of apartheid and the ruthlessness of the state in protecting it.

Walter's visit caused a storm within the executive. I undertook the task of personally conveying his apologies. I did not mention my secret request. Luthuli objected to the flouting of the ANC's code of conduct, and Professor Matthews expressed dismay about Walter visiting socialist countries. The executive was skeptical about Walter's motives, and questioned my explanation of the circumstances. A few wanted to formally censure Walter and me, but in the end did not.

Walter managed to reach China, where the leadership received him warmly. They conveyed their support of our struggle, but they were wary and cautious when he broached the idea of an armed struggle. They warned him that an armed struggle was an extremely grave undertaking and they questioned whether the liberation movement had matured sufficiently to justify such an endeavor. Walter came back with encouragement but no guns.

18

IN JOHANNESBURG, I had become a man of the city. I wore smart suits; I drove a colossal Oldsmobile, and I knew my way around the back alleys of the city. I commuted daily to a downtown office. But in fact I remained a country boy at heart, and there was nothing that lifted my spirits as much as blue skies, the open veld, and green grass. In September, with my bans ended, I decided to take advantage of my freedom and get a respite from the city. I took on a case in the little dorp of Villiers in the Orange Free State.

The drive to the Orange Free State from Johannesburg used to take several hours, and I set out on my journey from Orlando at 3 A.M., which has always been my favorite hour for departure. I am an early riser anyway, and at 3 A.M. the roads are empty and quiet, and one can be alone with one's thoughts. I like to see the coming of dawn, the change between day and night, which is always majestic. It was also a convenient hour for departure because the police were usually nowhere to be found.

The province of the Orange Free State has always had a magical effect on me, though some of the most racist elements of the white population call the Free State its home. With its flat dusty landscape as far as the eye can see, the great blue ceiling above, the endless stretches of yellow mealie fields, scrub and bushes, the Free State's landscape gladdens my heart no matter what my mood. When I am there I feel like nothing can shut me in, that my thoughts can roam as far and wide as the horizons.

The landscape bore the imprint of General Charles R. De Wet, the gifted Boer commander who outclassed the British in dozens of engagements during the final months of the Anglo-Boer War; fearless, proud, and shrewd, he would have been one of my heroes had he been fighting for the rights of all South Africans, not just Afrikaners. He demonstrated the courage and resourcefulness of the underdog, and the power of a less sophisticated but patriotic army against a tested war machine. As I drove, I imagined the hiding places of General De Wet's army and wondered whether they would someday shelter African rebels.

The drive to Villiers cheered me considerably, and I was laboring under a false sense of security when I entered the small courthouse on the morning of the third of September. I found a group of policemen waiting for me. With nary a word, they served me with an order under the Suppression of Communism Act requiring me to resign from the ANC, restricting me to the Johannesburg district, and prohibiting me from attending any meetings or gatherings for two years. I knew such measures would come, but I had not expected to receive my bans in the remote town of Villiers.

I was thirty-five years old and these new and more severe bans ended a period of nearly a decade of involvement with the ANC, years that had been the time of my political awakening and growth, and my gradual commitment to the struggle that had become my life. Henceforth, all of my actions and plans on behalf of the ANC and the liberation struggle would become secret and illegal. Once served, I had to return to Johannesburg immediately.

My bans drove me from the center of the struggle to the sidelines, from a role that was primary to one that was peripheral. Though I was often consulted and was able to influence the direction of events, I did so at a distance and only when expressly asked. I no longer felt like a vital organ of the body — the heart, lungs, or backbone — but a severed limb. Even freedom fighters, at least then, had to obey the laws, and at that point, imprisonment for violating my bans would have been useless to the ANC and to myself. We were not yet at the point where we were open revolutionaries, overtly fighting the system no matter what the cost. We believed then that it was better to organize underground than to go to prison. When I was forced to resign from the ANC, the organization had to replace me, and no matter what I might have liked, I could no longer wield the authority I once possessed. While driving back to Johannesburg, the Free State scenery did not have quite the same elevating effect on me as before.

19

WHEN I RECEIVED my banning, the Transvaal conference of the ANC was due to be held the following month, and I had already completed the draft of my presidential address. It was read to the conference by Andrew Kunene, a member of the executive. In that speech, which subsequently became known as "The No Easy Walk to Freedom" speech, a line taken from Jawaharlal Nehru, I said that the masses now had to be prepared for new forms of political struggle. The new laws and tactics of the government had made the old forms of mass protest — public meetings, press statements, stay-aways — extremely dangerous and self-destructive. Newspapers would not publish our statements; printing presses refused to print our leaflets, all for fear of prosecution under the Suppression of Communism Act. "These developments," I wrote, "require the evolution of new forms of political struggle. The old methods," I said, were now "suicidal."

"The oppressed people and the oppressors are at loggerheads. The day of reckoning between the forces of freedom and those of reaction is not very far off. I have not the slightest doubt that when that day comes truth and justice will prevail. . . . The feelings of the oppressed people have never been more bitter. The grave plight of the people compels them to resist to the death the stinking policies of the gangsters that rule our country. . . . To overthrow oppression has been sanctioned by humanity and is the highest aspiration of every free man."

In April of 1954, the Law Society of the Transvaal applied to the Supreme Court for my name to be struck off the roll of accredited attorneys on the ground that the political activities for which I was convicted in the Defiance case amounted to unprofessional and dishonorable conduct. This occurred at a time when Mandela and Tambo was flourishing and I was in court dozens of times a week.

The documents were served at my office, and as soon as the application against me had been made and publicized, I began to receive offers of support and help. I even received offers of help from a number of well-known Afrikaner lawyers. Many of these men were supporters of the National Party, but they believed that the application was biased and unfair. Their response suggested to me that even in racist South Africa professional solidarity can sometimes transcend color, and that there were still attorneys and judges who refused to be the rubber stamps of an immoral regime.

My case was ably defended by advocate Walter Pollack, Q.C., chairman of the Johannesburg Bar Council. At the time that I retained Walter Pollack, I was advised that I should also retain someone who was not connected with the struggle, as that would positively influence the Transvaal bar. To that end, we retained William Aaronsohn, as instructing attorney or barrister, who was head of one of the oldest law firms in Johannesburg. Both men acted for me without charge. We argued that the application was an affront to the idea of justice and that I had an inherent right to fight for my political beliefs, which was the right of all men in a state where the rule of law applied.

But the argument that had great weight was Pollack's use of the case of a man called Strijdom, who was detained during the Second World War together with B. J. Vorster (who later became prime minister). Both were interned for their pro-Nazi stance. Following a failed escape attempt, Strijdom had been found guilty of car theft. Later, after he was released, he applied to the bar for admission as an advocate. Despite his crimes and strong objections from the Bar Council, the court decided to admit him on the ground that his offense was political and that a man cannot be barred from practicing as an advocate for his political beliefs. Pollack said, "There are of course differences between Strijdom and Mandela. Mandela is not a Nationalist and Mandela is not a white."

Judge Ramsbottom, who heard the case, was an example of a judge who refused to be a mouthpiece for the Nationalists and upheld the independence of the judiciary. His judgment in the case completely upheld our claim that I had a right to campaign for my political beliefs even though they were opposed to the government, and he dismissed the Law Society's application. And in a rare instance the Law Society was ordered to pay its own costs.

20

THE ANTIREMOVAL CAMPAIGN in Sophiatown was a long-running battle. We held our ground, as did the state. Through 1954 and into 1955, rallies were held twice a week, on Wednesday and Sunday evenings. Speaker after speaker continued to decry the government's plans. The ANC and the Ratepayers Association, under the direction of Dr. Xuma, protested to the government in letters and petitions. We ran the antiremoval campaign on the slogan "Over Our Dead Bodies," a motto often shouted from the platforms and echoed by the audience. One night, it even roused the otherwise cautious Dr. Xuma to utter the electrifying slogan used to rally African warriors to battle in the previous century: *"Zemk' inkomo magwalandini!"* (The enemy has captured the cattle, you cowards!)

The government had scheduled the removal for February 9, 1955. As the day approached, Oliver and I were in the township daily, meeting local leaders, discussing plans, and acting in our professional capacity for those being forced out of the area or prosecuted. We sought to prove to the court that the government's documentation was often incorrect and that many orders to leave were therefore illegal. But this was only a temporary measure; the government would not let a few illegalities stand in their way.

Shortly before the scheduled removal, a special mass meeting was planned for Freedom Square. Ten thousand people gathered to hear Chief Luthuli speak. But upon his arrival in Johannesburg, he was served with a banning order forcing him to return to Natal.

The night before the removal, Joe Modise, one of the most dedicated of the local ANC leaders, addressed a tense meeting of more than five hundred youthful activists. They expected the ANC to give them an order to battle the police and the army. They were prepared to erect barricades overnight and engage the police with weapons and whatever came to hand the next day. They assumed our slogan meant what it said: that Sophiatown would be removed only over our dead bodies.

But after discussions with the ANC leadership, including myself, Joe told the youth to stand down. They were angry and felt betrayed. But we believed that violence would have been a disaster. We pointed out that an insurrection required careful planning or it would become an act of suicide. We were not yet ready to engage the enemy on its own terms.

In the hazy dawn hours of February 9, four thousand police and army troops cordoned off the township while workers razed empty houses and government trucks began moving families from Sophiatown to Meadowlands. The night before, the ANC had evacuated several families to prearranged accommodation with pro-ANC families in the interior of Sophiatown. But our efforts were too little and too late, and could only be a stopgap measure. The army and the police were relentlessly efficient. After a few weeks, our resistance collapsed. Most of our local leaders had been banned or arrested, and in the end, Sophiatown died not to the sound of gunfire but to the sound of rumbling trucks and sledgehammers.

One can always be correct about a political action one is reading about in the next day's newspaper, but when you are in the center of a heated political fight, you are given little time for reflection. We made a variety of mistakes in the Western Areas antiremoval campaign and learned a number of lessons. "Over Our Dead Bodies" was a dynamic slogan, but it proved as much a hindrance as a help. A slogan is a vital link between the organization and the masses it seeks to lead. It should synthesize a particular grievance into a succinct and pithy phrase, while mobilizing the people to combat it. Our slogan caught the imagination of the people, but it led them to believe that we would fight to the death to resist the removal. In fact, the ANC was not prepared to do that at all.

We never provided the people with an alternative to moving to Meadowlands. When the people in Sophiatown realized we could neither stop the government nor provide them with housing elsewhere, their own resistance waned and the flow of people to Meadowlands increased. Many tenants moved willingly, for they found they would have more space and cleaner housing in Meadowlands. We did not take into account the different situations of landlords and tenants. While the landlords had reasons to stay, many tenants had an incentive to leave. The ANC was criticized by a number of Africanist members who accused the leadership of protecting the interests of the landlords at the expense of the tenants.

The lesson I took away from the campaign was that in the end, we had no alternative to armed and violent resistance. Over and over again, we had used all the nonviolent weapons in our arsenal — speeches, deputations, threats, marches, strikes, stay-aways, voluntary imprisonment — all to no avail, for whatever we did was met by an iron hand. A freedom fighter learns the hard way that it is the oppressor who defines the nature of the struggle, and the oppressed is often left no recourse but to use methods that mirror those of the oppressor. At a certain point, one can only fight fire with fire.

Education is the great engine of personal development. It is through education that the daughter of a peasant can become a doctor, that the son of a mineworker can become the head of the mine, that a child of farmworkers can become the president of a great nation. It is what we make out of what we have, not what we are given, that separates one person from another.

Since the turn of the century, Africans owed their educational opportunities primarily to the foreign churches and missions that created and sponsored schools. Under the United Party, the syllabus for African secondary schools and white secondary schools was essentially the same. The mission schools provided Africans with Western-style English-language education, which I myself received. We were limited by lesser facilities but not by what we could read or think or dream.

Yet, even before the Nationalists came to power, the disparities in funding tell a story of racist education. The government spent about six times as much per white student as per African student. Education was not compulsory for Africans and was free only in the primary grades. Less than half of all African children of school age attended any school at all, and only a tiny number of Africans were graduated from high school.

Even this amount of education proved distasteful to the Nationalists. The Afrikaner has always been unenthusiastic about education for Africans. To him it was simply a waste, for the African was inherently ignorant and lazy and no amount of education could remedy that. The Afrikaner was traditionally hostile to Africans learning English, for English was a foreign tongue to the Afrikaner and the language of emancipation to us.

In 1953, the Nationalist-dominated Parliament passed the Bantu Education Act, which sought to put apartheid's stamp on African education. The act transferred control of African education from the Department of Education to the much loathed Native Affairs Department. Under the act, African primary and secondary schools operated by the church and mission bodies were given the choice of turning over their schools to the government or receiving gradually diminished subsidies; either the government took over education for Africans or there would be no education for Africans. African teachers were not permitted to criticize the government or any school authority. It was intellectual *"basskap,"* a way of institutionalizing inferiority.

Dr. Hendrik Verwoerd, the minister of Bantu education, explained that education "must train and teach people in accordance with their opportunities in life." His meaning was that Africans did not and would not have any opportunities, therefore, why educate them? "There is no place for the Bantu in the European community above the level of certain forms of labor," he said. In short, Africans should be trained to be menial workers, to be in a position of perpetual subordination to the white man.

To the ANC, the act was a deeply sinister measure designed to retard the progress of African culture as a whole and, if enacted, permanently set back the freedom struggle of the African people. The mental outlook of all future generations of Africans was at stake. As Professor Matthews wrote at the time, "Education for ignorance and for inferiority in Verwoerd's schools is worse than no education at all."

The act and Verwoerd's crude exposition of it aroused widespread indignation from both black and white. With the exception of the Dutch

Reform Church, which supported apartheid, and the Lutheran mission, all Christian churches opposed the new measure. But the unity of the opposition extended only to condemning the policy, not resisting it. The Anglicans, the most fearless and consistent critics of the new policy, had a divided policy. Bishop Ambrose Reeves of Johannesburg took the extreme step of closing his schools, which had a total enrollment of ten thousand children. But the archbishop of the church in South Africa, anxious to keep children out of the streets, handed over the rest of the schools to the government. Despite their protests, all the other churches did the same with the exception of the Roman Catholics, the Seventh-Day Adventists, and the United Jewish Reform Congregation — who soldiered on without state aid. Even my own church, the Wesleyan Church, handed over their two hundred thousand African students to the government. If all the other churches had followed the example of those who resisted, the government would have been confronted with a stalemate that might have forced a compromise. Instead, the state marched over us.

The transfer of control to the Native Affairs Department was set to take place on April 1, 1955, and the ANC began to discuss plans for a school boycott that would begin on that date. Our secret discussions among the executive turned on whether we should call on the people to stage a protest for a limited period or whether we should proclaim a permanent school boycott to destroy the Bantu Education Act before it could take root. The discussions were fierce and both sides had forceful advocates. The argument for an indefinite boycott was that Bantu Education was a poison one could not drink even at the point of death from thirst. To accept it in any form would cause irreparable damage. They argued that the country was in an explosive mood and the people were hungry for something more spectacular than a mere protest.

Although I had the reputation of being a firebrand, I always felt that the organization should never promise to do more than it was able, for the people would then lose confidence in it. I took the stance that our actions should be based not on idealistic considerations but on practical ones. An indefinite boycott would require massive machinery and vast resources that we did not possess, and our past campaigns showed no indication that we were up to such an undertaking. It was simply impossible for us to create our own schools fast enough to accommodate hundreds of thousands of pupils, and if we did not offer our people an alternative, we were offering next to nothing. Along with others, I urged a week's boycott.

The National Executive Committee resolved that a weeklong school boycott should begin on April 1. This was recommended at the annual conference in Durban in December of 1954, but the delegates rejected the recommendation and voted for an indefinite boycott. The conference was the supreme authority, even greater than the executive, and we found ourselves saddled with a boycott that would be almost impossible to effect. Dr. Verwoerd announced that the government would permanently close all schools that were boycotted and that children who stayed away would not be readmitted.

For this boycott to work, the parents and the community would have to step in and take the place of the schools. I spoke to parents and ANC members and told them that every home, every shack, every community structure, must become a center of learning for our children.

The boycott began on April 1 and had mixed results. It was often sporadic, disorganized, and ineffectual. On the east Rand it affected some seven thousand schoolchildren. Predawn marches called on parents to keep their children at home. Women picketed the schools and plucked out children who had wandered into them.

In Germiston, a township southeast of the city, Joshua Makue, chairman of our local branch, ran a school for eight hundred boycotting children that lasted for three years. In Port Elizabeth, Barrett Tyesi gave up a government teaching post and ran a school for boycotting children. In 1956, he presented seventy of these children for the Standard VI exams; all but three passed. In many places, improvised schools (described as "cultural clubs" in order not to attract the attention of the authorities) taught boycotting students. The government subsequently passed a law that made it an offense punishable by fine or imprisonment to offer unauthorized education. Police harassed these clubs, but many continued to exist underground. In the end, the community schools withered away and parents, faced with a choice between inferior education and no education at all, chose the former. My own children were at the Seventh-Day Adventist school, which was private and did not depend on government subsidies.

The campaign should be judged on two levels: whether the immediate objective was achieved, and whether it politicized more people and drew them into the struggle. On the first level, the campaign clearly failed. We did not close down African schools throughout the country nor did we rid ourselves of the Bantu Education Act. But the government was sufficiently rattled by our protest to modify the act, and at one point Verwoerd was compelled to declare that education should be the same for all. The government's November 1954 draft syllabus was a retreat from the original notion of modeling the school system on tribal foundations. In the end, we had no option but to choose between the lesser of two evils, and opt for a diminished education. But the consequences of Bantu Education came back to haunt the government in unforeseen ways. For it was Bantu Education that produced in the 1970s the angriest, most rebellious generation of black youth the country had ever seen. When these children of Bantu Education entered their late teens and early twenties, they rose up with a vehemence.

Several months after Chief Luthuli was elected president of the ANC, Professor Z. K. Matthews returned to South Africa after a year as a visiting professor in the U.S., armed with an idea that would reshape the liberation struggle. In a speech at the ANC annual conference in the Cape, Professor Matthews said, "I wonder whether the time has not come for the African National Congress to consider the question of convening a national convention, a congress of the people, representing all the people of this country irrespective of race or colour, to draw up a Freedom Charter for the democratic South Africa of the future."

Within months the ANC national conference accepted the proposal, and a Council of the Congress of the People was created, with Chief Luthuli as chairman and Walter Sisulu and Yusuf Cachalia as joint secretaries. The Congress of the People was to create a set of principles for the foundation of a new South Africa. Suggestions for a new constitution were to come from the people themselves, and ANC leaders all across the country were authorized to seek ideas in writing from everyone in their area. The charter would be a document born of the people.

The Congress of the People represented one of the two main currents of thought operating within the organization. It seemed inevitable that the government would ban the ANC, and many argued that the organization must be prepared to operate underground and illegally. At the same time, we did not want to give up on the important public policies and activities that brought the ANC attention and mass support. The Congress of the People would be a public display of strength.

Our dream for the Congress of the People was that it would be a landmark event in the history of the freedom struggle — a convention uniting all the oppressed and all the progressive forces of South Africa to create a clarion call for change. Our hope was that it would one day be looked upon with the same reverence as the founding convention of the ANC in 1912.

We sought to attract the widest possible sponsorship and invited some two hundred organizations — white, black, Indian, and Coloured — to send representatives to a planning conference at Tongaat, near Durban, in March of 1954. The National Action Council created there was composed of eight members from each of the four sponsoring organizations.

At the age of
nineteen, in Umtata,
Transkei. *(P. K. A.
Gaeshwe/Black Star)*

Oliver and I opened
the doors to our
office on Fox Street
in 1952; it was the
first black law
practice in
Johannesburg.
(Jurgen Schadeberg)

Opposite:
Under the Suppression of Communism Act, bans became a routine part of the life of a freedom fighter. *(Bailey's)*

Outside the courtroom with Dr. James Moroka and Yusuf Dadoo during the Defiance Campaign. *(Jurgen Schadeberg/Associated Press)*

With Patrick Moloa and Robert Resha at the Transvaal Supreme Court after receiving a nine-month suspended sentence. *(Jurgen Schadeberg)*

Dadoo, ex-president, SAIC.

Nelson Mandela, ex-president, Tvl. ANC.

James Phillips, ex-chairman, Tvl. CPAC.

Duma Nokwe, secretary, ANC Y.L.

Walter Sisulu, ex-secretary, ANC.

Albert Luthuli, president, ANC.

Cachalia, secretary, SAIC.

John B. Marks, ex-president, Tvl. ANC.

Stephen Sello, ex-Tvl. acting secretary.

David Bopape, ex-secretary, Tvl. ANC.

Moses Kotane, ex-leader, ANC.

Dr. Z. Njongwe, ex-chairman, ANC.

Im Amra, ex-leader, Indian C.

Dr. Silas M. Molema, ex-treasurer, ANC.

The Effects of New Laws: 2

BANNED MEN

DURING the last few months, nearly all the non-White leaders in South Africa have been restricted in their movements and activities. Most of them have been called upon to resign their positions in the African National Congress or the South African Indian Congress. Many of them have been forbidden to attend any gatherings, or to enter certain magisterial districts in the Union.

Albert Luthuli, for instance, president of the African National Congress, is forbidden to move away from his own district at Groutville, Natal. He cannot visit the shops in Durban, thirty miles away, or attend the cathedral there.

Most of the bans are in force for two years, after which time they may be renewed: some have already been renewed.

The bans take effect under the Suppression of Communism Act of 1950. This allows the Minister of Justice to prohibit from gatherings or organisations anyone suspected of furthering the aims of Communism. 'Communism' is defined under the act as aiming to bring about social, economic or political changes in the country.

Many of those convicted or 'named' under the Suppression of Communism Act are not 'Communists' in the usual sense of the term, but 'Statutory Communists' who come within the definition of the act.

Iliza Mji, ex-secretary, ANC.

Maulvi Cachalia, ex-secretary, Tvl. I.C.

uso, ex-Transvaal ANC leader.

Nana Sitha, ex-president, Transvaal I.C.

Dan Tlhoome, ex-leader, ANC.

Flag Boshielo, ex-leader, Transvaal ANC.

N. Thandray, ex-Tvl. secretary, I.C.

Hosia Seperepere, ex-leader, ANC.

Marquard, ex-t, Cape F.W.U.

Joseph Matthews, ex-president, ANC Y.L.

Robert Matji, ex-secretary, Cape ANC.

MacDon. Maseko, ex-leader, ANC.

Ismail Bhoola, ex-sec., Tvl. Indian YC.

Harrison Motlana, ex-secretary, Tvl. Y.L.

Dr. Moroka, after handing over the presidency of the ANC to Chief Albert Lutuli. *(G. R. Naidoo/Bailey's)*

Chief Lutuli giving the *"Afrika"* salute to ANC delegates at the forty-first annual congress in Queenstown. *(Bob Gosani/Bailey's)*

With youth leader Peter Nthite in 1955. *(Peter Magubane)*

Under the Group Areas Act, the vital township of Sophiatown was declared a "black spot"; removals to Meadowlands were scheduled to begin in 1955. *(Jurgen Schadeberg)*

One of the lessons I took away from the failed Western Areas antiremoval campaign was that it is the oppressor who defines the nature of the struggle; in the end, we would have no alternative but to resort to an armed resistance. *(Jurgen Schadeberg)*

Speaking to a group of women during their march to Pretoria Union Buildings to protest the pass laws. *(Peter Magubane/Associated Press)*

Tense times. 1956
(Ian Berry/Magnum)

The Treason Trial,
1956. The accused
were bused every day
from Johannesburg
to Pretoria. *(Peter
Magubane)*

We were forbidden from attending political gatherings of any kind, but so many leaders had been brought together for the Treason Trial that our afternoon breaks often felt like meetings of the National Executive Committee. *(Ian Berry/Magnum)*

Our supporters joined us in song outside the court in Pretoria, 1958. *(Peter Magubane)*

The chairman was Chief Luthuli, and the secretariat consisted of Walter Sisulu (later replaced by Oliver after Walter's banning forced him to resign), Yusuf Cachalia of the SAIC, Stanley Lollan of the South African Coloured People's Organization (SACPO), and Lionel Bernstein of the Congress of Democrats (COD).

Formed in Cape Town in September of 1953 by Coloured leaders and trade unionists, SACPO was the belated offspring of the struggle to preserve the Coloured vote in the Cape and sought to represent Coloured interests. SAPCO's founding conference was addressed by Oliver Tambo and Yusuf Cachalia. Inspired by the Defiance Campaign, the COD was formed in late 1952 as a party for radical, left-wing, antigovernment whites. The COD, though small and limited mainly to Johannesburg and Cape Town, had an influence disproportionate to its numbers. Its members, such as Michael Harmel, Bram Fischer, and Rusty Bernstein, were eloquent advocates of our cause. The COD closely identified itself with the ANC and the SAIC and advocated a universal franchise and full equality between black and white. We saw the COD as a means whereby our views could be put directly to the white public. The COD served an important symbolic function for Africans; blacks who had come into the struggle because they were antiwhite discovered that there were indeed whites of goodwill who treated Africans as equals.

The National Action Council invited all participating organizations and their followers to send suggestions for a freedom charter. Circulars were sent out to townships and villages all across the country. "IF YOU COULD MAKE THE LAWS . . . WHAT WOULD YOU DO?" they said. "HOW WOULD YOU SET ABOUT MAKING SOUTH AFRICA A HAPPY PLACE FOR ALL THE PEOPLE WHO LIVE IN IT?" Some of the flyers and leaflets were filled with the poetic idealism that characterized the planning:

WE CALL THE PEOPLE OF SOUTH AFRICA BLACK AND WHITE — LET US SPEAK TOGETHER OF FREEDOM! . . . LET THE VOICES OF ALL THE PEOPLE BE HEARD. AND LET THE DEMANDS OF ALL THE PEOPLE FOR THE THINGS THAT WILL MAKE US FREE BE RECORDED. LET THE DEMANDS BE GATHERED TOGETHER IN A GREAT CHARTER OF FREEDOM.

The call caught the imagination of the people. Suggestions came in from sports and cultural clubs, church groups, ratepayers' associations, women's organizations, schools, trade union branches. They came on serviettes, on paper torn from exercise books, on scraps of foolscap, on the backs of our own leaflets. It was humbling to see how the suggestions of ordinary people were often far ahead of the leaders'. The most commonly cited demand was for one-man-one-vote. There was a recognition that the country belongs to all those who have made it their home.

The ANC branches contributed a great deal to the process of writing the charter and in fact the two best drafts came from Durban and Pietermaritzburg. A combination of these drafts was then circulated to different regions and committees for comments and questions. The charter itself was drafted by a small committee of the National Action Council and reviewed by the ANC's National Executive Committee.

The charter would be presented at the Congress of the People and each of its elements submitted to the delegates for approval. In June, a few days before the congress was scheduled, a small group of us reviewed the draft. We made few changes, as there was little time and the document was already in good shape.

The Congress of the People took place at Kliptown, a multiracial village on a scrap of veld a few miles southwest of Johannesburg, on two clear, sunny days, June 25 and 26, 1955. More than three thousand delegates braved police intimidation to assemble and approve the final document. They came by car, bus, truck, and foot. Although the overwhelming number of delegates were black, there were more than three hundred Indians, two hundred Coloureds, and one hundred whites.

I drove to Kliptown with Walter. We were both under banning orders, so we found a place at the edge of the crowd where we could observe without mixing in or being seen. The crowd was impressive both in its size and in its discipline. "Freedom volunteers" wearing black, green, and yellow armbands met the delegates and arranged for their seating. There were old women and young wearing congress skirts, congress blouses, congress *doekies* (scarves); old men and young wearing congress armbands and congress hats. Signs everywhere said, "FREEDOM IN OUR LIFE-TIME, LONG LIVE THE STRUGGLE." The platform was a rainbow of colors: white delegates from the COD, Indians from the SAIC, Coloured representatives from SACPO all sat in front of a replica of a four-spoked wheel representing the four organizations in the Congress Alliance. White and African police and members of the Special Branch milled around, taking photographs, writing in notebooks, and trying unsuccessfully to intimidate the delegates.

There were dozens of songs and speeches. Meals were served. The atmosphere was both serious and festive. On the afternoon of the first day, the charter was read aloud, section by section, to the people in English, Sesotho, and Xhosa. After each section, the crowd shouted its approval with cries of *"Afrika!"* and *"Mayibuye!"* The first day of the congress was a success.

The second day was much like the first. Each section of the charter had been adopted by acclamation and at 3:30, the final approval was to be voted when a brigade of police and Special Branch detectives brandishing Sten guns swarmed onto the platform. In a gruff, Afrikaans-accented voice, one of the police took the microphone and announced that treason was suspected and that no one was to leave the gathering without police permission. The police began pushing people off the platform and confiscating documents and photographs, even signs such as "SOUP WITH MEAT" and "SOUP WITHOUT MEAT." Another group of constables armed with rifles formed a cordon around the crowd. The people responded magnificently by loudly singing *"Nkosi Sikelel' iAfrika."* The delegates were then allowed to leave one by one, each person interviewed by the police and his or her name taken down. I had been on the outskirts of the crowd when the police raid began, and while my instinct was to stay and help, discretion seemed the wiser course, because I would have immediately been arrested and tossed in jail. An emergency meeting had been called in Johannesburg and I made my way back there. As I returned to Johannesburg, I knew that this raid signaled a harsh new turn on the part of the government.

Though the Congress of the People had been broken up, the charter itself became a great beacon for the liberation struggle. Like other enduring political documents, such as the American Declaration of Independence, the French Declaration of the Rights of Man, and the Communist Manifesto, the Freedom Charter is a mixture of practical goals and poetic language. It extols the abolition of racial discrimination and the achievement of equal rights for all. It welcomes all who embrace freedom to participate in the making of a democratic, nonracial South Africa. It captured the hopes and dreams of the people and acted as a blueprint for the liberation struggle and the future of the nation. The preamble reads:

We, the people of South Africa, declare for all our country and the world to know: —

That South Africa belongs to all who live in it, black and white, and that no government can justly claim authority unless it is based on the will of the people;

That our people have been robbed of their birthright to land, liberty and peace by a form of government founded on injustice and inequality;

That our country will never be prosperous or free until all our people live in brotherhood, enjoying equal rights and opportunities;

That only a democratic state, based on the will of the people, can secure to all their birthright without distinction of colour, race, sex or belief;

And therefore, we, the people of South Africa, black and white, together — equals, countrymen and brothers — adopt this FREE-DOM CHARTER. And we pledge ourselves to strive together, sparing nothing of our strength and courage, until the democratic changes here set out have been won.

The charter then lays out the requirements for a free and democratic South Africa.

THE PEOPLE SHALL GOVERN!

Every man and woman shall have the right to vote for and stand as a candidate for all bodies which make laws.

All the people shall be entitled to take part in the administration of the country.

The rights of the people shall be the same regardless of race, colour or sex.

All bodies of minority rule, advisory boards, councils and authorities shall be replaced by democratic organs of self-government.

ALL NATIONAL GROUPS SHALL HAVE EQUAL RIGHTS!

There shall be equal status in the bodies of state, in the courts and in the schools for all national groups and races;

All national groups shall be protected by law against insults to their race and national pride;

All people shall have equal rights to use their own language and to develop their own folk culture and customs;

The preaching and practice of national, race or colour discrimination and contempt shall be a punishable crime;

All apartheid laws and practices shall be set aside.

THE PEOPLE SHALL SHARE IN THE COUNTRY'S WEALTH!

The national wealth of our country, the heritage of all South Africans, shall be restored to the people;

The mineral wealth beneath the soil, the banks and monopoly industry shall be transferred to the ownership of the people as a whole;

All other industries and trade shall be controlled to assist the well-being of the people;

All people shall have equal rights to trade where they choose, to manufacture and to enter all trades, crafts and professions.

THE LAND SHALL BE SHARED AMONG THOSE WHO WORK IT!

> Restriction of land ownership on racial basis shall be ended, and all the land re-divided amongst those who work it, to banish famine and land hunger. . . .

Some in the ANC, particularly the Africanist contingent, who were anti-Communist and antiwhite, objected to the charter as being a design for a radically different South Africa from the one the ANC had called for throughout its history. They claimed the charter favored a socialist order and believed the COD and white Communists had had a disproportionate influence on its ideology. In June 1956, in the monthly journal *Liberation,* I pointed out that the charter endorsed private enterprise and would allow capitalism to flourish among Africans for the first time. The charter guaranteed that when freedom came, Africans would have the opportunity to own their own businesses in their own names, to own their own houses and property, in short, to prosper as capitalists and entrepreneurs. The charter does not speak about the eradication of classes and private property, or public ownership of the means of production, or promulgate any of the tenets of scientific socialism. The clause discussing the possible nationalization of the mines, the banks, and monopoly industries was an action that needed to be taken if the economy was not to be solely owned and operated by white businessmen.

The charter was in fact a revolutionary document precisely because the changes it envisioned could not be achieved without radically altering the economic and political structure of South Africa. It was not meant to be capitalist or socialist but a melding together of the people's demands to end the oppression. In South Africa, to merely achieve fairness, one had to destroy apartheid itself, for it was the very embodiment of injustice.

21

IN EARLY SEPTEMBER 1955, my bans expired. I had last had a holiday in 1948 when I was an untested lightweight in the ANC with few responsibilities beyond attending meetings in the Transvaal executive and addressing the odd public gathering. Now, at the age of thirty-eight, I had reached the light heavyweight division and carried more pounds and more responsibility. I had been confined to Johannesburg for two years, chained to my legal and political work, and had neglected Mandela family affairs in the Transkei. I was keen to visit the countryside again, to be in the open veld and rolling valleys of my childhood. I was anxious to see my family and confer with Sabata and Daliwonga on certain problems involving the Transkei, while the ANC was eager that I confer with them on political matters. I was to have a working holiday, the only kind of holiday I knew how to take.

The night before I left, a number of friends gathered at my home to see me off. Duma Nokwe, the young and good-natured barrister who was then national secretary of the Youth League, was among them. Duma had accompanied Walter on his trip to the Youth Conference in Bucharest, and that night he entertained us with the Russian and Chinese songs he had learned on his trip. At midnight, as my guests were getting ready to leave, my daughter Makaziwe, then two, awoke and asked me if she could come along with me. I had been spending insufficient time with my family and Makaziwe's request provoked pangs of guilt. Suddenly, my enthusiasm for my trip vanished. But I carried her back to bed and kissed her good night and as she dropped off to sleep, I made my final preparations for my journey.

I was embarking on a fact-finding mission, which I would combine with the pleasures of seeing the countryside and old friends and comrades. I had been isolated from developments in other parts of the country and was eager to see for myself what was transpiring in the hinterlands. Although I read a variety of newspapers from around the country, newspapers are only a poor shadow of reality; their information is important to a freedom fighter not because it reveals the truth, but because it discloses the biases and perceptions of both those who produce the paper and those who read it. On this trip I wanted to talk firsthand with our people in the field.

I left shortly after midnight and within an hour I was on the highway to Durban. The roads were empty and I was accompanied only by the stars and gentle Transvaal breezes. Though I had not slept, I felt light-hearted and fresh. At daybreak I crossed from Volksrust to Natal, the country of Cetywayo, the last independent king of the Zulus, whose troops had defeated a British column at Isandhlwana in 1879. But the king was unable to withstand the firepower of the British and eventually surrendered his kingdom. Shortly after crossing the river on the Natal border I saw the Majuba Hills, the steep escarpment where a small Boer commando ambushed and defeated a garrison of British redcoats less than two years after the defeat of Cetywayo. At Majuba Hill the Afrikaner had stoutly defended his independence against British imperialism and struck a blow for nationalism. Now the descendants of those same freedom fighters were persecuting my people who were struggling for precisely the same thing the Afrikaners had once fought and died for. I drove through those historic hills thinking less of the ironies of history by which the oppressed becomes the oppressor, than of how the ruthless Afrikaners deserved their own Majuba Hill at the hands of my people.

This harsh reverie was interrupted by the happy music of Radio Bantu on my car radio. While I despised the conservative politics of Radio Bantu served up by the government-run South African Broadcasting Corporation, I reveled in its music. (In South Africa, African artists made the music, but white record companies made the money.) I was listening to a popular program called "Rediffusion Service," which featured most of the country's leading African singers: Miriam Makeba, Dolly Rathebe, Dorothy Masuku, Thoko Shukuma, and the smooth sound of the Manhattan Brothers. I enjoy all types of music, but the music of my own flesh and blood goes right to my heart. The curious beauty of African music is that it uplifts even as it tells a sad tale. You may be poor, you may have only a ramshackle house, you may have lost your job, but that song gives you hope. African music is often about the aspirations of the African people, and it can ignite the political resolve of those who might otherwise be indifferent to politics. One merely has to witness the infectious singing at African rallies. Politics can be strengthened by music, but music has a potency that defies politics.

I made a number of stops in Natal, meeting secretly with ANC leaders. Nearing Durban, I took the opportunity of stopping in Pietermaritzburg, where I spent the entire night with Dr. Chota Motale, Moses Mabhida, and others, reviewing the political situation in the country. I then traveled on to Groutville, spending the day with Chief Luthuli. Although he had been confined by banning orders for more than a year, the chief was well-informed about ANC activities. He was uneasy about what he saw as the increasing centralization of the ANC in Johannesburg and the declining power of the regions. I reassured him that we wanted the regions to remain strong.

My next stop was a meeting in Durban with Dr. Naicker and the Executive Committee of the Natal Indian Congress, where I raised the sensitive issue that the National Executive Committee believed that the Indian Congress had become inactive of late. I was reluctant to do this as Dr. Naicker was my senior and a man who had suffered far more than I, but we discussed ways to overcome government restrictions.

From Durban I drove south along the coast past Port Shepstone and Port St. Johns, small and lovely colonial towns that dotted the shimmering beaches fronting the Indian Ocean. While mesmerized by the beauty of the area, I was constantly rebuked by the buildings and streets that bear the names of white imperialists who suppressed the very people whose names belonged there. At this point, I turned inland and drove to

Umzumkulu to meet with Dr. Conco, the treasurer-general of the ANC, for further discussions and consultations.

With excitement mounting, I then set off for Umtata. When I turned into York Road, the main street of Umtata, I felt the rush of familiarity and fond memories one gets from coming home after a long exile. I had been away for thirteen years, and while there were no banners and fatted calves to greet this prodigal son upon his return, I was tremendously excited to see my mother, my humble home, and the friends of my youth. But my trip to the Transkei had a second motive: my arrival coincided with the meeting of a special committee appointed to oversee the transition of the Transkeian Bungha system to that of the Bantu Authorities.

The role of the Bungha, which consisted of 108 members, one-quarter of whom were white and three-quarters African, was to advise the government on legislation affecting Africans in the area and to regulate local matters like taxes and roads. While the Bungha was the most influential political body in the Transkei, its resolutions were advisory and its decisions subject to review by white magistrates. The Bungha was only as powerful as whites permitted it to be. Yet, the Bantu Authorities Act would replace it with an even more repressive system: a feudalistic order resting on hereditary and tribal distinctions as decided by the state. The government suggested that Bantu Authorities would free the people from the control of white magistrates, but this was a smoke screen for the state's undermining of democracy and promotion of tribal rivalries. The ANC regarded any acceptance of Bantu Authorities as a capitulation to the government.

On the night of my arrival, I met briefly with a number of Transkeian councillors and my nephew, K. D. Matanzima, whom I called Daliwonga. Daliwonga was playing a leading part in persuading the Bungha to accept Bantu Authorities, for the new order would reinforce and even increase his power as the chief of Emigrant Thembuland. Daliwonga and I were on separate sides of this difficult issue. We had grown apart: he had opted for a traditional leadership role and was cooperating with the system. But it was late, and rather than begin a lengthy discussion, we resolved to meet the following day.

I spent that night in a boardinghouse in town, rose early, and was joined for coffee in my room by two local chiefs to discuss their role in the new Bantu Authorities. In the middle of our conversation the mistress of the boardinghouse nervously ushered a white man into my room. "Are you Nelson Mandela?" he demanded.

"And who is asking?" I said.

He gave his name and rank as a detective sergeant in the security police.

"May I see your warrant, please?" I asked. It was obvious the sergeant resented my audacity, but he grudgingly produced an official document. Yes, I was Nelson Mandela, I told him. He informed me that the commanding officer wanted to see me. I replied that if he wanted to see me he knew where I was. He then ordered me to accompany him to the police station. I asked him whether I was under arrest, and he replied that I was not.

"In that case," I said, "I am not going." He was taken aback by my refusal but knew I was on firm legal ground. He proceeded to fire a succession of questions at me: when had I left Johannesburg? where had I visited? whom had I spoken with? did I have a permit to enter the Transkei and how long would I be staying? I informed him that the Transkei was my home and that I did not need a permit to enter it. The sergeant stomped out of the room.

The chiefs were taken aback by my behavior and upbraided me for my rudeness. I explained that I had merely treated him in the manner that he had treated me. The chiefs were unconvinced, and clearly thought I was a hotheaded young man who would get himself in trouble. These were men I was trying to persuade to reject Bantu Authorities, and it was apparent that I had not made a very good impression. The incident reminded me that I had returned to my homeland a different man from the one who had left thirteen years before.

The police were unsophisticated in the Transkei, and from the moment I left the boardinghouse, they followed me everywhere I went. After I talked to anyone, the police would confront the person and say, "If you talk with Mandela, we will come and arrest you."

I met briefly with a local ANC leader and was dismayed to learn of the organization's lack of funds, but at that moment, I was thinking less about the organization than my next stop: Qunu, the village where I was raised and where my mother still lived.

I roused my mother, who at first looked as though she was seeing a ghost. But she was overjoyed. I had brought some food — fruit, meat, sugar, salt, and a chicken — and my mother lit the stove to make tea. We did not hug or kiss; that was not our custom. Although I was happy to be back, I felt a sense of guilt at the sight of my mother living all alone in such poor circumstances. I tried to persuade her to come live with me in Johannesburg, but she swore that she would not leave the countryside she loved. I wondered — not for the first time — whether one was ever justified in neglecting the welfare of one's own family in order to fight for the welfare of others. Can there be anything more important than looking after one's aging mother? Is politics merely a pretext for shirking one's responsibilities, an excuse for not being able to provide in the way one wanted?

After an hour or so with my mother, I left to spend the night at Mqhekezweni. It was night when I arrived, and in my enthusiasm I started to blow the horn of my car. I had not considered how this noise might be interpreted and people emerged fearfully from their huts, thinking it might be the police. But when I was recognized, I was met with surprise and joy by a number of villagers.

But instead of sleeping like a child in my old bed, I tossed and turned that night wondering whether or not I had taken the right path. But I did not doubt that I had chosen correctly. I do not mean to suggest that the freedom struggle is of a higher moral order than taking care of one's family. It is not; they are merely different.

Returning to Qunu the next morning, I spent the day reminiscing with people, and walking the fields around the village. I also visited with my sister Mabel, the most practical and easygoing of my sisters and of whom I was very fond. Mabel was married, but her union involved an interesting tale. My sister Baliwe, who was older than Mabel, had been engaged to be married, and *lobola* had already been paid. But two weeks before the wedding, Baliwe, who was a spirited girl, ran away. We could not return the cattle, as they had already been accepted, so the family decided that Mabel would take Baliwe's place, and she did so.

I left late that afternoon to drive to Mqhekezweni. Again I arrived at night and announced my presence with loud hooting, only this time people emerged from their homes with the idea that Justice, their chief, had returned. Justice had been deposed from his chieftancy by the government and was then living in Durban. Though the government had appointed someone in his stead, a chief is a chief by virtue of his birth and wields authority because of his blood. They were happy to see me, but they would have been happier still welcoming home Justice.

My second mother, No-England, the widow of the regent, had been fast asleep when I arrived, but when she appeared in her nightdress and saw me, she became so excited she demanded I drive her immediately to a nearby relative to celebrate. She hopped into my car and we set off on a wild ride through the untamed veld, to get to the remote rondavel of her relative. There we woke up another family, and I finally went to sleep, tired and happy, just before dawn.

Over the next fortnight I moved back and forth between Qunu and Mqhekezweni, staying by turns with my mother and No-England, visiting and receiving friends and relatives. I ate the same foods I had eaten as a boy, I walked the same fields, and gazed at the same sky during the day, the same stars at night. It is important for a freedom fighter to remain in touch with his own roots, and the hurly-burly of city life has a way of erasing the past. The visit restored me and revived my feelings for the place in which I grew up. I was once again my mother's son in her house; I was once again the regent's charge in the Great Place.

The visit was also a way of measuring the distance I had come. I saw how my own people had remained in one place, while I had moved on and seen new worlds and gained new ideas. If I had not realized it before, I knew that I was right not to have returned to the Transkei after Fort Hare. If I had returned, my political evolution would have been stunted.

When the Special Committee considering the introduction of the Bantu Authorities had adjourned, Daliwonga and I went to visit Sabata in hospital in Umtata. I had hoped to talk with Sabata about the Bantu Authorities, but his health made it impossible. I wanted Sabata and his brother, Daliwonga, to begin talks on this issue as soon as Sabata was well enough to do so, and made this clear. I felt proud to be organizing a meeting between the descendants of Ngubengcuka, and mused for a moment on the irony that I was finally fulfilling the role of counselor to Sabata for which I'd been groomed so many years before.

From Umtata, Daliwonga and I drove to Qamata, where we met his younger brother George, who was then a practicing attorney. His two articled clerks were well known to me and I was pleased to see them both: A. P. Mda and Tsepo Letlaka. Both were still firm supporters of the organization who had given up teaching and decided to become lawyers. In Qamata, we all sat down to examine the issue of the proposed Bantu Authorities.

My mission was to persuade Daliwonga — a man destined to play a leading role in the politics of the Transkei — to oppose the imposition of the Bantu Authorities. I did not want our meeting to be a showdown, or even a debate; I did not want any grandstanding or faultfinding, but a serious discussion among men who all had the best interests of their people and their nation at heart.

In many ways, Daliwonga still regarded me as his junior, both in terms of my rank in the Thembu hierarchy and in my own political development. While I was his junior in the former realm, I believed I had advanced beyond my onetime mentor in my political views. Whereas his concerns focused on his own tribe, I had become involved with those who thought in terms of the entire nation. I did not want to complicate the discussion by introducing grand political theories; I would rely on common sense and the facts of our history. Before we began, Daliwonga invited Mda and Letlaka and his brother, George, to participate, but they demurred, preferring to listen to the two of us. "Let the nephew and the uncle conduct the debate," Mda said as a sign of respect. Etiquette dictated that I would make my case first and he would not interrupt; then he would answer while I listened.

In the first place, I said, the Bantu Authorities was impractical, because more and more Africans were moving out of the rural homelands to the cities. The government's policy was to try to put Africans into ethnic enclaves because they feared the power of African unity. The people, I said, wanted democracy, and political leadership based on merit not birth. The Bantu Authorities was a retreat from democracy.

Daliwonga's response was that he was trying to restore the status of his royal house that had been crushed by the British. He stressed the importance and vitality of the tribal system and traditional leadership, and did not want to reject a system that enshrined those things. He, too, wanted a free South Africa but he thought that goal could be achieved faster and more peacefully through the government's policy of separate development. The ANC, he said, would bring about bloodshed and bitterness. He ended by saying that he was startled and disturbed to learn that in spite of my own position in the Thembu royal house I did not support the principle of traditional leadership.

When Daliwonga finished, I replied that while I understood his personal position as a chief quite well, I believed that his own interests were in conflict with those of the community. I said that if I were in a similar position to his, I would try to subordinate my own interests to those of the people. I immediately regretted that last point because I have discovered that in discussions it never helps to take a morally superior tone to one's opponent. I noticed that Daliwonga stiffened when I made this point and I quickly shifted the discussion to more general issues.

We spoke the whole night, but came no closer to each other's position. As the sun was rising, we parted. We had embarked on different roads that put us in conflict with one another. This grieved me because few men had inspired me as Daliwonga had, and nothing would have given me greater joy than to fight beside him. But it was not to be. On family issues, we remained friends; politically, we were in opposite and antagonistic camps.

I returned to Qunu that morning and spent another few days there. I tramped across the veld to visit friends and relatives, but the magic world of my childhood had fled. One evening I bade my mother and sister farewell. I visited Sabata in hospital to wish him a speedy recovery, and by 3 A.M. I was on my way to Cape Town. The bright moonlight and crisp breeze kept me fresh all the way across the Kei River. The road winds up the rugged mountains, and as the sun rose my mood lifted. I had last been on that road eighteen years before, when Jongintaba had driven me to Healdtown.

I was driving slowly when I noticed a limping man at the side of the road raising his hand to me. I instinctively pulled over and offered him a ride. He was about my own age, of small stature, and rather unkempt; he had not bathed in quite a while. He told me that his car had broken down on the other side of Umtata and he had been walking for several days toward Port Elizabeth. I noticed a number of inconsistencies in his story, and I asked him the make of his car. A Buick, he replied. And the registration? I said. He told me a number. A few minutes later, I said, "What did you say that registration number was?" He told me a slightly different figure. I suspected he was a policeman, and I decided to say very little.

My reserve went unnoticed by my companion as he talked the entire way to Port Elizabeth. He pointed out various curiosities and was well versed in the history of the region. He never asked who I was and I did not tell him. But he was entertaining, and I found his conversation useful and interesting.

I made a stop in East London and spoke to a few ANC people. Before leaving I had a conversation with some other people in the township, one of whom struck me as an undercover policeman. My companion had learned my identity, and a few minutes after we were back in the car, he said to me, "You know, Mandela, I suspected that one chap at the end was a policeman." This raised my own suspicions, and I said to my companion, "Look here, how do I know you're not a policeman yourself? You must tell me who you are — otherwise I will dump you back on the road again."

He protested and said, "No, I will introduce myself properly." He confessed that he was a smuggler and had been carrying *dagga* (marijuana) from the Pondoland coast when he ran into a police roadblock. When he saw the roadblock, he jumped out of the car and tried to make a break for it. The police fired, wounding him in the leg. That explained his limp and his lack of transportation. He waved me down because he assumed the police were hunting for him.

I asked him why he had chosen such a dangerous livelihood. He had originally wanted to be a teacher, he told me, but his parents were too poor to send him to college. After school he had worked in a factory, but the wages were too meager for him to live on his own. He started to supplement them by smuggling *dagga,* and soon found it so profitable that he left the factory altogether. He said in any other country in the world he would have found an opportunity for his talents. "I saw white men who were my inferiors in ability and brains earning fifty times what I was." After a long pause, he announced in a solemn tone, "I am also a member of the ANC." He told me that he had defied during the 1952 Defiance Campaign and had served on various local committees in Port Elizabeth. I quizzed him on various personalities, all of whom he seemed to know, and later in Port Elizabeth I confirmed that he was telling me the truth. In fact, he had been one of the most reliable of those who went to jail during the Defiance Campaign. The doors of the liberation struggle are open to all who choose to walk through them.

As an attorney with a fairly large criminal practice, I was conversant with such tales. Over and over again, I saw men as bright and talented as my companion resort to crime in order to make ends meet. While I do think certain individuals are disposed to crime because of their genetic inheritance or an abusive upbringing, I am convinced that apartheid turned many otherwise law-abiding citizens into criminals. It stands to reason that an immoral and unjust legal system would breed contempt for its laws and regulations.

We reached Port Elizabeth at sunset, and Joe Matthews, Z. K. Matthews's son, arranged accommodation. The next morning I met with Raymond Mhlaba, Frances Baard, and Govan Mbeki, whom I was meeting for the first time. I knew his work, for as a student I had read his booklet "The Transkei in the Making." He had been running a cooperative store in the Transkei which he was soon to give up to become an editor of the weekly *New Age*. Govan was serious, thoughtful, and soft-spoken, equally at home in the world of scholarship and the world of political activism. He had been deeply involved in the planning of the Congress of the People and was destined for the highest levels of leadership in the organization.

I departed in the late morning for Cape Town, with only my radio for company. I had never before driven on roads between Port Elizabeth and Cape Town, and I was looking forward to many miles of entrancing scenery. It was hot, and the road was bordered by dense vegetation on either side. I had hardly left the city when I ran over a large snake slithering across the road. I am not superstitious and do not believe in omens, but the death of the snake did not please me. I do not like killing any living thing, even those creatures that fill some people with dread.

Once I passed Humansdorp, the forests became denser and for the first time in my life I saw wild elephants and baboons. A large baboon crossed the road in front of me, and I stopped the car. He stood and stared at me as intently as if he were a Special Branch detective. It was ironic that I, an African, was seeing the Africa of storybooks and legend for the first time. Such beautiful land, I thought, and all of it out of reach, owned by whites and untouchable for a black man. I could no more choose to live in such beauty than run for Parliament.

Seditious thoughts accompany a freedom fighter wherever he goes. At the town of Knysna, more than a hundred miles west of Port Elizabeth, I stopped to survey the surroundings. The road above the town affords a panoramic view as far as the eye can see. In every direction, I saw sprawling, dense forests and I dwelt not on the greenery but the fact that there were many places a guerrilla army could live and train undetected.

I arrived in Cape Town at midnight for what turned out to be a two-week stay. I stayed at the home of Reverend Walter Teka, a leader in the Methodist Church, but I spent most of my days with Johnson Ngwevela and Greenwood Ngotyana. Ngwevela was the chairman of the Cape western region of the ANC and Ngotyana a member of its executive. Both were Communists as well as leading members of the Wesleyan Church. I traveled every day to meet ANC officials in places like Worcester, Paarl, Stellenbosch, Simonstown, and Hermanus. I planned to work each day of my stay and when I asked what had been arranged for Sunday — a working day for me in the Transvaal — they informed me that the sabbath was reserved for churchgoing. I protested, but to no avail. Communism and Christianity, at least in Africa, were not mutually exclusive.

While I was walking in the city one day, I noticed a white woman in the gutter gnawing on some fish bones. She was poor and apparently homeless, but she was young and not unattractive. I knew of course that there were poor whites, whites who were every bit as poor as Africans, but one rarely saw them. I was used to seeing black beggars on the street, and it startled me to see a white one. While I normally did not give to African beggars, I felt the urge to give this woman money. In that moment I realized the tricks that apartheid plays on one, for the everyday travails that afflict Africans are accepted as a matter of course, while my heart immediately went out to this bedraggled white woman. In South Africa, to be poor and black was normal, to be poor and white was a tragedy.

As I was preparing to leave Cape Town, I went to the offices of New Age to see some old friends and discuss their editorial policy. New Age, the successor to earlier banned left-wing publications, was a friend of the ANC. It was early in the morning of the twenty-seventh of September, and as I walked up the steps I could hear angry voices inside the office and furniture being moved. I recognized the voice of Fred Carneson, the manager of the newspaper and its guiding spirit. I also heard the gruff voices of the security police who were in the process of searching the offices. I quietly left, and later discovered that this had not been an isolated incident but part of the largest nationwide raid undertaken in South African history. Armed with warrants authorizing the seizure of anything regarded as evidence of high treason, sedition, or violations of the Suppression of Communism Act, the police searched more than five hundred people in their homes and offices around the country. My office in Johannesburg was searched, as well as the homes of Dr. Moroka, Father Huddleston, and Professor Matthews.

The raid cast a shadow over my last day in Cape Town, for it signaled the first move in the state's new and even more repressive strategy. At the very least, a new round of bannings would take place, and I was certain to be among them. That evening, Reverend Teka and his wife had a number of people over to the house to bid me farewell, and led by the reverend, we knelt in prayer for the well-being of those whose homes had been raided. I left the house at my favored departure time of 3 A.M., and within half an hour I was on the road to Kimberley, the rough-and-ready mining town where the South African diamond business had begun in the last century.

I was to stay at the home of Dr. Arthur Letele for one night. Later to become the treasurer-general of the ANC, Arthur was a scrupulous medical practitioner. I had a cold, and when he greeted me on my arrival, he confined me to bed. He was a brave and dedicated man, and had led a small group of defiers to jail during the Defiance Campaign. This was a risky action for a doctor in a town where political action by blacks was rare. In Johannesburg, one has the support of hundreds and even thousands of others who are engaging in the same dangerous activities, but in a conservative place like Kimberley, with no liberal press or judiciary to oversee the police, such an action requires true valor. It was in Kimberley during the Defiance Campaign that one of the ANC's leading members was sentenced to lashes by the local magistrate.

Despite my cold, Arthur allowed me to address an ANC meeting in his house the following evening. I was preparing to leave the next morning at three o'clock, but Arthur and his wife insisted I remain for breakfast, which I did. I made good time on the way back to Johannesburg and arrived home just before supper, where I was met with excited cries from my children, who well knew that I was a father bearing gifts. One by one, I handed out the presents I had purchased in Cape Town and patiently answered their questions about the trip. Though not a true holiday, it had the same effect: I felt rejuvenated and ready to take up the fight once more.

22

IMMEDIATELY upon my return I reported on my trip to the Working Committee of the ANC. Their principal concern was whether or not the Congress Alliance was strong enough to halt the government's plans. I did not give them good news. I said the Transkei was not a well-organized

ANC area and the power of the security police would soon immobilize what little influence the ANC had.

I put forth an alternative that I knew would be unpopular. Why shouldn't the ANC participate in the new Bantu Authorities structures as a means of remaining in touch with the masses of people? In time, such participation would become a platform for our own ideas and policies.

Any suggestion of participating in apartheid structures in any way was automatically met with angry opposition. In my early days, I, too, would have strenuously objected. But my sense of the country was that relatively few people were ready to make the sacrifices to join the struggle. We should meet the people on their own terms, even if that meant appearing to collaborate. My idea was that our movement should be a great tent that included as many people as possible.

At the time, however, my report was given short shrift because of another related report with greater ramifications. The publication of the report of the Tomlinson Commission for the Socio-Economic Development of the Bantu Areas had set off a nationwide debate. The government-created commission proposed a plan for the development of the so-called Bantu Areas or bantustans. The result was in fact a blueprint for "separate development" or grand apartheid.

The bantustan system had been conceived by Dr. H. F. Verwoerd, the minister of native affairs, as a way of muting international criticism of South African racial policies but at the same time institutionalizing apartheid. The bantustans, or reserves as they were also known, would be separate ethnic enclaves or homelands for all African citizens. Africans, Verwoerd said, "should stand with both feet in the reserves" where they were to "develop along their own lines." The idea was to preserve the status quo where three million whites owned 87 percent of the land, and relegate the eight million Africans to the remaining 13 percent.

The central theme of the report was the rejection of the idea of integration between the races in favor of a policy of separate development of black and white. To that end, the report recommended the industrialization of the African areas, noting that any program of development that did not aim at providing opportunities for Africans in their own regions was doomed to failure. The commission pointed out that the present geographical configuration of the African areas was too fragmentary, and recommended instead a consolidation of African areas into what it termed seven "historical-logical" homelands of the principal ethnic groups.

But the creation of individual, self-contained bantustans, as proposed by the commission, was farcical. Transkei, the showpiece of the proposed homeland system, would be broken into three geographically separate blocks. The Swazi bantustan, Lebowa, and Venda were composed of three pieces each; Gazankule, four; the Ciskei, seventeen; Bophuthatswana, nineteen; and KwaZulu, twenty-nine. The Nationalists were creating a cruel jigsaw puzzle out of people's lives.

The government's intention in creating the homeland system was to keep the Transkei — and other African areas — as reservoirs of cheap labor for white industry. At the same time, the covert goal of the government was to create an African middle class to blunt the appeal of the ANC and the liberation struggle.

The ANC denounced the report of the Tomlinson Commission, despite some of its more liberal recommendations. As I told Daliwonga, separate development was a spurious solution to a problem that whites had no idea how to control. In the end, the government approved the report, but rejected a number of its recommendations as being too progressive.

Despite the encroaching darkness and my pessimism about the government's policies, I was thinking about the future. In February 1956, I returned to the Transkei to purchase a plot of land in Umtata. I have always thought a man should own a house near the place he was born, where he might find a restfulness that eludes him elsewhere.

With Walter, I journeyed down to the Transkei. Walter and I met with various ANC people in both Umtata and Durban, where we went first. Once again, we were clumsily shadowed by Special Branch police. In Durban, we paid a call on our colleagues at the Natal Indian Congress in an effort to boost activism in the area.

In Umtata, with Walter's help, I made a down payment to C. K. Sakwe for a plot of land he owned in town. Sakwe was a member of the Bunga and had served on the Natives Representative Council. While we were there he told us of an incident that had occurred the previous Saturday at Bumbhane, the Great Place of Sabata, at a meeting of government officials and chiefs about the introduction of the bantustans. A number of the chiefs objected to the government's policy and verbally attacked the magistrate. The meeting broke up in anger; this gave us some sense of the grassroots objections to the Bantu Authorities Act.

In March 1956, after several months of relative freedom, I received my third ban, which restricted me to Johannesburg for five years and prohibited me from attending meetings for that same period. For the next sixty months I would be quarantined in the same district, seeing the same streets, the same mine dumps on the horizon, the same sky. I would have to depend on newspapers and other people for reports on what was occurring outside of Johannesburg, another prospect I did not relish.

But this time my attitude toward my bans had changed radically. When I was first banned I abided by the rules and regulations of my persecutors. I had now developed contempt for these restrictions. I was not going to let my involvement in the struggle and the scope of my political activities be determined by the enemy I was fighting against. To allow my activities to be circumscribed by my opponent was a form of defeat, and I resolved not to become my own jailer.

I soon became involved in mediating a bitter political dispute right in Johannesburg. It pitted two sides against each other, both of which were seeking my support. Each side within this particular organization had legitimate grievances and each side was implacably opposed to the other. The altercation threatened to descend into an acrimonious civil war, and I did my best to prevent a rupture. I am speaking, of course, of the struggle at the boxing and weight lifting club at the Donaldson Orlando Community Center where I trained almost every evening.

I had joined the club in 1950, and on almost every free night I worked out at the Community Center. For the previous few years I had taken my son, Thembi, with me, and by 1956, when he was ten years old, he was a keen if spindly paperweight boxer. The club was managed by Johannes (Skipper Adonis) Molotsi, and its membership consisted of both professional and amateur boxers, as well as a variety of dedicated weight lifters. Our star boxer, Jerry (Uyinja) Moloi, later became the Transvaal lightweight champion and number one contender for the national title.

The gym was poorly equipped. We could not afford a ring and trained on a cement floor, which was particularly dangerous when a boxer was knocked down. We boasted a single punching bag and a few pairs of boxing gloves. We had no medicine or speed balls, no proper boxing trunks or shoes, and no mouth guards. Almost no one owned head guards. Despite the lack of equipment, the gym produced such champions as Eric (Black Material) Ntsele, bantamweight champion of South Africa, and Freddie (Tomahawk) Ngidi, the Transvaal flyweight champion, who spent his days working for me as an assistant at Mandela and Tambo. Altogether, we had perhaps twenty or thirty members.

Although I had boxed a bit at Fort Hare, it was not until I had lived in Johannesburg that I took up the sport in earnest. I was never an outstanding boxer. I was in the heavyweight division, and I had neither enough power to compensate for my lack of speed nor enough speed to make up for my lack of power. I did not enjoy the violence of boxing so much as the science of it. I was intrigued by how one moved one's body to protect oneself, how one used a strategy both to attack and retreat, how one paced oneself over a match. Boxing is egalitarian. In the ring, rank, age, color, and wealth are irrelevant. When you are circling your opponent, probing his strengths and weaknesses, you are not thinking about his color or social status. I never did any real fighting after I entered politics. My main interest was in training; I found the rigorous exercise to be an excellent outlet for tension and stress. After a strenuous workout, I felt both mentally and physically lighter. It was a way of losing myself in something that was not the struggle. After an evening's workout I would wake up the next morning feeling strong and refreshed, ready to take up the fight again.

I attended the gym for one and a half hours each evening from Monday through Thursday. I would go home directly after work, pick up Thembi, then drive to the Community Center. We did an hour of exercise, some combination of roadwork, skipping rope, calisthenics, or shadow boxing, followed by fifteen minutes of body work, some weight lifting and then sparring. If we were training for a fight or a tournament, we would extend the training time to two and a half hours.

We each took turns leading the training sessions in order to develop leadership, initiative, and self-confidence. Thembi particularly enjoyed leading these sessions. Things would get a bit rough for me on the nights that my son was in charge, for he would single me out for criticism. He was quick to chastise me whenever I got lazy. Everybody in the gym called me "Chief," an honorific he avoided, calling me "Mister Mandela," and occasionally, when he felt sympathy for his old man, "My bra," township slang meaning "My brother." When he saw me loafing, he would say in a stern voice, "Mister Mandela, you are wasting our time this evening. If you cannot keep up, why not go home and sit with the old women." Everyone enjoyed these jibes immensely, and it gave me pleasure to see my son so happy and confident.

The camaraderie of the club was shattered that year because of a spat between Skipper Molotsi and Jerry Moloi. Jerry and the other boxers felt that Skipper was not paying enough attention to the club. Skipper was a skillful coach, but was rarely present to impart his knowledge. He was a historian of boxing lore and could narrate all twenty-six rounds of Jack Johnson's famous bout in Havana in 1915 when the first black heavyweight champion of the world lost his title. But Skipper tended to appear only before a match or a tournament to collect the small fee that was his due. I myself was sympathetic to Jerry's point of view but did my best to patch up the quarrel in the interest of keeping harmony. In the end, even my son agreed with Jerry's criticism of Skipper and there was nothing I could do to prevent a rupture.

The boxers, under Jerry's leadership, threatened to secede from the club and start their own. I called a meeting for all the members and it was a lively session — conducted in Sesotho, Zulu, Xhosa, and English.

Shakespeare was even cited by Skipper in his attack against the rebellious boxers, accusing Jerry of double-crossing him as Brutus had betrayed Caesar. "Who are Caesar and Brutus?" my son asked. Before I could answer, someone said, "Aren't they dead?" To which Skipper replied, "Yes, but the truth about the betrayal is very much alive!"

The meeting resolved nothing and the boxers left for another venue while the weight lifters remained at the Community Center. I joined the boxers and for the first few weeks of the separation we trained at an uncomfortable place for a freedom fighter, the police gymnasium. Thereafter, the Anglican Church gave us premises at a reasonable rental in Orlando East, and we trained under Simon (Mshengu) Tshabalala, who later became one of the ANC's leading underground freedom fighters.

Our new facilities were no better than the old, and the club was never reconstituted. African boxers, like all black athletes and artists, were shackled by the twin handicaps of poverty and racism. What money an African boxer earned was typically used on food, rent, clothing, and whatever was left went to boxing equipment and training. He was denied the opportunity of belonging to the white boxing clubs that had the equipment and trainers necessary to produce a first-rate, world-class boxer. Unlike white professional boxers, African professional boxers had full-time day jobs. Sparring partners were few and poorly paid; without proper drilling and practice, the performance greatly suffered. Yet a number of African fighters were able to triumph over these difficulties and achieve great success. Boxers like Elijah (Maestro) Mokone, Enoch (Schoolboy) Nhlapo, Kangaroo Macto, one of the greatest stylists of the ring, Levi (Golden Boy) Madi, Nkosana Mgxaji, Mackeed Mofokeng, and Norman Sekgapane, all won great victories, while Jake Tuli, our greatest hero, won the British and Empire flyweight title. He was the most eloquent example of what African boxers could achieve if given the opportunity.

Part Five

———

TREASON

23

JUST AFTER DAWN, on the morning of December 5, 1956, I was awakened by a loud knocking on my door. No neighbor or friend ever knocks in such a peremptory way, and I knew immediately that it was the security police. I dressed quickly and found Head Constable Rousseau, a security officer who was a familiar figure in our area, and two policemen. He produced a search warrant, at which point the three of them immediately began to comb through the entire house looking for incriminating papers or documents. By this time the children were awake, and with a stern look I bade them to be calm. The children looked to me for reassurance. The police searched drawers and cabinets and closets, any place where contraband might have been hidden. After forty-five minutes, Rousseau matter-of-factly said, "Mandela, we have a warrant for your arrest. Come with me." I looked at the warrant, and the words leapt out at me: "HOOGVERRAAD — HIGH TREASON."

I walked with them to the car. It is not pleasant to be arrested in front of one's children, even though one knows that what one is doing is right. But children do not comprehend the complexity of the situation; they simply see their father being taken away by the white authorities without an explanation.

Rousseau drove and I sat next to him — without handcuffs — in the front seat. He had a search warrant for my office in town, where we were now headed after dropping off the two other policemen in a nearby area. To get to downtown Johannesburg, one had to travel along a desolate highway that cut through an unpopulated area. While we were motoring along this stretch, I remarked to Rousseau that he must be very confident to drive with me alone and unhandcuffed. He was silent.

"What would happen if I seized you and overpowered you?" I said.

Rousseau shifted uncomfortably. "You are playing with fire, Mandela," he said.

"Playing with fire is my game," I replied.

"If you continue speaking like this I will have to handcuff you," Rousseau said threateningly.

"And if I refuse?"

We continued this tense debate for a few more minutes, but as we passed into a populated area near the Langlaagte police station, Rousseau said to me: "Mandela, I have treated you well and I expect you to do the same to me. I don't like your jokes."

After a brief stop at the police station, we were joined by another officer and went to my office, which they searched for another forty-five minutes. From there, I was taken to Marshall Square, the rambling red-brick Johannesburg prison where I had spent a few nights in 1952 during the Defiance Campaign. A number of my colleagues were already there, having been arrested and booked earlier that morning. Over the next few hours, more friends and comrades began to trickle in. This was the swoop the government had long been planning. Someone smuggled in a copy of the afternoon edition of *The Star,* and we learned from its banner headlines that the raid had been countrywide and that the premier leaders of the Congress Alliance were all being arrested on charges of high treason and an alleged conspiracy to overthrow the state. Those who had been arrested in different parts of the country — Chief Luthuli, Monty Naicker, Reggie September, Lilian Ngoyi, Piet Beyleveld — were flown by military planes to Johannesburg, where they were to be arraigned. One hundred forty-four people had been arrested. The next day we appeared in court and we were formally charged. A week later, Walter Sisulu and eleven others were arrested, bringing the total to one hundred fifty-six. All told, there were one hundred five Africans, twenty-one Indians, twenty-three whites, and seven Coloureds. Almost the entire executive leadership of the ANC, both banned and unbanned, had been arrested. The government, at long last, had made its move.

We were soon transferred to the Johannesburg Prison, popularly known as the Fort, a bleak, castle-like structure located on a hill in the heart of the city. Upon admission we were taken to an outdoor quadrangle and ordered to strip completely and line up against the wall. We were forced to stand there for more than an hour, shivering in the breeze and feeling awkward — priests, professors, doctors, lawyers, businessmen, men of middle or old age, who were normally treated with deference and respect. Despite my anger, I could not suppress a laugh as I scrutinized the men around me. For the first time, the truth of the aphorism "clothes make the man" came home to me. If fine bodies and impressive physiques were essential to being a leader I saw that few among us would have qualified.

A white doctor finally appeared and asked whether any of us was ill. No one complained of any ailment. We were ordered to dress, and then escorted to two large cells with cement floors and no furniture. The cells had recently been painted and reeked of paint fumes. We were each given three thin blankets plus a sisal mat. Each cell had only one floor-level latrine, which was completely exposed. It is said that no one truly knows a nation until one has been inside its jails. A nation should not be judged by how it treats its highest citizens, but its lowest ones — and South Africa treated its imprisoned African citizens like animals.

We stayed in the Fort for two weeks, and despite the hardships, our spirits remained extremely high. We were permitted newspapers and read with gratification of the waves of indignation aroused by our arrests. Protest meetings and demonstrations were being held throughout South Africa; people carried signs declaring "We Stand by Our Leaders." We read of protests around the world over our incarceration.

Our communal cell became a kind of convention for far-flung freedom fighters. Many of us had been living under severe restrictions, making it illegal for us to meet and talk. Now, our enemy had gathered us all together under one roof for what became the largest and longest unbanned meeting of the Congress Alliance in years. Younger leaders met older leaders they had only read about. Men from Natal mingled with leaders from the Transvaal. We reveled in the opportunity to exchange ideas and experiences for two weeks while we awaited trial.

Each day, we put together a program of activities. Patrick Molaoa and Peter Nthite, both prominent Youth Leaguers, organized physical training. Talks on a variety of subjects were scheduled, and we heard Professor Matthews discourse on both the history of the ANC and the American Negro, Debi Singh lectured on the history of the SAIC, Arthur Letele discussed the African medicine man, while Reverend James Calata spoke on African music — and sang in his beautiful tenor voice. Every day, Vuyisile Mini, who years later was hanged by the government for political crimes, led the group in singing freedom songs. One of the most popular was: *"Nans' indod' emnyama Strijdom, Bhasobha nans' indod emnyama Strijdom"* (Here's the black man, Strijdom, beware the black man, Strijdom). We sang at the top of our lungs, and it kept our spirits high.

One time, Masabalala Yengwa (better known as M. B. Yengwa), the son of a Zulu laborer and the provincial secretary of the Natal ANC, contributed to a lecture on music by reciting a praise song in honor of Shaka, the legendary Zulu warrior and king. Yengwa draped himself with a blanket, rolled up a newspaper to imitate an assegai, and began to stride back and forth reciting the lines from the praise song. All of us, even those who did not understand Zulu, were entranced. Then he paused dramatically and called out the lines *"Inyoni edlezinya! Yathi isadlezinye, yadi ezinya!"* The lines liken Shaka to a great bird of prey that relentlessly slays its enemies. At the conclusion of these words, pandemonium broke out. Chief Luthuli, who until then had remained quiet, sprang to his feet, and bellowed, *"Ngu Shaka lowo!"* (That is Shaka!), and then began to dance and chant. His movements electrified us, and we all took to our feet. Accomplished ballroom dancers, sluggards who knew neither traditional nor Western dancing, all joined in the *indlamu,* the traditional Zulu war dance. Some moved gracefully, others resembled frozen mountaineers trying to shake off the cold, but all danced with enthusiasm and emotion. Suddenly there were no Xhosas or Zulus, no Indians or Africans, no rightists or leftists, no religious or political leaders; we were all nationalists and patriots bound together by a love of our common history, our culture, our country, and our people. In that moment, something stirred deep inside all of us, something strong and intimate, that bound us to one another. In that moment we felt the hand of the great past that made us what we were and the power of the great cause that linked us all together.

After the two weeks, we appeared for our preparatory examination on December 19 at the Drill Hall in Johannesburg, a military structure not normally used as a court of justice. It was a great bare barn of a building with a corrugated iron roof and was considered the only public building large enough to support a trial of so many accused.

We were taken in sealed police vans escorted by a half-dozen troop carriers filled with armed soldiers. One would have thought a full-scale civil war was under way from the precautions the state was taking with us. A massive crowd of our supporters was blocking traffic in Twist Street; we could hear them cheering and singing, and they could hear us answering from inside the van. The trip became a triumphal procession as the slow-moving van was rocked by the crowd. The entire perimeter of the hall was surrounded by gun-toting policemen and soldiers. The vans were brought to an area behind the hall and parked so that we alighted straight from the van into the courtroom.

Inside, we were met by another crowd of supporters, so that the hall seemed more like a raucous protest meeting than a staid court of law. We walked in with our thumbs raised in the ANC salute and nodded to our supporters sitting in the non-Whites Only section. The mood inside was more celebratory than punitive, as the accused mingled with reporters and friends.

The government was charging all one hundred fifty-six of us with high treason and a countrywide conspiracy to use violence to overthrow the present government and replace it with a Communist state. The period covered by the indictment was October 1, 1952, through December 13, 1956: it included the Defiance Campaign, the Sophiatown removal, and the Congress of the People. The South African law of high treason was based not on English law, but on Roman Dutch antecedents, and defined high treason as a hostile intention to disturb, impair, or endanger the independence or safety of the state. The punishment was death.

The purpose of a preparatory examination was to determine whether the government's charges were sufficient to put us on trial in the Supreme Court. There were two stages of giving evidence. The first stage took place in a magistrate's court. If the magistrate determined that there was sufficient evidence against the accused, the case would move to the Supreme Court and be tried before a judge. If the magistrate decided there was insufficient evidence, the defendants were discharged.

The magistrate was Mr. F. C. Wessel, the chief magistrate from Bloemfontein. That first day, when Wessel began to speak in his quiet voice it was impossible to hear him. The state had neglected to provide microphones and loudspeakers, and the court was adjourned for two hours while amplification was sought. We assembled in a courtyard and had what was very much like a picnic, with food sent in from the outside. The atmosphere was almost festive. Two hours later, court was recessed for the day because proper loudspeakers had not been found. To the cheers of the crowd, we were once again escorted back to the Fort.

The next day, the crowds outside were even larger, the police more tense. Five hundred armed police surrounded the Drill Hall. When we arrived, we discovered that the state had erected an enormous wire cage for us to sit in. It was made of diamond-mesh wire, attached to poles and scaffolding with a grille at the front and top. We were led inside and sat on benches, surrounded by sixteen armed guards.

In addition to its symbolic effect, the cage cut us off from communication with our lawyers, who were not permitted to enter. One of my colleagues scribbled on a piece of paper, which he then posted on the side of the cage: "Dangerous. Please Do Not Feed."

Our supporters and organization had assembled a formidable defense team, including Bram Fischer, Norman Rosenberg, Israel Maisels, Maurice Franks, and Vernon Berrangé. None of them had ever seen such a structure in court before. Franks lodged a powerful protest in open court against the state's humiliating his clients in such a "fantastic" fashion and treating them, he said, "like wild beasts." Unless the cage was removed forthwith, he announced, the entire defense team would walk out of court. After a brief adjournment, the magistrate decided that the cage would be pulled down; in the meantime, the front of it was removed.

Only then did the state begin its case. The chief prosecutor, Mr. Van Niekerk, began reading part of an 18,000-word address outlining the Crown case against us. Even with amplification he was barely audible against the shouting and singing outside, and at one point a group of policemen rushed out. We heard a revolver shot, followed by shouts and more gunfire. The court was adjourned while the magistrate held a meeting with counsel. Twenty people had been injured.

The reading of the charges continued for the next two days. Van Niekerk said that he would prove to the court that the accused, with help from other countries, were plotting to overthrow the existing government by violence and impose a Communist government on South Africa. This was the charge of high treason. The state cited the Freedom Charter as both proof of our Communist intentions and evidence of our plot to overthrow the existing authorities. By the third day, much of the cage had been dismantled. Finally, on the fourth day, we were released on bail. Bail was another example of the sliding scale of apartheid: £250 for whites; £100 for Indians; and £25 for Africans and Coloureds. Even treason was not color-blind. Well-wishers from diverse walks of life came forward to guarantee bail for each of the accused, gestures of support that later became the foundation for the Treason Trial Defense Fund started by Bishop Reeves, Alan Paton, and Alex Hepple. The fund was ably administered during the trial by Mary Benson and then Freda Levson. We were released provided we reported once a week to the police, and were forbidden from attending public gatherings. Court was to resume in early January.

The following day I was at my office bright and early. Oliver and I had both been in prison, and our caseload had mounted in the meantime. While trying to work that morning, I was visited by an old friend named Jabavu, a professional interpreter whom I had not seen for several months. Before the arrests I had deliberately cut down my weight, in anticipation of prison, where one should be lean and able to survive on little. In jail, I had continued my exercises, and was pleased to be so trim. But Jabavu eyed me suspiciously. "Madiba," he said, "why must you look so thin?" In African cultures, portliness is often associated with wealth and well-being. He burst out: "Man, you were scared of jail, that is all. You have disgraced us, we Xhosas!"

24

EVEN BEFORE THE TRIAL, my marriage to Evelyn had begun to unravel. In 1953, Evelyn had become set on upgrading her four-year certificate in general nursing. She enrolled in a midwifery course at King Edward VII Hospital in Durban that would keep her away from home for several months. This was possible because my mother and sister were staying with us and could look after the children. During her stay in Durban, I visited her on at least one occasion.

Evelyn returned, having passed her examinations. She was pregnant again and later that year, gave birth to Makaziwe, named after the daughter we had lost six years before. In our culture, to give a new child the name of a deceased child is considered a way of honoring the earlier child's memory and retaining a mystical attachment to the child who left too soon.

Over the course of the next year Evelyn became involved with the Watch Tower organization, part of the church of Jehovah's Witnesses. Whether this was due to some dissatisfaction with her life at the time, I do not know. The Jehovah's Witnesses took the Bible as the sole rule of faith and believed in a coming Armageddon between good and evil. Evelyn zealously began distributing their publication *The Watchtower,* and began to proselytize me as well, urging me to convert my commitment to the struggle to a commitment to God. Although I found some aspects of the Watch Tower's system to be interesting and worthwhile, I could not and did not share her devotion. There was an obsessional element to it that put me off. From what I could discern, her faith taught passivity and submissiveness in the face of oppression, something I could not accept.

My devotion to the ANC and the struggle was unremitting. This disturbed Evelyn. She had always assumed that politics was a youthful diversion, that I would someday return to the Transkei and practice there as a lawyer. Even as that possibility became remote, she never resigned herself to the fact that Johannesburg would be our home, or let go of the idea that we might move back to Umtata. She believed that once I was back in the Transkei, in the bosom of my family, acting as counselor to Sabata, I would no longer miss politics. She encouraged Daliwonga's efforts to persuade me to come back to Umtata. We had many arguments about this, and I patiently explained to her that politics was not a distraction but my lifework, that it was an essential and fundamental part of my being. She could not accept this. A man and a woman who hold such different views of their respective roles in life cannot remain close.

I tried to persuade her of the necessity of the struggle, while she attempted to persuade me of the value of religious faith. When I would tell her that I was serving the nation, she would reply that serving God was above serving the nation. We were finding no common ground, and I was becoming convinced that the marriage was no longer tenable.

We also waged a battle for the minds and hearts of the children. She wanted them to be religious, and I thought they should be political. She would take them to church at every opportunity and read them Watch

Tower literature. She even gave the boys *Watchtower* pamphlets to distribute in the township. I used to talk politics to the boys. Thembi was a member of the Pioneers, the juvenile section of the ANC, so he was already politically cognizant. I would explain to Makgatho in the simplest terms how the black man was persecuted by the white man.

Hanging on the walls of the house, I had pictures of Roosevelt, Churchill, Stalin, Gandhi, and the storming of the Winter Palace in St. Petersburg in 1917. I explained to the boys who each of the men was, and what he stood for. They knew that the white leaders of South Africa stood for something very different. One day, Makgatho came running into the house, and said, "Daddy, Daddy, there is Malan on the hill!" Malan had been the first Nationalist prime minister and the boy had confused him with a Bantu Education official, Willie Maree, who had announced that he would that day address a public meeting in the township. I went outside to see what Makgatho was talking about, for the ANC had organized a demonstration to ensure that the meeting did not succeed. As I went out, I saw a couple of police vans escorting Maree to the place he was meant to speak, but there was trouble from the start and Maree had fled without delivering his speech. I told Makgatho that it was not Malan but might as well have been.

My schedule in those days was relentless. I would leave the house very early in the morning and return late at night. After a day at the office, I would usually have meetings of one kind or another. Evelyn could not understand my meetings in the evening, and when I returned home late suspected I was seeing other women. Time after time, I would explain what meeting I was at, why I was there, and what was discussed. But she was not convinced. In 1955, she gave me an ultimatum: I had to choose between her and the ANC.

Walter and Albertina were very close to Evelyn, and their fondest wish was for us to stay together. Evelyn confided in Albertina. At one point, Walter intervened in the matter and I was very short with him, telling him it was none of his business. I regretted the tone I took, because Walter had always been a brother to me and his friendship and support had never faltered.

One day, Walter told me he wanted to bring someone over to the office for me to meet. He did not tell me that it was my brother-in-law, and I was surprised but not displeased to see him. I was pessimistic about the marriage and I thought it only fair to inform him of my feelings.

We were discussing this issue cordially among the three of us, when either Walter or I used a phrase like "Men such as ourselves," or something of that ilk. Evelyn's brother-in-law was a businessman, opposed to politics and politicians. He became very huffy and said, "If you chaps think you are in the same position as myself, that is ridiculous. Do not compare yourselves to me." When he left, Walter and I looked at each other and started laughing.

After we were arrested in December and kept in prison for two weeks, I had one visit from Evelyn. But when I came out of prison, I found that she had moved out and taken the children. I returned to an empty, silent house. She had even removed the curtains, and for some reason I found this small detail shattering. Evelyn had moved in with her brother, who told me, "Perhaps it is for the best; maybe when things will have cooled down you will come back together." It was reasonable advice, but it was not to be.

Evelyn and I had irreconcilable differences. I could not give up my life in the struggle, and she could not live with my devotion to something other than herself and the family. She was a very good woman, charming, strong, and faithful, and a fine mother. I never lost my respect and admiration for her, but in the end, we could not make our marriage work.

The breakup of any marriage is traumatic, especially for the children. Our family was no exception, and all of the children were wounded by our separation. Makgatho took to sleeping in my bed. He was a gentle child, a natural peacemaker and he tried to bring about some sort of reconciliation between me and his mother. Makaziwe was still very small, and I remember one day, when I was not in prison or in court, I visited her crèche (nursery school) unannounced. She had always been a very affectionate child, but that day, when she saw me, she froze. She did not know whether to run to me or retreat, to smile or frown. She had some conflict in her small heart, which she did not know how to resolve. It was very painful.

Thembi, who was ten at the time, was the most deeply affected. He stopped studying and became withdrawn. He had once been keen on English and Shakespeare, but after the separation he seemed to become apathetic about learning. The principal of his school spoke to me on one occasion, but there was little that I was able to do. I would take him to the gym whenever I could, and occasionally he would brighten a bit. There were many times when I could not be there and later, when I was underground, Walter would take Thembi with him along with his own son. One time, Walter took him to an event, and afterward Walter said to me, "Man, that chap is quiet." Following the breakup, Thembi would frequently wear my clothes, even though they were far too large for him; they gave him some kind of attachment to his too-often-distant father.

25

ON JANUARY 9, 1957, we once again assembled in the Drill Hall. It was the defense's turn to refute the state's charges. After summarizing the Crown's case against us, Vernon Berrangé, our lead counsel, announced our argument. "The defense," he said, "will strenuously repudiate that the terms of the Freedom Charter are treasonable or criminal. On the contrary, the defense will contend that the ideas and beliefs which are expressed in this charter, although repugnant to the policy of the present government, are such as are shared by the overwhelming majority of mankind of all races and colors, and also by the overwhelming majority of the citizens of this country." In consultation with our attorneys, we had decided that we were not merely going to prove that we were innocent of treason, but that this was a political trial in which the government was persecuting us for taking actions that were morally justified.

But the drama of the opening arguments was succeeded by the tedium of court logistics. The first month of the trial was taken up by the state's submission of evidence. One by one, every paper, pamphlet, document, book, notebook, letter, magazine, and clipping that the police had accumulated in the last three years of searches was produced and numbered; twelve thousand in all. The submissions ranged from the United Nations Declaration of Human Rights to a Russian cookbook. They even submitted the two signs from the Congress of the People: "SOUP WITH MEAT" and "SOUP WITHOUT MEAT."

During the preparatory examination, which was to last for months, we listened day after day as African and Afrikaner detectives read out their notes of ANC meetings, or transcripts of speeches. These recountings were always garbled, and often either nonsensical or downright false. Berrangé later revealed in his deft cross-examination that many of the African detectives were unable to understand or write English, the language in which the speeches were given.

To support the state's extraordinary allegation that we intended to replace the existing government with a Soviet-style state, the Crown relied on the evidence of Professor Andrew Murray, head of the Department of Political Science at the University of Cape Town. Murray labeled many of the documents seized from us, including the Freedom Charter itself, as communistic.

Professor Murray seemed, at the outset, relatively knowledgeable, but that was until Berrangé began his cross-examination. Berrangé said that he wanted to read Murray a number of passages from various documents and then have Murray label them communistic or not. Berrangé read him the first passage, which concerned the need for ordinary workers to co-operate with each other and not exploit one another. Communistic, Murray said. Berrangé then noted that the statement had been made by the former premier of South Africa, Dr. Malan. Berrangé proceeded to read him two other statements, both of which Professor Murray described as communistic. These passages had in fact been uttered by the American presidents Abraham Lincoln and Woodrow Wilson. The highlight came when Berrangé read Murray a passage that the professor unhesitatingly described as "communism straight from the shoulder." Berrangé then revealed that it was a statement that Professor Murray himself had written in the 1930s.

In the seventh month of the trial, the state said it would produce evidence of planned violence that occurred during the Defiance Campaign. The state called the first of their star witnesses, Solomon Ngubase, who offered sensational evidence that seemed to implicate the ANC. Ngubase was a soft-spoken fellow in his late thirties, with a shaky command of English, who was currently serving a sentence for fraud. In his opening testimony, Ngubase told the court he had obtained a bachelor of arts degree from Fort Hare, and that he was a practicing attorney. He said he became secretary of the Port Elizabeth branch of the ANC as well as a member of the National Executive Committee. He claimed to have been present at a meeting of the National Executive when a decision was made to send Walter Sisulu and David Bopape to the Soviet Union to procure arms for a violent revolution in South Africa. He said he was present at a meeting that planned the 1952 Port Elizabeth riot and that he had witnessed an ANC decision to murder all whites in the Transkei in the same manner as the Mau Mau in Kenya. Ngubase's dramatic testimony caused a stir in and out of court. Here at long last was evidence of a conspiracy.

But when Ngubase was cross-examined by Vernon Berrangé, it was revealed that he was equal parts madman and liar. Berrangé, whose cross-examination skills earned him the nickname Isangoma (a diviner or healer who exorcises an illness) among the accused, quickly established that Ngubase was neither a university graduate nor a member of the ANC, much less a member of the National Executive Committee. Berrangé showed that Ngubase had forged certificates for a university degree, had practiced law illegally for several years, and had a further case of fraud pending against him. At the time of the meeting he claimed to have attended to plan the Port Elizabeth riot, he was serving a sentence for fraud in a Durban jail. Almost none of Ngubase's testimony bore even a remote resemblance to the truth. At the end of his cross-examination, Berrangé asked the witness, "Do you know what a rogue is?" Ngubase said he did not. "You, sir, are a rogue!" Berrangé exclaimed.

Joe Slovo, one of the accused and a superb advocate, conducted his own defense. He was an irritant to the state because of his sharp questions and attempts to show that the state was the violator of laws, not the Congress. Slovo's cross-examination was often as devastating as Berrangé's. Detective Jeremiah Mollson, one of the few African members of the Special Branch, claimed to recall lines verbatim from ANC speeches that he attended. But what he reported was usually gibberish or outright fabrication.

Slovo: "Do you understand English?"

Mollson: "Not so well."

Slovo: "Do you mean to say that you reported these speeches in English but you don't understand English well?"

Mollson: "Yes, Your Worship."

Slovo: "Do you agree that your notes are a lot of rubbish?"

Mollson: "I don't know."

This last response caused an outbreak of laughter from the defendants. The magistrate scolded us for laughing, and said, "The proceedings are not as funny as they may seem."

At one point, Wessel told Slovo that he was impugning the integrity of the court and fined him for contempt. This provoked the fury of most of the accused, and it was only Chief Luthuli's restraining hand that kept a number of the defendants from being cited for contempt as well.

As the testimony continued, much of it tedious legal maneuvering, we began to occupy ourselves with other matters. I often brought a book to read or a legal brief to work on. Others read newspapers, did crossword puzzles, or played chess or Scrabble. Occasionally, the bench would reprimand us for not paying attention, and the books and puzzles would disappear. But, slowly, as the testimony resumed its snail's pace, the games and reading material reemerged.

As the preparatory examination continued, the state became increasingly desperate. It became more and more apparent that the state was gathering — often fabricating — evidence as it went along, to help in what seemed to be a lost cause.

Finally, on September 11, ten months after we had first assembled in the Drill Hall, the prosecutor announced that the state's case in the preparatory examination was completed. The magistrate gave the defense four months to sift through the eight thousand pages of typed evidence and twelve thousand documents to prepare its case.

The preparatory examination had lasted for the whole of 1957. Court adjourned in September, and the defense began reviewing the evidence. Three months later, without warning and without explanation, the Crown announced that charges against sixty-one of the accused were to be dropped. Most of these defendants were relatively minor figures in the ANC, but also among them were Chief Lutuli and Oliver Tambo. The Crown's release of Lutuli and Tambo pleased but bewildered us.

In January, when the government was scheduled to sum up its charges, the Crown brought in a new prosecutor, the formidable Oswald Pirow, Q.C. Pirow was a former minister of justice and of defense and a pillar of National Party politics. He was a longtime Afrikaner nationalist, and an outspoken supporter of the Nazi cause; he once described Hitler as the "greatest man of his age." He was a virulent anti-Communist. The appointment of Pirow was new evidence that the state was worried about the outcome and attached tremendous importance to a victory.

Before Pirow's summing-up, Berrangé announced he would apply for our discharge on the grounds that the state had not offered sufficient evidence against us. Pirow opposed this application for dismissal, and quoted from several inflammatory speeches by the accused, informing the court that the police had unearthed more evidence of a highly dangerous conspiracy. The country, he said portentously, was sitting on top of a volcano. It was an effective and highly dramatic performance. Pirow changed the atmosphere of the trial. We had become overconfident, and were reminded that we were facing a serious charge. Don't fool yourselves, counsel told us, you people might go to jail. Their warnings sobered us.

After thirteen months of the preparatory examination, the magistrate ruled that he had found "sufficient reason" for putting us on trial in the Transvaal Supreme Court for high treason. Court adjourned in January with the ninety-five remaining defendants committed to stand trial. When the actual trial would begin, we did not know.

26

ONE AFTERNOON, during a recess in the preparatory examination, I drove a friend of mine from Orlando to the medical school at the University of the Witwatersrand and went past Baragwanath Hospital, the premier black hospital in Johannesburg. As I passed a nearby bus stop, I noticed out of the corner of my eye a lovely young woman waiting for the bus. I was struck by her beauty, and I turned my head to get a better look at her, but my car had gone by too fast. This woman's face stayed with me — I even considered turning around to drive by her in the other direction — but I went on.

Some weeks thereafter, a curious coincidence occurred. I was at the office, and when I popped in to see Oliver, there was this same young woman with her brother, sitting in front of Oliver's desk. I was taken aback, and did my best not to show my surprise — or my delight — at this striking coincidence. Oliver introduced me to them and explained that they were visiting him on a legal matter.

Her name was Nomzamo Winnifred Madikizela, but she was known as Winnie. She had recently completed her studies at the Jan Hofmeyr School of Social Work in Johannesburg and was working as the first black female social worker at Baragwanath Hospital. At the time I paid little attention to her background or legal problem, for something in me was deeply stirred by her presence. I was thinking more of how I could ask her out than how our firm would handle her case. I cannot say for certain if there is such a thing as love at first sight, but I do know that the moment I first glimpsed Winnie Nomzamo, I knew that I wanted to have her as my wife.

Winnie was the sixth of eleven children of C. K. Madikizela, a school principal turned businessman. Her given name was Nomzamo, which means one who strives or undergoes trials, a name as prophetic as my own. She came from Bizana in Pondoland, an area adjacent to the part of the Transkei where I grew up. She is from the Phondo clan of amaNgutyana, and her great-grandfather was Madikizela, a powerful chief from nineteenth-century Natal who settled in the Transkei at the time of the iMfecane.

I telephoned Winnie the next day at the hospital and asked her for help in raising money for the Treason Trial Defense Fund from the Jan Hofmeyr School. It was merely a pretext to invite her to lunch, which I did. I picked her up where she was staying in town, and took her to an Indian restaurant near my office, one of the few places that served Africans and where I frequently ate. Winnie was dazzling, and even the fact that she had never before tasted curry and drank glass after glass of water to cool her palate only added to her charm.

After lunch I took her for a drive to an area between Johannesburg and Evaton, an open veld just past Eldorado Park. We walked on the long grass, grass so similar to that of the Transkei where we both had been raised. I told her of my hopes and of the difficulties of the Treason Trial. I knew right there that I wanted to marry her — and I told her so. Her spirit, her passion, her youth, her courage, her willfulness — I felt all of these things the moment I first saw her.

Over the next weeks and months we saw each other whenever we could. She visited me at the Drill Hall and at my office. She came to see me work out in the gym; she met Thembi, Makgatho, and Makaziwe. She came to meetings and political discussions; I was both courting her and politicizing her. As a student, Winnie had been attracted to the Non-European Unity Movement, for she had a brother who was involved with that party. In later years, I would tease her about this early allegiance, telling her that had she not met me, she would have married a leader of the NEUM.

Shortly after I filed for divorce from Evelyn, I told Winnie she should visit Ray Harmel, the wife of Michael Harmel, for a fitting for a wedding dress. In addition to being an activist, Ray was an excellent dressmaker. I asked Winnie how many bridesmaids she intended to have, and suggested she go to Bizana to inform her parents that we were to be married. Winnie has laughingly told people that I never proposed to her, but I always told her that I asked her on our very first date and that I simply took it for granted from that day forward.

The Treason Trial was in its second year and it put a suffocating weight on our law practice. Mandela and Tambo was falling apart as we could not be there, and both Oliver and I were experiencing grave financial difficulties. Since the charges against Oliver had been dropped, he was able to do some remedial work; but the damage had already been done. We had gone from a bustling practice that turned people away to one that was practically begging for clients. I could not even afford to pay the fifty-pound balance still owing on the plot of land that I had purchased in Umtata, and had to give it up.

I explained all this to Winnie. I told her it was more than likely that we would have to live on her small salary as a social worker. Winnie understood and said she was prepared to take the risk and throw in her lot with me. I never promised her gold and diamonds, and I was never able to give her them.

The wedding took place on June 14, 1958. I applied for a relaxation of my banning orders and was given six days' leave of absence from Johannesburg. I also arranged for *lobola,* the traditional brideprice, to be paid to Winnie's father.

The wedding party left Johannesburg very early on the morning of June 12, and we arrived in Bizana late that afternoon. My first stop, as always when one was banned, was the police station to report that I had arrived. At dusk, we then went to the bride's place, Mbongweni, as was customary. We were met by a great chorus of local women ululating with happiness, and Winnie and I were separated; she went to the bride's house, while I went with the groom's party to the house of one of Winnie's relations.

The ceremony itself was at a local church, after which we celebrated at the home of Winnie's eldest brother, which was the ancestral home of the Madikizela clan. The bridal car was swathed in ANC colors. There was dancing and singing, and Winnie's exuberant grandmother did a special dance for all of us. The entire executive of the ANC had been invited, but bans limited their attendance. Among those who came were Duma Nokwe, Lilian Ngoyi, Dr. James Njongwe, Dr. Wilson Conco, and Victor Tyamzashe.

The final reception was at the Bizana Town Hall. The speech I recall best was given by Winnie's father. He took note, as did everyone, that among the uninvited guests at the wedding were a number of security police. He spoke of his love for his daughter, my commitment to the country, and my dangerous career as a politician. When Winnie had first told him of the marriage, he had exclaimed, "But you are marrying a jailbird!" At the wedding, he said he was not optimistic about the future, and that such a marriage, in such difficult times, would be unremittingly tested. He told Winnie she was marrying a man who was already married to the struggle. He bade his daughter good luck, and ended his speech by saying, "If your man is a wizard, you must become a witch!" It was a way of saying that you must follow your man on whatever path he takes. After that, Constance Mbekeni, my sister, spoke on my behalf at the ceremony.

After the ceremony, a piece of the wedding cake was wrapped up for the bride to bring to the groom's ancestral home for the second part of the wedding. But it was never to be, for my leave of absence was up and we had to return to Johannesburg. Winnie carefully stored the cake in anticipation of that day. At our house, number 8115 Orlando West, a large party of friends and family were there to welcome us back. A sheep had been slaughtered and there was a feast in our honor.

There was no time or money for a honeymoon, and life quickly settled into a routine dominated by the trial. We woke very early in the morning, usually at about four. Winnie prepared breakfast before I left. I would then take the bus to the trial, or make an early morning visit to my office. As much as possible, afternoons and evenings were spent at my office attempting to keep our practice going and to earn some money. Evenings were often taken up with political work and meetings. The wife of a freedom fighter is often like a widow, even when her husband is not in prison. Though I was on trial for treason, Winnie gave me cause for hope. I felt as though I had a new and second chance at life. My love for her gave me added strength for the struggles that lay ahead.

27

THE MAJOR EVENT facing the country in 1958 was the general election — "general" only in the sense that three million whites could participate, but none of the thirteen million Africans. We debated whether or not to stage a protest. The central issue was: Did an election in which only whites could participate make any difference to Africans? The answer, as far as the ANC was concerned, was that we could not remain indifferent even when we were shut out of the process. We were excluded, but not unaffected: the defeat of the National Party would be in our interest and that of all Africans.

The ANC joined with the other congresses and SACTU, the South African Congress of Trade Unions, to call a three-day strike during the elections in April. Leaflets were distributed in factories and shops, at railway stations and bus stops, in beer halls and hospitals, and from house to house. "THE NATS MUST GO!" was the main slogan of this campaign. Our preparations worried the government; four days before the election, the state ruled that a gathering of more than ten Africans in any urban area was illegal.

The night before a planned protest, boycott, or stay-away, the leaders of the event would go underground in order to foil the police swoop that inevitably took place. The police were not yet monitoring us around the clock and it was easy to disappear for a day or two. The night before the strike, Walter, Oliver, Moses Kotane, J. B. Marks, Dan Tloome, Duma Nokwe, and I stayed in the house of Dr. Nthatho Motlana, my physician, in Orlando. Very early the next morning, we moved to another house in the same neighborhood where we were able to keep in touch by telephone with other leaders around the city. Communications were not very efficient in those days, particularly in the townships where few people owned telephones, and it was a frustrating task to oversee a strike. We dispatched men to strategic places around the townships to watch the trains, buses, and taxis in order to determine whether or not people were going to work. They returned with bad news: the buses and trains were filled; people were ignoring the strike. Only then did we notice that the gentleman in whose house we were staying was nowhere to be found — he had slipped out and gone to work. The strike was shaping up as a failure.

We resolved to call off the strike. A three-day strike that is canceled on the first day is only a one-day failure; a strike that fails three days running is a fiasco. It was humiliating to have to retreat, but we felt that it would have been more humiliating not to. Less than one hour after we had released a statement calling off the strike, the government-run South African Broadcasting Corporation read our announcement in full. Normally, the SABC ignored the ANC altogether; only in defeat did we make their broadcasts. This time, they even complimented us on calling off the strike. This greatly annoyed Moses Kotane. "To be praised by the SABC, that is too much," he said, shaking his head. Kotane questioned whether we had acted too hastily and played into the state's hands. It was a legitimate concern, but decisions should not be taken out of pride or embarrassment, but out of pure strategy — and strategy here suggested we call off the strike. The fact that the enemy had exploited our surrender didn't mean we were wrong to surrender.

But some areas did not hear that the strike was called off, while others spurned our call. In Port Elizabeth, an ANC stronghold, and other areas of the Cape, the response was better on the second and third days than the first. In general, however, we could not hide the fact that the strike was a failure. As if that were not enough, the Nationalists increased their popular vote in the election by more than 10 percent.

We had heated discussions about whether we ought to have relied on coercive measures. Should we have used pickets, which generally prevent people from entering their place of work? The hard-liners suggested that if we had deployed pickets, the strike would have been a success. But I have always resisted such methods. It is best to rely on the freely given support of the people; otherwise, that support is weak and fleeting. The organization should be a haven, not a prison. However, if the majority of the organization or the people support a decision, coercion can be used in certain cases against the dissident minority in the interests of the majority. A minority, however vocal, should not be able to frustrate the will of the majority.

In my own house, I attempted to use a different sort of coercion, but without success. Ida Mthimkhulu, a Sotho-speaking woman of my own age, was then our house assistant. Ida was more a member of the family than an employee and I called her Kgaitsedi, which means "Sister" and is a term of endearment. Ida ran the house with military efficiency, and Winnie and I took our orders willingly; I often ran out to do errands at her command.

The day before the strike, I was driving Ida and her twelve-year-old son home, and I mentioned that I needed her to wash and press some shirts for me the following day. A long and uncharacteristic silence followed. Ida then turned to me and said with barely concealed disdain, "You know very well that I can't do that."

"Why not?" I replied, surprised by the vehemence of her reaction.

"Have you forgotten that I, too, am a worker?" she said with some satisfaction. "I will be on strike tomorrow with my people and fellow workers!"

Her son saw my embarrassment and in his boyish way tried to ease the tension by saying that "Uncle Nelson" had always treated her as a sister not a worker. In irritation, she turned on her well-meaning son and said, "Boy, where were you when I was struggling for my rights in that house? If I had not fought hard against your 'Uncle Nelson' I would not today be treated like a sister!" Ida did not come to work the next day, and my shirts went unpressed.

28

FEW ISSUES touched a nerve as much as that of passes for women. The state had not weakened in its resolve to impose passes on women and women had not weakened in their resolve to resist. Although the government now called passes "reference books," women weren't fooled: they could still be fined ten pounds or imprisoned for a month for failing to produce their "reference book."

In 1957, spurred by the efforts of the ANC Women's League, women all across the country, in rural areas and in cities, reacted with fury to the state's insistence that they carry passes. The women were courageous, persistent, enthusiastic, indefatigable, and their protest against passes set a standard for antigovernment protest that was never equaled. As Chief Luthuli said, "When the women begin to take an active part in the struggle, no power on earth can stop us from achieving freedom in our lifetime."

All across the southeastern Transvaal, in Standerton, Heidelberg, Balfour, and other dorps, thousands of women protested. On recess from the Treason Trial, Frances Baard and Florence Matomela organized women to refuse passes in Port Elizabeth, their hometown. In Johannesburg, in October, a large group of women gathered at the central pass office, and chased away women who had come to collect passes and clerks who worked in the office, bringing the office to a standstill. Police arrested hundreds of the women.

Not long after these arrests, Winnie and I were relaxing after supper when she quietly informed me that she intended to join the group of Orlando women who would be protesting the following day at the pass office. I was a bit taken aback, and while I was pleased at her sense of commitment and admired her courage, I was also wary. Winnie had become increasingly politicized since our marriage, and had joined the Orlando West branch of the ANC's Women's League, all of which I encouraged.

I told her I welcomed her decision, but that I had to warn her about the seriousness of her action. It would, I said, in a single act, radically change her life. By African standards, Winnie was from a well-to-do family and had been shielded from some of the more unpleasant realities of life in South Africa. At the very least, she never had had to worry about where her next meal was coming from. Before our marriage, she had moved in circles of relative wealth and comfort, a life very different from the often hand-to-mouth existence of the freedom fighter.

I told her that if she was arrested she would be certain to be fired by her employer, the provincial administration — we both knew that it was her small income that was supporting the household — and that she could probably never work again as a social worker, since the stigma of imprisonment would make public agencies reluctant to hire her. Finally, she was pregnant, and I warned her of the physical hardship and humiliations of jail. My response may sound harsh, but I felt responsibility both as a husband and as a leader of the struggle, to be as clear as possible about the ramifications of her action. I, myself, had mixed emotions, for the concerns of a husband and a leader do not always coincide.

But Winnie is a determined person, and I suspect my pessimistic reaction only strengthened her resolve. She listened to all I said and informed me that her mind was made up. The next morning I rose early to make her breakfast, and we drove over to the Sisulus' house to meet Walter's wife, Albertina, one of the leaders of the protest. We then drove to the Phefeni station in Orlando, where the women would get the train into town. I embraced her before she boarded the train. Winnie was nervous yet resolute as she waved to me from the train, and I felt as though she were setting out on a long and perilous journey, the end of which neither of us could know.

Hundreds of women converged on the Central Pass Office in downtown Johannesburg. They were old and young; some carried babies on their backs, some wore tribal blankets, while others had on smart suits. They sang, marched, and chanted. Within minutes, they were surrounded by dozens of armed police, who arrested all of them, packed them into vans, and drove them to Marshall Square police station. The women were cheerful throughout; as they were being driven away, some called out to reporters, "Tell our madams we won't be at work tomorrow!" All told, more than one thousand women were arrested.

I knew this not because I was the husband of one of the detainees but because Mandela and Tambo had been called on to represent most of the women who had been arrested. I quickly made my way to Marshall Square to visit the prisoners and arrange bail. I managed to see Winnie, who beamed when she saw me and seemed as happy as one could be in a bare police cell. It was as if she had given me a great gift that she knew would please me. I told her I was proud of her, but I could not stay and talk as I had quite a lot of legal work to do.

By the end of the second day, the number of arrests had increased and nearly two thousand women were incarcerated, many of them remanded to the Fort to await trial. This created formidable problems not only for Oliver and me, but for the police and the prison authorities. There was simply not enough space to hold them all. There were too few blankets, too few mats and toilets, and too little food. Conditions at the Fort were cramped and dirty. While many in the ANC, including myself, were eager to bail out the women, Lilian Ngoyi, the national president of the Women's League, and Helen Joseph, secretary of the South African Women's Federation, believed that for the protest to be genuine and effective, the women should serve whatever time the magistrate ordered. I remonstrated with them but was told in no uncertain terms that the matter was the women's affair and that the ANC — as well as anxious husbands — should not meddle. I did tell Lilian that I thought she should discuss the issue with the women themselves before making a decision, and escorted her down to the cells where she could poll the prisoners. Many were desperate to be bailed out and had not been adequately prepared for what would await them in prison. As a compromise, I suggested to Lilian that the women spend a fortnight in prison, after which we would bail them out. Lilian accepted.

Over the next two weeks, I spent many hours in court arranging bail for the women. A few were frustrated and took their anger out on me. "Mandela, I am tired of this case of yours," one woman said to me. "If this does not end today I will not ever reappear in court." With the help of relatives and fund-raising organizations, we managed to bail them all out within two weeks.

Winnie did not seem the worse for wear from her prison experience. If she had suffered, she would not have told me anyway. While she was in prison Winnie became friendly with two teenaged Afrikaner ward-resses. They were sympathetic and curious, and after Winnie was released on bail, we invited them to visit us. They accepted and traveled by train to Orlando. We gave them lunch at the house and afterward Winnie took them for a tour of the township. Winnie and the two wardresses were about the same age and got on well. They laughed together as though they were all sisters. The two girls had an enjoyable day and thanked

Winnie, saying that they would like to return. As it turned out, this was not to be, for in traveling to Orlando they had, of necessity, sat in a non-White carriage. (There were no white trains to Orlando for the simple reason that no whites went to Orlando.) As a result, they attracted a great deal of attention and it was soon widely known that two Afrikaner wardresses from the Fort had visited Winnie and me. This was not a problem for us, but it proved to be one for them: the prison authorities dismissed them. We never saw nor heard from them again.

29

FOR SIX MONTHS — ever since the end of the preparatory hearings in January — we had been awaiting and preparing for our formal trial, which was to commence in August 1958. The government set up a special high court — Mr. Justice F. L. Rumpff, president of the three-man court, Mr. Justice Kennedy, and Mr. Justice Ludorf. The panel was not promising: it consisted of three white men, all with ties to the ruling party. While Judge Rumpff was an able man and better informed than the average white South African, he was rumored to be a member of the Broederbond, a secret Afrikaner organization whose aim was to solidify Afrikaner power. Judge Ludorf was a well-known member of the National Party, as was Judge Kennedy. Kennedy had a reputation as a hanging judge, having sent a group of twenty-three Africans to the gallows for the murder of two white policemen.

Shortly before the case resumed, the state played another unpleasant trick on us. They announced that the venue of the trial was to be shifted from Johannesburg to Pretoria, thirty-six miles away. The trial would be conducted in an ornate former synagogue that had been converted into a court of law. All of the accused as well as our defense team resided in Johannesburg, so we would be forced to travel each day to Pretoria. The trial would now take up even more of our time and money — neither of which we had in abundance. Those who had managed to keep their jobs had been able to do so because the court had been near their work. Changing the venue was also an attempt to crush our spirits by separating us from our natural supporters. Pretoria was the home of the National Party, and the ANC barely had a presence there.

Nearly all of the ninety-two accused commuted to Pretoria in a lumbering, uncomfortable bus, with stiff wooden slats for seats, which left every day at six in the morning and took two hours to reach the Old Synagogue. The round-trip took us nearly five hours — time far better spent earning money to pay for food, rent, and clothes for the children.

Once more we were privileged to have a brilliant and aggressive defense team, ably led by advocate Israel Maisels, and assisted by Bram Fischer, Rex Welsh, Vernon Berrangé, Sydney Kentridge, Tony O'Dowd, and G. Nicholas. On the opening day of the trial, they displayed their combativeness with a risky legal maneuver that a number of us had decided on in consultation with the lawyers. Issy Maisels rose dramatically and applied for the recusal of Judges Ludorf and Rumpff on the grounds that both had conflicts of interest that prevented them from being fair arbiters of our case. There was an audible murmur in the courtroom. The defense contended that Rumpff, as the judge at the 1952 Defiance Trial, had already adjudicated on certain aspects of the present indictment and therefore it was not in the interest of justice that he try this case. We argued that Ludorf was prejudiced because he had represented the government in 1954 as a lawyer for the police when Harold Wolpe had sought a court interdict to eject the police from a meeting of the Congress of the People.

This was a dangerous strategy, for we could easily win this legal battle but lose the war. Although we regarded both Ludorf and Rumpff as strong supporters of the National Party, there were far worse judges in the country who could replace them. In fact, while we were keen to have Ludorf step down, we secretly hoped that Rumpff, whom we respected as an honest broker, would decide not to recuse himself. Rumpff always stood for law, no matter what his own political opinions might be, and we were convinced that when it came to law, we could only be found innocent.

That Monday, the atmosphere was expectant when the three red-robed judges marched into the courtroom. Judge Ludorf announced that he would withdraw, adding that he had completely forgotten about the previous case. But Rumpff refused to recuse himself and instead offered the assurance that his judgment in the Defiance case would have no influence on him in this one. To replace Ludorf, the state appointed Mr. Justice Bekker, a man we liked right from the start and who was not linked to the National Party. We were happy about Rumpff's decision.

After the success of this first maneuver, we tried a second, nearly as risky. We began a long and detailed argument contesting the indictment itself. We claimed, among other things, that the indictment was vague and lacked particularity. We also argued that the planning of violence was necessary to prove high treason, and the prosecution needed to provide examples of its claim that we intended to act violently. It became apparent by the end of our argument that the three judges agreed. In August, the court quashed one of the two charges under the Suppression of Communism Act. On October 13, after two more months of legal wrangling, the Crown suddenly announced the withdrawal of the indictment altogether. This was extraordinary, but we were too well versed in the devious ways of the state to celebrate. A month later the prosecution issued a new, more carefully worded indictment and announced that the trial would proceed against only thirty of the accused; the others would be tried later. I was among the first thirty, all of whom were members of the ANC.

Under the new indictment, the prosecution was now required to prove the intention to act violently. As Pirow put it, the accused knew that the achievement of the goals of the Freedom Charter would "necessarily involve the overthrow of the State by violence." The legal sparring continued through the middle of 1959, when the court dismissed the Crown's indictment against the remaining sixty-one accused. For months on end, the activity in the courtroom consisted of the driest legal maneuvering imaginable. Despite the defense's successes in showing the shoddiness of the government's case, the state was obdurately persistent. As the minister of justice said, "This trial will be proceeded with, no matter how many millions of pounds it costs. What does it matter how long it takes?"

Just after midnight on the 4th of February, 1958, I returned home after a meeting to find Winnie alone and in pain, about to go into labor. I rushed her to Baragwanath Hospital, but was told that it would be many hours before her time. I stayed until I had to leave for the trial in Pretoria. Immediately after the session ended, I speeded back with Duma Nokwe to find mother and daughter doing extremely well. I held my newborn daughter in my arms and pronounced her a true Mandela. My relative, Chief Mdingi, suggested the name Zenani, which means "What have you brought to the world?" — a poetic name that embodies a challenge, suggesting that one must contribute something to society. It is a name one does not simply possess, but has to live up to.

My mother came from the Transkei to help Winnie, and planned to give Zenani a Xhosa baptism by calling in an *inyanga,* a tribal healer, to give the baby a traditional herbal bath. But Winnie was adamantly opposed, thinking it unhealthy and outdated, and instead smeared Zenani with olive oil, plastered her little body with Johnson's Baby Powder, and filled her stomach with shark oil.

As soon as Winnie was up and about, I undertook the task of teaching the new mother of the household how to drive. Driving, in those days, was a man's business; very few women, especially African women, were to be seen in the driver's seat. But Winnie was independent-minded and intent on learning, and it would be useful because I was gone so much of the time and could not drive her places myself. Perhaps I am an impatient teacher or perhaps I had a headstrong pupil, but when I attempted to give Winnie lessons along a relatively flat and quiet Orlando road, we could not seem to shift gears without quarreling. Finally, after she had ignored one too many of my suggestions, I stormed out of the car and walked home. Winnie seemed to do better without my tutelage than with it, for she proceeded to drive around the township on her own for the next hour. By that time, we were ready to make up, and it is a story we subsequently laughed about.

Married life and motherhood were an adjustment for Winnie. She was then a young woman of twenty-five who had yet to form her own character completely. I was already formed and rather stubborn. I knew that others often saw her as "Mandela's wife." It was undoubtedly difficult for her to create her own identity in my shadow. I did my best to let her bloom in her own right, and she soon did so without any of my help.

30

ON APRIL 6, 1959, on the anniversary of Jan Van Riebeeck's landing at the Cape, a new organization was born that sought to rival the ANC as the country's premier African political organization and repudiate the white domination that began three centuries before. With a few hundred delegates from around the country at the Orlando Communal Hall, the Pan Africanist Congress launched itself as an Africanist organization that expressly rejected the multiracialism of the ANC. Like those of us who had formed the Youth League fifteen years before, the founders of the new organization thought the ANC was insufficiently militant, out of touch with the masses, and dominated by non-Africans.

Robert Sobukwe was elected president and Potlako Leballo became national secretary, both of them former ANC Youth Leaguers. The PAC presented a manifesto and a constitution, along with Sobukwe's opening address, in which he called for a "government of the Africans by the Africans and for the Africans." The PAC declared that it intended to overthrow white supremacy and establish a government Africanist in origin, socialist in content, and democratic in form. They disavowed communism in all its forms and considered whites and Indians "foreign minority groups" or "aliens" who had no natural place in South Africa. South Africa was for Africans, and no one else.

The birth of the PAC did not come as a surprise to us. The Africanists within the ANC had been loudly voicing their grievances for more than three years. In 1957, the Africanists had called for a vote of no confidence in the Transvaal executive at the national conference, but had been defeated. They had opposed the election day stay-at-home of 1958, and their leader, Potlako Leballo, had been expelled from the ANC. At the November 1958 ANC conference, a group of Africanists had declared their opposition to the Freedom Charter, claiming it violated the principles of African nationalism.

The PAC claimed that they drew their inspiration from the principles surrounding the ANC's founding in 1912, but their views derived principally from the emotional African nationalism put forth by Anton Lembede and A. P. Mda during the founding of the Youth League in 1944. The PAC echoed the axioms and slogans of that time: Africa for the Africans and a United States of Africa. But the immediate cause for their breakaway was their objection to the Freedom Charter and the presence of whites and Indians in the Congress Alliance leadership. They were opposed to interracial cooperation, in large part because they believed that white communists and Indians had come to dominate the ANC.

The founders of the PAC were all well known to me. Robert Sobukwe was an old friend. He was the proverbial gentleman and scholar (his colleagues called him "Prof"). His consistent willingness to pay the penalty for his principles earned my enduring respect. Potlako Leballo, Peter Raboroko, and Zephania Mothopeng were all friends and colleagues. I was astonished and indeed somewhat dismayed to learn that my political mentor Gaur Radebe had joined the PAC. I found it curious that a former member of the Communist Party's Central Committee had decided to align himself with an organization that then explicitly rejected Marxism.

Many of those who cast their lot with the PAC did so out of personal grudges or disappointments and were not thinking of the advancement of the struggle, but of their own feelings of jealousy or revenge. I have always believed that to be a freedom fighter one must suppress many of the personal feelings that make one feel like a separate individual rather than part of a mass movement. One is fighting for the liberation of millions of people, not the glory of one individual. I am not suggesting that a man become a robot and rid himself of all personal feelings and motivations. But in the same way that a freedom fighter subordinates his own family to the family of the people, he must subordinate his own individual feelings to the movement.

I found the views and the behavior of the PAC immature. A philosopher once noted that something is odd if a person is not liberal when he is young and conservative when he is old. I am not a conservative, but one matures and regards some of the views of one's youth as undeveloped and callow. While I sympathized with the views of the Africanists and once shared many of them, I believed that the freedom struggle required one to make compromises and accept the kind of discipline that one resisted as a younger, more impulsive man.

The PAC put forward a dramatic and overambitious program that promised quick solutions. Their most dramatic — and naïve — promise was that liberation would be achieved by the end of 1963, and they urged Africans to ready themselves for that historic hour. "In 1960 we take our first step," they promised, "in 1963, our last towards freedom and independence." Although this prediction inspired hope and enthusiasm among people who were tired of waiting, it is always dangerous for an organization to make promises it cannot keep.

Because of the PAC's anticommunism, they became the darlings of the Western press and the American State Department, which hailed its birth as a dagger to the heart of the African left. Even the National Party saw a potential ally in the PAC: they viewed the PAC as mirroring their anticommunism and supporting their views on separate development. The Nationalists also rejected interracial cooperation, and both the National Party and the American State Department saw fit to exaggerate the size and importance of the new organization for their own ends.

While we welcomed anyone brought into the struggle by the PAC, the role of the organization was almost always that of a spoiler. They divided the people at a critical moment, and that was hard to forget. They would ask the people to go to work when we called a general strike, and make misleading statements to counter any pronouncement we would make. Yet the PAC aroused in me the hope that even though the founders were breakaway ANC men, unity between our two groups was possible. I thought that once the heated polemics had cooled, the essential commonality of the struggle would bring us together. Animated by this belief, I paid particular attention to their policy statement and activities, with the idea of finding affinities rather than differences.

The day after the PAC's inaugural conference, I approached Sobukwe for a copy of his presidential address, as well as the constitution and other policy material. Sobukwe, I thought, seemed pleased by my interest, and said he would make sure I received the requested material. I saw him again not long afterward and reminded him of my request and he said the material was on its way. I subsequently met Potlako Leballo and said, "Man, you chaps keep promising me your material, but no one has given it to me." He said, "Nelson, we have decided not to give it to you because we know you only want to use it to attack us." I disabused him of this notion, and he relented, giving me all that I had sought.

31

IN 1959, Parliament passed the Promotion of Bantu Self Government Act, which created eight separate ethnic bantustans. This was the foundation of what the state called *groot* or grand apartheid. At roughly the same time, the government introduced the deceptively named Extension of University Education Act, another leg of grand apartheid, which barred nonwhites from racially "open" universities. In introducing the Bantu Self Government Act, De Wet Nel, the minister of Bantu Administration and Development, said that the welfare of every individual and population group could best be developed within its own national community. Africans, he said, could never be integrated into the white community.

The immorality of the bantustan policy, whereby 70 percent of the people would be apportioned only 13 percent of the land, was obvious. Under the new policy, even though two-thirds of Africans lived in so-called white areas, they could only have citizenship in their own "tribal homelands." The scheme gave us neither freedom in "white" areas nor independence in what they deemed "our" areas. Verwoerd said the creation of the bantustans would engender so much goodwill that they would never become the breeding grounds of rebellion.

In reality, it was quite the opposite. The rural areas were in turmoil. Few areas fought so stubbornly as Zeerust, where Chief Abram Moilwa (with the able assistance of advocate George Bizos) led his people to resist the so-called Bantu Authorities. Such areas were usually invisible to the press, and the government used their inaccessibility to veil the cruelty of the state's actions. Scores of innocent people were arrested, prosecuted, jailed, banished, beaten, tortured, and murdered. The people of Sekhukhuneland also revolted, and the paramount chief, Moroamotsho Sekhukhune, Godfrey Sekhukhune, and other counselors were banished or arrested. A Sekhukhune chief, Kolane Kgoloko, who was perceived as a government lackey, was assassinated. By 1960, resistance in Sekhukhuneland had reached open defiance, and people were refusing to pay taxes.

In Zeerust and Sekhukhuneland, ANC branches played a prominent part in the protests. In spite of the severe repression, a number of new ANC branches sprang up in the Zeerust area, one of them having recruited about two thousand members. Sekhukhuneland and Zeerust were the first areas in South Africa where the ANC was banned by the government, evidence of our power in these remote areas.

Protest erupted in Eastern Pondoland, where government henchmen were assaulted and killed. Thembuland and Zululand fiercely resisted, and were among the last areas to yield. People were beaten, arrested, deported, and imprisoned. In Thembuland, resistance had been going on since 1955, with Sabata part of the forces of protest.

It was especially painful to me that in the Transkei, the wrath of the people was directed against my nephew and one-time mentor K. D. Matanzima. There was no doubt that Daliwonga was collaborating with the government. All the appeals I had made to him over the years had come to naught. There were reports that *impis* (traditional warriors) from Matanzima's headquarters had burned down villages that opposed him. There were several assassination attempts against him. Equally painful was the fact that Winnie's father was serving on Matanzima's council and was an unwavering supporter. This was terribly difficult for Winnie: her father and her husband were on opposite sides of the same issue. She loved her father, but she rejected his politics.

On a number of occasions, tribesmen and kinsmen from the Transkei visited me in Orlando to complain about chiefs collaborating with the government. Sabata was opposed to the Bantu Authorities and would not capitulate, but my visitors were afraid that Matanzima would depose him, which is eventually what happened. At one time, Daliwonga himself came to visit during the Treason Trial and I brought him with me to Pretoria. In the courtroom, Issy Maisels introduced him to the judges and they accorded him a seat of honor. But outside — among the accused — he was not treated so deferentially. He began aggressively to ask the various defendants, who regarded him as a sellout, why they objected to separate development. Lilian Ngoyi remarked: *"Tyhini, uyadelela lo mntu"* (Gracious, this man is provocative).

32

IT IS SAID that the mills of God grind exceedingly slowly, but even the Lord's machinations can't compete with those of the South African judicial system. On August 3, 1959, two years and eight months after our arrests, and after a full year of legal maneuvering, the actual trial commenced at the Old Synagogue in Pretoria. We were finally formally arraigned and all thirty of us pleaded not guilty.

Our defense team was once again led by Issy Maisels, and he was assisted by Sydney Kentridge, Bram Fischer, and Vernon Berrangé. This time, at long last, the trial was in earnest. During the first two months of the case, the Crown entered some two thousand documents into the record and called two hundred ten witnesses, two hundred of whom were members of the Special Branch. These detectives admitted to hiding in closets and under beds, posing as ANC members, perpetrating virtually any deception that would enable them to get information about our organization. Yet many of the documents the state submitted and the speeches they transcribed were public documents, public speeches, information available to all. As before, much of the Crown's evidence consisted of books, papers, and documents seized from the accused during numerous raids that took place between 1952 and 1956, as well as notes taken by the police at Congress meetings during this same period. As before, the reports by the Special Branch officers of our speeches were generally muddled. We used to joke that between the poor acoustics of the hall and the confused and inaccurate reports of the Special Branch detectives, we could be fined for what we did not say, imprisoned for what we could not hear, and hanged for what we did not do.

Each day at lunchtime we were permitted to sit outside in the spacious garden of a neighboring vicarage where we were supplied with a meal cooked by the redoubtable Mrs. Thayanagee Pillay and her friends. They prepared a spicy Indian lunch for us almost every day, and also tea, coffee, and sandwiches during the morning and afternoon breaks. These respites were like tiny vacations from court, and were a chance for us to discuss politics with each other. Those moments under the shade of the jacaranda trees on the vicarage lawn were the most pleasant of the trial, for in many ways the case was more a test of our endurance than a trial of justice.

On the morning of October 11, as we were preparing to go to court, we heard an announcement on the radio that the prosecutor, Oswald Pirow, had died suddenly from a stroke. His death was a severe setback to the government, and the effectiveness and aggressiveness of the Crown team diminished from that point on. In court that day, Judge Rumpff gave an emotional eulogy to Pirow, and praised his legal acumen and thoroughness. Although we would benefit from his absence, we did not rejoice at his death. We had developed a certain affection for our opponent, for despite Pirow's noxious political views, he was a humane man without the virulent personal racism of the government he was acting for. His habitual polite reference to us as "Africans" (even one of our own attorneys occasionally slipped and referred to us as "natives") contrasted with his supremacist political leanings. In a curious way, our small world inside the Old Synagogue seemed balanced when, each morning, we observed Pirow reading the right-wing *Nuwe Order* at his table and Bram Fischer reading the left-wing *New Age* at ours. His donation to us of the more than one hundred volumes of the preparatory examination free of charge was a generous gesture that saved the defense a great deal of money. Advocate De Vos became the new leader of the Crown's team and could not match the eloquence or acuity of his predecessor.

Shortly after Pirow's death, the prosecution concluded its submission of evidence. It was then that the prosecution began its examination of expert witnesses commencing with the long-suffering Professor Murray, its supposed expert in communism who had proved so inept in his subject during the preparatory examination. In a relentless cross-examination by Maisels, Murray admitted that the charter was in fact a humanitarian document that might well represent the natural reaction and aspirations of nonwhites to the harsh conditions in South Africa.

Murray was not the only Crown witness who did little to advance the state's case. Despite the voluminous amount of Crown evidence and the pages and pages of testimony from their expert witnesses, the prosecution had not managed to produce any valid evidence that the ANC plotted violence, and they knew it. Then, in March, the prosecution displayed a new burst of confidence. They were about to release their most damning evidence. With great fanfare and a long drumroll in the press, the state played for the court a secretly recorded speech of Robert Resha's. The speech was given in his capacity as Transvaal Volunteer-in-Chief to a roomful of Freedom Volunteers in 1956, a few weeks before we were all to be arrested. The courtroom was very quiet, and despite the static of the recording and the background din, one could make out Robert's words very clearly.

> When you are disciplined and you are told by the organization not to be violent, you must not be violent . . . but if you are a true volunteer and you are called upon to be violent, you must be absolutely violent, you must murder! Murder! That is all.

The prosecution believed it had sealed its case. Newspapers prominently featured Resha's words and echoed the sensibilities of the state. To the Crown, the speech revealed the ANC's true and secret intent, unmasking the ANC's public pretense of nonviolence. But in fact, Resha's words were an anomaly. Robert was an excellent if rather excitable platform speaker, and his choice of analogy was unfortunate. But as the defense would show, he was merely emphasizing the importance of discipline and that the volunteer must do whatever he is ordered, however unsavory. Over and over, our witnesses would show that Resha's speech was not only taken out of context but did not represent ANC policy.

*　　　*　　　*

The prosecution concluded its case on March 10, 1960, and we were to call our first witness for the defense four days later. We had been in the doldrums for months, but as we started to prepare ourselves for our testimony, we were eager to go on the offensive. We had been parrying the enemy's attacks for too long.

There had been much speculation in the press that our first witness would be Chief Luthuli. The Crown apparently believed that as well, for there was great consternation among the prosecution when, on March 14, our first witness was not Luthuli but Dr. Wilson Conco.

Conco was the son of a Zulu cattle farmer from the beautiful Ixopo district of Natal. In addition to being a practicing physician, he had been one of the founders of the Youth League, an active participant in the Defiance Campaign, and the treasurer of the ANC. As a preparation for his testimony, he was asked about his brilliant academic record at the University of the Witwatersrand, where he graduated first in his medical school class, ahead of all the sons and daughters of white privilege. As Conco's credentials were cited, I got the distinct impression that Justice Kennedy, who was also from Natal, seemed proud. Natalians are noted for their loyalty to their region, and these peculiar bonds of attachment can sometimes even transcend color. Indeed, many Natalians thought of themselves as white Zulus. Justice Kennedy had always seemed to be a fair-minded man, and I sensed that through Wilson Conco's example, he began to see us not as heedless rabble-rousers but men of worthy ambitions who could help their country if their country would only help them. At the end of Conco's testimony, when Conco was cited for some medical achievement, Kennedy said in Zulu, a language in which he was fluent, *"Sinjalo thina maZulu,"* which means, "We Zulus are like that." Dr. Conco proved a calm and articulate witness who reaffirmed the ANC's commitment to nonviolence.

Chief Luthuli was next. With his dignity and sincerity, he made a deep impression on the court. He was suffering from high blood pressure, and the court agreed to sit only in the mornings while he gave evidence. His evidence-in-chief lasted several days and he was cross-examined for nearly three weeks. He carefully outlined the evolution of the ANC's policy, putting things simply and clearly, and his former positions as teacher and chief imparted an added gravity and authority to his words. As a devout Christian, he was the perfect person to discuss how the ANC had sincerely strived for racial harmony.

The chief testified to his belief in the innate goodness of man and how moral persuasion plus economic pressure could well lead to a change of heart on the part of white South Africans. In discussing the ANC's policy of nonviolence, he emphasized that there was a difference between nonviolence and pacifism. Pacifists refused to defend themselves even when violently attacked, but that was not necessarily the case with those who espoused nonviolence. Sometimes men and nations, even when nonviolent, had to defend themselves when they were attacked.

As I listened to Conco and Luthuli, I thought that here, probably for the first time in their lives, the judges were listening not to their domestic servants who said only what they knew their masters would like to hear, but to independent and articulate Africans spelling out their political beliefs and how they hoped to realize them.

The chief was cross-examined by Advocate Trengrove, who doggedly attempted to get him to say the ANC was dominated by Communists and had a dual policy of nonviolence intended for the public and a secret plan of waging violent revolution. The chief steadfastly refuted the implications of what Trengrove was suggesting. He himself was the soul of moderation, particularly as Trengrove seemed to lose control. At one point, Trengrove accused the chief of hypocrisy. The chief ignored Trengrove's aspersion and calmly remarked to the bench, "My Lord, I think the Crown is running wild."

But on March 21, the chief's testimony was interrupted by a shattering event outside the courtroom. On that day, the country was rocked by an occurrence of such magnitude that when Chief Luthuli returned to testify a month later, the courtroom — and all of South Africa — was a different place.

33

THE DECEMBER 1959 ANC annual conference was held in Durban during that city's dynamic antipass demonstrations. The conference unanimously voted to initiate a massive countrywide antipass campaign beginning March 31 and climaxing on June 26 with a great bonfire of passes.

The planning began immediately. On March 31, deputations were sent to local authorities. ANC officials toured the country, talking to the branches about the campaign. ANC field-workers spread the word in townships and factories. Leaflets, stickers, and posters were printed and circulated and posted in trains and buses.

The mood of the country was grim. The state was threatening to ban the organization, with cabinet ministers warning the ANC that it would soon be battered with "an ungloved fist." Elsewhere in Africa, the freedom struggle was marching on: the emergence of the independent republic of Ghana in 1957 and its pan-Africanist, anti-apartheid leader, Kwame Nkrumah, had alarmed the Nationalists and made them even more intent on clamping down on dissent at home. In 1960, seventeen former colonies in Africa were scheduled to become independent states. In February, British Prime Minister Harold Macmillan visited South Africa and gave a speech before Parliament in which he talked of "winds of change" sweeping Africa.

The PAC at the time appeared lost; they were a leadership in search of followers, and they had yet to initiate any action that put them on the political map. They knew of the ANC's antipass campaign and had been invited to join, but instead of linking arms with the Congress movement, they sought to sabotage us. The PAC announced that it was launching its own antipass campaign on March 21, ten days before ours was to begin. No conference had been held by them to discuss the date, no organizational work of any significance had been undertaken. It was a blatant case of opportunism. Their actions were motivated more by a desire to eclipse the ANC than to defeat the enemy.

Four days before the scheduled demonstration, Sobukwe invited us to join with the PAC. Sobukwe's offer was not a gesture of unity but a tactical move to prevent the PAC from being criticized for not including us. He made the offer at the eleventh hour, and we declined to participate. On the morning of March 21, Sobukwe and his executive walked to the Orlando police station to turn themselves in for arrest. The tens of thousands of people going to work ignored the PAC men. In the magistrate's court, Sobukwe announced the PAC would not attempt to defend itself, in accordance with their slogan "No bail, no defense, no fine." They believed the defiers would receive sentences of a few weeks. But Sobukwe was sentenced not to three weeks' but to three years' imprisonment without the option of a fine.

The response to the PAC's call in Johannesburg was minimal. No demonstrations at all took place in Durban, Port Elizabeth, or East London. But in Evaton, Z. B. Molete, ably assisted by Joe Molefi and Vusumuzi Make, mustered the support of the entire township as several hundred men presented themselves for arrest without passes. Cape Town saw one of the biggest antipass demonstrations in the history of the city. In Langa township, outside Cape Town, some thirty thousand people, led by the young student Philip Kgosana, gathered and were spurred to rioting by a police baton-charge. Two people were killed. But the last of the areas where demonstrations took place was the most calamitous and the one whose name still echoes with tragedy: Sharpeville.

Sharpeville was a small township about thirty-five miles south of Johannesburg in the grim industrial complex around Vereeniging. PAC activists had done an excellent job of organizing the area. In the early afternoon, a crowd of several thousand surrounded the police station. The demonstrators were controlled and unarmed. The police force of seventy-five was greatly outnumbered and panicky. No one heard warning shots or an order to shoot, but suddenly, the police opened fire on the crowd and continued to shoot as the demonstrators turned and ran in fear. When the area had cleared, sixty-nine Africans lay dead, most of them shot in the back as they were fleeing. All told, more than seven hundred shots had been fired into the crowd, wounding more than four hundred people, including dozens of women and children. It was a massacre, and the next day press photos displayed the savagery on front pages around the world.

The shootings at Sharpeville provoked national turmoil and a government crisis. Outraged protests came in from across the globe, including one from the American State Department. For the first time, the U.N. Security Council intervened in South African affairs, blaming the government for the shootings and urging it to initiate measures to bring about racial equality. The Johannesburg stock exchange plunged and capital started to flow out of country. South African whites began making plans to emigrate. Liberals urged Verwoerd to offer concessions to Africans. The government insisted Sharpeville was the result of a Communist conspiracy.

The massacre at Sharpeville created a new situation in the country. In spite of the amateurishness and opportunism of their leaders, the PAC rank and file displayed great courage and fortitude in their demonstrations at Sharpeville and Langa. In just one day, they had moved to the front lines of the struggle, and Robert Sobukwe was being hailed inside and outside the country as the savior of the liberation movement. We in the ANC had to make rapid adjustments to this new situation, and we did so.

A small group of us — Walter, Duma Nokwe, Joe Slovo, and myself — held an all-night meeting in Johannesburg to plan a response. We knew we had to acknowledge the events in some way and give the people an outlet for their anger and grief. We conveyed our plans to Chief Luthuli, and he readily accepted them. On March 26, in Pretoria, the chief publicly burned his pass, calling on others to do the same. He announced a nationwide stay-at-home on March 28, a national Day of Mourning and protest for the atrocities at Sharpeville. In Orlando, Duma Nokwe and I then burned our passes before hundreds of people and dozens of press photographers.

Two days later, on the twenty-eighth, the country responded magnificently as several hundred thousand Africans observed the chief's call. Only a truly mass organization could coordinate such activities, and the

ANC did so. In Cape Town a crowd of fifty thousand met in Langa township to protest the shootings. Rioting broke out in many areas. The government declared a State of Emergency, suspending habeas corpus and assuming sweeping powers to act against all forms of subversion. South Africa was now under martial law.

34

AT 1:30 IN THE MORNING, on March 30, I was awakened by sharp, unfriendly knocks at my door, the unmistakable signature of the police. "The time has come," I said to myself as I opened the door to find half-a-dozen armed security policemen. They turned the house upside down, taking virtually every piece of paper they could find, including the transcripts I had recently been making of my mother's recollections of family history and tribal fables. I was never to see them again. I was then arrested without a warrant, and given no opportunity to call my lawyer. They refused to inform my wife as to where I was to be taken. I simply nodded at Winnie; it was no time for words of comfort.

Thirty minutes later we arrived at Newlands police station, which was familiar to me from the many occasions when I had visited clients there. The station was located in Sophiatown, or rather, what was left of it, for the once bustling township was now a ruin of bulldozed buildings and vacant lots. Inside I found a number of my colleagues who had been similarly rousted out of bed, and over the course of the night, more arrived; by morning we totaled forty in all. We were put in a cramped yard with only the sky as a roof and a dim bulb for light, a space so small and dank that we remained standing all night.

At 7:15, we were taken into a tiny cell with a single drainage hole in the floor which could be flushed only from the outside. We were given no blankets, no food, no mats, and no toilet paper. The hole regularly became blocked and the stench in the room was insufferable. We issued numerous protests, among them the demand to be fed. These were met with surly rejoinders, and we resolved that the next time the door opened, we would surge out into the adjacent courtyard and refuse to return to the cell until we had been fed. The young policeman on duty took fright and left as we stampeded through the door. A few minutes later, a burly no-nonsense sergeant entered the courtyard and commanded us to return to the cell. "Go inside!" he yelled. "If you don't, I'll bring in fifty men with batons and we'll break your skulls!" After the horrors of Sharpeville, the threat did not seem empty.

The station commander approached the gate of the courtyard to observe us, and then came over and berated me for standing with my hands in my pockets. "Is that the way you act around an officer?" he yelled. "Take your bloody hands out of your pockets!" I kept my hands firmly rooted in my pockets as if I were taking a walk on a chilly day. I told him that I might condescend to remove my hands if we were fed.

At 3 P.M., more than twelve hours after most of us had arrived, we were delivered a container of thin mealie pap and no utensils. Normally, I would have considered this unfit for consumption, but we reached in with our unwashed hands and ate as though we had been provided with the most delicious delicacies under the sun. After our meal, we elected a committee to represent us, which included Duma Nokwe and Z. B. Molete, the publicity secretary of the Pan Africanist Congress, and me. I was elected spokesman. We immediately drew up a petition protesting the unfit conditions and demanding our immediate release on the grounds that our detention was illegal.

At six o'clock we received sleeping mats and blankets. I do not think words can do justice to a description of the foulness and filthiness of this bedding. The blankets were encrusted with dried blood and vomit, ridden with lice, vermin, and cockroaches, and reeked with a stench that actually competed with the odiousness of the drain.

Near midnight, we were told we were to be called out, but for what we did not know. Some of the men smiled at the expectation of release. Others knew better. I was the first to be called and I was ushered over to the front gate of the prison where I was briefly released in front of a group of police officers. But before I could move, an officer shouted.

"Name!"

"Mandela," I said.

"Nelson Mandela," the officer said, "I arrest you under the powers vested in me by the Emergency Regulations." We were not to be released at all, but rearrested under the terms of what we only then discovered was a State of Emergency. Each of us in turn was released for mere seconds, and then rearrested. We had been arrested illegally before the State of Emergency; now we were being properly arrested under the State of Emergency that came into force at midnight. We drafted a memorandum to the commander asking to know our rights.

The next morning, I was called to the commander's office, where I found my colleague Robert Resha, who had been arrested and was being interrogated by the station commander. When I walked into the room, Resha asked the commander why he had erupted at me the previous night. His answer was that of the typical white *baas:* "Mandela was cheeky." I responded, "I'm not bound to take my hands out of my pockets for the likes of you, then or now." The commander jumped out of his chair, but was restrained by other officers. At this moment, Special Branch Detective Sergeant Helberg entered the office and said, "Hello, Nelson!" in a pleasant way. To which I shot back, "I am not Nelson to you, I am Mr. Mandela." The room was on the brink of becoming a full-scale battle when we were informed that we had to leave to attend the Treason Trial in Pretoria. I did not know whether to laugh or despair, but in the midst of this thirty-six hours of mistreatment and the declaration of a State of Emergency, the government still saw fit to bring us back to Pretoria to continue their desperate and now seemingly outdated case against us. We were taken straight to Pretoria Local Prison, where we were detained.

35

IN THE MEANTIME, court resumed, in our absence, on March 31, but the witness box was conspicuously empty. Those who did attend were the accused whom the police had failed to pick up under the State of Emergency. Chief Luthuli had been in the middle of his evidence, and Judge Rumpff asked for an explanation for his absence. He was informed that the chief had been taken into custody the night before. Judge Rumpff expressed irritation with the explanation and said he did not see why the State of Emergency should stand in the way of his trial. He demanded that the police bring the chief to court so that he could resume his testimony, and court was adjourned.

Later we discovered that after the chief's arrest, he had been assaulted. He had been walking up some stairs when he was jostled by a warder, causing his hat to fall to the floor. As he bent to pick it up, he was smacked across the head and face. This was hard for us to take. A man of immense dignity and achievement, a lifelong devout Christian, and a man with a dangerous heart condition, was treated like a barnyard animal by men who were not fit to tie his shoes.

When we were called back into session that morning, Judge Rumpff was informed that the police refused to bring the chief to court. The judge then adjourned court for the day, and we expected to go home. But as they were leaving the court grounds to find transportation, we were all once again rearrested.

But the police, with their usual disorganized overzealousness, made a comical mistake. Wilton Mkwayi, one of the accused and a longtime union leader and ANC man, had traveled to Pretoria for the trial from Port Elizabeth. Somehow he had gotten separated from his colleagues and when he approached the gate and saw the commotion of his fellow accused being arrested, he asked a policeman what was going on. The policeman ordered him to leave. Wilton stood there. The policeman again ordered him to leave, whereupon Wilton informed the officer he was one of the accused. The officer called him a liar, and threatened to arrest him for obstruction of justice. The officer then angrily ordered him to leave the area. Wilton shrugged his shoulders, walked out of the gate, and that was the last anyone saw of Wilton in court. He went underground for the next two months, successfully evading arrest, and then was smuggled out of the country, soon emerging as a foreign representative for the Congress of Trade Unions and later going for military training in China.

That night, we were joined by detainees from other parts of the Transvaal. The countrywide police raid had led to the detention without trial of more than two thousand people. These men and women belonged to all races and all anti-apartheid parties. A call-up of soldiers had been announced, and units of the army had been mobilized and stationed in strategic areas around the country. On April 8, both the ANC and the PAC were declared illegal organizations, under the Suppression of Communism Act. Overnight, being a member of the ANC had become a felony punishable by a term in jail and a fine. The penalty for furthering the aims of the ANC was imprisonment for up to ten years. Now even nonviolent law-abiding protests under the auspices of the ANC were illegal. The struggle had entered a new phase. We were now, all of us, outlaws.

For the duration of the State of Emergency we stayed at Pretoria Local, where the conditions were as bad as those at Newlands. Groups of five prisoners were pressed into cells measuring nine feet by seven feet; the cells were filthy, with poor lighting and worse ventilation. We had a single sanitary pail with a loose lid and vermin-infested blankets. We were allowed outside for an hour a day.

On our second day in Pretoria, we sent a deputation to complain about the conditions to the prison's commanding officer, Colonel Snyman. The colonel's response was rude and abrupt. He demanded that we produce evidence, calling our complaints lies. "You have brought the vermin into my prison from your filthy homes," he sneered.

I said we also required a room that was quiet and well lit so that we could prepare for our case. The colonel was again contemptuous: "Government regulations do not require prisoners to read books, if you can read at all." Despite the colonel's disdainful attitude, the cells were soon painted and fumigated and we were supplied with fresh blankets and sanitary pails. We were permitted to stay out in the yard for much of the day, while those of us involved in the Treason Trial were provided with a large cell for consultations, in which we were also permitted to keep legal books.

Pretoria Local would be our home for the foreseeable future. We would leave for the trial in the morning and return to the prison in the afternoon. The prison, according to apartheid dictates, separated detainees by color. We were of course already separated from our white colleagues, but the separation from our Indian and Coloured comrades within the same non-White facility seemed like madness. We demanded to be accommodated together, and were given all sorts of absurd explanations why this was impossible. When the proverbial inflexibility of red tape is combined with the petty small-mindedness of racism, the result can be mind-boggling. But the authorities eventually yielded, allowing the Treason Trialists to be kept together.

Although we were kept together, our diet was fixed according to race. For breakfast, Africans, Indians, and Coloureds received the same quantities, except that Indians and Coloureds received a half-teaspoonful of sugar, which we did not. For supper, the diets were the same, except that Indians and Coloureds received four ounces of bread while we received none. This latter distinction was made on the curious premise that Africans did not naturally like bread, which was a more sophisticated or "Western" taste. The diet for white detainees was far superior to that for Africans. So color-conscious were the authorities that even the type of sugar and bread supplied to whites and nonwhites differed: white prisoners received white sugar and white bread, while Coloured and Indian prisoners were given brown sugar and brown bread.

We complained vociferously about the inferior quality of the food, and as a result, our advocate Sydney Kentridge made a formal complaint in court. I stated that the food was unfit for human consumption. Judge Rumpff agreed to sample the food himself and that day went out to do so. Samp and beans was the best meal that the prison prepared, and in this case, the authorities put in more beans and gravy than usual. Judge Rumpff ate a few spoonfuls and pronounced the food well cooked and tasty. He did allow that it should be served warm. We laughed among ourselves at the idea of "warm" jail food; it was a contradiction in terms. Eventually, the authorities supplied the detainees with what they called an Improved Diet: Africans received bread, while Indians and Coloureds received the same food provided to white prisoners.

I enjoyed one extraordinary privilege during our detention: weekend trips to Johannesburg. These were not a vacation from prison but a busman's holiday. Shortly before the State of Emergency, Oliver left South Africa on the instructions of the ANC. We had long suspected a clamp-down was coming, and the Congress decided that certain members needed to leave the country to strengthen the organization abroad in anticipation of the time it would be banned entirely.

Oliver's departure was one of the most well-planned and fortunate actions ever taken by the movement. At the time we hardly suspected how absolutely vital the external wing would become. With his wisdom and calmness, his patience and organizational skills, his ability to lead and inspire without stepping on toes, Oliver was the perfect choice for this assignment.

Before leaving, Oliver had retained a mutual friend of ours, Hymie Davidoff, a local attorney, to close up our office and wind up our practice. Davidoff made a special request to Colonel Prinsloo to permit me to come to Johannesburg on weekends to help him put things in order. In a fit of generosity, Colonel Prinsloo agreed, allowing me to be driven to Johannesburg on Friday afternoons to work in the office all weekend and then be driven back to the trial on Monday morning. Sergeant Kruger and I would leave after court adjourned at one o'clock on Friday, and after arriving at my office, I would work with Davidoff and our accountant Nathan Marcus. I would spend the nights in Marshall Square prison and the days at the office.

Sergeant Kruger was a tall and imposing fellow who treated us with fairness. On the way from Pretoria to Johannesburg, he would often stop the car and leave me inside while he went into a shop to buy biltong, oranges, and chocolate for both of us. I thought about jumping out of the car, especially on Fridays, when the sidewalks and streets were busy and one could get lost in a crowd.

While at the office, I could walk downstairs to the ground-floor café to buy incidentals, and he turned his head aside on one or two occasions when Winnie came to visit me. We had a kind of gentleman's code between us: I would not escape and thereby get him into trouble, while he permitted me a degree of freedom.

36

ON APRIL 25, the day before the trial was to resume, Issy Maisels called us together to discuss the grave effect the State of Emergency was having on the conduct of the trial. Because of the Emergency Regulations, consultations between the accused and our lawyers had become virtually impossible. Our lawyers, who were based in Johannesburg, had trouble seeing us in prison and were unable to prepare our case. They would often drive up and be informed that we were not available. Even when we were able to see them, consultations were harassed and cut short. More important, Maisels explained that under the Emergency Regulations, those already in detention would be exposing themselves to further detention merely by testifying, for they would inevitably make statements regarded as "subversive," thereby subjecting themselves to greater penalties. Defense witnesses who were not imprisoned now risked detainment if they testified.

The defense team proposed that they withdraw from the case in protest. Maisels explained the serious implications of such a withdrawal and the consequences of our conducting our own defense in a capital case. Under the hostile atmosphere at the time, he said, the judges might see fit to give us longer terms of imprisonment. We discussed the proposal among ourselves, and each of the twenty-nine accused — we were now minus Wilton Mkwayi — was able to express his opinion. The resolution was unanimously endorsed, and it was agreed that Duma Nokwe and I would help in preparing the case in the absence of our lawyers. I was in favor of this dramatic gesture, for it highlighted the iniquities of the State of Emergency.

On April 26, Duma Nokwe, the first African advocate in the Transvaal, rose in court and made the sensational announcement that the accused were instructing defense counsel to withdraw from the case. Maisels then said simply, "We have no further mandate and we will consequently not trouble Your Lordships any further," after which the defense team silently filed out of the synagogue. This shocked the three-judge panel, who warned us in direst terms about the dangers of conducting our own defense. But we were angry and eager to take on the state. For the next five months, until the virtual end of the Emergency, we conducted our own defense.

Our strategy was simple and defensive in nature: to drag out the case until the State of Emergency was lifted and our lawyers could return. The case had gone on so long already that it did not seem to matter if we stretched it out even further. In practice, this strategy became rather comical. Under the law, each one of us was now entitled to conduct his own defense and was able to call as a witness each of the other accused; and each of the accused was entitled to cross-examine each witness. We were arranged in alphabetical order according to the docket and accused number one was Farid Adams, of the Transvaal Indian Youth Congress. Farid would open his case by calling accused number two, Helen Joseph, as his first witness. After being examined by Farid, Helen would then be cross-examined by the twenty-seven other co-accused. She would then be cross-examined by the Crown and reexamined by accused number one. Adams would then proceed to call accused number three, and so on, and the whole procedure would duplicate itself until every accused was called in this fashion. At that rate, we would be at trial until the millennium.

It is never easy to prepare a case from prison, and in this instance we were hampered by the customary apartheid barriers. All of the accused needed to be able to meet together but prison regulations prohibited meetings between male and female prisoners, and between black and white, so we were not permitted to consult with Helen Joseph, Leon Levy, Lilian Ngoyi, and Bertha Mashaba.

Helen, as the first witness to be called, needed to prepare her evidence in the presence of Duma, myself, and Farid Adams, who would be examining her. After protracted negotiations with the prison authorities, we were permitted to have consultations under very strict conditions. Helen Joseph, Lilian, Leon, and Bertha were to be brought from their various prisons and sections (separated by race and gender) to the African men's prison. The first stipulation was that there could be no physical contact between white and black prisoners, and between male and female prisoners. The authorities erected an iron grille to separate Helen and Leon (as whites) from us and a second partition to separate them from Lilian, who was also participating in the preparations. Even a master architect would have had trouble designing such a structure. In prison we were separated from each other by this elaborate metal contraption, while in court we all mingled freely.

We first needed to coach Farid in the art of courtroom etiquette, and rehearse Helen's testimony. To help Helen, I was playing the role that Farid would play in court. I assumed the proper courtroom manner and began the examination.

"Name?" I said.

"Helen Joseph," she replied.

"Age?"

Silence. I repeated, "Age?"

Helen pursed her lips and waited. Then, after some moments, she scowled at me and said sharply, "What has my age to do with this case, Nelson?"

Helen was as charming as she was courageous, but she also had an imperious side. She was a woman of a certain age, and sensitive about it. I explained that it was customary to note down the witness's particulars, such as name, age, address, and place of birth. A witness's age helps the court to weigh her testimony and influences sentencing.

I continued: "Age?"

Helen stiffened. "Nelson," she said, "I will cross that bridge when I come to it in court, but not until then. Let us move on."

I then asked her a series of questions that she might expect from the Crown in a manner perhaps too realistic for her, because at one point Helen turned to me and said, "Are you Mandela or are you the prosecutor?"

There were other light moments, some of which were quite encouraging.

I was permitted to visit Helen Joseph on weekends and bring her records of the proceedings. On these occasions I met other women detainees and consulted with them as possible witnesses. I was always very cordial with the white wardresses, and I noticed that my visits caused considerable interest. The wardresses had never known there was even such a species as an African lawyer or doctor, and regarded me as an exotic creature. But as I became more familiar they became more friendly and at ease, and I joked with them that I would handle any of their legal problems. Seeing prominent and educated white women discussing serious matters with a black man on the basis of perfect equality could only lead to the weakening of the wardresses' apartheid assumptions.

Once during a long interview with Helen, I turned to the wardress who was required to sit in on our conversation and said, "I'm sorry to bore you with this endless consultation." "No," she said, "you are not boring me at all, I am enjoying it." I could see she was following our conversation, and once or twice she even offered small suggestions. I saw this as one of the side benefits of the trial. Most of these wardresses had no idea why we were in prison, and gradually began to discover what we were fighting for and why we were willing to risk jail in the first place.

This is precisely why the National Party was violently opposed to all forms of integration. Only a white electorate indoctrinated with the idea of the black threat, ignorant of African ideas and policies, could support the monstrous racist philosophy of the National Party. Familiarity, in this case, would not breed contempt, but understanding, and even, eventually, harmony.

The light moments in prison could not make up for the low ones. Winnie was allowed to visit on a number of occasions while I was in Pretoria, and each time she brought Zenani, who was then beginning to walk and talk. I would hold her and kiss her if the guards permitted me, and toward the end of the interview, hand her back to Winnie. As Winnie was saying good-bye, and the guards were ushering them out, Zeni would often motion for me to come with them, and I could see on her small puzzled face that she did not understand why I could not.

In court, Farid Adams deftly led Helen through her evidence-in-chief. He argued frequently and fairly competently with the judges. We were now energized: no longer was anyone doing crossword puzzles to pass the time. As the accused took turns cross-examining the witnesses, the Crown and the prosecution began to get a sense for the first time of the true caliber of the men and women on trial.

According to South African law, since we were in the Supreme Court, Duma, as an advocate, was the only one permitted to address the judges directly. I, as an attorney, could instruct him, but I was not technically permitted to address the court, and neither were any of the other defendants. We dismissed our advocates under the correct assumption that an accused, in the absence of representation, would be permitted to address the court. I addressed the court and Justice Rumpff, trying to frustrate us, interrupted me. "You appreciate the fact, Mr. Mandela," he said, "that Mr. Nokwe, as an advocate, is the only lawyer who is permitted to address the court." To which I replied, "Very well, My Lord, I believe we are all prepared to abide by that as long as you are prepared to pay Mr. Nokwe his fees." From then on no one objected to any of the accused addressing the court.

While Farid was questioning Helen and the subsequent witnesses, Duma and I sat on either side of him, supplying him with questions, helping him to deal with legal issues as they arose. In general, he did not need much prompting. But one day, when we were under constant pressure, we were whispering suggestions to him every few seconds. Farid seemed weary, and Duma and I were running out of material. Then, without consulting us, Farid suddenly asked the judges for a postponement, saying he was fatigued. The judges refused his application, saying it was not sufficient reason for a postponement and reiterating the warning they gave us the day our lawyers withdrew.

That afternoon there was no singing as we returned to prison, and everyone sat with sullen faces. A crisis was brewing among the accused. Upon our arrival in prison, a handful of the accused demanded a meeting. I called all the men together, and J. Nkampeni, a businessman from Port Elizabeth who had helped out the families of defiers during the Defiance Campaign, led what turned out to be an attack.

"Madiba," he said, using my clan name as a sign of respect, "I want you to tell us why you drove away our lawyers." I reminded him that the lawyers were not released by any one individual; their withdrawal had been approved by all, including himself. "But what did we know about court procedure, Madiba?" he said. "We relied on you lawyers."

A substantial number of men shared Nkampeni's misgivings. I warned them against the dangers of being disheartened and insisted we were doing quite well. I said that today was a minor setback, and that we would face worse difficulties. Our case was far more than a trial of legal issues between the Crown and a group of people charged with breaking the law. It was a trial of strength, a test of the power of a moral idea versus an immoral one, and I said we needed to worry about more than just the legal technique of our advocates. The protest abated.

After Helen Joseph had been cross-examined and reexamined, accused number three, Ahmed Kathrada, opened his case. It was during the testimony of Kathy's second witness, accused number four, Stanley Lollan, a member of the executive of the Coloured People's Congress, that Prime Minister Verwoerd announced that the State of Emergency would soon be lifted. The Emergency had never been intended to be permanent, and the government believed that it had successfully stifled the liberation struggle. At this point, our defense lawyers returned, to the general relief of all of us, though we remained in prison for another few weeks. We had been kept in detention and had functioned without our lawyers for more than five months.

My own testimony began on August 3. I felt well prepared through my preparation of the others. After three years of silence, banning, and internal exile, I looked forward to the chance to speak out before the people attempting to judge me. During my evidence-in-chief I preached moderation and reaffirmed the ANC's commitment to nonviolent struggle. In answer to a question as to whether democracy could be achieved through gradual reforms, I suggested it could.

> We demand universal adult franchise and we are prepared to exert economic pressure to attain our demands. We will launch defiance campaigns, stay-at-homes, either singly or together, until the Government should say, "Gentlemen, we cannot have this state of affairs, laws being defied, and this whole situation created by stay-at-homes. Let's talk." In my own view I would say, "Yes, let us talk" and the Government would say, "We think that the Europeans at present are not ready for a type of government where they might be dominated by non-Europeans. We think we should give you 60 seats. The African population to elect 60 Africans to represent them in Parliament. We will leave the matter over for five years and we will review it at the end of five years." In my view, that would be a victory, My Lords; we would have taken a significant step toward the attainment of universal adult suffrage for Africans, and we would then for the five years say, We will suspend civil disobedience.

The state was determined to prove that I was a dangerous, violence-spouting Communist. While I was not a Communist or a member of the party, I did not want to be seen as distancing myself from my Communist allies. Although I could have been sent back to jail for voicing such views, I did not hesitate to reaffirm the tremendous support the Communists had given us. At one point, the bench posed the question as to whether or not I thought a one-party state was a viable option for South Africa.

> NM: My Lord, it is not a question of form, it is a question of democracy. If democracy would be best expressed by a one-party system then I would examine the proposition very carefully. But if a democracy could best be expressed by a multiparty system then I would examine that carefully. In this country, for example, we have a multiparty system at present, but so far as the non-Europeans are concerned this is the most vicious despotism that you could think of.

I became testy with Judge Rumpff when he fell into the same mistake made by so many white South Africans about the idea of a universal franchise. Their notion was that to exercise this responsibility, voters must be "educated." To a narrow-thinking person, it is hard to explain that to be "educated" does not only mean being literate and having a B.A., and that an illiterate man can be a far more "educated" voter than someone with an advanced degree.

> JUSTICE RUMPFF: What is the value of participation in the Government of a state of people who know nothing?
> NM: My Lord, what happens when illiterate whites vote . . .
> JUSTICE RUMPFF: Are they not subject as much to the influence of election leaders as children would be?
> NM: No, My Lord, this is what happens in practice. A man stands up to contest a seat in a particular area; he draws up a manifesto, and he says, "These are the ideas for which I stand"; it is a rural area and he says, "I am against stock limitation"; then, listening to the policy of this person, you decide whether this man will advance your interests if you return him to Parliament, and on that basis you vote for a candidate. It has nothing to do with education.
> JUSTICE RUMPFF: He only looks to his own interests?
> NM: No, a man looks at a man who will be able to best present his point of view and votes for that man.

I told the court that we believed we could achieve our demands without violence, through our numerical superiority.

> We had in mind that in the foreseeable future it will be possible for us to achieve these demands, and we worked on the basis that Europeans themselves in spite of the wall of prejudice and hostility which we

encountered, that they can never remain indifferent indefinitely to our demands, because we are hitting them in the stomach with our policy of economic pressure. The Europeans dare not look at it with indifference. They would have to respond to it and indeed, My Lord, they are responding to it.

The Emergency was lifted on the last day of August. We would be going home for the first time in five months. When people in Johannesburg heard about the end of the Emergency, they drove up on the chance that we might be released; when we were let go, we were met with a jubilant reception from friends and family. Winnie had gotten a ride to Pretoria and our reunion was joyous. I had not held my wife in five months or seen her smile with joy. For the first time in five months, I slept in my own bed that night.

After one has been in prison, it is the small things that one appreciates: being able to take a walk whenever one wants, going into a shop and buying a newspaper, speaking or choosing to remain silent. The simple act of being able to control one's person.

Even after the end of the Emergency, the trial continued for another nine months until March 29, 1961. In many ways, these were the glory days for the accused, for our own people were on the stand fearlessly enunciating ANC policy. Robert Resha forcefully disputed the government's absurd contention that the ANC wanted to induce the government to use violence so we could use violence in return. Gert Sibande eloquently told the court of the miseries of African farmworkers. Venerable Isaac Behndy of Ladysmith, eighty-one years old, a lay preacher of the African Native Mission Church, explained why we opted for stay-at-homes instead of strikes.

In October, the redoubtable Professor Matthews was called as our final witness. He was imperturbable on the witness stand and treated the prosecutors as though they were errant students who needed stern admonishment. Often he would reply to the overmastered prosecutor with some version of the following: "What you really want me to say is that the speech which you allege is violent represents the policy of my organization. First, your contention is incorrect and second, I am not going to say that."

He explained in beautiful language that the African people knew that a nonviolent struggle would entail suffering but had chosen it because they prized freedom above all else. People, he said, will willingly undergo the severest suffering in order to free themselves from oppression. With

Professor Matthews in the dock, the defense ended on a high note. After he finished testifying, Justice Kennedy shook his hand and expressed the hope that they would meet again under better circumstances.

37

AFTER THE LIFTING of the Emergency, the National Executive Committee met secretly in September to discuss the future. We had had discussions in jail during the trial, but this was our first formal session. The state was arming itself not for an external threat but an internal one. We would not disband but carry on from underground. We would have to depart from the democratic procedures outlined in the ANC's constitution, of holding conferences, branch meetings, and public gatherings. New structures had to be created for communication with unbanned Congress organizations. But all of these new structures were illegal and would subject the participants to arrest and imprisonment. The executive committee and its subordinate structures would have to be severely streamlined to adapt to illegal conditions. Of necessity, we dissolved the ANC Youth League and Women's League. Some fiercely resisted these changes; but the fact was that we were now an illegal organization. For those who would continue to participate, politics went from being a risky occupation to a truly perilous one.

Though Mandela and Tambo had closed its doors and settled its remaining accounts, I continued to do whatever legal work I could. Numerous colleagues readily made their offices, staff, and phone facilities available to me, but most of the time I preferred to work from Ahmed Kathrada's flat, number 13 Kholvad House. Although my practice had dissolved, my reputation as a lawyer was undimmed. Soon, the lounge of number 13 and the hallway outside were crammed with clients. Kathy would return home and discover to his dismay that the only room in which he could be alone was his kitchen.

During this period, I hardly had time for meals and saw very little of my family. I would stay late in Pretoria preparing for our case, or rush back to handle another case. When I could actually sit down to supper with my family, the telephone would ring and I would be called away. Winnie was pregnant again and infinitely patient. She was hoping her husband might actually be at the hospital when she gave birth. But it was not to be.

During the Christmas adjournment in 1960, I learned that Makgatho was ill in the Transkei where he was at school and I violated my banning orders and went down to see him. I drove the entire night, stopping only for petrol. Makgatho required surgery, and I decided to bring him back with me to Johannesburg. I again drove all night, and took Makgatho to his mother's place while I went to arrange for his surgery. When I returned, I learned that Winnie had already gone into labor. I rushed to the non-European wing of Bridgman Memorial Hospital to find that mother and daughter were already in residence. The newborn girl was fine, but Winnie was very weak.

We named our new daughter Zindziswa, after the daughter of the poet laureate of the Xhosa people, Samuel Mqhayi, who had inspired me so many years before at Healdtown. The poet returned home after a very long trip to find that his wife had given birth to a daughter. He had not known that she was pregnant and assumed that the child had been fathered by another man. In our culture, when a woman gives birth, the husband does not enter the house where she is confined for ten days. In this case, the poet was too enraged to observe this custom, and he stormed into the house with an assegai, ready to stab both mother and daughter. But when he looked at the baby girl and saw that she was the image of himself, he stepped back, and said, *"u zindzile,"* which means, "You are well established." He named her Zindziswa, the feminine version of what he had said.

38

THE CROWN took over a month to do its summing up, which was often interrupted by interjections from the bench pointing out lapses in the argument. In March, it was our turn. Issy Maisels categorically refuted the charges of violence. "We admit that there is a question of noncooperation and passive resistance," he said. "We shall say quite frankly that if noncooperation and passive resistance constitute high treason, then we are guilty. But these are plainly not encompassed in the law of treason."

Maisels's argument was continued by Bram Fischer, but on March 23, the bench cut short Bram's concluding argument. We still had weeks of argument ahead, but the judges asked for a week's adjournment. This was irregular, but we regarded it as a hopeful sign, for it suggested the judges had already formed their opinion. We were to return to court six days later for what we presumed would be the verdict. In the meantime, I had work to do.

My bans were due to expire two days after the adjournment. I was almost certain that the police would not be aware of this, as they rarely kept track of when bans ended. It would be the first time in nearly five years that I would be free to leave Johannesburg, free to attend a meeting. That weekend was the long-planned All-in Conference in Pietermaritzburg. Its aim was to agitate for a national constitutional convention for all South Africans. I was secretly scheduled to be the main speaker at the conference. I would make the three-hundred-mile drive down to Pietermaritzburg the night before I was scheduled to speak.

The day before I was to leave, the National Working Committee met secretly to discuss strategy. After many meetings in prison and outside, we had decided that we would work from underground, adopting a strategy along the lines of the M-Plan. The organization would survive clandestinely. It was decided that if we were not convicted I would go underground to travel about the country organizing the proposed national convention. Only someone operating full-time from underground would be free from the paralyzing restrictions imposed by the enemy. It was decided that I would surface at certain events, hoping for a maximum of publicity, to show that the ANC was still fighting. It was not a proposal that came as a surprise to me, nor was it one I particularly relished, but it was something I knew I had to do. This would be a hazardous life, and I would be apart from my family, but when a man is denied the right to live the life he believes in, he has no choice but to become an outlaw.

When I returned home from the meeting it was as if Winnie could read my thoughts. Seeing my face, she knew that I was about to embark on a life that neither of us wanted. I explained what had transpired and that I would be leaving the next day. She took this stoically, as if she had expected it all along. She understood what I had to do, but that did not make it any easier for her. I asked her to pack a small suitcase for me. I told her that friends and relatives would look after her while I was gone. I did not tell her how long I would be gone and she did not ask. It was just as well, because I did not know the answer. I would return to Pretoria for what would probably be the verdict on Monday. No matter the result, I would not be returning home: if we were convicted, I would go directly to prison; if we were discharged, I would immediately go underground.

My elder son, Thembi, was in school in the Transkei, so I could not say good-bye to him, but that afternoon I fetched Makgatho and my daughter Makaziwe from their mother in Orlando East. We spent some hours together, walking on the veld outside town, talking and playing. I said good-bye to them, not knowing when I would see them again. The children of a freedom fighter also learn not to ask their father too many questions, and I could see in their eyes that they understood that something serious was occurring.

At home, I kissed the two girls good-bye and they waved as I got in the car with Wilson Conco and began the long drive to Natal.

*   *   *

Fourteen hundred delegates from all over the country representing one hundred fifty different religious, social, cultural, and political bodies converged on Pietermaritzburg for the All-in Conference. When I walked out onstage on Saturday evening, March 25, in front of this loyal and enthusiastic audience, it had been nearly five years since I had been free to give a speech on a public platform. I was met with a joyous reaction. I had almost forgotten the intensity of the experience of addressing a crowd.

In my speech I called for a national convention in which all South Africans, black and white, Indian and Coloured, would sit down in brotherhood and create a constitution that mirrored the aspirations of the country as a whole. I called for unity, and said we would be invincible if we spoke with one voice.

The All-in Conference called for a national convention of elected representatives of all adult men and women on an equal basis to determine a new nonracial democratic constitution for South Africa. A National Action Council was elected, with myself as honorary secretary, to communicate this demand to the government. If the government failed to call such a convention, we would call a countrywide three-day stay-away beginning on May 29 to coincide with the declaration of South Africa as a republic. I had no illusions that the state would agree to our proposal.

In October 1960, the government had held an all-white referendum on whether South Africa should become a republic. This was one of the long-cherished dreams of Afrikaner nationalism, to cast off ties to the country they had fought against in the Anglo-Boer War. The pro-republic sentiment won with 52 percent of the vote, and the proclamation of the republic was set for May 31, 1961. We set our stay-at-home on the date of the proclamation to indicate that such a change for us was merely cosmetic.

Directly after the conference I sent Prime Minister Verwoerd a letter in which I formally enjoined him to call a national constitutional convention. I warned him that if he failed to call the convention we would stage the country's most massive three-day strike ever, beginning on May 29. "We have no illusions about the counter-measures your government might take," I wrote. "During the last twelve months we have gone through a period of grim dictatorship." I also issued press statements affirming that the strike was a peaceful and nonviolent stay-at-home. Verwoerd did not reply, except to describe my letter in Parliament as "arrogant." The government instead began to mount one of the most intimidating displays of force ever assembled in the country's history.

39

EVEN BEFORE the doors of the Old Synagogue opened on the morning of March 29, 1961, the day of the long-anticipated verdict in the Treason Trial, a crowd of supporters and press people jostled to get inside. Hundreds were turned away. When the judges brought the court to order, the visitors' gallery and the press bench were packed. Moments after Justice Rumpff pounded his gavel, the Crown made an extraordinary application to change the indictment. This was the fifty-ninth minute of the eleventh hour, and it was two years too late. The court rebuffed the prosecution and the gallery murmured its approval.

"Silence in the court!" the orderly yelled, and Judge Rumpff announced that the three-judge panel had reached a verdict. Silence now reigned. In his deep, even voice, Judge Rumpff reviewed the court's conclusions. Yes, the African National Congress had been working to replace the government with a "radically and fundamentally different form of state"; yes, the African National Congress had used illegal means of protest during the Defiance Campaign; yes, certain ANC leaders had made speeches advocating violence; and yes, there was a strong left-wing tendency in the ANC that was revealed in its anti-imperialist, anti-West, pro-Soviet attitudes, but —

> On all the evidence presented to this court and on our finding of fact it is impossible for this court to come to the conclusion that the African National Congress had acquired or adopted a policy to overthrow the state by violence, that is, in the sense that the masses had to be prepared or conditioned to commit direct acts of violence against the state.

The court said the prosecution had failed to prove that the ANC was a Communist organization or that the Freedom Charter envisioned a Communist state. After speaking for forty minutes, Justice Rumpff said, "The accused are accordingly found not guilty and are discharged."

The spectators' gallery erupted in cheers. We stood and hugged each other, and waved to the happy courtroom. All of us then paraded into the courtyard, smiling, laughing, crying. The crowd yelled and chanted as we emerged. A number of us hoisted our defense counsels on our shoulders, which was no easy task in the case of Issy Maisels, for he was such a large man. Flashbulbs were popping all around us. We looked around for friends, wives, relatives. Winnie had come up and I hugged her in joy, though I knew that while I might be free for this moment, I would not be able to savor that freedom. When we were all outside together, the Treason Trialists and the crowd all began to sing *"Nkosi Sikelel' iAfrika."*

After more than four years in court and dozens of prosecutors, thousands of documents and tens of thousands of pages of testimony, the state had failed in its mission. The verdict was an embarrassment to the government, both at home and abroad. Yet the result only embittered the state against us even further. The lesson they took away was not that we had legitimate grievances but that they needed to be far more ruthless.

I did not regard the verdict as a vindication of the legal system or evidence that a black man could get a fair trial in a white man's court. It was the right verdict and a just one, but it was largely as a result of a superior defense team and the fair-mindedness of the panel of these particular judges.

The court system, however, was perhaps the only place in South Africa where an African could possibly receive a fair hearing and where the rule of law might still apply. This was particularly true in courts presided over by enlightened judges who had been appointed by the United Party. Many of these men still stood by the rule of law.

As a student, I had been taught that South Africa was a place where the rule of law was paramount and applied to all persons, regardless of their social status or official position. I sincerely believed this and planned my life based on that assumption. But my career as a lawyer and activist removed the scales from my eyes. I saw that there was a wide difference between what I had been taught in the lecture room and what I learned in the courtroom. I went from having an idealistic view of the law as a sword of justice to a perception of the law as a tool used by the ruling class to shape society in a way favorable to itself. I never expected justice in court, however much I fought for it, and though I sometimes received it.

In the case of the Treason Trial, the three judges rose above their prejudices, their education, and their background. There is a streak of goodness in men that can be buried or hidden and then emerge unexpectedly. Justice Rumpff, with his aloof manner, gave the impression throughout the proceedings that he shared the point of view of the ruling white minority. Yet in the end, an essential fairness dominated his judgment. Kennedy was less conservative than his colleagues and seemed attracted by the idea of equality. Once, for example, he and Duma Nokwe flew on the same plane from Durban to Johannesburg, and when the airline bus to town refused to take Duma, Kennedy refused to ride in it as well. Judge Bekker always struck me as open-minded and seemed aware that the accused before him had suffered a great deal at the hands of the state. I commended these three men as individuals, not as representatives of the court or of the state or even of their race, but as exemplars of human decency under adversity.

Judge Bekker's wife was a person sensitive to the needs of others. During the State of Emergency, she collected goods which she brought to the accused.

But the consequence of the government's humiliating defeat was that the state decided never to let it happen again. From that day forth they were not going to rely on judges whom they had not themselves appointed. They were not going to observe what they considered the legal niceties that protected terrorists or permitted convicted prisoners certain rights in jail. During the Treason Trial, there were no examples of individuals being isolated, beaten, and tortured in order to elicit information. All of those things became commonplace shortly thereafter.

Part Six

THE BLACK PIMPERNEL

40

I DID NOT return home after the verdict. Although others were in a festive mood, and eager to celebrate, I knew the authorities could strike at any moment, and I did not want to give them the opportunity. I was anxious to be off before I was banned or arrested, and I spent the night in a safe house in Johannesburg. It was a restless night in a strange bed, and I started at the sound of every car, thinking it might be the police.

Walter and Duma saw me off on the first leg of my journey, which was to take me to Port Elizabeth. In P.E., I met with Govan Mbeki and Raymond Mhlaba to discuss the new underground structures of the organization. We met at the house of Dr. Masla Pather, who would later be sentenced to two years in prison for allowing us to meet at his home. At safe houses arranged by the organization, I met the editor of the liberal *Port Elizabeth Morning Post* to discuss the campaign for a national convention, a goal several newspapers subsequently endorsed. I later visited Patrick Duncan, the editor and publisher of the liberal weekly *Contact,* a founding member of the Liberal Party, and one of the first white defiers during the Defiance Campaign. His newspaper had repeatedly been decrying ANC policy as being dictated by Communists, but when he saw me the first thing he said was that a close reading of the Treason Trial record had disabused him of that notion and he would correct it in his paper.

That night I addressed a meeting of African township ministers in Cape Town. I mention this because the opening prayer of one of the ministers has stayed with me over these many years and was a source of strength at a difficult time. He thanked the Lord for His bounty and goodness, for His mercy and His concern for all men. But then he took the liberty of reminding the Lord that some of His subjects were more downtrodden than others, and that it sometimes seemed as though He was not paying attention. The minister then said that if the Lord did not show a little more initiative in leading the black man to salvation, the black man would have to take matters into his own two hands. Amen.

On my last morning in Cape Town, I was leaving my hotel in the company of George Peake, a founding member of the South African Coloured People's Organization, and I stopped to thank the Coloured manager of the hotel for looking after me so well. He was grateful, but also curious. He had discovered my identity and told me that the Coloured community feared that under an African government they would be just as oppressed as under the present white government. He was a middle-class businessman who probably had little contact with Africans, and feared them in the same way as whites did. This was a frequent anxiety on the part of the Coloured community, especially in the Cape, and though I was running late, I explained the Freedom Charter to this fellow and stressed our commitment to nonracialism. A freedom fighter must take every opportunity to make his case to the people.

The following day I joined a secret meeting of the ANC National Executive Committee and the joint executives of the Congress movement in Durban to discuss whether the planned action should take the form of a stay-at-home or a full-fledged strike with organized pickets and demonstrations. Those who argued for the strike said that the stay-at-home strategy we had used since 1950 had outlasted its usefulness, that at a time when the PAC was appealing to the masses, more militant forms of the struggle were necessary. The alternative view, which I advocated, was that stay-at-homes allowed us to strike at the enemy while preventing him from striking back. I argued that the confidence of the people in our campaigns had grown precisely because they realized that we were not reckless with their lives. Sharpeville, I said, for all the heroism of the demonstrators, allowed the enemy to shoot down our people. I argued for stay-at-homes even though I was aware that our people around the country were becoming impatient with passive forms of struggle, but I did not think we should depart from our proven tactics without comprehensive planning, and we had neither the time nor the resources to do so. The decision was for a stay-at-home.

Living underground requires a seismic psychological shift. One has to plan every action, however small and seemingly insignificant. Nothing is innocent. Everything is questioned. You cannot be yourself; you must fully inhabit whatever role you have assumed. In some ways, this is not much of an adaptation for a black man in South Africa. Under apartheid, a black man lived a shadowy life between legality and illegality, between openness and concealment. To be a black man in South Africa meant not to trust anything, which was not unlike living underground for one's entire life.

I became a creature of the night. I would keep to my hideout during the day, and would emerge to do my work when it became dark. I operated mainly from Johannesburg, but I would travel as necessary. I stayed in empty flats, in people's houses, wherever I could be alone and inconspicuous. Although I am a gregarious person, I love solitude even more. I welcomed the opportunity to be by myself, to plan, to think, to plot. But one can have too much of solitude. I was terribly lonesome for my wife and family.

The key to being underground is to be invisible. Just as there is a way to walk in a room in order to make yourself stand out, there is a way of walking and behaving that makes you inconspicuous. As a leader, one often seeks prominence; as an outlaw, the opposite is true. When underground I did not walk as tall or stand as straight. I spoke more softly, with less clarity and distinction. I was more passive, more unobtrusive; I did not ask for things, but instead let people tell me what to do. I did not shave or cut my hair. My most frequent disguise was as a chauffeur, a chef, or a "garden boy." I would wear the blue overalls of the field-worker and often wore round, rimless glasses known as Mazzawati tea-glasses. I had a car and I wore a chauffeur's cap with my overalls. The pose of chauffeur was convenient because I could travel under the pretext of driving my master's car.

During those early months, when there was a warrant for my arrest and I was being pursued by the police, my outlaw existence caught the imagination of the press. Articles claiming that I had been here and there were on the front pages. Roadblocks were instituted all over the country, but the police repeatedly came up empty-handed. I was dubbed the Black Pimpernel, a somewhat derogatory adaptation of Baroness Orczy's fictional character the Scarlet Pimpernel, who daringly evaded capture during the French Revolution.

I traveled secretly about the country; I was with Muslims in the Cape; with sugar-workers in Natal; with factory workers in Port Elizabeth; I moved through townships in different parts of the country attending secret meetings at night. I would even feed the mythology of the Black Pimpernel by taking a pocketful of "tickeys" 20 (threepenny pieces) and phoning individual newspaper reporters from telephone boxes and relaying to them stories of what we were planning or of the ineptitude of the police. I would pop up here and there to the annoyance of the police and to the delight of the people.

There were many wild and inaccurate stories about my experiences underground. People love to embellish tales of daring. I did have a number of narrow escapes, however, which no one knew about. On one occasion, I was driving in town and I stopped at a traffic light. I looked to my left and in an adjacent car saw Colonel Spengler, the chief of the Witwatersrand Security Branch. It would have been a great plum for him to catch the Black Pimpernel. I was wearing a workman's cap, my blue overalls, and my glasses. He never looked my way, but even so the seconds I spent waiting for the light to change seemed like hours.

One afternoon, when I was in Johannesburg posing as a chauffeur and wearing my long duster and cap, I was waiting on a corner to be picked up and I saw an African policeman striding deliberately toward me. I looked around to see if I had a place to run, but before I did, he smiled at me and surreptitiously gave me the thumbs-up ANC salute and was gone. Incidents like this happened many times, and I was reassured when I saw that we had the loyalty of many African policemen. There was a black sergeant who used to tip off Winnie as to what the police were doing. He would whisper to her, "Make sure Madiba is not in Alexandra on Wednesday night because there is going to be a raid." Black policemen have often been severely criticized during the struggle, but many have played covert roles that have been extremely valuable.

When I was underground, I remained as unkempt as possible. My overalls looked as if they had been through a lifetime of hard toil. The police had one picture of me with a beard, which they widely distributed, and my colleagues urged me to shave it off. But I had become attached to my beard, and I resisted all efforts to get me to shave.

Not only was I not recognized, I was sometimes snubbed. Once, I was planning to attend a meeting in a distant area of Johannesburg and a well-known priest arranged with friends of his to put me up for the night. I arrived at the door, and before I could announce who I was, the elderly lady who answered exclaimed, "No, we don't want such a man as you here!" and shut the door.

41

MY TIME UNDERGROUND was mainly taken up in planning the May 29 stay-at-home. It was shaping up to be a virtual war between the state and the liberation movement. Late in May, the government staged countrywide raids on opposition leaders. Meetings were banned; printing presses were seized; and legislation was rushed through Parliament permitting the police to detain charged prisoners for twelve days without bail.

Verwoerd declared that those supporting the strike, including sympathetic newspapers, were "playing with fire," an ominous declaration given the ruthlessness of the state. The government urged industries to provide sleeping accommodations for workers so that they would not have to return home during the strike. Two days before the stay-at-home, the government staged the greatest peacetime show of force in South African history. The military exercised its largest call-up since the war. Police holidays were canceled. Military units were stationed at the entrances and exits of townships. While Saracen tanks rumbled through the dirt streets of the townships, helicopters hovered above, swooping down to break up any gathering. At night, the helicopters trained searchlights on houses.

The English-language press had widely publicized the campaign until a few days before it was to begin. But on the eve of the stay-at-home the entire English-language press crumbled and urged people to go to work. The PAC played the role of saboteur and released thousands of flyers telling people to oppose the stay-at-home, and denouncing the ANC leaders as cowards. The PAC's actions shocked us. It is one thing to criticize, and that we can accept, but to attempt to break a strike by calling upon the people to go to work directly serves the interests of the enemy.

The night before the stay-at-home, I was scheduled to meet the Johannesburg leadership of the ANC at a safe house in Soweto. To avoid police roadblocks, I entered Soweto through Kliptown, which was normally not patrolled. But as I went around a blind corner I drove straight into what I had been trying to avoid: a roadblock. A white policeman motioned for me to stop. I was dressed in my usual costume of overalls and chauffeur's cap. He squinted through the window at me and then stepped forward and searched the car on his own. Normally, this was the duty of the African police. After he found nothing, he demanded my pass. I told him that I had left it at home by mistake, and casually recited a fictitious pass number. This seemed to satisfy him and he motioned for me to drive through.

On Monday, May 29, the first day of the stay-at-home, hundreds of thousands of people risked their jobs and livelihoods by not going to work. In Durban, Indian workers walked out of factories while in the Cape thousands of Coloured workers stayed home. In Johannesburg, more than half of employees stayed home and in Port Elizabeth the rate was even higher. I praised the response as "magnificent" to the press, lauding our people for "defying unprecedented intimidation by the state." The white celebration of Republic Day was drowned out by our protest.

Although reports on the first day of the stay-at-home suggested strong reactions in various parts of the country, the response as a whole appeared less than we had hoped. Communication was difficult, and bad news always seems to travel more efficiently than good news. As more reports came in, I felt let down and disappointed by the reaction. That evening, feeling demoralized and a bit angry, I had a conversation with Benjamin Pogrund of the *Rand Daily Mail* in which I suggested that the days of nonviolent struggle were over.

On the second day of the stay-at-home, after consultations with my colleagues, I called it off. I met that morning in a safe flat in a white suburb with various members of the local and foreign press, and I once again called the stay-at-home "a tremendous success." But I did not mask the fact that I believed a new day was dawning. I said, "If the government reaction is to crush by naked force our nonviolent struggle, we will have to reconsider our tactics. In my mind we are closing a chapter on this question of a nonviolent policy." It was a grave declaration, and I knew it. I was criticized by our executive for making that remark before it was discussed by the organization, but sometimes one must go public with an idea to push a reluctant organization in the direction you want it to go.

The debate on the use of violence had been going on among us since early 1960. I had first discussed the armed struggle as far back as 1952 with Walter. Now, I again conferred with him and we agreed that the organization had to set out on a new course. The Communist Party had secretly reconstituted itself underground and was now considering forming its own military wing. We decided that I should raise the issue of the armed struggle within the Working Committee, and I did so in a meeting in June of 1961.

I had barely commenced my proposal when Moses Kotane, the secretary of the Communist Party and one of the most powerful figures in the ANC executive, staged a counterassault, accusing me of not having thought out the proposal carefully enough. He said that I had been outmaneuvered and paralyzed by the government's actions, and now in desperation I was resorting to revolutionary language. "There is still room," he stressed, "for the old methods if we are imaginative and determined enough. If we embark on the course Mandela is suggesting, we will be exposing innocent people to massacres by the enemy."

Moses spoke persuasively and I could see that he had defeated my proposal. Even Walter did not speak on my behalf, and I backed down. Afterward I spoke with Walter and voiced my frustration, chiding him for not coming to my aid. He laughed and said it would have been as foolish as attempting to fight a pride of angry lions. Walter is a diplomat and extremely resourceful. "Let me arrange for Moses to come and see you privately," he said, "and you can make your case that way." I was underground, but Walter managed to put the two of us together in a house in the township and we spent the whole day talking.

I was candid and explained why I believed we had no choice but to turn to violence. I used an old African expression: *Sebatana ha se bokwe ka diatla* (The attacks of the wild beast cannot be averted with only bare hands). Moses was an old-line Communist, and I told him that his opposition was like the Communist Party in Cuba under Batista. The party had insisted that the appropriate conditions had not yet arrived, and waited because they were simply following the textbook definitions of Lenin and Stalin. Castro did not wait, he acted — and he triumphed. If you wait for textbook conditions, they will never occur. I told Moses point-blank that his mind was stuck in the old mold of the ANC's being a legal organization. People were already forming military units on their own, and the only organization that had the muscle to lead them was the ANC. We have always maintained that the people were ahead of us, and now they were.

We talked the entire day, and at the end, Moses said to me, "Nelson, I will not promise you anything, but raise the issue again in committee, and we will see what happens." A meeting was scheduled in a week's time, and once again I raised the issue. This time, Moses was silent, and the general consensus of the meeting was that I should make the proposal to the National Executive Committee in Durban. Walter simply smiled.

The executive meeting in Durban, like all ANC meetings at the time, was held in secret and at night in order to avoid the police. I suspected I would encounter difficulties because Chief Luthuli was to be in attendance and I knew of his moral commitment to nonviolence. I was also wary because of the timing: I was raising the issue of violence so soon after the Treason Trial, where we had contended that for the ANC nonviolence was an inviolate principle, not a tactic to be changed as conditions warranted. I myself believed precisely the opposite: that nonviolence was a tactic that should be abandoned when it no longer worked.

At the meeting I argued that the state had given us no alternative to violence. I said it was wrong and immoral to subject our people to armed attacks by the state without offering them some kind of alternative. I mentioned again that people on their own had taken up arms. Violence would begin whether we initiated it or not. Would it not be better to guide this violence ourselves, according to principles where we save lives by attacking symbols of oppression, and not people? If we did not take the lead now, I said, we would soon be latecomers and followers to a movement we did not control.

The chief initially resisted my arguments. For him, nonviolence was not simply a tactic. But we worked on him the whole night; and I think that in his heart he realized that we were right. He ultimately agreed that a military campaign was inevitable. When someone later insinuated that perhaps the chief was not prepared for such a course, he retorted, "If anyone thinks I'm a pacifist, let him try to take my chickens, and he will know how wrong he is!"

The National Executive formally endorsed the preliminary decision of the Working Committee. The chief and others suggested that we should treat this new resolution as if the ANC had not discussed it. He did not want to jeopardize the legality of our unbanned allies. His idea was that a military movement should be a separate and independent organ, linked to the ANC and under the overall control of the ANC, but fundamentally autonomous. There would be two separate streams of the struggle. We readily accepted the chief's suggestion. The chief and others warned against this new phase becoming an excuse for neglecting the essential tasks of organization and the traditional methods of struggle. That, too, would be self-defeating because the armed struggle, at least in the beginning, would not be the centerpiece of the movement.

The following night a meeting of the joint executives was scheduled in Durban. This would include the Indian Congress, the Colored People's Congress, the South African Congress of Trade Unions, and the Congress of Democrats. Although these other groups customarily accepted ANC decisions, I knew that some of my Indian colleagues would strenuously oppose the move toward violence.

The meeting had an inauspicious beginning. Chief Luthuli, who was presiding, announced that even though the ANC had endorsed a decision on violence, "it is a matter of such gravity, I would like my colleagues here tonight to consider the issue afresh." It was apparent that the chief was not fully reconciled to our new course.

We began our session at 8 P.M. and it was tumultuous. I made the identical arguments that I had been making all along, and many people expressed reservations. Yusuf Cachalia and Dr. Naicker pleaded with us not to embark on this course, arguing that the state would slaughter the whole liberation movement. J. N. Singh, an effective debater, uttered words that night which still echo in my head. "Nonviolence has not failed us," he said, "we have failed nonviolence." I countered by saying that in fact nonviolence had failed us, for it had done nothing to stem the violence of the state nor change the heart of our oppressors.

We argued the entire night, and in the early hours of the morning I began to feel we were making progress. Many of the Indian leaders were now speaking in a sorrowful tone about the end of nonviolence. But then suddenly M. D. Naidoo, a member of the South African Indian Congress, burst forth and said to his Indian colleagues, "Ah, you are afraid of going to jail, that is all!" His comment caused pandemonium in the meeting. When you question a man's integrity, you can expect a fight. The entire debate went back to square one. But toward dawn, there was a resolution. The congresses authorized me to go ahead and form a new military organization, separate from the ANC. The policy of the ANC would still be that of nonviolence. I was authorized to join with whomever I wanted or needed to create this organization and would not be subject to the direct control of the mother organization.

This was a fateful step. For fifty years, the ANC had treated nonviolence as a core principle, beyond question or debate. Henceforth, the ANC would be a different kind of organization. We were embarking on a new and more dangerous path, a path of organized violence, the results of which we did not and could not know.

42

I, WHO HAD NEVER been a soldier, who had never fought in battle, who had never fired a gun at an enemy, had been given the task of starting an army. It would be a daunting task for a veteran general much less a military novice. The name of this new organization was Umkhonto we Sizwe (The Spear of the Nation) — or MK for short. The symbol of the spear was chosen because with this simple weapon Africans had resisted the incursions of whites for centuries.

Although the executive of the ANC did not allow white members, MK was not thus constrained. I immediately recruited Joe Slovo, and along with Walter Sisulu, we formed the High Command with myself as chairman. Through Joe, I enlisted the efforts of white Communist Party members who had resolved on a course of violence and had already executed acts of sabotage like cutting government telephone and communication lines. We recruited Jack Hodgson, who had fought in World War II with the Springbok Legion, and Rusty Bernstein, both party members. Jack became our first demolitions expert. Our mandate was to wage acts of violence against the state — precisely what form those acts would take was yet to be decided. Our intention was to begin with what was least violent to individuals but most damaging to the state.

I began the only way I knew how, by reading and talking to experts. What I wanted to find out were the fundamental principles for starting a revolution. I discovered that there was a great deal of writing on this very subject, and I made my way though the available literature on armed warfare and in particular guerrilla warfare. I wanted to know what circumstances were appropriate for a guerrilla war; how one created, trained, and maintained a guerrilla force; how it should be armed; where it gets its supplies — all basic and fundamental questions.

Any and every source was of interest to me. I read the report of Blas Roca, the general secretary of the Communist Party of Cuba, about their years as an illegal organization during the Batista regime. In *Commando,* by Deneys Reitz, I read of the unconventional guerrilla tactics of the Boer generals during the Anglo-Boer War. I read works by and about Che Guevara, Mao Tse-tung, Fidel Castro. In Edgar Snow's brilliant *Red Star*

Over China I saw that it was Mao's determination and nontraditional thinking that led him to victory. I read *The Revolt* by Menachem Begin and was encouraged by the fact that the Israeli leader had led a guerrilla force in a country with neither mountains nor forests, a situation similar to our own. I was eager to know more about the armed struggle of the people of Ethiopia against Mussolini, and of the guerrilla armies of Kenya, Algeria, and the Cameroons.

I went into the South African past. I studied our history both before and after the white man. I probed the wars of African against African, of African against white, of white against white. I made a survey of the country's chief industrial areas, the nation's transportation system, its communication network. I accumulated detailed maps and systematically analyzed the terrain of different regions of the country.

On June 26, 1961, our Freedom Day, I released a letter to South African newspapers from underground, which commended the people for their courage during the recent stay-at-home, once more calling for a national constitutional convention. I again proclaimed that a countrywide campaign of noncooperation would be launched if the state failed to hold such a convention. My letter read in part:

> I am informed that a warrant for my arrest has been issued, and that the police are looking for me. The National Action Council has given full and serious consideration to this question . . . and they have advised me not to surrender myself. I have accepted this advice, and will not give myself up to a Government I do not recognize. Any serious politician will realize that under present day conditions in the country, to seek for cheap martyrdom by handing myself to the police is naive and criminal. . . .
>
> I have chosen this course which is more difficult and which entails more risk and hardship than sitting in gaol. I have had to separate myself from my dear wife and children, from my mother and sisters to live as an outlaw in my own land. I have had to close my business, to abandon my profession, and live in poverty, as many of my people are doing. . . . I shall fight the Government side by side with you, inch by inch, and mile by mile, until victory is won. What are you going to do? Will you come along with us, or are you going to co-operate with the Government in its efforts to suppress the claims and aspirations of your own people? Are you going to remain silent and neutral in a matter of life and death to my people, to our people? For my own part I have made my choice. I will not leave South Africa, nor will I surrender. Only

through hardship, sacrifice and militant action can freedom be won. The struggle is my life. I will continue fighting for freedom until the end of my days.

43

DURING THOSE FIRST few months underground I lived for a few weeks with a family on Market Street, after which I shared a one-room ground-floor bachelor flat with Wolfie Kodesh in Berea, a quiet white suburb a short distance north of downtown. Wolfie was a member of the Congress of Democrats, a reporter for *New Age,* and had fought in North Africa and Italy during World War II. His knowledge of warfare and his firsthand battle experience were extremely helpful to me. At his suggestion I read the Prussian general Karl von Clausewitz's classic work *On War.* Clausewitz's central thesis, that war was a continuation of diplomacy by other means, dovetailed with my own instincts. I relied on Wolfie to procure reading material for me and I fear that I took over his life, infringing on both his work and pleasure. But he was such an amiable, modest fellow that he never complained.

I spent nearly two months in his flat, sleeping on a campaign stretcher, staying inside during the day with the blinds drawn reading and planning, leaving only for meetings or organizing sessions at night. I annoyed Wolfie every morning, for I would wake up at five, change into my sweat clothes, and run in place for more than an hour. Wolfie eventually surrendered to my regimen and began working out with me in the morning before he left for town.

MK was then practicing setting off explosions. One night, I accompanied Wolfie to an old brickworks on the outskirts of town for a demonstration. It was a security risk, but I wanted to attend MK's first test of an explosive device. Explosions were common at the brickworks, for companies would use dynamite to loosen the clay before the great machines scooped it up to make bricks. Jack Hodgson had brought along a paraffin tin filled with nitroglycerin; he had created a timing device that used the inside of a ball-point pen. It was dark and we had only a small light, and we stood to the side as Jack worked. When it was ready, we stood back and counted down to thirty seconds; there was a great roar and much displaced earth. The explosion had been a success, and we all quickly returned to our cars and went off in different directions.

*   *   *

I felt safe in Berea. I did not go outside, and because it was a white area, the police would probably not think to look for me there. While I was reading in the flat during the day, I would often place a pint of milk on the windowsill to allow it to ferment. I am very fond of this sour milk, which is known as *amasi* among the Xhosa people and is greatly prized as a healthy and nourishing food. It is very simple to make and merely involves letting the milk stand in the open air and curdle. It then becomes thick and sour, rather like yogurt. I even prevailed upon Wolfie to try it, but he grimaced when he tasted it.

One evening, after Wolfie had returned, we were chatting in the flat when I overheard a conversation going on near the window. I could hear two young black men speaking in Zulu, but I could not see them, as the curtains were drawn. I motioned Wolfie to be quiet.

"What is 'our milk' doing on that window ledge?" one of the fellows said.

"What are you talking about?" replied the other fellow.

"The sour milk — *amasi* — on the window ledge," he said. "What is it doing there?" Then there was silence. The sharp-eyed fellow was suggesting that only a black man would place milk on the ledge like that and what was a black man doing living in a white area? I realized then that I needed to move on. I left for a different hideout the next night.

I stayed at a doctor's house in Johannesburg, sleeping in the servants' quarters at night, and working in the doctor's study during the day. Whenever anyone came to the house during the day, I would dash out to the backyard and pretend to be the gardener. I then spent about a fortnight on a sugar plantation in Natal living with a group of African laborers and their families in a small community called Tongaat, just up the coast from Durban. I lived in a hostel and posed as an agricultural demonstrator who had come at the behest of the government to evaluate the land.

I had been equipped by the organization with a demonstrator's tools and I spent part of each day testing the soil and performing experiments. I little understood what I was doing and I do not think I fooled the people of Tongaat. But these men and women, who were mostly farmworkers, had a natural kind of discretion and did not question my identity, even when they began seeing people arriving at night in cars, some of them well-known local politicians. Often I was at meetings all night and would sleep all day — not the normal schedule of an agricultural demonstrator. But even though I was involved in other matters I felt a closeness with the community. I would attend services on Sunday, and I enjoyed the old-fashioned, Bible-thumping style of these Zionist Christian ministers. Shortly before I was planning to leave, I thanked one elderly fellow for having looked after me. He said, "You are of course welcome, but, Kwedeni [young man], please tell us, what does Chief Luthuli want?" I was taken aback but I quickly responded. "Well, it would be better to ask him yourself and I cannot speak for him, but as I understand it, he wants our land returned, he wants our kings to have their power back, and he wants us to be able to determine our own future and run our own lives as we see fit."

"And how is he going to do that if he does not have an army?" the old man said.

I wanted very much to tell the old man that I was busy attempting to form that army, but I could not. While I was encouraged by the old man's sentiments, I was nervous that others had discovered my mission as well. Again I had stayed too long in one place, and the following night I left as quietly as I had arrived.

44

MY NEXT ADDRESS was more of a sanctuary than a hideout: Liliesleaf Farm, located in Rivonia, a bucolic northern suburb of Johannesburg, and I moved there in October. In those days Rivonia consisted mainly of farms and smallholdings. The farmhouse and property had been purchased by the movement for the purpose of having a safe house for those underground. It was an old house that needed work and no one lived there.

I moved in under the pretext that I was the houseboy or caretaker who would look after the place until my master took possession. I had taken the alias David Motsamayi, the name of one of my former clients. At the farm, I wore the simple blue overalls that were the uniform of the black male servant. During the day, the place was busy with workers, builders, and painters who were repairing the main house and extending the outbuildings. We wanted to have a number of small rooms added to the house so more people could stay. The workers were all Africans from Alexandra township and they called me "waiter" or "boy" (they never bothered to ask my name). I prepared breakfast for them and made them tea in the late morning and afternoon. They also sent me on errands about the farm, or ordered me to sweep the floor or pick up trash.

One afternoon, I informed them that I had prepared tea in the kitchen. They came in and I passed around a tray with cups, tea, milk and sugar. Each man took a cup, and helped himself. As I was carrying the tray I came to one fellow who was in the middle of telling a story. He took a cup of tea, but he was concentrating more on his story than on me, and he simply held his teaspoon in the air while he was talking, using it to gesture and tell his tale rather than help himself to some sugar. I stood there for what seemed like several minutes and finally, in mild exasperation, I started to move away. At that point he noticed me, and said sharply, "Waiter, come back here, I didn't say you could leave."

Many people have painted an idealistic picture of the egalitarian nature of African society, and while in general I agree with this portrait, the fact is that Africans do not always treat each other as equals. Industrialization has played a large role in introducing the urban African to the perceptions of status common to white society. To those men, I was an inferior, a servant, a person without a trade, and therefore to be treated with disdain. I played the role so well that none of them suspected I was anything other than what I seemed.

Every day, at sunset, the workers would return to their homes and I would be alone until the next morning. I relished these hours of quiet, but on most evenings I would leave the property to attend meetings, returning in the middle of the night. I often felt uneasy coming back at such hours to a place I did not know well and where I was living illegally under an assumed name. I recall being frightened one night when I thought I saw someone lurking in the bushes; although I investigated, I found nothing. An underground freedom fighter sleeps very lightly.

After a number of weeks I was joined at the farm by Raymond Mhlaba, who had journeyed up from Port Elizabeth. Ray was a staunch trade unionist, a member of the Cape executive and the Communist Party, and the first ANC leader to be arrested in the Defiance Campaign. He had been chosen by the ANC to be one of the first recruits for Umkhonto we Sizwe. He had come to prepare for his departure, with three others, for military training in the People's Republic of China; we had renewed the contacts that Walter had made back in 1952. Ray stayed with me for a fortnight and provided me with a clearer picture of the problems the ANC was having in the eastern Cape. I also enlisted his assistance in writing the MK constitution. We were joined by Joe Slovo as well as Rusty Bernstein, who both had hands in drafting it.

After Raymond left, I was joined for a brief time by Michael Harmel, a key figure in the underground Communist Party, a founding member of the Congress of Democrats, and an editor of the magazine *Liberation*. Michael was a brilliant theorist and was working on policy matters for the Communist Party and needed a quiet and safe place to work on this full-time.

During the day, I kept my distance from Michael as it would have seemed exceedingly curious if a white professional man and an African houseboy were having regular conversations. But at night, after the workers left, we had long conversations about the relationship between the Communist Party and the ANC. One night I returned to the farm late after a meeting. When I was there alone, I made sure that all the gates were locked and the lights were out. I took quite a few precautions because a black man driving a car into a smallholding in Rivonia in the middle of the night would attract unwanted questions. But I saw that the house lights were on, and as I approached the house I heard a radio blaring. The front door was open and I walked in and found Michael in bed fast asleep. I was furious at this breach of security, and I woke him up and said, "Man, how can you leave the lights on and the radio playing!" He was groggy but angry. "Nel, must you disturb my sleep? Can't this wait until tomorrow?" I said it couldn't, it was a matter of security, and I reprimanded him for his lax conduct.

Soon after this Arthur Goldreich and his family moved into the main house as official tenants and I took over the newly built domestic workers' cottage. Arthur's presence provided a safe cover for our activities. Arthur was an artist and designer by profession, a member of the Congress of Democrats and one of the first members of MK. His politics were unknown to the police and he had never before been questioned or raided. In the 1940s, Arthur had fought with the Palmach, the military wing of the Jewish National Movement in Palestine. He was knowledgeable about guerrilla warfare and helped fill many gaps in my knowledge. Arthur was a flamboyant person and he gave the farm a buoyant atmosphere.

The final addition to the regular group at the farm was Mr. Jelliman, an amiable white pensioner and old friend of the movement who became the farm foreman. Mr. Jelliman brought in several young workers from Sekhukhuneland, and the place soon appeared to be like any other smallholding in the country. Jelliman was not a member of the ANC, but he was loyal, discreet, and hardworking. I used to prepare breakfast for him as well as supper, and he was unfailingly gracious. Much later, Jelliman risked his own life and livelihood in a courageous attempt to help me.

The loveliest times at the farm were when I was visited by my wife and family. Once the Goldreichs were in residence, Winnie would visit me on weekends. We were careful about her movements, and she would be picked up by one driver, dropped off at another place, and then picked up by a second driver before finally being delivered to the farm. Later, she would drive herself and the children, taking the most circuitous route possible. The police were not yet following her every move.

On these weekends time would sometimes seem to stop as we pretended that these stolen moments together were the rule not the exception of our lives. Ironically, we had more privacy at Liliesleaf than we ever had at home. The children could run about and play, and we were secure, however briefly, in this idyllic bubble.

Winnie brought me an old air rifle that I had in Orlando and Arthur and I would use it for target practice or hunting doves on the farm. One day, I was on the front lawn of the property and aimed the gun at a sparrow perched high in a tree. Hazel Goldreich, Arthur's wife, was watching me and jokingly remarked that I would never hit my target. But she had hardly finished the sentence when the sparrow fell to the ground. I turned to her and was about to boast, when the Goldreich's son Paul, then about five years old, turned to me with tears in his eyes and said, "David, why did you kill that bird? Its mother will be sad." My mood immediately shifted from one of pride to shame; I felt that this small boy had far more humanity than I did. It was an odd sensation for a man who was the leader of a nascent guerrilla army.

45

IN PLANNING the direction and form that MK would take, we considered four types of violent activities: sabotage, guerrilla warfare, terrorism, and open revolution. For a small and fledgling army, open revolution was inconceivable. Terrorism inevitably reflected poorly on those who used it, undermining any public support it might otherwise garner. Guerrilla warfare was a possibility, but since the ANC had been reluctant to embrace violence at all, it made sense to start with the form of violence that inflicted the least harm against individuals: sabotage.

Because it did not involve loss of life it offered the best hope for reconciliation among the races afterward. We did not want to start a blood feud between white and black. Animosity between Afrikaner and Englishman was still sharp fifty years after the Anglo-Boer War; what would race relations be like between white and black if we provoked a civil war? Sabotage had the added virtue of requiring the least manpower.

Our strategy was to make selective forays against military installations, power plants, telephone lines, and transportation links; targets that would not only hamper the military effectiveness of the state, but frighten National Party supporters, scare away foreign capital, and weaken the economy. This we hoped would bring the government to the bargaining table. Strict instructions were given to members of MK that we would countenance no loss of life. But if sabotage did not produce the results we wanted, we were prepared to move on to the next stage: guerrilla warfare and terrorism.

The structure of MK mirrored that of the parent organization. The National High Command was at the top; below it were Regional Commands in each of the provinces, and below that there were local commands and cells. Regional Commands were set up around the country, and an area like the eastern Cape had over fifty cells. The High Command determined tactics and general targets and was in charge of training and finance. Within the framework laid down by the High Command, the Regional Commands had authority to select local targets to be attacked. All MK members were forbidden to go armed into an operation and were not to endanger life in any way.

One problem we encountered early on was the question of divided loyalties between MK and the ANC. Most of our recruits were ANC members who were active in the local branches, but we found that once they were working for MK, they stopped doing the local work they had been performing before. The secretary of the local branch would find that certain men were no longer attending meetings. He might approach one and say, "Man, why were you not at the meeting last night?" and the fellow would say, "Ah, well, I was at another meeting."

"What kind of meeting?" the secretary would say.

"Oh, I cannot say."

"You cannot tell me, your own secretary?" But the secretary would soon discover the member's other loyalty. After some initial misunderstandings, we decided that if we recruited members from a branch, the secretary must be informed that one of his members was now with MK.

One warm December afternoon, while I sat in the kitchen at Liliesleaf Farm, I listened on the radio to the announcement that Chief Luthuli had been awarded the Nobel Peace Prize at a ceremony in Oslo. The government had issued him a ten-day visa to leave the country and accept the award. I was — we all were — enormously pleased. It was, first of all, an acknowledgment of our struggle, and of the achievements of the chief as the leader of that struggle and as a man. It represented a recognition in the West that our struggle was a moral one, one too long ignored by the great powers. The award was an affront to the Nationalists, whose propaganda portrayed Luthuli as a dangerous agitator at the head of a Communist conspiracy. Afrikaners were dumbfounded; to them the award was another example of the perversity of Western liberals and their bias against white South Africans. When the award was announced, the chief was in the third year of a five-year ban restricting him to the district of Stanger in Natal. He was also unwell; his heart was strained and his memory was poor. But the award cheered him and all of us as well.

The honor came at an awkward time for it was juxtaposed against an announcement that seemed to call the award itself into question. The day after Luthuli returned from Oslo, MK dramatically announced its emergence. On the orders of the MK High Command, in the early morning hours of December 16 — the day white South Africans used to celebrate as Dingane's Day — homemade bombs were exploded at electric power stations and government offices in Johannesburg, Port Elizabeth, and Durban. One of our men, Petrus Molife, was inadvertently killed, the first death of an MK soldier. Death in war is unfortunate, but unavoidable. Every man who joined MK knew that he might be called on to pay the ultimate sacrifice.

At the time of the explosions, thousands of leaflets with the new MK Manifesto were circulated all over the country announcing the birth of Umkhonto we Sizwe.

> Units of Umkhonto we Sizwe today carried out planned attacks against government installations, particularly those connected with the policy of apartheid and race discrimination. Umkhonto we Sizwe is a new, independent body, formed by Africans. It includes in its ranks South Africans of all races. . . . Umkhonto we Sizwe will carry on the struggle for freedom and democracy by new methods, which are necessary to complement the actions of the established national liberation movement. . . .
>
> The time comes in the life of any nation when there remain only two choices: submit or fight. That time has now come to South Africa. We shall not submit and we have no choice but to hit back by all means within our power in defence of our people, our future and our freedom. . . .
>
> We of Umkhonto have always sought — as the liberation movement has sought — to achieve liberation without bloodshed and civil clash. We hope, even at this late hour, that our first actions will awaken everyone to a realization of the disastrous situation to which the Nationalist policy is leading. We hope that we will bring the government and its supporters to their senses before it is too late, so that both the government and its policies can be changed before matters reach the desperate stage of civil war. . . .

We chose December 16, Dingane's Day, for a reason. On that day, white South Africans celebrate the defeat of the great Zulu leader Dingane at the Battle of Blood River in 1838. Dingane, the half brother of Shaka, then ruled the most powerful African state that ever existed south of the Limpopo River. That day, the bullets of the Boers were too much for the assegais of the Zulu *impis* and the water of the nearby river ran red with their blood. Afrikaners celebrate December 16 as the triumph of the Afrikaner over the African and the demonstration that God was on their side; while Africans mourned this day of the massacre of their people. We chose December 16 to show that the African had only begun to fight, and that we had righteousness — and dynamite — on our side.

The explosions took the government by surprise. They condemned the sabotage as heinous crimes while at the same time deriding it as the work of foolish amateurs. The explosions also shocked white South Africans into the realization that they were sitting on top of a volcano. Black South Africans realized that the ANC was no longer an organization of passive resistance, but a powerful spear that would take the struggle to the heart of white power. We planned and executed another set of explosions two weeks later on New Year's Eve. The combined sound of bells tolling and sirens wailing seemed not just a cacophonous way to ring in the new year, but a sound that symbolized a new era in our freedom struggle.

The announcement of Umkhonto spurred a vicious and unrelenting government counteroffensive on a scale that we had never before seen. The Special Branch of the police now made it their number one mission to capture members of MK, and they would spare no effort to do so. We had shown them we were not going to sit back any longer; they would show us that nothing would stop them from rooting out what they saw as the greatest threat to their own survival.

46

WHEN WINNIE VISITED, I had the illusion, however briefly, that the family was still intact. Her visits were becoming less frequent, as the police were becoming more vigilant. Winnie would bring Zindzi and Zenani to Rivonia, but they were too young to know that I was in hiding. Makgatho, then eleven, was old enough to know and he had been instructed never to reveal my real name in front of anyone. I could tell that he was determined, in his own small way, to keep my identity a secret.

But one day, toward the end of that year, he was at the farm playing with Nicholas Goldreich, Arthur's eleven-year-old son. Winnie had brought me a copy of the magazine *Drum*, and Makgatho and Nicholas stumbled upon it while they were playing. They began paging through it when suddenly Makgatho stopped at a picture of me taken before I had gone underground. "That's my father," he exclaimed. Nicholas did not believe him, and his skepticism made Makgatho even keener to prove it was true. Makgatho then told his friend that my real name was Nelson Mandela. "No, your father's name is David," Nicholas replied. The boy then ran to his mother and asked her whether or not my name was David. She replied that yes, it was David. Nicholas then explained to his mother that Makgatho had told him that his father's real name was Nelson. This alarmed Hazel and I soon learned of this lapse. Once again I had the feeling that I had remained too long in one place. But I stayed put, for in a little over a week I was to leave on a mission that would take me to places that I had only ever dreamed of. Now, the struggle would for the first time take me outside the borders of my country.

In December, the ANC received an invitation from the Pan African Freedom Movement for East, Central, and Southern Africa (PAFMECSA) to attend its conference in Addis Ababa in February 1962. PAFMECSA, which later became the Organization of African Unity, aimed to draw together the independent states of Africa and promote the liberation movements on the continent. The conference would furnish important connections for the ANC and be the first and best chance for us to enlist support, money, and training for MK.

The underground executive asked me to lead the ANC delegation to the conference. Although I was eager to see the rest of Africa and meet freedom fighters from my own continent, I was greatly concerned that I would be violating the promise I had made not to leave the country but to operate from underground. My colleagues, including Chief Luthuli, insisted that I go, but were adamant that I return immediately afterward. I decided to make the trip.

My mission in Africa was broader than simply attending the conference; I was to arrange political and economic support for our new military force and, more important, military training for our men in as many places on the continent as possible. I was also determined to boost our reputation in the rest of Africa where we were still relatively unknown. The PAC had launched its own propaganda campaign and I was delegated to make our case wherever possible.

Before leaving, I secretly drove to Groutville to confer with the chief. Our meeting — at a safe house in town — was disconcerting. As I have related, the chief was present at the creation of MK, and was as informed as any member of the National Executive Committee about its development. But the chief was not well and his memory was not what it had once been. He chastised me for not consulting with him about the formation of MK. I attempted to remind the chief of the discussions that we had in Durban about taking up violence, but he did not recall them. This is in large part why the story has gained currency that Chief Luthuli was not informed about the creation of MK and was deeply opposed to the ANC taking up violence. Nothing could be further from the truth.

*   *   *

I had spent the night before my departure with Winnie at the house of white friends in the northern suburbs and she brought me a new suitcase that she had packed. She was anxious about my leaving the country, but once again remained stoic. She behaved as much like a soldier as a wife.

The ANC had to arrange for me to travel to Dar es Salaam in Tanganyika. The flight to Addis Ababa would originate in Dar es Salaam. The plan was for Walter, Kathrada, and Duma Nokwe to meet me at a secret rendezvous in Soweto and bring me my credentials for the trip. It would also be a moment for last-minute consultations before I left the country.

Ahmed Kathrada arrived at the appointed hour, but Walter and Duma were extremely late. I finally had to make alternative arrangements and Kathy managed to locate someone to drive me to Bechuanaland, where I would charter a plane. I later learned that Walter and Duma had been arrested on their way.

The drive to Bechuanaland was trying, as I was nervous both about the police and the fact that I had never crossed the boundaries of my country before. Our destination was Lobatse, near the South African border. We passed through the border without a problem and arrived in Lobatse in the late afternoon, where there was a telegram for me from Dar es Salaam postponing my trip for a fortnight. I put up with my fellow Treason Trialist Fish Keitsing, who had since moved to Lobatse.

That afternoon I met with Professor K. T. Motsete, the president of the Bechuanaland People's Party, which had been formed mainly by ex-ANC members. I now had unexpected spare time, which I used for reading, preparing my speech for the conference, and hiking the wild and beautiful hills above the town. Although I was not far outside my own country's borders, I felt as though I were in an exotic land. I was often accompanied by Max Mlonyeni, the son of a friend from the Transkei and a young member of the PAC. It was as though we were on safari, for we encountered all manner of animals, including a battalion of sprightly baboons, which I followed for some time, admiring their military-like organization and movements.

I was soon joined by Joe Matthews, who had come from Basutoland, and I insisted we should make haste for Dar es Salaam. An ANC colleague in Lobatse had recently been kidnapped by the South African police and I thought the sooner we could leave, the better. A plane was arranged, and our first destination was a town in northern Bechuanaland called Kasane, strategically situated near a point where the borders of four countries met — Bechuanaland, Northern and Southern Rhodesia, and South West Africa, as these colonies were then known. The landing strip at Kasane was waterlogged and we came in at a drier strip several miles

away in the middle of the bush. The manager of a local hotel came to
fetch us armed with rifles and reported that he had been delayed by a
herd of rogue elephants. He was in an open van and Joe and I sat in the
back, and I watched a lioness lazily emerge from the bush. I felt far from
my home streets of Johannesburg; I was in the Africa of myth and legend
for the first time.

Early the next morning we left for Mbeya, a Tanganyikan town near
the Northern Rhodesian border. We flew near Victoria Falls and then
headed north through a mountain range. While over the mountains, the
pilot tried to contact Mbeya, but there was no answer. "Mbeya, Mbeya!"
he kept saying into the microphone. The weather had changed and the
mountains were full of air pockets that made the plane bounce up and
down like a cork on a rough sea. We were now flying through clouds and
mists and in desperation the pilot descended and followed a twisting road
through the mountains. By this time the mist had become so thick we
could not see the road and when the pilot abruptly turned the plane I
realized that we narrowly missed a mountain that seemed to rear up out
of nowhere. The emergency alarm went off, and I remember saying to
myself, "That's the end of us." Even the ever-loquacious Joe was stone
silent. But then just as we could see no farther in the clouds and I imagined
we were about to crash into a mountain, we emerged from the bad weather
into a gloriously clear sky. I have never enjoyed flying much, and while
this was the most frightening episode I have ever had on a plane, I
am sometimes adept at appearing brave and I pretended that I was
unconcerned.

We booked in a local hotel and found a crowd of blacks and whites
sitting on the veranda making polite conversation. Never before had I
been in a public place or hotel where there was no color bar. We were
waiting for Mr. Mwakangale of the Tanganyika African National Union,
a member of Parliament, and unbeknown to us he had already called
looking for us. An African guest approached the white receptionist.
"Madam, did a Mr. Mwakangale inquire after these two gentlemen?" he
asked, pointing to us. "I'm sorry, sir," she replied. "He did but I forgot
to tell them."

"Please be careful, madam," he said in a polite but firm tone. "These
men are our guests and we would like them to receive proper attention."
I then truly realized that I was in a country ruled by Africans. For the
first time in my life, I was a free man. Though I was a fugitive and wanted
in my own land, I felt the burden of oppression lifting from my shoulders.
Everywhere I went in Tanganyika my skin color was automatically accepted
rather than instantly reviled. I was being judged for the first time not by

the color of my skin but by the measure of my mind and character. Although I was often homesick during my travels, I nevertheless felt as though I were truly home for the first time.

We arrived in Dar es Salaam the next day and I met with Julius Nyerere, the newly independent country's first president. We talked at his house, which was not at all grand, and I recall that he drove himself in a simple car, a little Austin. This impressed me, for it suggested that he was a man of the people. Class, Nyerere always insisted, was alien to Africa; socialism indigenous.

I reviewed our situation for him, ending with an appeal for help. He was a shrewd, soft-spoken man who was well-disposed to our mission, but his perception of the situation surprised and dismayed me. He suggested we postpone the armed struggle until Sobukwe came out of prison. This was the first of many occasions when I learned of the PAC's appeal in the rest of Africa. I described the weakness of the PAC, and argued that a postponement would be a setback for the struggle as a whole. He suggested I seek the favor of Emperor Haile Selassie and promised to arrange an introduction.

I was meant to meet Oliver in Dar, but because of my delay he was unable to wait and left a message for me to follow him to Lagos, where he was to attend the Lagos Conference of Independent States. On the flight to Accra I ran into Hymie Basner and his wife. Basner, who had once been my employer, had been offered a position in Accra. His radical politics and left-wing activities in South Africa had made him persona non grata there and he was seeking political asylum in Ghana.

The plane stopped in Khartoum and we lined up to go through customs. Joe Matthews was first, then myself, followed by Basner and his wife. Because I did not have a passport, I carried with me a rudimentary document from Tanganyika that merely said, "This is Nelson Mandela, a citizen of the Republic of South Africa. He has permission to leave Tanganyika and return here." I handed this paper to the old Sudanese man behind the immigration counter and he looked up with a smile and said, "My son, welcome to the Sudan." He then shook my hand and stamped my document. Basner was behind me and handed the old man the same type of document. The old man looked at it for a moment, and then said in a rather agitated manner: "What is this? What is this piece of paper? It is not official!"

Basner calmly explained it was a document he had been given in Tanganyika because he did not have a passport. "Not have a passport?" the immigration official said with disdain. "How can you not have a passport — you are a white man!" Basner replied that he was persecuted in his own country because he fought for the rights of blacks. The Sudanese looked skeptical: "But you are a white man!" Joe looked at me and knew what I was thinking: he whispered to me not to intervene, as we were guests in the Sudan and did not want to offend our host's hospitality. But apart from being my employer, Basner was one of those whites who had truly taken risks on the behalf of black emancipation, and I could not desert him. Instead of leaving with Joe, I remained and stood close to the official and every time Basner said something, I simply bowed and nodded to the official as if to verify what he was saying. The old man realized what I was doing, softened his manner, and finally stamped his document and said quietly, "Welcome to the Sudan."

I had not seen Oliver in nearly two years, and when he met me at the airport in Accra I barely recognized him. Once clean shaven and conservatively groomed, he now had a beard and longish hair and affected the military-style clothing characteristic of freedom fighters around the continent. (He probably had exactly the same reaction to me.) It was a happy reunion, and I complimented him on the tremendous work he had done abroad. He had already established ANC offices in Ghana, England, Egypt, and Tanganyika, and had made valuable contacts for us in many other countries. Everywhere I subsequently traveled, I discovered the positive impression Oliver had made on diplomats and statesmen. He was the best possible ambassador for the organization.

The goal of the Lagos Conference of Independent States was to unite all African states, but it eventually disintegrated into bickering about which states to include or exclude. I kept a low profile and avoided the conference, for we did not want the South African government to know that I was abroad until I appeared at the PAFMECSA conference in Addis.

On the plane from Accra to Addis, we found Gaur Radebe, Peter Molotsi, and other members of the PAC who were also on their way to PAF-MECSA. They were all surprised to see me, and we immediately plunged into discussions concerning South Africa. The atmosphere was enjoyable and relaxed. Though I had been dismayed to learn of Gaur's leaving the ANC, that did not diminish my pleasure in seeing him. High above the ground and far from home, we had much more that united us than separated us.

We put down briefly in Khartoum, where we changed to an Ethiopian Airways flight to Addis. Here I experienced a rather strange sensation. As I was boarding the plane I saw that the pilot was black. I had never seen a black pilot before, and the instant I did I had to quell my panic.

How could a black man fly an airplane? But a moment later I caught myself: I had fallen into the apartheid mind-set, thinking Africans were inferior and that flying was a white man's job. I sat back in my seat, and chided myself for such thoughts. Once we were in the air, I lost my nervousness and studied the geography of Ethiopia, thinking how guerrilla forces hid in these very forests to fight the Italian imperialists.

47

FORMERLY KNOWN as Abyssinia, Ethiopia, according to tradition, was founded long before the birth of Christ, supposedly by the son of Solomon and the queen of Sheba. Although it had been conquered dozens of times, Ethiopia was the birthplace of African nationalism. Unlike so many other African states, it had fought colonialism at every turn. Menelik had rebuffed the Italians in the last century, though Ethiopia failed to halt them in this one. In 1930, Haile Selassie became emperor and the shaping force of contemporary Ethiopian history. I was seventeen when Mussolini attacked Ethiopia, an invasion that spurred not only my hatred of that despot but of fascism in general. Although Selassie was forced to flee when the Italians conquered Ethiopia in 1936, he returned after Allied forces drove the Italians out in 1941.

Ethiopia has always held a special place in my own imagination and the prospect of visiting Ethiopia attracted me more strongly than a trip to France, England, and America combined. I felt I would be visiting my own genesis, unearthing the roots of what made me an African. Meeting the emperor himself would be like shaking hands with history.

Our first stop was Addis Ababa, the Imperial City, which did not live up to its title, for it was the opposite of grand, with only a few tarred streets, and more goats and sheep than cars. Apart from the Imperial Palace, the university, and the Ras Hotel, where we stayed, there were few structures that could compare with even the least impressive buildings of Johannesburg. Contemporary Ethiopia was not a model when it came to democracy, either. There were no political parties, no popular organs of government, no separation of powers; only the emperor, who was supreme.

Before the opening of the conference, the delegates assembled at the tiny town of Debra Zaid. A grandstand had been erected in the central square and Oliver and I sat off to the side, away from the main podium. Suddenly we heard the distant music of a lone bugle and then the strains of a brass band accompanied by the steady beating of African drums.

As the music came closer, I could hear — and feel — the rumbling of hundreds of marching feet. From behind a building at the edge of the square, an officer appeared brandishing a gleaming sword; at his heels marched five hundred black soldiers in rows four across, each carrying a polished rifle against his uniformed shoulder. When the troops had marched directly in front of the grandstand, an order rang out in Amharic, and the five hundred soldiers halted as one man, spun around, and executed a precise salute to an elderly man in a dazzling uniform, His Highness the Emperor of Ethiopia, Haile Selassie, the Lion of Judah.

Here, for the first time in my life, I was witnessing black soldiers commanded by black generals applauded by black leaders who were all guests of a black head of state. It was a heady moment. I only hoped it was a vision of what lay in the future for my own country.

On the morning after the parade, Oliver and I attended a meeting where each organization had to apply for accreditation. We were unpleasantly surprised to find that our application was blocked by a delegate from Uganda who complained that we were a tribal organization of Xhosas. My impulse was to dismiss this claim contemptuously, but Oliver's notion was that we should simply explain that our organization was formed to unite Africans and our membership was drawn from all sections of the people. This I did, adding that the president of our organization, Chief Luthuli, was a Zulu. Our application was accepted. I realized that many people on the continent only knew about the ANC from the PAC's description of us.

The conference was officially opened by our host, His Imperial Majesty, who was dressed in an elaborate brocaded army uniform. I was surprised by how small the emperor appeared, but his dignity and confidence made him seem like the African giant that he was. It was the first time I had witnessed a head of state go through the formalities of his office, and I was fascinated. He stood perfectly straight, and inclined his head only slightly to indicate that he was listening. Dignity was the hallmark of all his actions.

I was scheduled to speak after the emperor, the only other speaker that morning. For the first time in many months, I flung aside the identity of David Motsamayi and became Nelson Mandela. In my speech, I reviewed the history of the freedom struggle in South Africa and listed the brutal massacres that had been committed against our people, from Bulhoek in 1921, when the army and police killed one hundred eighty-three unarmed peasants, to Sharpeville forty years later. I thanked the assembled nations for exerting pressure on South Africa, citing in particular Ghana, Nigeria, and Tanganyika, who spearheaded the successful drive to oust South Africa from the British Commonwealth. I retraced the birth of Umkhonto we Sizwe, explaining that all opportunities for peaceful struggle had been closed to us. "A leadership commits a crime against its own people if it hesitates to sharpen its political weapons where they have become less effective. . . . On the night of 16 December last year, the whole of South Africa vibrated under the heavy blows of Umkhonto we Sizwe." I had no sooner said this than the chief minister of Uganda cried out: "Give it to them again!"

I then related my own experience:

I have just come out of South Africa, having for the last ten months lived in my own country as an outlaw, away from family and friends. When I was compelled to lead this sort of life, I made a public statement in which I announced that I would not leave the country but would continue working underground. I meant it and I will honor that undertaking.

The announcement that I would return to South Africa was met with loud cheers. We had been encouraged to speak first so PAFMECSA could evaluate our cause and decide how much support to give it. There was a natural reluctance among many African states to support violent struggles elsewhere; but the speech convinced people that freedom fighters in South Africa had no alternative but to take up arms.

Oliver and I had a private discussion with Kenneth Kaunda, the leader of the United National Independence Party of Northern Rhodesia and the future president of Zambia. Like Julius Nyerere, Kaunda was worried about the lack of unity among South African freedom fighters and suggested that when Sobukwe emerged from jail, we might all join forces. Among Africans, the PAC had captured the spotlight at Sharpeville in a way that far exceeded their influence as an organization. Kaunda, who had once been a member of the ANC, told us he was concerned about our alliance with white Communists and indicated that this reflected poorly on us in Africa. Communism was suspect not only in the West but in Africa. This came as something of a revelation to me, and it was a view that I was to hear over and over during my trip.

When I attempted to make the case that UNIP's support of the PAC was misguided, Kaunda put his hand on my shoulder and said, "Nelson, speaking to me on this subject is like carrying coals to Newcastle. I am your supporter and a follower of Chief Luthuli. But I am not the sole voice of UNIP. You must speak to Simon Kapwepwe. If you persuade him you will make my job easier." Kapwepwe was the second in command of UNIP, and I made arrangements to see him the following day. I asked Oliver to join me but he said, "Nel, you must see him on your own. Then you can be completely frank."

I spent the entire day with Kapwepwe and heard from him the most astonishing tale. "We were mightily impressed by your speech," he said, "and indeed by your entire ANC delegation. If we were to judge your organization by these two things, we would certainly be in your camp. But we have heard disturbing reports from the PAC to the effect that Umkhonto we Sizwe is the brainchild of the Communist Party and the Liberal Party, and that the idea of the organization is merely to use Africans as cannon fodder."

I was nonplussed, and I blurted out that I was astounded that he could not see himself how damnably false this story was. "First of all," I said, "it is well known that the Liberal Party and the Communist Party are archenemies and could not come together to form a game of cards. Second, I am here to tell you at the risk of immodesty that I myself was the prime mover behind MK's formation." Finally, I said I was greatly disappointed in the PAC for spreading such lies.

By the end of the day, I had converted Kapwepwe, and he said he would call a meeting and make our case himself — and he did so. But it was another example of both the lack of knowledge about South Africa in the rest of Africa and the extraordinary lengths the PAC would go to besmirch the ANC. Kapwepwe bade me good luck, for the conference was now over. It had been successful, but we had our work cut out for us.

As a student, I had fantasized about visiting Egypt, the cradle of African civilization, the treasure chest of so much beauty in art and design, about seeing the pyramids and the sphinx, and crossing the Nile, the greatest of African rivers. From Addis, Oliver, Robert Resha — who was to accompany me on the rest of my travels — and I flew to Cairo. I spent the whole morning of my first day in Cairo at the museum, looking at art, examining artifacts, making notes, learning about the type of men who founded the ancient civilization of the Nile Valley. This was not amateur archaeological interest; it is important for African nationalists to be armed with evidence to dispute the fictitious claims of whites that Africans are without a civilized past that compares with that of the West. In a single morning, I discovered that Egyptians were creating great works of art and architecture when whites were still living in caves.

Egypt was an important model for us, for we could witness firsthand the program of socialist economic reforms being launched by President Nasser. He had reduced private ownership of land, nationalized certain sectors of the economy, pioneered rapid industrialization, democratized education, and built a modern army. Many of these reforms were precisely the sort of things that we in the ANC someday hoped to enact. At that time, however, it was more important to us that Egypt was the only African state with an army, navy, and air force that could in any way compare with those of South Africa.

After a day, Oliver left for London, promising to join Robbie and me in Ghana. Before Robbie and I left on our tour, we discussed the presentation we would make in each country. My inclination was to explain the political situation as truthfully and objectively as possible and not omit the accomplishments of the PAC. In each new country, I would initially seal myself away in our hotel familiarizing myself with information about the country's policies, history, and leadership. Robbie did the opposite. A natural extrovert, he would leave the hotel as soon as we arrived and hit the streets, learning by seeing and talking to people. We were an odd couple, for I affected the informal dress I had gotten used to underground and wore khakis and fatigues, while Robbie was always smartly turned out in a suit.

In Tunis, our first stop, we met with the minister of defense, who bore a striking resemblance to Chief Luthuli. But I'm afraid that is where the similarity ended, for when I was explaining to him the situation in our country with PAC leaders such as Robert Sobukwe in jail, he interrupted me and said, "When that chap returns, he will finish you!" Robbie raised his eyebrows at this (later he said, "Man, you were putting the case for the PAC better than they could!"), but I insisted on giving the minister the full picture. When we met the following day with President Habib Bourguiba, his response was utterly positive and immediate: he offered training for our soldiers and five thousand pounds for weapons.

Rabat in Morocco, our next stop, with its ancient and mysterious walls, its fashionable shops, and its medieval mosques, seemed a charming mixture of Africa, Europe, and the Middle East. Apparently freedom fighters thought so as well, for Rabat was the crossroads of virtually every liberation movement on the continent. While there, we met with freedom fighters from Mozambique, Angola, Algeria, and Cape Verde. It was also the headquarters of the Algerian revolutionary army, and we spent several days with Dr. Mustafa, head of the Algerian mission in Morocco, who briefed us on the history of the Algerian resistance to the French.

The situation in Algeria was the closest model to our own in that the rebels faced a large white settler community that ruled the indigenous majority. He related how the FLN had begun their struggle with a handful of guerrilla attacks in 1954, having been heartened by the defeat of the French at Dien Bien Phu in Vietnam. At first, the FLN believed they could defeat the French militarily, Dr. Mustafa said, then realized that a pure military victory was impossible.

Instead, they resorted to guerrilla warfare. Guerrilla warfare, he explained, was not designed to win a military victory so much as to unleash political and economic forces that would bring down the enemy. Dr. Mustafa counseled us not to neglect the political side of war while planning the military effort. International public opinion, he said, is sometimes worth more than a fleet of jet fighters.

At the end of three days, he sent us to Oujda, a dusty little town right across the border from Algeria and the headquarters of the Algerian army in Morocco. We visited an army unit at the front, and at one point I took a pair of field glasses and could actually see French troops across the border. I confess I imagined that I was looking at the uniforms of the South African Defense Force.

A day or two later I was a guest at a military parade in honor of Ahmed Ben Bella, who was to become the first prime minister of independent Algeria and who had recently emerged from a French prison. A far cry from the military parade I had witnessed in Addis Ababa, this parade was not the crisp, well-drilled, handsomely uniformed force of Ethiopia but a kind of walking history of the guerrilla movement in Algeria.

At its head sauntered proud, battle-hardened veterans in turbans, long tunics, and sandals, who had started the struggle many years before. They carried the weapons they had used: sabers, old flintlock rifles, battle-axes, and assegais. They were followed in turn by younger soldiers, all carrying modern arms and equally proud. Some held heavy antitank and anti-aircraft guns. But even these soldiers did not march with the smartness and precision of the Ethiopians. This was a guerrilla force, and they were soldiers who had won their stripes in the fire of battle, who cared more about fighting and tactics than dress uniforms and parades. As inspired as I was by the troops in Addis, I knew that our own force would be more like these troops here in Oujda, and I could only hope they would fight as valiantly.

At the rear was a rather ragtag military band that was led by a man called Sudani. Tall, well built, and confident, he was as black as the night. He was swinging a ceremonial mace, and when we saw him, our whole party stood up and started clapping and cheering. I looked around and noticed others staring at us, and I realized that we were only cheering because this fellow was a black man and black faces were quite rare in Morocco. Once again I was struck by the great power of nationalism and ethnicity. We reacted instantly, for we felt as though we were seeing a brother African. Later, our hosts informed us that Sudani had been a legendary soldier, and had even reputedly captured an entire French unit single-handedly. But we were cheering him because of his color, not his exploits.

From Morocco, I flew across the Sahara to Bamako, the capital of Mali, and then on to Guinea. The flight from Mali to Guinea was more like a local bus than an airplane. Chickens wandered the aisles; women walked back and forth carrying packages on their heads and selling bags of peanuts and dried vegetables. It was flying democratic-style and I admired it very much.

My next stop was Sierra Leone, and when I arrived, I discovered that Parliament was in session and decided to attend the proceedings. I entered as any tourist would and was given a seat not far from the Speaker. The clerk of the House approached me and asked me to identify myself. I whispered to him, "I am the representative of Chief Luthuli of South Africa." He shook my hand warmly and proceeded to report to the Speaker. The clerk then explained that I had inadvertently been given a seat not normally allowed to visitors, but in this case it was an honor for them to make an exception.

Within an hour there was an adjournment, and as I stood among the members and dignitaries drinking tea, a queue formed in front of me and I saw to my amazement that the entire Parliament had lined up to shake hands with me. I was very gratified, until the third or fourth person in line mumbled something to the effect of, "It is a great honor to shake the hand of the revered Chief Luthuli, winner of the Nobel Peace Prize." I was an impostor! The clerk had misunderstood. The prime minister, Sir Milton Margai, was then brought over to meet me, and the clerk introduced me as the chief. I immediately attempted to inform the clerk that I was not Chief Luthuli, but the fellow would have none of it, and I decided that in the interests of hospitality I would continue the charade. I later met with the president, explained the case of mistaken identity, and he offered generous material assistance.

In Liberia, I met with President Tubman, who not only gave me five thousand dollars for weapons and training, but said in a quiet voice, "Have you any pocket money?" I confessed that I was a bit low, and instantly an aide came back with an envelope containing four hundred dollars in cash. From Liberia, I went to Ghana, where I was met by Oliver and entertained by Guinea's resident minister, Abdoulaye Diallo. When I told him that I had not seen Sékou Touré when I was in Guinea, he arranged for us to return immediately to that arid land. Oliver and I were impressed with Touré. He lived in a modest bungalow, and wore an old faded suit that could have used a visit to the dry cleaners. We made our case to him, explained the history of the ANC and MK, and asked for five thousand dollars for the support of MK. He listened very carefully, and replied in a rather formal way. "The government and the people of Guinea," he said, as though giving a speech, "fully support the struggle of our brothers in South Africa, and we have made statements at the U.N. to that effect." He went to the bookcase where he removed two books of his, which he autographed to Oliver and me. He then said thank you, and we were dismissed.

Oliver and I were annoyed: we had been called back from another country, and all he gave us were signed copies of his book? We had wasted our time. A short while later, we were in our hotel room, when an official from the Foreign Affairs Department knocked on our door and presented us with a suitcase. We opened it and it was filled with banknotes; Oliver and I looked at each other in glee. But then Oliver's expression changed. "Nelson, this is Guinean currency," he said. "It is worthless outside of here; it is just paper." But Oliver had an idea: we took the money to the Czech embassy, where he had a friend who exchanged it for a convertible currency.

The gracefulness of the slender fishing boats that glided into the harbor in Dakar was equaled only by the elegance of the Senegalese women who sailed through the city in flowing robes and turbaned heads. I wandered through the nearby marketplace, intoxicated by the exotic spices and perfumes. The Senegalese are a handsome people and I enjoyed the brief time that Oliver and I spent in their country. Their society showed how disparate elements — French, Islamic, and African — can mingle to create a unique and distinctive culture.

On our way to a meeting with President Leopold Senghor, Oliver suffered a severe attack of asthma. He refused to return to the hotel, and I carried him on my back up the stairs to the president's office. Senghor was greatly concerned by Oliver's condition and insisted that he be attended to by his personal physician.

I had been told to be wary of Senghor, for there were reports that Senegalese soldiers were serving with the French in Algeria, and that President Senghor was a bit too taken with the customs and charms of the ancien régime. There will always be, in emerging nations, an enduring attraction to the ways of the colonizer — I myself was not immune to it. President Senghor was a scholar and a poet, and he told us he was collecting research material on Shaka, flattering us by asking numerous questions about that great South African warrior. We summarized the situation in South Africa and made our request for military training and money. Senghor replied that his hands were tied until Parliament met.

In the meantime, he wanted us to talk with the minister of justice, a Mr. Daboussier, about military training, and the president introduced me to a beautiful white French girl who, he explained, would interpret for me in my meeting with him. I said nothing, but was disturbed. I did not feel comfortable discussing the very sensitive issues of military training in front of a young woman I did not know and was not sure I could trust. Senghor sensed my uneasiness, for he said, "Mandela, do not worry, the French here identify themselves completely with our African aspirations."

When we reached the minister's office, we found some African secretaries in the reception area. One of the black secretaries asked the French woman what she was doing here. She said she had been sent by the president to interpret. An argument ensued and in the middle of it, one of the African secretaries turned to me and said, "Sir, can you speak English?" I said I could, and she replied, "The minister speaks English and you can talk with him directly. You don't need an interpreter." The French girl, now quite miffed, stood aside as I went in to speak to the minister, who promised to fulfill our requests. In the end, although Senghor did not then provide us with what we asked for, he furnished me with a diplomatic passport and paid for our plane fares from Dakar to our next destination: London.

48

I CONFESS TO being something of an Anglophile. When I thought of Western democracy and freedom, I thought of the British parliamentary system. In so many ways, the very model of the gentleman for me was an Englishman. Despite Britain being the home of parliamentary democracy, it was that democracy that had helped inflict a pernicious system of iniquity on my people. While I abhorred the notion of British imperialism, I never rejected the trappings of British style and manners.

I had several reasons for wanting to go to England, apart from my desire to see the country I had so long read and heard about. I was concerned about Oliver's health and wanted to persuade him to receive treatment. I very much wanted to see Adelaide, his wife, and their children, as well as Yusuf Dadoo, who was now living there and representing the Congress movement. I also knew that in London I would be able to obtain literature on guerrilla warfare that I had been unable to acquire elsewhere.

I resumed my old underground ways in London, not wanting word to leak back to South Africa that I was there. The tentacles of South African security forces reached all the way to London. But I was not a recluse; my ten days there were divided among ANC business, seeing old friends, and occasional jaunts as a conventional tourist. With Mary Benson, a British friend who had written about our struggle, Oliver and I saw the sights of the city that had once commanded nearly two-thirds of the globe: Westminster Abbey, Big Ben, the Houses of Parliament. While I gloried in the beauty of these buildings, I was ambivalent about what they represented. When we saw the statue of General Smuts near Westminster Abbey, Oliver and I joked that perhaps someday there would be a statue of us in its stead.

I had been informed by numerous people that the *Observer* newspaper, run by David Astor, had been tilting toward the PAC in its coverage, editorializing that the ANC was the party of the past. Oliver arranged for me to meet Astor at his house, and we talked at length about the ANC. I do not know if I had an effect on him, but the coverage certainly changed. He also recommended that I talk to a number of prominent politicians, and in the company of Labour MP Denis Healey, I met with Hugh Gaitskell, the leader of the Labour Party, and Jo Grimond, the leader of the Liberal Party.

It was only toward the end of my stay that I saw Yusuf, but it was not a happy reunion. Oliver and I had encountered a recurring difficulty in our travels: one African leader after another had questioned us about our relations with white and Indian communists, sometimes suggesting that they controlled the ANC. Our nonracialism would have been less of a problem had it not been for the formation of the explicitly nationalistic and antiwhite PAC. In the rest of Africa, most African leaders could understand the views of the PAC better than those of the ANC. Oliver had discussed these things with Yusuf, who was unhappy about Oliver's conclusions. Oliver had resolved that the ANC had to appear more independent, taking certain actions unilaterally without the involvement of the other members of the alliance, and I agreed.

I spent my last night in London discussing these issues with Yusuf. I explained that now that we were embarking on an armed struggle we would be relying on other African nations for money, training, and support, and therefore had to take their views into account more than we did in the past. Yusuf believed that Oliver and I were changing ANC policy, that we were preparing to depart from the nonracialism that was the core of the Freedom Charter. I told him he was mistaken; we were not rejecting nonracialism, we were simply saying the ANC must stand more on its own and make statements that were not part of the Congress Alliance. Often, the ANC, the South African Indian Congress, and the Coloured People's Congress would make a collective statement on an issue affecting only Africans. That would have to change. Yusuf was unhappy about this. "What about policy?" he kept asking. I told him I was not talking about policy, I was talking about image. We would still work together, only the ANC had to appear to be the first among equals.

*   *   *

Although I was sad to leave my friends in London, I was now embarking on what was to be the most unfamiliar part of my trip: military training. I had arranged to receive six months of training in Addis Ababa. I was met there by Foreign Minister Yefu, who warmly greeted me and took me to a suburb called Kolfe, the headquarters of the Ethiopian Riot Battalion, where I was to learn the art and science of soldiering. While I was a fair amateur boxer, I had very little knowledge of even the rudiments of combat. My trainer was a Lieutenant Wondoni Befikadu, an experienced soldier, who had fought with the underground against the Italians. Our program was strenuous: we trained from 8 A.M. until 1 P.M., broke for a shower and lunch, and then again from 2 P.M. to 4 P.M. From 4 P.M. into the evening, I was lectured on military science by Colonel Tadesse, who was also assistant commissioner of police and had been instrumental in foiling a recent coup attempt against the emperor.

I learned how to shoot an automatic rifle and a pistol and took target practice both in Kolfe with the Emperor's Guard, and at a shooting range about fifty miles away with the entire battalion. I was taught about demolition and mortar-firing and I learned how to make small bombs and mines — and how to avoid them. I felt myself being molded into a soldier and began to think as a soldier thinks — a far cry from the way a politician thinks.

What I enjoyed most were the "fatigue marches" in which you are equipped with only a gun, bullets, and some water, and you must reach a distant point within a certain time. During these marches I got a sense of the landscape, which was very beautiful, with dense forests and spare highlands. The country was extremely backward: people used wooden plows and lived on a very simple diet supplemented by home-brewed beer. Their existence was similar to the life in rural South Africa; poor people everywhere are more alike than they are different.

In my study sessions, Colonel Tadesse discussed matters such as how to create a guerrilla force, how to command an army, and how to enforce discipline. One evening, during supper, Colonel Tadesse said to me, "Now, Mandela, you are creating a liberation army not a conventional capitalist army. A liberation army is an egalitarian army. You must treat your men entirely differently than you would in a capitalist army. When you are on duty, you must exercise your authority with assurance and control. That is no different from a capitalist command. But when you are off duty, you must conduct yourself on the basis of perfect equality, even with the lowliest soldier. You must eat what they eat; you must not take your food in your office, but eat with them, drink with them, not isolate yourself."

All of this seemed admirable and sensible, but while he was talking to me, a sergeant came into the hall and asked the colonel where he could find a certain lieutenant. The colonel regarded him with ill-concealed contempt and said, "Can't you see that I am talking to an important individual here? Don't you know not to interrupt me when I am eating? Now, get out of my sight!" Then he continued with his discussion in the same didactic tone as before.

The training course was meant to be six months, but after eight weeks I received a telegram from the ANC urgently requesting that I return home. The internal armed struggle was escalating and they wanted the commander of MK on the scene.

Colonel Tadesse rapidly arranged for me to take an Ethiopian flight to Khartoum. Before I left, he presented me with a gift: an automatic pistol and two hundred rounds of ammunition. I was grateful, both for the gun and his instruction. Despite my fatigue marches, I found it wearying to carry around all that ammunition. A single bullet is surprisingly heavy: hauling around two hundred is like carrying a small child on one's back.

In Khartoum, I was met by a British Airways official who told me that my connecting flight to Dar es Salaam would not leave until the following day and they had taken the liberty of booking me into a posh hotel in town. I was dismayed, for I would have preferred to stay in a less conspicuous third-class hotel.

When I was dropped off, I had to walk across the hotel's long and elegant veranda, where several dozen whites were sitting and drinking. This was long before metal detectors and security checks, and I was carrying my pistol in a holster inside my jacket and the two hundred rounds wrapped around my waist inside my trousers. I also had several thousand pounds in cash. I had the feeling that all of these well-dressed whites had X-ray vision and that I was going to be arrested at any moment. But I was escorted safely to my room, where I ordered room service; even the footsteps of the waiters put me on edge.

From Khartoum I went directly to Dar es Salaam, where I greeted the first group of twenty-one Umkhonto recruits who were headed to Ethiopia to train as soldiers. It was a proud moment, for these men had volunteered for duty in an army I was then attempting to create. They were risking their lives in a battle that was only just beginning, a battle that would be most dangerous for those who were its first soldiers. They were young men, mainly from the cities, and they were proud and eager. We had a dinner in Addis: the men slaughtered a goat in my honor, and I addressed them about my trip and told them of the necessity of good behavior and discipline abroad, because they were representatives of the South African freedom struggle. Military training, I said, must go hand in hand with political training, for a revolution is not just a question of pulling a trigger; its purpose is to create a fair and just society. It was the first time that I was ever saluted by my own soldiers.

President Nyerere gave me a private plane to Mbeya, and I then flew directly to Lobatse. The pilot informed me that we would be landing in Kanye. This concerned me: why was the plan altered? In Kanye, I was met by the local magistrate and a security man, both of whom were white. The magistrate approached me and asked me my name. David Motsamayi, I replied. No, he said, please tell me your real name. Again, I said David Motsamayi. The magistrate said, "Please tell me your real name because I was given instructions to meet Mr. Mandela here and provide him with help and transportation. If you are not Mr. Nelson Mandela, I am afraid I will have to arrest you for you have no permit to enter the country. Are you Nelson Mandela?"

This was a quandary; I might be arrested either way. "If you insist that I am Nelson Mandela and not David Motsamayi," I said, "I will not challenge you." He smiled and said simply, "We expected you yesterday." He then offered me a lift to where my comrades would be waiting for me. We drove to Lobatse, where I met Joe Modise and an ANC supporter named Jonas Matlou, who was then living there. The magistrate told me that the South African police were aware that I was returning, and he suggested that I leave tomorrow. I thanked him for his help and advice, but when I arrived at Matlou's house, I said that I would leave tonight. I was to drive back to South Africa with Cecil Williams, a white theater director and member of MK. Posing as his chauffeur, I got behind the wheel and we left that night for Johannesburg.

Part Seven

———

RIVONIA

49

AFTER CROSSING THE BORDER, I breathed in deeply. The air of one's home always smells sweet after one has been away. It was a clear winter night and somehow even the stars looked more welcoming here than from elsewhere on the continent. Though I was leaving a world where I experienced freedom for the first time and returning to one where I was a fugitive, I was profoundly relieved to be back in the land of my birth and destiny.

Between Bechuanaland and the northwestern Transvaal, dozens of unmarked roads transverse the border, and Cecil knew just which ones to take. During the drive, he filled me in on many of the events I had missed. We drove all night, slipping across the border just after midnight and reaching Liliesleaf Farm at dawn. I was still wearing my beat-up khaki training uniform.

Once at the farm, I did not have time for rest and reflection because the following night we held a secret meeting for me to brief the Working Committee on my trip. Walter, Moses Kotane, Govan Mbeki, Dan Tloome, J. B. Marks, and Duma Nokwe all arrived at the farm, a rare reunion. I first gave a general overview of my travels, itemizing the money we had received and the offers of training. At the same time, I reported in detail the reservations I had encountered about the ANC's cooperation with whites, Indians, particularly Communists. Still ringing in my ears was my final meeting with the Zambian leaders who told me that while they knew the ANC was stronger and more popular than the PAC, they understood the PAC's pure African nationalism but were bewildered by the ANC's nonracialism and Communist ties. I informed them that Oliver and I believed the ANC had to appear more independent to reassure our new allies on the continent, for they were the ones who would be financing and training Umkhonto we Sizwe. I proposed reshaping the Congress Alliance so that the ANC would clearly be seen as the leader, especially on issues directly affecting Africans.

This was a serious proposition, and the entire leadership had to be consulted. The Working Committee urged me to go down to Durban and brief the chief. All agreed except Govan Mbeki, who was not then living at Liliesleaf Farm but was present as part of the High Command of MK. He urged me to send someone else. It was simply too risky, he said, and the organization should not jeopardize my safety, especially as

I was newly returned and ready to push ahead with MK. This wise advice was overruled by everyone, including myself.

I left the next night from Rivonia in the company of Cecil, again, posing as his chauffeur. I had planned a series of secret meetings in Durban, the first of which was with Monty Naicker and Ismail Meer to brief them about my trip and to discuss the new proposal. Monty and Ismail were extremely close to the chief, and the chief trusted their views. I wanted to be able to tell Luthuli I had spoken to his friends and convey their reaction. Ismail and Monty, however, were disturbed by my belief that the ANC needed to take the lead among the Congress Alliance and make statements on its own concerning affairs that affected Africans. They were against anything that unraveled the alliance.

I was taken to Groutville, where the chief lived, and we met in the house of an Indian lady in town. I explained the situation to the chief at some length, and he listened without speaking. When I was done, he said he did not like the idea of foreign politicians dictating policy to the ANC. He said we had evolved the policy of nonracialism for good reasons and he did not think that we should alter our policy because it did not suit a few foreign leaders.

I told the chief that these foreign politicians were not dictating our policy, but merely saying that they did not understand it. My plan, I told him, was simply to effect essentially cosmetic changes in order to make the ANC more intelligible — and more palatable — to our allies. I saw this as a defensive maneuver, for if African states decided to support the PAC, a small and weak organization could suddenly become a large and potent one.

The chief did not make decisions on the spur of the moment. I could see he wanted to think about what I had said and talk to some of his friends about it. I said farewell, and he advised me to be careful. I still had a number of clandestine meetings in the city and townships that evening. My last meeting that evening was with the MK Regional Command in Durban.

The Durban Command was led by a sabotage expert named Bruno Mtolo, whom I had never met before, but would meet again under dramatically different circumstances. I briefed them on my trip to Africa, about the support we had received and the offers of training. I explained that for the moment MK was limited to sabotage, but that if sabotage did not have the desired effect we would probably move on to guerrilla warfare.

Later that same evening, at the home of the photojournalist G. R. Naidoo, where I was staying, I was joined by Ismail and Fatima Meer,

Monty Naicker, and J. N. Singh for what was a combination welcome-home party and going-away party, for I was leaving the next day for Johannesburg. It was a pleasant evening and my first night of relaxation in a long while. I slept well and I met Cecil on Sunday afternoon — the fifth of August — for the long drive back to Johannesburg in his trusty Austin.

I wore my chauffeur's white dust-coat and sat next to Cecil as he drove. We often took turns spelling each other behind the wheel. It was a clear, cool day and I reveled in the beauty of the Natal countryside; even in winter, Natal remains green. Now that I was returning to Johannesburg I would have some time to see Winnie and the children. I had often wished that Winnie could share with me the wonders of Africa, but the best I could do was to tell her what I had seen and done.

Once we left the industrial precincts of Durban, we moved through hills that offered majestic views of the surrounding valleys and the blue-black waters of the Indian Ocean. Durban is the principal port for the country's main industrial area, and the highway that leads to Johannesburg runs parallel to the railway line for a great distance. I went from contemplating the natural beauty to ruminating on the fact that the railway line, being so close to the highway, offered a convenient place for sabotage. I made a note of this in the small notebook I always carried with me.

Cecil and I were engrossed in discussions of sabotage plans as we passed through Howick, twenty miles northwest of Pietermaritzburg. At Cedara, a small town just past Howick, I noticed a Ford V-8 filled with white men shoot past us on the right. I instinctively turned round to look behind and I saw two more cars filled with white men. Suddenly, in front of us, the Ford was signaling us to stop. I knew in that instant that my life on the run was over; my seventeen months of "freedom" were about to end.

As Cecil slowed down he turned to me and said, "Who are these men?" I did not answer because we both knew full well who they were. They had chosen their hiding-spot well; to the left of us was a steep wooded bank they could have forced us into had we tried to elude them. I was in the left-hand passenger seat, and for a moment I thought about jumping out and making an escape into the woods, but I would have been shot in a matter of seconds.

When our car stopped, a tall slender man with a stern expression on his face came directly over to the window on the passenger side. He was unshaven and it appeared that he had not slept in quite a while. I immediately assumed he had been waiting for us for several days. In a calm voice, he introduced himself as Sergeant Vorster of the Pietermaritzburg police and produced an arrest warrant. He asked me to identify myself.

I told him my name was David Motsamayi. He nodded, and then, in a very proper way, he asked me a few questions about where I had been and where I was going. I parried these questions without giving him much information. He seemed a bit irritated and then, he said, "Ag, you're Nelson Mandela, and this is Cecil Williams, and you are under arrest!"

He informed us that a police major from the other car would accompany us back to Pietermaritzburg. The police were not yet so vigilant in those days, and Sergeant Vorster did not bother searching me. I had my loaded revolver with me, and again, I thought of escape, but I would have been greatly outnumbered. I secretly put the revolver — and my notebook — in the upholstery between my seat and Cecil's. For some reason, the police never found the gun or the small notebook, which was fortunate, for many more people would have been arrested if they had.

At the police station I was led into Sergeant Vorster's office, where I saw a number of officers, one of whom was Warrant Officer Truter, who had testified in the Treason Trial. Truter had made a favorable impression on the accused because he had accurately explained the policy of the ANC, and had not exaggerated or lied. We greeted each other in a friendly way.

I had still not admitted to anything other than the name David Motsamayi, and Truter said to me, "Nelson, why do you keep up this farce? You know I know who you are. We all know who you are." I told him simply that I had given a name and that is the name I was standing by. I asked for a lawyer and was curtly refused. I then declined to make a statement.

Cecil and I were locked in separate cells. I now had time to ruminate on my situation. I had always known that arrest was a possibility, but even freedom fighters practice denial, and in my cell that night I realized I was not prepared for the reality of capture and confinement. I was upset and agitated. Someone had tipped off the police about my whereabouts; they had known I was in Durban and that I would be returning to Johannesburg. For weeks before my return the police believed that I was already back in the country. In June, newspaper headlines blared "RETURN OF THE BLACK PIMPERNEL" while I was still in Addis Ababa. Perhaps that had been a bluff?

The authorities had been harassing Winnie in the belief that she would know whether or not I was back. I knew that they had followed her and searched the house on a number of occasions. I guessed they had figured I would visit Chief Lutuli directly upon my return, and they were correct. But I also suspected they had information that I was in Durban at that time. The movement had been infiltrated with informers, and even well-intentioned people were generally not as tight-lipped as they should have been. I had also been lax. Too many people had known I was in Durban. I had even had a party the night before I left, and I chastised myself for letting down my guard. My mind ricocheted among the possibilities. Was it an informer in Durban? Someone from Johannesburg? Someone from the movement? Or even a friend or member of the family? But such speculation about unknowns is futile, and with the combination of mental and physical exhaustion, I soon fell deeply asleep. At least on this night — August 5, 1962 — I did not have to worry about whether the police would find me. They already had.

In the morning, I felt restored and I braced myself for the new ordeal that lay ahead of me. I would not, under any circumstances, seem despairing or even disappointed to my captors. At 8:30 I appeared before the local magistrate and was formally remanded to Johannesburg. It was low-key, and the magistrate seemed no more concerned than if he were handling a traffic summons. The police had not taken elaborate precautions for the trip back to Johannesburg or for my security, and I merely sat in the backseat of a sedan, un-handcuffed, with two officers riding in front. My arrest had been discovered by my friends; Fatima Meer brought some food to the jail for me and I shared it with the two officers in the car. We even stopped at Volksrust, a town along the way, and they allowed me to take a brief walk to stretch my legs. I did not contemplate escape when people were kind to me; I did not want to take advantage of the trust they placed in me.

But as we approached Johannesburg, the atmosphere changed. I heard an announcement over the police radio of my capture and the order to fold up the roadblocks to and from Natal. At sunset, on the outskirts of Johannesburg, we were met by a sizable police escort. I was abruptly handcuffed, taken from the car, and placed in a sealed police van with small opaque windows reinforced with wire netting. The motorcade then took a circuitous and unfamiliar route to Marshall Square as if they were concerned we might be ambushed.

I was locked in a cell by myself. In the quiet of the cell I was planning my strategy for the next day, when I heard a cough from a nearby cell. I did not realize a prisoner was close by, but more than that, there was something about this cough, something that struck me as curiously familiar. I sat up in sudden recognition and called out, "Walter?"

"Nelson, is that you?" he said, and we laughed with an indescribable mixture of relief, surprise, disappointment, and happiness. Walter, I learned, had been arrested shortly after my own arrest. We did not think that the arrests were unrelated. While this was not the most auspicious place for a meeting of the National Working Committee, it was certainly convenient and the night sped by as I gave him a full account of my arrest, as well as my meetings in Durban.

The next day I appeared in court before a senior magistrate for formal remand. Harold Wolpe and Joe Slovo had come to court after hearing of my arrest, and we conferred in the basement. I had appeared before this magistrate on numerous occasions in my professional capacity and we had grown to respect one another. A number of attorneys were also present, some of whom I knew quite well. It is curious how one can be easily flattered in certain situations by otherwise insignificant incidents. I am by no means immune to flattery in normal circumstances, but there I was, a fugitive, number one on the state's Most Wanted list, a hand-cuffed outlaw who had been underground for more than a year, and yet the judge, the other attorneys, and the spectators all greeted me with deference and professional courtesy. They knew me as Nelson Mandela attorney-at-law, not Nelson Mandela, outlaw. It lifted my spirits immensely.

During the proceedings, the magistrate was diffident and uneasy, and would not look at me directly. The other attorneys also seemed embarrassed, and at that moment, I had something of a revelation. These men were not only uncomfortable because I was a colleague brought low, but because I was an ordinary man being punished for his beliefs. In a way I had never quite comprehended before, I realized the role I could play in court and the possibilities before me as a defendant. I was the symbol of justice in the court of the oppressor, the representative of the great ideals of freedom, fairness, and democracy in a society that dishonored those virtues. I realized then and there that I could carry on the fight even within the fortress of the enemy.

When I was asked the name of my counsel, I announced that I would represent myself, with Joe Slovo as legal adviser. By representing myself I would enhance the symbolism of my role. I would use my trial as a showcase for the ANC's moral opposition to racism. I would not attempt to defend myself so much as put the state itself on trial. That day, I answered only the questions as to my name and choice of counsel. I listened silently to the charges: inciting African workers to strike and leaving the country without valid travel documents. In apartheid South Africa, the penalties for these "crimes" could be as much as ten years in prison. Yet the charges were something of a relief: the state clearly did not have enough evidence to link me with Umkhonto we Sizwe or ı would have been charged with the far more serious crimes of treason or sabotage.

Only as I was leaving the courtroom, did I see Winnie in the spectators'

Sparring with Jerry
Moloi at his gym
in Orlando. *(Bob
Gosani/Bailey's)*

With Ruth First outside the court. *(Peter Magubane)*

Opposite, above: After the second trial I went underground, becoming known for a time as "the black pimpernel." (*photographer unknown*)

A triumphant moment with Moses Kotane outside the court; we had just learned that the Crown was withdrawing its indictment. But the victory was to be short-lived: three months later, in 1959, twenty-nine of us found ourselves on trial once again. *(Jurgen Schadeberg)*

Opposite, below: Oliver Tambo and Robert Resha at the Dar es Salaam airport after the banning of the ANC, 1962. *(Associated Press)*

In hiding after my return from abroad, 1962. *(Eli Weinberg/ Camera Press Ltd.)*

At work sewing clothes in prison in Pretoria, before being sent to Robben Island. *(Archive Photos)*

The books I kept in my cell during my years on Robben Island. *(Archive Photos)*

Opposite, above: With Walter in the prison yard, 1966. *(Archive Photos)*

Opposite, below: The prison yard at Robben Island. *(Archive Photos)*

Opposite:
Walter and I had
been imprisoned
together on Robben
Island for nearly two
decades; in the
Bishop's Court
Gardens Residence of
Archbishop Tutu in
Capetown, we gave
the *"Afrika"* salute
and prepared to take
up the battle on the
outside once again.
*(Gideon Mendel/
Magnum)*

Freedom. February
1990. *(Gideon Mendel,
Magnum)*

At home in Orlando.
(Peter Magubane)

Above, left:
A private exchange
between old
comrades. *(Peter
Magubane)*

Above:
In December of 1990
Oliver Tambo
returned home to
South Africa after
more than thirty
years in exile.
(Associated Press)

Left:
Oliver's welcome
home rally in
Johannesburg.
(Associated Press)

gallery. She looked distressed and gloomy; she was undoubtedly considering the difficult months and years ahead, of life on her own, raising two small children, in an often hard and forbidding city. It is one thing to be told of possible hardships ahead, it is entirely another to actually have to confront them. All I could do, as I descended the steps to the basement, was to give her a wide smile, as if to show her that I was not worried and that she should not be either. I cannot imagine that it helped very much.

From the court, I was taken to the Johannesburg Fort. When I emerged from the courthouse to enter the sealed van, there was a crowd of hundreds of people cheering and shouting *"Amandla!"* followed by *"Ngawethu,"* a popular ANC call-and-response meaning "Power!" and "The power is ours!" People yelled and sang and pounded their fists on the sides of the van as the vehicle crawled out of the courthouse exit. My capture and case had made headlines in every paper: "POLICE SWOOP ENDS TWO YEARS ON THE RUN" was one; "NELSON MANDELA UNDER ARREST" was another. The so-called Black Pimpernel was no longer at large.

A few days later Winnie was granted permission to visit me. She had gotten dressed up and now, at least on the face of it, appeared less glum than before. She brought me a new pair of expensive pajamas and a lovely silk gown more appropriate to a salon than a prison. I did not have the heart to tell her it was wholly inappropriate for me to wear such things in jail. I knew, however, that the parcel was a way of expressing her love and a pledge of solidarity. I thanked her, and although we did not have much time we quickly discussed family matters, especially how she would support herself and the children. I mentioned the names of friends who would help her and also clients of mine who still owed me money. I told her to tell the children the truth of my capture, and how I would be away for a long time. I said we were not the first family in this situation, and that those who underwent such hardships came out the stronger. I assured her of the strength of our cause, the loyalty of our friends, and how it would be her love and devotion that would see me through whatever transpired. The officer supervising the visit turned a blind eye, and we embraced and clung to each other with all the strength and pent-up emotion inside each of us, as if this were to be the final parting. In a way, it was, for we were to be separated for much longer than either of us could then have imagined. The warrant officer allowed me to accompany Winnie part of the way to the main gate where I was able to watch her, alone and proud, disappear around the corner.

50

AT THE FORT I was being supervised by Colonel Minnaar, a courtly Afrikaner considered something of a liberal by his more *verkrampte* (hard-line) colleagues. He explained that he was placing me in the prison hospital because it was the most comfortable area and I would be able to have a chair and table on which I could prepare my case. While the hospital was indeed comfortable — I was able to sleep in a proper bed, something I had never done before in prison — the real reason for his generosity was that the hospital was the safest place to keep me. To reach it one had to pass through two impregnable walls, each with armed guards; and once inside, four massive gates had to be unlocked before one even reached the area where I was kept. There was speculation in the press that the movement was going to attempt to rescue me, and the authorities were doing their utmost to prevent it.

There had also been wild speculations, in the press and within the ANC, that I had been betrayed by someone in the movement. I knew that some people blamed G. R. Naidoo, my Durban host, a suggestion I believe was unfounded. The press trumpeted the notion that I had been betrayed by white and Indian Communists who were unsettled by my suggestions that the ANC must become more Africanist-oriented. But I believed these stories were planted by the government to divide the Congress movement, and I regarded it as malicious mischief. I later discussed the matter not only with Walter, Duma, Joe Slovo, and Ahmed Kathrada, but with Winnie, and I was gratified to see that they shared my feelings. Winnie had been invited to open the annual conference of the Transvaal Indian Youth Congress, and at my instigation she repudiated these rumors in no uncertain terms. The newspapers were filled with stories of her beauty and eloquence. "We shall not waste time looking for evidence as to who betrayed Mandela," she told the audience. "Such propaganda is calculated to keep us fighting one another instead of uniting to combat Nationalist oppression."

The most oft-cited story was that an American consular official with connections to the CIA had tipped off the authorities. This story has never been confirmed and I have never seen any reliable evidence as to the truth of it. Although the CIA has been responsible for many contemptible activities in its support of American imperialism, I cannot lay my capture at their door. In truth, I had been imprudent about maintaining the secrecy of my movements. In retrospect, I realized that the authorities could have had a myriad of ways of locating me on my trip to Durban. It was a wonder in fact that I wasn't captured sooner.

I spent only a few days in the Fort's hospital before being transferred to Pretoria. There had been no restrictions on visits in Johannesburg, and I had had a continuous stream of people coming to see me. Visitors keep one's spirits up in prison, and the absence of them can be disheartening. In transferring me to Pretoria, the authorities wanted to get me away from my home turf to a place where I would have fewer friends dropping by.

I was handcuffed and taken to Pretoria in an old van in the company of another prisoner. The inside of the van was filthy and we sat on a greasy spare tire, which slid from side to side as the van rumbled its way to Pretoria. The choice of companion was curious: his name was Nkadimeng and he was a member of one of Soweto's fiercest gangs. Normally, officials would not permit a political prisoner to share the same vehicle with a common-law criminal, but I suspect they were hoping I would be intimidated by Nkadimeng, who I assumed was a police informer. I was dirty and annoyed by the time I reached prison, and my irritation was aggravated by the fact that I was put in a single cell with this fellow. I demanded and eventually received separate space so that I could prepare my case.

I was now permitted visitors only twice a week. Despite the distance, Winnie came regularly and always brought clean clothes and delicious food. This was another way of showing her support, and every time I put on a fresh shirt I felt her love and devotion. I was aware of how difficult it must have been to get to Pretoria in the middle of the day in the middle of the week with two small children at home. I was visited by many others who brought food, including the ever-faithful Mrs. Pillay who supplied me with a spicy lunch every day.

Because of the generosity of my visitors I had an embarrassment of riches and wanted to share my food with the other prisoners on my floor. This was strictly forbidden. In order to circumvent the restrictions, I offered food to the warders, who might then relent. With this in mind I presented a shiny red apple to an African warder who looked at it and stonily rebuffed me with the phrase *"Angiyifuni"* (I don't want it). African warders tend to be either much more sympathetic than white warders, or even more severe, as though to outdo their masters. But, a short while later, the black warder saw a white warder take the apple he had rejected, and changed his mind. Soon I was supplying all my fellow prisoners with food.

Through the prison grapevine, I learned that Walter had been brought to Pretoria as well, and although we were isolated from each other we did manage to communicate. Walter had applied for bail — a decision I fully supported. Bail has long been a sensitive issue within the ANC. There are those who believed we should always reject bail, as it could be interpreted that we were fainthearted rebels who accepted the racist strictures of the legal system. I did not think this view should be universally applied and believed we should examine the issue on a case-by-case basis. Ever since Walter had become secretary-general of the ANC, I had felt that every effort should be made to bail him out of prison. He was simply too vital to the organization to allow him to languish in jail. In his case, bail was a practical not a theoretical issue. It was different in my own case. I had been underground; Walter had not. I had become a public symbol of rebellion and struggle; Walter operated behind the scenes. He agreed that no application for bail should be made in my case. For one thing, it would not have been granted and I did not want to do anything that might suggest that I was not prepared for the consequences of the underground life I had chosen.

Not long after Walter and I reached this decision I was again transferred back to the hospital at the Fort. A hearing had been set for October. Little can be said in favor of prison, but enforced isolation is conducive to study. I had begun correspondence studies for my LL.B., a bachelor of laws degree allowing one to practice as an advocate. One of the first things I had done after arriving at Pretoria Local was to send a letter to the authorities notifying them of my intention to study and requesting permission to purchase a copy of the Law of Torts, part of my syllabus.

A few days later, Colonel Aucamp, commanding officer of Pretoria Local and one of the more notorious of prison officials, marched into my cell and in a gloating manner said, "Mandela, we have got you now!" Then he said, "Why do you want a book about torches, man, unless you plan to use it for your damn sabotage?" I had no idea what he was talking about, until he produced my letter requesting a book about what he called "the Law of Torches." I smiled at this and he became angry that I was not taking him seriously. The Afrikaans word for "torch" is *toort,* very similar to tort, and I explained to him that in English *tort* was a branch of law not a burning stick of wood that could be used to set off a bomb. He went away in a huff.

One day I was in the prison courtyard at the Fort doing my daily exercises, which consisted of jogging, running in place, push-ups, and sit-ups, when I was approached by a tall, handsome Indian fellow named Moosa Dinath whom I had known slightly as a prosperous, even flamboyant businessman. He was serving a two-year sentence for fraud. On the outside we would have remained acquaintances, but prison is an incubator of friendship. Dinath would often accompany me on my jogs around the courtyard.

One day he asked whether I had any objection if he obtained permission from the commanding officer to be near me in the prison hospital. I told him that I would welcome it, but I thought to myself that the authorities would never permit it. I was wrong.

It was exceedingly odd that a convicted prisoner like Dinath was permitted to stay together with a political prisoner awaiting trial. But I said nothing, as I was glad to have company. Dinath was wealthy and had a private payroll for the prison authorities. In return for his money, he received many privileges: he wore clothes meant for white prisoners, ate their diet, and did no jail work at all.

One night, to my astonishment, I observed Colonel Minnaar, who was the head of prison, and a well-known Afrikaner advocate come to fetch him. Dinath then left prison for the night and did not come back again until the morning. If I had not seen it with my own eyes I would not have believed it.

Dinath regaled me with tales of financial shenanigans and corruption among cabinet ministers, which I found fascinating. It confirmed to me how apartheid was a poison that bred moral decay in all areas. I scrupulously avoided discussing with him any matters of a political or sensitive nature on the grounds that he might also have been an informer. He once asked me to tell him about my African trip and I simply glossed over it. In the end, Dinath pulled enough strings to speed up his release and left after serving only four months of his two-year sentence.

Escape serves a double purpose: it liberates a freedom fighter from jail so that he can continue to fight, but offers a tremendous psychological boost to the struggle and a great publicity blow against the enemy. As a prisoner, I always contemplated escape, and during my various trips to and from the commanding officer's office, I carefully surveyed the walls, the movements of the guards, the types of keys and locks used in the doors. I made a detailed sketch of the prison grounds with particular emphasis on the exact location of the prison hospital and the gates leading out of it. This map was smuggled out to the movement with instructions to destroy it immediately after it was perused.

There were two plans, one hatched by Moosa Dinath, which I ignored; the second was conceived by the ANC and communicated to me by Joe Slovo. It involved bribes, copies of keys, and even a false beard that was to be sewn into the shoulder pad of one of my jackets brought to me in prison. The idea was that I would don the beard after I had made my escape. I carefully considered the escape plan and concluded that it was premature, and the likelihood of its failure was unacceptably high. Such a failure would be fatal to the organization. During a meeting with Joe,

I passed him a note communicating my views. I wrote that MK was not ready for such an operation; even an elite and trained force would probably not be able to accomplish such a mission. I suggested that such a gambit be postponed until I was a convicted prisoner and the authorities were less cautious. At the end, I wrote, "Please destroy this after you have finished reading it." Joe and the others took my advice about not attempting the escape, but he decided the note should be saved as a historical document, and it later turned up at a very unfortunate time.

51

THE INITIAL HEARING was set for Monday, October 15, 1962. The organization had set up a Free Mandela Committee and launched a lively campaign with the slogan "Free Mandela." Protests were held throughout the country and the slogan began to appear scrawled on the sides of buildings. The government retaliated by banning all gatherings relating to my imprisonment, but this restriction was ignored by the liberation movement.

In preparation for Monday's hearing, the Free Mandela Committee had organized a mass demonstration at the courthouse. The plan was to have people line both sides of the road along the route my van would take. From press reports, conversations with visitors, and even the remarks of prison guards, I learned that a large and vociferous turnout was expected.

On Saturday, while I was preparing myself for the Monday hearing, I was ordered to pack my things immediately: the hearing had been shifted to Pretoria. The authorities had made no announcement, and had I not managed to get word out through a sympathetic jailer, no one would have known that I had left Johannesburg.

But the movement reacted quickly, and by the time my case began on Monday morning, the Old Synagogue was packed with supporters. The synagogue was like a second home to me after four years of the Treason Trial. My legal adviser, Joe Slovo, could not be present as he was confined to Johannesburg by bans and I was ably assisted instead by Bob Hepple.

I entered the court that Monday morning wearing a traditional Xhosa leopard-skin kaross instead of a suit and tie. The crowd of supporters rose as one and with raised, clenched fists shouted *"Amandla!"* and *"Ngaw-ethu!"* The kaross electrified the spectators, many of whom were friends and family, some of whom had come all the way from the Transkei. Winnie also wore a traditional beaded headdress and an ankle-length Xhosa skirt.

I had chosen traditional dress to emphasize the symbolism that I was a black African walking into a white man's court. I was literally carrying on my back the history, culture, and heritage of my people. That day, I felt myself to be the embodiment of African nationalism, the inheritor of Africa's difficult but noble past and her uncertain future. The kaross was also a sign of contempt for the niceties of white justice. I well knew the authorities would feel threatened by my kaross as so many whites feel threatened by the true culture of Africa.

When the crowd had quieted down and the case was called, I formally greeted the prosecutor, Mr. Bosch, whom I had known from my attorney days, and the magistrate, Mr. Von Heerden, who was also familiar to me. I then immediately applied for a two-week remand on the grounds that I had been transferred to Pretoria without being given the opportunity of notifying my attorneys. I was granted a week's postponement.

When I was on my way back to my cell, a very nervous white warder said that the commanding officer, Colonel Jacobs, had ordered me to hand over the kaross. I said, "You can tell him that he is not going to have it." This warder was a weak fellow, and he started trembling. He practically begged me for it and said he would be fired if he did not bring it back. I felt sorry for him and I said, "Look, here, just tell your commanding officer that it is Mandela speaking, not you." A short while later Colonel Jacobs himself appeared and ordered me to turn over what he referred to as my "blanket." I told him that he had no jurisdiction over the attire I chose to wear in court and if he tried to confiscate my kaross I would take the matter all the way to the Supreme Court. The colonel never again tried to take my "blanket," but the authorities would permit me to wear it only in court, not on my way to or from court for fear it would "incite" other prisoners.

When the case resumed a week later I was given permission to address the court before I was asked to plead. "I hope to be able to indicate," I explained, "that this case is a trial of the aspirations of the African people, and because of that I thought it proper to conduct my own defense." I wanted to make it clear to the bench, the gallery, and the press that I intended to put the state on trial. I then made application for the recusal of the magistrate on the grounds that I did not consider myself morally bound to obey laws made by a Parliament in which I had no representation. Nor was it possible to receive a fair trial from a white judge:

> Why is it that in this courtroom I am facing a white magistrate, confronted by a white prosecutor, escorted by white orderlies? Can anybody honestly and seriously suggest that in this type of atmosphere the scales of justice are evenly balanced? Why is it that no African in the history

of this country has ever had the honor of being tried by his own kith and kin, by his own flesh and blood? I will tell Your Worship why: the real purpose of this rigid color bar is to ensure that the justice dispensed by the courts should conform to the policy of the country, however much that policy might be in conflict with the norms of justice accepted in judiciaries throughout the civilized world. . . . Your Worship, I hate racial discrimination most intensely and in all its manifestations. I have fought it all my life. I fight it now, and I will do so until the end of my days. I detest most intensely the set-up that surrounds me here. It makes me feel that I am a black man in a white man's court. This should not be.

During the trial the prosecutor called more than one hundred witnesses from all over the country, including the Transkei and South West Africa. They were policemen, journalists, township superintendents, printers. Most of them gave technical evidence to show that I left the country illegally and that I had incited African workers to strike during the three-day stay-at-home in May 1961. It was indisputable — and in fact I did not dispute — that I was technically guilty of both charges.

The prosecutor had called Mr. Barnard, the private secretary to the prime minister, to testify to the letter I had sent the prime minister demanding that he call a national convention and informing him that if he did not, we would organize a three-day strike. In my cross-examination of Mr. Barnard I first read the court the letter I sent requesting that the prime minister call a national convention for all South Africans to write a new nonracial constitution.

NM: Did you place this letter before your prime minister?
WITNESS: Yes.
NM: Now was any reply given to this letter by the prime minister?
WITNESS: He did not reply to the writer.
NM: He did not reply to the letter. Now, will you agree that this letter raises matters of vital concern to the vast majority of the citizens of this country?
WITNESS: I do not agree.
NM: You don't agree? You don't agree that the question of human rights, of civil liberties, is a matter of vital importance to the African people?
WITNESS: Yes, that is so, indeed.
NM: Are these things mentioned here?
WITNESS: Yes, I think so.
NM: . . . You have already agreed that this letter raises questions like the rights of freedom, civil liberties, and so on?

WITNESS: Yes, the letter raises it.

NM: Now, you know of course that Africans don't enjoy the rights demanded in this letter? They are denied these rights of government.

WITNESS: Some rights.

NM: No African is a member of Parliament?

WITNESS: That is right.

NM: No African can be a member of the provincial council, of the municipal councils.

WITNESS: Yes.

NM: Africans have no vote in this country?

WITNESS: They have got no vote as far as Parliament is concerned.

NM: Yes, that is what I am talking about, I am talking about Parliament and other government bodies of the country, the provincial councils, the municipal councils. They have no vote?

WITNESS: That is right.

NM: Would you agree with me that in any civilized country in the world it would be scandalous for a prime minister to fail to reply to a letter raising vital issues affecting the majority of the citizens of that country. Would you agree with that?

WITNESS: I don't agree with that.

NM: You don't agree that it would be irregular for a prime minister to ignore a letter raising vital issues affecting the vast majority of the citizens of that country?

WITNESS: This letter has not been ignored by the prime minister.

NM: Just answer the question. Do you regard it proper for a prime minister not to respond to pleas made in regard to vital issues by the vast majority of the citizens of the country? You say that is wrong?

WITNESS: The prime minister did respond to the letter.

NM: Mr. Barnard, I don't want to be rude to you. Will you confine yourself to answering my questions. The question I am putting to you is, do you agree that it is most improper on the part of a prime minister not to reply to a communication raising vital issues affecting the vast majority of the country?

Mr. Barnard and I never did agree. In the end, he simply said that the tone of the letter was aggressive and discourteous and for that reason the prime minister did not answer it.

Throughout the proceedings the prosecutor and the magistrate repeatedly inquired about the number of witnesses I intended to call. I would always reply, "I plan to call as many witnesses as the state, if not more." When the state finally concluded its case, there was a stillness in the courtroom in anticipation of the beginning of my defense. I rose and instead of calling my first witness, I declared quite matter-of-factly that I was not calling any witnesses at all, at which point I abruptly closed my case. There was a murmur in the courtroom and the prosecutor could not help exclaiming, "Lord!"

I had misled the court from the beginning because I knew the charge was accurate and the state's case was solid, and I saw no point in attempting to call witnesses and defend myself. Through my cross-examination and attempts to force the judge to recuse himself, I had made the statements I wanted about the unfairness of the court. I saw no advantage in calling witnesses to try to disprove something that was incontrovertible.

The magistrate was taken by surprise by my action and asked me with some incredulity, "Have you anything more to say?"

"Your Worship, I submit that I am guilty of no crime."

"Is that all you have to say?"

"Your Worship, with respect, if I had something more to say I would have said it."

The prosecutor then shuffled through his papers attempting to get ready for an address he did not expect to have to make. He briefly addressed the court and asked the magistrate to find me guilty on both counts. The court was then adjourned until the following day, when I would have a chance to address the court in what is known as the plea in mitigation before the magistrate gave his sentence.

The following morning, before court was called into session, I was in an office off the courtroom talking with Bob Hepple, who had been advising me on the case, and we were praising the fact that the day before, the General Assembly of the U.N. had voted in favor of sanctions against South Africa for the first time. Bob also told me that acts of sabotage in Port Elizabeth and Durban had occurred, both celebrating the U.N. vote and protesting my trial. We were in the midst of this discussion when the prosecutor, Mr. Bosch, entered the room and then asked Bob to excuse himself.

"Mandela," he said, after Bob had left, "I did not want to come to court today. For the first time in my career, I despise what I am doing. It hurts me that I should be asking the court to send you to prison." He then reached out and shook my hand, and expressed the hope that everything would turn out well for me. I thanked him for his sentiments, and assured him that I would never forget what he had said.

The authorities were on alert that day. The crowd inside the courtroom seemed even larger than on the first day of the case. All one hundred fifty "non-European" seats were filled. Winnie was present, in Xhosa dress, as well as a number of my relatives from the Transkei. Hundreds of demonstrators stood a block from the courthouse, and there seemed to be as many policemen as spectators.

When I walked in the courtroom, I raised my right fist and called out *"Amandla!"* which was met by a mighty *"Ngawethu!"* The magistrate pounded his gavel and cried for order. When the court was quiet, he summed up the charges, after which I had my opportunity to speak. My plea in mitigation lasted over an hour. It was not a judicial appeal at all but a political testament. I wanted to explain to the court how and why I had become the man I was, why I had done what I had done, and why, if given the chance, I would do it again.

Many years ago, when I was a boy brought up in my village in the Transkei, I listened to the elders of the tribe telling stories about the good old days before the arrival of the white man. Then our people lived peacefully, under the democratic rule of their kings and their *amapakati* [literally "insiders," but meaning those closest in rank to the king], and moved freely and confidently up and down the country without let or hindrance. The country was our own, in name and right. We occupied the land, the forests, the rivers; we extracted the mineral wealth beneath the soil and all the riches of this beautiful country. We set up and operated our own government, we controlled our own arms and we organized our trade and commerce. The elders would tell tales of the wars fought by our ancestors in defense of the Fatherland, as well as the acts of valor by generals and soldiers during these epic days. . . .

The structure and organization of early African societies in this country fascinated me very much and greatly influenced the evolution of my political outlook. The land, then the main means of production, belonged to the whole tribe and there was no individual ownership whatsoever. There were no classes, no rich or poor and no exploitation of man by man. All men were free and equal and this was the foundation of government. Recognition of this general principle found expression in the constitution of the council, variously called "Imbizo" or "Pitso" or "Kgotla," which governs the affairs of the tribe. The council was so completely democratic that all members of the tribe could participate in its deliberations. Chief and subject, warrior and medicine man, all took part and endeavored to influence its decisions. It was so weighty and influential a body that no step of any importance could ever be taken by the tribe without reference to it.

There was much in such a society that was primitive and insecure and it certainly could never measure up to the demands of the present epoch. But in such a society are contained the seeds of revolutionary democracy in which none will be held in slavery or servitude, and in which poverty, want and insecurity shall be no more. This is the history which, even today, inspires me and my colleagues in our political struggle.

I told the court how I had joined the African National Congress and how its policy of democracy and nonracialism reflected my own deepest convictions. I explained how as a lawyer I was often forced to choose between compliance with the law and accommodating my conscience.

I would say that the whole life of any thinking African in this country drives him continuously to a conflict between his conscience on the one hand and the law on the other. This is not a conflict peculiar to this country. The conflict arises for men of conscience, for men who think and who feel deeply in every country. Recently in Britain, a peer of the realm, Earl [Bertrand] Russell, probably the most respected philosopher of the Western world, was sentenced and convicted for precisely the type of activities for which I stand before you today — for following his conscience in defiance of the law, as a protest against the nuclear weapons policy being pursued by his own government. He could do no other than to oppose the law and to suffer the consequences for it. Nor can I. Nor can many Africans in this country. The law as it is applied, the law as it has been developed over a long period of history, and especially the law as it is written and designed by the Nationalist government is a law which, in our views, is immoral, unjust, and in-tolerable. Our consciences dictate that we must protest against it, that we must oppose it and that we must attempt to alter it. . . . Men, I think, are not capable of doing nothing, of saying nothing, of not reacting to injustice, of not protesting against oppression, of not striving for the good society and the good life in the ways they see it.

I recounted in detail the numerous times the government had used the law to hamper my life, career, and political work, through bannings, restrictions, and trials.

I was made, by the law, a criminal, not because of what I had done, but because of what I stood for, because of what I thought, because of my conscience. Can it be any wonder to anybody that such conditions make a man an outlaw of society? Can it be wondered that such a man, having been outlawed by the government, should be prepared to lead the life of an outlaw, as I have led for some months, according to the evidence before this court?

It has not been easy for me during the past period to separate myself from my wife and children, to say good-bye to the good old days when, at the end of a strenuous day at an office I could look forward to joining my family at the dinnertable, and instead to take up the life of a man hunted continuously by the police, living separated from those who are closest to me, in my own country, facing continually the hazards of detection and of arrest. This has been a life infinitely more difficult than serving a prison sentence. No man in his right senses would voluntarily choose such a life in preference to the one of normal, family, social life which exists in every civilized community.

But there comes a time, as it came in my life, when a man is denied the right to live a normal life, when he can only live the life of an outlaw because the government has so decreed to use the law to impose a state of outlawry upon him. I was driven to this situation, and I do not regret having taken the decisions that I did take. Other people will be driven in the same way in this country, by this very same force of police persecution and of administrative action by the government, to follow my course, of that I am certain.

I enumerated the many times that we had brought our grievances before the government and the equal number of times that we were ignored or shunted aside. I described our stay-away of 1961 as a last resort after the government showed no signs of taking any steps to either talk with us or meet our demands. It was the government that provoked violence by employing violence to meet our nonviolent demands. I explained that because of the government's actions we had taken a more militant stance. I said that I had been privileged throughout my political life to fight alongside colleagues whose abilities and contributions were far greater than my own. Many others had paid the price of their beliefs before me, and many more would do so after me.

Before sentencing, I informed the court that whatever sentence the state imposed, it would do nothing to change my devotion to the struggle.

I do not believe, Your Worship, that this court, in inflicting penalties on me for the crimes for which I am convicted should be moved by the belief that penalties will deter men from the course that they believe is right. History shows that penalties do not deter men when their conscience is aroused, nor will they deter my people or the colleagues with whom I have worked before.

I am prepared to pay the penalty even though I know how bitter and desperate is the situation of an African in the prisons of this country.

I have been in these prisons and I know how gross is the discrimination, even behind the prison wall, against Africans. . . . Nevertheless these considerations do not sway me from the path that I have taken nor will they sway others like me. For to men, freedom in their own land is the pinnacle of their ambitions, from which nothing can turn men of conviction aside. More powerful than my fear of the dreadful conditions to which I might be subjected in prison is my hatred for the dreadful conditions to which my people are subjected outside prison throughout this country. . . .

Whatever sentence Your Worship sees fit to impose upon me for the crime for which I have been convicted before this court, may it rest assured that when my sentence has been completed I will still be moved, as men are always moved, by their conscience; I will still be moved by my dislike of the race discrimination against my people when I come out from serving my sentence, to take up again, as best I can, the struggle for the removal of those injustices until they are finally abolished once and for all. . . .

I have done my duty to my people and to South Africa. I have no doubt that posterity will pronounce that I was innocent and that the criminals that should have been brought before this court are the members of the government.

When I had finished, the magistrate ordered a ten-minute recess to consider the sentence. I turned and looked out at the crowd before exiting the courtroom. I had no illusions about the sentence I would receive. Exactly ten minutes later, in a courtroom heavy with tension, the magistrate pronounced sentence: three years for inciting people to strike and two years for leaving the country without a passport; five years in all, with no possibility of parole. It was a stern sentence and there was wailing among the spectators. As the court rose, I turned to the gallery and again made a clenched fist, shouting *"Amandla!"* three times. Then, on its own, the crowd began to sing our beautiful anthem, *"Nkosi Sikelel' iAfrika."* People sang and danced and the women ululated as I was led away. The uproar among the gallery made me forget for a moment that I would be going to prison to serve what was then the stiffest sentence yet imposed in South Africa for a political offense.

Downstairs, I was permitted a brief good-bye to Winnie, and on this occasion she was not at all grim: she was in high spirits and shed no tears. She seemed confident, as much a comrade as a wife. She was determined to brace me. As I was driven away in the police van I could still hear the people outside singing *"Nkosi Sikelel' iAfrika."*

52

PRISON NOT ONLY robs you of your freedom, it attempts to take away your identity. Everyone wears the same uniform, eats the same food, follows the same schedule. It is by definition a purely authoritarian state that tolerates no independence or individuality. As a freedom fighter and as a man, one must fight against the prison's attempt to rob one of these qualities.

From the courthouse, I was taken directly to Pretoria Local, the gloomy red-brick monstrosity that I knew so well. But I was now a convicted prisoner, not an awaiting-trial prisoner, and was treated without even that little deference that is afforded to the latter. I was stripped of my clothes and Colonel Jacobs was finally able to confiscate my kaross. I was issued the standard prison uniform for Africans: a pair of short trousers, a rough khaki shirt, a canvas jacket, socks, sandals, and a cloth cap. Only Africans are given short trousers, for only African men are deemed "boys" by the authorities.

I informed the authorities that I would under no circumstances wear shorts and told them I was prepared to go to court to protest. Later, when I was brought dinner, stiff cold porridge with a half teaspoonful of sugar, I refused to eat it. Colonel Jacobs pondered this and came up with a solution: I could wear long trousers and have my own food, if I agreed to be put in isolation. "We were going to put you with the other politicals," he said, "but now you will be alone, man. I hope you enjoy it." I assured him that solitary confinement would be fine as long as I could wear and eat what I chose.

For the next few weeks, I was completely and utterly isolated. I did not see the face or hear the voice of another prisoner. I was locked up for twenty-three hours a day, with thirty minutes of exercise in the morning and again in the afternoon. I had never been in isolation before, and every hour seemed like a year. There was no natural light in my cell; a single bulb burned overhead twenty-four hours a day. I did not have a wristwatch and I often thought it was the middle of the night when it was only late afternoon. I had nothing to read, nothing to write on or with, no one to talk to. The mind begins to turn in on itself, and one desperately wants something outside of oneself on which to fix one's attention. I have known men who took half-a-dozen lashes in preference to being locked up alone. After a time in solitary, I relished the company even of the insects in my cell, and found myself on the verge of initiating conversations with a cockroach.

I had one middle-aged African warder whom I occasionally was able to see, and one day I tried to bribe him with an apple to get him to talk to me. *"Baba,"* I said, which means Father, and is a term of respect, "can I give you an apple?" He turned away, and met all my subsequent overtures with silence. Finally, he said, "Man, you wanted long trousers and better food, and now you have them and you are still not happy." He was right. Nothing is more dehumanizing than the absence of human companionship. After a few weeks, I was ready to swallow my pride and tell Colonel Jacobs that I would trade my long trousers for some company.

During those weeks I had plenty of time to ponder my fate. The place of a freedom fighter is beside his people, not behind bars. The knowledge and contacts I had recently made in Africa were going to be locked away rather than used in the struggle. I cursed the fact that my expertise would not be put to use in creating a freedom army.

I soon began to protest vigorously against my circumstances and demanded to be put with the other political prisoners at Pretoria Local. Among them was Robert Sobukwe. My request was ultimately granted, accompanied by a stern warning from Colonel Jacobs that serious consequences would result if I returned to my impudent ways. I don't think I ever looked forward to eating cold mealie pap so much in my life.

Apart from my desire for company, I was keen to talk with Sobukwe and the others, most of whom were PAC, because I thought that in prison we might forge a unity that we could not on the outside. Prison conditions have a way of tempering polemics, and making individuals see more what unites them than what divides them.

When I was taken to the courtyard with the others, we greeted each other warmly. Besides Sobukwe, there was also John Gaetsewe, a leading member of the South African Congress of Trade Unions; Aaron Molete, an ANC member who worked for *New Age;* and Stephen Tefu, a prominent Communist, trade unionist, and PAC member. Robert asked me to give them an account of my African tour, which I did gladly. I was candid about how both the PAC and the ANC were perceived in the rest of Africa. At the end of my narrative I said there were issues that I wanted us to examine. But after initially allowing Sobukwe and me a certain proximity, the authorities took pains to keep us apart. We lived in single cells along a corridor and he and I were given cells at opposite ends.

Occasionally, we did have a chance to talk as we sat next to each other on the ground of the prison courtyard sewing and patching up shabby old mailbags. I have always respected Sobukwe, and found him a balanced and reasonable man. But we differed markedly about the principal subject at hand: prison conditions. Sobukwe believed that to fight poor conditions would be to acknowledge the state's right to have him in prison in the first place. I responded that it was always unacceptable to live in degrading conditions and that political prisoners throughout history had considered it part of their duty to fight to improve prison conditions. Sobukwe responded that prison conditions would not change until the country changed. I completely agreed with this, but I did not see why that ought to prevent us from fighting in the only realm in which we now could fight. We never resolved this issue, but we did make some progress when we submitted a joint letter to the commanding officer setting out our complaints about prison conditions.

Sobukwe never broke in prison. But in Pretoria he was a bit sensitive and testy, and I attribute this to Stephen Tefu. Tefu had become a kind of goad to Sobukwe, teasing, taunting, and challenging him. Even at the best of times, Tefu was a difficult fellow: dyspeptic, argumentative, overbearing. He was also articulate, knowledgeable, and an expert in Russian history. Above all, he was a fighter, but he would fight everyone, even his friends. Tefu and Sobukwe quarreled every day.

I was keen to discuss policy issues with Sobukwe, and one of the matters I took up with him was the PAC slogan "Freedom in 1963." It was already 1963 and freedom was nowhere to be seen. "My brother," I said to Sobukwe, "there is nothing so dangerous as a leader making a demand that he knows cannot be achieved. It creates false hopes among the people."

I said this in a most respectful manner, but Tefu jumped in and started to berate Sobukwe. "Bob," he said, "you have met your match with Mandela. You know he is right." Tefu continued in this vein, annoying Sobukwe to the point where he would tell Tefu, "Leave me alone." But Tefu would not stop. "Bob, the people are waiting for you. They are going to kill you because you have deceived them. You are just an amateur, Bob. You are not a real politician."

Tefu did his best to alienate me as well. Every morning, when we were visited by the warders, he would complain to them about something — the food, the conditions, the heat or the cold. One day, an officer said to Tefu: "Look, man, why do you complain every morning?"

"I complain because it is my duty to complain," Steve said.

"But, look at Mandela," the officer said, "he does not complain every day."

"Ah," said Tefu with disgust, "Mandela is a little boy who is afraid of the white man. I don't even know who he is. One morning, I woke up and found every newspaper saying, 'Mandela, Mandela, Mandela,' and I said to myself, 'Who is this Mandela?' I will tell you who Mandela is. He is a chap built up by you people for some reason that I don't understand. That is who Mandela is!"

We were joined for two weeks by Walter, who had been on trial in Johannesburg for incitement to strike while I had been in Pretoria. He was sentenced to six years. We had a number of opportunities to talk in jail and we discussed Walter's application for bail while his appeal was pending, a move I wholeheartedly supported. After two weeks he was released on bail, and he was instructed by the movement to go underground, from where he was to continue to lead the struggle, which he ably did.

Not long after Walter left, I was walking to the prison hospital with Sobukwe when I spotted Nana Sita in the courtyard about twenty-five yards away. Sita, the distinguished Indian campaigner who had led our defiance at Boksburg in 1952, had just been convicted by a Pretoria magistrate for refusing to vacate his house — the house he had lived in for more than forty years — which was in a precinct that had been proclaimed "white" in terms of the Group Areas Act. He was hunched over, and the fact that he was barefoot despite an acute arthritic condition made me uncomfortable in my own sandals. I wanted to go over to greet him, but we were marching under the eyes of a half-dozen warders.

Suddenly and without warning, I suffered a blackout. I crumpled to the concrete and sustained a deep gash above my left eye, which required three stitches. I had been diagnosed back in the Fort with high blood pressure and had been given certain pills. The cause of the blackout was evidently an overdose of these pills; I was taken off them, and put on a low-salt diet, which solved the problem.

That afternoon was my first scheduled visit from Winnie since I had been sentenced. Stitches or no stitches, I was not going to miss it. She was extremely concerned when she saw me but I assured her I was fine and explained what happened. Even so, rumors circulated that my health had broken down.

53

IN OCTOBER 1962, during my trial, the ANC held its first annual conference since 1959. Because the organization was illegal, the conference took place in Lobatse, just over the border in Bechuanaland. The conference was a milestone, for it explicitly linked the ANC and MK. Although the National Executive Committee stated, "Our emphasis still remains mass political action," Umkhonto was referred to as the "military wing of our struggle." This was done in part to try to quell the more irresponsible acts of terrorism then being committed by Poqo. Poqo, Xhosa for "independent" or "standing alone," was loosely linked to the PAC, and their acts of terrorism targeted both African collaborators and whites. The ANC wanted the people to see its new militancy, but also to see that it was controlled and responsible.

The government had decided to accelerate the program of "separate development" to show the world that apartheid allowed races their individual "freedom." The prototype would be the Transkei. In January 1962, Verwoerd had announced that South Africa intended to grant the Transkei "self-government." In 1963, the Transkei became a "self-governing" homeland. In November 1963, an election was held for the Transkei legislative assembly. But by a margin of more than three to one, Transkei voters elected members opposed to the homeland policy.

The bantustan system was nevertheless instituted; the voters had opposed it, but participated in it simply by voting. Though I abhorred the bantustan system, I felt the ANC should use both the system and those within it as a platform for our policies, particularly as so many of our leaders were now voiceless through imprisonment, banning, or exile.

Terrorism against the Bantu Authorities increased. As acts of sabotage mounted, so did the government's vigilance. John Vorster, the new minister of justice, who had himself been detained during World War II for opposing the government's support of the Allies, was a man unsentimental in the extreme. For him, the iron fist was the best and only answer to subversion.

On May 1, 1963, the government enacted legislation designed "to break the back" of Umkhonto, as Vorster put it. The General Law Amendment Act, better known as the Ninety-Day Detention Law, waived the right of habeas corpus and empowered any police officer to detain any person without a warrant on grounds of suspicion of a political crime. Those arrested could be detained without trial, charge, access to a lawyer, or protection against self-incrimination for up to ninety days. The ninety-day detention could be extended, as Vorster ominously explained, until "this side of eternity." The law helped transform the country into a police state; no dictator could covet more power than the Ninety-Day Detention Law gave to the authorities. As a result, the police became more savage: prisoners were routinely beaten and we soon heard reports of electric shock, suffocation, and other forms of torture. In Parliament, Helen Suzman, the representative of the liberal Progressive Party, cast the lone vote against the act.

Increased penalties were ordered for membership in illegal organizations; sentences from five years to the death penalty were instituted for "furthering the aims" of communism or of other banned organizations. Political prisoners were redetained as I found out in May 1963, when Sobukwe's three-year sentence was up; instead of releasing him, the government simply redetained him without charging him, and then sent him to Robben Island.

Vorster also championed the Sabotage Act of June 1962, which allowed for house arrests and more stringent bannings not subject to challenge in the court, restricting the liberties of citizens to those in the most extreme fascist dictatorships. Sabotage itself now carried a minimum penalty of five years without parole and a maximum of death. Because the wording of the act was so broad, even activities such as trespassing or illegal possession of weapons could constitute sabotage. Another act of Parliament prohibited the reproduction of any statement made by a banned person. Nothing I said or had ever said could be reported in the newspapers. *New Age* was banned at the end of 1962, and possession of a banned publication became a criminal offense, punishable by up to two years in prison. Provision was also made for house arrest, the most well-known use of which was imposed on the white political activist Helen Joseph.

54

ONE NIGHT, toward the end of May, a warder came to my cell and ordered me to pack my things. I asked him why, but he did not answer. In less than ten minutes, I was escorted down to the reception office where I found three other political prisoners: Tefu, John Gaetsewe, and Aaron Molete. Colonel Aucamp curtly informed us that we were being transferred. Where? Tefu asked. Someplace very beautiful, Aucamp said. Where? said Tefu. *"Die Eiland,"* said Aucamp. The island. There was only one. Robben Island.

The four of us were shackled together and put in a windowless van that contained only a sanitary bucket. We drove all night to Cape Town, and arrived at the city's docks in the late afternoon. It is not an easy or pleasant task for men shackled together to use a sanitary bucket in a moving van.

The docks at Cape Town were swarming with armed police and nervous plainclothes officials. We had to stand, still chained, in the hold of the old wooden ferry, which was difficult as the ship rocked in the swells off the coast. A small porthole above was the only source of light and air. The porthole served another purpose as well: the warders enjoyed urinating on us from above. It was still light when we were led on deck and we saw the island for the first time. Green and beautiful, it looked at first more like a resort than a prison.

Esiquithini. At the island. That is how the Xhosa people describe the narrow, windswept outcrop of rock that lies eighteen miles off the coast of Cape Town. Everyone knows which island you are referring to. I first heard about the island as a child. Robben Island was well known among the Xhosas after Makanna (also known as Nxele), the six foot six inch commander of the Xhosa army in the Fourth Xhosa War, was banished there by the British after leading ten thousand warriors against Grahamstown in 1819. He tried to escape from Robben Island by boat, but drowned before reaching shore. The memory of that loss is woven into the language of my people who speak of a "forlorn hope" by the phrase *"Ukuza kuka Nxele."*

Makanna was not the first African hero confined on the island. In 1658, Autshumao, known to European historians as Harry the Strandloper, was banished by Jan Van Riebeeck during a war between the Khoi Khoi and the Dutch. I took solace in the memory of Autshumao, for he is reputed to be the first and only man to ever escape from Robben Island, and he did so by rowing to the mainland in a small boat.

The island takes its name from the Dutch word for seal, hundreds of which once cavorted in the icy Benguela currents that wash the shores. Later the island was turned into a leper colony, a lunatic asylum, and a naval base. The government had only recently turned the island back into a prison.

We were met by a group of burly white warders shouting: *"Dis die Eiland! Hier julle gaan vrek!"* (This is the island. Here you will die.) Ahead of us was a compound flanked by a number of guardhouses. Armed guards lined the path to the compound. It was extremely tense. A tall, red-faced warder yelled at us: *"Hier ek is you baas!"* (Here I am your boss!) He was one of the notorious Kleynhans brothers, known for their brutality to prisoners. The warders always spoke in Afrikaans. If you replied in English they would say, *"Ek verstaan nie daardie kaffirboetie se taal nie."* (I don't understand that kaffir-lover's language.)

As we walked toward the prison, the guards shouted "Two-two! Two-two!" — meaning we should walk in pairs, two in front, two behind. I linked up with Tefu. The guards started screaming, *"Haak! . . . Haak!"* The word *haak* means "move" in Afrikaans, but it is customarily reserved for cattle.

The warders were demanding that we jog, and I turned to Tefu and under my breath said that we must set an example; if we gave in now we would be at their mercy. Tefu nodded his head in agreement. We had to show them that we were not everyday criminals but political prisoners being punished for our beliefs.

I motioned to Tefu that we two should walk in front, and we took the lead. Once in front, we actually decreased the pace, walking slowly and deliberately. The guards were incredulous. "Listen," Kleynhans said, "this is not Johannesburg, this is not Pretoria, this is Robben Island, and we will tolerate no insubordination here. *Haak! Haak!*" But we continued at our stately pace. Kleynhans ordered us to halt, and stood in front of us: "Look, man, we will kill you, we are not fooling around, your wives and children and mothers and fathers will never know what happened to you. This is the last warning. *Haak! Haak!*"

To this I said: "You have your duty and we have ours." I was determined that we would not give in, and we did not, for we were already at the cells. We were ushered into a rectangular stone building and taken to a large open room. The floor was covered with water a few inches deep. The guards yelled: *"Trek uit! Trek uit!"* (Undress! Undress!) As we removed each item of clothing, the guards would grab it, search it quickly, and then throw it in the water. Jacket off, searched, thrown in the water. Then the guards commanded us to get dressed, by which they meant for us to put on our soaking clothes.

Two officers entered the room. The less senior of the two was a captain whose name was Gericke. From the start, we could see that he was intent on manhandling us. The captain pointed to Aaron Molete, the youngest of the four of us and a very mild and gentle person, and said, "Why is your hair so long?" Aaron said nothing. The captain shouted, "I'm talking to you! Why is your hair so long? It is against regulations. Your hair should have been cut. Why is it long . . ." and then he paused and turned to look at me, and said, ". . . like this boy's!" pointing at me. I began to speak: "Now, look here, the length of our hair is determined by the regulations . . ."

Before I could finish, he shouted in disbelief: "Never talk to me that way, boy!" and began to advance. I was frightened; it is not a pleasant sensation to know that someone is about to hit you and you are unable to defend yourself.

When he was just a few feet from me, I said, as firmly as I could, "If you so much as lay a hand on me, I will take you to the highest court in the land and when I finish with you, you will be as poor as a church mouse." The moment I began speaking, he paused, and by the end of my speech, he was staring at me with astonishment. I was a bit surprised myself. I had been afraid, and spoke not from courage, but out of a kind of bravado. At such times, one must put up a bold front despite what one feels inside.

"Where's your ticket?" he asked, and I handed it to him. I could see he was nervous. "What's your name?" he said. I nodded my head toward the ticket, and said, "It is written there." He said, "How long are you in for?" I said again, gesturing toward the ticket, "It is written there." He looked down and said, "Five years! You are in for five years and you are so arrogant! Do you know what it means to serve five years?" I said, "That is my business. I am ready to serve five years but I am not prepared to be bullied. You must act within the law."

No one had informed him who we were, or that we were political prisoners, or that I was a lawyer. I had not noticed it myself, but the other officer, a tall, quiet man, had vanished during our confrontation; I later discovered that he was Colonel Steyn, the commanding officer of Robben Island. The captain then left, much quieter than he had entered.

We were then by ourselves and Steve, his nerves jangling, could not stop speaking. "We have provoked the Boere," he said. "Now we are in for a rough time." He was in the midst of speaking when a stocky fellow named Lieutenant Pretorius walked in. To our surprise, Pretorius spoke to us in Xhosa, which he seemed to know quite well. "We have looked at your records and they are not so bad. All except this one," he said, nodding toward Steve. "Your record is filthy."

Steve exploded. "Who are you to talk to me like that? You say I have a filthy record. You have read my files, eh. Well, you will find that all those convictions were for cases I was fighting for the rights of my people. I am not a criminal; you are the criminal." The lieutenant then warned Steve that he would charge him if he ever addressed him in that way again. Before leaving, the lieutenant said he was placing us in a single large cell with windows that faced outside and then added, rather ominously, "But I don't want you to talk to anyone through those windows, especially you, Mandela."

We were then taken to our cell, one of the best I had ever seen. The windows were large and within easy reach. From one set of windows we could see other prisoners and warders as they walked past. It was spacious, certainly large enough for the four of us, and had its own toilets and showers.

It had been an exhausting day and a short while later, after a supper of cold porridge, the others went to sleep. I was lying on my blanket on the floor, when I heard a tapping at the window. I looked up and saw a white man, beckoning me to come to the glass. I remembered the lieutenant's admonition and stayed put.

Then I heard the fellow whisper: "Nelson, come here." The fact that he knew my name intrigued me and I decided to take a chance. I went over to the window and looked at him. He must have realized that I thought he was white, because the first thing he whispered was, "I'm a Coloured warder from Bloemfontein." He then gave me news of my wife. There had been a report in the Johannesburg newspapers that my wife had come to see me at Pretoria Local, but that they had not informed her that I had been taken to Robben Island. I thanked him for the information.

"Do you smoke?" he said. I told him that I did not and he seemed disappointed. I then got the idea: "Yes, but my comrades do." He brightened at this and said he would return in a few minutes with tobacco and sandwiches. Everyone was now awake. Tefu and John Gaetsewe smoked, and I split the pouch of tobacco between them, and we all divided the sandwiches.

For the next few weeks the Coloured warder came almost every night with tobacco and sandwiches. And each night I would divide up the tobacco evenly between Tefu and Gaetsewe. The warder was taking great risks, and he warned me that he was only prepared to deal directly with me, or the arrangement was off.

When we arrived on the island we had no idea how many other prisoners were there. Within a few days we learned there were about a thousand men, all Africans, all recent arrivals. Most of these men were common-law prisoners, but I knew there would be some political prisoners among them. I wanted to contact them, but we were completely isolated. For the first few days we were kept locked in our cell and not even permitted outside. We demanded to be taken to work like the other prisoners, and this was soon granted, but we were taken out alone, supervised by Kleynhans. Our first job was covering up some newly laid pipe and we were on a small hill and could see some of the island, which was wild and lovely.

We worked hard that first day, but on each succeeding day Kleynhans pushed us harder. He did this crudely, as one would urge on a horse or cow. *"Nee, man. Kom aan! Gaan aan!"* (No, man. Come on. Go on.) At one point, Steve, who was older than the rest of us, put down his shovel and was immediately threatened by Kleynhans. But Steve, in Afrikaans, responded: "You ignoramus who cannot even speak your own language properly — you cannot tell me what to do. I will work at my own rate, that is what I am prepared to do, and that is all I can do." Then, with great dignity, he picked up his shovel and resumed work. Steve had been a teacher of Afrikaans, and he not only spoke perfect Afrikaans but its antecedent, High Dutch. Steve would speak to the warders in a condescending and grandiloquent style that they probably did not understand. But they knew better than to engage him in a verbal battle.

There were two Kleynhans brothers on the island, both reputed to have viciously assaulted prisoners. We were looked after by the older brother, who must have been warned to restrain himself, for he never touched us. The younger one was under no such constraints. One day, we were walking back from work along a road and passed a workspan of several hundred prisoners carting sand in wheelbarrows. They were non-political prisoners and both of our groups were ordered to halt while the two brothers had a chat; the younger brother ordered one of his men to polish his boots while he talked. I recognized some of the men in the other workspan as those who had been sentenced to death in the Sekhukhuneland peasant revolt of 1958, and I turned around to get a better look at them. The younger brother rudely ordered me to look the other way. I do not know how I would have reacted had I not been standing in full view of the other prisoners, but my pride was now at stake. I refused to turn around. The younger Kleynhans advanced with the obvious intent of assaulting me, but when he was a few steps away, his brother ran over, grabbed him, whispered a few words, and the incident passed.

One day we were visited by the head of prison, who was responsible for running all of Robben Island and had come to hear our complaints. Theron was a sour fellow who did not like to deal with prisoners face to face. I did not want to alienate him but I was not going to cringe. "We are grateful that you have come to see us," I said, speaking for the group, "because we have a number of problems which I am certain you will be able to sort out." I enumerated the problems and when I finished, he said, "I will see what I can do."

Perhaps he thought he had given in too easily because as he was walking out he turned to Tefu, who had a large belly, and said, *"Jou groot pens sal in die plek verbruin,"* Afrikaans for "That great stomach of yours is going to disappear here in prison." *Pens* means stomach, but is used to refer to the stomach of animals like sheep or cattle. The word for the stomach of a human being is *maag*.

Steve did not take kindly to the prison head's jab, and he was incapable of letting an insult go unanswered. "You know, Captain," he said, "there is nothing you can do to me that can truly affect me for I am a member of the most revolutionary political organization in the world, the Communist Party, which has a distinguished record of service to oppressed people around the globe. You and your poor National Party will be on the ash-heap of history while we are ruling the world. I am better known

internationally than your witless state president. Who are you? A small
functionary not even worth paying attention to. By the time I leave prison
I won't even know your name." Theron turned on his heel and left.

The nightly visits of our Coloured warder went a long way to mitigate
the harshness of the island. But even with this luxury, Steve was still
dissatisfied. Tefu was a heavy smoker; he would sometimes puff away the
entire night, leaving himself no tobacco for the next day. Gaetsewe, however, conserved his tobacco, and never ran out. One evening, in a particularly irritable mood, Tefu confronted me. "Nelson," he said, "you are
shortchanging me. You are giving Gaetsewe more tobacco than me."

This was not true, but I thought I would play a game with him. "Very
well then," I said. "Every night when I get the tobacco I will first divide
it into two portions and then I will let you choose which one you want."
That night, and each night afterward, I separated the tobacco into equal
piles and said to Steve, "Choose."

Tefu would be in an agony of indecision. He would look at both piles,
his head swinging back and forth between the two. Finally, in frustration,
he would grab one of the piles and go off and begin to smoke. Though
this process seemed to me eminently fair — and also humorous — Tefu
was still unhappy. He began to hover about when the warder came to the
window in order to make sure that I was not hoarding the tobacco. This
made the warder uncomfortable. "Look," he said to me, "I only deal with
you. It is a question of security." I said I understood, and told Tefu that
he could not be around when I was dealing with the warder.

The next night, however, when the warder came to the window, Tefu
strode up to the bars and said to him, "From now on I want my own
tobacco. Just give it to me directly." The warder panicked. "Mandela,"
he said, "you have broken our agreement. No more. I won't be bringing
you these things." I shooed Tefu away and remonstrated with the warder.
I said, "Look, man, this is an old chap," meaning Tefu. "And he's not
very normal," I said pointing to my head. "Make an exception." So he
softened and gave me the supplies, but warned if it happened again, that
would be the end.

That night, I thought it necessary to punish Tefu. I said, "Now, look,
you have jeopardized our supplies. You are not going to have any tobacco
or sandwiches tonight. You have almost lost us these privileges. So we're
cutting you off until you improve." Tefu was silent.

We stayed in one corner of the cell that night, eating our sandwiches
and reading the paper the warder also brought for us. Tefu sat by himself
in the opposite corner. Eventually we drifted off to sleep. At about mid-

night, I felt an arm on my shoulder, jostling me awake. "Nelson . . . Nelson." It was Tefu.

"Nelson," he said, speaking softly, "you have hit me in a weak spot. You have deprived me of my tobacco. I am an old man. I have suffered for my commitment to my people. You are the leader here in jail, and you are punishing me like this. It is not fair, Nelson."

He had hit *me* in a weak spot. I felt as though I had abused my power. He had indeed suffered, far more than I had. I had not eaten half my sandwich, and I immediately gave it to him. I roused Gaetsewe — I had given him all the tobacco — and asked him if he would share it with Tefu. Tefu was always difficult, but from that point on he behaved much better.

Once we started working, I got some sense of what life was like for other prisoners on the island. The authorities also moved some young political prisoners from the PAC into the cells opposite ours. At night, we were able to talk with them through the barred door. Among these young men, I discovered, was Nqabeni Menye, a nephew of mine from Mqhe-kezweni whom I had last seen when he was a baby in 1941.

We conversed about the Transkei and caught up on family history. One night, while his friends were gathered around him, he said, "Uncle, what organization do you belong to?" The ANC, I said, of course. My response caused consternation among those young men and suddenly their faces disappeared from the window. After some time, my nephew reappeared and asked me whether or not I had ever been a member of the PAC. I replied that I had not. He then said he had understood that I joined the PAC during my Africa tour. I told him that I had not, that I had always been a member of the ANC, and that I always would be. This again caused dismay among them and they vanished.

I later learned that PAC propaganda claimed that I had joined the organization when I was traveling elsewhere on the continent. Although I was not pleased to hear this, it did not surprise me. In politics, one can never underestimate how little people know about a situation. A short while later my nephew was back and asked me if I had met and talked with Sobukwe at Pretoria Local. I said that I had and that we had very good discussions. This pleased them and they said good night, and that was the last I saw of them.

A few hours later that same evening a captain came to our cell and com-manded the four of us to pack our belongings. Within minutes my com-rades were taken away, leaving me in the cell by myself. In prison, one counts oneself lucky to be able to wave good-bye to one's comrades. One can be in extraordinarily intimate circumstances with someone for months, and then never see the person again. It is dehumanizing, for it forces one to adapt by becoming more self-contained and insulated.

Now that I was alone, I was also somewhat anxious. There is sometimes safety in numbers; when you are alone, there are no witnesses. I realized I had not been served any food, and banged on the door: "Warder, I have not received my supper."

"You must call me *baas*," he yelled. I went hungry that night.

Very early the next morning I was taken back to Pretoria. The Department of Prisons released a statement to the press that I had been removed from the island for my own safety because PAC prisoners were planning to assault me. This was patently false; they had brought me back me to Pretoria for their own motives, which soon became clear.

I was kept in solitary confinement at Pretoria Local. But prisoners are resourceful and I was soon receiving secret notes and other communications from some of the ANC people there. I had a communication from Henry Fazzie, one of the MK cadres who had undergone military training in Ethiopia and been arrested while attempting to return to South Africa. They were among the first ANC members to be tried under the Sabotage Act.

Through the prison grapevine, I attempted to help them with their defense and suggested they contact Harold Wolpe. I later heard that Wolpe was in police detention. This was my first intimation that something had gone seriously wrong. One day, as I was being led away from the courtyard after exercise, I saw Andrew Mlangeni. I had last seen him in September of 1961 when he was leaving the country for military training. Wolpe, Mlangeni — who else was under arrest?

Early in 1961, Winnie had been banned for two years. I heard from another prisoner that Winnie had recently been charged with violating her bans, which could lead to imprisonment or house arrest. Winnie was headstrong; a banning order was just the type of thing that would make her angry. I had no doubt that she violated her orders, and I would never counsel her not to do so, but it concerned me greatly that she might spend time in prison.

One morning in July 1963, as I was walking along the passage to my cell, I saw Thomas Mashifane, who had been the foreman at Liliesleaf Farm. I greeted him warmly, though I realized that the authorities had undoubtedly led him to my passage to see if I recognized or acknowledged him. I could not help but do otherwise. His presence there could mean only one thing: the authorities had discovered Rivonia.

A day or two later I was summoned to the prison office where I found Walter; Govan Mbeki; Ahmed Kathrada; Andrew Mlangeni; Bob Hepple;

Raymond Mhlaba, a member of the MK High Command who had recently returned from training in China; Elias Motsoaledi, also a member of MK; Dennis Goldberg, an engineer and a member of the Congress of Democrats; Rusty Bernstein, an architect and also a member of the COD; and Jimmy Kantor, an attorney who was Harold Wolpe's brother-in-law. We were all charged with sabotage, and scheduled to appear in court the next day. I had served just nine months of my five-year sentence.

In bits and pieces, I learned what had happened. On the afternoon of July 11, a dry cleaner's van entered the long driveway of the farm. No one at Liliesleaf had ordered a delivery. The vehicle was stopped by a young African guard, but he was overwhelmed when dozens of armed policemen and several police dogs sprang from the vehicle. They surrounded the property and a handful of officers entered the main building and the principal outbuilding. In the latter they found a dozen men around a table discussing a document. Walter jumped out a window but was cut off by a snarling police dog. The arrests also included Arthur Goldreich, who had driven into the farm as the police raid was in progress.

The police searched the entire farm and confiscated hundreds of documents and papers, though they found no weapons. One of the most important documents remained right on the table: Operation Mayibuye, a plan for guerrilla warfare in South Africa. In one fell swoop, the police had captured the entire High Command of Umkhonto we Sizwe. Everyone was detained under the new Ninety-Day Detention Law.

Joe Slovo and Bram Fischer were fortunately not there at the time of the raid. But Joe and Bram often went to the farm two or three times a day. In hindsight, it is extraordinary that Liliesleaf was not discovered sooner. The regime had become stricter and more sophisticated. Wiretaps had become common, as was twenty-four-hour surveillance. The raid was a coup for the state.

On our first day in court we were not given the opportunity to instruct counsel. We were brought before a magistrate and charged with sabotage. A few days later we were allowed to meet with Bram, Vernon Berrangé, Joel Joffe, George Bizos, and Arthur Chaskalson, all of whom were acting for us. I was still being kept separately as I was a convicted prisoner, and these sessions were my first opportunity to talk with my colleagues.

Bram was very somber. In his quiet voice, he told us that we were facing an extremely serious trial and that the state had formally advised him they would ask for the supreme penalty permitted by law, the death sentence. Given the climate of the times, Bram said, this result was a very real possibility. From that moment on we lived in the shadow of the gallows. The mere possibility of a death sentence changes everything. From the start, we considered it the most likely outcome of the trial. Far lesser crimes than ours had recently been punished by life sentences.

Prison officials never let you forget that you might hang. That night, a warder rapped on my cell door at bedtime. "Mandela, you don't have to worry about sleep," he said. "You are going to sleep for a long, long time." I waited a moment and said, "All of us, you included, are going to sleep for a long, long time." It was small consolation.

55

ON OCTOBER 9, 1963, we were picked up in a heavily fortified police van. It had a steel divider running along the center, segregating the white prisoners from the Africans. We were driven to the Palace of Justice in Pretoria, where the Supreme Court sits, for the opening of *The State versus the National High Command and others,* what later became known as *The State versus Nelson Mandela and others,* and is still better known as the Rivonia Trial. Near the court stands a statue of Paul Kruger, the president of the Republic of the Transvaal who fought against British imperialism in the nineteenth century. Underneath this Afrikaner hero is a quotation from one of his speeches. The inscription reads, "In confidence we lay our cause before the whole world. Whether we win or whether we die, freedom will rise in Africa like the sun from the morning clouds."

Our van was in the center of a convoy of police trucks. At the front of this motorcade were limousines carrying high police officials. The Palace of Justice was teeming with armed policemen. To avoid the enormous crowd of our supporters, who had grouped in front of the building, we were driven into the rear of the building and taken in through great iron gates. All around the building police officers with machine guns stood at attention. As we descended from the van, we could hear the great crowd singing and chanting. Once inside, we were held in cells below the courtroom before the opening of what was depicted in the newspapers at home and around the world as the most significant political trial in the history of South Africa.

As we emerged from the cells, each of the accused was accompanied by two armed warders. When we entered the ornate, high-ceilinged courtroom, we each turned to the crowd and made a clenched-fist ANC salute. In the visitors' gallery our supporters shouted *"Amandla Ngawethu!"* and *"Mayibuye Afrika!"* This was inspiring, but dangerous: the police took the names and addresses of all the spectators in the galleries, and photographed them as they left the court. The courtroom was filled with domestic and international journalists, and dozens of representatives of foreign governments.

After we filed in, a group of police officers formed a tight cordon between us and the spectators. I was disgusted to have to appear in court wearing my prison clothes of khaki shorts and flimsy sandals. As a convicted prisoner, I did not have the choice of wearing proper clothes. Many people later commented on how poorly I looked, and not just because of my wardrobe. I had been in and out of solitary confinement for months and I had lost more than twenty-five pounds. I took pains to smile at the gallery when I walked into the courtroom, and seeing our supporters was the best medicine I could have had.

Security was particularly tight as only a few weeks before Arthur Goldreich, Harold Wolpe, Mosie Moola, and Abdulhay Jassat had bribed a young guard and escaped from jail. Arthur and Harold made their way to Swaziland disguised as priests, then flew to Tanganyika. Their escape came at a time of hysteria about the underground and was greeted with blaring newspaper headlines. It was an embarrassment to the government and a boost to our morale.

Our judge in the Rivonia Trial was Mr. Quartus de Wet, judge-president of the Transvaal, who sat in his flowing red robes beneath a wooden canopy. De Wet was one of the last judges appointed by the United Party before the Nationalists came to power and was not considered a government lackey. He was a poker-faced judge who did not suffer fools gladly. The prosecutor was Dr. Percy Yutar, deputy attorney general of the Transvaal, whose ambition was to become attorney general of South Africa. He was a small, bald, dapper fellow, whose voice squeaked when he became angry or emotional. He had a flair for the dramatic and for high-flown if imprecise language.

Yutar rose and addressed the court: "My Lord, I call the case of the state against the National High Command and others." I was accused number one. Yutar handed in the indictment and authorized that we be charged immediately and tried summarily. This was the first time we were given a copy of the indictment. The prosecution had kept it from us, though they gave it to the *Rand Daily Mail,* which had splashed it all over that day's edition of the paper. The indictment charged eleven of us with complicity in over two hundred acts of sabotage aimed at facilitating violent revolution and an armed invasion of the country. The state contended that we were actors in a conspiracy to overthrow the government.

We were charged with sabotage and conspiracy rather than high treason because the law does not require a long preparatory examination (which is highly useful to the defense) for sabotage and conspiracy as it does for treason. Yet the supreme penalty — death by hanging — is the same. With high treason, the state must prove its case beyond a reasonable doubt and needs two witnesses to testify to each charge. Under the Sabotage Law, the onus was on the defense to prove the accused innocent.

Bram Fischer stood up and asked the court for a remand on the grounds that the defense had not had time to prepare its case. He noted that a number of the accused had been held in solitary confinement for unconscionable lengths of time. The state had been preparing for three months, but we had only received the indictment that day. Justice de Wet gave us a three-week adjournment until October 29.

I was disturbed to discover that first day that Winnie was unable to attend. Because of her banning and her restriction to Johannesburg, she needed police permission to come to court. She had applied and been refused. I also learned that our house had been raided and the police had detained a young relative of Winnie's. Winnie was not the only wife being harassed. Albertina Sisulu and Caroline Motsoaledi were detained under the Ninety-Day Detention Act, and Walter's young son Max was also arrested. This was one of the state's most barbarous techniques of applying pressure: imprisoning the wives and children of freedom fighters. Many men in prison were able to handle anything the authorities did to them, but the thought of the state doing the same thing to their families was almost impossible to bear.

Winnie subsequently appealed to the minister of justice, who granted her permission to attend the trial on the condition that she did not wear traditional dress. Ironically, the same government that was telling us to embrace our culture in the homelands forbade Winnie from wearing a Xhosa gown into court.

During the next three weeks, we were permitted to spend our days together preparing our case. I was now among my fellow accused, and the company of my colleagues was a tonic. As awaiting-trial prisoners we were entitled to two half-hour visits a week, and one meal a day could be sent in from the outside. I soon gained back my lost weight with Mrs. Pillay's delicious dinners.

While we were preparing our defense, the government was trying the case in the newspapers. Normally, a case that is sub judice cannot be commented upon in public or in the press. But since the men arrested at Rivonia were Ninety-Day detainees, and therefore not technically charged with a crime, this judicial principle went by the wayside. We were publicly branded as violent revolutionaries by everyone from the minister of justice on down. Newspapers regularly featured headlines like "REVOLUTION ON MILITARY BASIS."

On October 29, we again entered the Palace of Justice; again the crowds were large and excited; again the security was extremely tight; again the court was filled with dignitaries from many foreign embassies. After three weeks with my comrades I felt rejuvenated, and I was far more comfortable in court this time in a suit. Our attorneys had objected to our having to come to court in prison garb and we had won the right to wear our own clothes. We again raised clenched fists to the gallery, and were warned that if we did it again, we would be forced to come to court in our prison khakis. To prevent such outbursts, the authorities reversed the normal order of the prisoners preceding the judge into the courtroom. After that first day, the judge entered first so that court would already be in session when we entered.

We went on the attack immediately — Bram Fischer criticized the state's indictment as shoddy, poorly drawn, and containing absurdities such as the allegation that I had participated in certain acts of sabotage on dates when I was in Pretoria Local. Yutar was flummoxed. Judge de Wet looked to him to reply to Bram's argument, and instead of offering particulars he began to give what the judge derided as "a political speech." De Wet was impatient with Yutar's fumbling and told him so. "The whole basis of your argument as I understand it, Mr. Yutar, is that you are satisfied that the accused are guilty." De Wet then quashed the indictment and gaveled the session to a close.

For that moment we were technically free, and there was pandemonium in the court. But we were rearrested even before Judge de Wet left his seat. Lieutenant Swanepoel clapped each of us on the shoulder and said, "I am arresting you on a charge of sabotage," and we were herded back to our cells. Even so, this was a blow to the government, for they now had to go back to the drawing board in the case they were calling the trial to end all trials.

The state redrew their indictment and we were back in court in early December. We all sensed that in the interim Justice de Wet had grown more hostile to us. We suspected his previous independence had brought down the wrath of the government and pressure had been applied. The new charges were read: we were alleged to have recruited persons for sabotage and guerrilla warfare for the purpose of starting a violent revolution; we had allegedly conspired to aid foreign military units to invade the republic in order to support a Communist revolution; and we had solicited and received funds from foreign countries for this purpose. The orders for munitions on the part of the accused, said Yutar melodramatically, were enough to blow up Johannesburg.

The registrar then requested our pleas. We had agreed not to plead in the traditional manner but to use the moment to show our disdain for the proceedings.

"Accused number one, Nelson Mandela, do you plead guilty or not guilty?"

I rose and said, "My Lord, it is not I, but the government that should be in the dock. I plead not guilty."

"Accused number two, Walter Sisulu, do you plead guilty or not guilty?"

Sisulu: "The government is responsible for what has happened in this country. I plead not guilty."

Justice de Wet said he was not interested in hearing political speeches, that we should merely plead not guilty or guilty. But his direction was ignored. Each of the accused suggested that it was the government that was criminal before pleading not guilty.

To enhance the drama of the proceedings, the state had made arrangements for a live broadcast of Yutar's speech on the South African Broadcasting System. Microphones had been placed on the prosecution table as well as in front of the judge. But just as Yutar was clearing his throat, Bram Fischer rose and made an application to the court for the removal of the microphones on the grounds that the broadcasts would unfairly prejudice the case and were not in keeping with the dignity of the court. Despite Yutar's shrill plea for their retention, Justice de Wet ordered them removed.

In his address, Yutar argued that from the time the ANC had been driven underground, the organization had embarked on a policy of violence designed to lead from sabotage through guerrilla warfare to an armed invasion of the country. He asserted that we planned to deploy thousands of trained guerrilla units throughout the country, and these units were to spearhead an uprising that would be followed by an armed invasion by military units of a foreign power. "In the midst of the resulting chaos, turmoil, and disorder," Yutar proclaimed, "it was planned by the accused to set up a Provisional Revolutionary Government to take over the administration and control of the country." The engine of this grand plan was Umkhonto we Sizwe, under the political direction of the ANC and the Communist Party, and the headquarters of Umkhonto was Rivonia.

In his orotund prose, Yutar described how we recruited members for MK, how we planned our national uprising for 1963 (here he was confusing us with the PAC), how we erected a powerful radio transmitter at Rivonia, and how we were collectively responsible for two hundred twenty-two acts of sabotage. He said Elias Motsoaledi and Andrew Mlangeni were in charge of recruiting members and that Dennis Goldberg ran a special school for recruits in the Cape. He detailed the production of various bombs, as well as the solicitation of money abroad.

Over the next three months, the state produced one hundred seventy-three witnesses and entered into the record thousands of documents and photographs, including standard works on Marxism, histories of guerrilla warfare, maps, blueprints, and a passport made out to one David Motsamayi. The first witness was a police photographer who had taken pictures of Rivonia, and the next witnesses were domestic workers for the Goldreich family, who had been held in detention all this time even though they had no connection to the politics of the household. These servants identified most of us by pointing to us in the dock, but old Mr. Jelliman, in a brave attempt to help me, pretended that he did not see me when he was asked to point to accused number one. Look again, the prosecutor said, go over all the faces carefully. "I do not think he is here," Jelliman said quietly.

We wondered what evidence the state had to prove my guilt. I had been out of the country and in prison while much of the planning at Rivonia had taken place. When I saw Walter in Pretoria Local just after my sentencing, I urged him to make sure that all my books and notes were removed from the farm. But during the first week of the trial, when Rusty Bernstein applied for bail, Percy Yutar dramatically produced the sketch of the Fort and the accompanying note about escape that I had made while detained there. Yutar exclaimed that this was evidence that all of the accused meant to escape. It was a sign that nothing of mine had been removed from Rivonia. Later, I was told that my colleagues at Rivonia had decided to preserve my escape note because they thought it would be historic in the future. But in the present, it cost Rusty Bernstein his bail.

The state's star witness was Bruno Mtolo, or "Mr. X" as he was known in court. In introducing "Mr. X," Yutar informed the court that the interrogation would take three days and then, in theatrical tones, he added that the witness was "in mortal danger." Yutar asked that the evidence be given in camera, but that the press be included provided that they not identify the witness.

Mtolo was a tall, well-built man with an excellent memory. A Zulu from Durban, he had become the leader of the Natal region of MK. He was an experienced saboteur, and had been to Rivonia. I had met him only once, when I addressed his group of MK cadres in Natal after my return from the continent. His evidence concerning me in particular made me realize that the state would certainly be able to convict me.

He began by saying that he was an MK saboteur who had blown up a municipal office, a power pylon, and an electricity line. With impressive precision, he explained the operation of bombs, land mines, and grenades, and how MK worked from underground. Mtolo said that while he had never lost faith in the ideals of the ANC, he did lose faith in the organization when he realized that it and MK were instruments of the Communist Party.

His testimony was given with simplicity and what seemed like candor, but Mtolo had gone out of his way to embellish his evidence. This was undoubtedly done on police instructions. He told the court that during my remarks to the Natal Regional Command I had stated that all MK cadres ought to be good Communists but not to disclose their views publicly. In fact, I never said anything of the sort, but his testimony was meant to link me and MK to the Communist Party. His memory appeared so precise the ordinary person would assume that it was accurate in all instances. But this was not so.

I was bewildered by Mtolo's betrayal. I never ruled out the possibility of even senior ANC men breaking down under police torture. But by all accounts, Mtolo was never touched. On the stand, he went out of his way to implicate people who were not even mentioned in the case. It is possible, I know, to have a change of heart, but to betray so many others, many of whom were quite innocent, seemed to me inexcusable.

During cross-examination we learned that Mtolo had been a petty criminal before joining MK and had been imprisoned three previous times for theft. But despite these revelations, he was an extremely damaging witness, for the judge found him reliable and believable, and his testimony incriminated nearly all of us.

The keystone of the state's case was the six-page Plan of Action confiscated in the Rivonia raid. The leaders of the High Command had had this very document before them on the table when the police stormed the farm. Operation Mayibuye sketches out in general form the plan for the possible commencement of guerrilla operations, and how it might spark a mass armed uprising against the government. It envisions an initial landing of small guerrilla forces in four different areas of South Africa and the attacking of preselected targets. The document set a goal of seven thousand MK recruits in the country who would meet the initial outside force of one hundred twenty trained guerrillas.

The prosecution's case rested in large part on their contention that Operation Mayibuye had been approved by the ANC executive and had become the operating plan of MK. We insisted that Operation Mayibuye had not yet been formally adopted and was still under discussion at the time of the arrests. As far as I was concerned, Operation Mayibuye was a draft document that was not only not approved, but was entirely unrealistic in its goals and plans. I did not believe that guerrilla warfare was a viable option at that stage.

The plan had been drafted in my absence so I had very little knowledge of it. Even among the Rivonia Trialists there was disagreement as to whether the plan had been adopted as ANC policy. Govan, who had drafted the document with Joe Slovo, insisted that it had been agreed upon and felt that it was wrong for us to argue in court that it was still under discussion. But all the other accused contended that the document, while drawn up by the High Command, had not been approved by the ANC executive or even seen by Chief Luthuli.

Although a capital trial can be quite grim, our spirits were generally high. There was a good deal of gallows humor among us. Dennis Goldberg, the youngest of the accused, had an irrepressible sense of humor and often had us laughing when we should not have been. When one of the prosecution witnesses described how Raymond Mhlaba had worn a clerical collar as a disguise, Dennis took to calling him Reverend Mhlaba.

In our consulting room downstairs, we often communicated through notes, which we would then burn and throw in the wastebasket. One of the Special Branch officers who looked after us was Lieutenant Swanepoel, a burly, red-faced fellow who was convinced we were always putting one over on him. One day, while Swanepoel was observing us from the door, Govan Mbeki began to write a note in a conspicuously secretive manner. With similar drama he handed me the note. I read it, nodded my head sagely, and passed it to Kathy, who ostentatiously took out his matches as if to burn the note when Swanepoel swooped into the room, grabbed the paper out of Kathy's hands, and said something about the dangers of lighting matches indoors. He then left the room to read his prize; a few seconds later, he stormed back saying, "I will get all of you for this!" Govan had written in capital letters: "ISN'T SWANEPOEL A FINE-LOOKING CHAP?"

We were locked up in prison and on trial for our lives, but outside new life was blossoming. Jimmy Kantor's wife was to give birth any day. Jimmy was an attorney who had been roped into the trial by the state for no other reason than that he was Harold Wolpe's brother-in-law.

One morning, when we were sitting in the dock, a note was passed down to me from the other end.

Barbara and I have discussed godfathers at length and we have come to the conclusion that, whether the baby is a girl or boy, we would consider it an honour if you would agree to accept this office as an adjunct to the more disreputable positions you have held in the past.

By return mail I sent Jimmy back a note.

I would be more than delighted, and the honour is mine, not the baby's. Now they dare not hang me.

56

THE STATE CASE continued through the Christmas season of 1963, ending on February 29, 1964. We had a little over a month to examine the evidence and prepare our defense. We were not all equally affected by the evidence. There was no evidence against James Kantor; he was not even a member of our organization and should not have been on trial at all. For Rusty Bernstein, Raymond Mhlaba, and Ahmed Kathrada, the evidence of involvement in conspiracy was slight and we decided they should not incriminate themselves. In Rusty's case, the evidence was negligible; he had merely been found at Rivonia with the others. The remaining six of us would make admissions of guilt on certain charges.

Bram was deeply pessimistic. He avowed that even if we proved that guerrilla war had not been approved and our policy of sabotage was designed not to sacrifice human life, the state could still impose the death sentence. The defense team was divided on whether or not we should testify. Some asserted that it would hurt our case if we testified. George Bizos, though, suggested that unless we gave evidence and convinced the judge that we had not decided on guerrilla warfare, he would certainly impose the supreme penalty.

Right from the start we had made it clear that we intended to use the trial not as a test of the law but as a platform for our beliefs. We would not deny, for example, that we had been responsible for acts of sabotage. We would not deny that a group of us had turned away from nonviolence. We were not concerned with getting off or lessening our punishment, but with having the trial strengthen the cause for which we were all struggling — at whatever cost to ourselves. We would not defend ourselves in a legal sense so much as in a moral sense. We saw the trial as a continuation of the struggle by other means. We would readily admit what was known by the state to be true but refuse to give away any information we thought might implicate others.

We would dispute the state's central contention that we had embarked on guerrilla warfare. We would admit that we had made contingency plans to undertake guerrilla warfare in the event sabotage failed. But we would claim it had not yet failed, for it had not been sufficiently attempted. We would deny the claims of murder and damage to innocent bystanders that the state alleged; either these claims were outright lies, or the incidents were the work of someone else. We had never contemplated the intervention of foreign military forces. In order to make these claims, we believed we would have to explain Operation Mayibuye to the court.

In my own case, the court had sufficient evidence for a conviction. Documents in my handwriting showed that I had left the country illegally, had arranged for military training for our men, and had been behind the formation of Umkhonto we Sizwe. There was also a document in my handwriting called "How to be a good Communist," which the state suggested was proof that I was a card-carrying Communist. In fact the document's title was taken from the work of a Chinese theoretician named Liu Shao Chi, and was written by me to prove a point to Moses Kotane. We had been engaged in a running debate about the appeal of communism to ordinary South Africans. I had long argued that Communist literature was, for the most part, dull, esoteric, and Western-centered, but ought to be simple, clear, and relevant to the African masses. Moses insisted it could not be done. To prove my point, I had taken Liu's essay and rewritten it for an African audience.

I would be the first witness and therefore set the tone for the defense. In South African courts, evidence from the witness box can be given only in the form of an answer to a question. I did not want to be limited to that format. We decided that instead of giving testimony, I would read a statement from the dock, while the others would testify and go through cross-examination.

Because a witness making a statement from the dock does not submit to cross-examination or questions from the bench, the statement does not have the same legal weight as ordinary testimony. Those who choose to make such a statement usually do so to avoid cross-examination. Our attorneys warned me that it would put me in a more precarious legal situation; anything I said in my statement regarding my own innocence would be discounted by the judge. But that was not our highest priority. We believed it was important to open the defense with a statement of our politics and ideals, which would establish the context for all that followed. I wanted very much to cross swords with Percy Yutar, but it was more important that I use the platform to highlight our grievances.

All of this was agreed upon in consultation, mainly through notes because the consultation room was bugged. We even used the state's eavesdropping to our advantage by supplying them with disinformation. We gave every indication that I was going to testify so that they would spend their time planning their cross-examination. In a staged conversation, I told our attorney Joel Joffe that I would need the Treason Trial record to prepare my testimony. We smiled at the notion of Yutar poring over the hundred or so volumes of Treason Trial transcripts.

I spent about a fortnight drafting my address, working mainly in my cell in the evenings. When I was finished, I read it first to my comrades and fellow accused. They approved of it, suggesting a few changes, and then I asked Bram Fischer to look it over. Bram became concerned after reading it and had a respected advocate named Hal Hanson read it. Hanson told Bram, "If Mandela reads this in court they will take him straight out in back of the courthouse and string him up." That confirmed Bram's anxieties and he came to me the next day and urged me to modify the speech. I felt we were likely to hang no matter what we said, so we might as well say what we truly believed. The atmosphere at the time was extremely grim, with newspapers routinely speculating that we would receive the death sentence. Bram begged me not to read the final paragraph, but I was adamant.

On Monday, the twentieth of April, under the tightest of security, we were taken to the Palace of Justice, this time to begin our defense. Winnie was there with my mother, and I nodded to them as we entered the court, which was again full.

Bram announced that certain parts of the state's evidence would be conceded by the accused, and there was a buzz in the court. But he went on to say that the defense would deny a number of the state's assertions, including the contention that Umkhonto we Sizwe was the military wing of the ANC. He said that the leaders of MK and the ANC "endeavored to keep these two organizations entirely separate. They did not always succeed in this," he said, "but . . . every effort was made to achieve that object." He emphatically denied that the ANC took orders from the Communist Party. He said the defense would challenge the allegation that Goldberg, Kathrada, Bernstein, and Mhlaba were members of Umkhonto. He stated that the defense would show that Umkhonto had not in fact adopted Operation Mayibuye, and that MK had not embarked on preparations for guerrilla warfare.

"That will be denied?" asked Justice de Wet incredulously.

"That will be denied," replied Bram. "The evidence will show that while preparations for guerrilla warfare were being made, no plan was ever adopted. It was hoped throughout that such a step could be avoided."

Then, in his soft voice, Bram said, "The defense case, My Lord, will commence with a statement from the dock by accused number one, who personally took part in the establishment of Umkhonto, and who will be able to inform the court of the beginnings of that organization."

At this, Yutar popped up from the table and cried, "My Lord! My Lord!" He was distressed that I would not be testifying for he had undoubtedly prepared for my cross-examination. "My Lord," he said rather despondently, "a statement from the dock does not carry the same weight as evidence under oath."

"I think, Dr. Yutar," Justice de Wet responded dryly, "that counsel for the defense have sufficient experience to advise their clients without your assistance." Yutar sat down.

"Neither we nor our clients are unaware of the provisions of the criminal code," replied Bram. "I call on Nelson Mandela."

I rose and faced the courtroom and read slowly.

I am the first accused.

I hold a Bachelor's degree in Arts, and practiced as an attorney in Johannesburg for a number of years in partnership with Mr. Oliver Tambo. I am a convicted prisoner, serving five years for leaving the country without a permit and for inciting people to go on strike at the end of May 1961.

I admit immediately that I was one of the persons who helped to form Umkhonto we Sizwe and that I played a prominent role in its affairs until I was arrested in August 1962.

At the outset, I want to say that the suggestion made by the state in its opening that the struggle in South Africa is under the influence of foreigners or Communists is wholly incorrect. I have done whatever I did, both as an individual and as a leader of my people, because of my experience in South Africa, and my own proudly felt African background, and not because of what any outsider might have said.

In my youth in the Transkei, I listened to the elders of my tribe telling stories of the old days. Amongst the tales they related to me were those of wars fought by our ancestors in defense of the fatherland. The names of Dingane and Bambatha, Hintsa and Makanna, Squngthi and Dalasile, Moshoeshoe and Sekhukhuni, were praised as the pride and glory of the entire African nation. I hoped then that life might offer me the opportunity to serve my people and make my own humble contribution to their freedom struggle. This is what has motivated me in all that I have done in relation to the charges made against me in this case.

Having said this, I must deal immediately and at some length with the question of violence. Some of the things so far told the court are true and some are untrue. I do not, however, deny that I planned sabotage. I did not plan it in a spirit of recklessness nor because I have any love of violence. I planned it as a result of a calm and sober assessment of the political situation that had arisen after many years of tyranny, exploitation, and oppression of my people by whites.

I wanted to impress upon the court that we had not acted irresponsibly or without thought to the ramifications of taking up violent action. I laid particular emphasis on our resolve to cause no harm to human life.

We of the ANC have always stood for a nonracial democracy, and we shrank from any action which might drive the races further apart than they already were. But the hard facts were that fifty years of nonviolence had brought the African people nothing but more repressive legislation, and fewer and fewer rights. It may not be easy for this court to understand, but it is a fact that for a long time the people had been talking of violence — of the day when they would fight the white man and win back their country, and we, the leaders of the ANC, had nevertheless always prevailed upon them to avoid violence and to use peaceful methods. While some of us discussed this in May and June of 1961, it could not be denied that our policy to achieve a nonracial state by nonviolence had achieved nothing, and that our followers were beginning to lose confidence in this policy and were developing disturbing ideas of terrorism. . . .

Umkhonto was formed in November 1961. When we took this decision, and subsequently formulated our plans, the ANC heritage of nonviolence and racial harmony was very much with us. We felt that the country was drifting towards a civil war in which blacks and whites would fight each other. We viewed the situation with alarm. Civil war would mean the destruction of what the ANC stood for; with civil war racial peace would be more difficult than ever to achieve. We already have examples in South African history of the results of war. It has taken more than fifty years for the scars of the South African [Anglo-Boer] War to disappear. How much longer would it take to eradicate the scars of interracial civil war, which could not be fought without a great loss of life on both sides?

Sabotage, I said, offered the best hope for future race relations. The reaction of the white rulers to our first efforts were swift and brutal: sabotage was declared to be a crime punishable by death. We did not want civil war, I said, but we needed to be prepared for it.

Experience convinced us that rebellion would offer the government limitless opportunities for the indiscriminate slaughter of our people. But it was precisely because the soil of South Africa is already drenched with the blood of innocent Africans that we felt it our duty to make preparations as a long-term undertaking to use force in order to defend ourselves against force. If war were inevitable, we wanted the fight to be conducted on terms most favorable to our people. The fight which held out prospects best for us and the least risk of life to both sides was guerrilla warfare. We decided, therefore, in our preparations for the future, to make provision for the possibility of guerrilla warfare.

All whites undergo compulsory military training, but no such training was given to Africans. It was in our view essential to build up a nucleus of trained men who would be able to provide the leadership which would be required if guerrilla warfare started. We had to prepare for such a situation before it became too late to make proper preparations.

I explained that at this stage in our discussions I left the country to attend the PAFMECSA conference and undergo military training. I said that I underwent training because if there was to be a guerrilla war, I wanted to be able to stand and fight beside my own people. Even so, I believed that the possibilities of sabotage were far from exhausted and should be pursued with vigor.

I told the court of the dividing line between the ANC and MK, and how we made good-faith attempts to keep the two separate. This was our policy, but in practice, it was not so simple. Because of bannings and imprisonment, people often had to work in both organizations. Though this might have sometimes blurred the distinction, it did not abolish it. I disputed the allegations of the state that the aims and objects of the ANC and the Communist Party were one and the same.

Experience convinced us that rebellion would offer the government

The ideological creed of the ANC is, and always has been, the creed of African Nationalism. It is not the concept of African Nationalism expressed in the cry, "Drive the white man into the sea." The African Nationalism for which the ANC stands is the concept of freedom and fulfillment for the African people in their own land. The most important political document ever adopted by the ANC is the Freedom Charter. It is by no means a blueprint for a socialist state. . . . The ANC has never at any period of its history advocated a revolutionary change in the economic structure of the country, nor has it, to the best of my recollection, ever condemned capitalist society. . . .

The ANC, unlike the Communist Party, admitted Africans only as members. Its chief goal was, and is, for the African people to win unity and full political rights. The Communist Party's main aim, on the other hand, was to remove the capitalists and to replace them with a working-class government. The Communist Party sought to emphasize class distinctions whilst the ANC seeks to harmonize them.

It is true that there has often been close cooperation between the ANC and the Communist Party. But cooperation is merely proof of a common goal — in this case the removal of white supremacy — and is not proof of a complete community of interests. The history of the world is full of similar examples. Perhaps the most striking illustration is to be found in the cooperation between Great Britain, the United States of America and the Soviet Union in the fight against Hitler. Nobody but Hitler would have dared to suggest that such cooperation turned Churchill or Roosevelt into Communists or Communist tools, or that Britain and America were working to bring about a Communist world. . . .

It is perhaps difficult for white South Africans, with an ingrained prejudice against communism, to understand why experienced African politicians so readily accepted Communists as their friends. But to us the reason is obvious. Theoretical differences amongst those fighting against oppression is a luxury we cannot afford at this stage. What is more, for many decades Communists were the only political group in South Africa who were prepared to treat Africans as human beings and their equals; who were prepared to eat with us; talk with us, live with and work with us. Because of this, there are many Africans who, today, tend to equate freedom with communism.

I told the court that I was not a Communist and had always regarded myself as an African patriot. I did not deny that I was attracted by the idea of a classless society, or that I had been influenced by Marxist thought. This was true of many leaders of the newly independent states of Africa, who accepted the need for some form of socialism to enable their people to catch up with the advanced countries of the West.

From my reading of Marxist literature and from conversations with Marxists, I have gained the impression that Communists regard the parliamentary system of the West as undemocratic and reactionary. But, on the contrary, I am an admirer of such a system.

The Magna Carta, the Petition of Rights and the Bill of Rights, are documents which are held in veneration by democrats throughout the world. I have great respect for British political institutions, and for the country's system of justice. I regard the British Parliament as the most democratic institution in the world, and the independence and impartiality of its judiciary never fail to arouse my admiration. The American Congress, the country's doctrine of separation of powers, as well as the independence of its judiciary, arouse in me similar sentiments.

I detailed the terrible disparities between black and white life in South Africa. In education, health, income, every aspect of life, blacks were barely at a subsistence level while whites had the highest standards in the world — and aimed to keep it that way. Whites, I said, often claim that Africans in South Africa were better off than Africans in the rest of the continent. Our complaint, I said, was not that we were poor by comparison with the people in the rest of Africa, but that we were poor by comparison with the whites in our country, and that we were prevented by legislation from righting that imbalance.

> The lack of human dignity experienced by Africans is the direct result of the policy of white supremacy. White supremacy implies black inferiority. Legislation designed to preserve white supremacy entrenches this notion. Menial tasks in South Africa are invariably performed by Africans. When anything has to be carried or cleaned the white man looks around for an African to do it for him, whether the African is employed by him or not. . . .
>
> Poverty and the breakdown of family life have secondary effects. Children wander about the streets of the townships because they have no schools to go to, or no money to enable them to go to school, or no parents at home to see that they go to school, because both parents (if there be two) have to work to keep the family alive. This leads to a breakdown in moral standards, to an alarming rise in illegitimacy and to growing violence which erupts, not only politically, but everywhere. . . .
>
> Africans want a just share in the whole of South Africa; they want security and a stake in society. Above all, we want equal political rights, because without them our disabilities will be permanent. I know this sounds revolutionary to the whites in this country, because the majority of voters will be Africans. This makes the white man fear democracy. . . .
>
> This then is what the ANC is fighting for. Their struggle is a truly national one. It is a struggle of the African people, inspired by their own suffering and their own experience. It is a struggle for the right to live.

I had been reading my speech, and at this point I placed my papers on the defense table, and turned to face the judge. The courtroom became extremely quiet. I did not take my eyes off Justice de Wet as I spoke from memory the final words.

> During my lifetime I have dedicated myself to this struggle of the African people. I have fought against white domination, and I have fought against black domination. I have cherished the ideal of a democratic and free society in which all persons live together in harmony and with equal opportunities. It is an ideal which I hope to live for and to achieve. But if needs be, it is an ideal for which I am prepared to die.

The silence in the courtroom was now complete. At the end of the address, I simply sat down. I did not turn and face the gallery, though I felt all their eyes on me. The silence seemed to stretch for many minutes. But in fact it lasted probably no more than thirty seconds, and then from the gallery I heard what sounded like a great sigh, a deep, collective "ummmm," followed by the cries of women.

I had read for over four hours. It was a little after four in the afternoon, the time court normally adjourned. But Justice de Wet, as soon as there was order in the courtroom, asked for the next witness. He was determined to lessen the impact of my statement. He did not want it to be the last and only testimony of the day. But nothing he did could weaken its effect. When I finished my address and sat down, it was the last time that Justice de Wet ever looked me in the eye.

The speech received wide publicity in both the local and foreign press, and was printed, virtually word for word, in the *Rand Daily Mail*. This despite the fact that all my words were banned. The speech both indicated our line of defense and disarmed the prosecution, which had prepared its entire case based on the expectation that I would be giving evidence denying responsibility for sabotage. It was now plain that we would not attempt to use legal niceties to avoid accepting responsibility for actions we had taken with pride and premeditation.

Accused number two, Walter Sisulu, was next. Walter had to bear the brunt of the cross-examination that Yutar had prepared for me. Walter withstood a barrage of hostile questions and rose above Yutar's petty machinations to explain our policy in clear and simple terms. He asserted that Operation Mayibuye and the policy of guerrilla warfare had not been adopted as ANC policy. In fact, Walter told the court that he had personally opposed its adoption on the grounds that it was premature.

Govan followed Walter in the witness box and proudly related to the court his longtime membership in the Communist Party. The prosecutor asked Govan why, if he admitted many of the actions in the four counts against him, he did not simply plead guilty to the four counts? "First," Govan said, "I felt I should come and explain under oath some of the reasons that led me to join these organizations. There was a sense of moral duty attached to it. Secondly, for the simple reason that to plead guilty would to my mind indicate a sense of moral guilt. I do not accept there is moral guilt attached to my answers."

Like Govan, Ahmed Kathrada and Rusty Bernstein testified to their membership of the Communist Party as well as the ANC. Although Rusty was captured at Rivonia during the raid, the only evidence of a direct nature that the state had against him was that he had assisted in the erection of a radio aerial at the farm. Kathy, in his sharp-witted testimony, denied committing acts of sabotage or inciting others to do so, but he said he supported such acts if they advanced the struggle.

We had all been surprised when accused number eight, James Kantor, had been arrested and grouped with us. Apart from being the brother-in-law and legal partner of Harold Wolpe, who performed a number of transactions for us through his office, he had no involvement whatsoever with the ANC or MK. There was virtually no evidence against him, and I assumed the only reason the state kept up the charade of prosecuting him in prison was to intimidate progressive lawyers.

On the day that Justice de Wet was to rule on Jimmy's case, we were waiting in the cells underneath the court and I said to Jimmy, "Let us exchange ties for good luck." But when he saw the wide, old-fashioned tie I gave him compared to the lovely, silk tie he gave me, he probably thought I was merely trying to improve my wardrobe. Jimmy was something of a clotheshorse, but he wore the tie to court and when Justice de Wet dismissed the charges against him, he lifted the tie up to me as a kind of salute and farewell.

Raymond Mhlaba was one of the leading ANC and MK figures in the eastern Cape, but because the state did not have much evidence against him, he denied he was a member of MK and that he knew anything about sabotage. We all decided that neither Elias Motsoaledi, accused number nine, nor Andrew Mlangeni, accused number ten, should testify. They were low-level members of MK, and could not add much to what had already been said. Elias Motsoaledi, despite having been beaten and tortured in prison, never broke down. Andrew Mlangeni, the last accused, made an unsworn statement admitting that he carried messages and instructions for MK and had disguised himself as a priest to facilitate this work. He, too, informed the court that he had been assaulted while in prison, and subjected to electric shock treatment. Andrew was the last witness. The defense rested. All that remained were the final arguments and then judgment.

On the twentieth of May, Yutar handed out a dozen blue leather-bound volumes of his final speech to the press and one to the defense. Despite its handsome packaging, Yutar's address was a garbled summary of the prosecution's case and did not explain the indictment or assess the evidence. It was filled with ad hominem insults. "The deceit of the accused is amazing," he said at one point. "Although they represented scarcely 1% of the Bantu population they took it upon themselves to tell the world that the Africans in South Africa are suppressed, oppressed and depressed." Even Judge de Wet seemed mystified by Yutar's speech, and at one point interrupted him to say, "Mr. Yutar, you do concede that you failed to prove guerrilla warfare was ever decided upon, do you not?"

Yutar was stunned. He had assumed precisely the opposite. We were surprised as well, for the judge's question gave us hope. Yutar haltingly told the court that preparations for guerrilla warfare were indeed made.

"Yes, I know that," de Wet replied impatiently, "the defense concedes that. But they say that prior to their arrest they took no decision to engage in guerrilla warfare. I take it that you have no evidence contradicting that and that you accept it?"

"As Your Worship wishes," Yutar said in a strangled voice.

Yutar finished by saying that the case was not only one of high treason "par excellence," but of murder and attempted murder — neither of which was mentioned in the indictment. In a fit of bluster, he proclaimed, "I make bold to say that every particular allegation in the indictment has been proved." He knew, even as he uttered those words, that they were patently false.

Defense counsel Arthur Chaskalson rose first to deal with some of the legal questions raised by the prosecution. He rejected Yutar's statement that the trial had anything to do with murder, and reminded the court that MK's express policy was that there should be no loss of life. When Arthur began to explain that other organizations committed acts of sabotage for which the accused were blamed, de Wet interrupted to say he already accepted that as a fact. This was another unexpected victory.

Bram Fischer spoke next and was prepared to tackle the state's two most serious contentions: that we had undertaken guerrilla warfare and that the ANC and MK were the same. Though de Wet had said he believed that guerrilla warfare had not yet begun, we were taking no chances. But as Bram launched into his first point, de Wet interjected somewhat testily,

"I thought I made my attitude clear. I accept that no decision or date was fixed upon for guerrilla warfare."

When Bram began his second point, de Wet again interrupted him to say that he also conceded the fact that the two organizations were separate. Bram, who was usually prepared for anything, was hardly prepared for de Wet's response. He then sat down; the judge had accepted his arguments even before he made them. We were jubilant — that is, if men facing the death sentence can be said to be jubilant. Court was adjourned for three weeks while de Wet considered the verdict.

57

THE WORLD had been paying attention to the Rivonia Trial. Nightlong vigils were held for us at St. Paul's Cathedral in London. The students of London University elected me president of their Students' Union, in absentia. A group of experts at the U.N. urged a national convention for South Africa that would lead to a truly representative parliament, and recommended an amnesty for all opponents of apartheid. Two days before Judge de Wet was due to give his decision, the U.N. Security Council (with four abstentions, including Great Britain and the United States) urged the South African government to end the trial and grant amnesty to the defendants.

In the days before we were due to reconvene, I wrote papers for a set of London University examinations for my LL.B. It might seem odd that I was taking law exams a few days before the verdict. It certainly seemed bizarre to my guards, who said I would not need a law degree where I was going. But I had continued my studies through the trial and I wanted to take the examination. I was single-minded about it, and I later realized that it was a way to keep myself from thinking negatively. I knew I would not be practicing law again very soon, but I did not want to consider the alternative. I passed the exams.

On Thursday, June 11, we reassembled in the Palace of Justice for the verdict. We knew that for at least six of us, there could be no verdict but guilty. The question was the sentence.

De Wet wasted no time in getting down to business. He spoke in low, rapid tones. "I have recorded the reasons for the conclusions I have come to. I do not propose to read them out.

"Accused number one is found guilty on all four counts. Accused number two is found guilty on all four counts. Accused number three is found guilty on all four counts. . . ."

De Wet pronounced each of the main accused guilty on all counts. Kathy was found guilty on only one of four counts, and Rusty Bernstein was found not guilty and discharged.

"I do not propose to deal with the question of sentence today," de Wet said. "The state and the defense will be given opportunities to make any submission they want tomorrow morning at ten o'clock." Court was then adjourned.

We had hoped that Kathy and Mhlaba might escape conviction, but it was another sign, if one was necessary, that the state was taking a harsh line. If he could convict Mhlaba on all four counts with little evidence, could the death sentence be far behind for those of us against whom the evidence was overwhelming?

That night, after a discussion among ourselves, Walter, Govan, and I informed counsel that whatever sentences we received, even the death sentence, we would not appeal. Our decision stunned our lawyers. Walter, Govan, and I believed an appeal would undermine the moral stance we had taken. We had from the first maintained that what we had done, we had done proudly, and for moral reasons. We were not now going to suggest otherwise in an appeal. If a death sentence was passed, we did not want to hamper the mass campaign that would surely spring up. In light of the bold and defiant line we had taken all along, an appeal would seem anticlimactic and even disillusioning. Our message was that no sacrifice was too great in the struggle for freedom.

Counsel were unhappy about our decision, and wanted to talk about an appeal. But Walter, Govan, and I wanted to discuss the mechanics of the sentencing procedure the next day. If we were sentenced to death, what would then happen? We were told that after de Wet pronounced the death sentence, he would ask me, as the first accused, "Have you any reason to advance why the sentence of death should not be passed?" I told Bram, Joel, and Vernon that in that case I would have quite a lot to say. I would tell de Wet that I was prepared to die secure in the knowledge that my death would be an inspiration to the cause for which I was giving my life. My death — our deaths — would not be in vain; if anything we might serve the cause greater in death as martyrs than we ever could in life. Counsel said that such a speech would not be very helpful for an appeal, and I reaffirmed that we would not be appealing.

Even if — especially if — we did not receive the death penalty, there were practical reasons not to appeal. For one thing, we might lose. An appellate court might decide that de Wet had been too lenient and that we deserved the death penalty. An appeal would forestall international pressure to release us.

For the state, a death sentence would be the most practical verdict. We had heard that John Vorster, the minister of justice, had told friends that Prime Minister Smuts's greatest blunder during the Second World War was not hanging him for his treason. The Nationalists, he said, would not make the same mistake.

I was prepared for the death penalty. To be truly prepared for something, one must actually expect it. One cannot be prepared for something while secretly believing it will not happen. We were all prepared, not because we were brave but because we were realistic. I thought of the line from Shakespeare: "Be absolute for death; for either death or life shall be the sweeter."

58

ON FRIDAY, JUNE 12, 1964, we entered court for the last time. Nearly a year had passed since the fateful arrests at Rivonia. Security was extraordinarily high. Our convoy raced through the streets with sirens wailing. All the roads leading to the courthouse had been blocked off to normal traffic. The police checked the identification of anyone attempting to go near the Palace of Justice. They had even set up checkpoints at the local bus and railway stations. Despite the intimidation, as many as two thousand people assembled in front of the courthouse holding banners and signs such as "WE STAND BY OUR LEADERS." Inside, the spectators' gallery was full, and it was standing room only for the local and foreign press.

I waved hello to Winnie and my mother. It was heartening to see them there; my mother had journeyed all the way from the Transkei. It must be a very odd sensation to come to a courtroom to see whether or not your son will be sentenced to death. Though I suspect my mother did not understand all that was going on, her support never wavered. Winnie was equally stalwart, and her strength gave me strength.

The registrar called out the case: "The State against Mandela and others." Before the sentence was to be passed, there were two pleas in mitigation. One was delivered by Harold Hanson and the other by the author Alan Paton, who was also national president of the Liberal Party. Hanson spoke eloquently, saying that a nation's grievances cannot be suppressed, that people will always find a way to give voice to those grievances. "It was not their aims which had been criminal," said Hanson, "only the means to which they had resorted." Hanson said the judge would do well to recall that his own people, the Afrikaners, had struggled violently for their freedom.

Though Paton did not himself support violence, he said the accused had had only two alternatives: "to bow their heads and submit, or to resist by force." The defendants should receive clemency, he said, otherwise the future of South Africa would be bleak.

But de Wet did not seem to be listening to either man. He neither looked up nor took any notes while they spoke. He seemed absorbed in his own thoughts. He had obviously already decided; he was merely waiting for the moment to reveal his decision.

He nodded for us to rise. I tried to catch his eye, but he was not even looking in our direction. His eyes were focused on the middle distance. His face was very pale, and he was breathing heavily. We looked at each other and seemed to know: it would be death, otherwise why was this normally calm man so nervous? And then he began to speak.

> I have heard a great deal during the course of this case about the grievances of the non-European population. The accused have told me and their counsel have told me that the accused who were all leaders of the non-European population were motivated entirely by a desire to ameliorate these grievances. I am by no means convinced that the motives of the accused were as altruistic as they wish the court to believe. People who organize a revolution usually take over the government and personal ambition cannot be excluded as a motive.

He paused for a moment as if to catch his breath. De Wet's voice, which was muted before, was now barely audible.

> The function of this court as is the function of the court in any other country is to enforce law and order and to enforce the laws of the state within which it functions. The crime of which the accused have been convicted, that is the main crime, the crime of conspiracy, is in essence one of high treason. The state has decided not to charge the crime in this form. Bearing this in mind and giving the matter very serious consideration I have decided not to impose the supreme penalty which in a case like this would usually be the proper penalty for the crime, but consistent with my duty that is the only leniency which I can show. The sentence in the case of all the accused will be one of life imprisonment.

We looked at each other and smiled. There had been a great collective gasp in the courtroom when de Wet announced that he was not sentencing us to death. But there was consternation among some spectators because they had been unable to hear de Wet's sentence. Dennis Goldberg's wife called to him, "Dennis, what is it!?"

"Life!," he yelled back, grinning. "Life! To live!"

I turned and smiled broadly to the gallery, searching out Winnie's face and that of my mother, but it was extremely confused in the court, with people shouting, police pushing the crowd this way and that. I could not see them. I flashed the thumbs-up ANC salute as many of the spectators were dashing outside to tell the crowd the verdict. Our police guardians began to hustle us out of the dock and toward the door leading underground, and although I looked again for Winnie's face, I was not able to see her before I ducked through the door leading to the cells below.

We were kept handcuffed in the cells underneath the courthouse. The police were extremely nervous about the crowd outside. They kept us underground for more than half an hour, hoping people would disperse. We were taken through the back of the building and entered the black van. We could hear the motorcycle escort revving up beside us. To avoid the crowd, the van took a different course, but even so, we could hear the crowd shouting *"Amandla!,"* and the slow beautiful rhythms of *"Nkosi Sikelel' iAfrika."* We made clenched fists through the bars of the window, hoping the crowd could see us, not knowing if they could.

All of us were now convicted prisoners. We were separated from Dennis Goldberg because he was white and he was taken to a different facility. The rest of us were locked up in cells in Pretoria Local away from all the other prisoners. Instead of shouts and songs, we now heard only the clanging of doors and gates.

That night, as I lay on my mat on the floor of my cell, I ran over the reasons for de Wet's decision. The demonstrations throughout South Africa and the international pressure undoubtedly weighed on his mind. International trade unions had protested the trial. Dockworkers' unions around the world threatened not to handle South African goods. The Russian prime minister, Leonid Brezhnev, wrote to Dr. Verwoerd asking for leniency. Members of the United States Congress protested. Fifty members of the British Parliament had staged a march in London. Alex Douglas-Home, the British foreign secretary, was rumored to be working behind the scenes to help our cause. Adlai Stevenson, the U.S. representative at the U.N., wrote a letter saying that his government would do everything it could to prevent a death sentence. I thought that once de Wet had accepted that we had not yet initiated guerrilla warfare and that the ANC and MK were separate entities, it would have been difficult to impose the death penalty; it would have seemed excessive.

Verwoerd told Parliament that the judgment had not been influenced by the telegrams of protest and representations that had come in from around the world. He boasted that he had tossed into the wastebasket all the telegrams from socialist nations.

Towards the end of the proceedings, Judge de Wet had remarked in passing to Bram Fischer that the defense had generated a great deal of worldwide propaganda in the case. This was perhaps his own way of acknowledging the pressure. He knew that if we were executed, the great majority of the people would regard him as our killer.

Yet he was under even greater pressure from his own people. He was a white Afrikaner, a creature of the South African system and mind-set. He had no inclination to go against the belief system that had formed him. He had succumbed to these pressures by sentencing us to life and resisted them by not giving us death.

I was surprised and displeased by the sentences de Wet imposed on Kathrada, Motsoaledi, and Mlangeni. I had expected him to discharge Kathy, and to give Elias and Andrew lighter sentences. The latter two were comparatively junior members of MK, and the combined offenses of the three of them could hardly be compared with those of the rest of us. But by not appealing, we undoubtedly cost Kathy, Andrew, and Elias: an appeals court might have cut down their sentences.

Every evening, in Pretoria Local, before lights were out, the jail would echo to African prisoners singing freedom songs. We too would sing in this great swelling chorus. But, each evening, seconds before the lights were dimmed, as if in obedience to some silent command, the hum of voices would stop and the entire jail would become silent. Then, from a dozen places throughout the prison, men would yell *"Amandla!"* This would be met by hundreds of voices replying *"Ngawethu!"* Often, we would start this call-and-response ourselves, but that night, other nameless prisoners took the initiative, and the voices from around the prison seemed uncommonly strong as though steeling us for what lay ahead.

Part Eight

ROBBEN ISLAND: THE DARK YEARS

59

AT MIDNIGHT, I was awake and staring at the ceiling — images from the trial were still rattling around in my head — when I heard steps coming down the hallway. I was locked in my own cell, away from the others. There was a knock at my door and I could see Colonel Aucamp's face at the bars. "Mandela," he said in a husky whisper, "are you awake?"

I told him I was. "You are a lucky man," he said. "We are taking you to a place where you will have your freedom. You will be able to move around; you'll see the ocean and the sky, not just gray walls."

He intended no sarcasm, but I well knew that the place he was referring to would not afford me the freedom I longed for. He then remarked rather cryptically, "As long as you don't make trouble, you'll get everything you want."

Aucamp then woke the others, all of whom were in a single cell, ordering them to pack their things. Fifteen minutes later we were making our way through the iron labyrinth of Pretoria Local, with its endless series of clanging metal doors echoing in our ears.

Once outside, the seven of us — Walter, Raymond, Govan, Kathy, Andrew, Elias, and myself — were handcuffed and piled into the back of a police van. It was well after midnight, but none of us was tired, and the atmosphere was not at all somber. We sat on the dusty floor, singing and chanting, reliving the final moments of the trial. The warders provided us with sandwiches and cold drinks and Lieutenant Van Wyck was perched in the back with us. He was a pleasant fellow, and during a lull in the singing, he offered his unsolicited opinion on our future. "Well," he said, "you chaps won't be in prison long. The demand for your release is too strong. In a year or two, you will get out and you will return as national heroes. Crowds will cheer you, everyone will want to be your friend, women will want you. Ag, you fellows have it made." We listened without comment, but I confess his speech cheered me considerably. Unfortunately, his prediction turned out to be off by nearly three decades.

We were departing quietly, secretly, under a heavy police escort, in the middle of the night, and in less than half an hour we found ourselves at a small military airport outside the city. We were hustled onto a Dakota, a large military transport plane that had seen better days. There was no heat, and we shivered in the belly of the plane. Some of the others had never flown before and they seemed more anxious about our voyage than our destination; bumping up and down in a plane at fifteen thousand feet seemed far more perilous than being locked in a cell behind high walls.

After about an hour in the air, dawn lightened the terrain below. The plane had portholes, and as soon as we could see in the half-light, my comrades pressed their faces to the glass. We flew southeast, over the dry, flat plains of the Orange Free State and the green and mountainous Cape peninsula. I, too, craned to see out the portholes, examining the scenery not as a tourist but as a strategist, looking for areas where a guerrilla army might hide itself.

There had been a running argument since the formation of MK as to whether the countryside of South Africa could support a guerrilla army. Most of the High Command thought that it could not. When we flew over a wooded, mountainous area called Matroosberg in the Cape, I yelled to my colleagues that here was terrain where we could fight. The men became excited and craned to get a better look, and indeed, the heavily forested area appeared as though it could shelter a nascent guerrilla force.

Minutes later we approached the outskirts of Cape Town. Soon, we could see the little matchbox houses of the Cape Flats, the gleaming towers of downtown, and the horizontal top of Table Mountain. Then, out in Table Bay, in the dark blue waters of the Atlantic, we could make out the misty outline of Robben Island.

We landed on an airstrip on one end of the island. It was a grim, over-cast day, and when I stepped out of the plane, the cold winter wind whipped through our thin prison uniforms. We were met by guards with automatic weapons; the atmosphere was tense but quiet, unlike the bois-terous reception I had received on my arrival on the island two years before.

We were driven to the old jail, an isolated stone building, where we were ordered to strip while standing outside. One of the ritual indignities of prison life is that when you are transferred from one prison to another, the first thing that happens is that you change from the garb of the old prison to that of the new. When we were undressed, we were thrown the plain khaki uniforms of Robben Island.

Apartheid's regulations extended even to clothing. All of us, except Kathy, received short trousers, an insubstantial jersey, and a canvas jacket. Kathy, the one Indian among us, was given long trousers. Normally Africans would receive sandals made from car tires, but in this instance we were given shoes. Kathy, alone, received socks. Short trousers for Africans were meant to remind us that we were "boys." I put on the short trousers that day, but I vowed that I would not put up with them for long.

The warders pointed with their guns where they wanted us to go, and barked their orders in simple one-word commands: "Move!" "Silence!" "Halt!" They did not threaten us in the swaggering way that I recalled from my previous stay, and betrayed no emotion.

The old jail was only temporary quarters for us. The authorities were in the process of finishing an entirely separate maximum-security structure for political prisoners. While there, we were not permitted to go outside or have any contact with other prisoners.

The fourth morning we were handcuffed and taken in a covered truck to a prison within a prison. This new structure was a one-story rectangular stone fortress with a flat cement courtyard in the center, about one hundred feet by thirty feet. It had cells on three of the four sides. The fourth side was a twenty-foot-high wall with a catwalk patrolled by guards with German shepherds.

The three lines of cells were known as sections A, B, and C, and we were put in section B, on the easternmost side of the quadrangle. We were each given individual cells on either side of a long corridor, with half the cells facing the courtyard. There were about thirty cells in all. The total number of prisoners in the single cells was usually about twenty-four. Each cell had one window, about a foot square, covered with iron bars. The cell had two doors: a metal gate or grille with iron bars on the inside and a thick wooden door outside of that. During the day, only the grille was locked; at night, the wooden door was locked as well.

The cells had been constructed hurriedly, and the walls were perpetually damp. When I raised this with the commanding officer, he told me our bodies would absorb the moisture. We were each issued three blankets so flimsy and worn they were practically transparent. Our bedding consisted of a single sisal, or straw, mat. Later we were given a felt mat, and one placed the felt mat on top of the sisal one to provide some softness. At that time of year, the cells were so cold and the blankets provided so little warmth that we always slept fully dressed.

I was assigned a cell at the head of the corridor. It overlooked the courtyard and had a small eye-level window. I could walk the length of my cell in three paces. When I lay down, I could feel the wall with my feet and my head grazed the concrete at the other side. The width was about six feet, and the walls were at least two feet thick. Each cell had a white card posted outside of it with our name and our prison service number. Mine read, "N Mandela 466/64," which meant I was the 466th prisoner admitted to the island in 1964. I was forty-six years old, a political prisoner with a life sentence, and that small cramped space was to be my home for I knew not how long.

We were immediately joined by a number of prisoners who had been held in the general section of the prison, a squat brick building not far from Section B. The general prison, known as sections F and G, contained about a thousand mostly common-law prisoners. As many as a quarter of them were political prisoners, and a handful of those men were put with us in Section B. We were isolated from the general prisoners for two reasons: we were considered risky from a security perspective, but even more dangerous from a political standpoint. The authorities were concerned we might "infect" the other prisoners with our political views.

Among the men put with us was George Peake, one of the founders of the South African Coloured People's Organization, a Treason Trialist, and most recently a member of the Cape Town City Council. He had been sentenced for planting explosives outside a Cape Town prison. Dennis Brutus, another Coloured political activist, was a poet and writer from Port Elizabeth imprisoned for violating his bans. We were also joined by Billy Nair, a longtime member of the Natal Indian Congress, sentenced for sabotage as a member of Umkhonto we Sizwe.

Within a few days we had more company, including Neville Alexander, a prominent Coloured intellectual and member of the Non-European Unity Movement, who had formed a tiny radical offshoot called the Yu Chi Chan Club in Cape Town which studied guerrilla warfare. Neville had a B.A. from the University of Cape Town and a doctorate in German literature from Tubingen University in Germany. Along with Neville, there was Fikile Bam, a law student of the University of Cape Town and another member of the Yu Chi Chan Club; and Zephania Mothopeng, a member of the PAC National Executive. Zeph had been a teacher in Orlando, and was a staunch opponent of Bantu Education, and one of the most level-headed of the PAC's leaders. Three aged peasants from the Transkei, sentenced for plotting to assassinate K. D. Matanzima, now the chief minister of the "self-governing" Transkei, were also imprisoned with us.

This became our core group of about twenty prisoners. Some I knew, some I had heard of, while others I did not know at all. Normally, in prison, one of the few festive times is seeing old friends and new faces, but the atmosphere in those first few weeks was so oppressive we were not even able to greet each other. We had as many guards as prisoners, and they enforced every regulation with threats and intimidation.

*   *   *

That first week we began the work that would occupy us for the next few months. Each morning, a load of stones about the size of volleyballs was dumped by the entrance to the courtyard. Using wheelbarrows, we moved the stones to the center of the yard. We were given either four-pound hammers or fourteen-pound hammers for the larger stones. Our job was to crush the stones into gravel. We were divided into four rows, about a yard-and-a-half apart, and sat cross-legged on the ground. We were each given a thick rubber ring, made from tires, in which to place the stones. The ring was meant to catch flying chips of stone, but hardly ever did so. We wore makeshift wire masks to protect our eyes.

Warders walked among us to enforce the silence. During those first few weeks, warders from other sections and even other prisons came to stare at us as if we were a collection of rare caged animals. The work was tedious and difficult; it was not strenuous enough to keep us warm but it was demanding enough to make all our muscles ache.

June and July were the bleakest months on Robben Island. Winter was in the air, and the rains were just beginning. It never seemed to go above forty degrees Fahrenheit. Even in the sun, I shivered in my light khaki shirt. It was then that I first understood the cliché of feeling the cold in one's bones. At noon we would break for lunch. That first week all we were given was soup, which stank horribly. In the afternoon, we were permitted to exercise for half an hour under strict supervision. We walked briskly around the courtyard in single file.

On one of our first days pounding rocks, a warder commanded Kathy to take a wheelbarrow filled with gravel to the truck parked by the entrance. Kathy was a slender fellow unused to hard physical labor. He could not budge the wheelbarrow. The warders yelled: *"Laat daardie kruiwa loop!"* (Let that wheelbarrow move!) As Kathy managed to nudge it forward, the wheelbarrow looked as if it would tip over, and the warders began to laugh. Kathy, I could see, was determined not to give them cause for mirth. I knew how to maneuver the wheelbarrows, and I jumped up to help him. Before being ordered to sit down, I managed to tell Kathy to wheel it slowly, that it was a matter of balance not strength. He nodded and then carefully moved the wheelbarrow across the courtyard. The warders stopped smiling.

The next morning, the authorities placed an enormous bucket in the courtyard and announced that it had to be half full by the end of the week. We worked hard and succeeded. The following week, the warder in charge announced that we must now fill the bucket three-quarters of the way. We worked with great diligence and succeeded. The next week we were ordered to fill the bucket to the top. We knew we could not tolerate this much longer, but said nothing. We even managed to fill the bucket all the way, but the warders had provoked us. In stolen whispers we resolved on a policy: no quotas. The next week we initiated our first go-slow strike on the island: we would work at less than half the speed we had before to protest the excessive and unfair demands. The guards immediately saw this and threatened us, but we would not increase our pace, and we continued this go-slow strategy for as long as we worked in the courtyard.

Robben Island had changed since I had been there for a fortnight's stay in 1962. In 1962, there were few prisoners; the place seemed more like an experiment than a fully-fledged prison. Two years later, Robben Island was without question the harshest, most iron-fisted outpost in the South African penal system. It was a hardship station not only for the prisoners but for the prison staff. Gone were the Coloured warders who had supplied cigarettes and sympathy. The warders were white and over-whelmingly Afrikaans-speaking, and they demanded a master-servant relationship. They ordered us to call them *"baas,"* which we refused. The racial divide on Robben Island was absolute: there were no black warders, and no white prisoners.

Moving from one prison to another always requires a period of adjustment. But journeying to Robben Island was like going to another country. Its isolation made it not simply another prison, but a world of its own, far removed from the one we had come from. The high spirits with which we left Pretoria had been snuffed out by its stern atmosphere; we were face to face with the realization that our life would be unredeemably grim. In Pretoria, we felt connected to our supporters and our families; on the island, we felt cut off, and indeed we were. We had the consolation of being with each other, but that was the only consolation. My dismay was quickly replaced by a sense that a new and different fight had begun.

From the first day, I had protested about being forced to wear short trousers. I demanded to see the head of the prison and made a list of complaints. The warders ignored my protests, but by the end of the second week, I found a pair of old khaki trousers unceremoniously dumped on the floor of my cell. No pin-striped three-piece suit has ever pleased me as much. But before putting them on I checked to see if my comrades had been issued trousers as well.

They had not, and I told the warder to take them back. I insisted that all African prisoners must have long trousers. The warder grumbled, "Mandela, you say you want long pants and then you don't want them when we give them to you." The warder balked at touching trousers worn by a black man, and finally the commanding officer himself came to my cell to pick them up. "Very well, Mandela," he said, "you are going to have the same clothing as everyone else." I replied that if he was willing to give me long trousers, why couldn't everyone else have them? He did not have an answer.

60

AT THE END of our first two weeks on the island, we were informed that our lawyers, Bram Fischer and Joel Joffe, were going to be visiting the following day. When they arrived, we were escorted to the visiting area to meet them. The purpose of their visit was twofold: to see how we had settled in, and to verify that we still did not want to appeal our sentences. It had only been a few weeks since I had seen them, but it felt like an eternity. They seemed like visitors from another world.

We sat in an empty room, a major just outside supervising the consultation. I felt like hugging them, but I was restrained by the presence of the major. I told them that all of us were well, and explained that we were still opposed to an appeal for all the reasons we had previously enunciated, including the fact that we did not want our appeal to interfere with the cases of other ANC defendants. Bram and Joel seemed resigned to this, though I knew Bram believed we should mount an appeal.

When we were winding up our conversation, I briefly asked Bram about Molly, his wife. No sooner had I pronounced Molly's name than Bram stood up, turned away, and abruptly walked out of the room. A few minutes later, he returned, once again composed, and resumed the conversation, but without answering my question.

Our meeting ended shortly afterward, and when we were walking back to our cells with the major, he said to me, "Mandela, were you struck by the behavior of Bram Fischer?" I said that I had been. He told me that Molly had died in a car accident the previous week. Bram, he said, had been driving and had swerved to avoid an animal in the road, and the car had plunged into a river. Molly had drowned.

We were devastated by the news. Molly was a wonderful woman, generous and unselfish, utterly without prejudice. She had supported Bram in more ways than it was possible to know. She had been wife, colleague, and comrade. Bram had already experienced disaster in his life: his son, a diabetic, had died in adolescence.

The act of turning away when I asked about Molly was typical of Bram's character. He was a stoic, a man who never burdened his friends with his own pain and troubles. As an Afrikaner whose conscience forced him to reject his own heritage and be ostracized by his own people, he showed a level of courage and sacrifice that was in a class by itself. I fought only against injustice, not my own people.

I informed the major that I intended to write Bram a condolence letter, and he responded that I could do so. The rules governing letter-writing were then extremely strict. We were only permitted to write to our immediate families, and just one letter of five hundred words every six months. I was therefore surprised and pleased when the major did not oppose my writing Bram. But he didn't live up to his agreement. I wrote the letter and handed it over to the major, but it was never posted.

Within a few months, our life settled into a pattern. Prison life is about routine: each day like the one before; each week like the one before it, so that the months and years blend into each other. Anything that departs from this pattern upsets the authorities, for routine is the sign of a well-run prison.

Routine is also comforting for the prisoner, which is why it can be a trap. Routine can be a pleasant mistress whom it is hard to resist, for routine makes the time go faster. Watches and timepieces of any kind were barred on Robben Island, so we never knew precisely what time it was. We were dependent on bells and warders' whistles and shouts. With each week resembling the one before, one must make an effort to recall what day and month it is. One of the first things I did was to make a calendar on the wall of my cell. Losing a sense of time is an easy way to lose one's grip and even one's sanity.

Time slows down in prison; the days seem endless. The cliché of time passing slowly usually has to do with idleness and inactivity. But this was not the case on Robben Island. We were busy almost all the time, with work, study, resolving disputes. Yet, time nevertheless moved glacially. This is partially because things that took a few hours or days outside would take months or years in prison. A request for a new toothbrush might take six months or a year to be filled. Ahmed Kathrada once said that in prison the minutes can seem like years, but the years go by like minutes. An afternoon pounding rocks in the courtyard might seem like forever, but suddenly it is the end of the year, and you do not know where all the months went.

The challenge for every prisoner, particularly every political prisoner, is how to survive prison intact, how to emerge from prison undiminished, how to conserve and even replenish one's beliefs. The first task in accomplishing that is learning exactly what one must do to survive. To that end, one must know the enemy's purpose before adopting a strategy to undermine it. Prison is designed to break one's spirit and destroy one's resolve. To do this, the authorities attempt to exploit every weakness, demolish every initiative, negate all signs of individuality — all with the idea of stamping out that spark that makes each of us human and each of us who we are.

Our survival depended on understanding what the authorities were attempting to do to us, and sharing that understanding with each other. It would be very hard if not impossible for one man alone to resist. I do not know that I could have done it had I been alone. But the authorities' greatest mistake was keeping us together, for together our determination was reinforced. We supported each other and gained strength from each other. Whatever we knew, whatever we learned, we shared, and by sharing we multiplied whatever courage we had individually. That is not to say that we were all alike in our responses to the hardships we suffered. Men have different capacities and react differently to stress. But the stronger ones raised up the weaker ones, and both became stronger in the process. Ultimately, we had to create our own lives in prison. In a way that even the authorities acknowledged, order in prison was preserved not by the warders but by ourselves.

As a leader, one must sometimes take actions that are unpopular, or whose results will not be known for years to come. There are victories whose glory lies only in the fact that they are known to those who win them. This is particularly true of prison, where one must find consolation in being true to one's ideals, even if no one else knows of it.

I was now on the sidelines, but I also knew that I would not give up the fight. I was in a different and smaller arena, an arena for whom the only audience was ourselves and our oppressors. We regarded the struggle in prison as a microcosm of the struggle as a whole. We would fight inside as we had fought outside. The racism and repression were the same; I would simply have to fight on different terms.

Prison and the authorities conspire to rob each man of his dignity. In and of itself, that assured that I would survive, for any man or institution that tries to rob me of my dignity will lose because I will not part with it at any price or under any pressure. I never seriously considered the possibility that I would not emerge from prison one day. I never thought that a life sentence truly meant life and that I would die behind bars. Perhaps I was denying this prospect because it was too unpleasant to contemplate. But I always knew that someday I would once again feel the grass under my feet and walk in the sunshine as a free man.

I am fundamentally an optimist. Whether that comes from nature or nurture, I cannot say. Part of being optimistic is keeping one's head pointed toward the sun, one's feet moving forward. There were many dark moments when my faith in humanity was sorely tested, but I would not and could not give myself up to despair. That way lay defeat and death.

61

WE WERE AWAKENED at 5:30 each morning by the night warder, who clanged a brass bell at the head of our corridor and yelled, *"Word wakker! Staan op!"* (Wake up! Get up!) I have always been an early riser and this hour was not a burden to me. Although we were roused at 5:30, we were not let out of our cells until 6:45, by which time we were meant to have cleaned our cells and rolled up our mats and blankets. We had no running water in our cells and instead of toilets had iron sanitary buckets known as "ballies." The ballies had a diameter of ten inches and a concave porcelain lid on the top that could contain water. The water in this lid was meant to be used for shaving and to clean our hands and faces.

At 6:45, when we were let out of our cells, the first thing we did was to empty our ballies. The ballies had to be thoroughly cleansed in the sinks at the end of the hallway or they created a stench. The only pleasant thing about cleaning one's ballie was that this was the one moment in those early days when we could have a whispered word with our colleagues. The warders did not like to linger when we cleaned them, so it was a chance to talk softly.

During those first few months, breakfast was delivered to us in our cells by prisoners from the general section. Breakfast consisted of mealie pap porridge, cereal made from maize or corn, which the general prisoners would slop in a bowl and then spin through the bars of our cells. It was a clever trick and required a deft hand so as not to spill any of the porridge.

After a few months, breakfast was delivered to us in the courtyard in old metal oil drums. We would help ourselves to pap using simple metal bowls. We each received a mug of what was described as coffee, but which was in fact ground-up maize, baked until it was black, and then brewed with hot water. Later, when we were able to go into the courtyard to serve ourselves, I would go out into the courtyard and jog around the perimeter until breakfast arrived.

Like everything else in prison, diet is discriminatory.

In general, Coloureds and Indians received a slightly better diet than Africans, but it was not much of a distinction. The authorities liked to say that we received a balanced diet; it was indeed balanced — between the unpalatable and the inedible. Food was the source of many of our protests, but in those early days, the warders would say, "Ag, you kaffirs are eating better in prison than you ever ate at home!"

In the midst of breakfast, the guards would yell, *"Val in! Val in!"* (Fall in! Fall in!), and we would stand outside our cells for inspection. Each prisoner was required to have the three buttons of his khaki jacket properly buttoned. We were required to doff our hats as the warder walked by. If our buttons were undone, our hats unremoved, or our cells untidy, we were charged with a violation of the prison code and punished with either solitary confinement or the loss of meals.

After inspection we would work in the courtyard hammering stones until noon. There were no breaks; if we slowed down, the warders would yell at us to speed up. At noon, the bell would clang for lunch and another metal drum of food would be wheeled into the courtyard. For Africans, lunch consisted of boiled mealies, that is, coarse kernels of corn. The Indian and Coloured prisoners received samp, or mealie rice, which consisted of ground mealies in a souplike mixture. The samp was sometimes served with vegetables whereas our mealies were served straight.

For lunch we often received *phuzamandla,* which means "drink of strength," a powder made from mealies and a bit of yeast. It is meant to be stirred into water or milk and when it is thick, it can be tasty, but the prison authorities gave us so little of the powder that it barely colored the water. I would usually try to save my powder for several days until I had enough to make a proper drink, but if the authorities discovered that you were hoarding food, the powder was confiscated and you were punished.

After lunch we worked until four, when the guards blew shrill whistles and we once again lined up to be counted and inspected. We were then permitted half an hour to clean up. The bathroom at the end of our corridor had two seawater showers, a saltwater tap, and three large galvanized metal buckets, which were used as bathtubs. There was no hot water. We would stand or squat in these buckets, soaping ourselves with the brackish water, rinsing off the dust from the day. To wash yourself with cold water when it is cold outside is not pleasant, but we made the best of it. We would sometimes sing while washing, which made the water seem less icy. In those early days, this was one of the only times that we could converse.

Precisely at 4:30, there would be a loud knock on the wooden door at the end of our corridor, which meant that supper had been delivered. Common law prisoners were used to dish out the food to us and we would return to our cells to eat it. We again received mealie pap porridge, sometimes with the odd carrot or piece of cabbage or beetroot thrown in — but one usually had to search for it. If we did get a vegetable, we would usually have the same one for weeks on end, until the carrots or cabbage were old and moldy and we were thoroughly sick of them. Every other day, we received a small piece of meat with our porridge. The meat was usually mostly gristle.

For supper, Coloured and Indian prisoners received a quarter loaf of bread (known as a *katkop,* that is, a cat's head, after the shape of the bread) and a slab of margarine. Africans, it was presumed, did not care for bread as it was a "European" type of food.

Typically, we received even less than the meager amounts stipulated in the regulations. This was because the kitchen was rife with smuggling. The cooks — all of whom were common-law prisoners — kept the best food for themselves or their friends. Often they would lay aside the tastiest morsels for the warders in exchange for favors or preferential treatment.

At 8 P.M., the night warder would lock himself in the corridor with us, passing the key through a small hole in the door to another warder outside. The warder would then walk up and down the corridor, ordering us to go to sleep. No cry of "lights out" was ever given on Robben Island because the single mesh-covered bulb in our cell burned day and night. Later, those studying for higher degrees were permitted to read until ten or eleven.

The acoustics along the corridor were quite good, and we would try to chat a bit to each other before going to sleep. But if we could hear a whisper quite clearly, so could the warder, who would yell, *"Stilte in die gang!"* (Quiet in the passage!) The warder would walk up and down a few times to make sure we were not reading or writing. After a few months, we would sprinkle a handful of sand along the corridor so that we could hear the warder's footsteps and have time to stop talking or hide any contraband. Only when we were quiet did he take a seat in the small office at the end of the passage where he dozed until morning.

62

ONE MORNING, several days after my meeting with Bram and Joel, we were taken to the head office. The head office was only about a quarter of a mile away and was a simple stone structure that resembled our own section. Once there, we were lined up to have our fingerprints taken, which was routine prison service business. But while waiting, I noticed a warder with a camera. After our fingerprints had been taken, the chief warder ordered us to line up for photographs. I motioned to my colleagues not to move, and I addressed the warder: "I would like you to produce the document from the commissioner of prisons authorizing our pictures to be taken." Photographs of prisoners required such authorization.

It was always valuable to be familiar with regulations, because the warders themselves were often ignorant of them and could be intimidated by one's superior knowledge. The warder was taken aback by my request and was unable to offer any explanation or produce anything in writing from the commissioner of prisons. He threatened to charge us if we did not consent to have our photographs taken, but I said that if there was no authorization, there would be no pictures, and that is where the matter remained.

As a rule, we objected to having our pictures taken in prison on the grounds that it is generally demeaning to be seen as a prisoner. But there was one photograph I did consent to, the only one I ever agreed to while on Robben Island.

One morning, a few weeks later, the chief warder, instead of handing us hammers for our work in the courtyard, gave us each needles and thread and a pile of worn prison jerseys. We were instructed to repair the garments, but we discovered that most of these jerseys were frayed beyond repair. This struck us as a curious task, and we wondered what had provoked the change. Later that morning, at about eleven o'clock, the front gate swung open, revealing the commanding officer with two men in suits. The commanding officer announced that the two visitors were a reporter and photographer from the *Daily Telegraph* in London. He related this as if visiting members of the international press were a regular diversion for us.

Although these men were our first official visitors, we regarded them skeptically. Firstly, they were brought in under the auspices of the government, and second, we were aware that the *Telegraph* was a conservative newspaper unlikely to be sympathetic to our cause. We well knew that there was great concern in the outside world about our situation and that it was in the government's interest to show that we were not being mistreated.

The two journalists walked slowly around the courtyard, surveying us. We kept our heads down concentrating on our work. After they had made one circuit, one of the guards plucked me by the shoulder and said, "Mandela, come, you will talk now." In those early days, I often spoke on behalf of my fellow prisoners. The prison service regulations were explicit that each prisoner was permitted to speak only for himself. This was done to negate the power of organization and to neutralize our collective strength. We objected to this rule, but made little headway. We were not even permitted to use the word *we* when we made complaints.

But during the first few years, when the authorities needed one prisoner to speak on behalf of others, that individual would be me.

I talked to the reporter, whose name was Mr. Newman, for about twenty minutes, and was candid about both prison and the Rivonia Trial. He was an agreeable fellow, and at the end of our talk, he said he would like the photographer to take my picture. I was reluctant, but in this case relented because I knew the photograph would only be published overseas, and might serve to help our cause if the article was even the least bit friendly. I told him I would agree provided Mr. Sisulu could join me. The image shows the two of us talking in the courtyard about some matter that I can no longer remember. I never saw the article or heard anything about it. The reporters were barely out of sight when the warders removed the jerseys and gave us back our hammers.

The men from the *Telegraph* were the first of a small stream of visitors during those early months. While the Rivonia Trial still resonated in people's minds, the government was eager to show the international community that we were being treated properly. There were stories in the press about the inhuman conditions on the island, about how we were being assaulted and tortured. These allegations embarrassed the government, and to combat them they brought in a string of outsiders meant to rebut these critical stories.

We were briefly visited by a British lawyer who had argued for Namibian independence before the World Court, after which we were informed that a Mr. Hynning, a representative of the American Bar Association, would be coming to see us. Americans were then a novelty in South Africa, and I was curious to meet a representative of so august a legal organization.

On the day of Mr. Hynning's visit we were called into the courtyard. The American arrived in the company of General Steyn, the commissioner of prisons, who rarely made appearances on the island. General Steyn was that unusual thing in the prison service, a polished and sophisticated man. His suits were always of a fine quality and a fashionable cut. He was courtly, and referred to us as "gentlemen," even doffing his hat to us, something no one else in the prison service ever did. Yet General Steyn oppressed us by omission rather than commission. He basically turned a blind eye to what was happening on the island. His habitual absence emboldened the more brutal prison officials and gave them carte blanche to do whatever they wanted. In his most gracious manner, the general introduced our guest and said, "Gentlemen, please select your spokesman." A number of the prisoners called out my name.

General Steyn nodded in my direction, and I stood up. In contrast to

General Steyn, Mr. Hynning was a heavyset, unkempt man. I thanked him for visiting us and said we were honored by his presence. I then summarized our complaints, beginning with the central and most important one, that we were political prisoners, not criminals, and that we should be treated as such. I enumerated our grievances about the food, our living conditions, and the work detail. But as I was speaking, Mr. Hynning kept interrupting me. When I made a point about the long hours doing mindless work, he declared that as prisoners we had to work and were probably lazy to boot.

When I started to detail the problems with our cells, he interjected that the conditions in backward American prisons were far worse than Robben Island, which was a paradise by comparison. He added that we had been justly convicted and were lucky not to have received the death penalty, which we probably deserved.

Mr. Hynning perspired a great deal and there were those among us who thought he was not altogether sober. He spoke in what I assumed was a southern American accent, and had a curious habit of spitting when he talked, something none of us had ever seen before.

Finally, I had heard enough, and I interrupted him, "No, sir, you misunderstand the points that I am making." Hynning took offense that I was now contradicting him, while General Steyn watched and listened without comment. Under the circumstances, it was difficult to keep tempers down. The men were angered by Mr. Hynning's remarks and annoyed that he had been permitted to see us at all. Normally, a visit of any kind lifted our spirits but the visit of Mr. Hynning was demoralizing. Perhaps that is what the authorities wanted. To meet someone with so impressive an affiliation and so little understanding was depressing. Hynning finally just turned and walked away without so much as a good-bye. We were not sorry to see him go.

We discussed Mr. Hynning for years afterward and many of the men imitated the way he spoke to comic effect. We never heard about him again, and he certainly did not win any friends on Robben Island for the American Bar Association.

63

IN JAIL, all prisoners are classified by the authorities as one of four categories: A, B, C, or D. A is the highest classification and confers the most privileges; D is the lowest and confers the least. All political prisoners, or what the authorities called "security prisoners," were automatically classified as D on admission. The privileges affected by these classifications included visits and letters, studies, and the opportunity to buy groceries and incidentals — all of which are the lifeblood of any prisoner. It normally took years for a political prisoner to raise his status from D to C.

We disdained the classification system. It was corrupt and demeaning, another way of repressing prisoners in general and political prisoners in particular. We demanded that all political prisoners be in one category. Although we criticized it, we could not ignore it: the classification system was an inflexible feature of prison life. If you protested that, as a D Group prisoner, you could receive only one letter every six months, the authorities would say, Improve your behavior, become a C Group prisoner, and you will be able to receive two letters every six months. If you complained that you did not receive enough food, the authorities would remind you that if you were in A Group, you would be able to receive money orders from the outside and purchase extra food at the prison canteen. Even a freedom fighter benefits from the ability to buy groceries and books.

The classifications generally ran parallel to the length of one's sentence. If you were sentenced to eight years, you would generally be classified as D for the first two years, C for the next two, B for the following two, and A for the last two. But the prison authorities wielded the classification system as a weapon against political prisoners, threatening to lower our hard-won classifications in order to control our behavior.

Though I had been in prison for nearly two years before I was taken to Robben Island, I was still in D Group when I arrived. While I desired the privileges that came with higher classifications, I refused to compromise my conduct. The fastest way to raise one's classification was to be docile and not complain. "Ag, Mandela, you are a trouble-maker," the warders would say. "You will be in D Group for the rest of your life."

Every six months, prisoners were called before the prison board to have their classifications evaluated. The board was meant to assess our behavior in terms of prison regulations, but we found that it preferred to act as a political tribunal rather than a mere evaluator of behavior. During my first meeting with the board, the officials asked me questions about the ANC and my beliefs. Although this had nothing to with the classification system, I was vain enough to answer and think that I might convert them to my beliefs. It was one of the few times we were treated as human beings, and I for one responded. Later I realized that this was simply a technique on the part of the authorities to glean information from us, and I had fallen for it. Shortly afterward, we agreed among ourselves not to discuss politics with the prison board.

*   *   *

As a D Group prisoner, I was entitled to have only one visitor, and to write and receive only one letter every six months. I found this one of the most inhumane restrictions of the prison system. Communication with one's family is a human right; it should not be restricted by the artificial gradations of a prison system. But it was one of the facts of prison life.

Visits and letters were restricted to "first degree" relatives. This was a restriction we not only found irksome but racist. The African sense of immediate family is far different from that of the European or Westerner. Our family structures are larger and more inclusive; anyone who claims descent from a common ancestor is deemed part of the same family.

In prison, the only thing worse than bad news about one's family is no news at all. It is always harder to cope with the disasters and tragedies one imagines than with the reality, however grim or disagreeable. A letter with ill tidings was always preferable to no letter at all.

But even this miserable restriction was abused by the authorities. The anticipation of mail was overwhelming. Mail call took place once a month, and sometimes six months would go by without a letter. To be allowed one letter in six months and then not to receive it is a great blow. One wonders: What has happened to my wife and children, to my mother and my sisters? When I did not receive a letter I felt as dry and barren as the Great Karroo desert. Often the authorities would withhold mail out of spite. I can remember warders saying, "Mandela, we have received a letter for you, but we cannot give it to you." No explanation of why, or whom the letter was from. It required all my self-discipline not to explode at such times. Afterward, I would protest through the proper channels, and sometimes get it.

When letters did arrive, they were cherished. A letter was like the summer rain that could make even the desert bloom. When I was handed a letter by the authorities, I would not rush forward and grab it as I felt like doing, but take it in a leisurely manner. Though I yearned to tear it open and read it on the spot, I would not give the authorities the satisfaction of seeing my eagerness, and I would return slowly to my cell as though I had many things to occupy me before opening a letter from my family.

During the first few months, I received one letter from Winnie, but it was so heavily censored that not much more than the salutation was left. The island's censors would black out the offending passages in ink, but they later changed this when they realized we could wash away the ink and see what was underneath. They began to use razors to slice out whole paragraphs. Since most letters were written on both sides of a single piece of paper, the material on the other side would also be excised.

They seemed to relish delivering letters in tatters. The censorship delayed the delivery of mail because warders, some of whom were not proficient in English, might take as long as a month to censor a letter. The letters we wrote were censored as well; they were often as cut up as the letters we received.

At the end of August, after I had been on the island less than three months, I was informed by the authorities that I would have a visitor the following day. They would not tell me who it was. Walter was informed that he, too, would have a visitor, and I suspected, I hoped, I wished — I believed — that it would be a visit from Winnie and Albertina.

From the moment Winnie learned we had been brought to the island, she had been trying to arrange a visit. As a banned person, Winnie had to receive a special dispensation from the minister of justice, for she was technically not permitted to communicate with me.

Even with the help of the authorities, visiting Robben Island was not an easy proposition. Visits were a maximum of thirty minutes long, and political prisoners were not permitted contact visits, in which the visitor and prisoner were in the same room.

Visits did not seem to be planned in advance by the authorities. One day, they would contact your wife and say, "You have permission to visit your husband tomorrow." This was enormously inconvenient, and often had the effect of making visits impossible. If a family member was able to plan a visit in advance, the authorities would sometimes deliberately delay issuing a permit until after the plane had departed. Since most of the men's families lived far from the Cape and had very little money, visits by family members were often far beyond their means. Some men who came from poor families did not see their wives for many years at a time, if at all. I knew of men who spent a decade or more on Robben Island without a single visit.

The visiting room for noncontact visits was cramped and windowless. On the prisoner's side, there was a row of five cubicles with small square pieces of glass that looked out on identical cubicles on the other side. One sat in a chair and looked through the thick, smudged glass that had a few small holes drilled into it to permit conversation. One had to talk very loudly to be heard. Later the authorities installed microphones and speakers in front of the glass, a marginal improvement.

Walter and I were called to the visitors' office in the late morning and took seats at the far end of the room. I waited with some anxiety, and suddenly, filling out the glass on the other side of the window was Winnie's lovely face. Winnie always dressed up for prison visits, and tried to wear something new and elegant. It was tremendously frustrating not to be able to touch my wife, to speak tenderly to her, to have a private moment together. We had to conduct our relationship at a distance under the eyes of people we despised.

I could see immediately that Winnie was under tremendous strain. Seeing me in such circumstances must have been trying. Just getting to the island itself was difficult, and added to that were the harsh rituals of the prison, the undoubted indignities of the warders, and the impersonality of the contact.

Winnie, I later discovered, had recently received a second banning order and had been terminated from her job at the Child Welfare Office as a result. Her office was searched by the police shortly before she was fired. The authorities were convinced that Winnie was in secret communication with me. Winnie loved her job as a social worker. It was the hands-on end of the struggle: placing babies with adoptive parents, finding work for the unemployed and medical help for the uninsured. The banning and harassment of my wife greatly troubled me: I could not look after her and the children, and the state was making it difficult for her to look after herself. My powerlessness gnawed at me.

Our conversation was awkward at first, and was not made easier by the presence of two warders standing directly behind her and three behind me. Their role was not only to monitor but to intimidate. Regulations dictated that conversation had to be in either English or Afrikaans — African languages were forbidden — and could involve family matters only. Any line of talk that departed from the family and verged on the political might mean the abrupt termination of the visit. If one mentioned a name unfamiliar to the warders, they would interrupt the conversation, and ask who the person was and the nature of the relationship. This happened often, as the warders were generally unfamiliar with the variety and nature of African names. It was frustrating to spend precious minutes of one's visit explaining to a warder the different branches of one's family tree. But their ignorance also worked in our favor: it allowed us to invent code names for people we wanted to talk about and pretend that we were referring to family members.

That first visit was important, for I knew that Winnie was anxious about my health: she had heard stories that we were being physically abused. I quickly informed her that I was fine and she could see that I was fit, though a bit thinner than before. She, too, was thinner, something I always attributed to stress. After a visit in which Winnie's face looked drawn or tense, I would urge her to put on a bit of weight. She was always dieting, and I was always telling her not to. I inquired one by one about all the children, about my mother and sisters, and Winnie's own family.

Suddenly, I heard the warder behind me say, "Time up! Time up!" I turned and looked at him with incredulity. It was impossible that half an hour had passed. But, in fact, he was right; visits always seemed to go by in the blink of an eye. For all the years that I was in prison, I never failed to be surprised when the warder called, "Time up!" Winnie and I were both hustled from our chairs and we waved a quick farewell. I always felt like lingering after Winnie left, just to retain the sense of her presence, but I would not let the warders see such emotion. As I walked back to the cell, I reviewed in my head what we had talked about. Over the next days, weeks, and months, I would return to that one visit again and again. I knew I would not be able to see my wife again for at least six months. As it turned out, Winnie was not able to visit me for another two years.

64

ONE MORNING in early January, as we lined up to be counted before beginning work in the courtyard, we were instead marched outside and ordered into a covered truck. It was the first time that we had left our compound. No announcement was made as to our destination, but I had an idea of where we were headed. A few minutes later we emerged from the truck in a place that I had first seen when I was on the island in 1962: the lime quarry.

The lime quarry looked like an enormous white crater cut into a rocky hillside. The cliffs and the base of the hillside were blindingly white. At the top of the quarry were grass and palm trees, and at the base was a clearing with a few old metal sheds.

We were met by the commanding officer, Colonel Wessels, a rather colorless fellow who cared only about strict adherence to prison regulations. We stood at attention as he told us that the work we would be doing would last six months and afterward we would be given light tasks for the duration of our terms. His timing was considerably off. We remained at the quarry for the next thirteen years.

After the C.O.'s speech, we were handed picks and shovels and given rudimentary instructions as to the mining of lime. Mining lime is not a simple task. That first day, we were clumsy with our new tools and extracted little. The lime itself, which is the soft, calcified residue of seashells and coral, is buried in layers of rock, and one had to break through to it with a pick, and then extract the seam of lime with a shovel. This was far more strenuous than the work in the courtyard, and after our first few days on the quarry we fell asleep immediately after our supper at 4:30 in the afternoon. We woke the next morning aching and still tired.

The authorities never explained why we had been taken from the court-yard to the quarry. They may simply have needed extra lime for the island's roads. But when we later discussed the transfer, we assumed it was another way of enforcing discipline, of showing us that we were not different from the general prisoners — who worked in the island's stone quarry — and that we had to pay for our crimes just as they did. It was an attempt to crush our spirits.

But those first few weeks at the quarry had the opposite effect on us. Despite blistered and bleeding hands, we were invigorated. I much pre-ferred being outside in nature, being able to see grass and trees, to observe birds flitting overhead, to feel the wind blowing in from the sea. It felt good to use all of one's muscles, with the sun at one's back, and there was simple gratification in building up mounds of stone and lime.

Within a few days, we were walking to the quarry, rather than going by truck, and this too was a tonic. During our twenty-minute march to the quarry, we got a better sense of the island, and could see the dense brush and tall trees that covered our home, and smell the eucalyptus blossoms, spot the occasional springbok or kudu grazing in the distance. Although some of the men regarded the march as drudgery, I never did.

Although our work at the quarry was meant to show us that we were no different from the other prisoners, the authorities still treated us like the lepers who once populated the island. Sometimes we would see a group of common-law prisoners working by the side of the road, and their warders would order them into the bushes so they would not see us as we marched past. It was as if the mere sight of us might somehow affect their discipline. Sometimes out of the corner of an eye we could see a prisoner raise his fist in the ANC salute.

Near the quarry, the dirt road diverged, and to the right the general prisoners trooped off to the rock quarry. This crossroads was later to become an important site of communications with them. Where the road branched, we could see in the brush the small white cottage where Robert Sobukwe lived. The house had been built for a black warder years before, and now Sobukwe lived in it by himself. It was a tiny plot, unkempt and overgrown, and one would not even know that anyone lived there, except for the guard who stood in front.

Sobukwe's sentence had ended in 1963, but under what became known as the Sobukwe clause of the General Law Amendment Act of 1963, the minister of justice could hold political prisoners indefinitely without charge. That is precisely what they did with Bob. For six years, Sobukwe lived a kind of half-life on the island; he was a free man who was denied his liberty. Sometimes we were able to get a glimpse of him in his garden, but that was all.

After arriving in the morning, we would fetch our picks, shovels, hammers, and wheelbarrows from a zinc shed at the top of the quarry. Then we would array ourselves along the quarry face, usually in groups of three or four. Warders with automatic weapons stood on raised platforms watching us. Unarmed warders walked among us, urging us to work harder. *"Gaan aan! Gaan aan!"* (Go on! Go on!), they would shout, as if we were oxen.

By eleven, when the sun was high in the sky, we would begin to flag. By that time, I would already be drenched in sweat. The warders would then drive us even harder. *"Nee, man! Kom aan! Kom aan!"* (No, man! Come on! Come on!), they would shout. Just before noon, when we would break for lunch, we would pile the lime into wheelbarrows and cart it over to the truck, which would take it away.

At midday, a whistle would blow, and we would make our way to the bottom of the hill. We sat on makeshift seats under a simple zinc shed shielding us from the sun. The warders ate at a larger shed with tables and benches. Drums of boiled mealies were delivered to us. Hundreds of seagulls, screaming and swooping, circled above us as we ate, and a well-aimed dropping could sometimes spoil a man's lunch.

We worked until four, when we again carted the lime to the waiting truck. By the end of the day, our faces and bodies were caked with white dust. We looked like pale ghosts except where rivulets of sweat had washed away the lime. When we returned to our cells, we would scrub ourselves in the cold water, which never seemed to completely rinse away the dust.

Worse than the heat at the quarry was the light. Our backs were protected from the sun by our shirts, but the sun's ray's would be reflected into our eyes by the lime itself. The glare hurt our eyes and, along with the dust, made it difficult to see. Our eyes teared and our faces became fixed in a permanent squint. It would take a long time after each day's work for our eyes to adjust to the diminished light.

After our first few days at the quarry, we made an official request for sunglasses. The authorities refused. This was not unexpected, for we were then not even permitted reading glasses. I had previously pointed out to the commanding officer that it did not make sense to permit us to read books but not permit us glasses to read them with.

During the following weeks and months, we requested sunglasses again and again. But it was to take us almost three years before we were allowed to have them, and that was only after a sympathetic physician agreed that the glasses were necessary to preserve our eyesight. Even then, we had to purchase the glasses ourselves.

For us, such struggles — for sunglasses, long trousers, study privileges, equalized food — were corollaries to the struggle we waged outside prison. The campaign to improve conditions in prison was part of the apartheid struggle. It was, in that sense, all the same; we fought injustice wherever we found it, no matter how large, or how small, and we fought injustice to preserve our own humanity.

Shortly after we started working at the quarry, we were joined in Section B by a number of other prominent political prisoners. Several were MK men who had been arrested in July of 1964 and convicted of more than fifty acts of sabotage in what became known as the "little Rivonia Trial." These included Mac Maharaj, a member of the SACP and one of the sharpest minds in the struggle; Laloo Chiba, also a member of the MK High Command, and a stalwart colleague who proved a great asset in prison; and Wilton Mkwayi, the Treason Trialist who had been mistakenly let go during a moment of confusion when the State of Emergency was declared in 1960. He had left South Africa secretly, received military training, and become commander-in-chief of MK after the Rivonia Trial. We were also joined by Eddie Daniels, a Coloured member of the Liberal Party, who had been convicted for sabotage operations undertaken by the African Resistance Movement, a small sabotage group composed of members of the Liberal Party. Eddie was to become one of my greatest friends in prison.

To counterbalance the effect of these new political allies, the authorities also put a handful of common-law prisoners in our section. These men were hardened criminals, convicted of murder, rape, and armed robbery. They were members of the island's notorious criminal gangs, either the Big Fives or the Twenty-Eights, which terrorized other prisoners. They were brawny and surly, and their faces bore the scars of the knife fights that were common among gang members. Their role was to act as agents provocateurs, and they would attempt to push us around, take our food, and inhibit any political discussions we tried to have. One of these fellows was known as Bogart, after the American tough-guy movie actor. He had a cell opposite Walter's and Walter used to complain that he would demand Walter's breakfast from him each morning, and that he was too scared to refuse.

The gang members worked in their own clique apart from us at the quarry. One day, they began singing what sounded like a work song. In fact, it was a famous work song with their own adapted lyrics: *"Benifunani eRivonia?,"* which means "What did you want at Rivonia?" The next line was something like "Did you think that you would become the government?" They sang exuberantly and with a mocking tone. They had obviously been encouraged by the warders, who were hoping that the song would provoke us.

Although the more hotheaded among us wanted to confront them, instead, we decided to fight fire with fire. We had far more and better singers among us than they had, and we huddled together and planned our response. Within a few minutes, we were all singing the song *"Stimela,"* a rousing anthem about a train making its way down from Southern Rhodesia. *"Stimela"* is not a political song, but in the context, it became one, for the implication was that the train contained guerrillas coming down to fight the South African army.

For a number of weeks our two groups sang as we worked, adding songs and changing lyrics. Our repertoire increased, and we were soon singing overt political songs, such as *"Amajoni,"* a song about guerrilla soldiers, the title of which was a corruption of the English slang word for soldier, Johnny; and *"Tshotsholoza,"* a song that compares the struggle to the motion of an oncoming train. (If you say the title over and over, it mimics the sound of the train.) We sang a song about the Freedom Charter, and another about the Transkei, whose lyrics said, "There are two roads, one road is the Matanzima road, and one road is the Mandela road, which one will you take?"

The singing made the work lighter. A few of the fellows had extraordinary voices, and I often felt like putting my pick down and simply listening. The gang members were no competition for us; they soon became quiet while we continued singing. But one of the warders was fluent in Xhosa and understood the content of our songs, and we were soon ordered to stop singing. (Whistling was also banned.) From that day on we worked in silence.

I saw the gang members not as rivals but as raw material to be converted. There was a nonpolitical prisoner among us, nicknamed Joe My Baby, who later joined the ANC and proved invaluable in helping us smuggle material in and out of prison.

One day we heard that Bogart had been savagely beaten by a warder at the quarry. I did not see the assault, but I saw the results. His face cut and badly bruised, Bogart approached me in our corridor and asked for help. I immediately agreed to take up his case.

We were always looking for ways to stand up to the authorities, and the report of a beating was the kind of incident we could raise with the head office. Shortly before this, we had learned that a certain PAC man named Ganya had been beaten by a warder. In my role as an attorney, I wrote a letter to the commissioner of prisons protesting on behalf of Ganya. I was brought to the Head Office, where I was confronted by prison officials. In the same breath they denied that the beating had occurred and wanted to know how I had heard about it. I insisted that the warder who had beaten Ganya be removed from the island. They refused, saying there was no evidence against him. But shortly afterward the warder in question was transferred off the island.

I had been emboldened by this case, so when Bogart asked for help I immediately demanded to see the commanding officer. The next day I was summoned to the head office, where the commander blandly informed me that the case had been investigated and dismissed. "That's a violation of regulations," I said. "The case must be tried."

"No," he said, "we have attempted to interview the so-called complainant and he denies that he was ever assaulted."

"That's impossible," I said. "I spoke to him only yesterday." The commander gestured to a lieutenant and said, "Then see for yourself." The lieutenant led Bogart into the room. His face was covered with bandages. The commander asked him whether or not he had been beaten. "No, baas," he said quietly, without meeting my gaze, "I was never assaulted." He was then dismissed.

"Well, Mandela," the commander said. "The case is closed." The commander had succeeded in humiliating me. He had obviously bribed Bogart with extra food and tobacco to drop his charges. From that point on, I demanded a signed and written statement from a prisoner before I agreed to take up his case.

65

ONE DAY in the summer of 1965, we discovered some fat glistening on our porridge at breakfast and chunks of fresh meat with our pap at supper. The next day some of the men received new shirts. The guards at the quarry and the warders in our section seemed a bit more deferential. All of us were suspicious; in prison, no improvement happens without a reason. A day later we were notified that the International Red Cross would be arriving the following day.

This was a crucial occasion, more important than any of our previous visitors. The Red Cross was responsible and independent, an international organization to whom the Western powers and the United Nations paid attention. The prison authorities respected the Red Cross — and by re-spected, I mean feared, for the authorities respected only what they were afraid of. The prison service distrusted all organizations that could affect world opinion, and regarded them not as legitimate investigators to be dealt with honestly but as meddling interlopers to be hoodwinked if possible. Avoiding international condemnation was the authorities' prin-cipal goal.

In those early years, the International Red Cross was the only orga-nization that both listened to our complaints and responded to them. This was vital, because the authorities ignored us. Regulations required that the authorities provide some official procedure for acknowledging our complaints. They did so, but only in the most perfunctory manner. Every Saturday morning, the chief warder would come into our section and call out, *"Klagtes and Versoeke! Klagtes and Versoeke!"* (Complaints and Requests! Complaints and Requests!) Those of us with *klagtes* and *versoeke* — which was nearly everyone — lined up to see the chief warder. One by one, we would make formal complaints about food, or clothing, or visits. To each, the chief warder would nod his head and simply say, *"Ja, ja,"* and then, "Next!" He did not even write down what we said. If we tried to speak for our organizations, the warders would yell, "No ANC or PAC here! *Verstaan?"* (Understand?)

Shortly before the Red Cross's visit we had submitted a formal list of complaints to the commissioner of prisons. At the time we were only permitted paper and pencil to write letters. We had secretly consulted with each other at the quarry and in the lavatory, and put together a list. We submitted it to our chief warder, who did not want to take it and accused us of violating regulations by making such a list. One of our complaints to the Red Cross would be that the authorities did not listen to our complaints.

On the day of their visit, I was called to the head office to meet with the Red Cross representative. That year, and for the following few years, the representative was a Mr. Senn, a former director of prisons in his native Sweden who had emigrated to Rhodesia. Senn was a quiet, rather nervous man in his mid-fifties who did not seem at all comfortable in his surroundings.

The meeting was not monitored, a critical difference from nearly all of our other visitors. He asked to hear all of our complaints and grievances, and listened very carefully, taking extensive notes. He was very courteous and thanked me for all that I told him. Even so, that first visit was rather tense. Neither of us yet knew what to expect from the other.

I complained quite vociferously about our clothing, affirming that we did not want to wear short trousers and needed proper clothing including socks and underwear, which we were not then given. I recounted our grievances regarding food, visits, letters, studies, exercise, hard labor, and the behavior of warders. I made certain requests I knew the authorities would never satisfy, such as our desire to be transferred to prisons nearer our homes.

After our session, Senn met with the commissioner of prisons and his staff while I waited. I assumed that he relayed our complaints to the authorities, indicating the ones he thought were reasonable. Not long after Senn's visit our clothing did improve and we were given long trousers. But Senn was not a progressive fellow by any means; his years in Rhodesia seemed to have acclimatized him to racism. Before I had returned to my cell, I reminded him of our complaint that African prisoners did not receive bread. Mr. Senn appeared flustered, and glanced over at the colonel, who was head of the prison. "Bread is very bad for your teeth, you know, Mandela," Mr. Senn said. "Mealies are much better for you. They make your teeth strong."

In later years, the International Red Cross sent more liberal men who wholeheartedly fought for improvements. The organization also played a critical role in an area that was less obvious but no less important to us. They often provided money to wives and relatives who would not otherwise have been able to visit us on the island.

After we had been sent to Robben Island, there was concern among our supporters that we would not be permitted to study. Within a few months of our arrival, the authorities announced that those who wanted to study could apply for permission. Most of the men did so and even though they were D Group prisoners, permission was granted. The state, after the Rivonia Trial, was feeling confident and thought giving us study privileges would be harmless. Later, they came to regret it. Postgraduate study was not permitted, but they made an exception in my case because I had established a precedent when I was in Pretoria.

Very few of the men in our section had B.A.'s and many registered for university-level courses. Quite a few did not have high school degrees and elected courses to qualify for that degree. Some of the men were already well educated, like Govan Mbeki and Neville Alexander, but others had not gone past Standard V or VI. Within months, virtually all of us were studying for one degree or another. At night, our cell block seemed more like a study hall than a prison.

But the privilege of studying came with a host of conditions. Certain subjects, such as politics and military history, were prohibited. For years, we were not permitted to receive funds except from our families, so that poor prisoners rarely had money for books or tuition. This made the opportunity to study a function of how much money one had. Nor were we permitted to lend books to other prisoners, which would have enabled our poorer colleagues to study.

There was always controversy about whether or not we should accept study privileges. Some members of the Unity Movement at first felt that we were accepting a handout from the government, which compromised our integrity. They argued that studying should not be a conditional privilege but an unfettered right. While I agreed, I could not accept that we should therefore disavow studying. As freedom fighters and political prisoners, we had an obligation to improve and strengthen ourselves, and study was one of the few opportunities to do so.

Prisoners were permitted to enroll at either the University of South Africa (UNISA) or Rapid Results College, which was for those studying for their high school qualification. In my own case, studying under the auspices of the University of London was a mixed blessing. On the one hand I was assigned the sorts of stimulating books that would not have been on a South African reading list; on the other, the authorities inevitably regarded many of them as unsuitable and thus banned them.

Receiving books at all was often a challenge. You might make an application to a South African library for a book on contract law. They would process your request and then send you the book by post. But because of the vagaries of the mail system, the remoteness of the island, and the often deliberate slowness of the censors, the book would reach you after the date that it needed to be returned. If the date had passed, the warders would typically send the book back without even showing it to you. Given the nature of the system, you might receive a late fine without ever having received the book.

In addition to books, we were permitted to order publications necessary to our studies. The authorities were extremely strict about this, and the only kind of publication that would pass muster might be a quarterly on actuarial science for a prisoner studying accounting. But one day, Mac Maharaj told a comrade who was studying economics to request *The Economist*. We laughed and said we might as well ask for *Time* magazine, because *The Economist* was also a newsweekly. But Mac simply smiled and said the authorities won't know that; they judge a book by its title. Within a month, we were receiving *The Economist* and reading the news we hungered for. But the authorities soon discovered their mistake and ended the subscription.

Once most of the men began to study, we complained that we did not even have the minimum facilities necessary for studying, such as desks and chairs. I made this complaint to the International Red Cross. Finally, the authorities built in each cell a kind of stand-up desk, a simple wooden board that jutted out from the wall at about chest-level.

This was not precisely what we had envisaged. After a tedious day at the quarry, one did not much feel like working at a stand-up desk. A number of us complained about the desks, and Kathy was the most vociferous. He informed the commanding officer that not only was it an imposition to have stand-up desks, but that they sloped so steeply that the books fell off. The commanding officer made a surprise visit to Kathy's cell, asked for a book, and plunked it on his desk. It did not move. He asked Kathy for another and placed it on top of the first one; again, nothing happened. Finally, after placing four books on the desk, he turned to a sheepish Kathy and said, "Ag, there's nothing wrong with these desks," and walked out. But about six months later, the authorities relented and we were given three-legged wooden stools and the stand-up desks were lowered.

One complaint I voiced to the International Red Cross concerned the arbitrary way we were charged by the warders. To be "charged" meant that a warder claimed that a prisoner had violated a specific regulation, which could be punished by isolation or by loss of meals and privileges. Warders generally did not treat this lightly, for when a prisoner was charged he was allowed a judicial hearing and, depending on the seriousness of the offense, a magistrate was brought in from Cape Town. At the time, the authorities were refusing to permit hearings. When I complained to the International Red Cross about this, I had yet to experience the problem myself. But that situation was soon remedied.

On weekends, during our first year on the island, we were kept inside our cells all day except for a half hour of exercise. One Saturday, after returning from exercise in the courtyard, I noticed that a warder had left a newspaper on the bench at the end of the corridor. He had become rather friendly to us, and I assumed that he had not left the newspaper there by accident.

Newspapers were more valuable to political prisoners than gold or diamonds, more hungered for than food or tobacco; they were the most precious contraband on Robben Island. News was the intellectual raw material of the struggle. We were not allowed any news at all, and we craved it. Walter, even more than myself, seemed bereft without news. The authorities attempted to impose a complete blackout; they did not want us to learn anything that might raise our morale or reassure us that people on the outside were still thinking about us.

We regarded it as our duty to keep ourselves current on the politics of the country, and we fought long and hard for the right to have newspapers. Over the years, we devised many ways of obtaining them, but back then we were not so adept. One of the advantages of going to the quarry was that warders' sandwiches were wrapped in newspaper and they would often discard these newsprint wrappers in the trash, where we secretly retrieved them. We would distract the warders' attention, pluck the papers out of the garbage, and slide them into our shirts.

One of the most reliable ways to acquire papers was through bribery, and this was the only area where I tolerated what were often unethical means of obtaining information. The warders always seemed to be short of money, and their poverty was our opportunity.

When we did get hold of a paper, it was far too risky to pass around. Possession of a newspaper was a serious charge. Instead, one person would read the paper, usually Kathy or, later, Mac Maharaj. Kathy was in charge of communications, and he had thought of ingenious ways for us to pass information. Kathy would go through the paper and make cuttings of relevant stories, which were then secretly distributed to the rest of us. Each of us would write out a summary of the story we were given; these summaries were then passed among us, and later smuggled to the general section. When the authorities were particularly vigilant, Kathy or Mac would write out his summary of the news and then destroy the paper, usually by tearing it into small pieces and placing it in his ballie, which the warders never inspected.

When I noticed the newspaper lying on the bench, I quickly left my cell, walked to the end of the corridor, looked in both directions, and then plucked the newspaper off the bench and slipped it into my shirt. Normally, I would have hidden the newspaper somewhere in my cell and taken it out only after bedtime. But like a child who eats his sweet before his main course, I was so eager for news that I opened the paper in my cell immediately.

I don't know how long I was reading; I was so engrossed in the paper that I did not hear any footsteps. Suddenly, an officer and two other warders appeared and I did not even have time to slide the paper under my bed. I was caught black-and-white-handed, so to speak. "Mandela," the officer said, "we are charging you for possession of contraband, and you will pay for this." The two warders then began a thorough search of my cell to see if they could turn up anything else.

Within a day or two a magistrate was brought in from Cape Town and

I was taken to the room at headquarters that was used as the island's court. In this instance, the authorities were willing to call in an outside magistrate because they knew they had an open-and-shut case. I offered no defense, and was sentenced to three days in isolation and deprivation of meals.

I do not think that I was set up by the warder who left the newspaper on the bench, though some assumed I had been. At the hearing, the authorities grilled me as to how I got the newspaper, and I refused to answer. If I had been railroaded, the authorities would have known how I'd gotten it.

The isolation cells were in our same complex, but in another wing. Although just across the courtyard, they felt enormously distant. In isolation, one was deprived of company, exercise, and even food: one received only rice water three times a day for three days. (Rice water is simply water in which rice has been boiled.) By comparison, our normal ration of pap seemed like a feast.

The first day in isolation was always the most painful. One grows accustomed to eating regularly and the body is not used to being deprived. I found that by the second day I had more or less adjusted to the absence of food, and the third passed without much craving at all. Such deprivation was not uncommon among Africans in everyday life. I myself had gone without food for days at a time in my early years in Johannesburg.

As I have already mentioned, I found solitary confinement the most forbidding aspect of prison life. There is no end and no beginning; there is only one's own mind, which can begin to play tricks. Was that a dream or did it really happen? One begins to question everything. Did I make the right decision, was my sacrifice worth it? In solitary, there is no distraction from these haunting questions.

But the human body has an enormous capacity for adjusting to trying circumstances. I have found that one can bear the unbearable if one can keep one's spirits strong even when one's body is being tested. Strong convictions are the secret of surviving deprivation; your spirit can be full even when your stomach is empty.

In those early years, isolation became a habit. We were routinely charged for the smallest infractions and sentenced to isolation. A man might lose his meals for a sidelong glance or be sentenced for failing to stand when a warder entered the room. Some PAC prisoners, who often flouted the rules simply for the sake of doing so, spent a great deal of time in isolation. The authorities believed that isolation was the cure for our defiance and rebelliousness.

The second time I was charged and spent time in isolation occurred shortly after the first. As I have mentioned, we were having great difficulty making our complaints heard. The remoteness of the prison made the authorities feel they could ignore us with impunity. They believed that if they turned a deaf ear to us, we would give up in frustration and the people on the outside would forget about us.

One day we were working at the lime quarry when the commanding officer came to observe us, accompanied by a gentleman whom we at first did not recognize. One of my colleagues whispered to me that it was Brigadier Aucamp from the Head Office, our commanding officer's commanding officer. (He is not to be confused with the Aucamp of Pretoria Local, who looked after us during the Rivonia Trial.) The two men stood at a distance, watching us.

Aucamp was a short, heavyset fellow in a suit rather than a military uniform. He normally came to the island on biannual inspections. On those occasions, we were ordered to stand at attention at the grille of our cells and hold up our prison cards as he walked by.

I decided that Aucamp's unexpected appearance was a singular opportunity to present our grievances to the man who had the power to remedy them. I put down my pick and began to walk over to them. The warders immediately became alarmed and moved toward me. I knew that I was violating regulations, but I hoped the warders would be so surprised by the novelty of my action that they would do nothing to stop me. That proved to be the case.

When I reached the two men, the commanding officer said bluntly, "Mandela, go back to your place. No one called you." I disregarded him and addressed Aucamp, saying I had taken this extraordinary action because our complaints were being ignored. The C.O. interrupted me: "Mandela, I order you back to your place." I turned to him and said in a measured tone, "I am here already, I will not go back." I was hoping that Aucamp would agree to hear me out, but he studied me coldly and then turned to the warders and said calmly, "Charge him."

I continued to speak as the guards led me away. "Take him back to the cells," the C.O. said. I was charged and, once again, I had no defense. The punishment this time was four days in isolation. There was a lesson in what I had done, a lesson I already knew but had disobeyed out of desperation. No one, least of all prison officials, ever likes to have his authority publicly challenged. In order to respond to me, Aucamp would have had to humiliate his subordinate. Prison officials responded much better to private overtures. The best way to effect change on Robben Island was to attempt to influence officials privately rather than publicly. I was sometimes condemned for appearing to be too accommodating to prison officials, but I was willing to accept the criticism in exchange for the improvement.

66

THE MOST IMPORTANT PERSON in any prisoner's life is not the minister of justice, not the commissioner of prisons, not even the head of prison, but the warder in one's section. If you are cold and want an extra blanket, you might petition the minister of justice, but you will get no response. If you go to the commissioner of prisons, he will say, "Sorry, it is against regulations." The head of prison will say, "If I give you an extra blanket, I must give one to everyone." But if you approach the warder in your corridor, and you are on good terms with him, he will simply go to the stockroom and fetch a blanket.

I always tried to be decent to the warders in my section; hostility was self-defeating. There was no point in having a permanent enemy among the warders. It was ANC policy to try to educate all people, even our enemies: we believed that all men, even prison service warders, were capable of change, and we did our utmost to try to sway them.

In general we treated the warders as they treated us. If a man was considerate, we were considerate in return. Not all of our warders were ogres. We noticed right from the start that there were some among them who believed in fairness. Yet, being friendly with warders was not an easy proposition, for they generally found the idea of being courteous to a black man abhorrent. Because it was useful to have warders who were well disposed toward us, I often asked certain men to make overtures to selected warders. No one liked to take on such a job.

We had one warder at the quarry who seemed particularly hostile to us. This was troublesome, for at the quarry we would hold discussions among ourselves, and a warder who did not permit us to talk was a great hindrance. I asked a certain comrade to befriend this fellow so that he would not interrupt our talks. The warder was quite crude, but he soon began to relax a bit around this one prisoner. One day, the warder asked this comrade for his jacket so that he could lay it on the grass and sit on it. Even though I knew it went against the comrade's grain, I nodded to him to do it.

A few days later, we were having our lunch under the shed when this warder wandered over. The warder had an extra sandwich, and he threw it on the grass near us and said, "Here." That was his way of showing friendship.

This presented us with a dilemma. On the one hand, he was treating us as animals to whom he could toss a bit of slop, and I felt it would undermine our dignity to take the sandwich. On the other hand, we were hungry, and to reject the gesture altogether would humiliate the warder we were trying to befriend. I could see that the comrade who had befriended the warder wanted the sandwich, and I nodded for him to take it.

The strategy worked, for this warder became less wary around us. He even began to ask questions about the ANC. By definition, if a man worked for the prison service he was probably brainwashed by the government's propaganda. He would have believed that we were terrorists and Communists who wanted to drive the white man into the sea. But as we quietly explained to him our nonracialism, our desire for equal rights, and our plans for the redistribution of wealth, he scratched his head and said, "It makes more bloody sense than the Nats."

Having sympathetic warders facilitated one of our most vital tasks on Robben Island: communication. We regarded it as our duty to stay in touch with our men in F and G, which was where the general prisoners were kept. As politicians, we were just as intent on fortifying our organization in prison as we had been outside. Communication was essential if we were to coordinate our protests and complaints. Because of the greater numbers of prisoners coming and going in the general section, the men in F and G tended to have more recent information about not only what was happening in the movement, but about our friends and families.

Communication between sections was a serious violation of regulations. We found many effective ways around the ban. The men who delivered our drums of food were from the general section, and in the early months we managed to have whispered conversations with them in which we conveyed brief messages. We formed a clandestine communications committee, composed of Kathy, Mac Maharaj, Laloo Chiba, and several others, and their job was to organize all such practices.

One of the first techniques was engineered by Kathy and Mac, who had noticed that on our walks to the quarry, the warders often tossed away empty matchboxes. They began secretly collecting them, and Mac had the idea of constructing a false bottom to the box and placing in it a tiny written message. Laloo Chiba, who once trained as a tailor, wrote out minuscule coded messages that would be placed in the converted matchbox. Joe Gqabi, another MK soldier who was with us, would carry the matchboxes on our walks to the quarry and drop them at a strategic crossing where we knew the general prisoners would pass. Through whispered conversations at food deliveries, we explained the plan. Designated prisoners from F and G would pick up the matchboxes on their walks, and we retrieved messages in the same fashion. It was far from perfect, and we could easily be foiled by something as simple as the rain. We soon evolved more efficient methods.

We looked for moments when the warders were inattentive. One such time was during and after meals. We helped ourselves to our food, and we worked out a scheme whereby comrades from the general section who worked in the kitchen began placing letters and notes wrapped in plastic at the bottom of the food drums. We sent return communication in a similar way, wrapping notes in the same plastic and placing them at the bottom of the mounds of dirty dishes that were routed back to the kitchen. We would do our best to create a mess, scattering food all over the plates. The warders even complained about the disarray, but never bothered to investigate.

Our toilets and showers were adjacent to the isolation section. Prisoners from the general section were often sentenced to isolation there and would use the same set of toilets we did, though at different times. Mac devised a method of wrapping notes in plastic and then taping them inside the rim of the toilet bowl. We encouraged our political comrades in the general section to be charged and placed in isolation so that they could retrieve these notes and send replies. The warders never bothered to search there.

In order not to have our notes read or understood by the authorities if they were found, we devised ways of writing that could not easily be seen or deciphered. One way was to write messages with milk. The milk would dry almost immediately, and the paper would look blank. But the disinfectant we were given to clean our cells, when sprayed on the dried milk, made the writing reappear. Unfortunately, we did not regularly receive milk. After one of us was diagnosed with an ulcer, we used his.

Another technique was to write in tiny, coded script on toilet paper. The paper was so small and easily hidden that this became a popular way of smuggling out messages. When the authorities discovered a number of these communications, they took the extraordinary measure of rationing toilet paper. Govan was then ailing and not going to the quarry, and he was given the task of counting out eight squares of toilet paper for each prisoner per day.

But even with all these ingenious methods, one of the best ways was also the easiest: getting sent to the prison hospital. The island had one hospital, and it was difficult to segregate us from the general prisoners while we were there. Sometimes prisoners from the different sections even shared the same wards, and men from Section B and prisoners from F and G mingled and exchanged information about political organizations, strikes, go-slows, whatever the current prison issues were.

Communication with the outside world was accomplished in two ways: through prisoners whose sentences were completed and who were leaving the island, and through contact with visitors. Prisoners who were leaving would smuggle out letters in their clothes or baggage. With outside visitors, the situation was even more dangerous, because the risks were also borne by the visitor. When lawyers visited us, warders were not permitted in the room and we would sometimes pass a letter to the lawyer to be taken out. Lawyers were not searched. In these meetings, we could also communicate by writing as we had during the Rivonia Trial. Because the room was bugged, we might say, "Please tell . . ." and then pause and write "O.T.," meaning Oliver Tambo, on a piece of paper, "that we approve of his plan to cut down the size of the . . ." and then write, "National Executive."

Through a plastic-wrapped note hidden in our food drums, we learned in July of 1966 that the men in the general section had embarked on a hunger strike to protest poor conditions. The note was imprecise, and we did not know exactly when the strike had started or exactly what it was about. But we would support any strike of prisoners for whatever reason they were striking. Word was passed among us, and we resolved to initiate a sympathetic strike beginning with our next meal. A hunger strike consists of one thing: not eating.

Because of the time lag in communications, the general prisoners probably did not learn of our participation for a day or so. But we knew that the news would hearten them. The authorities would be telling them that we were not participating in the strike, that we were gorging ourselves on gourmet meals. This was standard operating procedure; in a crisis, the authorities inevitably started a disinformation campaign to play one section against the other. In this case, while the ANC unanimously supported the strike, some PAC men in the general section did not.

During the first day of our strike, we were served our normal rations and refused to take them. On the second day, we noticed that our portions were larger and a few more vegetables accompanied our pap. On the third day, juicy pieces of meat were served with supper. By the fourth day, the porridge was glistening with fat, and great hunks of meat and colorful vegetables were steaming on top. The food was positively mouthwatering. The warders smiled when we passed up the food. The temptation was great, but we resisted, even though we were being driven especially hard at the quarry. We heard that in the main section, prisoners were collapsing and being taken away in wheelbarrows.

I was called to the Head Office for an interview with Colonel Wessels. Such sessions were delicate, as my fellow prisoners knew that the authorities would attempt to influence me to call off the strike. Wessels was a direct man and demanded to know why we were on a hunger strike. I explained that as political prisoners we saw protest to alter prison conditions as an extension of the anti-apartheid struggle. "But you don't even know why they are striking in F and G," he said. I said that did not matter, that the men in F and G were our brothers and that our struggle was indivisible. He snorted, and dismissed me.

The following day we learned of an extraordinary course of events: the warders had gone on their own food boycott, refusing to go to their own cafeteria. They were not striking in support of us, but had decided that if we could do such a thing, why couldn't they? They were demanding better food and improved living conditions. The combination of the two strikes was too much for the authorities. They settled with the warders and then, a day or two later, we learned the authorities had gone to the general section and asked for three representatives to negotiate changes. The general prisoners declared victory and called off the hunger strike. We followed suit a day later.

That was the first and most successful of the hunger strikes on the island. As a form of protest, they did not have a high success rate and the rationale behind them always struck me as quixotic. In order for a hunger strike to succeed, the outside world must learn of it. Otherwise, prisoners will simply starve themselves to death and no one will know. Smuggled-out information that we were on a hunger strike would elicit newspaper stories, which in turn would generate pressure from advocacy groups. The problem, particularly in the early years, was that it was next to impossible to alert people on the outside that we were waging a hunger strike inside.

For me, hunger strikes were altogether too passive. We who were already suffering were threatening our health, even courting death. I have always favored a more active, militant style of protest such as work strikes, go-slow strikes, or refusing to clean up; actions that punished the authorities, not ourselves. They wanted gravel and we produced no gravel. They wanted the prison yard clean and it was untidy. This kind of behavior distressed and exasperated them, whereas I think they secretly enjoyed watching us go hungry.

But when it came to a decision, I was often outvoted. My colleagues even jokingly accused me of not wanting to miss a meal. The proponents of hunger strikes argued that it was a traditionally accepted form of protest that had been waged all over the world by such prominent leaders as Mahatma Gandhi. Once the decision was taken, however, I would support it as wholeheartedly as any of its advocates. In fact, during the strikes I was often in the position of remonstrating with some of my more wayward colleagues who did not want to abide by our agreement. "Madiba, I want my food," I remember one man saying. "I don't see why I should go without. I have served the struggle for many years."

Comrades would sometimes eat on the sly. We knew this for a simple reason: by the second day of a hunger strike, no one needs to use the toilet. Yet one morning you might see a fellow going to the toilet. We had our own internal intelligence service because we knew that certain men were weak in this regard.

67

IN THE MIDST of the July 1966 hunger strike I had my second visit from my wife. It was almost exactly two years after the first visit, and it nearly did not happen at all. Winnie had been under constant harassment since her first visit in 1964. Her sisters and brother were persecuted by the police, and the authorities attempted to forbid anyone in her family from living with her. Some of this I learned at the time, much of it I found out later. Some of the nastiest items were known to me because when I would return from the quarry, I often would find neatly cut clippings about Winnie that had been anonymously placed on my bed by the warders.

In small and spiteful ways, the authorities did their best to make Winnie's journeys as unpleasant as possible. For the previous two years, her visits had been stymied by local magistrates and by the repeated bannings that prevented her from traveling. I had recently heard through counsel that Winnie had been informed by the police that she could visit me only if she carried a pass. Winnie, who had been protesting the government's policy regarding women's passes since the 1950s, rightly refused to carry the hated document. The authorities were clearly attempting to humiliate her and me. But I thought it was more important that we see each other than to resist the petty machinations of the authorities, and Winnie consented to carry a pass. I missed her enormously and needed the reassurance of seeing her, and we also had vital family matters to discuss.

The regulations governing each of Winnie's visits were long and complicated. She was barred from taking a train or car and had to fly, making the trip much more expensive. She was required to take the shortest route from the airport to Caledon Square, the Cape Town police station, where she was required to sign various documents. She had to report to the same station on the way back and sign more documents.

I had also learned from a newspaper clipping that a Special Branch officer broke into our Orlando house while Winnie was dressing and she reacted angrily, pushing the officer out of the bedroom. The lieutenant laid a charge of assault against her, and I asked my friend and colleague George Bizos to defend her, which he ably did. We had seen stories about this in the newspapers, and some of the men even joked with me about Winnie's bellicosity. "You are not the only boxer in the family, Madiba," they said.

This second visit was for only half an hour, and we had much to discuss. Winnie was a bit agitated from the rough treatment in Cape Town and the fact that, as always, she had to ride in the hold of the ferry where the fumes from the engine made her ill. She had taken pains to dress up for me, but she looked thin and drawn.

We reviewed the education of the children, the health of my mother, which was not very good, and our finances. A critical issue was the education of Zeni and Zindzi. Winnie had placed the girls in a school designated as Indian, and the authorities were harassing the principal on the grounds that it was a violation of the law for the school to accept African pupils. We made the difficult decision to send Zeni and Zindzi to boarding school in Swaziland. This was hard on Winnie, who found her greatest sustenance in the two girls. I was consoled by the fact that their education would probably be superior there, but I worried about Winnie. She would be lonely and prey for people who sought to undermine her under the guise of being her friends. If anything, Winnie was too trusting of people's motives.

To get around the restrictions on discussing nonfamily matters, we used names whose meaning was clear to us, but not to the warders. If I wanted to know how Winnie was really doing, I might say, "Have you heard about Ngutyana recently; is she all right?" Ngutyana is one of Winnie's clan names, but the authorities were unaware of that. Then Winnie could talk about how and what Ngutyana was doing. If the warder asked who Ngutyana was, we would say she was a cousin. If I wanted to know about how the external mission of the ANC was faring, I would ask, "How is the church?" Winnie would discuss "the church" in appropriate terms, and I might then ask, "How are the priests? Are there any new sermons?" We improvised and managed to exchange a great deal of information that way.

As always, when the warder yelled, "Time up!," I thought only a few minutes had passed. I wanted to kiss the glass good-bye, but restrained myself. I always preferred for Winnie to leave first so she would not have to see me led away by the warders, and I watched as she whispered a good-bye, hiding her pain from the warders.

After the visit, I replayed all the details in my mind, what Winnie wore, what she said, what I said. I then wrote her a letter going over some of what we had discussed, and reminding her of how much I cared for her, how unshakable our bond was, how courageous she was. I saw my letters to her both as love letters and as the only way I could give her the emotional support she needed.

Soon after the visit, I learned that Winnie had been charged for failing to report to the police on her arrival in Cape Town as well as refusing to furnish the police with her address when she left. Having already given her address at the ferry, she was asked again when she returned, and refused, saying she had done so earlier.

Winnie was arrested and released on bail. She was tried and sentenced to a year's imprisonment, which was suspended except for four days. Winnie was subsequently dismissed from her second job as a social worker because of the incident, and lost her main source of income.

The state did its utmost to harass me in ways they thought I would be powerless to resist. Toward the end of 1966, the Transvaal Law Society, at the instigation of the minister of justice, made a motion to strike me off the roll of practicing attorneys as a result of my conviction in the Rivonia Trial. Apparently they were not discouraged by the earlier unsuccessful attempt to remove my name from the roll because of my conviction in the Defiance Campaign.

I found out about the Law Society's action only after it had been initiated. The Transvaal Law Society was an extremely conservative organization, and they were seeking to punish me at a time when they assumed I would be unable to defend myself. It is not easy for a prisoner on Robben Island to defend himself in court, but that is precisely what I intended to do.

I informed the authorities that I planned to contest the action and would prepare my own defense. I told prison officials that in order to prepare adequately, I would need to be exempt from going to the quarry and would also require a proper table, chair, and reading light to work on my brief. I said I needed access to a law library and demanded to be taken to Pretoria.

My strategy was to overwhelm the prison authorities and the courts with legitimate requests, which I knew they would have a difficult time satisfying. The authorities always found it distressing when I wanted to defend myself in court because the accompanying publicity would show that I was still fighting for the same values I always had.

Their first response was, "Mandela, why don't you retain a lawyer to defend you? He will be able to handle the case properly. Why put yourself out?" I went ahead and applied to the registrar of the Supreme Court for the records, documents, and books that I would need. I also requested a list of the state's witnesses and summaries of their prospective testimony.

I received a letter stating that before the court would grant my requests they would need to know the nature of my defense. This was extraordinary. To ask the nature of a lawyer's defense before the trial? No defendant can be compelled to reveal his defense before he is actually in court. I wrote back to tell them that the nature of my defense would become clear to them when I filed my papers — and not until then.

This was the beginning of a flurry of correspondence between me and the registrar as well as the state attorney, who was representing the Law Society. I would not back down on any of my requests. The authorities were equally intransigent: I could not be taken off quarry detail, I could not have a table and chair, and under no circumstances would I be able to go to Pretoria to use the law library.

I continued to bedevil the Law Society and registrar with demands, which they continued to deflect. Finally, several months and many letters later, without any fanfare and with just a cursory notification to me, they dropped the entire matter. The case was becoming more than they had bargained for. They had reckoned I would not have the initiative or where-withal to defend myself; they were mistaken.

I was able to read in detail about the official reactions to my opposition to the Law Society's actions because we were receiving a daily newspaper just as if it were delivered to our door. In effect, it was.

The warder who supervised us at night was a quiet, elderly Jehovah's Witness whom Mac Maharaj had befriended. One night, he wandered over to Mac's cell and told him that he wanted to enter a newspaper contest that required an essay. Would Mac, he wondered, be willing to assist him in writing it? The old warder hinted that if Mac helped him, there would be a reward. Mac agreed, and duly wrote the essay. A fortnight later, the old man came to Mac very excited. He was now a finalist in the competition; would Mac write him another essay? The warder promised Mac a cooked chicken in return. Mac told the old warder that he would think about it.

The next day, Mac came to Walter and me and explained the situation. While Walter encouraged Mac to accept the food, I appreciated his re-luctance to do so, because it would appear that he was getting special treatment. That night, he told the warder he would write the essay in exchange for a pack of cigarettes. The old warder agreed, and the following evening presented Mac with a newly bought pack of cigarettes.

The next day, Mac told us that he now had the leverage he wanted over the old warder. How? we asked. "Because I have his fingerprints on the cigarette pack," Mac said, "and I can blackmail him." Walter exclaimed that that was immoral. I did not criticize Mac, but asked what he would blackmail him for. Mac raised his eyebrow: "Newspapers," he said. Walter and I looked at each other. I think Walter was the only man on Robben Island who relished newspapers as much as I did. Mac had already discussed his plan with the communications committee, and although we both had reservations about Mac's technique, we did not stop him.

That night Mac told the warder that he had his fingerprints on the pack of cigarettes and that if the old man did not cooperate, he would expose him to the commanding officer. Terrified of being fired and losing his pension, the warder agreed to do whatever Mac wanted. For the next six months, until the warder was transferred, the old man would smuggle that day's newspaper to Mac. Mac would then summarize the news and reduce it to a single small piece of paper, which would circulate among us. The unfortunate warder did not win the contest, either.

It would be hard to say what we did more of at the quarry: mine lime or talk. By 1966, the warders had adopted a laissez-faire attitude: we could talk as much as we wanted as long as we worked. We would cluster in small groups, four or five men in a rough circle, and talk all day long, about every subject under the sun. We were in a perpetual conversation with each other on topics both solemn and trifling.

There is no prospect about prison which pleases — with the possible exception of one. One has time to think. In the vortex of the struggle, when one is constantly reacting to changing circumstances, one rarely has the chance to carefully consider all the ramifications of one's decisions or policies. Prison provided the time — much more than enough time — to reflect on what one had done and not done.

We were constantly engaged in political debates. Some were dispatched in a day, others were disputed for years. I have always enjoyed the cut-and-thrust of debating, and was a ready participant. One of our earliest and longest debates concerned the relationship between the ANC and the Communist Party. Some of the men, especially those MK soldiers who had been trained in socialist countries, believed that the ANC and the party were one and the same. Even some very senior ANC colleagues, such as Govan Mbeki and Harry Gwala, subscribed to this theory.

The party did not exist as a separate entity on Robben Island. In prison, there was no point in making the distinction between the ANC and the party that existed on the outside. My own views on the subject had not altered in many years. The ANC was a mass liberation movement that welcomed all those with the same objectives.

Over time, the debate concerning the ANC and the party grew progressively acrimonious. A number of us proposed one way to resolve it: we would write to the ANC in exile in Lusaka. We prepared a secret twenty-two-page document on the subject with a covering letter from myself to be sent to Lusaka. It was a risky maneuver to prepare and smuggle out such a document. In the end, Lusaka confirmed the separation of the ANC and the party and the argument eventually withered away.

Another recurrent political discussion was whether or not the ANC leadership should come exclusively from the working class. Some argued that because the ANC was a mass organization made up mainly of ordinary workers, the leadership should come from those same ranks. My argument was that it was as undemocratic to specify that the leaders had to be from the working class as to declare that they should be bourgeois intellectuals. If the movement had insisted on such a rule, most of its leaders, men such as Chief Luthuli, Moses Kotane, Dr. Dadoo, would have been ineligible. Revolutionaries are drawn from every class.

Not all debates were political. One issue that provoked much discussion was circumcision. Some among us maintained that circumcision as practiced by the Xhosa and other tribes was not only an unnecessary mutilation of the body, but a reversion to the type of tribalism that the ANC was seeking to overthrow. It was not an unreasonable argument, but the prevailing view, with which I agreed, was that circumcision was a cultural ritual that had not only a salutary health benefit but an important psychological effect. It was a rite that strengthened group identification and inculcated positive values.

The debate continued for years, and a number of men voted in favor of circumcision in a very direct way. A prisoner working in the hospital who had formerly practiced as an *ingcibi* set up a secret circumcision school, and a number of the younger prisoners from our section were circumcised there. Afterward, we would organize a small party of tea and biscuits for the men, and they would spend a day or two walking around in blankets, as was the custom.

One subject we hearkened back to again and again was the question of whether there were tigers in Africa. Some argued that although it was popularly assumed that tigers lived in Africa, this was a myth and they were native to Asia and the Indian subcontinent. Africa had leopards in abundance, but no tigers. The other side argued that tigers were native to Africa and some still lived there. Some claimed to have seen with their own eyes this most powerful and beautiful of cats in the jungles of Africa.

I maintained that while there were no tigers to be found in contemporary Africa, there was a Xhosa word for tiger, a word different from the one for leopard, and that if the word existed in our language, the creature must have once existed in Africa. Otherwise, why would there be a name for it? This argument went round and round, and I remember Mac retorting that hundreds of years ago there was a Hindi word for a craft that flew in the air, long before the airplane was invented, but that did not mean that airplanes existed in ancient India.

68

"ZITHULELE," the Quiet One, was what we called the tolerant, soft-spoken warder in charge of us at the quarry. He routinely stood a great distance from us while we worked and did not appear to care what we did as long as we were orderly. He never berated us when he found us leaning on our spades and talking.

We responded in kind. One day, in 1966, he came to us and said, "Gentlemen, the rains have washed away the lines on the roads, we need twenty kilos of lime today. Can you help?" Although we were working very little at the time, he had approached us as human beings, and we agreed to assist him.

That spring, we had felt a certain thawing on the part of the authorities, a relaxation of the iron-fisted discipline that had prevailed on the island. The tension between prisoners and warders had lessened somewhat.

But this lull proved to be short-lived and came to an abrupt end one morning in September. We had just put down our picks and shovels on the quarry face and were walking to the shed for lunch. As one of the general prisoners wheeled a drum of food toward us, he whispered, "Verwoerd is dead." That was all. The news quickly passed among us. We looked at each other in disbelief and glanced over at the warders, who seemed unaware that anything momentous had occurred.

We did not know how the prime minister had died. Later, we heard about the obscure white parliamentary messenger who stabbed Verwoerd to death, and we wondered at his motives. Although Verwoerd thought Africans were beneath animals, his death did not yield us any pleasure. Political assassination is not something I or the ANC has ever supported. It is a primitive way of contending with an opponent.

Verwoerd had proved to be both the chief theorist and master builder of grand apartheid. He had championed the creation of the bantustans and Bantu Education. Shortly before his death he had led the Nationalists in the general election of 1966, in which the party of apartheid had increased its majority, winning 126 seats to the 39 achieved by the United Party, and the single seat won by the Progressive Party.

As often happened on the island, we had learned significant political news before our own guards. But by the following day, it was obvious the warders knew, for they took out their anger on us. The tension that had taken months to abate was suddenly at full force. The authorities began a crackdown against political prisoners as though we had held the knife that stabbed Verwoerd.

The authorities always imagined that we were secretly linked with all kinds of powerful forces on the outside. The spate of successful guerrilla attacks against the South African police forces in Namibia by the South-West African People's Organization (SWAPO) — an ally of the ANC — had also unnerved them. I suppose we should have been flattered that the government thought our nascent military ability was sophisticated enough to successfully eliminate their head of state. But their suspicions merely reflected the insecurities of narrow, shortsighted men who blamed their problems not on their own misguided policies but on an opponent by the name of the ANC.

The punishment against us was never enunciated as an official policy, but it was a renewal of the harsh atmosphere that prevailed upon our arrival on the island. The Quiet One was replaced with a man who was a vicious martinet. His name was Van Rensburg and he had been flown to the island on twenty-four hours' notice after the assassination. His reputation preceded him, for his name was a byword among prisoners for brutality.

Van Rensburg was a big, clumsy, brutish fellow who did not speak but shouted. During his first day on the job we noticed he had a small swastika tattooed on his wrist. But he did not need this offensive symbol to prove his cruelty. His job was to make our lives as wretched as possible, and he pursued that goal with great enthusiasm.

Each day over the next few months, Van Rensburg would charge one of us for insubordination or malingering. Each morning, he and the other warders would discuss who would be charged that afternoon. It was a policy of selective intimidation, and the decision on who would be charged was taken regardless of how hard that prisoner had worked that day. When we were trudging back to our cells, Van Rensburg would read from a list, "Mandela [or Sisulu or Kathrada], I want to see you immediately in front of the head of prison."

The island's administrative court began working overtime. In response, we formed our own legal committee made up of myself, Fikile Bam, and Mac Maharaj. Mac had studied law and was adept at putting the authorities on the defensive. Fiks, who was working toward a law degree, was a bright, resourceful fellow who had become the head of the prisoners' committee in our section. The job of our legal committee was to advise our comrades on how to conduct themselves in the island's administrative court.

Van Rensburg was not a clever fellow, and while he would lord it over us at the quarry, we could outwit him in court. Our strategy was not to argue with him in the field, but to contest the charges in court where we would have a chance to make our case before slightly more enlightened officers. In administrative court, the charge would be read by the presiding magistrate. "Malingering at the quarry," he might say, at which Van Rensburg would look smug. After the charge had been read in full, I always advised my colleagues to do one thing and one thing only: ask the court for "further particulars." This was one's right as a defendant, and though the request became a regular occurrence, Van Rensburg would almost always be stumped. Court would then have to be adjourned while Van Rensburg went out to gather "further particulars."

Van Rensburg was vindictive in large ways and small. When our lunch arrived at the quarry and we would sit down to eat — we now had a simple wooden table — Van Rensburg would inevitably choose that moment to urinate next to our food. I suppose we should have been grateful that he did not urinate directly on our food, but we lodged a protest against the practice anyway.

One of the few ways prisoners can take revenge on warders is through humor, and Van Rensburg became the butt of many of our jokes. Among ourselves we called him "Suitcase." Warders' lunch boxes were known as "suitcases" and normally a warder would designate a prisoner, usually his favorite, to carry his "suitcase," and then reward him with half a sandwich. But we always refused to carry Van Rensburg's "suitcase," hence, the nickname. It was humiliating for a warder to carry his own lunch pail.

One day, Wilton Mkwayi inadvertently referred to "Suitcase" within Van Rensburg's hearing. "Who is Suitcase?" Van Rensburg bellowed. Wilton paused for a moment and then blurted out, "It's you!"

"Why do you call me Suitcase?" Van Rensburg asked. Wilton paused. "Come, man," Van Rensburg said. "Because you carry your own 'suitcase,'" Wilton replied tentatively. "The general prisoners carry the 'suitcases' of their warders, but we won't carry yours — so we call you Suitcase."

Van Rensburg considered this for a moment, and instead of getting angry, announced, "My name is not Suitcase, it's Dik Nek." There was silence for a moment, and then all of us burst into laughter. In Afrikaans, Dik Nek literally means "Thick Neck"; it suggests someone who is stubborn and unyielding. Suitcase, I suspect, was too thick to know that he had been insulted.

One day at the quarry, we resumed our discussion of whether or not the tiger was native to Africa. We were not able to talk as freely during Van Rensburg's tenure as we had been before, but we were able to talk nonetheless while we worked.

The principle advocate of those who argued that the tiger was not native to Africa was Andrew Masondo, an ANC leader from the Cape who had also been a lecturer at Fort Hare. Masondo could be a volatile fellow, and he was vehement in his assertions that no tigers had ever been found in Africa. The argument was going back and forth and the men had put down their picks and shovels in the heat of the argument. This attracted the attention of the warders, and they shouted at us to get back to work. But we were so absorbed in the argument that we ignored the warders. A few of the lower-ranking warders ordered us to go back to work, but we paid them no attention. Finally, Suitcase marched over and bellowed at us in English, a language in which he was not expert: "You talk too much, but you work too few!"

The men now did not pick up their tools because they were bent over in laughter. Suitcase's grammatical mistake struck everyone as extremely comical. But Suitcase was not at all amused. He immediately sent for Major Kellerman, the commanding officer.

Kellerman arrived on the scene a few minutes later to find us in much the same state as we had been before. Kellerman was relatively new to the island, and was determined to set the right tone. One of the warders then reported to Kellerman that Andrew Masondo and I had not been working, and we were to be charged with malingering and insubordination. Under Kellerman's authority, we were then handcuffed and taken to isolation.

From that point on, Suitcase seemed to hold a special grudge against me. One day, while he was supervising us at the quarry, I was working next to Fikile Bam. We were off by ourselves, on the far side of the quarry. We worked diligently, but since we were both studying law at the time, we were discussing what we had read the night before. At the end of the day, Van Rensburg stood in front of us and said, "Fikile Bam and Nelson Mandela, I want to see you in front of the head of prison."

We were brought before the lieutenant, who was the head of prison, and Van Rensburg announced, "These men did not work the whole day. I'm charging them for defying orders." The lieutenant asked if we had anything to say. "Lieutenant," I responded, "we dispute the charge. We have been working and, in fact, we have evidence that we have been working, and it is essential to our defense." The lieutenant scoffed at this. "All you men work in the same area," he said. "How is it possible to have evidence?" I explained that Fiks and I had been working apart from the others and that we could show exactly how much work we had done. Suitcase naively confirmed that we had been off by ourselves, and the lieutenant agreed to have a look. We drove back to the quarry.

Once there, Fiks and I walked to the area where we had been working. I pointed to the considerable pile of rocks and lime that we had built up and said, "There, that is what we have done today." Suitcase had never even bothered to examine our work and was rattled by the quantity of it. "No," he said to the lieutenant, "that is the result of a week's work." The lieutenant was skeptical. "All right, then," he said to Suitcase, "show me the small pile that Mandela and Bam put together today." Suitcase had no reply, and the lieutenant did something I have rarely seen a superior officer do: he chastised his subordinate in the presence of prisoners. "You are telling lies," he said, and dismissed the charges on the spot.

One morning in early 1967, during Suitcase's tenure, we were preparing to walk to the quarry when Suitcase informed us that an order had come down from Major Kellerman forbidding us to talk. Not only was conversation banned on our walks; henceforth, there would be no conversation permitted at the quarry. "From now on, silence!" he yelled.

This command was greeted by profound dismay and outrage. Talking and discussing issues were the only things that made the work at the quarry tolerable. Of course, we could not discuss it on the way to the quarry because we were ordered not to talk, but during our lunch break the ANC leadership and the heads of the other political groups managed secretly to hash out a plan.

While we were surreptitiously hatching our plan, Major Kellerman himself appeared and walked into our lunch shed. This was highly unusual; we had never had such a high-ranking visitor in our lowly shed. With a cough of embarrassment, he announced that his order had been a mistake and that we could resume talking at the quarry, just as long as we did it quietly. He then told us to carry on and spun on his heel and was gone. We were glad the order was rescinded, but suspicious as to why.

For the remainder of the day, we were not forced to work very hard. Suitcase did his best to be friendly, and said that as a gesture of goodwill he had decided to withdraw all pending charges against us.

That afternoon, I discovered that my cell had been moved from number 4, near the entrance of the passageway, to number 18, at the back. All of my belongings had been dumped into the new cell. As always, there was no explanation.

We guessed that we were to have a visitor and I had been moved because the authorities did not want me to be the first among the prisoners to talk to whoever was coming. If each prisoner in turn voiced his complaints, the authorities could yell "Time up!" before a visitor reached cell 18. We resolved that in the interest of unity, each individual along the passageway would inform any visitor that while everyone had individual complaints, the prisoner in number 18 would speak for all.

The following morning, after breakfast, we were informed by Suitcase that we would not be going to the quarry. Then Major Kellerman appeared to say that Mrs. Helen Suzman, the lone member of the liberal Progressive Party in Parliament and the only voice of true opposition to the Nationalists in Parliament, would be arriving shortly. In less than fifteen minutes, Mrs. Suzman — all five feet two inches of her — came through the door of our passageway, accompanied by General Steyn, the commissioner of prisons. As she was introduced to each prisoner, she asked him whether or not he had any complaints. Each man replied the same way: "I have many complaints, but our spokesman is Mr. Nelson Mandela at the end of the corridor." To General Steyn's dismay, Mrs. Suzman was soon at my cell. She firmly shook my hand and cordially introduced herself.

Unlike judges and magistrates, who were automatically permitted access to prisons, members of Parliament had to request permission to visit a prison. Mrs. Suzman was one of the few, if not the only, members of Parliament who took an interest in the plight of political prisoners. Many stories were circulating about Robben Island, and Mrs. Suzman had come to investigate for herself.

As this was Mrs. Suzman's first visit to Robben Island, I attempted to put her at ease. But she was remarkably confident and utterly unfazed by her surroundings, and proposed that we get down to business right away. General Steyn and the commanding officer stood by her, but I did not mince words. I told her of our desire to have the food improved and equalized and to have better clothing; the need for facilities for studying; our right to information such as newspapers; and many more things. I told her of the harshness of the warders, and mentioned Van Rensburg in particular. I pointed out that he had a swastika tattooed on his forearm. Helen reacted like a lawyer. "Well, Mr. Mandela," she said, "we must not take that too far because we don't know when it was made. Perhaps, for example, his parents had it tattooed on him?" I assured her that was not the case.

Normally, I would not complain about an individual warder. One learns in prison that it is better to fight for general principles than to battle each individual case. However callous a warder may be, he is usually just carrying out prison policy. But Van Rensburg was in a class by himself, and we believed that if he were gone, it would make a disproportionate difference for all of us.

Mrs. Suzman listened attentively, jotting down what I said in a small notebook, and promised to take these matters up with the minister of justice. She then made an inspection of our cells, and talked a bit with some of the other men. It was an odd and wonderful sight to see this courageous woman peering into our cells and strolling around our courtyard. She was the first and only woman ever to grace our cells.

Van Rensburg was exceedingly nervous during Mrs. Suzman's visit. According to Kathy, while Mrs. Suzman and I were talking, Van Rensburg apologized for all his past actions. But his contrition did not last long, for the next day he informed us he was reinstating all the charges against us. We later learned that Mrs. Suzman had taken up our case in Parliament, and within a few weeks of her visit, Suitcase was transferred off the island.

69

I NEVER IMAGINED the struggle would be either short or easy. The first few years on the island were difficult times both for the organization outside and those of us in prison. After Rivonia, much of the movement's underground machinery had been destroyed. Our structures had been discovered and uprooted; those who were not captured were scrambling to stay one step ahead of the enemy. Virtually every one of the ANC's senior leaders was either in jail or in exile.

In the years after Rivonia, the ANC's External Mission, formerly responsible for fund-raising, diplomacy, and establishing a military training program, took up the reins of the organization as a whole. The External Mission not only had to create an organization in exile, but had the even more formidable task of trying to revitalize the underground ANC inside South Africa.

The state had grown stronger. The police had become more powerful, their methods more ruthless, their techniques more sophisticated. The South African Defense Force was expanding. The economy was stable, the white electorate untroubled. The South African government had powerful allies in Great Britain and the United States who were content to maintain the status quo.

But elsewhere the struggle against imperialism was on the march. In the middle to late 1960s, armed struggles were being fought throughout southern Africa. In Namibia (then South-West Africa), SWAPO was making its first incursions in the Caprivi Strip; in Mozambique and Angola, the guerrilla movement was growing and spreading. In Zimbabwe (then Rhodesia), the battle against white minority rule was advancing. Ian Smith's white government was bolstered by the South African Defense Force, and the ANC regarded the battle in Zimbabwe as an extension of our struggle at home. In 1967, we learned that the ANC had forged an alliance with the Zimbabwe African People's Union (ZAPU), which had been formed by Joshua Nkomo.

That year, a group of MK soldiers who had been training in Tanzania and Zambia crossed the Zambezi River into Rhodesia with the intention of making their way home. This first group of MK soldiers was christened the Luthuli Detachment and they were the spearhead of the armed struggle. In August, as the Luthuli Detachment, accompanied by ZAPU troops, moved southward, they were spotted by the Rhodesian army. Over the next few weeks, fierce battles were fought and both sides sustained casualties. Finally, our troops were overpowered by the superior numbers of the Rhodesian forces. Some were captured, and others retreated into Bechuanaland — which had become independent Botswana. By the beginning of 1968, another larger ANC detachment had entered Rhodesia and fought not only the Rhodesian army but South African policemen who had been posted to Rhodesia.

We heard of this months later by rumor, but did not learn the full story until some of the men who had fought there were imprisoned with us. Though our forces were not victorious, we quietly celebrated the fact that our MK cadres had engaged the enemy in combat on their own terms. It was a milestone in the struggle. "Justice" Panza, one of the commanders of the Luthuli Detachment, was later imprisoned with us. He briefed us on the detachment's military training, political education, and valor in the field. As a former commander-in-chief of MK, I was terribly proud of our soldiers.

Before receiving the news of MK's battles abroad, we also learned of Chief Luthuli's death at home in July 1967. The circumstances were curious: he had been hit by a train in an area near his farm where he often walked. I was granted permission to write a letter to his widow. Luthuli's death left a great vacuum in the organization; the chief was a Nobel Prize winner, a distinguished, internationally known figure, a man who commanded respect from both black and white. For these reasons, he was irreplaceable. Yet in Oliver Tambo, who was acting president-general of the ANC, the organization found a man who could fill the chief's shoes. Like Luthuli, he was articulate yet not showy, confident but humble. He too epitomized Chief Luthuli's precept: "Let your courage rise with danger."

We organized a small memorial service for the chief in Section B and permitted everyone who wanted to speak to do so. It was a quiet, respectful service, with only one sour note. When Neville Alexander of the Unity Movement rose to speak, it was apparent that he had come not to praise the chief but to bury him. Without even perfunctory regrets at the man's passing, he accused Luthuli of being a patsy of the white man, mainly on the grounds that the chief had accepted the Nobel Peace Prize.

Apart from its wrong-headedness, Neville's speech was entirely contrary to the climate of cooperation between organizations we were trying to create on the island. From the moment I arrived on the island, I had made it my mission to seek some accommodation with our rivals in the struggle. I saw Robben Island as an opportunity to patch up the long and often bitter differences between the PAC and the ANC. If we could unite the two organizations on the island, that could set a precedent for uniting them in the liberation struggle as a whole.

Yet from the beginning, relations with the PAC had been more competitive than cooperative. Some of the PAC men had already been on the island, and saw our arrival as an encroachment on their territory. We heard from some of our men that the most senior PAC prisoners had expressed regret that we had not been hanged.

In 1962, when I had first been on the island, the PAC had greatly outnumbered the ANC. In 1967, the numbers were reversed. Yet this seemed to harden the PAC in their positions. They were unashamedly anti-Communist and anti-Indian. In the early years, I had talks with Zeph Mothopeng, who had been on the PAC's National Executive Committee. Zeph argued that the PAC was more militant than the ANC, and that in prison, the ANC should follow the PAC's lead. The PAC maintained that negotiations with the authorities were a betrayal, but that did not stop them from taking advantage of the benefits that resulted from negotiations. In 1967, I held talks with Selby Ngendane on the question of unity. Outside of prison, Ngendane had been violently opposed to the Freedom Charter, but in prison, particularly when sent to our section, Selby mellowed. We eventually wrote separate letters to our respective organizations in the general section advocating the idea of unity. The ANC also worked well with Clarence Makwetu, who later became president of the PAC. Makwetu, who had once been a member of the ANC Youth League, was in our section and was a balanced, sensible man. We had many fruitful discussions about the unity of our two organizations, but after Makwetu was released and was succeeded in the PAC leadership on Robben Island by John Pokela, the talks foundered.

The PAC's insecurity occasionally had comical results. At one point, an order came from Pretoria that I was to be isolated from all other prisoners at the quarry. I would work separately, eat separately, and have my own guard. We noticed that this new ruling caused some agitation among the PAC. Several days later, the PAC decided that their leader, Zeph Mothopeng, would also be isolated, and on their own they had him work and eat separately from everyone else for as long as I did.

The PAC often refused to participate in meetings that had no overt party affiliation. When we called meetings to discuss our grievances and later had news sessions to discuss what we had learned from the paper, the PAC boycotted these gatherings. I found this greatly annoying. The PAC, we learned, were ignorant of changes in their own organization on the outside. At the time, the PAC members on the island refused to believe our claims that the exiled PAC had opened its doors to whites and Indians as members. That was heresy. Yet we had read in the paper that the white activist Patrick Duncan had become a member of the PAC executive. The PAC members derided this at the time as ANC propaganda.

The ANC formed its own internal organization on the island. Known as the High Command, or more officially, the High Organ, it consisted of the most senior ANC leaders on Robben Island, the men who had been members of the National Executive Committee: Walter Sisulu, Govan Mbeki, Raymond Mhlaba, and myself. I served as the head of the High Organ.

From its inception, we decided the High Organ would not try to influence external ANC policy. We had no reliable way of evaluating the situation in the country, and concluded it would neither be fair nor wise for us to offer guidance on matters about which we were uninformed. Instead, we made decisions about such matters as prisoners' complaints, strikes, mail, food — all of the day-to-day concerns of prison life. We would, when possible, convene a general members meeting, which we regarded as vital to the health of our organization. But as these meetings were extremely dangerous and thus infrequent, the High Organ would often take decisions that were then communicated to all the other members. The High Organ also operated a cell system, with each cell consisting of three members.

In the first few years on the island, the High Organ also acted as a representative committee for all the political prisoners in our section. In 1967, we organized a petition demanding better treatment that was signed by virtually everyone, including members of the PAC, the Unity Movement, and the Liberal Party, represented by Eddie Daniels. This arrangement was acceptable to all until Neville Alexander complained that the High Organ was neither democratic nor truly representative, and that some other body ought to be created.

Neville's original suggestion eventually turned into a prisoners' committee composed of people from all political parties. There was fear among the other organizations that the ANC would attempt to dominate it, and the committee's rules were crafted so that its powers were purely consultative and its decisions not binding. Even so, it was still difficult to agree on a common approach to problems. We suggested that Fikile Bam, a member of the Yu Chi Chan Club, preside over meetings. Later, the committee leadership would rotate. Eventually the committee became known as Ulundi, and acted as a disciplinary committee for all political prisoners.

The High Organ was the source of some controversy because of its ethnic composition: all four permanent members were from Xhosa backgrounds. This was a matter of coincidence rather than design; the senior ANC leadership on the island, the only four to have served on the National Executive Committee, happened to be Xhosa. It would not have been proper to take a less senior comrade and put him on the High Organ simply because he was not a Xhosa. But the fact that the High Organ was Xhosa-dominated disturbed me because it seemed to reinforce the mistaken perception that we were a Xhosa organization.

I have always found this criticism to be vexing and based on both ignorance of ANC history and maliciousness. I would refute it by noting that the presidents of the ANC have been Zulus, Mosothos, Pedis, and Tswanas, and the executive has always been a mixture of tribal groups. I recall once working in our courtyard on a sunny afternoon, while some men from the general section were working on the roof above me. They shouted at me, "*Mdala!* [Old man!], why do you only talk to Xhosas?" The accusation stung me. I looked up and said, "How can you accuse me of discrimination? We are one people." They seemed satisfied by that, but their perception stuck in my mind. From then on, whenever I knew I would be walking in front of men from the general section, I would try to converse with Kathy or Eddie Daniels, or someone who was not a Xhosa.

We subsequently decided that there should be a fifth, rotating member of the High Organ. This member was usually not a Xhosa; Kathy, for example, was the fifth member of the High Organ for more than five years. Laloo Chiba also served for a time, and in the end, the criticism died a slow and unremarkable death.

I did not by any means dominate the High Organ, and in fact, a number of proposals that I felt strongly about were rejected. This is as it should be, but I sometimes found it frustrating. There were two issues regarding the authorities about which I could never persuade my colleagues. Prison regulations stated that prisoners must stand in the presence of a senior officer. I advocated that we should remain seated, as it was demeaning to have to recognize the enemy when he did not recognize us as political prisoners. My comrades believed this was a trivial matter and the negative consequences of resistance would outweigh any benefits.

The second issue was rejected by the High Organ on similar grounds. The warders called us by either our surnames or our Christian names. Each, I felt, was degrading, and I thought we should insist on the honorific "Mister." I pressed for this for many years, without success. Later, it even became a source of humor as my colleagues would occasionally call me "Mr." Mandela.

70

TIME MAY SEEM to stand still for those of us in prison, but it did not halt for those outside. I was reminded of this when I was visited by my mother in the spring of 1968. I had not seen her since the end of the Rivonia Trial. Change is gradual and incremental, and when one lives in the midst of one's family, one rarely notices differences in them. But when one doesn't see one's family for many years at a time, the transformation can be striking. My mother suddenly seemed very old.

She had journeyed all the way from the Transkei, accompanied by my son Makgatho, my daughter Makaziwe, and my sister Mabel. Because I had four visitors and they had come a great distance, the authorities extended the visiting time from a half an hour to forty-five minutes.

I had not seen my son and daughter since before the trial and they had become adults in the interim, growing up without me. I looked at them with amazement and pride. But though they had grown up, I am afraid I still treated them more or less as the children they had been when I went to prison. They may have changed, but I hadn't.

My mother had lost a great deal of weight, which concerned me. Her face appeared haggard. Only my sister Mabel seemed unchanged. While it was a great pleasure to see all of them and to discuss family issues, I was uneasy about my mother's health.

I spoke with Makgatho and Maki about my desire for them both to pursue further schooling and asked Mabel about relatives in the Transkei. The time passed far too quickly. As with most visits, the greatest pleasure often lies in the recollection of it, but this time, I could not stop worrying about my mother. I feared that it would be the last time I would ever see her.

Several weeks later, after returning from the quarry, I was told to go to the Head Office to collect a telegram. It was from Makgatho, informing me that my mother had died of a heart attack. I immediately made a request to the commanding officer to be permitted to attend her funeral in the Transkei, which he turned down. "Mandela," he said, "while I know you are a man of your word and would not try to escape, I cannot trust your own people, and we fear that they would try to kidnap you." It added to my grief that I was not able to bury my mother, which was my responsibility as her eldest child and only son.

Over the next few months I thought about her a great deal. Her life had been far from easy. I had been able to support her when I was practicing as an attorney, but once I went to prison, I was unable to help her. I had never been as attentive as I should have been.

A mother's death causes a man to look back on and evaluate his own life. Her difficulties, her poverty, made me question once again whether I had taken the right path. That was always the conundrum: Had I made the right choice in putting the people's welfare even before that of my own family? For a long time, my mother had not understood my commitment to the struggle. My family had not asked for or even wanted to be involved in the struggle, but my involvement penalized them.

But I came back to the same answer. In South Africa, it is hard for a man to ignore the needs of the people, even at the expense of his own family. I had made my choice, and in the end, she had supported it. But that did not lessen the sadness I felt at not being able to make her life more comfortable, or the pain of not being able to lay her to rest.

In the early hours of the morning of May 12, 1969, the security police awakened Winnie at our home in Orlando and detained her without charge under the 1967 Terrorism Act, which gave the government unprecedented powers of arrest and detention without trial. The raid, I later learned, was part of a nationwide crackdown in which dozens of others were detained, including Winnie's sister. The police dragged Winnie away while Zeni and Zindzi clung to her skirts. She was placed in solitary confinement in Pretoria, where she was denied bail and visitors; over the next weeks and months, she was relentlessly and brutally interrogated.

When Winnie was finally charged — six months later — I managed to send instructions that she be represented by Joel Carlson, a longtime antiapartheid lawyer. Winnie and twenty-two others were charged under the Suppression of Communism Act for attempting to revive the ANC. Later,

George Bizos and Arthur Chaskalson, both members of the Rivonia team, joined the defense. In October, seventeen months after her arrest, the state withdrew its case without explanation, and Winnie was released. Within two weeks, she was again banned, and placed under house arrest. She immediately applied for permission to visit me and was rebuffed.

There was nothing I found so agonizing in prison as the thought that Winnie was in prison too. I put a brave face on the situation, but inwardly I was deeply disturbed and worried. Nothing tested my inner equilibrium as much as the time that Winnie was in solitary confinement. Although I often urged others not to worry about what they could not control, I was unable to take my own advice. I had many sleepless nights. What were the authorities doing to my wife? How would she bear up? Who was looking after our daughters? Who would pay the bills? It is a form of mental torture to be constantly plagued by such questions and not have the means to answer them.

Brigadier Aucamp allowed me to send letters to Winnie, and relayed one or two from her. Normally, prisoners awaiting trial are not permitted mail, but Aucamp permitted it as a favor to me. I was grateful, but knew the authorities had not granted permission out of altruism: they were reading our letters, hoping to glean some information that would assist their case against Winnie.

During this time I experienced another grievous loss. One cold morning in July of 1969, three months after I learned of Winnie's incarceration, I was called to the main office on Robben Island and handed a telegram. It was from my youngest son, Makgatho, and it was only a sentence long. He informed me that his older brother, my first and oldest son, Madiba Thembekile, whom we called Thembi, had been killed in a motorcar accident in the Transkei. Thembi was then twenty-five years old, and the father of two small children.

What can one say about such a tragedy? I was already overwrought about my wife, I was still grieving for my mother, and then to hear such news . . . I do not have words to express the sorrow, or the loss I felt. It left a hole in my heart that can never be filled.

I returned to my cell and lay on my bed. I do not know how long I stayed there, but I did not emerge for dinner. Some of the men looked in, but I said nothing. Finally, Walter came to me and knelt beside my bed, and I handed him the telegram. He said nothing, but only held my hand. I do not know how long he remained with me. There is nothing that one man can say to another at such a time.

I asked permission of the authorities to attend my son's funeral. As a father, it was my responsibility to make sure that my son's spirit would rest peacefully. I told them they could send a security cordon with me, and that I would give my word that I would return. Permission was denied. All I was permitted to do was write a letter to Thembi's mother, Evelyn, in which I did my best to comfort her and tell her that I shared her suffering.

I thought back to one afternoon when Thembi was a boy and he came to visit me at a safe house in Cyrildene that I used for secret ANC work. Between my underground political work and legal cases, I had not been able to see him for some time. I surprised him at the house and found him wearing an old jacket of mine that came to his knees. He must have taken some comfort and pride in wearing his father's clothing, just as I once did with my own father's. When I had to say good-bye again, he stood up tall, as if he were already grown, and said, "I will look after the family while you are gone."

Part Nine

ROBBEN ISLAND:
BEGINNING TO HOPE

71

THE GRAPH of improvement in prison was never steady. Progress was halting, and typically accompanied by setbacks. An advancement might take years to win, and then be rescinded in a day. We would push the rock up the hill, only to have it tumble down again. But conditions did improve. We had won a host of small battles that added up to a change in the atmosphere of the island. While we did not run the island, the authorities could not run it without us, and in the aftermath of Van Rensburg's departure, our life became more tolerable.

Within our first three years on the island we were all given long trousers. By 1969, we received our own individual prison uniforms, instead of being issued a different set each week. These uniforms actually fit us and we were allowed to wash them ourselves. We were permitted out in the courtyard at all hours during the weekend. Although our food was not yet equalized, African prisoners would occasionally receive bread in the morning. We were allowed to pool our food anyway, so that the differences did not matter. We had been given board games and cards, which we often played on Saturdays and Sundays. At the quarry, our talk was rarely interrupted. If the commanding officer was coming, the warders on duty would blow a whistle to warn us to pick up our tools. We had neutralized the worst warders and befriended the more reasonable ones, though the authorities realized this and rotated warders every few months.

We were able to meet among ourselves virtually whenever we wanted. Meetings of the High Organ, general members' meetings, and meetings of Ulundi were generally not broken up unless they were too conspicuous. The inmates seemed to be running the prison, not the authorities.

Stern and God-fearing, the Afrikaner takes his religion seriously. The one inflexible event on our weekly schedule was Sunday morning religious services. This was an observance the authorities considered mandatory. It was as if they believed their own mortal souls would be in peril if they did not give us the benefit of worship on Sunday.

Every Sunday morning, a minister from a different denomination would preach to us. One Sunday it would be an Anglican priest, the next a Dutch Reform predicant, the next a Methodist minister. The clerics were recruited by the prison service, whose one edict was that they must preach exclusively on religious matters. Warders were present at all services and if the minister strayed from religion, he was not invited back.

During the first two years on the island, we were not even permitted to leave our cells for Sunday services. The minister would preach from the head of our corridor. By our third year, services were held in the courtyard, which we preferred. In those years, this was the only time we were permitted in the courtyard on Sunday, except for our half hour of exercise. Few of our men were religious, but no one minded long sermons; we enjoyed being outside.

Once services were held outside, we were given the option of attending. Some men only attended services in their own denomination. Though I am a Methodist, I would attend each different religious service.

One of our first ministers was an Anglican priest by the name of Father Hughes, a gruff, burly Welshman who had served as a chaplain in the submarine corps during the Second World War. When he first arrived, he was perturbed by having to preach in the corridor, which he found inimical to the contemplation of God. On his first visit, instead of preaching to us, he recited passages of Winston Churchill's wartime radio addresses in his beautiful baritone: "We shall fight on the beaches, we shall fight on the landing grounds, we shall fight in the fields and in the streets, we shall fight in the hills; we shall never surrender."

Father Hughes soon preached to us in the courtyard and we found his sermons splendid. He made a point of discreetly inserting bits and pieces of news into his sermons, something we appreciated. He might say, for example, that like the pharaoh of ancient Egypt, the prime minister of South Africa was raising an army.

We always sang hymns at the end of services, and I think Father Hughes visited us so frequently just to hear us sing. He brought along a portable organ, and he would play for us. He praised our singing, saying that it was the only singing that matched the choirs in his native Wales.

The Methodist minister was a Reverend Jones, a nervous and gloomy fellow who had been based in the Congo during its revolution. His experience there seemed to be the source of his melancholy. Over and over, he preached the importance of reconciliation — implying that it was we who needed to reconcile ourselves to the whites.

One Sunday, during the reverend's one-sided message, I noticed Eddie Daniels shifting uneasily. Finally, Eddie could take it no longer. "You're preaching reconciliation to the wrong people," Eddie called out. "We've been seeking reconciliation for the last seventy-five years." This was enough for Reverend Jones and we never saw him again.

Reverend Jones was not the only minister Eddie scared away. We were visited by a Coloured minister known as Brother September. One Sunday, a prisoner named Hennie Ferris, who was an eloquent speaker, volunteered to lead a prayer. Brother September was pleased to recognize such devotion. Hennie began speaking in lofty language, and at one point, asked the congregation to close its eyes and pray. Everyone, including Brother September, obliged. Eddie then tiptoed to the front, opened Brother September's briefcase, and removed the *Sunday Times* of that day. No one suspected anything at the time, but Brother September never brought newspapers again.

Reverend Andre Scheffer was a minister of the Dutch Reformed Mission Church in Africa, a sister church of the Dutch Reformed Church, the faith of nearly all the Afrikaner people. The Mission Church catered only to Africans. Reverend Scheffer was a crusty, conservative fellow who usually preached to the general prisoners. One Sunday, he wandered over to our section and we asked him why he didn't preach to us. "You men think you are freedom fighters," he said contemptuously. "You must have been drunk on liquor or high on *dagga* [marijuana] when you were arrested. Freedom fighters, my foot!" But we challenged him to come to preach to us, and eventually, in the late 1960s, he responded.

Reverend Scheffer was unorthodox in one respect: he took a scientific approach to religion. I found this very appealing. Many people use science to debunk religion, but Reverend Scheffer enlisted science to bolster his beliefs. I recall one sermon in which he talked about the three Wise Men from the East who followed a star until it led them to Bethlehem. "This is not just a superstition or a myth," he said, and then cited evidence from astronomers that at that time in history there was a comet that followed the path outlined in the Bible.

As Reverend Scheffer became familiar with us, he became more sympathetic. He had a dry sense of humor and liked to poke fun at us. "You know," he would say, "the white man has a more difficult task than the black man in this country. Whenever there is a problem, we have to find a solution. But whenever you blacks have a problem, you have an excuse. You can simply say, '*Ingabilungu.*'" We burst into laughter not only because his pronunciation was unintentionally comical, but also because we were amused by the idea. "*Ngabelungu*" is a Xhosa expression that means, "It is the whites." He was saying that we could always blame all of our troubles on the white man. His message was that we must also look within ourselves and become responsible for our actions — sentiments with which I wholeheartedly agreed.

What Sundays were to the rest of the week, Christmas was to the rest of the year. It was the one day when the authorities showed any goodwill toward men. We did not have to go to the quarry on Christmas Day, and we were permitted to purchase a small quantity of sweets. We did not have a traditional Christmas meal, but we were given an extra mug of coffee for supper.

The authorities permitted us to organize a concert, hold competitions, and put on a play. The concert was the centerpiece. Our choirmaster was Selby Ngendane of the PAC. Selby had been a member of the ANC Youth League before switching allegiance to the Pan Africanist Congress. He was a natural entertainer with a lovely voice and a fine ear.

Selby chose the songs, arranged the harmonies, selected the soloists, and conducted the performance. The concert took place on Christmas morning in the courtyard. We would mix in traditional English Christmas songs with African ones, and include a few protest songs — the authorities did not seem to mind or perhaps know the difference. The warders were our audience, and they enjoyed our singing as much as we did.

Before coming to prison, Ngendane was perceived as something of a political lightweight. But in prison, Selby showed his mettle. In prison, one likes to be around men who have a sunny disposition, and Selby had one.

Prison was a kind of crucible that tested a man's character. Some men, under the pressure of incarceration, showed true mettle, while others revealed themselves as less than what they had appeared to be.

In addition to the concerts, we held a chess and draughts (or checkers) tournament, and also played Scrabble and bridge. Every year, I competed in the draughts competition, and some years, I won the grand prize, which was usually a candy bar. My style of play was slow and deliberate; my strategy conservative. I carefully considered the ramifications of every option and took a long time between moves. I resist such analogies, but it is my preferred mode of operating not only in draughts but in politics.

Most of my opponents played more swiftly, and often lost patience with my manner of play. One of my most frequent opponents was Don Davis. A member of the Non-European Unity Movement, Don had grown up in the diamond-mining area of Kimberley and was a rugged, fearless fellow who was also highly strung. Don was an excellent draughts player, but his style contrasted with mine. When Don played, perspiration would flow down his face. He became tense and agitated as he played, and made his moves rapidly as though points were awarded for speed. Several times Don and I found ourselves in the finals of the annual tournament.

Don called me Qhipu because of a habit I had when playing draughts. I would ponder each possibility, and then when I was about to move, I would call out, *"Qhipu!"* — which means "I strike!" — and then move the piece. Don found this frustrating and he called me Qhipu more in irritation than in amity.

Don and I played in many tournaments, and even if he won, he would come back within a few minutes, challenging me to another match. Don always wanted to play draughts, and did not seem satisfied until I responded. Soon I was spending so much time playing with Don that my other pursuits languished. When I once failed to pass an exam in my studies, a few colleagues asked me why, and I responded, to much laughter, "Don Davis!"

Our amateur drama society made its yearly offering at Christmas. My thespian career, which had lain dormant since I played John Wilkes Booth while at Fort Hare, had a modest revival on Robben Island. Our productions were what might now be called minimalist: no stage, no scenery, no costumes. All we had were the words of the play.

I only performed in a few dramas, but I had one memorable role: that of Creon, the king of Thebes, in Sophocles' *Antigone*. I had read some of the classic Greek plays in prison, and found them enormously elevating. What I took out of them was that character was measured by facing up to difficult situations and that a hero was a man who would not break even under the most trying circumstances.

When *Antigone* was chosen as the play, I volunteered my services, and was asked to play Creon, an elderly king fighting a civil war over the throne of his beloved city-state. At the outset of the play, Creon is sincere and patriotic, and there is wisdom in his early speeches when he suggests that experience is the foundation of leadership and that obligations to the people take precedence over loyalty to an individual.

> Of course you cannot know a man completely,
> his character, his principles, sense of judgment,
> not till he's shown his colors, ruling the people,
> making laws. Experience, there's the test.

But Creon deals with his enemies mercilessly. He has decreed that the body of Polynices, Antigone's brother, who had rebelled against the city, does not deserve a proper burial. Antigone rebels, on the grounds that there is a higher law than that of the state. Creon will not listen to Antigone, nor does he listen to anyone but his own inner demons. His inflexibility and blindness ill become a leader, for a leader must temper justice with mercy. It was Antigone who symbolized our struggle; she was, in her own way, a freedom fighter, for she defied the law on the grounds that it was unjust.

72

SOME OF THE WARDERS began to engage us in conversation. I never initiated conversations with warders, but if they addressed a question to me, I tried to answer. It is easier to educate a man when he wants to learn. Usually, these questions were posed with a kind of exasperation: "All right, Mandela, what is it you really want?" Or, "Look, you have a roof over your head and enough food, why are you causing so much trouble?" I would then calmly explain our policies to the warders. I wanted to demystify the ANC for them, to peel away their prejudices.

In 1969 a young warder arrived who seemed particularly eager to get to know me. I had heard rumors that our people on the outside were organizing an escape for me, and had infiltrated a warder onto the island who would assist me. Gradually, this fellow communicated to me that he was planning my escape.

In bits and pieces he explained the plan: one night, he would drug the warders on duty at the lighthouse to allow for the landing of a boat on the beach. He would furnish me with a key to get out of our section so that I could meet the boat. On the boat I was to be equipped with underwater diving gear, which I would use to swim into the harbor at Cape Town. From Cape Town, I would be taken to a local airport and flown out of the country.

I listened to the plan in its entirety and did not communicate to him how far-fetched and unreliable it sounded. I consulted with Walter, and we agreed that this fellow was not to be trusted. I never told him that I would not do it, but I never took any of the actions required to implement the plan. He must have gotten the message, for he was soon transferred off the island.

As it turned out, my mistrust was justified, for we later learned that the warder was an agent of the Bureau of State Security (BOSS), South Africa's secret intelligence agency. The plot was that I was to be successfully taken off the island, but killed in a dramatic shootout with security forces at the airport as I tried to leave the country. The entire plan had been dreamed up by BOSS, even the rumors that reached me about the ANC's planning an escape. It was not the last time they would try to eliminate me.

The term of a commanding officer was usually no more than three years, and we had been through several by 1970. That year, Robben Island's commanding officer was Colonel Van Aarde, a rather amiable, harmless fellow who allowed us free rein. But at the end of the year, the authorities concluded that they wanted a different atmosphere on the island, and Colonel Piet Badenhorst was named the new C.O. of Robben Island.

This was an ominous development. Badenhorst was reputed to be one of the most brutal and authoritarian officers in the entire prison service. His appointment indicated one thing: the government believed that discipline on the island was too lax, and that a strong hand was needed to keep us in line. Badenhorst would supposedly make us yearn for the days of Suitcase.

Whenever a new commanding officer was appointed, I requested a meeting with him. I did this in order to impress upon him the seriousness of our cause and also to evaluate his character. I requested a meeting with Colonel Badenhorst and was turned down. He was the first commanding officer to spurn such a meeting.

We felt the effects of his regime before we ever saw him. A number of the newer regulations regarding study and free time were immediately rescinded. It was obvious that he intended to roll back every privilege we had won over the years. Our old warders were transferred off the island and replaced by Badenhorst's handpicked guards. They were younger, coarser men who enforced every niggling regulation, whose job was to harass and demoralize us. Within days of Badenhorst's appointment, our cells were raided and searched; books and papers were confiscated; meals were suspended without warning; and men were jostled on the way to the quarry.

Badenhorst attempted to turn back the clock to the way the island was in the early 1960s. The answer to every question was always no. Prisoners who requested to see their lawyers were given solitary confinement instead. Complaints were completely ignored. Visits were canceled without explanation. The food deteriorated. Censorship increased.

About a week after Badenhorst arrived, we were working at the quarry one morning when, without introduction or fanfare, Badenhorst and his driver pulled up in the commander's car. He got out and surveyed us from a distance. We paused to look at our new commander. Badenhorst returned my glance and called out, "Mandela, *Jy moet jou vinger uit jou gat trek*" (You must pull your finger out of your arse). I did not care for this expression at all, and without thinking, I started advancing toward Badenhorst. He was still a distance away, and before I got close he had returned to his car and driven away.

From his car, Badenhorst radioed a command to his staff, and within minutes a truck had arrived to transport us back to Section B. We were commanded to be silent in the truck, and when we arrived at the courtyard, we were ordered to stand at attention. Badenhorst appeared in front of us, pacing back and forth. He seemed incapable of uttering a sentence without including an oath or swearword. *"Jou ma se moer,"* was his favorite expression. "Your mother is a *moer"* — *moer* being a vulgar term for an intimate part of a woman's anatomy.

In his guttural voice, he told us he was disgusted to have observed our laziness at the quarry. As a result, he said, he was arbitrarily dropping all of our classifications by one notch. Though we despised the classification system, most of the men had by that time risen to at least C level, where they were permitted to study. D level prisoners were not allowed to study. The authorities rued the fact that they had allowed us study privileges, and Badenhorst was determined to rectify that mistake.

Later, after my anger abated, I realized that Badenhorst's crude remark to me at the quarry was a calculated one. He had been brought to Robben Island to restore order, and he had singled out the individual he assumed was the source of the disorder. Like a teacher who takes over a rowdy class, he sought to discipline the student he regarded as the principal troublemaker.

73

IN LATE MAY of 1971, a number of men from SWAPO (the South-West African People's Organization), an ally of the ANC fighting for independence in Namibia, were brought to the isolation section. They were led by Andimba Toivo ja Toivo, a founder of SWAPO and a formidable freedom fighter. We learned that they had embarked on a hunger strike to protest their isolation, and we immediately decided to join in. This angered Badenhorst and the authorities who regarded this as unacceptable insubordination.

Late on the night of May 28, we were awakened by shouts and fierce knocking on our cell doors. "Get up! Get up!" the warders yelled. We were ordered to strip and then line up against the wall of the courtyard. The warders were obviously drunk and were yelling and taunting us. They were led by a sadistic fellow named Fourie, whom we privately called Gangster.

It was a bitterly cold night, and for the next hour, while we stood at attention naked and shivering, our cells were searched one by one. Warders kept up their abuse for the entire time. Toward the end of the hour, Govan experienced severe chest pains and collapsed. This seemed to scare Fourie, and he ordered us to return to our cells.

The warders searched high and low, and found nothing. But the search seemed only an excuse for Fourie's sadistic impulses. Only later did we learn that Fourie was reputed to have molested prisoners in the general section. The following day we discovered that the warders had brutally beaten some general prisoners before they came to us, and afterward, assaulted Toivo ja Toivo, who hit back and knocked down the warder who was beating him. Toivo was severely punished for this.

We filed a formal complaint about our treatment, but it was ignored. The incident stands out in my memory, but it was by no means unique; incidents like it were the rule rather than the exception during Badenhorst's command.

We were determined not to let conditions deteriorate entirely under Badenhorst. We smuggled messages to our people on the outside to agitate for his dismissal. At the same time, we resolved to create a delegation among ourselves to see Badenhorst. We discussed this for months and gradually decided on its composition; Walter and I represented the ANC, and each of the other parties had two representatives as well.

Badenhorst agreed to meet us, and at our parley we threatened work stoppages, go-slows, hunger strikes — every weapon at our disposal — unless he reformed his ways and restored many of the privileges that he had rescinded. He merely said he would take what we said under consideration. We regarded this confrontation as a victory, for he was wary of us and knew that we had alerted people on the outside of our complaints. These efforts soon produced a response.

A few weeks later, we knew an important visit must be imminent because when it rained that day at the quarry we were allowed to take shelter instead of continuing to work. The following day we were informed that a troika of judges were coming to the island. The authorities asked us to nominate a spokesman to express our grievances, and I was chosen.

As I was preparing for my meeting with the judges, I was informed by a reliable source that a prisoner in the general section had recently been severely beaten by a guard. The three judges were Justices Jan Steyn, M. E. Theron, and Michael Corbett of the Cape provincial division of the Supreme Court. They were escorted by the commissioner of prisons, General Steyn, and accompanied by Colonel Badenhorst. I met them that day outside, where we were working.

General Steyn introduced me to the judges and explained that I had been selected to represent the other prisoners. The judges then indicated that as a matter of course they would talk with me privately. I replied that I had nothing to hide and that in fact I welcomed the presence of General Steyn and the colonel. I could see that they were taken aback by my statement, and I added that it would be only proper for them to have the opportunity to reply to my charges. The judges reluctantly acquiesced.

I began by recounting the recent assault in the general section. I told them the details that had been reported to me, the viciousness of the beating, and the cover-up of the crime. I had barely begun to speak when I noticed Badenhorst shifting uncomfortably. When I had finished describing the incident, Badenhorst interjected in a gruff, aggressive manner: "Did you actually witness this assault?" I replied calmly that I had not but that I trusted the people who had told me of it. He snorted and wagged his finger in my face. "Be careful, Mandela," he said. "If you talk about things you haven't seen, you will get yourself in trouble. You know what I mean."

I ignored Badenhorst's remarks and turned to the judges and said, "Gentlemen, you can see for yourselves the type of man we are dealing with as commanding officer. If he can threaten me here, in your presence, you can imagine what he does when you are not here." Judge Corbett then turned to the others and said, "The prisoner is quite right."

I spent the remainder of the meeting enumerating complaints about our diet, work, and studying. Inwardly Badenhorst must have been fuming, but outwardly he seemed chastened. At the end of the session, the judges thanked me, and I bade them good-bye.

I have no idea what the judges said or did after the meeting, but over the next few months, Badenhorst seemed to have his hands tied. The harshness abated, and within three months of the judges' visit, we received word that Badenhorst was to be transferred.

A few days before Badenhorst's departure, I was called to the main office. General Steyn was visiting the island and wanted to know if we had any complaints. Badenhorst was there as I went through a list of demands. When I had finished, Badenhorst spoke to me directly. He told me that he would be leaving the island, and added, "I just want to wish you people good luck." I do not know if I looked dumbfounded, but I was amazed. He spoke these words like a human being, and showed a side of himself we had never seen before. I thanked him for his good wishes, and wished him luck in his endeavors.

I thought about this moment for a long time afterward. Badenhorst had perhaps been the most callous and barbaric commanding officer we had had on Robben Island. But that day in the office, he had revealed that there was another side to his nature, a side that had been obscured but that still existed. It was a useful reminder that all men, even the most seemingly cold-blooded, have a core of decency, and that if their heart is touched, they are capable of changing. Ultimately, Badenhorst was not evil; his inhumanity had been foisted upon him by an inhuman system. He behaved like a brute because he was rewarded for brutish behavior.

74

IT WAS ANNOUNCED that Colonel Willemse would succeed Colonel Badenhorst as commanding officer. I requested a meeting with the colonel after his appointment and visited with him shortly after his arrival. While he was obviously not a progressive man, he was courteous and reasonable, in marked contrast to his predecessor. Badenhorst's tenure, we hoped, would simply be a dip on the graph of the steady improvement of our conditions.

The aggressive young warders departed with Badenhorst as well, and we quickly resumed our customary behavior at the quarry and in our section. Willemse may have been a reasonable man, but when he saw that we spent more time at the quarry talking than working, he was shocked.

He had been on the island for only a few weeks when I was summoned to his office for a meeting. "Mandela," he said frankly, "you must help me." I asked him how. "Your men are not working. They don't listen to orders. They only do what they want to do. This is a prison. There must be some discipline. It is not only good for us but good for you. We must have some order or they will bring back someone like the previous head of prison."

What the colonel said made sense. I listened and told him that his request was a legitimate one, but before I could respond to him, I would need to meet with all my men. At that time, a meeting of all prisoners in the single cells was something that was expressly forbidden. By asking him to permit such a meeting, I was asking him for a significant extension of the rules. He knew this as well as I did, and he wanted some time to consider it.

Within days, I received a communication from Willemse saying he would allow it. All of us met one afternoon in the courtyard, without guards watching over us. I told the men what Willemse said, and noted that by compromising a bit now, we would be making our conditions better in the long run. We decided that we would at least appear to be working, but what work we did would be at a pace that suited us. From then on, that is what we did, and we heard no more complaints from the commanding officer.

During the early part of Willemse's tenure, in 1971–2, there was a steady influx of captured MK soldiers. These men had seen combat, and were well informed about the state of the exile movement. While I was never happy to see ANC men imprisoned, I was keen to debrief them after they arrived. I was extremely eager to know about Oliver, about the training camps, about MK's successes and failures.

The men were extremely militant, and they did not take to prison life easily. One of the first of these men was Jimmy April, an MK officer who had trained under Joe Slovo and had fought against the enemy in Rhodesia. MK had been slowly infiltrating men back into the country with forged identity documents. Jimmy had been one of them and he was arrested in South Africa.

Jimmy regaled us with war stories, but I also took him aside and asked him about MK's problems. As I was founder of MK and its first commander-in-chief, Jimmy and the others were more candid with me than they were with the others. He told me stories of discontent in the camps, and of abuses by MK officers. I asked him to keep the matter to himself, and I managed to smuggle a letter out to Oliver suggesting that some reforms must be made in the camps.

One day, I was at the Head Office meeting with Colonel Willemse when I saw Jimmy outside the office of another official. He turned to me and said in some agitation, "They are refusing to give me my letter."

"On what ground?" I replied.

"They claim it contains matter which I am not allowed to see," he said. I entered the office to discuss the matter, but before I could even open my mouth, Jimmy had barged in and loudly said to the official, "Give me my letter!" Jimmy began to push me aside to get to the officer's desk and take the letter himself. At this point, the official took the letter and moved behind me as if for protection from Jimmy. It might have been a comical scene in a film, but at the time it was nerve-racking. I turned to Jimmy and said quietly but sternly, "Please don't do this. Calm down. I'll sort out this matter and see to it that you get your letter. Now, please leave."

My speech had the intended effect, and Jimmy left the office. I then turned to the officer, who was extremely rattled. It was, for me, an odd position. I was not opposing the authorities but mediating between my own people and the men I had so long fought against. The militancy of those who were coming to the island put me in this position more and more frequently. While we were encouraged by their radicalism, these men sometimes made our day-to-day life more burdensome.

Within a week, the officer handed me Jimmy's letter.

With Walter and
Winnie in 1990.
*(Gideon Mendel/
Magnum)*

Cyril Ramaphosa
and Joe Slovo in
Johannesburg, during
preparatory talks for
a new constitution.
(Associated Press)

Left:
At the Chris Hani memorial at Orlando Stadium, Soweto, with Tokyo Sexwale (right) and Charles Ngekule (left). *(Magnum)*

Below:
In 1993, I revisited Robben Island. *(Copyright Island Pictures)*

Opposite, above:
The cell in which I lived for eighteen of my twenty-seven years in prison. *(Copyright Island Pictures)*

Opposite, below:
The waters of Table Bay separate Robben Island from Cape Town. In the distance is Table Mountain. *(Copyright Island Pictures)*

With Archbishop
Tutu. *(Peter
Magubane)*

With F. W. de Klerk.
(Peter Magubane)

Casting my vote in
South Africa's first
general election.
(Peter Magubane)

Singing the national
anthem at my
inauguration with
Thabo Mbeki and
my daughter Zinani.
(Ian Berry/Magnum)

A warm embrace
with Bishop Tutu
after the ceremony.
(Ian Berry/Magnum)

With my children
Zindzi, Zinani,
Makaziwe, and
Makgatho. *(Peter
Magubane)*

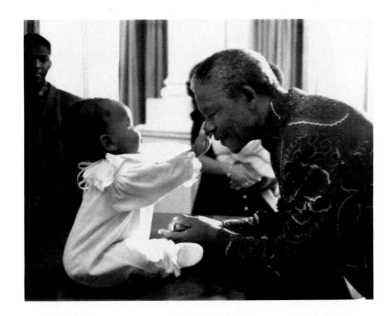

Left:
With my great-granddaughter in September 1994. *(Peter Magubane)*

My family. *(Peter Magubane)*

With my grandson
Bambata. *(Peter Magubane)*

75

ONE MORNING, instead of walking to the quarry, we were ordered into the back of a truck. It rumbled off in a new direction, and fifteen minutes later we were ordered to jump out. There in front of us, glinting in the morning light, we saw the ocean, the rocky shore, and in the distance, winking in the sunshine, the glass towers of Cape Town. Although it was surely an illusion, the city, with Table Mountain looming behind it, looked agonizingly close, as if one could almost reach out and grasp it.

The senior officer explained to us that we had been brought to the shore to collect seaweed. We were instructed to pick up the large pieces that had washed up on the beach, and wade out to collect seaweed attached to rocks or coral. The seaweed itself was long and slimy and brownish-green in color. Sometimes the pieces were six to eight feet in length and thirty pounds in weight. After fishing out the seaweed from the shallows, we lined it up in rows on the beach. When it was dry, we loaded it into the back of truck. We were told it was then shipped to Japan, where it was used as a fertilizer.

The work did not seem too taxing to us that day, but in the coming weeks and months, we found it could be quite strenuous. But that hardly mattered because we had the pleasures and distractions of such a panoramic tableau: we watched fishing ships trawling, stately oil tankers moving slowly across the horizon; we saw gulls spearing fish from the sea and seals cavorting on the waves; we laughed at the colony of penguins, which resembled a brigade of clumsy, flat-footed soldiers; and we marveled at the daily drama of the weather over Table Mountain, with its shifting canopy of clouds and sun.

In the summer, the water felt wonderful, but in winter, the icy Benguela currents made wading out into the waves a torture. The rocks on and around the shore were jagged, and we often cut and scraped our legs as we worked. But we preferred the sea to the quarry, although we never spent more than a few days there at a time.

The ocean proved to be a treasure chest. I found beautiful pieces of coral and elaborate shells, which I sometimes brought back to my cell. Once someone discovered a bottle of wine stuck in the sand that was still corked. I am told it tasted like vinegar. Jeff Masemola of the PAC was an extremely talented artist and sculptor, and the authorities allowed him to harvest pieces of driftwood, which he carved into fantastic figures, some of which the warders offered to buy. He constructed a bookcase for me, which I used for many years. The authorities told visitors that they had provided me with it.

The atmosphere at the shore was more relaxed than at the quarry. We also relished the seaside because we ate extremely well there. Each morning when we went to the shore, we would take a large drum of fresh water. Later, we would bring along a second drum, which we would use to make a kind of Robben Island seafood stew. For our stew we would pick up clams and mussels. We also caught crayfish, which hid themselves in the crevices of rocks. Capturing a crayfish was tricky; one had to grab it firmly between its head and tail or it would wiggle free.

Abalone, or what we call *perlemoen,* was my favorite dish. Abalones are mollusks that cling tenaciously to rocks, and one has to pry them loose. They are stubborn creatures, difficult to open, and if they are the slightest bit overcooked, they are too tough to eat.

We would take our catch and pile it into the second drum. Wilton Mkwayi was the chef among us and he would concoct the stew. When it was ready, the warders would join us and we would all sit down on the beach and have a kind of picnic lunch. In 1973, in a smuggled newspaper, we read about the wedding of Princess Anne and Mark Phillips, and the story detailed the bridal luncheon of rare and delicate dishes. The menu included mussels, crayfish, and abalone, which made us laugh; we were dining on such delicacies every day.

One afternoon, we were sitting on the beach eating our stew when Lieutenant Terblanche, who was then head of prison, made a surprise visit. We quickly pretended to be working, but we had not fooled him. He soon discovered the second drum containing a mussel stew bubbling over the fire. The lieutenant opened the pot and looked inside. He then speared a mussel, ate it, and pronounced it *"Smaaklik,"* Afrikaans for "tasty."

76

IN THE STRUGGLE, Robben Island was known as the University. This is not only because of what we learned from books, or because prisoners studied English, Afrikaans, art, geography, and mathematics, or because so many of our men, such as Billy Nair, Ahmed Kathrada, Mike Dingake, and Eddie Daniels, earned multiple degrees. Robben Island was known as the University because of what we learned from each other. We became our own faculty, with our own professors, our own curriculum, our own courses. We made a distinction between academic studies, which were official, and political studies, which were not.

Our university grew up partly out of necessity. As young men came to the island, we realized that they knew very little about the history of the ANC. Walter, perhaps the greatest living historian of the ANC, began to tell them about the genesis of the organization and its early days. His teaching was wise and full of understanding. Gradually, this informal history grew into a course of study, constructed by the High Organ, which became known as Syllabus A, involving two years of lectures on the ANC and the liberation struggle. Syllabus A included a course taught by Kathy, "A History of the Indian Struggle." Another comrade added a history of the Coloured people. Mac, who had studied in the German Democratic Republic, taught a course in Marxism.

Teaching conditions were not ideal. Study groups would work together on the quarry and station themselves in a circle around the leader of the seminar. The style of teaching was Socratic in nature; ideas and theories were elucidated through the leaders asking and answering questions.

It was Walter's course that was at the heart of all the education on the island. Many of the young ANC members who came to the island had no idea that the organization had even been in existence in the 1920s and 1930s. Walter guided them from the founding of the ANC in 1912 through to the present day. For many of these young men, it was the only political education they had ever received.

As these courses became known in the general section, we began to get queries from our men on the other side. This started what became a kind of correspondence course with the prisoners in the general section. The teachers would smuggle lectures over to them and they would respond with questions and comments.

This was beneficial for us as well as for them. These men had little formal education, but a great knowledge of the hardships of the world. Their concerns tended to be practical rather than philosophical. If one of the lectures stated that a tenet of socialism is "From each according to his ability and to each according to his need," we might receive a question back that said, "Yes, but what does that mean in practice? If I have land and no money, and my friend has money but no land, which of us has a greater need?" Such questions were immensely valuable and forced one to think hard about one's views.

For a number of years, I taught a course in political economy. In it, I attempted to trace the evolution of economic man from the earliest times up to the present, sketching out the path from ancient communal societies to feudalism to capitalism and socialism. I am by no means a scholar and not much of a teacher, and I would generally prefer to answer questions than to lecture. My approach was not ideological, but it was biased in favor of socialism, which I saw as the most advanced stage of economic life then evolved by man.

In addition to my informal studies, my legal work continued. I sometimes considered hanging a shingle outside my cell, because I was spending many hours a week preparing judicial appeals for other prisoners, though this was forbidden under prison service regulations. Prisoners from all different political stripes sought my help.

South African law does not guarantee a defendant the right to legal representation, and thousands upon thousands of indigent men and women went to prison every year for lack of such representation. Few Africans could afford a lawyer, and most had no choice but to accept whatever verdict the court handed down. Many men in the general section had been sentenced without benefit of counsel, and a number of them sought me out to make an appeal. For most of these men, it was the first time they had ever dealt with an attorney.

I would receive a smuggled note from a prisoner in F or G asking for help. I would then request the particulars of the case, the charge, the evidence, and the testimony. Because of the clandestine nature of these exchanges, information would come slowly in bits and pieces. A consultation that would last no more than half an hour in my old Mandela and Tambo office might take a year or more on the island.

I advised my "clients" to write a letter to the registrar of the Supreme Court asking for a record of their case. I told the prisoner to inform the registrar that he had limited funds and would like the record at no charge. Sometimes the registrars were kind enough to supply that material gratis.

Once I had the record of the case, I could put together an appeal, usually based on some judicial irregularity such as bias, incorrect procedure, or insufficient evidence. I drafted a letter to the judge or magistrate in my own handwriting, and then sent it to the other side. Because it was a violation of regulations for me to prepare a man's case, I would instruct the prisoner to copy the document in his own hand. If he could not write, and many prisoners could not, I told him to find someone who could.

I enjoyed keeping my legal skills sharp, and in a few cases verdicts were overturned and sentences reduced. These were gratifying victories; prison is contrived to make one feel powerless, and this was one of the few ways to move the system. Often I never met the men I worked for, and sometimes, out of the blue, a man who was serving us pap for lunch would whisper a thank-you to me for the work I had done on his behalf.

77

THE OPPRESSION of my wife did not let up. In 1972, security policemen kicked down the door of 8115 Orlando West. Bricks were hurled through the window. Gunshots were fired at the front door. In 1974, Winnie was charged with violating her banning orders, which restricted her from having any visitors apart from her children and her doctor. She was then working at a lawyer's office, and a friend brought Zeni and Zindzi to see her during her lunch hour. For this, Winnie was charged and then sentenced to six months' imprisonment. She was put in Kroonstad Prison, in the Orange Free State, but her experience there was not as horrendous as her previous stay in Pretoria. Winnie wrote to me that she felt liberated in prison this time, and it served to reaffirm her commitment to the struggle. The authorities permitted Zindzi and Zeni to visit her on Sundays.

When Winnie was released in 1975, we managed, through letters and communications with our lawyers, to work out a plan for me to see Zindzi. Prison regulations stated that no child between the ages of two and sixteen may visit a prisoner. When I went to Robben Island, all my children were in this legal limbo of age restrictions. The reasoning behind the rule is not pernicious: the lawmakers presumed that a prison visit would negatively affect the sensitive psyches of children. But the effect on prisoners was perhaps equally damaging. It is a source of deep sorrow not to be able to see one's children.

In 1975, Zindzi turned fifteen. The plan was for her mother to alter Zindzi's birth documents to show that the girl was turning sixteen, not fifteen, and therefore able to see me. Birth records are not kept in a very uniform or organized way for Africans, and Winnie found that it was not hard to modify her documents to show that Zindzi was born a year earlier. She applied for a permit, and it was approved.

A few weeks before Zindzi's scheduled visit in December, I had a previously arranged visit with Winnie's mother. When I was seated across from her in the visiting area, I said to her, "Well, Ma, I'm very excited because I'm going to see Zindzi." My mother-in-law, who was a former teacher, regarded me with some surprise and then said in a rather peevish way, "No, Zindzi cannot come and see you because she is not yet sixteen."

I realized immediately that no one had told her about our gambit. There was a warder behind each of us, and I decided I would simply gloss over what she had said, and mumbled, "Ah, well, Ma, it is nothing."

But my mother-in-law is a stubborn woman and she did not let it pass. "Well, Mkonyanisi" — an affectionate term for son-in-law in Xhosa, which is what she always called me — "you have made a serious error because Zindzi is only fifteen."

I widened my eyes in a gesture of alarm and she must have gotten the message because she did not mention Zindzi again.

I had not seen Zindzi since she was three years old. She was a daughter who knew her father from old photographs rather than memory. I put on a fresh shirt that morning, and took more trouble than usual with my appearance: it is my own vanity, but I did not want to look like an old man for my youngest daughter.

I had not seen Winnie for over a year, and I was gratified to find that she looked well. But I was delighted to behold what a beautiful woman my youngest daughter had become and how closely she resembled her equally beautiful mother.

Zindzi was shy and hesitant at first. I am sure it was not easy for her finally to see a father she had never really known, a father who could love her only from a distance, who seemed to belong not to her but to the people. Somewhere deep inside her she must have harbored resentment and anger for a father who was absent during her childhood and adolescence. I could see right away that she was a strong and fiery young woman like her own mother had been when she was Zindzi's age.

I knew she would be feeling uncomfortable, and I did my best to lighten the atmosphere. When she arrived I said to her, "Have you met my guard of honor?," gesturing to the warders who followed me everywhere. I asked her questions about her life, her schooling, and her friends, and then tried to take her back to the old days that she barely remembered. I told her how I often recalled Sunday mornings at home when I dandled her on my knee while Mum was in the kitchen making a roast. I recollected small incidents and adventures in Orlando when she was a baby, and how she had rarely cried even when she was small. Through the glass, I could see her holding back her tears as I talked.

The one tragic note of the visit was when I learned from Winnie that Bram Fischer had died of cancer shortly after being let out of prison. Bram's death affected me deeply. Although the government left no fingerprints on Bram's body, it was the state's relentless harassment of him that brought on the final illness that took him too soon. They hounded him even after death — the state confiscated his ashes after his cremation.

Bram was a purist, and after the Rivonia Trial, he decided he could best serve the struggle by going underground and living the life of an outlaw. It burdened him that the men whom he was representing in court were going to prison while he lived freely. During the trial, I advised Bram not to take this route, stressing that he served the struggle best in the courtroom, where people could see this Afrikaner son of a judge president fighting for the rights of the powerless. But he could not let others suffer while he remained free. Like the general who fights side by side with his troops at the front, Bram did not want to ask others to make a sacrifice that he was unwilling to make himself.

Bram went underground while out on bail and was captured in 1965, and sentenced to life imprisonment for conspiracy to commit sabotage. I had tried to write him in prison, but regulations forbade prisoners from corresponding with each other. After he had been diagnosed with cancer, a newspaper campaign calling for his release on humanitarian grounds had influenced the government. It was just a few weeks after the authorities released him, still under house arrest, to his brother's house in Bloemfontein that he died.

In many ways, Bram Fischer, the grandson of the prime minister of the Orange River Colony, had made the greatest sacrifice of all. No matter what I suffered in my pursuit of freedom, I always took strength from the fact that I was fighting with and for my own people. Bram was a free man who fought against his own people to ensure the freedom of others.

A month after this visit I received word from Winnie that her most recent request for a visit had been turned down by the authorities on the absurd grounds that I did not wish to see her. I immediately made an appointment with Lieutenant Prins, who was then head of prison, to lodge a protest.

Prins was not what one would call a sophisticated man. When I went in to see him I explained the situation evenly and without animosity. But I said the situation as it stood was unacceptable and my wife must be permitted to visit.

Prins did not appear to be listening, and when I had finished he said, "Ag, Mandela, your wife is only seeking publicity." I told him that I resented his remark, and before I had even finished, he uttered something so offensive and uncomplimentary about my wife that I immediately lost my temper.

I rose from my chair and started to move around the desk toward the lieutenant. Prins began to retreat, but I soon checked myself. Instead of assaulting him with my fists, as I felt like doing, I pummeled him with words. I am not a man who approves of oaths or curses, but that day I violated my own principle. I finished by telling him that he was a contemptible man without honor, and that if he ever repeated those same words I would not hold myself back as I had that day.

When I had finished, I turned and stormed out of his office. As I was leaving, I saw Kathy and Eddie Daniels outside but I did not even greet them as I walked back to my cell. Even though I had silenced Prins, he had caused me to violate my self-control and I consider that a defeat at the hands of my opponent.

After breakfast the following morning, two warders entered my cell and said I was wanted at the Head Office. When I reached the office, I was surrounded by a half-dozen armed warders. Off to one side was Lieutenant Prins and in the center of this circle was a warrant officer who was the prison prosecutor. The atmosphere was tense.

"Well, Mandela," the prosecutor said, "I hear you had yourself a nice time yesterday, but today will not be so pleasant. I am charging you for having insulted and threatened the head of prison. It is a grave charge." He then handed me the summons.

"Do you have anything to say?" he asked.

"No," I replied. "You can speak with my attorney." I then asked to be taken back to my cell. Prins did not say a word.

I knew immediately what I would do: prepare a countersuit charging everyone from the lieutenant all the way up to the minister of justice with misconduct. I would indict the prison system as a whole as a racist institution that sought to perpetuate white supremacy. I would make the case a cause célèbre, and make them regret they had ever charged me in the first place.

I asked George Bizos to represent me, and a meeting was soon arranged. Before George's visit I informed the authorities that I would be giving him written instructions. They asked me why and I replied frankly that I assumed the consultation room was bugged. The authorities then refused permission for me to give a written statement; I must make an oral one. I told them that they had no right to withhold permission, and the fact that they did only confirmed my suspicions.

The truth was that the authorities were afraid George would leak a written statement to the press. This was indeed part of our strategy. They were also concerned that I was using George as a conduit to communicate with Oliver in Lusaka, and assumed that the written statement would contain sensitive information. I had previously used George for such purposes, but the document in question did not contain such material.

A date was set for the island's disciplinary court, and a magistrate from Cape Town was assigned. A day before the hearing, I was told that my attorney would be arriving the following day and I would be free to give him my written statement. I met George at the head office in the morning and we briefly consulted before court was called into session. But the hearing had no sooner started than the prosecutor announced that the prison was withdrawing its case. The judge gaveled the session to a close and abruptly left the room. George and I looked at each other in surprise, and congratulated one another on an apparent victory. I was putting away my papers when another warrant officer came over and, pointing to my written statement, said, "Hand me that file."

I refused, saying it was a confidential matter between myself and my attorney. I called over the prosecutor and said: "Inform this man that these documents are protected by attorney-client privilege, and that I do not have to turn them over." The prosecutor replied that they were, but that the case was over, court was no longer in session, and the only authority in the room was that of the warrant officer. The officer plucked the document off the table. There was nothing I could do to stop him. I believe the authorities dropped the case simply to get hold of that document — which, as they discovered, contained nothing they did not already know.

As unlikely a prospect as it may have seemed, I nevertheless thought about escape the entire time I was on the island. Mac Maharaj and Eddie Daniels, both brave and resourceful men, were always hatching plans and discussing possibilities. Most were far too dangerous, but that did not stop us from considering them.

We had made certain advances. Jeff Masemola, our master craftsman, had managed to make a passkey that unlocked most of the doors in and around our section. One day, a warder had left his key on the desk in the office at the end of our corridor. Jeff took a piece of soap and made an imprint of the key. Using that outline, he took a piece of metal and filed it into the shape of the key. This key gave us access to some of the storerooms behind our cells as well as to the isolation section. But we never used it to leave our section. It was the sea, after all, that was the uncrossable moat around Robben Island.

In 1974, Mac had an idea how to cross that barrier. He had recently been taken to the dentist in Cape Town and discovered that the dentist himself was related by marriage to a well-known political prisoner. The dentist was sympathetic; he had refused to treat Mac unless Mac's leg irons were first removed. Mac had also noticed that the window in the dentist's second-floor waiting room was just a short drop to a small side-street where we might make a run for it.

When Mac returned, he met with a few of us and urged us to make appointments at the dentist. We did so, and learned that a day had been arranged for Mac, Wilton Mkwayi, me, and one other prisoner to go to

Cape Town. The three of us were willing to make the attempt, but when Mac contacted the fourth man, he refused. We had doubts about this man's loyalty, and it concerned me that he knew what we were planning.

The three of us were taken by boat to Cape Town and then to the dentist's office under heavy guard. All three of us had trained as soldiers and we probably had the best chance of actually executing an escape. Mac was also carrying a knife, and was prepared to use it. At the dentist's office, the guards first cleared away all the other patients. We demanded to have our leg irons removed, and with the support of the dentist, our guards took them off.

Mac led us over to the window and pointed out the street that was our escape route. But something about the street bothered Mac as soon as he saw it: we were in the center of Cape Town in the middle of the day, and yet the street was empty. When he had been here before, the street had been filled with traffic. "It's a setup," Mac whispered. I, too, had the sense that something was not right, and I agreed with Mac. Wilton, whose adrenaline was flowing, said Mac was talking nonsense. "Madiba, you're losing your nerve," he said. But I agreed with Mac, and the three of us simply ended up having our teeth examined. The dentist was curious as to why I had come, because my teeth were fine.

While Mac considered the most practical escape plans, Eddie Daniels hatched the most imaginative ones. During the early years, airplanes were not permitted to fly over the island. But by the mid-1970s, we noticed that not only were planes flying over our heads, but helicopters on their way to and from the tankers that sailed off the coast. Eddie came to me with a plan that would involve the organization using a helicopter, painted with the South African military colors, to pick me up on the island and then deposit me on the roof of a friendly foreign embassy in Cape Town where I would seek asylum. It was not an ill-conceived plan, and I told Eddie he should smuggle out the suggestion to Oliver in Lusaka. Eddie did manage to get his idea to Lusaka, but we never received a response.

78

BIRTHDAY CELEBRATIONS were bare-bones affairs on Robben Island. In lieu of cake and gifts, we would pool our food and present an extra slice of bread or cup of coffee to the birthday honoree. Fikile Bam and I were born on the same date, July 18, and I would save a few sweets that I had purchased at Christmas for the two of us to share on our mutual anniversary. My fiftieth birthday had passed without much notice in 1968, but in 1975, when I turned fifty-seven, Walter and Kathy approached me with a long-term plan that would make my sixtieth birthday more memorable.

One of the issues that always concerned us was how to keep the idea of the struggle before the people. During the previous decade, the government had silenced most of the radical press, and there remained a prohibition on publishing the words or pictures of any banned or imprisoned individuals. An editor could go to jail and his newspaper be shuttered for publishing so much as a snapshot of me or my colleagues.

One day, Kathy, Walter, and myself were talking in the courtyard when they suggested that I ought to write my memoirs. Kathy noted that the perfect time for such a book to be published would be on my sixtieth birthday. Walter said that such a story, if told truly and fairly, would serve to remind people of what we had fought and were still fighting for. He added that it could become a source of inspiration for young freedom fighters. The idea appealed to me, and during a subsequent discussion, I agreed to go ahead.

When I decide to do something, I like to start immediately, and I threw myself into this new project. I adopted a rather unorthodox work schedule: I would write most of the night and sleep during the day. During the first week or two, I would take a nap after dinner, awake at ten o'clock, and then write until it was time for breakfast. After working at the quarry, I would then sleep until dinner, and the process would begin again. After a few weeks of this, I notified the authorities that I was not feeling well and would not be going to the quarry. They did not seem to care, and from then on I was able to sleep most of the day.

We created an assembly line to process the manuscript. Each day I passed what I wrote to Kathy, who reviewed the manuscript, and then read it to Walter. Kathy then wrote their comments in the margins. Walter and Kathy have never hesitated to criticize me, and I took their suggestions to heart, often incorporating their changes. This marked-up manuscript was then given to Laloo Chiba, who spent the next night transferring my writing to his own almost microscopic shorthand, reducing ten pages of foolscap to a single small piece of paper. It would be Mac's job to smuggle the manuscript to the outside world.

The warders grew suspicious. They went to Mac and said, "What is Mandela up to? Why is he sitting up late at night?" But Mac merely shrugged his shoulders and said he had no idea. I wrote rapidly, completing a draft in four months. I did not hesitate over choosing a word or phrase. I covered the period from my birth through the Rivonia Trial, and ended with some notes about Robben Island.

I relived my experiences as I wrote about them. Those nights, as I wrote in silence, I could once again experience the sights and sounds of my youth in Qunu and Mqhekezweni; the excitement and fear of coming to Johannesburg; the tempests of the Youth League; the endless delays of the Treason Trial; the drama of Rivonia. It was like a waking dream and I attempted to transfer it to paper as simply and truthfully as I could.

Mac ingeniously hid the transcribed version of the manuscript inside the binding of a number of notebooks he used for his studies. In this way, he was able to safeguard the entire text from the authorities and smuggle it out when he was released in 1976. The arrangement was that Mac would secretly communicate when the manuscript was safely out of the country; only then would we destroy the original. In the meantime, we still had to dispose of a five-hundred-page manuscript. We did the only thing we could do: we buried it in the garden in the courtyard. Surveillance in the courtyard had become careless and sporadic. The warders usually sat in an office at the northern end talking among themselves. From that office, they could not see the southern end next to the isolation area where there was a small garden. I had casually inspected this area on my early morning walks, and it was there that I decided to bury the manuscript.

In order not to have to dig a great hole, we decided to bury the manuscript in three separate places. We divided it into two smaller segments and one larger one, wrapped each in plastic, and placed them inside empty cocoa containers. The work would have to be done quickly, and I asked Jeff Masemola to fashion some digging tools. Within a few days I was equipped with several sharp iron stakes.

One morning, after breakfast, Kathy, Walter, Eddie Daniels, and I drifted over to the garden at the southern end of the courtyard where we appeared to be having a political discussion. We were each hiding portions of the manuscript in our shirts. At a signal from me, we dropped down and began digging. I dug in the center, near a manhole cover that led to a drainpipe. When I reached the pipe, I carved out a space beneath it, and it was there that I placed the largest of the three containers. The others dug two shallower holes for their portions.

We finished just in time to line up for our march to the quarry. As I walked that morning, I felt a sense of relief that the manuscript was safely hidden. I then thought no more about it.

A few weeks later, just after our wake-up call, I heard a sound in the courtyard that made me uneasy: it was the thud of picks and shovels on the ground. When we were allowed out of our cells for wash-up, I walked to the front of the corridor and managed to peer out the door and around

the corner. There, at the south end of the courtyard, was a work crew
from the general section. To my alarm, they were digging in the area
where the manuscript was buried.

The authorities had decided to build a wall in front of the isolation
section because they had discovered that the prisoners in isolation were
able to communicate with us in the courtyard. The work crew was
digging a shallow trench for the concrete foundation of the wall.

While washing up I managed to inform Walter and Kathy about the
digging outside. Kathy thought that the main part of the manuscript,
which was buried under the pipe, would probably be safe, but that the
other two were vulnerable. When the drums of breakfast porridge were
wheeled into the courtyard, the warders commanding the work crew
ordered the men out of the yard. This was done to prevent any frater-
nization with the political prisoners.

With our bowls of porridge in hand, I led Walter and Kathy over to
the south end of the courtyard as though I wanted to confer with them
privately. The beginnings of the trench were already perilously close to
the two smaller containers. At the same time, we were joined by Eddie
Daniels, who immediately recognized the problem.

There was only one thing to do: as inconspicuously as possible, the
four of us began digging in the area where the two smaller pieces of
manuscript would be. We managed to unearth the two containers rather
quickly, and covered the area again with soil. To rescue the chunk of
manuscript under the pipe would require more time, but we were confident that they would not find the manuscript because they would not
dislodge the pipe in order to build the wall.

We hid the manuscript in our shirts as we walked back to our cells.
Eddie was not going to the quarry that day, and we gave the containers
to him, instructing him to destroy them as soon as possible. At great
personal risk, Eddie agreed to do so. I breathed easier knowing that we
had salvaged the two containers, and tried not to dwell on the remaining
piece of manuscript as I worked that day.

When we returned from the quarry that afternoon, instead of washing
up, which I normally did, I strolled over to the far end of the courtyard.
I attempted to appear as casual as possible, but I was alarmed by what I
saw. The prisoners had dug a trench that ran parallel to the wall of the
isolation section and had actually removed the pipe altogether. They could
not help but have uncovered the manuscript.

I must have flinched or reacted in some way that was noticeable. Unknown to me, I was being watched by a number of warders, who later
said that my reaction confirmed that I knew a manuscript had been there.

I returned to the corridor to wash up and told Walter and Kathy that I suspected the manuscript had been discovered. Eddie had meanwhile successfully disposed of the other two pieces.

Early the next morning, I was summoned to the office to see the commanding officer. Next to him stood a high prison official who had just arrived from Pretoria. Without any greeting whatsoever, the commanding officer announced: "Mandela, we have found your manuscript."

I did not reply. The commanding officer then reached behind his desk and produced a sheaf of papers.

"This is your handwriting, is it not?" he demanded. Again, I remained silent.

"Mandela," the commander said in some exasperation. "We know this is your work."

"Well," I replied, "you must produce some proof of that." They scoffed at this, and said they knew the notations in the margin were made by Walter Sisulu and Ahmed Kathrada. Again, I said that they must furnish evidence if they were going to impose any penalties.

"We do not need evidence," the commander said. "We have the evidence."

Although he did not impose a penalty that day, a short while later, Walter, Kathy, and I were called before General Rue, the deputy commissioner of prisons, who told us that we had abused our study privileges in order to illegally write the manuscript. For that offense, our study privileges were being suspended indefinitely. As it turned out, we lost study privileges for four years.

After Mac was released in December, he sent the notebooks overseas to England. He spent the next six months under house arrest in South Africa before slipping out of the country and going first to Lusaka to see Oliver, and then to London. He stayed there for six months; with a typist he reconstructed the manuscript and put together a typescript. He then returned to Lusaka and presented Oliver with a copy.

From there, the trail grows cold. I heard nothing from Lusaka about the manuscript and still do not know precisely what Oliver did with it. Although it was not published while I was in prison, it forms the spine of this memoir.

79

IN 1976, I RECEIVED an extraordinary visit: Jimmy Kruger, the minister of prisons, a prominent member of the prime minister's cabinet, came to see me. Kruger was not only influential about prisons policy but he was critical to the government's handling of the liberation struggle.

I had an inkling as to why he had come. The government was then engaged in a massive effort to make a success of its separate development policy, and "quasi-independent" homelands. The showpiece of separate development was the Transkei, led by my nephew and one-time benefactor, K. D. Matanzima, who had successfully repressed almost all legitimate opposition to his rule. I recalled that the commanding officer had recently said to me in a bantering way, "Mandela, you ought to retire to the Transkei and take a good long rest."

As it turned out, that was precisely what Jimmy Kruger was proposing as well. He was a stout, blunt man, not nearly as polished as I would have expected from a cabinet minister. I approached the meeting as another opportunity to present our grievances, and at first he seemed content to listen. I began by reminding him of the letter we had sent him in 1969, which had gone unanswered. He merely shrugged. I then detailed the poor conditions on the island, reiterating once more that we were political prisoners, not criminals, and expected to be treated as such. But Kruger scoffed at this, saying, "Nah, you are all violent Communists!"

I then began to tell him a bit about the history of our organization and why we had turned to violence. It was clear that he knew almost nothing about the ANC, and what he did know was gleaned from the propaganda of the right-wing press. When I told him the organization was far older than the National Party, he was dumbfounded. I said that if he considered us Communists he should reread the Freedom Charter. He looked at me blankly. He had never heard of the Freedom Charter. I found it extraordinary that a cabinet minister should be so uninformed. Yet I should not have been surprised; Nationalist politicians routinely condemned what they didn't understand.

I raised the question of our release and reminded him of the case of the 1914 Afrikaner rebels, who had resorted to violence though they were represented in Parliament, could hold meetings, and could even vote. Even though General de Wet and Major Kemp had led a force of twelve thousand and occupied towns and caused many deaths, they were both released soon after their convictions for high treason. I mentioned the case of Robey Leibbrandt, who set up an underground organization during the Second World War to oppose South Africa's support for the Allies; he was sentenced to life imprisonment but soon pardoned. Kruger seemed as ignorant of these episodes in the history of his own people as he was of the Freedom Charter. It is difficult to negotiate with those who do not share the same frame of reference.

Kruger waved all of this aside. "That is ancient history," he said. He came armed with a specific offer. Despite his reputation for brusqueness, he made his proposal in a deferential manner. He stated the matter simply: if I recognized the legitimacy of the Transkei government and was willing to move there, my sentence would be dramatically reduced.

I listened respectfully until he had finished. First, I said, I wholly rejected the bantustan policy, and would do nothing to support it, and second, I was from Johannesburg, and it was to Johannesburg that I would return. Kruger remonstrated with me, but to no avail. A month later he returned with the same proposal, and again I turned him down. It was an offer only a turncoat could accept.

80

AS DILIGENT AS WE WERE in gathering news and information, our knowledge of current events was always sketchy. Happenings in the outside world were muffled by the fact that we heard of them first through rumor; only later might they be confirmed by a newspaper account or an outside visitor.

In June of 1976, we began to hear vague reports of a great uprising in the country. The whispers were fanciful and improbable: the youth of Soweto had overthrown the military and the soldiers had dropped their guns and fled. It was only when the first young prisoners who had been involved in the June 16 uprising began to arrive on Robben Island in August that we learned what truly happened.

On June 16, 1976, fifteen thousand schoolchildren gathered in Soweto to protest the government's ruling that half of all classes in secondary schools must be taught in Afrikaans. Students did not want to learn and teachers did not want to teach in the language of the oppressor. Pleadings and petitions by parents and teachers had fallen on deaf ears. A detachment of police confronted this army of earnest schoolchildren and without warning opened fire, killing thirteen-year-old Hector Pieterson and many others. The children fought with sticks and stones, and mass chaos ensued, with hundreds of children wounded, and two white men stoned to death.

The events of that day reverberated in every town and township of South Africa. The uprising triggered riots and violence across the country. Mass funerals for the victims of state violence became national rallying points. Suddenly the young people of South Africa were fired with the spirit of protest and rebellion. Students boycotted schools all across the country. ANC organizers joined with students to actively support the protest. Bantu Education had come back to haunt its creators, for these angry and audacious young people were its progeny.

In September, the isolation section was filled with young men who had been arrested in the aftermath of the uprising. Through whispered conversations in an adjacent hallway we learned firsthand what had taken place. My comrades and I were enormously cheered; the spirit of mass protest that had seemed dormant through the 1960s was erupting in the 1970s. Many of these young people had left the country to join our own military movement, and then smuggled themselves back home. Thousands of them were trained in our camps in Tanzania, Angola, and Mozambique. There is nothing so encouraging in prison as learning that the people outside are supporting the cause for which you are inside.

These young men were a different breed of prisoner than we had ever seen before. They were brave, hostile, and aggressive; they would not take orders, and shouted *"Amandla!"* at every opportunity. Their instinct was to confront rather than cooperate. The authorities did not know how to handle them, and they turned the island upside down. During the Rivonia Trial, I remarked to a security policeman that if the government did not reform itself, the freedom fighters who would take our place would someday make the authorities yearn for us. That day had indeed come on Robben Island.

In these young men we saw the angry revolutionary spirit of the times. I had had some warning. At a visit with Winnie a few months before, she had managed to tell me through our coded conversation that there was a rising class of discontented youth who were militant and Africanist in orientation. She said they were changing the nature of the struggle and that I should be aware of them.

The new prisoners were appalled by what they considered the barbaric conditions of the island, and said they could not understand how we could live in such a way. We told them that they should have seen the island in 1964. But they were almost as skeptical of us as they were of the authorities. They chose to ignore our calls for discipline and thought our advice feeble and unassertive.

It was obvious that they regarded us, the Rivonia Trialists, as moderates. After so many years of being branded a radical revolutionary, to be perceived as a moderate was a novel and not altogether pleasant feeling. I knew that I could react in one of two ways: I could scold them for their impertinence or I could listen to what they were saying. I chose the latter.

When some of these men, such as Strini Moodley of the South African Students' Organization and Saths Cooper of the Black People's Convention, came into our section, I had them give us papers on their movement and philosophy. I wanted to know what had brought them to the struggle, what motivated them, what their ideas were for the future.

Shortly after their arrival on the island, the commanding officer came to me and asked me as a favor to address the young men. He wanted me to tell them to restrain themselves, to recognize the fact that they were in prison and to accept the discipline of prison life. I told him that I was not prepared to do that. Under the circumstances, they would have regarded me as a collaborator of the oppressor.

These fellows refused to conform to even basic prison regulations. One day I was at the Head Office conferring with the commanding officer. As I was walking out with the major, we came upon a young prisoner being interviewed by a prison official. The young man, who was no more than eighteen years old, was wearing his prison cap in the presence of senior officers, a violation of regulations. Nor did he stand up when the major entered the room, another violation.

The major looked at him and said, "Please, take off your cap." The prisoner ignored him. Then in an irritated tone, the major said, "Take off your cap." The prisoner turned and looked at the major, and said, "What for?"

I could hardly believe what I had just heard. It was a revolutionary question: What for? The major also seemed taken aback, but managed a reply. "It is against regulations," he said. The young prisoner responded, "Why do you have this regulation? What is the purpose of it?" This questioning on the part of the prisoner was too much for the major, and he stomped out of the room, saying, "Mandela, you talk to him." But I would not intervene on his behalf, and simply bowed in the direction of the prisoner to let him know that I was on his side.

This was our first exposure to the Black Consciousness Movement. With the banning of the ANC, PAC, and Communist Party, the Black Consciousness Movement helped fill a vacuum among young people. Black Consciousness was less a movement than a philosophy and grew out of the idea that blacks must first liberate themselves from the sense of psychological inferiority bred by three centuries of white rule. Only then could the people rise up in confidence and truly liberate themselves from repression. While the Black Consciousness Movement advocated a nonracial society, they excluded whites from playing a role in achieving that society.

These concepts were not unfamiliar to me: they closely mirrored ideas I myself held at the time of the founding of the ANC Youth League a quarter-century before. We, too, were Africanists; we, too, stressed ethnic pride and racial self-confidence; we, too, rejected white assistance in the struggle. In many ways, Black Consciousness represented the same response to the same problem that had never gone away.

But just as we had outgrown our Youth League outlook, I was confident that these young men would transcend some of the strictures of Black Consciousness. While I was encouraged by their militancy, I thought that their philosophy, in its concentration on blackness, was exclusionary, and represented an intermediate view that was not fully mature. I saw my role as an elder statesman who might help them move on to the more inclusive ideas of the Congress Movement. I knew also that these young men would eventually become frustrated because Black Consciousness offered no program of action, no outlet for their protest.

Although we viewed the ranks of the BCM as a fertile ground for the ANC, we did not attempt to recruit these men. We knew that this would alienate both them and the other parties on the island. Our policy was to be friendly, to take an interest, to compliment them on their achievements, but not to proselytize. If they came to us and asked questions — "What is the ANC policy on the bantustans?" "What does the Freedom Charter say about nationalization?" — we would answer them — and a great many of them did come to us with questions.

I myself contacted some of these men through smuggled notes. I spoke with some who were from the Transkei and asked questions about my old home. Some of the men who arrived were already well known in the struggle. I had heard reports of the bravery of Patrick "Terror" Lekota, a leader of the South African Students' Association, and sent him a note of welcome to Robben Island.

Terror's nickname comes from his prowess on the soccer field, but he was just as formidable in a debate. He disagreed with some of his colleagues on the issue of racial exclusiveness and inched closer to the ideas of the ANC. Once on the island, Terror decided that he wanted to join us, but we discouraged him — not because we did not want him but because we thought such a maneuver would create tensions in the general section.

But Terror would not take no for an answer and publicly switched his allegiance to the ANC. One day, not long afterward, he was assaulted with a garden fork by disgruntled BC members. After he was treated, the authorities charged the attackers and planned to put them on trial. But in the interest of harmony, we advised Terror not to lodge a complaint. He agreed, and refused to testify against those who had hurt him. The case was dropped. Such a trial, I felt, would only play into the hands of the authorities. I wanted these young men to see that the ANC was a great tent that could accommodate many different views and affiliations.

After that incident, the floodgates seemed to open and dozens of BC men decided to join the ANC, including some of those who had planned the attack on Terror. Terror rose to the top of the ANC hierarchy in the general section, and was soon teaching ANC policies to other prisoners. The courage and vision of men like Lekota confirmed to us that our views remained potent, and still represented the best hope for unifying the liberation struggle as a whole.

Political feuding continued in F and G. We learned of a clash among the ANC, the PAC, and the BCM in the general section. A number of ANC people had been beaten. A large number of ANC members were charged by the authorities, and a trial was set for the island's administrative court. The ANC men brought in an outside lawyer to handle the case. Although I had not witnessed the fight, I was asked to be a character witness. This was a troubling prospect. While I was more than willing to give testimonials for my comrades, I did not want to take any action that would heighten the bitterness between the ANC, the PAC, and the BCM.

I regarded my role in prison not just as the leader of the ANC, but as a promoter of unity, an honest broker, a peacemaker, and I was reluctant to take a side in this dispute, even if it was the side of my own organization. If I testified on behalf of the ANC, I would jeopardize my chances of bringing about reconciliation among the different groups. If I preached unity, I must act like a unifier, even at the risk of perhaps alienating some of my own colleagues.

I decided not to testify. This disappointed some of my colleagues, but I thought the issue was serious enough to risk their displeasure. It was more important to show the young Black Consciousness men that the struggle was indivisible and that we all had the same enemy.

81

IN THEIR ANXIOUSNESS to deal with these young lions, the authorities more or less let us fend for ourselves. We were in the second year of a go-slow strike at the quarry, demanding a complete end to all manual labor. Our requirement was for the right to do something useful with our days, like studying or learning a trade. We no longer even went through the motions of working at the quarry; we simply talked among ourselves. In early 1977, the authorities announced the end of manual labor. Instead, we could spend our days in our section. They arranged some type of work for us to do in the courtyard, but it was merely a fig leaf to hide their capitulation.

This victory was the combined result of our own unceasing protests and simple logistics. The authorities normally preferred to have a ratio of one warder for every three prisoners. Even before the arrival of the post-Soweto prisoners, there was a shortage of warders, and the rebellious young men required even greater supervision. They were so bold that each man seemed to require his own warder. If we remained in our section, we required less supervision.

The end of manual labor was liberating. I could now spend the day reading, writing letters, discussing issues with my comrades, or formulating legal briefs. The free time allowed me to pursue what became two of my favorite hobbies on Robben Island: gardening and tennis.

To survive in prison, one must develop ways to take satisfaction in one's daily life. One can feel fulfilled by washing one's clothes so that they are particularly clean, by sweeping a hallway so that it is empty of dust, by organizing one's cell to conserve as much space as possible. The same pride one takes in more consequential tasks outside of prison one can find in doing small things inside prison.

Almost from the beginning of my sentence on Robben Island, I asked the authorities for permission to start a garden in the courtyard. For years, they refused without offering a reason. But eventually they relented, and we were able to cut out a small garden on a narrow patch of earth against the far wall.

The soil in the courtyard was dry and rocky. The courtyard had been constructed over a landfill, and in order to start my garden, I had to excavate a great many rocks to allow the plants room to grow. At the time, some of my comrades jested that I was a miner at heart, for I spent my days at the quarry and my free time digging in the courtyard.

The authorities supplied me with seeds. I initially planted tomatoes, chilies, and onions — hardy plants that did not require rich earth or constant care. The early harvests were poor, but they soon improved. The authorities did not regret giving permission, for once the garden began to flourish, I often provided the warders with some of my best tomatoes and onions.

While I have always enjoyed gardening, it was not until I was behind bars that I was able to tend my own garden. My first experience in the garden was at Fort Hare where, as part of the university's manual labor requirement, I worked in one of my professors' gardens and enjoyed the contact with the soil as an antidote to my intellectual labors. Once I was in Johannesburg studying and then working, I had neither the time nor the space to cultivate a garden.

I began to order books on gardening and horticulture. I studied different gardening techniques and types of fertilizer. I did not have many of the materials that the books discussed, but I learned through trial and error. For a time, I attempted to grow peanuts, and used different soils and fertilizers, but finally I gave up. It was one of my only failures.

A garden was one of the few things in prison that one could control. To plant a seed, watch it grow, to tend it and then harvest it, offered a simple but enduring satisfaction. The sense of being the custodian of this small patch of earth offered a small taste of freedom.

In some ways, I saw the garden as a metaphor for certain aspects of my life. A leader must also tend his garden; he, too, plants seeds, and then watches, cultivates, and harvests the result. Like the gardener, a leader must take responsibility for what he cultivates; he must mind his work, try to repel enemies, preserve what can be preserved, and eliminate what cannot succeed.

I wrote Winnie two letters about a particularly beautiful tomato plant, how I coaxed it from a tender seedling to a robust plant that produced deep red fruit. But, then, either through some mistake or lack of care, the plant began to wither and decline, and nothing I did would bring it back to health. When it finally died, I removed the roots from the soil, washed them, and buried them in a corner of the garden.

I narrated this small story at great length. I do not know what she read into that letter, but when I wrote it I had a mixture of feelings: I did not want our relationship to go the way of that plant, and yet I felt that I had been unable to nourish many of the most important relationships in my life. Sometimes there is nothing one can do to save something that must die.

One unanticipated result of ending manual labor was that I began to gain weight. Though we were doing barely enough labor at the quarry to work up a sweat, the walk there and back was enough to keep me trim.

I have aways believed that exercise is not only a key to physical health but to peace of mind. Many times in the old days I unleashed my anger and frustration on a punching bag rather than taking it out on a comrade or even a policeman. Exercise dissipates tension, and tension is the enemy of serenity. I found that I worked better and thought more clearly when I was in good physical condition, and so training became one of the inflexible disciplines of my life. In prison, having an outlet for one's frustrations was absolutely essential.

Even on the island, I attempted to follow my old boxing routine of doing roadwork and muscle-building from Monday through Thursday and then resting for the next three days. On Monday through Thursday, I would do stationary running in my cell in the morning for up to forty-five minutes. I would also perform one hundred fingertip push-ups, two hundred sit-ups, fifty deep knee-bends, and various other calisthenics.

In my letters to my children, I regularly urged them to exercise, to play some fast-moving sport like basketball, soccer, or tennis to take their mind off whatever might be bothering them. While I was not always successful with my children, I did manage to influence some of my more sedentary colleagues. Exercise was unusual for African men of my age and generation. After a while, even Walter began to take a few turns around the courtyard in the morning. I know that some of my younger comrades looked at me and said to themselves, "If that old man can do it, why can't I?" They too began to exercise.

From the very first meetings I had with outside visitors and the International Red Cross, I stressed the importance of having the time and facilities for proper exercise. Only in the mid-1970s, under the auspices of the International Red Cross, did we begin to receive things like volleyball equipment and a Ping-Pong table.

At roughly the same time we finished working at the quarry, one of the warders had the idea of converting our courtyard into a tennis court. Its dimensions were perfect. Prisoners from the general section painted the cement surface green and then fashioned the traditional configuration of white lines. A few days later a net was put up and suddenly we had our own Wimbledon in our front yard.

I had played a bit of tennis when I was at Fort Hare, but I was by no means an expert. My forehand was relatively strong, my backhand regrettably weak. But I pursued the sport for exercise, not style; it was the best and only replacement for the walks to and from the quarry. I was one of the first in our section to play regularly. I was a back-court player, only rushing the net when I had a clean slam.

Once manual labor ended, I had much more time for reading, but the books I had been using were now out-of-bounds. When my studies were canceled, I was still in the midst of pursuing my LL.B. at the University of London. I had started studying for the LL.B. during the Rivonia Trial and the suspension of study privileges for four years would undoubtedly assure me of the university record for the most number of years pursuing that degree.

But the suspension of study privileges had an unintended benefit, and that was that I began to read books that I would not otherwise have read. Instead of poring over tomes about contract law, I was now absorbed by novels.

I did not have an unlimited library to choose from on Robben Island. We had access to many unremembered mysteries and detective novels and all the works of Daphne du Maurier, but little more. Political books were off-limits. Any book about socialism or communism was definitely out. A request for a book with the word *red* in the title, even if it was *Little Red Riding Hood,* would be rejected by the censors. *War of the Worlds* by H. G. Wells, though it is a work of science fiction, would be turned down because the word *war* appeared in its title.

From the first, I tried to read books about South Africa or by South African writers. I read all the unbanned novels of Nadine Gordimer and learned a great deal about the white liberal sensibility. I read many American novels, and recall especially John Steinbeck's *The Grapes of Wrath,* in which I found many similarities between the plight of the migrant workers in that novel and our own laborers and farmworkers.

One book that I returned to many times was Tolstoy's great work, *War and Peace.* (Although the word *war* was in the title, this book was permitted.) I was particularly taken with the portrait of General Kutuzov, whom everyone at the Russian court underestimated. Kutuzov defeated Napoleon precisely because he was not swayed by the ephemeral and superficial values of the court, and made his decisions on a visceral understanding of his men and his people. It reminded me once again that to truly lead one's people one must also truly know them.

82

IN THE WAKE of the Soweto student uprising, I learned that Winnie, along with my old friend and physician, Dr. Nthatho Motlana, had become involved with the Black Parents Association, an organization of concerned local professionals and church leaders who acted as a guiding hand and intermediary for the students. The authorities seemed to be as wary of the parents association as of the young rebels. In August, less than two months after the student revolt, Winnie was detained under the Internal Security Act and imprisoned without charge in the Fort in Johannesburg, where she was held for five months. During that time, I was able to write to her and my daughters, who were at boarding school in Swaziland, expressing support and solidarity. I was greatly distressed by her imprisonment, though she was apparently not mistreated this time and emerged from jail in December even firmer in her commitment to the struggle.

Though banned, Winnie picked up where she left off, and the authorities were dismayed about her popularity with the young radicals of Soweto. They were determined to lessen her influence and did it with a brazen and shameless act: they sent her into internal exile. On the night of May 16, 1977, police cars and a truck pulled up outside of the house in Orlando West and began loading furniture and clothing into the back of the truck. This time Winnie was not being arrested, or detained, or interrogated; she was being banished to a remote township in the Free State called Brandfort. I discovered the details from Kathy, who had been given the information from a visiting Hindu priest.

Brandfort is about two hundred fifty miles southwest of Johannesburg, just north of Bloemfontein, in the Free State. After a long and rough ride, Winnie, Zindzi, and all their possessions were dumped in front of a three-room tin-roofed shack in Brandfort's bleak African township, a desperately poor and backward place where the people were under the thumb of the local white farmers. Winnie was regarded with wariness and trepidation. The local language was Sesotho, which Winnie did not speak.

Her new circumstances saddened and angered me. At least when she was home in Soweto, I could picture her cooking in the kitchen or reading in the lounge, I could imagine her waking up in the house I knew so well. That was a source of comfort to me. In Soweto, even if she was banned, there were friends and family nearby. In Brandfort she and Zindzi would be alone.

I had passed through this township once on my way to Bloemfontein, and took no notice of it. There was nothing memorable in its all too typical poverty and desolateness. I did not know at the time how familiar the address — house number 802, Brandfort — would one day become to me. Once again, I felt as though Winnie and I were in prison at the same time.

Life in Brandfort was hard, as I learned from Winnie's letters. They had no heat, no toilet, no running water. The township had no shops and the stores in town were hostile to African customers. The whites for the most part were Afrikaans-speaking and deeply conservative.

Winnie and Zindzi were under constant police surveillance and intermittent harassment. Within a few months Zindzi — who was not banned — was upset by the security police's intimidation. In September, with the help of Winnie's lawyers, I brought an urgent application for an interdict against the local Brandfort security police to restrain them from harassing my daughter. Affidavits filed before the judge described policemen bursting into the house and threatening Zindzi. The judge ruled that Zindzi could receive visitors in peace.

Winnie is a resilient person, and within a relatively short time, she had won over the people of the township, including some sympathetic whites in the vicinity. She supplied food to the people in the township with the help of Operation Hunger, started a crèche or nursery school for the township's children, and raised funds to create a medical clinic in a place where few people had ever seen a doctor.

In 1978, Zeni, my second-youngest daughter and my first child with Winnie, married Prince Thumbumuzi, a son of King Sobhuza of Swaziland. They had met while Zeni was away at school. Being in prison, I was not able to fulfill the father's traditional duties. In our culture, the father of the bride must interview the prospective groom and assess his prospects. He must also determine *lobola,* the brideprice, which is paid by the groom to the bride's family. On the wedding day itself, the father gives away his daughter. Although I had no doubts about the young man, I asked my friend and legal adviser George Bizos to be a stand-in for me. I instructed George to interview the prince about how he intended to look after my daughter.

George met with the prince in his office and then arranged to consult with me on Robben Island. Because Zeni was under twenty-one years of age, it was necessary for me to give my legal consent for her to marry. I met George in the consulting room and he was surprised to find a warder in the consulting room with us. I explained that this was according to regulations because this was considered a family visit not a legal one. I jestingly reassured George by saying that I had no secrets from my guards.

George reported how much the two children loved one another and the bright prospects of my future son-in-law. His father, King Sobhuza, was an enlightened traditional leader and also a member of the ANC. As George relayed to me some of the requirements made by the young man's family, he was at pains to point out that the boy was a Swazi prince. I told George to tell the young man that he was getting a Thembu princess.

There was a tremendous advantage in Zeni's becoming a member of the Swazi royal family: she was immediately granted diplomatic privileges and could visit me virtually at will. That winter, after she and Thumbumuzi were married, they came to see me, along with their newborn baby daughter. Because of the prince's status, we were allowed to meet one another in the consulting room, not the normal visiting area where one is separated from one's family by thick walls and glass. I waited for them with some nervousness.

It was a truly wondrous moment when they came into the room. I stood up, and when Zeni saw me, she practically tossed her tiny daughter to her husband and ran across the room to embrace me. I had not held my now-grown daughter virtually since she was about her own daughter's age. It was a dizzying experience, as though time had sped forward in a science fiction novel, to suddenly hug one's fully grown child. I then embraced my new son and he handed me my tiny granddaughter whom I did not let go of for the entire visit. To hold a newborn baby, so vulnerable and soft in my rough hands, hands that for too long had held only picks and shovels, was a profound joy. I don't think a man was ever happier to hold a baby than I was that day.

The visit had a more official purpose and that was for me to choose a name for the child. It is a custom for the grandfather to select a name, and the one I had chosen was Zaziwe — which means "Hope." The name had special meaning for me, for during all my years in prison hope never left me — and now it never would. I was convinced that this child would be a part of a new generation of South Africans for whom apartheid would be a distant memory — that was my dream.

83

I DO NOT KNOW whether it was the upheaval inside the prison after the Soweto uprising or the upheaval in my family's life outside of prison, but in the year or two following 1976 I was in a dreamy, nostalgic state of mind. In prison, one has time to review the past, and memory becomes both friend and foe. My memory transported me into moments of both great joy and sadness. My dream life became very rich, and I seemed to pass entire nights reliving the high and low times of the old days.

I had one recurring nightmare. In the dream, I had just been released from prison — only it was not Robben Island, but a jail in Johannesburg. I walked outside the gates into the city and found no one there to meet me. In fact, there was no one there at all, no people, no cars, no taxis. I would then set out on foot toward Soweto. I walked for many hours before arriving in Orlando West, and then turned the corner toward 8115. Finally, I would see my home, but it turned out to be empty, a ghost house, with all the doors and windows open, but no one at all there.

But not all my dreams of release were so dark. In 1976 I wrote to Winnie of a happier vision.

The night of 24 February, I dreamt arriving at 8115 finding the house full of youth dancing away to a mixture of jive and infiba. I caught all of them by surprise as I walked in unexpectedly. Some greeted me warmly, whilst others simply melted away shyly. I found the bedroom equally full with members of the family and close friends. You were relaxing in bed, with Kgatho [my son Makgatho], looking young and sleeping against the opposite wall.

Perhaps in that dream I was recalling the two weeks in December 1956 when he was six and when I left Makhulu [Evelyn's mother] alone in the house. He was living with his mother in O.E. [Orlando East] then, but a few days before I came back he joined Makhulu and slept in my bed. He was missing me very much and using the bed must have relieved the feeling of longing a bit.

While I took joy from dwelling on happy moments, I rued the pain I had often caused my family through my absence. Here is another letter from 1976.

As I woke up on the morning of 25 February I was missing you and the children a great deal as always. These days I spend quite some time thinking of you both as Dadewethu [Sister], Mum, pal and mentor. What you perhaps don't know is how I often think and actually picture in my mind all that makes you up physically and spiritually — the loving remarks which came daily and the blind eye you've always turned against those numerous irritations that would have frustrated another woman. . . . I even remember a day when you were bulging with Zindzi, struggling to cut your nails. I now recall those incidents with a sense of shame. I could have done it for you. Whether or not I was conscious of it, my attitude was: I've done my duty, a second brat is on the way, the difficulties you are now facing as a result of your physical condition are all yours. My only consolation is the knowledge that I then led a life where I'd hardly enough time even to think. Only I wonder what it'll be like when I return. . . .

Your beautiful photo still stands about two feet above my left shoulder as I write this note. I dust it carefully every morning, for to do so gives me the pleasant feeling that I'm caressing you as in the old days. I even touch your nose with mine to recapture the electric current that used to flush through my blood whenever I did so. Nolitha stands on the table directly opposite me. How can my spirits ever be down when I enjoy the fond attentions of such wonderful ladies.

Nolitha was the one person who was not a member of the family whose photo I kept. I revealed the secret of her identity to my daughter Zindzi in another letter from 1976.

By the way, has Mum ever told you about Nolitha, the other lady in my cell from the Andaman Islands? She keeps you, Zeni, Ndindi and Nandi, Mandla [these last three are grandchildren], Maki and Mum company. It's one matter over which Mum's comments are surprisingly economic. She regards the pygmy beauty as some sort of rival and hardly suspects that I took her picture out of the *National Geographic*.

I thought continually of the day when I would walk free. Over and over, I fantasized about what I would like to do. This was one of the pleasantest ways to pass the time. I put my daydreams on paper, again in 1976.

I wish I could drive you on a long, long journey just as I did on 12/6/58, with the one difference that this time I'd prefer us to be alone. I've been away from you for so long that the very first thing I would like to do on my return would be to take you away from that suffocating atmosphere, drive you along carefully, so that you could have the opportunity of breathing fresh and clean air, seeing the beauty spots of South Africa, its green grass and trees, colourful wild flowers, sparkling streams, animals grazing in the veld and be able to talk to the simple people we meet along the road. Our first stop would be to the place where Ma Radebe and CK [Winnie's mother and father] sleep. I hope they lie next to each other. Then I would be able to pay my respects to those who have made it possible for me to be as happy and free as I am now. Perhaps the stories I've so much wanted to tell you all these years would begin there. The atmosphere should probably sharpen your ears and restrain me to concentrate on those aspects which are tasty, edifying and constructive. Thereafter, we would adjourn and resume next to Mphakanyiswa and Nosekeni [my parents] where the environment would be similar. I believe we would then be fresh and solid as we drive back to 8115.

When the authorities began to allow us to receive photographs of immediate family members in the early 1970s, Winnie sent me an album. Whenever I received a photograph of Winnie, the children, or the grandchildren, I would carefully paste it in. I cherished this album; it was the one way that I could see those I loved whenever I wanted.

But in prison no privilege comes without some accompanying impediment. Though I was permitted to receive pictures and to keep the album, warders would often search my cell and confiscate pictures of Winnie. Eventually, however, the practice of seizing pictures ceased, and I built up my album so that it was thick with pictures of my entire family.

I do not remember who first asked to borrow my photo album, but it was undoubtedly someone in my section. I happily loaned it, and someone else asked, and then someone else. Soon it became so widely known that I possessed a photo album that I was receiving requests from men in F and G.

The men of F and G rarely received visitors or even letters, and it would have been ungenerous to deny them this window on the world. But before long I found that my precious photo album was in tatters, and that many of my irreplaceable photographs had been removed. These men were desperate to have something personal in their cells and could not help themselves. Each time this happened, I resolved to build up my album once more.

Sometimes men would just ask me for a photograph rather than the album. I recall one day a young BC fellow from the general section who was bringing us food took me aside and said, "Madiba, I would like a photograph." I said fine, I would send him one. "When?" he said rather brusquely. I replied that I would try to send it that weekend. This seemed to satisfy him, and he began to walk away, but suddenly he turned round and said, "Look, don't send me a photograph of the old lady. Send me one of the young girls, Zindzi or Zeni — remember, not the old lady!"

84

IN 1978, after we had spent almost fifteen years agitating for the right to receive news, the authorities offered us a compromise. Instead of permitting us to receive newspapers or listen to radio, they started their own radio news service, which consisted of a daily canned summary of the news read over the prison's intercom system.

The broadcasts were far from objective or comprehensive. Several of the island's censors would compile a brief news digest from other daily radio bulletins. The broadcasts consisted of good news for the government and bad news for all its opponents.

The first broadcast opened with a report about the death of Robert Sobukwe. Other early reports concerned the victories of Ian Smith's troops in Rhodesia and detentions of government opponents in South

Africa. Despite the slanted nature of the news, we were glad to have it, and prided ourselves on reading between the lines and making educated guesses based on the obvious omissions.

That year, we learned via the intercom that P. W. Botha had succeeded John Vorster as prime minister. What the warders did not tell us was that Vorster resigned as a result of press revelations about the Department of Information's misuse of government funds. I knew little about Botha apart from the fact that he had been an aggressive defense minister and had supported a military strike into Angola in 1975. We had no sense that he would be a reformer in any way.

I had recently read an authorized biography of Vorster (this was one of the books the prison library did have) and found that he was a man willing to pay for his beliefs; he went to prison for his support of Germany during the Second World War. We were not sorry to see Vorster go. He had escalated the battle against freedom to new heights of repression.

But even without our expurgated radio broadcast, we had learned what the authorities did not want us to know. We learned of the successful liberation struggles in Mozambique and Angola in 1975 and their emergence as independent states with revolutionary governments. The tide was turning our way.

In keeping with the increased openness on the island, we now had our own cinema. Almost every week, we watched films on a sheet in a large room adjacent to our corridor. Later, we had a proper screen. The films were a wonderful diversion, a vivid escape from the bleakness of prison life.

The first films we saw were silent, black-and-white Hollywood action movies and westerns that were even before my time. I recall one of the first ones was the *The Mark of Zorro,* with the swashbuckling Douglas Fairbanks, a movie that was made in 1920. The authorities seemed to have a weakness for historical films, particularly ones with a stern moral message. Among the early films we saw — now in color, with dialogue — were *The Ten Commandments* with Charlton Heston as Moses, *The King and I,* with Yul Brynner, and *Cleopatra,* with Richard Burton and Elizabeth Taylor.

We were intrigued by *The King and I,* for to us it depicted the clash between the values of East and West, and seemed to suggest that the West had much to learn from the East. *Cleopatra* proved controversial; many of my comrades took exception to the fact that the queen of Egypt was depicted by a raven-haired, violet-eyed American actress, however beautiful. The detractors asserted that the movie was an example of Western propaganda that sought to erase the fact that Cleopatra was an African woman. I related how on my trip to Egypt I saw a splendid sculpture of a young, ebony-skinned Cleopatra.

Later, we also saw local South African films with black stars whom we all knew from the old days. On those nights, our little makeshift theater echoed with the shouts, whistles, and cheers that greeted the appearance of an old friend on screen. Later, we were permitted to select documentaries — a form that I preferred — and I began to skip the conventional films. (Although I would never miss a movie with Sophia Loren in it.) The documentaries were ordered from the state library and usually selected by Ahmed Kathrada, who was our section's librarian. I was particularly affected by a documentary we saw about the great naval battles of World War II, which showed newsreel footage of the sinking of the H.M.S. *Prince of Wales* by the Japanese. What moved me most was a brief image of Winston Churchill weeping after he heard the news of the loss of the British vessel. The image stayed in my memory a long time, and demonstrated to me that there are times when a leader can show sorrow in public, and that it will not diminish him in the eyes of his people.

One of the documentaries we watched concerned a controversial American motorcycle group, the Hell's Angels. The film depicted the Hell's Angels as reckless, violent, and antisocial, and the police as decent, upstanding, and trustworthy. When the film ended, we immediately began to discuss its meaning. Almost without exception the men criticized the Hell's Angels for their lawless ways. But then Strini Moodley, a bright, young Black Consciousness member, stood up and accused the assembled group of being out of touch with the times, for the bikers represented the equivalent of the Soweto students of 1976 who rebelled against the authorities. He reproached us for being elderly middle-class intellectuals who identified with the movie's right-wing authorities instead of with the bikers.

Strini's accusations caused a furor, and a number of men rose to speak against him, saying the Hell's Angels were indefensible and it was an insult to compare our struggle with this band of amoral sociopaths. But I considered what Strini said, and while I did not agree with him, I came to his defense. Even though the Hell's Angels were unsympathetic, they were the rebels against the authorities, unsavory rebels though they were.

I was not interested in the Hell's Angels, but the larger question that concerned me was whether we had, as Strini suggested, become stuck in a mind-set that was no longer revolutionary. We had been in prison for more than fifteen years; I had been in prison for nearly eighteen. The world that we left was long gone. The danger was that our ideas had become frozen in time. Prison is a still point in a turning world, and it is very easy to remain in the same place in jail while the world moves on.

I had always attempted to remain open to new ideas, not to reject a position because it was new or different. During our years on the island we kept up a continuing dialogue about our beliefs and ideas; we debated them, questioned them, and thereby refined them. I did not think we had stayed in one place; I believe we had evolved.

Although Robben Island was becoming more open, there was as yet still no sign that the state was reforming its views. Even so, I did not doubt that I would someday be a free man. We may have been stuck in one place, but I was confident the world was moving toward our position, not away from it. The movie reminded me once again that on the day I did walk out of prison, I did not want to appear to be a political fossil from an age long past.

It took fifteen years, but in 1979, the authorities announced over the intercom system that the diet for African, Coloured, and Indian prisoners would henceforth be the same. But just as justice delayed is justice denied, a reform so long postponed and so grudgingly enacted was hardly worth celebrating.

All prisoners were to receive the same amount of sugar in the morning: a spoonful and a half. But instead of simply increasing the African quota, the authorities reduced the amount of sugar that Coloured and Indian prisoners received by half a spoonful, while adding that amount for African prisoners. A while before, African prisoners had begun to receive bread in the morning, but that made little difference. We had been pooling bread for years.

Our food had already improved in the previous two years, but not because of the authorities. In the wake of the Soweto uprising, the authorities had decided that the island would become the exclusive home of South Africa's "security prisoners." The number of general prisoners had been drastically reduced. As a result, political prisoners were recruited to work in the kitchen for the first time. Once political prisoners were in the kitchen, our diet improved dramatically. This was not because they were better chefs, but because the smuggling of food immediately stopped. Instead of siphoning off food for themselves or to bribe the warders, the new cooks used all the food allotted us. Vegetables became more abundant, and chunks of meat began to appear in our soups and stews. Only then did we realize we should have been eating such food for years.

85

IN THE SUMMER OF 1979, I was playing tennis in the courtyard, when my opponent hit a cross-court shot that I strained to reach. As I ran across the court, I felt a pain in my right heel that was so intense I had to stop playing. For the next few days I walked with a severe limp.

I was examined by a doctor on the island who decided I should go to Cape Town to see a specialist. The authorities had become more solicitous of our health, afraid that if we died in prison they would be condemned by the international community.

Although under normal circumstances I and the other men would relish a visit to Cape Town, going as a prisoner was altogether different. I was handcuffed and kept in a remote corner of the boat surrounded by five armed warders. The sea was rough that day, and the boat shuddered at every wave. About midway between the island and Cape Town, I thought we were in danger of capsizing. I spied a lifejacket behind two warders young enough to be my grandsons. I said to myself, "If this boat goes under, I will commit my last sin on earth and run over those two boys to get that lifejacket." But in the end, it was unnecessary.

On the docks, we were met by more armed guards and a small crowd. It is a humiliating experience to watch the fear and disgust on ordinary citizens' faces when they watch a convict go by. My inclination was to duck down and hide, but one could not do that.

I was examined by a young surgeon who asked if I had ever before injured my heel. In fact, I had when I was at Fort Hare. One afternoon, I was playing soccer when I attempted to steal the ball and felt a searing pain in my heel. I was taken to the local hospital, the first time in my life I had ever been to a hospital or seen a doctor. Where I grew up, there was no such thing as an African doctor, and going to see a white doctor was unheard of.

The Fort Hare doctor examined my heel and said he would need to operate. The diagnosis alarmed me, and I abruptly told him that I did not want him to touch me. At that stage in my life I regarded seeing a doctor as unmanly and having a medical procedure seemed even worse. "Suit yourself," he said, "but when you are old this thing will worry you."

The Cape Town surgeon X-rayed my heel and discovered bone fragments that had probably been there since Fort Hare. He said he could remove them in a procedure that could be performed with a local anesthetic right in his office. I immediately agreed.

The surgery went well, and when it was over, the doctor was explaining to me how to care for my heel. He was abruptly interrupted by the head warder, who said that I had to return immediately to Robben Island. The surgeon was incensed by this and in his most authoritative manner said that it was necessary for Mr. Mandela to remain in hospital overnight and that he would not release me under any circumstances. The warder was intimidated and acquiesced.

My first night in a proper hospital turned out to be quite pleasant. The nurses fussed over me a good deal. I slept very well, and in the morning, a group of nurses came in and said that I should keep the pajamas and dressing gown that I had been given. I thanked them and told them that I would be the envy of all my comrades.

I found the trip instructive in another way because in that hospital I sensed a thawing in the relationship between black and white. The doctor and nurses had treated me in a natural way as though they had been dealing with blacks on a basis of equality all their lives. This was something new and different to me, and an encouraging sign. It reaffirmed my long-held belief that education was the enemy of prejudice. These were men and women of science, and science had no room for racism.

My only regret was that I did not have the opportunity to contact Winnie before I went into hospital. Rumors had appeared in newspapers that I was at death's door and she had become quite concerned. But when I returned, I wrote to her to dispel her fears.

In 1980, we were granted the right to buy newspapers. This was a victory, but as always, each new privilege contained within it a catch. The new regulation stated that A Group prisoners were granted the right to buy one English-language newspaper and one Afrikaans newspaper a day. But the annoying caveat was that any A Group prisoner found sharing his newspaper with a non–A Group prisoner would lose his newspaper privileges. We protested against this restriction, but to no avail.

We received two daily newspapers: the *Cape Times* and *Die Burger*. Both were conservative papers, especially the latter. Yet prison censors went through each of those newspapers every day with scissors, clipping articles that they deemed unsafe for us to see. By the time we received them, they were filled with holes. We were soon able to supplement these papers with copies of the *Star*, the *Rand Daily Mail*, and the Sunday *Times*, but these papers were even more heavily censored.

One story I was certainly not able to read was in the *Johannesburg Sunday Post* in March 1980. The headline was "FREE MANDELA!" Inside was a petition that people could sign to ask for my release and that of my fellow political prisoners. While newspapers were still barred from printing my picture or any words I had ever said or written, the *Post*'s campaign ignited a public discussion of our release.

The idea had been conceived in Lusaka by Oliver and the ANC, and the campaign was the cornerstone of a new strategy that would put our cause in the forefront of people's minds. The ANC had decided to personalize the quest for our release by centering the campaign on a single figure. There is no doubt that the millions of people who subsequently became supporters of this campaign had no idea of precisely who Nelson Mandela was. (I am told that when "Free Mandela" posters went up in London, most young people thought my Christian name was Free.) There were a handful of dissenting voices on the island who felt that personalizing the campaign was a betrayal of the collectivity of the organization, but most people realized that it was a technique to rouse the people.

The previous year I had been awarded the Jawaharlal Nehru Human Rights Award in India, another bit of evidence of the resurgence of the struggle. I was of course refused permission to attend the ceremony, as was Winnie, but Oliver accepted the award in my absence. We had a sense of a reviving ANC. Umkhonto we Sizwe was stepping up its sabotage campaign, which had become far more sophisticated. In June, MK set off bombs at the vast Sasolburg refinery just south of Johannesburg. MK was orchestrating an explosion a week at some strategic site or another. Bombs exploded at power stations in the eastern Transvaal, at police stations in Germiston, Daveyton, New Brighton, and elsewhere, and at the Voortrekkerhoogte military base outside Pretoria. These were all strategically significant locations, places that would attract attention and worry the state. The defense minister, General Magnus Malan, backed by P. W. Botha, introduced a policy known as "total onslaught," which was a militarization of the country to combat the liberation struggle.

The Free Mandela campaign had its lighter side as well. In 1981, I learned that the students at the University of London had nominated me as a candidate for the honorific post of university chancellor. This was a wonderful honor, to be sure, and my rivals were none other than Princess Anne and the trade union leader Jack Jones. In the end, I polled 7,199 votes and lost to the daughter of the queen. I wrote to Winnie in Brandfort that I hoped the voting might have for a moment turned her humble shack into a castle, making its tiny rooms as grand as the ballroom at Windsor.

The campaign for our release rekindled our hopes. During the harsh days of the early 1970s, when the ANC seemed to sink into the shadows, we had to force ourselves not to give into despair. In many ways, we had miscalculated; we had thought that by the 1970s we would be living in a democratic, nonracial South Africa. Yet as we entered the new decade my hopes for that South Africa rose once again. Some mornings I walked out into the courtyard and every living thing there, the seagulls and wagtails, the small trees, and even the stray blades of grass seemed to smile and shine in the sun. It was at such times when I perceived the beauty of even this small, closed-in corner of the world, that I knew that someday my people and I would be free.

86

LIKE MY FATHER BEFORE ME, I had been groomed to be a counselor to the king of the Thembu. Although I had chosen a different path, I tried in my own fashion to live up to the responsibilities of the role for which I had been schooled. From prison, I did my best to remain in contact with the king and advise him as best I could. As I grew older, my thoughts turned more and more often to the green hills of the Transkei. Although I would never move there under the government's auspices, I dreamed of one day returning to a free Transkei. Thus, it was with great dismay that I learned in 1980 that the king, Sabata Dalindyebo, the paramount chief of the Thembu, had been deposed by my nephew, K. D. Matanzima, the prime minister of the Transkei.

A group of Thembu chiefs requested an urgent visit with me, which was approved by the authorities, who were usually willing to countenance visits by traditional leaders — believing that the more involved I was in tribal and Transkei matters, the less committed I would be to the struggle.

The government promoted the power of traditional leaders as a counterpoint to the ANC. While many of my comrades thought we should disavow those leaders, my inclination was to reach out to them. There is no contradiction between being a traditional leader and a member of the ANC. This spurred one of the longest and most delicate debates we had on the island: whether or not the ANC should participate in government-sponsored institutions. Many of the men considered this collaborationist. Once again, I thought it necessary to draw a distinction between principle and tactics. To me, the critical question was a tactical one: Will our organization emerge stronger through participating in these organizations or by boycotting them? In this case, I thought we would emerge stronger by participating.

I met with the chiefs in a large room in the visiting area, and they explained their dilemma. Although their hearts were with Sabata, they feared Matanzima. After listening to their presentation, I advised them to throw their support to Sabata against Matanzima, who was illegally and shamefully usurping power from the king. I sympathized with their situation, but I could not condone Matanzima's actions. I asked them to convey my support to Sabata and my disapproval to Matanzima.

Matanzima had also proposed a visit to discuss Sabata and family matters. As my nephew, he had actually been requesting such a visit for a number of years. Although Matanzima claimed to want to discuss family matters, such a visit would have political consequences. From the moment of Matanzima's first request, I referred the matter to the High Organ and the ANC men in our section. Some simply shrugged their shoulders and said, "He's your nephew; he has a right to visit." Raymond, Govan, and Kathy, however, insisted that although such a visit could be explained away as a family matter, it would be interpreted by many people inside and outside as a sign of my endorsement of the man and his policies. That was the reason why Matanzima wanted to visit, and the reason such a visit was unacceptable.

I understood and in large part agreed with their arguments, but I wanted to meet with my nephew. I have always had perhaps too high a regard for the importance of face-to-face meetings and of my own ability in such a meeting to persuade men to change their views. I was hoping I could convince Matanzima to modify his policies.

Eventually, the ANC men in our section decided not to object to a visit. In the interests of democracy, we then consulted with our men in F and G on the matter, and they were adamantly opposed. Steve Tshwete, who was one of the leading ANC figures in the general section, said such a visit would help Matanzima politically and was therefore out of the question. Many of them noted that Matanzima had already tried to coopt my approval by making Winnie's father, Columbus Madikizela, the minister of agriculture in his government. This was bad enough, they said, without Madiba agreeing to see him. I bowed to the views of the membership in the general section and regretfully informed the authorities that I would not accept a visit from my nephew.

In March of 1982, I was told by the prison authorities that my wife had been in a car accident, and that she was in hospital. They had very little information, and I had no idea of her condition or what her circumstances were. I accused the authorities of holding back information, and I made an urgent application for my attorney to visit me. The authorities used information as a weapon, and it was a successful one. I was preoccupied with my wife's health until I was visited on March 31 by Winnie's attorney and my friend Dullah Omar.

Dullah quickly eased my mind about Winnie. She had been in a car that overturned but she was all right. Our visit was brief, and as I was led back to Section B my mind was still dwelling on Winnie, and I was plagued by the feeling of powerlessness and my inability to help her.

I had not been in my cell long when I was visited by the commanding officer and a number of other prison officials. This was highly unusual; the commanding officer did not generally pay calls on prisoners in their cells. I stood up when they arrived, and the commander actually entered my cell. There was barely room for the two of us.

"Mandela," he said, "I want you to pack up your things."

I asked him why.

"We are transferring you," he said simply.

Where?

"I cannot say," he replied.

I demanded to know why. He told me only that he had received instructions from Pretoria that I was to be transferred off the island immediately. The commanding officer left and went in turn to the cells of Walter, Raymond Mhlaba, and Andrew Mlangeni and gave them the same order.

I was disturbed and unsettled. What did it mean? Where were we going? In prison, one can only question and resist an order to a certain point, then one must succumb. We had no warning, no preparation. I had been on the island for over eighteen years, and to leave so abruptly?

We were each given several large cardboard boxes in which to pack our things. Everything that I had accumulated in nearly two decades could fit in these few boxes. We packed in little more than half an hour.

There was a commotion in the corridor when the other men learned we were leaving, but we had no time to say a proper good-bye to our comrades of many years. This is another one of the indignities of prison. The bonds of friendship and loyalty with other prisoners count for nothing with the authorities.

Within minutes we were on board the ferry headed for Cape Town. I looked back at the island as the light was fading, not knowing whether or not I would ever see it again. A man can get used to anything, and I had grown used to Robben Island. I had lived there for almost two decades and while it was never a home — my home was in Johannesburg — it had become a place where I felt comfortable. I have always found change difficult, and leaving Robben Island, however grim it had been at times, was no exception. I had no idea what to look forward to.

At the docks, surrounded by armed guards, we were hustled into a windowless truck. The four of us stood in the dark while the truck drove for what seemed considerably longer than an hour. We passed through various checkpoints, and finally came to a stop. The back doors swung open, and in the dark we were marched up some concrete steps and through metal doors into another security facility. I managed to ask a guard where we were.

"Pollsmoor Prison," he said.

Part Ten

TALKING WITH THE ENEMY

87

POLLSMOOR MAXIMUM SECURITY PRISON is located on the edge of a prosperous white suburb of green lawns and tidy houses called Tokai, a few miles southeast of Cape Town. The prison itself is set amidst the strikingly beautiful scenery of the Cape, between the mountains of Constantiaberge to the north and hundreds of acres of vineyards to the south. But this natural beauty was invisible to us behind Pollsmoor's high concrete walls. At Pollsmoor I first understood the truth of Oscar Wilde's haunting line about the tent of blue that prisoners call the sky.

Pollsmoor had a modern face but a primitive heart. The buildings, particularly the ones for the prison staff, were clean and contemporary; but the housing for the prisoners was archaic and dirty. With the exception of ourselves, all men at Pollsmoor were common-law prisoners, and their treatment was backward. We were kept separately from them and treated differently.

It was not until the next morning that we got a proper sense of our surroundings. The four of us had been given what was in effect the prison's penthouse: a spacious room on the third and topmost floor of the prison. We were the only prisoners on the entire floor. The main room was clean, modern, and rectangular, about fifty feet by thirty, and had a separate section with a toilet, urinal, two sinks, and two showers. There were four proper beds, with sheets, and towels, a great luxury for men who had spent much of the last eighteen years sleeping on thin mats on a stone floor. Compared to Robben Island, we were in a five-star hotel.

We also had our own L-shaped terrace, an open, outdoor section that was as long as half a soccer field, where we were allowed out during the day. It had white concrete walls about twelve feet high, so that we could see only the sky, except in one corner where we could make out the ridges of the Constantiaberge mountains, in particular a section known as the Elephant's Eye. I sometimes thought of this bit of mountain as the tip of the iceberg of the rest of the world.

It was greatly disorienting to be uprooted so suddenly and without explanation. One must be prepared for precipitate movements in prison, but one does not ever get used to them. Though we were now on the mainland, we felt more isolated. For us, the island had become the locus of the struggle. We took solace in each other's company, and spent those early weeks speculating on why we had been transferred. We knew the authorities had long resented and feared the influence we had on younger prisoners. But the reason seemed to be more strategic: we believed the authorities were attempting to cut off the head of the ANC on the island by removing its leadership. Robben Island itself was becoming a sustaining myth in the struggle, and they wanted to rob it of some of its symbolic import by removing us. Walter, Raymond, and I were members of the High Organ, but the one piece that did not fit was the presence of Mlangeni. Andrew was not a member of the High Organ and had not been in the forefront of the island leadership, although we considered the possibility that the authorities did not know this. Their intelligence about the organization was often inexact.

One of our hypotheses seemed to be confirmed a few months later when we were joined by Kathy, who had indeed been a member of the High Organ. More important, Kathy had been our chief of communications, and it was because of his work that we were able to communicate with new young prisoners.

A few weeks after Kathy arrived, we were also joined by a man we did not know who had not even come from Robben Island. Patrick Maqubela was a young lawyer and ANC member from the eastern Cape. He had been articled to Griffiths Mxenge, a highly respected attorney who had appeared for many detained ANC men and who had been assassinated near Durban the year before. Maqubela was serving a twenty-year sentence for treason and had been transferred to Pollsmoor from Diepkloof in Johannesburg, where he had made waves by organizing prisoners.

At first, we were skeptical of this new arrival, and wondered if he could perhaps be a security plant by the authorities. But we soon saw that this was not the case. Patrick was a bright, amiable, undaunted fellow with whom we got along very well. It could not have been easy for him bunking in with a group of old men set in their ways who had been together for the previous two decades.

We were now in a world of concrete. I missed the natural splendor of Robben Island. But our new home had many consolations. For one thing, the food at Pollsmoor was far superior; after years of eating pap three meals a day, Pollsmoor's dinners of proper meat and vegetables were like a feast. We were permitted a fairly wide range of newspapers and magazines, and could receive such previously contraband publications as *Time* magazine and *The Guardian* weekly from London. This gave us a window on the wider world. We also had a radio, but one that received only local stations, not what we really wanted: the BBC World Service. We were allowed out on our terrace all day long, except between twelve and two when the warders had their lunch. There was not even a pretense that we had to work. I had a small cell near our large one that functioned as a study, with a chair, desk, and bookshelves, where I could read and write during the day.

On Robben Island I would do my exercises in my own cramped cell, but now I had room to stretch out. At Pollsmoor, I would wake up at five and do an hour and a half of exercise in our communal cell. I did my usual regimen of stationary running, skipping rope, sit-ups, and fingertip press-ups. My comrades were not early risers and my program soon made me a very unpopular fellow in our cell.

I was visited by Winnie shortly after arriving at Pollsmoor and was pleased to find that the visiting area was far better and more modern than the one on Robben Island. We had a large glass barrier through which one could see the visitor from the waist up and far more sophisticated microphones so that we did not have to strain to hear. The window gave at least the illusion of greater intimacy, and in prison, illusions can offer comfort.

It was far easier for my wife and family to get to Pollsmoor than Robben Island, and this made a tremendous difference. The supervision of visits also became more humane. Often, Winnie's visits were overseen by Warrant Officer James Gregory, who had been a censor on Robben Island. I had not known him terribly well, but he knew us, because he had been responsible for reviewing our incoming and outgoing mail.

At Pollsmoor I got to know Gregory better and found him a welcome contrast to the typical warder. He was polished and soft-spoken, and treated Winnie with courtesy and deference. Instead of barking, "Time up!" he would say, "Mrs. Mandela, you have five more minutes."

The Bible tells us that gardens preceded gardeners, but that was not the case at Pollsmoor, where I cultivated a garden that became one of my happiest diversions. It was my way of escaping from the monolithic concrete world that surrounded us. Within a few weeks of surveying all the empty space we had on the building's roof and how it was bathed in sun the whole day, I decided to start a garden and received permission to do so from the commanding officer. I requested that the prison service supply me with sixteen 44-gallon oil drums that I had them slice in half. The authorities then filled each half with rich, moist soil, creating in effect thirty-two giant flowerpots.

I grew onions, eggplant, cabbage, cauliflower, beans, spinach, carrots, cucumbers, broccoli, beetroot, lettuce, tomatoes, peppers, strawberries, and much more. At its height, I had a small farm with nearly nine hundred plants; a garden far grander than the one I had on Robben Island.

Some of the seeds I purchased and some — for example, broccoli and carrots — were given to me by the commanding officer, Brigadier Munro, who was particularly fond of these vegetables. Warders also gave me seeds of vegetables they liked, and I was supplied with excellent manure to use as fertilizer.

Each morning, I put on a straw hat and rough gloves and worked in the garden for two hours. Every Sunday, I would supply vegetables to the kitchen so that they could cook a special meal for the common-law prisoners. I also gave quite a lot of my harvest to the warders, who used to bring satchels to take away their fresh vegetables.

At Pollsmoor, our problems tended to be less consequential than those we experienced on Robben Island. Brigadier Munro was a decent, helpful man, who took extra pains to make sure we had what we wanted. Nevertheless, small problems sometimes got blown out of proportion. In 1983, during a visit with Winnie and Zindzi, I mentioned to my wife that I had been given shoes that were a size too small and were pinching my toe. Winnie was concerned, and I soon learned that there were press reports that I was having a toe amputated. Because of the difficulty of communication, information from prison often becomes exaggerated in the outside world. If I had simply been able to telephone my wife and tell her that my foot was fine, such confusion would not have happened. A short while later, Helen Suzman was permitted to visit, and she inquired about my toe. I thought the best answer was a demonstration: I took off my socks, held my bare foot up to the glass, and wiggled my toes.

We complained about the dampness in our cell, which was causing us to catch colds. Later, I heard reports that South African newspapers were writing that our cell was flooded. We asked for contact with other prisoners, and in general made the same basic complaint that we always had: to be treated as political prisoners.

In May of 1984, I found some consolation that seemed to make up for all the discomforts. At a scheduled visit from Winnie, Zeni, and her youngest daughter, I was escorted down to the visiting area by Sergeant Gregory, who instead of taking me to the normal visiting area, ushered me into a separate room where there was only a small table, and no dividers of any kind. He very softly said to me that the authorities had made a change. That day was the beginning of what were known as "contact" visits.

He then went outside to see my wife and daughter and asked to speak to Winnie privately. Winnie actually got a fright when Gregory took her aside, thinking that I was perhaps ill. But Gregory escorted her around the door and before either of us knew it, we were in the same room and in each other's arms. I kissed and held my wife for the first time in all these many years. It was a moment I had dreamed about a thousand times.

It was as if I were still dreaming. I held her to me for what seemed like an eternity. We were still and silent except for the sound of our hearts. I did not want to let go of her at all, but I broke free and embraced my daughter and then took her child into my lap. It had been twenty-one years since I had even touched my wife's hand.

88

AT POLLSMOOR, we were more connected to outside events. We were aware that the struggle was intensifying, and that the efforts of the enemy were similarly increasing. In 1981, the South African Defense Force launched a raid on ANC offices in Maputo, Mozambique, killing thirteen of our people, including women and children. In December 1982, MK set off explosions at the unfinished Koeberg nuclear power plant outside Cape Town and placed bombs at many other military and apartheid targets around the country. That same month, the South African military again attacked an ANC outpost in Maseru, Lesotho, killing forty-two people, including a dozen women and children.

In August of 1982, activist Ruth First was opening her mail in Maputo, where she was living in exile, when she was murdered by a letter bomb. Ruth, the wife of Joe Slovo, was a brave anti-apartheid activist who had spent a number of months in prison. She was a forceful, engaging woman whom I first met when I was studying at Wits, and her death revealed the extent of the state's cruelty in combating our struggle.

MK's first car bomb attack took place in May of 1983, and was aimed at an air force and military intelligence office in the heart of Pretoria. This was an effort to retaliate for the unprovoked attacks the military had launched on the ANC in Maseru and elsewhere and was a clear escalation of the armed struggle. Nineteen people were killed and more than two hundred injured.

The killing of civilians was a tragic accident, and I felt a profound horror at the death toll. But as disturbed as I was by these casualties, I knew that such accidents were the inevitable consequence of the decision to embark on a military struggle. Human fallibility is always a part of war, and the price for it is always high. It was precisely because we knew that such incidents would occur that our decision to take up arms had been so grave and reluctant. But as Oliver said at the time of the bombing, the armed struggle was imposed upon us by the violence of the apartheid regime.

Both the government and the ANC were working on two tracks: military and political. On the political front, the government was pursuing its standard divide-and-rule strategy in attempting to separate Africans from Coloureds and Indians. In a referendum of November 1983, the white electorate endorsed P. W. Botha's plan to create a so-called tricameral Parliament, with Indian and Coloured chambers in addition to the white Parliament. This was an effort to lure Indians and Coloureds into the system, and divide them from Africans. But the offer was merely a "toy telephone," as all parliamentary action by Indians and Coloureds was subject to a white veto. It was also a way of fooling the outside world into thinking that the government was reforming apartheid. Botha's ruse did not fool the people, as more than 80 percent of eligible Indian and Coloured voters boycotted the election to the new houses of Parliament in 1984.

Powerful grassroots political movements were being formed inside the country that had firm links to the ANC, the principal one being the United Democratic Front, of which I was named a patron. The UDF had been created to coordinate protest against the new apartheid constitution in 1983, and the first elections to the segregated tricameral Parliament in 1984. The UDF soon blossomed into a powerful organization that united over six hundred anti-apartheid organizations — trade unions, community groups, church groups, student associations.

The ANC was experiencing a new birth of popularity. Opinion polls showed that the Congress was far and away the most popular political organization among Africans even though it had been banned for a quarter of a century. The anti-apartheid struggle as a whole had captured the attention of the world; in 1984, Bishop Desmond Tutu was awarded the Nobel Peace Prize. (The authorities refused to send Bishop Tutu my letter of congratulations.) The South African government was under growing international pressure, as nations all across the globe began to impose economic sanctions on Pretoria.

The government had sent "feelers" to me over the years, beginning with Minister Kruger's efforts to persuade me to move to the Transkei. These were not efforts to negotiate, but attempts to isolate me from my organization. On several other occasions, Kruger said to me: "Mandela, we can work with you, but not your colleagues. Be reasonable." Although I did not respond to these overtures, the mere fact that they were talking rather than attacking could be seen as a prelude to genuine negotiations.

The government was testing the waters. In late 1984 and early 1985, I had visits from two prominent Western statesmen, Lord Nicholas Bethell, a member of the British House of Lords and the European Parliament, and Samuel Dash, a professor of law at Georgetown University and a former counsel to the U.S. Senate Watergate Committee. Both visits were authorized by the new minister of justice, Kobie Coetsee, who appeared to be a new sort of Afrikaner leader.

I met Lord Bethell in the prison commander's office, which was dominated by a large photograph of a glowering President Botha. Bethell was a jovial, rotund man and when I first met him, I teased him about his stoutness. "You look like you are related to Winston Churchill," I said as we shook hands, and he laughed.

Lord Bethell wanted to know about our conditions at Pollsmoor and I told him. We discussed the armed struggle and I explained to him it was not up to us to renounce violence, but the government. I reaffirmed that we aimed for hard military targets, not people. "I would not want our men to assassinate, for instance, the major here," I said, pointing to Major Fritz van Sittert, who was monitoring the talks. Van Sittert was a good-natured fellow who did not say much, but he started at my remark.

In my visit with Professor Dash, which quickly followed that of Lord Bethell, I laid out what I saw as the minimum for a future nonracial South Africa: a unitary state without homelands; nonracial elections for the central Parliament; and one-person-one-vote. Professor Dash asked me whether I took any encouragement from the government's stated intention of repealing the mixed-marriage laws and certain other apartheid statutes. "This is a pinprick," I said. "It is not my ambition to marry a white woman or swim in a white pool. It is political equality that we want." I told Dash quite candidly that at the moment we could not defeat the government on the battlefield, but could make governing difficult for them.

I had one not-so-pleasant visit from two Americans, editors of the conservative newspaper the *Washington Times*. They seemed less intent on finding out my views than on proving that I was a Communist and a terrorist. All of their questions were slanted in that direction, and when I reiterated that I was neither a Communist nor a terrorist, they attempted to show that I was not a Christian either by asserting that the Reverend Martin Luther King never resorted to violence. I told them that the conditions in which Martin Luther King struggled were totally different from my own: the United States was a democracy with constitutional guarantees of equal rights that protected nonviolent protest (though there was still prejudice against blacks); South Africa was a police state with a constitution that enshrined inequality and an army that responded to nonviolence with force. I told them that I was a Christian and had always been a Christian. Even Christ, I said, when he was left with no alternative, used force to expel the moneylenders from the temple. He was not a man of violence, but had no choice but to use force against evil. I do not think I persuaded them.

Faced with trouble at home and pressure from abroad, P. W. Botha offered a tepid, halfway measure. On January 31, 1985, in a debate in Parliament, the state president publicly offered me my freedom if I "unconditionally rejected violence as a political instrument." This offer was extended to all political prisoners. Then, as if he were staking me to a public challenge, he added, "It is therefore not the South Africa government which now stands in the way of Mr. Mandela's freedom. It is he himself."

I had been warned by the authorities that the government was going to make a proposal involving my freedom, but I had not been prepared for the fact that it would be made in Parliament by the state president. By my reckoning, it was the sixth conditional offer the government had made for my release in the past ten years. After I listened to the speech on radio, I made a request to the commander of the prison for an urgent visit by my wife and my lawyer, Ismail Ayob, so that I could dictate my response to the state president's offer.

Winnie and Ismail were not given permission to visit for a week, and in the meantime I wrote a letter to the foreign minister, Pik Botha, rejecting the conditions for my release, while also preparing a public response. I was keen to do a number of things in this response, because Botha's offer was an attempt to drive a wedge between me and my colleagues by tempting me to accept a policy the ANC rejected. I wanted to reassure the ANC in general and Oliver in particular that my loyalty to the organization was beyond question. I also wished to send a message to the government that while I rejected its offer because of the conditions attached to it, I nevertheless thought negotiation, not war, was the path to a solution.

Botha wanted the onus of violence to rest on my shoulders and I wanted to reaffirm to the world that we were only responding to the violence done to us. I intended to make it clear that if I emerged from prison into the same circumstances in which I was arrested, I would be forced to resume the same activities for which I was arrested.

I met with Winnie and Ismail on a Friday; on Sunday, a UDF rally was to be held in Soweto's Jabulani Stadium, where my response would be made public. Some guards with whom I was not familiar supervised the visit, and as we began discussing my response to the state president, one of the warders, a relatively young fellow, interrupted to say that only family matters were permitted to be discussed. I ignored him, and he returned minutes later with a senior warder whom I barely knew. This warder said that I must cease discussing politics, and I told him that I was dealing with a matter of national importance involving an offer from the state president. I warned him that if he wanted to halt the discussion he must get direct orders from the state president himself. "If you are not willing to telephone the state president to get those orders," I said coldly, "then kindly do not interrupt us again." He did not.

I gave Ismail and Winnie the speech I had prepared. In addition to responding to the government, I wanted to thank publicly the UDF for its fine work and to congratulate Bishop Tutu on his prize, adding that his award belonged to all the people. On Sunday, February 10, 1985, my daughter Zindzi read my response to a cheering crowd of people who had not been able to hear my words legally anywhere in South Africa for more than twenty years.

Zindzi was a dynamic speaker like her mother, and said that her father should be at the stadium to speak the words himself. I was proud to know that it was she who spoke my words.

I am a member of the African National Congress. I have always been a member of the African National Congress and I will remain a member of the African National Congress until the day I die. Oliver Tambo is more than a brother to me. He is my greatest friend and comrade for nearly fifty years. If there is any one amongst you who cherishes my freedom, Oliver Tambo cherishes it more, and I know that he would give his life to see me free. . . .

I am surprised at the conditions that the government wants to impose on me. I am not a violent man. . . . It was only then, when all other forms of resistance were no longer open to us, that we turned to armed struggle. Let Botha show that he is different to Malan, Strijdom and Verwoerd. Let him renounce violence. Let him say that he will dismantle apartheid. Let him unban the people's organization, the African National Congress. Let him free all who have been imprisoned, banished or exiled for their opposition to apartheid. Let him guarantee free political activity so that people may decide who will govern them.

I cherish my own freedom dearly, but I care even more for your freedom. Too many have died since I went to prison. Too many have suffered for the love of freedom. I owe it to their widows, to their orphans, to their mothers, and to their fathers who have grieved and wept for them. Not only I have suffered during these long, lonely, wasted years. I am not less life-loving than you are. But I cannot sell my birthright, nor am I prepared to sell the birthright of the people to be free. . . .

What freedom am I being offered while the organization of the people remains banned? What freedom am I being offered when I may be arrested on a pass offense? What freedom am I being offered to live my life as a family with my dear wife who remains in banishment in Brandfort? What freedom am I being offered when I must ask for permission to live in an urban area? . . . What freedom am I being offered when my very South African citizenship is not respected?

Only free men can negotiate. Prisoners cannot enter into contracts. . . . I cannot and will not give any undertaking at a time when I and you, the people, are not free. Your freedom and mine cannot be separated. I will return.

89

IN 1985 after a routine medical examination with the prison doctor, I was referred to a urologist, who diagnosed an enlarged prostate gland and recommended surgery. He said the procedure was routine. I consulted with my family and decided to go ahead with the operation.

I was taken to Volks Hospital in Cape Town, under heavy security. Winnie flew down and was able to see me prior to the surgery. But I had another visitor, a surprising and unexpected one: Kobie Coetsee, the minister of justice. Not long before, I had written to Coetsee pressing him for a meeting to discuss talks between the ANC and the government. He did not respond. But that morning, the minister dropped by the hospital unannounced as if he were visiting an old friend who was laid up for a few days. He was altogether gracious and cordial, and for the most part we simply made pleasantries. Though I acted as though this was the most normal thing in the world, I was amazed. The government, in its slow and tentative way, was reckoning that they had to come to some accommodation with the ANC. Coetsee's visit was an olive branch.

Although we did not discuss politics, I did bring up one sensitive issue, and that was the status of my wife. In August, shortly before I entered the hospital, Winnie had gone to Johannesburg to receive medical treatment. The only trips she was permitted from Brandfort were to visit either me or her doctor. While in Johannesburg, her house in Brandfort and the clinic behind it were firebombed and destroyed. Winnie had no place in which to reside, and she decided to remain in Johannesburg despite the fact that the city was off-limits to her. Nothing happened for a few weeks, and then the security police wrote to inform her that the house in Brandfort had been repaired and she must return. But she refused to do so. I asked Coetsee to allow Winnie to remain in Johannesburg and not force her to return to Brandfort. He said he could promise nothing, but he would indeed look into it. I thanked him.

I spent several days in hospital recuperating from the surgery. When I was discharged, I was fetched at the hospital by Brigadier Munro. Commanding officers do not usually pick up prisoners at the hospital, so my suspicions were immediately aroused.

On the ride back, Brigadier Munro said to me in a casual way, as though he were simply making conversation, "Mandela, we are not taking you back to your friends now." I asked him what he meant. "From now on, you are going to be alone." I asked him why. He shook his head. "I don't know. I've just been given these instructions from headquarters." Once again, there was no warning and no explanation.

Upon my return to Pollsmoor I was taken to a new cell on the ground floor of the prison, three floors below and in an entirely different wing. I was given three rooms, and a separate toilet, with one room to be used for sleeping, one across the hall for studying, and another for exercise. By prison standards, this was palatial, but the rooms were damp and musty and received very little natural light. I said nothing to the brigadier, for I knew the decision had not been his. I wanted time to consider the ramifications of the move. Why had the state taken this step?

It would be too strong to call it a revelation, but over the next few days and weeks I came to a realization about my new circumstances. The change, I decided, was not a liability but an opportunity. I was not happy to be separated from my colleagues and I missed my garden and the sunny terrace on the third floor. But my solitude gave me a certain liberty, and I resolved to use it to do something I had been pondering for a long while: begin discussions with the government. I had concluded that the time had come when the struggle could best be pushed forward through negotiations. If we did not start a dialogue soon, both sides would be plunged into a dark night of oppression, violence, and war. My solitude would give me an opportunity to take the first steps in that direction, without the kind of scrutiny that might destroy such efforts.

We had been fighting against white minority rule for three-quarters of a century. We had been engaged in the armed struggle for more than two decades. Many people on both sides had already died. The enemy was strong and resolute. Yet even with all their bombers and tanks, they must have sensed they were on the wrong side of history. We had right on our side, but not yet might. It was clear to me that a military victory was a distant if not impossible dream. It simply did not make sense for both sides to lose thousands if not millions of lives in a conflict that was unnecessary. They must have known this as well. It was time to talk.

This would be extremely sensitive. Both sides regarded discussions as a sign of weakness and betrayal. Neither would come to the table until the other made significant concessions. The government asserted over and over that we were a terrorist organization of Communists, and that they would never talk to terrorists or Communists. This was National Party dogma. The ANC asserted over and over that the government was fascistic and racist and that there was nothing to talk about until they unbanned the ANC, unconditionally released all political prisoners, and removed the troops from the townships.

A decision to talk to the government was of such import that it should only have been made in Lusaka. But I felt that the process needed to begin, and that I had neither the time nor the means to communicate fully with Oliver. Someone from our side needed to take the first step, and my new isolation gave me both the freedom to do so and the assurance, at least for a while, of the confidentiality of my efforts.

I was now in a kind of splendid isolation. Though my colleagues were only three floors above me, they might as well have been in Johannesburg. In order to see them, I had to put in a formal request for a visit, which had to be approved by the Head Office in Pretoria. It often took weeks to receive a response. If it was approved, I would then meet them in the visiting area. This was a novel experience: my comrades and fellow prisoners were now official visitors. For years, we had been able to talk for hours a day; now we had to make official requests and appointments, and our conversations were monitored.

After I had been in my new cell for a few days, I asked the commanding officer to arrange such a meeting. He did so, and the four of us discussed the issue of my transfer. Walter, Kathy, and Ray were angry that we had been separated. They wanted to lodge a strong protest, and demand that we be reunited. My response was not what they expected. "Look, chaps," I said, "I don't think we should oppose this thing." I mentioned that my new accommodations were superior, and maybe this would set a precedent for all political prisoners. I then added somewhat ambiguously, "Perhaps something good will come of this. I'm now in a position where the government can make an approach to us." They did not care too much for this latter explanation, as I knew they would not.

I chose to tell no one of what I was about to do. Not my colleagues upstairs or those in Lusaka. The ANC is a collective, but the government had made collectivity in this case impossible. I did not have the security or the time to discuss these issues with my organization. I knew that my colleagues upstairs would condemn my proposal, and that would kill my initiative even before it was born. There are times when a leader must move out ahead of the flock, go off in a new direction, confident that he is leading his people the right way. Finally, my isolation furnished my organization with an excuse in case matters went awry: the old man was alone and completely cut off, and his actions were taken by him as an individual, not a representative of the ANC.

90

WITHIN A FEW WEEKS of my move, I wrote to Kobie Coetsee to propose talks about talks. As before, I received no response. I wrote once more, and again there was no response. I found this peculiar and de-moralizing, and I realized I had to look for another opportunity to be heard. That came in early 1986.

At a meeting of the British Commonwealth in Nassau in October 1985, the leaders could not reach agreement on whether to participate in international sanctions against South Africa. This was mainly because British Prime Minister Margaret Thatcher was adamantly opposed. To resolve the deadlock, the assembled nations agreed that a delegation of "eminent persons" would visit South Africa and report back on whether sanctions were the appropriate tool to help bring about the end of apartheid. In early 1986, the seven-member Eminent Persons Group, led by General Olusegun Obasanjo, the former military leader of Nigeria, and former Australian Prime Minister Malcolm Fraser, arrived in South Africa on their fact-finding mission.

In February, I was visited by General Obasanjo to discuss the nature of the delegation's brief. He was eager to facilitate a meeting between me and the full group. With the government's permission, such a meeting was scheduled for May. The group would be talking with the cabinet after they saw me, and I viewed this as a chance to raise the subject of negotiations.

The government regarded my session with the group as something extraordinary. Two days before the meeting I was visited by Brigadier Munro, who had brought along a tailor. "Mandela," the commander said, "we want you to see these people on an equal footing. We don't want you to wear those old prison clothes, so this tailor will take your mea-surements and outfit you with a proper suit." The tailor must have been some kind of wizard, for the very next day I tried on a pinstriped suit that fit me like a glove. I was also given a shirt, tie, shoes, socks, and underwear. The commander admired my new attire. "Mandela, you look like a prime minister now, not a prisoner," he said and smiled.

*   *   *

At the meeting between myself and the Eminent Persons Group, we were joined by two significant observers: Kobie Coetsee and Lieutenant General W. H. Willemse, the commissioner of prisons. Like the tailor, these two men were there to take my measure. But, curiously, they left shortly after the session started. I pressed them to remain, saying I had nothing to hide, but they left anyway. Before they took their leave, I told them the time had come for negotiations, not fighting, and that the government and the ANC should sit down and talk.

The Eminent Persons Group had come with many questions involving the issues of violence, negotiations, and international sanctions. At the outset, I set the ground rules for our discussions. "I am not the head of the movement," I told them. "The head of the movement is Oliver Tambo in Lusaka. You must go and see him. You can tell him what my views are, but they are my personal views alone. They don't even represent the views of my colleagues here in prison. All that being said, I favor the ANC beginning discussions with the government."

Various members of the group had concerns about my political ideology and what a South Africa under ANC leadership might look like. I told them I was a South African nationalist, not a Communist, that nationalists came in every hue and color, and that I was firmly committed to a nonracial society. I told them I believed in the Freedom Charter, that the charter embodied principles of democracy and human rights, and that it was not a blueprint for socialism. I spoke of my concern that the white minority feel a sense of security in any new South Africa. I told them I thought many of our problems were a result of lack of communication between the government and the ANC and that some of these could be resolved through actual talks.

They questioned me extensively on the issue of violence, and while I was not yet willing to renounce violence, I affirmed in the strongest possible terms that violence could never be the ultimate solution to the situation in South Africa and that men and women by their very nature required some kind of negotiated understanding. While I once again reiterated that these were my views and not those of the ANC, I suggested that if the government withdrew the army and the police from the townships, the ANC might agree to a suspension of the armed struggle as a prelude to talks. I told them that my release alone would not stem the violence in the country or stimulate negotiations.

After the group finished with me, they planned to see both Oliver in Lusaka and government officials in Pretoria. In my remarks, I had sent messages to both places. I wanted the government to see that under the right circumstances we would talk and I wanted Oliver to know that my position and his were the same.

In May, the Eminent Persons Group was scheduled to see me one last time. I was optimistic as they had been to both Lusaka and Pretoria, and I hoped that the seed of negotiations had been planted. But the day before we were to meet, the South African government took a step that sabotaged whatever goodwill had been engendered by the Commonwealth visitors. On the day the Eminent Persons Group was scheduled to meet with cabinet ministers, the South African Defense Force, under the orders of President Botha, launched air raids and commando attacks on ANC bases in Botswana, Zambia, and Zimbabwe. This utterly poisoned the talks, and the Eminent Persons Group immediately left South Africa. Once again, I felt my efforts to move negotiations forward had stalled.

Oliver Tambo and the ANC had called for the people of South Africa to render the country ungovernable, and the people were obliging. The state of unrest and political violence was reaching new heights. The anger of the masses was unrestrained; the townships were in upheaval. International pressure was growing stronger every day. On June 12, 1986, the government imposed a State of Emergency in an attempt to keep a lid on protest. In every outward way, the time seemed inauspicious for negotiations. But often, the most discouraging moments are precisely the time to launch an initiative. At such times people are searching for a way out of their dilemma. That month I wrote a very simple letter to General Willemse, the commissioner of prisons. In it, I merely said, "I wish to see you on a matter of national importance." I handed the letter to Brigadier Munro on a Wednesday.

That weekend, I was told by the commanding officer to be prepared to see General Willemse, who was coming down from Pretoria. This meeting was not treated in the usual fashion. Instead of conferring with the general in the visiting area, I was taken to his residence on the grounds of Pollsmoor itself.

Willemse is a direct fellow and we got down to business immediately. I told him I wanted to see Kobie Coetsee, the minister of justice. He asked me why. I hesitated for a moment, reluctant to discuss political matters with a prison official. But I responded with frankness: "I want to see the minister in order to raise the question of talks between the government and the ANC."

He pondered this for a moment, and then said, "Mandela, as you know, I am not a politician. I cannot discuss such issues myself, for they are beyond my authority." He then paused, as if something had just occurred to him. "It just so happens," he said, "that the minister of justice is in Cape Town. Perhaps you can see him. I will find out."

The general then telephoned the minister and the two spoke for a few moments. After putting down the phone, the general turned to me and said, "The minister said, 'Bring him round.' " Minutes later, we left the general's residence in his car bound for the minister's house in Cape Town. Security was light; only one other car accompanied the general's vehicle. The ease and rapidity with which this meeting was set up made me suspect that the government might have planned this rendezvous ahead of time. Whether they had or not was immaterial; it was an opportunity to take the first step toward negotiations.

At his official residence in the city, Coetsee greeted me warmly and we settled down on comfortable chairs in his lounge. He apologized that I had not had a chance to change out of my prison clothes. I spent three hours in conversation with him and was struck by his sophistication and willingness to listen. He asked knowledgeable and relevant questions — questions that reflected a familiarity with the issues that divided the government and the ANC. He asked me under what circumstances would we suspend the armed struggle; whether or not I spoke for the ANC as a whole; whether I envisioned any constitutional guarantees for minorities in a new South Africa. His questions went to the heart of the issues dividing the government and the ANC.

After responding in much the same way as I did to the Eminent Persons Group, I sensed that Coetsee wanted some resolution. What is the next step? he asked. I told him I wanted to see the state president and the foreign minister, Pik Botha. Coetsee noted this on a small pad he had kept beside him, and said he would send my request through the proper channels. We then shook hands, and I was driven back to my solitary cell on the ground floor of Pollsmoor prison.

I was greatly encouraged. I sensed the government was anxious to overcome the impasse in the country, that they were now convinced they had to depart from their old positions. In ghostly outline, I saw the beginnings of a compromise.

I told no one of my encounter. I wanted the process to be under way before I informed anyone. Sometimes it is necessary to present one's colleagues with a policy that is already a fait accompli. I knew that once they examined the situation carefully, my colleagues at Pollsmoor and in Lusaka would support me. But again, after this promising start, nothing happened. Weeks and then months passed without a word from Coetsee. In some frustration, I wrote him another letter.

91

ALTHOUGH I DID NOT GET a direct response from Kobie Coetsee, there were other signs that the government was preparing me for a different kind of existence. On the day before Christmas, Lieutenant Colonel Gawie Marx, the deputy commander of Pollsmoor, wandered by my cell after breakfast and said quite casually, "Mandela, would you like to see the city?" I was not exactly certain what he had in mind, but I thought there was no harm in saying yes. Good, he said, come along. I walked with the colonel through the fifteen locked metal doors between my cell and the entrance, and when we emerged, I found his car waiting for us.

We drove into Cape Town along the lovely road that runs parallel to the coast. He had no destination in mind and simply meandered around the city in a leisurely fashion. It was absolutely riveting to watch the simple activities of people out in the world: old men sitting in the sun, women doing their shopping, people walking their dogs. It is precisely those mundane activities of daily life that one misses most in prison. I felt like a curious tourist in a strange and remarkable land.

After an hour or so, Colonel Marx stopped the car in front of a small shop on a quiet street. "Would you like a cold drink?" he asked me. I nodded, and he disappeared inside the shop. I sat there alone. For the first few moments, I did not think about my situation, but as the seconds ticked away, I became more and more agitated. For the first time in twenty-two years, I was out in the world and unguarded. I had a vision of opening the door, jumping out, and then running and running until I was out of sight. Something inside was urging me to do just that. I noticed a wooded area near the road where I could hide. I was extremely tense and began to perspire. Where was the colonel? But then I took control of myself; such an action would be unwise and irresponsible, not to mention dangerous. It was possible that the whole situation was contrived to try to get me to escape, though I do not think that was the case. I was greatly relieved a few moments later when I saw the colonel walking back to the car with two cans of Coca-Cola.

As it turned out, that day in Cape Town was the first of many excursions. Over the next few months, I went out again with the colonel not only to Cape Town but to some of the sights around the city, its beautiful beaches and lovely cool mountains. Soon, more junior officers were permitted to take me around. One of the places I regularly visited with these junior officers was known as the "gardens," a series of small holdings on the edge of the prison grounds where crops were grown for the prison's kitchen. I enjoyed being out in nature, being able to see the horizon and feel the sun on my shoulders.

One day I went to the gardens with a captain, and after walking in the fields we strolled over to the stables. There were two young white men in overalls working with the horses. I walked over to them, praised one of the animals, and said to the fellow, "Now, what is this horse's name?" The young man seemed quite nervous and did not look at me. He then mumbled the name of the horse, but to the captain, not me. I then asked the other fellow in turn what the name of his horse was, and he had precisely the same reaction.

As I was walking back to the prison with the captain, I commented on what I thought was the curious behavior of the two young men. The captain laughed. "Mandela, don't you know what those two chaps were?" I said I did not. "They were white prisoners. They had never been questioned by a native prisoner in the presence of a white officer before."

Some of the younger warders took me quite far afield, and we would walk on the beach and even stop at a café and have tea. At such places, I often tried to see if people recognized me, but no one ever did; the last published picture of me had been taken in 1962.

These trips were instructive on a number of levels. I saw how life had changed in the time I had been away, and because we mainly went to white areas, I saw the extraordinary wealth and ease that whites enjoyed. Though the country was in upheaval and the townships were on the brink of open warfare, white life went on placidly and undisturbed. Their lives were unaffected. Once, one of the warders, a very pleasant young man named Warrant Officer Brand, actually took me to his family's flat and introduced me to his wife and children. From then on, I sent his children Christmas cards every year.

As much as I enjoyed these little adventures, I well knew that the authorities had a motive other than keeping me diverted. I sensed that they wanted to acclimatize me to life in South Africa and perhaps at the same time, get me so used to the pleasures of small freedoms that I might be willing to compromise in order to have complete freedom.

92

IN 1987, I RESUMED CONTACT with Kobie Coetsee. I had several private meetings with him at his residence, and later that year the government made its first concrete proposal. Coetsee said the government would like to appoint a committee of senior officials to conduct private discussions with me. This would be done with the full knowledge of the state president, Coetsee said. Coetsee himself would be head of the committee, and it would include General Willemse, the commissioner of prisons; Fanie van der Merwe, the director general of the Prisons Department; and Dr. Niel Barnard, a former academic who was then head of the National Intelligence Service. The first three individuals were associated with the prison system, so if talks foundered or were leaked to the press, both sides would be able to cover up and say we were discussing prison conditions and nothing more.

The presence of Dr. Barnard, however, disturbed me. He was the head of South Africa's equivalent of the CIA, and was also involved with military intelligence. I could justify to my organization discussions with the other officials, but not Barnard. His presence made the talks more problematic and suggested a larger agenda. I told Coetsee that I would like to think about the proposal overnight.

That night I considered all the ramifications. I knew that P. W. Botha had created something called the State Security Council, a shadowy secretariat of security experts and intelligence officials. He had done this, according to the press, to circumvent the authority of the cabinet and increase his own power. Dr. Barnard was a key player in this inner council and was said to be a protégé of the president. I thought that my refusing Barnard would alienate Botha, and I decided that such a tack was too risky. If the state president was not brought on board, nothing would happen. In the morning, I sent word to Coetsee that I accepted his offer.

I knew that I had three crucial matters that I needed to address: first, I wanted to sound out my colleagues on the third floor before I proceeded any further; second, it was essential to communicate with Oliver in Lusaka about what was occurring; and finally, I intended to draft a memorandum to P. W. Botha laying out my views and those of the ANC on the vital issues before the country. This memorandum would create talking points for any future discussion.

I requested a meeting with my colleagues, and to my surprise, the authorities summarily refused. This was remarkable, and I assumed it reflected a great deal of nervousness about the prospect of secret talks between myself and the government. I took my complaints to more senior officials. Finally, the request was approved, with the proviso that I could see my colleagues one by one, not together.

I met them in the visiting area. I had resolved to leave out a few details; I would seek their counsel about the idea of having talks with the government without mentioning that an actual committee had been formed. Walter was first. I told him about my letter to the commissioner of prisons and my meeting with Coetsee. I said that I had discussed with Coetsee the idea of beginning talks with the government and that the government seemed interested. What were his views on the matter?

I have been through thick and thin with Walter. He was a man of reason and wisdom, and no man knew me better than he did. There was no one whose opinion I trusted or valued more. Walter considered what I told him. I could see he was uncomfortable, and at best, lukewarm. "In principle," he said, "I am not against negotiations. But I would have wished that the government initiated talks with us rather than us initiating talks with them."

I replied that if he was not against negotiations in principle, what did it matter who initiated them? What mattered was what they achieved, not how they started. I told Walter that I thought we should move forward with negotiations and not worry about who knocked on the door first. Walter saw that my mind was made up and he said he would not stop me, but that he hoped I knew what I was doing.

Next was Raymond Mhlaba. I explained the entire situation to him as I had to Walter. Ray was always a man of few words, and for several moments he digested what I had said. He then looked at me and said, "Madiba, what have you been waiting for? We should have started this years ago." Andrew Mlangeni's reaction was virtually the same as Ray's. The last man was Kathy. His response was negative; he was as resolutely against what I was suggesting as Raymond and Andrew were in favor. Even more strongly than Walter, he felt that by initiating talks it would appear that we were capitulating. Like Walter, he said he was not in principle against negotiations, and I responded exactly as I had with Walter. But Kathy was adamant; he felt I was going down the wrong path. But, despite his misgivings, he said he would not stand in my way.

Not long after this I received a note from Oliver Tambo that was smuggled in to me by one of my lawyers. He had heard reports that I was having secret discussions with the government and he was concerned. He said he knew I had been alone for some time and separated from my colleagues. He must have been wondering: What is going on with Mandela? Oliver's note was brief and to the point: What, he wanted to know, was I discussing with the government? Oliver could not have believed that I was selling out, but he might have thought I was making an error in judgment. In fact, the tenor of his note suggested that.

I replied to Oliver in a very terse letter saying that I was talking to the government about one thing and one thing only: a meeting between the

National Executive Committee of the ANC and the South African government. I would not spell out the details, for I could not trust the confidentiality of the communication. I simply said the time had come for such talks and that I would not compromise the organization in any way.

Although the ANC had called for talks with the government for decades, we had never been confronted with the actual prospect of such talks. It is one thing to consider them in theory, and quite another to engage in them. As I was writing my response to Oliver, I was also beginning to draft my memorandum to P. W. Botha. I would make sure that Oliver saw this as well. I knew that when Oliver and the National Executive read my memo, their fears that I had gone off the road would be allayed.

93

THE FIRST FORMAL MEETING of the secret working group took place in May 1988, at a posh officers' club within the precincts of Pollsmoor. While I knew both Coetsee and Willemse, I had never before met van der Merwe and Dr. Barnard. Van der Merwe was a quiet, levelheaded man who spoke only when he had something important to say. Dr. Barnard was in his mid-thirties and was exceedingly bright, a man of controlled intelligence and self-discipline.

The initial meeting was quite stiff, but in subsequent sessions we were able to talk more freely and directly. I met with them almost every week for a few months, and then the meetings occurred at irregular intervals, sometimes not for a month, and then suddenly every week. The meetings were usually scheduled by the government, but sometimes I would request a session.

During our early meetings, I discovered that my new colleagues, with the exception of Dr. Barnard, knew little about the ANC. They were all sophisticated Afrikaners, and far more open-minded than nearly all of their brethren. But they were the victims of so much propaganda that it was necessary to straighten them out about certain facts. Even Dr. Barnard, who had made a study of the ANC, had received most of his information from police and intelligence files, which were in the main inaccurate and sullied by the prejudices of the men who had gathered them. He could not help but be infected by the same biases.

I spent some time in the beginning sketching out the history of the ANC and then explaining our positions on the primary issues that divided the organization from the government. After these preliminaries, we focused on the critical issues: the armed struggle, the ANC's alliance with the Communist Party, the goal of majority rule, and the idea of racial reconciliation.

The first issue to arise was in many ways the most crucial, and that was the armed struggle. We spent a number of months discussing it. They insisted that the ANC must renounce violence and give up the armed struggle before the government would agree to negotiations — and before I could meet President Botha. Their contention was that violence was nothing more than criminal behavior that could not be tolerated by the state.

I responded that the state was responsible for the violence and that it is always the oppressor, not the oppressed, who dictates the form of the struggle. If the oppressor uses violence, the oppressed have no alternative but to respond violently. In our case it was simply a legitimate form of self-defense. I ventured that if the state decided to use peaceful methods, the ANC would also use peaceful means. "It is up to you," I said, "not us, to renounce violence."

I think I advanced their understanding on this point, but the issue soon moved from a philosophical question to a practical one. As Minister Coetsee and Dr. Barnard pointed out, the National Party had repeatedly stated that it would not negotiate with any organization that advocated violence: therefore, how could it suddenly announce talks with the ANC without losing its credibility? In order for us to begin talks, they said, the ANC must make some compromise so that the government would not lose face with its own people.

It was a fair point and one that I could well understand, but I would not offer them a way out. "Gentlemen," I said, "it is not my job to resolve your dilemma for you." I simply told them that they must tell their people that there can be no peace and no solution to the situation in South Africa without sitting down with the ANC. People will understand, I said.

The ANC's alliance with the Communist Party seemed to trouble them almost as much as the armed struggle. The National Party accepted the most hidebound of 1950s cold war ideology and regarded the Soviet Union as the evil empire and communism as the work of the devil. There was nothing that one could do to disabuse them of this notion. They maintained that the Communist Party dominated and controlled the ANC and that in order for negotiations to begin we must break with the party.

First of all, I said, no self-respecting freedom fighter would take orders from the government he is fighting against or jettison a longtime ally in the interest of pleasing an antagonist. I then explained at great length that the party and the ANC were separate and distinct organizations that shared the same short-term objectives, the overthrow of racial oppression and the birth of a nonracial South Africa, but that our long-term interests were not the same.

This discussion went on for months. Like most Afrikaners, they thought that because many of the Communists in the ANC were white or Indian, they were controlling the blacks in the ANC. I cited many occasions when the ANC and the CP had differed on policy and the ANC had prevailed, but this did not seem to impress them. Finally, in exasperation, I said to them, "You gentlemen consider yourselves intelligent, do you not? You consider yourselves forceful and persuasive, do you not? Well, there are four of you and only one of me, and you cannot control me or get me to change my mind. What makes you think the Communists can succeed where you have failed?"

They were also concerned about the idea of nationalization, insisting that the ANC and the Freedom Charter supported blanket nationalization for the South African economy. I explained that we were for a more even distribution of the rewards of certain industries, industries that were already monopolies, and that nationalization might occur in some of those areas. But I referred them to an article I wrote in 1956 for *Liberation* in which I said that the Freedom Charter was not a blueprint for socialism but for African-style capitalism. I told them I had not changed my mind since then.

The other main area of discussion was the issue of majority rule. They felt that if there was majority rule, the rights of minorities would be trampled. How would the ANC protect the rights of the white minority? they wanted to know. I said that there was no organization in the history of South Africa to compare with the ANC in terms of trying to unite all the people and races of South Africa. I referred them to the preamble of the Freedom Charter: "South Africa belongs to all who live in it, black and white." I told them that whites were Africans as well, and that in any future dispensation the majority would need the minority. We do not want to drive you into the sea, I said.

94

THE MEETINGS had a positive effect: I was told in the winter of 1988 that President Botha was planning to see me before the end of August. The country was still in turmoil. The government had reimposed a State of Emergency in both 1987 and 1988. International pressure mounted.

More companies left South Africa. The American Congress had passed a sweeping sanctions bill.

In 1987, the ANC celebrated its seventy-fifth anniversary and held a conference at the end of the year in Tanzania attended by delegates from more than fifty nations. Oliver declared that the armed struggle would intensify until the government was prepared to negotiate the abolition of apartheid. Two years before, at the ANC's Kabwe conference in Zambia marking the thirtieth anniversary of the Freedom Charter, members of other races were elected to the National Executive Committee for the first time, and the NEC pledged that no discussions with the government could be held until all ANC leaders were released from prison.

Although violence was still pervasive, the National Party had never been stronger. In the white general election of May 1987, the Nationalists won an overwhelming majority. Worse still, the liberal Progressive Federal Party had been replaced as the official opposition by the Conservative Party, which was to the right of the Nationalists and campaigned on the theme that the government was too lenient with the black opposition.

Despite my optimism about the secret talks, it was a difficult time. I had recently had a visit from Winnie and I learned that 8115 Orlando West, the house in which we had been married and which I considered home, had been burned down by arsonists. We had lost invaluable family records, photographs, and keepsakes — even the slice of wedding cake Winnie was saving for my release. I had always thought that someday when I left prison I would be able to recapture the past when looking over those pictures and letters, and now they were gone. Prison had robbed me of my freedom but not my memories, and now I felt some enemies of the struggle had tried to rob me of even those.

I was also suffering from a bad cough that I could not seem to shake, and I often felt too weak to exercise. I had continued to complain about the dampness of my cell, but nothing had been done about it. One day, during a meeting in the visiting area with my attorney, Ismail Ayob, I felt ill and vomited. I was taken back to my cell, examined by a doctor, and I soon recovered. A few days later, however, I was in my cell after dinner when a number of warders and a doctor arrived. The physician gave me a cursory examination, and then one of the warders told me to get dressed. "We are taking you to hospital in Cape Town," I was told. Security was tight; I went in a convoy of cars and military vehicles accompanied by at least a dozen warders.

I was taken to Tygerberg Hospital, on the campus of the University of Stellenbosch, in a rich and verdant area of the Cape. As I later discovered, they had nearly chosen a different facility because the authorities feared

I might attract sympathetic attention at a university hospital. The warders went in first and cleared everyone out of the entrance area. I was then escorted up to a floor that had been entirely emptied. The hall of the floor was lined with more than a dozen armed guards.

While sitting on a table in the examining room, I was looked at by a young and amiable doctor who was also a professor at the university medical school. He inspected my throat, tapped my chest, took some cultures, and in no time pronounced me fit. "There is nothing wrong with you," he said with a smile. "We should be able to release you tomorrow." I was anxious not to be diverted from my talks with the government, so I was pleased with his diagnosis.

After the examination, the doctor asked me if I would like some tea. I said I would and a few minutes later, a tall young Coloured nurse came in with a tray. The presence of all the armed guards and warders so frightened her that she dropped the tray on my bed, spilling the tea, before rushing out.

I spent the night in the empty ward under heavy guard. The first thing the next morning, even before I had breakfast, I was visited by an older doctor who was head of internal medicine at the hospital. He was a no-nonsense fellow and had far less of a bedside manner than the cordial young physician of the night before. Without any preliminaries, he tapped me roughly on my chest and then said gruffly, "There is water in your lung." I told him that the previous doctor had done tests and said I was fine. With a hint of annoyance, he said, "Mandela, take a look at your chest." He pointed out that one side of my chest was actually larger than the other, and said that it was probably filled with water.

He asked a nurse to bring him a syringe, and without further ado he poked it into my chest and drew out some brownish liquid. "Have you had breakfast?" he said. No, I replied. "Good," he said, "we are taking you to the operating theater immediately." He told me I had a great deal of water on my lung and he wanted to draw it out right away.

In the operating room I was given anesthesia, and the next thing I recalled was waking up in a room with the doctor present. I was groggy, but I concentrated on what he said: he had removed two liters of water from my chest and when the liquid was analyzed, a tuberculosis germ had been discovered. He said it was in the very early stages of the illness, and that the germ had done no damage to the lung. While full-blown tuberculosis normally took six months to cure, he said, I should be better in two months. The doctor agreed that it was probably the damp cell that had helped cause my illness.

*　　　*　　　*

I spent the next six weeks at Tygerberg recuperating and receiving treatment. In December, I was moved to the Constantiaberge Clinic, a luxurious facility near Pollsmoor that had never had a black patient before. My first morning there, I had an early visit from Kobie Coetsee, who was accompanied by Major Marais, a deputy commander responsible for looking after me. We had barely exchanged greetings when the orderly brought in my breakfast.

Because of my recent illness and my history of high blood pressure, I had been put on a strict low-cholesterol diet. That order had apparently not yet been conveyed to the clinic's kitchen, for the breakfast tray contained scrambled eggs, three rashers of bacon, and several pieces of buttered toast. I could not remember the last time I had tasted bacon and eggs, and I was ravenous. Just as I was about to take a delicious forkful of egg, Major Marais said, "No, Mandela, that is against the orders of your physician," and he reached over to take the tray. I held it tightly, and said, "Major, I am sorry. If this breakfast will kill me, then today I am prepared to die."

Once I was ensconced at Constantiaberge, I again began to meet with Kobie Coetsee and the secret committee. While I was still at the clinic Coetsee said he wanted to put me in a situation that was halfway between confinement and freedom. While he did not spell out what this meant, I had a notion of what he was talking about, and I merely nodded. I would not be so naïve as to consider his proposal to be freedom, but I knew that it was a step in that direction.

In the meantime, the clinic was extremely comfortable and for the first time I actually enjoyed a hospital convalescence. The nurses — who were white or Coloured, no black nurses were permitted — spoiled me; they brought extra desserts and pillows and were constantly visiting, even during their time off.

One day, one of the nurses came to me and said, "Mr. Mandela, we are having a party tonight and we would like you to come." I said I'd be honored to attend, but that the authorities would undoubtedly have something to say about it. The prison authorities refused permission for me to go, which nettled the nurses, and as a result, they decided to hold their party in my room, insisting they could not have their party without me.

That night, a dozen or so of these young ladies in party frocks descended on my room with cake and punch and gifts. The guards seemed befuddled, but they could hardly consider these vivacious young girls a security risk. In fact, when one of the guards attempted to prevent some of the nurses from entering my room, I jestingly accused him of being jealous of an old man receiving so much attention from such beautiful young ladies.

95

IN EARLY DECEMBER 1988, security on my ward was tightened and the officers on duty were more alert than usual. Some change was imminent. On the evening of December 9, Major Marais came into my room, and told me to prepare myself to leave. Where to? I asked him. He could not say. I packed my things and looked around for some of my loyal nurses; I was disappointed at not being able to thank them and bid them farewell.

We left in a rush, and after about an hour on the road we entered a prison whose name I recognized: Victor Verster. Located in the lovely old Cape Dutch town of Paarl, Victor Verster is thirty-five miles northeast of Cape Town in the province's wine-growing region. The prison had the reputation of being a model facility. We drove through the entire length of the prison, and then along a winding dirt road through a rather wild, wooded area at the rear of the property. At the end of the road we came to an isolated, whitewashed one-story cottage set behind a concrete wall and shaded by tall fir trees.

I was ushered into the house by Major Marais and found a spacious lounge, next to a large kitchen, with an even larger bedroom at the back of the house. The place was sparsely but comfortably furnished. It had not been cleaned or swept before my arrival, and the bedroom and living room were teeming with all kinds of exotic insects, centipedes, monkey spiders, and the like, some of which I had never seen before. That night, I swept the insects off my bed and windowsill and slept extremely well in what was to be my new home.

The next morning I surveyed my new abode and discovered a swimming pool in the backyard, and two smaller bedrooms. I walked outside and admired the trees that shaded the house and kept it cool. The entire place felt removed, isolated. The only thing spoiling the idyllic picture was that the walls were topped with razor wire, and there were guards at the entrance to the house. Even so, it was a lovely place and situation; a halfway house between prison and freedom.

That afternoon I was visited by Kobie Coetsee, who brought a case of Cape wine as a housewarming gift. The irony of a jailer bringing his prisoner such a gift was not lost on either of us. He was extremely solicitous and wanted to make sure that I liked my new home. He surveyed the house himself, and the only thing he recommended was that the walls outside the house be raised — for my privacy, he said. He told me that the cottage at Victor Verster would be my last home before becoming a free man. The reason behind this move, he said, was that I should have a place where I could hold discussions in privacy and comfort.

The cottage did in fact give one the illusion of freedom. I could go to sleep and wake up as I pleased, swim whenever I wanted, eat when I was hungry — all were delicious sensations. Simply to be able to go outside during the day and take a walk when I desired was a moment of private glory. There were no bars on the windows, no jangling keys, no doors to lock or unlock. It was altogether pleasant, but I never forgot that it was a gilded cage.

The prison service provided me with a cook, Warrant Officer Swart, a tall, quiet Afrikaner who had once been a warder on Robben Island. I did not remember him, but he said he sometimes drove us to the quarry and purposely steered the truck over bumps to give us a rocky ride. "I did that to you," he said sheepishly, and I laughed. He was a decent, sweet-tempered fellow without any prejudice and he became like a younger brother to me.

He arrived at seven in the morning and left at four, and would make my breakfast, lunch, and dinner. I had a diet outlined by my physician and he would follow it in his preparations. He was a lovely cook, and when he went home at four, he would leave me supper to heat up in the microwave oven, a device that was new to me.

Warrant Officer Swart baked bread, made home-brewed ginger beer and assorted other delicacies. When I had visitors, which was increasingly often, he would prepare gourmet meals. They always praised the food and I daresay my chef was the envy of all my visitors. When the authorities began to permit some of my ANC comrades and members of the United Democratic Front (UDF) and the Mass Democratic Movement (MDM) to visit me, I accused them of coming only for the food.

One day, after a delicious meal prepared by Mr. Swart, I went into the kitchen to wash the dishes. "No," he said, "that is my duty. You must return to the sitting room." I insisted that I had to do something, and that if he cooked, it was only fair for me to do the dishes. Mr. Swart protested, but finally gave in. He also objected to the fact that I would make my bed in the morning, saying it was his responsibility to do so. But I had been making my own bed for so long it had become a reflex.

We also traded off in another respect. Like many Afrikaans-speaking warders, he was keen to improve his English. I was always looking for ways to improve my Afrikaans. We made an agreement: he would speak to me in English and I would answer in Afrikaans, and in that way we both practiced the language at which we were weakest.

I would occasionally ask him to make certain dishes for me. I sometimes requested samp and beans, which I used to eat as a boy. One day, I said to him, "You know, I would like you to cook me some brown rice." To my astonishment, he said, "What is brown rice?" Swart was a young man, and I explained to him that brown rice was the unrefined rice kernel, and we used to eat it during the war when white rice was unavailable. I said it was far healthier than white rice. He was skeptical, but managed to find me some. He cooked it and I enjoyed it very much. But Mr. Swart could not abide the taste and vowed that if I ever wanted it again, I would have to cook it myself.

Even though I was not a drinker, I wanted to be a proper host and serve wine to my guests. I would occasionally take a sip of wine in order to make my guests feel comfortable, but the only wine I can stomach is a South African semisweet wine, which is actually very sweet.

Before my guests came I would ask Mr. Swart to get a certain type of Nederburg wine, which I had tasted before and knew was a semisweet. One day, I was expecting my friends and lawyers for lunch, Dullah Omar, George Bizos, and Ismail Ayob, and asked Mr. Swart to purchase some Nederburg wine should George Bizos, not a Muslim, want some with his meal. I noticed that he grimaced when I said this, and asked him what was wrong.

"Mr. Mandela," he said. "I always buy that wine for you because you ask me to, but it is cheap stuff and not very nice." I reminded him that I did not like dry wines and I was sure George could not tell the difference anyway. Mr. Swart smiled at this and proposed a compromise: he would go out and buy two bottles, a dry wine and my Nederburg, and then he would ask my guest which wine he preferred. "Fine," I said, "let us try your experiment."

When all four of us were seated for lunch, Swart came out holding the two bottles and turned to the guests and said, "Gentlemen, which wine would you like?" Without even looking at me, George pointed to the bottle of dry white. Warrant Officer Swart just smiled.

96

THE MEETINGS with the committee continued, and we stalled on the same issues that had always prevented us from moving forward: the armed struggle, the Communist Party, and majority rule. I was still pressing Coetsee for a meeting with P. W. Botha. By this time, the authorities permitted me to have rudimentary communications with my comrades at Pollsmoor and Robben Island and also the ANC in Lusaka. Although I knew I was going out ahead of my colleagues, I did not want to go too far ahead and find that I was all alone.

In January 1989, I was visited by my four comrades from Pollsmoor and we discussed the memorandum I was planning to send to the state president. The memorandum reiterated most of the points I had made in our secret committee meetings, but I wanted to make sure the state president heard them directly from me. He would see that we were not wild-eyed terrorists, but reasonable men.

"I am disturbed," I wrote to Mr. Botha in the memorandum, sent to him in March, "as many other South Africans no doubt are, by the specter of a South Africa split into two hostile camps — blacks on one side . . . and whites on the other, slaughtering one another." To avert this and prepare the groundwork for negotiations, I proposed to deal with the three demands made of the ANC by the government as a precondition to negotiations: renouncing violence; breaking with the SACP; and abandoning the call for majority rule.

On the question of violence I wrote that the refusal of the ANC to renounce violence was not the problem: "The truth is that the government is not yet ready . . . for the sharing of political power with blacks." I explained our unwillingness to cast aside the SACP, and reiterated that we were not under its control. "Which man of honour," I wrote, "will desert a lifelong friend at the insistence of a common opponent and still retain a measure of credibility with his people?" I said the rejection of majority rule by the government was a poorly disguised attempt to preserve power. I suggested he must face reality. "Majority rule and internal peace are like the two sides of a single coin, and white South Africa simply has to accept that there will never be peace and stability in this country until the principle is fully applied."

At the end of the letter, I offered a very rough framework for negotiations.

> Two political issues will have to be addressed; firstly, the demand for majority rule in a unitary state, secondly, the concern of white South Africa over this demand, as well as the insistence of whites on structural guarantees that majority rule will not mean domination of the white minority by blacks. The most crucial tasks which will face the government and the ANC will be to reconcile these two positions.

I proposed that this be done in two stages, the first being a discussion to create the proper conditions for negotiations, the second being the actual negotiations themselves. "I must point out that the move I have taken provides you with the opportunity to overcome the current deadlock, and to normalize the country's political situation. I hope you will seize it without delay."

But delay there was. In January, P. W. Botha suffered a stroke. While it did not incapacitate the president, it did weaken him and, according to his cabinet, made him even more irascible. In February, Botha unexpectedly resigned as head of the National Party, but kept his position as state president. This was an unparalleled situation in the country's history: in the South African parliamentary system, the leader of the majority party becomes the head of state. President Botha was now head of state but not of his own party. Some saw this as a positive development: that Botha wanted to be "above party politics" in order to bring about true change in South Africa.

Political violence and international pressure continued to intensify. Political detainees all across the country had held a successful hunger strike, persuading the minister of law and order to release over nine hundred of them. In 1989, the UDF formed an alliance with the Congress of South African Trade Unions (COSATU) to form the Mass Democratic Movement (MDM), which then began organizing a countrywide "defiance campaign" of civil disobedience to challenge apartheid institutions. On the international front, Oliver held talks with the governments of Great Britain and the Soviet Union, and in January 1987 met with the U.S. secretary of state, George Shultz, in Washington. The Americans recognized the ANC as an indispensable element of any solution in South Africa. Sanctions against South Africa remained in force and even increased.

Political violence also had its tragic side. As the violence in Soweto intensified, my wife permitted a group of young men to act as her bodyguards as she moved around the township. These young men were untrained and undisciplined and became involved in activities that were unbecoming to a liberation struggle. Winnie subsequently became legally entangled in the trial of one of her bodyguards who was convicted of murdering a young comrade. This situation was deeply disconcerting to me, for such a scandal only served to divide the movement at a time when unity was essential. I wholly supported my wife and maintained that while she had shown poor judgment, she was innocent of any serious charges.

That July, for my seventy-first birthday, I was visited at the cottage at Victor Verster by nearly my entire family. It was the first time I had ever had my wife and children and grandchildren all in one place, and it was a grand and happy occasion. Warrant Officer Swart outdid himself in preparing a feast, and he did not even get upset when I permitted some of the grandchildren to eat their sweets before their main course. After the meal, the grandchildren went into my bedroom to watch a video of a horror movie while the adults stayed outside gossiping in the lounge. It was a deep, deep pleasure to have my whole family around me, and the only pain was the knowledge that I had missed such occasions for so many years.

97

ON JULY 4, I was visited by General Willemse, who informed me that I was being taken to see President Botha the following day. He described the visit as a "courtesy call," and I was told to be ready to leave at 5:30 A.M. I told the general that while I was looking forward to the meeting, I thought it appropriate that I have a suit and tie in which to see Mr. Botha. (The suit from the visit of the Eminent Persons Group had long since vanished.) The general agreed, and a short while later, a tailor appeared to take my measurements. That afternoon I was delivered a new suit, tie, shirt, and shoes. Before leaving, the general also asked me my blood type, just in case anything untoward should happen the following day.

I prepared as best I could for the meeting. I reviewed my memo and the extensive notes I had made for it. I looked at as many newspapers and publications as I could to make sure I was up to date. After President Botha's resignation as head of the National Party, F. W. de Klerk had been elected in his place, and there was said to be considerable jockeying between the two men. Some might interpret Botha's willingness to meet me as his way of stealing thunder from his rival, but that did not concern me. I rehearsed the arguments that the state president might make and the ones I would put in return. In every meeting with an adversary, one must make sure one has conveyed precisely the impression one intends to.

I was tense about seeing Mr. Botha. He was known as *die Groot Krokodil* — the Great Crocodile — and I had heard many accounts of his ferocious temper. He seemed to me to be the very model of the old-fashioned, stiff-necked, stubborn Afrikaner who did not so much discuss matters with black leaders as dictate to them. His recent stroke had apparently only exacerbated this tendency. I resolved that if he acted in that finger-wagging fashion with me I would have to inform him that I found such behavior unacceptable, and I would then stand up and adjourn the meeting.

*   *   *

At precisely 5:30 in the morning, Major Marais, the commander of Victor Verster, arrived at my cottage. He came into the lounge where I stood in front of him in my new suit for inspection. He walked around me, and then shook his head from side to side.

"No, Mandela, your tie," he said. One did not have much use for ties in prison, and I realized that morning when I was putting it on that I had forgotten how to tie it properly. I made a knot as best I could and hoped no one would notice. Major Marais unbuttoned my collar, loosened and then removed my tie, and then, standing behind me, tied it in a double Windsor knot. He then stood back to admire his handiwork. "Much better," he said.

We drove from Victor Verster to Pollsmoor, to the residence of General Willemse, where we were served breakfast by the general's wife. After breakfast, in a small convoy, we drove to Tuynhuys, the official presidential office, and parked in an underground garage where we would not be seen. Tuynhuys is a graceful, nineteenth-century Cape Dutch-style building, but I did not get a proper look at it that day. I was essentially smuggled into the presidential suite.

We took an elevator to the ground floor and emerged in a grand, wood-paneled lobby in front of the president's office. There we were met by Kobie Coetsee and Niel Barnard, and a retinue of prison officials. I had spoken extensively with both Coetsee and Dr. Barnard about this meeting, and they had always advised me to avoid controversial issues with the president. While we were waiting, Dr. Barnard looked down and noticed that my shoelaces were not properly tied and he quickly kneeled down to tie them for me. I realized just how nervous they were, and that did not make me any calmer. The door then opened and I walked in expecting the worst.

From the opposite side of his grand office, P. W. Botha walked toward me. He had planned his march perfectly, for we met exactly halfway. He had his hand out and was smiling broadly, and in fact, from that very first moment, he completely disarmed me. He was unfailingly courteous, deferential, and friendly.

We very quickly posed for a photograph of the two of us shaking hands, and then were joined at a long table by Kobie Coetsee, General Willemse, and Dr. Barnard. Tea was served and we began to talk. From the first, it was not as though we were engaged in tense political arguments but a lively and interesting tutorial. We did not discuss substantive issues, so much as history and South African culture. I mentioned that I had recently read an article in an Afrikaans magazine about the 1914 Afrikaner Rebellion, and I mentioned how they had occupied towns in the Free

State. I said I saw our struggle as parallel to this famous rebellion, and we discussed this historical episode for quite a while. South African history, of course, looks very different to the black man than to the white man. Their view was that the rebellion had been a quarrel between brothers, whereas my struggle was a revolutionary one. I said that it could also be seen as a struggle between brothers who happen to be different colors.

The meeting was not even half an hour, and was friendly and breezy until the end. It was then that I raised a serious issue. I asked Mr. Botha to release unconditionally all political prisoners, including myself. That was the only tense moment in the meeting, and Mr. Botha said that he was afraid that he could not do that.

There was then a brief discussion as to what we should say if news of the meeting leaked out. We very quickly drafted a bland statement saying that we had met for tea in an effort to promote peace in the country. When this was agreed upon, Mr. Botha rose and shook my hand, saying what a pleasure it had been. Indeed, it had been. I thanked him, and left the way we had come.

While the meeting was not a breakthrough in terms of negotiations, it was one in another sense. Mr. Botha had long talked about the need to cross the Rubicon, but he never did it himself until that morning at Tuynhuys. Now, I felt, there was no turning back.

A little more than a month later, in August 1989, P. W. Botha went on national television to announce his resignation as state president. In a curiously rambling farewell address, he accused cabinet members of a breach of trust, of ignoring him and of playing into the hands of the African National Congress. The following day, F. W. de Klerk was sworn in as acting president and affirmed his commitment to change and reform.

To us, Mr. de Klerk was a cipher. When he became head of the National Party, he seemed to be the quintessential party man, nothing more and nothing less. Nothing in his past seemed to hint at a spirit of reform. As education minister, he had attempted to keep black students out of white universities. But as soon as he took over the National Party, I began to follow him closely. I read all of his speeches, listened to what he said, and began to see that he represented a genuine departure from his predecessor. He was not an ideologue, but a pragmatist, a man who saw change as necessary and inevitable. On the day he was sworn in, I wrote him a letter requesting a meeting.

In his inaugural address, Mr. de Klerk said his government was committed to peace and that it would negotiate with any other group committed to peace. But his commitment to a new order was demonstrated only after his inauguration when a march was planned in Cape Town to protest police brutality. It was to be led by Archbishop Tutu and the Reverend Allan Boesak. Under President Botha, the march would have been banned, marchers would have defied that ban, and violence would have resulted. The new president lived up to his promise to ease restrictions on political gatherings and permitted the march to take place, only asking that the demonstrators remain peaceful. A new and different hand was on the tiller.

98

EVEN AS DE KLERK became president, I continued to meet with the secret negotiating committee. We were joined by Gerrit Viljoen, the minister of constitutional development, a brilliant man with a doctorate in classics, whose role was to bring our discussions into a constitutional framework. I pressed the government to display evidence of its good intentions, urging the state to show its bona fides by releasing my fellow political prisoners at Pollsmoor and Robben Island. While I told the committee that my colleagues had to be released unconditionally, I said the government could expect disciplined behavior from them after their release. That was demonstrated by the conduct of Govan Mbeki, who had been unconditionally released at the end of 1987.

On October 10, 1989, President de Klerk announced that Walter Sisulu and seven of my former Robben Island comrades, Raymond Mhlaba, Ahmed Kathrada, Andrew Mlangeni, Elias Motsoaledi, Jeff Masemola, Wilton Mkwayi, and Oscar Mpetha, were to be released. That morning, I had been visited by Walter, Kathy, Ray, and Andrew, who were still at Pollsmoor, and I was able to say good-bye. It was an emotional moment, but I knew I would not be too far behind. The men were released five days later from Johannesburg Prison. It was an action that rightly evoked praise here and abroad, and I conveyed my appreciation to Mr. de Klerk.

But my gratitude paled compared to my unalloyed joy that Walter and the others were free. It was a day we had yearned for and fought for over so many years. De Klerk had lived up to his promise, and the men were released under no bans; they could speak in the name of the ANC. It was clear that the ban on the organization had effectively expired, a vindication of our long struggle and our resolute adherence to principle.

De Klerk began a systematic dismantling of many of the building blocks of apartheid. He opened South African beaches to people of all colors, and stated that the Reservation of Separate Amenities Act would soon be repealed. Since 1953 this act had enforced what was known as "petty apartheid," segregating parks, theaters, restaurants, buses, libraries, toilets, and other public facilities, according to race. In November, he announced that the National Security Management System, a secret structure set up under P. W. Botha to combat anti-apartheid forces, would be dissolved.

In early December, I was informed that a meeting with de Klerk was set for the twelfth of that month. By this time I was able to consult with my colleagues new and old, and I had meetings at the cottage with my old colleagues, and the leaders of the Mass Democratic Movement and the UDF. I received ANC people from all of the regions, as well as delegates from the UDF and COSATU. One of these young men was Cyril Ramaphosa, the general secretary of the National Union of Mine Workers and one of the ablest of the new generation of leadership. I also had visits from colleagues of mine from Robben Island, including Terror Lekota and Tokyo Sexwale, who stayed to lunch. They are both men with large appetites, and the only complaint I heard about them was from Warrant Officer Swart, who said, "Those fellows will eat us out of house and home!"

With guidance from a number of colleagues, I then drafted a letter to de Klerk not unlike the one I had sent to P. W. Botha. The subject was talks between the government and the ANC. I told the president that the current conflict was draining South Africa's lifeblood and talks were the only solution. I said the ANC would accept no preconditions to talks, especially not the precondition that the government wanted: the suspension of the armed struggle. The government asked for an "honest commitment to peace" and I pointed out that our readiness to negotiate was exactly that.

I told Mr. de Klerk how impressed I was by his emphasis on reconciliation, enunciated in his inaugural address. His words had imbued millions of South Africans and people around the world with the hope that a new South Africa was about to be born. The very first step on the road to reconciliation, I said, was the complete dismantling of apartheid and all the measures used to enforce it.

But I said that the spirit of that speech had not been much in evidence of late. The government's policies were perceived by many as a continuation of apartheid by other means. The government, I said, had spent too much time talking with black homeland leaders and others coopted by the system; these men, I asserted, were the agents of an oppressive past that the mass of black South Africans rejected.

I reiterated my proposal that talks take place in two stages. I told him I fully supported the guidelines the ANC had adopted in the Harare Declaration of 1989, which put the onus on the government to eliminate the obstacles to negotiations that the state itself had created. Those demands included the release of all political prisoners, the lifting of all bans on restricted organizations and persons, the end to the State of Emergency, and the removal of all troops from the townships. I stressed that a mutually agreed-upon cease-fire to end hostilities ought to be the first order of business, for without that, no business could be conducted. The day before our meeting the letter was delivered to Mr. de Klerk.

On the morning of December 13, I was again taken to Tuynhuys. I met de Klerk in the same room where I had had tea with his predecessor. Mr. de Klerk was accompanied by Kobie Coetsee, General Willemse, Dr. Barnard, and his colleague Mike Louw. I congratulated Mr. de Klerk on becoming president and expressed the hope that we would be able to work together. He was extremely cordial and reciprocated these sentiments.

From the first I noticed that Mr. de Klerk listened to what I had to say. This was a novel experience. National Party leaders generally heard what they wanted to hear in discussions with black leaders, but Mr. de Klerk seemed to be making an attempt to truly understand.

One of the issues I emphasized that day was the National Party's recently introduced five-year plan, which contained the concept of "group rights." The idea of "group rights" was that no racial or ethnic group could take precedence over any other. Although they defined "group rights" as a way of protecting the freedom of minorities in a new South Africa, in fact their proposal was a means of preserving white domination. I told Mr. de Klerk that this was unacceptable to the ANC.

I added that it was not in his interest to retain this concept, for it gave the impression that he wanted to modernize apartheid without abandoning it; this was damaging his image and that of the National Party in the eyes of the progressive forces in this country and around the world. An oppressive system cannot be reformed, I said, it must be entirely cast aside. I mentioned an editorial that I had recently read in *Die Burger*, the mouthpiece of the National Party in the Cape, implying that the group rights concept was conceived as an attempt to bring back apartheid through the back door. I told Mr. de Klerk that if that was how his party's paper perceived group rights, how did he think we regarded it? I added that the ANC had not struggled against apartheid for seventy-five years only to yield to a disguised form of it and that if it was his true intention to preserve apartheid through the Trojan horse of group rights, then he did not truly believe in ending apartheid.

Mr. de Klerk, I saw that day, does not react quickly to things. It was a mark of the man that he listened to what I had to say and did not argue with me. "You know," he said, "my aim is no different than yours. Your memo to P. W. Botha said the ANC and the government should work together to deal with white fears of black domination, and the idea of 'group rights' is how we propose to deal with it." I was impressed with this response, but said that the idea of "group rights" did more to increase black fears than allay white ones. De Klerk then said, "We will have to change it, then."

I then brought up the question of my freedom and said that if he expected me to go out to pasture upon my release he was greatly mistaken. I reaffirmed that if I was released into the same conditions under which I had been arrested I would go back to doing precisely those things for which I had been imprisoned. I made the case to him that the best way to move forward was to unban the ANC and all other political organizations, to lift the State of Emergency, to release political prisoners, and to allow the exiles to return. If the government did not unban the ANC, as soon as I was out of prison I would be working for an illegal organization. "Then," I said, "you must simply rearrest me after I walk through those gates."

Again, he listened carefully to what I had to say. My suggestions certainly came as no surprise to him. He said he would take all that I said under consideration, but that he would make no promises. The meeting was an exploratory one and I understood that nothing was going to be resolved that day. But it was extremely useful, for I had taken the measure of Mr. de Klerk just as I did with new prison commanders when I was on Robben Island. I was able to write to our people in Lusaka that Mr. de Klerk seemed to represent a true departure from the National Party politicians of the past. Mr. de Klerk, I said, echoing Mrs. Thatcher's famous description of Mr. Gorbachev, was a man we could do business with.

99

ON FEBRUARY 2, 1990, F. W. de Klerk stood before Parliament to make the traditional opening speech and did something no other South African head of state had ever done: he truly began to dismantle the apartheid system and lay the groundwork for a democratic South Africa. In dramatic fashion, Mr. de Klerk announced the lifting of the bans on the ANC, the PAC, the South African Communist Party, and thirty-one other illegal organizations; the freeing of political prisoners incarcerated for nonviolent activities; the suspension of capital punishment; and the lifting of various restrictions imposed by the State of Emergency. "The time for negotiation has arrived," he said.

It was a breathtaking moment, for in one sweeping action he had virtually normalized the situation in South Africa. Our world had changed overnight. After forty years of persecution and banishment, the ANC was now a legal organization. I and all my comrades could no longer be arrested for being a member of the ANC, for carrying its green, yellow, and black banner, for speaking its name. For the first time in almost thirty years, my picture and my words, and those of all my banned comrades, could freely appear in South African newspapers. The international community applauded de Klerk's bold actions. Amidst all the good news, however, the ANC objected to the fact that Mr. de Klerk had not completely lifted the State of Emergency or ordered the troops out of the townships.

On February 9, seven days after Mr. de Klerk's speech opening Parliament, I was informed that I was again going to Tuynhuys. I arrived at six o'clock in the evening. I met a smiling Mr. de Klerk in his office and as we shook hands, he informed me that he was going to release me from prison the following day. Although the press in South Africa and around the world had been speculating for weeks that my release was imminent, Mr. de Klerk's announcement nevertheless came as a surprise to me. I had not been told that the reason Mr. de Klerk wanted to see me was to tell me that he was making me a free man.

I felt a conflict between my blood and my brain. I deeply wanted to leave prison as soon as I could, but to do so on such short notice would not be wise. I thanked Mr. de Klerk, and then said that at the risk of appearing ungrateful I would prefer to have a week's notice in order that my family and my organization could be prepared for my release. Simply to walk out tomorrow, I said, would cause chaos. I asked Mr. de Klerk to release me a week from that day. After waiting twenty-seven years, I could certainly wait another seven days.

De Klerk was taken aback by my response. Instead of replying, he continued to relate the plan for my release. He said that the government would fly me to Johannesburg and officially release me there. Before he went any further, I told him that I strongly objected to that. I wanted to walk out of the gates of Victor Verster and be able to thank those who looked after me and greet the people of Cape Town. Though I was from Johannesburg, Cape Town had been my home for nearly three decades. I would make my way back to Johannesburg, but when I chose to, not when the government wanted me to. "Once I am free," I said, "I will look after myself."

De Klerk was again nonplused. But this time my objections caused a reaction. He excused himself and left his office to consult with others. After ten minutes he returned with a rather long face and said, "Mr. Mandela, it is too late to change the plan now." I replied that the plan was unacceptable and that I wanted to be released a week hence and at Victor Verster, not Johannesburg. It was a tense moment and, at the time, neither of us saw any irony in a prisoner asking not to be released and his jailer attempting to release him.

De Klerk again excused himself and left the room. After ten minutes he returned with a compromise: yes, I could be released at Victor Verster, but, no, the release could not be postponed. The government had already informed the foreign press that I was to be set free tomorrow and felt they could not renege on that statement. I felt I could not argue with that. In the end, we agreed on the compromise, and Mr. de Klerk poured a tumbler of whisky for each of us to drink in celebration. I raised the glass in a toast, but only pretended to drink; such spirits are too strong for me.

I did not get back to my cottage until shortly before midnight, whereupon I immediately sent word to my colleagues in Cape Town that I was to be released the following day. I managed to get a message to Winnie and I telephoned Walter in Johannesburg. They would all fly in on a chartered plane the next day. That evening, a number of ANC people on what was known as the National Reception Committee came to the cottage to draft a statement that I would make the following day. They left in the early hours of the morning, and despite my excitement, I had no trouble falling asleep.

Part Eleven

———

FREEDOM

100

I AWOKE ON THE DAY of my release after only a few hours' sleep at 4:30 A.M. February 11 was a cloudless, end-of-summer Cape Town day. I did a shortened version of my usual exercise regimen, washed, and ate breakfast. I then telephoned a number of people from the ANC and the UDF in Cape Town to come to the cottage to prepare for my release and work on my speech. The prison doctor came by to give me a brief checkup. I did not dwell on the prospect of my release, but on all the many things I had to do before then. As so often happens in life, the momentousness of an occasion is lost in the welter of a thousand details.

There were numerous matters that had to be discussed and resolved with very little time to do so. A number of comrades from the reception committee, including Cyril Ramaphosa and Trevor Manuel, were at the house bright and early. I wanted initially to address the people of Paarl, who had been very kind to me during my incarceration, but the reception committee was adamant that that would not be a good idea: it would look curious if I gave my first speech to the prosperous white burghers of Paarl. Instead, as planned, I would speak first to the people of Cape Town at the Grand Parade in Cape Town.

One of the first questions to be resolved was where I would spend my first night of freedom. My inclination was to spend the night in the Cape Flats, the bustling black and Coloured townships of Cape Town, in order to show my solidarity with the people. But my colleagues and, later, my wife argued that for security reasons I should stay with Archbishop Desmond Tutu in Bishop's Court, a plush residence in a white suburb. It was not an area where I would have been permitted to live before I went to prison, and I thought it would send the wrong signal to spend my first night of freedom in a posh white area. But the members of the committee explained that Bishop's Court had become multiracial under Tutu's tenure, and symbolized an open, generous nonracialism.

The prison service supplied me with boxes and crates for packing. During my first twenty or so years in prison, I accumulated very few possessions, but in the last few years I had amassed enough property — mainly books and papers — to make up for previous decades. I filled over a dozen crates and boxes.

My actual release time was set for 3 P.M., but Winnie and Walter and the other passengers from the chartered flight from Johannesburg did not arrive until after two. There were already dozens of people at the house, and the entire scene took on the aspect of a celebration. Warrant Officer Swart prepared a final meal for all of us, and I thanked him not only for the food he had provided for the last two years but the companionship. Warrant Officer James Gregory was also there at the house, and I embraced him warmly. In the years that he had looked after me from Pollsmoor through Victor Verster, we had never discussed politics, but our bond was an unspoken one and I would miss his soothing presence. Men like Swart, Gregory, and Warrant Officer Brand reinforced my belief in the essential humanity even of those who had kept me behind bars for the previous twenty-seven and a half years.

There was little time for lengthy farewells. The plan was that Winnie and I would be driven in a car to the front gate of the prison. I had told the authorities that I wanted to be able to say good-bye to the guards and warders who had looked after me and I asked that they and their families wait for me at the front gate, where I would be able to thank them individually.

At a few minutes after three, I was telephoned by a well-known SABC presenter who requested that I get out of the car a few hundred feet before the gate so that they could film me walking toward freedom. This seemed reasonable, and I agreed to do it. This was my first inkling that things might not go as calmly as I had imagined.

By 3:30, I began to get restless, as we were already behind schedule. I told the members of the reception committee that my people had been waiting for me for twenty-seven years and I did not want to keep them waiting any longer. Shortly before four, we left in a small motorcade from the cottage. About a quarter of a mile in front of the gate, the car slowed to a stop and Winnie and I got out and began to walk toward the prison gate.

At first, I could not really make out what was going on in front of us, but when I was within one hundred fifty feet or so, I saw a tremendous commotion and a great crowd of people: hundreds of photographers and television cameras and newspeople as well as several thousand well-wishers. I was astounded and a little bit alarmed. I had truly not expected such a scene; at most, I had imagined that there would be several dozen people, mainly the warders and their families. But this proved to be only the beginning; I realized we had not thoroughly prepared for all that was about to happen.

Within twenty feet or so of the gate, the cameras started clicking, a noise that sounded like some great herd of metallic beasts. Reporters started shouting questions; television crews began crowding in; ANC supporters were yelling and cheering. It was a happy, if slightly disorienting chaos. When a television crew thrust a long, dark, furry object at me, I recoiled slightly, wondering if it were some newfangled weapon developed while I was in prison. Winnie informed me that it was a microphone.

When I was among the crowd I raised my right fist and there was a roar. I had not been able to do that for twenty-seven years and it gave me a surge of strength and joy. We stayed among the crowd for only a few minutes before jumping back into the car for the drive to Cape Town. Although I was pleased to have such a reception, I was greatly vexed by the fact that I did not have a chance to say good-bye to the prison staff. As I finally walked through those gates to enter a car on the other side, I felt — even at the age of seventy-one — that my life was beginning anew. My ten thousand days of imprisonment were over.

Cape Town was thirty-five miles to the southwest, but because of the unexpected crowds at the gate, the driver elected to take a different path to the city. We drove round to the back of the prison, and our convoy took small roads and byways into town. We drove through beautiful green vineyards and manicured farms, and I relished the scenery around me.

The countryside was lush and well cared for, but what surprised me was how many white families were standing beside the road to get a glimpse of our motorcade. They had heard on the radio that we were taking an alternate route. Some, perhaps a dozen, even raised their clenched right fists in what had become the ANC power salute. This astonished me; I was tremendously encouraged by these few brave souls from a conservative farming area who expressed their solidarity. At one point, I stopped and got out of the car to greet and thank one such white family and tell them how inspired I was by their support. It made me think that the South Africa I was returning to was far different from the one I had left.

As we entered the outskirts of the city, I could see people streaming toward the center. The reception committee had organized a rally at the Grand Parade in Cape Town, a great open square that stretched out in front of the old City Hall. I would speak to the crowd from the balcony of that building, which overlooked the entire area. We heard sketchy reports that a great sea of people had been waiting there since morning. The plan was for our motorcade to avoid the crowd and drive around to the back of City Hall, where I would quietly enter the building.

The drive to Cape Town took forty-five minutes, and as we neared the Grand Parade we could see an enormous crowd. The driver was meant to turn right and skirt its edges, but instead, he inexplicably plunged straight into the sea of people. Immediately the crowd surged forward and enveloped the car. We inched forward for a minute or two but were then forced to stop by the sheer press of bodies. People began knocking on the windows, and then on the boot and the bonnet. Inside it sounded like a massive hailstorm. Then people began to jump on the car in their excitement. Others began to shake it and at that moment I began to worry. I felt as though the crowd might very well kill us with their love.

The driver was even more anxious than Winnie and I, and he was clamoring to jump out of the car. I told him to stay calm and remain inside, that others from the cars behind us would come to our rescue. Allan Boesak and others began to attempt to clear a way for our vehicle and push the people off the car, but with little success. We sat inside — it would have been futile to even attempt to open the door, so many people were pressing on it — for more than an hour, imprisoned by thousands of our own supporters. The scheduled beginning of the speech had long passed.

Several dozen marshals eventually came to the rescue and managed slowly to clear an exit path. When we finally broke free, the driver set off at great speed in the opposite direction from City Hall. "Man, where are you going?" I asked him in some agitation. "I don't know!" he said, his voice tense with anxiety. "I've never experienced anything like that before," he said, and then continued driving without any destination in mind.

When he began to calm down I gave him directions to the house of my friend and attorney Dullah Omar, who lived in the Indian area of the city. We could go there, I said, and relax for a few minutes. This appealed to him. Fortunately, Dullah and his family were home, but they were more than a bit surprised to see us. I was a free man for the first time in twenty-seven years, but instead of greeting me, they said with some concern, "Aren't you meant to be at the Grand Parade?"

We were able to sip some cold drinks at Dullah's, but we had only been there a few minutes when Archbishop Tutu telephoned. How he knew we were there I do not know. He was quite distressed and said, "Nelson, you must come back to the Grand Parade immediately. The people are growing restless. If you do not return straightaway I cannot vouch for what will happen. I think there might be an uprising!" I said I would return at once.

Our problem was the driver: he was deeply reluctant to return to the Grand Parade. But I remonstrated with him and soon we were on our way back to City Hall. The building was surrounded by people on all sides, but it was not as dense in the back, and the driver managed to make his way through to the rear entrance. It was almost dusk when I was led up to the top floor of this stately building whose halls had always been filled with shuffling white functionaries. I walked out onto the balcony and saw a boundless sea of people cheering, holding flags and banners, clapping, and laughing.

I raised my fist to the crowd and the crowd responded with an enormous cheer. Those cheers fired me anew with the spirit of the struggle. *"Amandla!"* I called out. *"Ngawethu!"* they responded. *"iAfrika!"* I yelled; *"Mayibuye!"* they answered. Finally, when the crowd had settled down a bit, I took out my speech and then reached into my breast pocket for my glasses. They were not there; I had left them at Victor Verster. I knew Winnie's glasses were a similar prescription and I borrowed hers.

> Friends, comrades and fellow South Africans. I greet you all in the name of peace, democracy and freedom for all! I stand here before you not as a prophet but as a humble servant of you, the people. Your tireless and heroic sacrifices have made it possible for me to be here today. I therefore place the remaining years of my life in your hands.

I spoke from the heart. I wanted first of all to tell the people that I was not a messiah, but an ordinary man who had became a leader because of extraordinary circumstances. I wanted immediately to thank the people all over the world who had campaigned for my release. I thanked the people of Cape Town, and I saluted Oliver Tambo and the African National Congress, Umkhonto we Sizwe, the South African Communist Party, the UDF, the South African Youth Congress, COSATU, the Mass Democratic Movement, the National Union of South African Students, and the Black Sash, a group formed by women that had long been a voice of conscience. I also publicly expressed my gratitude to my wife and family, saying, "I am convinced that [their] pain and suffering was far greater than my own."

I told the crowd in no uncertain terms that apartheid had no future in South Africa, and that the people must not let up their campaign of mass action. "The sight of freedom looming on the horizon should encourage us to redouble our efforts." I felt it was important publicly to explain my talks with the government. "Today," I said, "I wish to report to you that my talks with the government have been aimed at normalizing the political situation in the country. I wish to stress that I myself have at no time entered into negotiations about the future of our country except to insist on a meeting between the ANC and the government."

I said I hoped that a climate conducive to a negotiated settlement could soon be achieved, ending the need for the armed struggle. The steps to achieving such a climate, I said, had been outlined in the ANC's 1989 Harare Declaration. As a condition to real negotiations, I said, the government must immediately end the State of Emergency and free all political prisoners.

I told the people that de Klerk had gone further than any other Nationalist leader to normalize the situation and then, in words that came back to haunt me, I called Mr. de Klerk "a man of integrity." These words were flung back at me many times when Mr. de Klerk seemed not to live up to them.

It was vital for me to show my people and the government that I was unbroken and unbowed, and that the struggle was not over for me but beginning anew in a different form. I affirmed that I was "a loyal and disciplined member of the African National Congress." I encouraged the people to return to the barricades, to intensify the struggle, and we would walk the last mile together.

It was evening by the time my speech was finished, and we were hustled back into our cars for the trip to Bishop's Court. As we entered its pristine environs, I saw hundreds of black faces waiting to greet me. When they saw us, the people burst into song. When I greeted Archbishop Tutu, I enveloped him in a great hug; here was a man who had inspired an entire nation with his words and his courage, who had revived the people's hope during the darkest of times. We were led inside the house where more family and friends met us, but for me, the most wonderful moment was when I was told that I had a telephone call from Stockholm. I knew immediately who it was. Oliver's voice was weak, but unmistakable, and to hear him after all those years filled me with great joy. Oliver was in Sweden recuperating from a debilitating stroke he had suffered in August 1989. We agreed that we would meet as soon as possible.

My dream upon leaving prison was to take a leisurely drive down to the Transkei, and visit my birthplace, the hills and streams where I had played as a boy, and the burial ground of my mother, which I had never seen. But my dream had to be deferred, for I learned very quickly of the extensive plans that the ANC had for me, and none of them involved a relaxing journey to the Transkei.

101

I WAS SCHEDULED to hold a press conference the afternoon after my release, and in the morning I met with a number of my colleagues to talk about scheduling and strategy. A small mountain of telegrams and messages of congratulations had arrived, and I tried to review as many of these as possible. There were telegrams from all around the world, from presidents and prime ministers, but I remember one in particular from a white Cape Town housewife that amused me greatly. It read: "I am very glad that you are free, and that you are back among your friends and family, but your speech yesterday was very boring."

Before I went to prison I never held such a press conference as I did that day. In the old days there were no television cameras, and most ANC press conferences were conducted clandestinely. That afternoon, there were so many journalists, from so many different countries, I did not know whom to speak with. I was pleased to see a high percentage of black journalists among the throng. At the press conference I was once again keen to reassert a number of themes: first, that I was a loyal and disciplined member of the ANC. I was mindful of the fact that the most senior ANC people would be watching my release from abroad, and attempting to gauge my fidelity from a distance. I was aware that they had heard rumors that I had strayed from the organization, that I was compromised, so at every turn I sought to reassure them. When asked what role I would play in the organization, I told the press that I would play whatever role the ANC ordered.

I told the reporters that there was no contradiction between my continuing support for the armed struggle and my advocating negotiations. It was the reality and the threat of the armed struggle that had brought the government to the verge of negotiations. I added that when the state stopped inflicting violence on the ANC, the ANC would reciprocate with peace. Asked about sanctions, I said the ANC could not yet call for the relaxation of sanctions, because the situation that caused sanctions in the first place — the absence of political rights for blacks — was still the status quo. I might be out of jail, I said, but I was not yet free.

I was asked as well about the fears of whites. I knew that people expected me to harbor anger toward whites. But I had none. In prison, my anger toward whites decreased, but my hatred for the system grew. I wanted South Africa to see that I loved even my enemies while I hated the system that turned us against one another.

I wanted to impress upon the reporters the critical role of whites in any new dispensation. I have tried never to lose sight of this. We did not want to destroy the country before we freed it, and to drive the whites away would devastate the nation. I said that there was a middle ground between white fears and black hopes, and we in the ANC would find it. "Whites are fellow South Africans," I said, "and we want them to feel safe and to know that we appreciate the contribution that they have made toward the development of this country." Any man or woman who abandons apartheid will be embraced in our struggle for a democratic, nonracial South Africa; we must do everything we can to persuade our white compatriots that a new, nonracial South Africa will be a better place for all.

From my very first press conference I noticed that journalists were as eager to learn about my personal feelings and relationships as my political thoughts. This was new to me; when I went to prison, a journalist would never have thought of asking questions about one's wife and family, one's emotions, one's most intimate moments. While it was understandable that the press might be interested in these things, I nevertheless found their curiosity difficult to satisfy. I am not and never have been a man who finds it easy to talk about his feelings in public. I was often asked by reporters how it felt to be free, and I did my best to describe the indescribable, and usually failed.

After the press conference, Archbishop Tutu's wife telephoned us from Johannesburg to say that we must fly there straightaway. Winnie and I had hoped to spend a few days in Cape Town relaxing, but the message we were getting was that the people of Johannesburg were getting restless and there might be chaos if I did not return directly. We flew to Johannesburg that evening, but I was informed that there were thousands of people surrounding our old home, 8115 Orlando West, which had been reconstructed, and that it would be unwise to go there. I reluctantly acceded; I yearned to spend my second night of freedom under my own roof. Instead, Winnie and I stayed in the northern suburbs at the home of an ANC supporter.

The following morning we flew by helicopter to the First National Bank Stadium in Soweto. We were able to make an aerial tour of Soweto, the teeming metropolis of matchbox houses, tin shanties, and dirt roads, the mother city of black urban South Africa, the only home I ever knew as a man before I went to prison. While Soweto had grown, and in some places prospered, the overwhelming majority of the people remained dreadfully poor, without electricity or running water, eking out an existence that was shameful in a nation as wealthy as South Africa. In many places, the poverty was far worse than when I went to prison.

We circled over the stadium, overflowing with 120,000 people, and landed in the center. The stadium was so crowded, with people sitting or standing in every inch of space, that it looked as though it would burst. I expressed my delight to be back among them, but I then scolded the people for some of the crippling problems of urban black life. Students, I said, must return to school. Crime must be brought under control. I told them that I had heard of criminals masquerading as freedom fighters, harassing innocent people and setting alight vehicles; these rogues had no place in the struggle. Freedom without civility, freedom without the ability to live in peace, was not true freedom at all.

Today, my return to Soweto fills my heart with joy. At the same time I also return with a deep sense of sadness. Sadness to learn that you are still suffering under an inhuman system. The housing shortage, the schools crisis, unemployment and the crime rate still remain. . . . As proud as I am to be part of the Soweto community, I have been greatly disturbed by the statistics of crime that I read in the newspapers. Although I understand the deprivations our people suffer I must make it clear that the level of crime in the township is unhealthy and must be eliminated as a matter of urgency.

I ended by opening my arms to all South Africans of goodwill and good intentions, saying that "no man or woman who has abandoned apartheid will be excluded from our movement toward a nonracial, united and democratic South Africa based on one-person one-vote on a common voters' roll." That was the ANC's mission, the goal that I had always kept before me during the many lonely years in prison, the goal that I would work toward during the remaining years of my life. It was the dream I cherished when I entered prison at the age of forty-four, but I was no longer a young man, I was seventy-one, and I could not afford to waste any time.

That night, I returned with Winnie to number 8115 in Orlando West. It was only then that I knew in my heart that I had left prison. For me, 8115 was the centerpoint of my world, the place marked with an X in my mental geography. The house had been soundly rebuilt after the fire. When I saw the four-roomed house, I was surprised by how much smaller and humbler it was than I remembered it being. Compared to my cottage at Victor Verster, number 8115 could have been the servants' quarters at the back. But any house in which a man is free is a castle when compared to even the plushest prison.

That night, as happy as I was to be home, I had a sense that what I most wanted and longed for was going to be denied me. I yearned to resume a normal and ordinary life, to pick up some of the old threads from my life as a young man, to be able to go to my office in the morning and return to my family in the evening, to be able to pop out and buy some toothpaste at the pharmacy, to visit in the evening with old friends. These ordinary things are what one misses most in prison, and dreams about doing when one is free. But I quickly realized that such things were not going to be possible. That night, and every night for the next weeks and months, the house was surrounded by hundreds of well-wishers. People sang and danced and called out, and their joy was infectious. These were my people, and I had no right and no desire to deny myself to them. But in giving myself to my people I could see that I was once again taking myself away from my family.

We did not sleep much that night, as the singing continued until the early hours, when members of the ANC and UDF who were guarding the house begged the crowd to remain quiet and allow us to rest. There were many in the ANC who advised me to move to the home a few blocks distant, in Diepkloof extension, that Winnie had built while I was in prison. It was a grand place by Soweto standards, but it was a house that held no meaning or memories for me. Moreover, it was a house that because of its size and expense seemed somehow inappropriate for a leader of the people. I rejected that advice for as long as I could. I wanted not only to live among my people, but like them.

102

MY FIRST RESPONSIBILITY was to report to the leadership of the ANC, and on February 27, when I had been out of prison a little over two weeks, I flew to Lusaka for a meeting of the National Executive Committee. It was a wonderful reunion to be with old comrades whom I had not seen in decades. A number of African heads of state were also in attendance, and I had brief talks with Robert Mugabe of Zimbabwe, Kenneth Kaunda of Zambia, José Eduardo Dos Santos of Angola, Quett Masire of Botswana, Joaquim Chissano of Mozambique, and Yoweri Musaveni of Uganda.

While the members of the executive were pleased that I had been freed, they were also eager to evaluate the man who had been released. I could see the questions in their eyes. Was Mandela the same man who went to prison twenty-seven years before, or was this a different Mandela, a re-formed Mandela? Had he survived or had he been broken? They had heard reports of my conversations with the government and they were rightly concerned. I had not only been out of touch with the situation on the ground — since 1984 I had not even been able to communicate with my colleagues in prison.

I carefully and soberly explained the nature of my talks with the government. I described the demands I had made, and the progress that had been achieved. They had seen the memoranda I had written to Botha and de Klerk, and knew that these documents adhered to ANC policy. I knew that over the previous few years some of the men who had been released had gone to Lusaka and whispered, "Madiba has become soft. He has been bought off by the authorities. He is wearing three-piece suits, drinking wine, and eating fine food." I knew of these whispers, and I intended to refute them. I knew that the best way to disprove them was simply to be direct and honest about everything that I had done.

At that session of the NEC I was elected deputy president of the organization while Alfred Nzo, the organization's secretary-general, was named acting president while Oliver was recuperating. At a press conference after our meeting, I was asked about a suggestion made by Dr. Kaunda, the president of Zambia and a longtime supporter of the Congress, that the ANC should suspend armed operations inside South Africa now that I had been released. I replied that while we valued Mr. Kaunda's wisdom and support, it was too soon to suspend the armed struggle, for we had not yet achieved the goal for which we took up arms; it was not the ANC's job, I said, to help Mr. de Klerk placate his right-wing supporters.

I began a tour of Africa, which included many countries. During the first six months after my release, I spent more time abroad than at home. Nearly everywhere I went there were great enthusiastic crowds so that even if I felt weary the people buoyed me. In Dar es Salaam I was met by a crowd estimated at half a million.

I enjoyed my travels immensely. I wanted to see new — and old — sights, taste different foods, speak with all manner of people. I very quickly had to acclimatize myself to a world radically different from the one I had left. With changes in travel, communication, and mass media, the world had accelerated; things now happened so fast it was sometimes difficult to keep up with them. Winnie tried to get me to slow down, but there was simply too much to do; the organization wanted to make sure we took advantage of the euphoria generated by my release.

In Cairo, the day after a private meeting with the Egyptian president, Hosni Mubarak, I was scheduled to address a large meeting in a local hall. When I arrived, the crowd seemed to be spilling out of the building and there was precious little security. I mentioned to a policeman that I thought he needed reinforcements but he merely shrugged. Winnie and I waited in a room behind the hall, and at the appointed hour, a policeman motioned for me to go in. I told him to escort the rest of my delegation in first because I feared that when I went in there would be pandemonium and they would be cut off. But the policeman urged me to go first, and indeed as soon as I was in the hall, the crowd surged forward and overcame the cordon of policemen. In their enthusiasm, I was jostled and a bit shaken, and at one point I lost my shoe in the general confusion. When things began to calm down a few minutes later, I found that neither my shoe nor my wife could be located. Finally, after nearly half an hour, Winnie was brought onto the stage with me, quite cross that she had been lost. I was not able to even address the crowd, for they were shouting "Mandela! Mandela!" so furiously that I could not be heard above the din, and finally I left, without my shoe and with an uncharacteristically silent wife.

While in Cairo I held a press conference at which I said the ANC was "prepared to consider a cessation of hostilities." This was a signal to the government. Both the ANC and the government were engaged in creating a climate whereby negotiations would succeed. While the ANC was demanding that the government normalize the situation in the country by ending the State of Emergency, releasing all political prisoners, and repealing all apartheid laws, the government was intent on first persuading the ANC to suspend the armed struggle. While we were not yet ready to announce such a suspension, we wanted to provide Mr. de Klerk with enough encouragement to pursue his reformist strategies. We knew that we would eventually suspend the armed struggle, in part to facilitate more serious negotiations and in part to allow Mr. de Klerk to go to his own constituency, the white voters of South Africa, and say, "Look, here are the fruits of my policy."

After my last stop in Africa, I flew to Stockholm to visit Oliver. Seeing my old friend and law partner was the reunion I most looked forward to. Oliver was not well, but when we met we were like two young boys in the veld who took strength from our love for each other. We began by talking of old times, but when we were alone, the first subject he raised was the leadership of the organization. "Nelson," he said, "you must now take over as president of the ANC. I have been merely keeping the job warm for you." I refused, telling him that he had led the organization in exile far better than I ever could have. It was neither fair nor democratic for a transfer to occur in such a manner. "You have been elected by the organization as the president," I said. "Let us wait for an election; then the organization can decide." Oliver protested, but I would not budge. It was a sign of his humility and selflessness that he wanted to appoint me president, but it was not in keeping with the principles of the ANC.

In April 1990, I flew to London to attend a concert at Wembley, held in my honor. Many international artists, most of whom I never knew, were performing and the event was to be televised worldwide. I took advantage of this to thank the world's anti-apartheid forces for the tremendous work they had done in pressing for sanctions, for the release of myself and fellow political prisoners, and for the genuine support and solidarity they had shown the oppressed people of my country.

103

WHEN I EMERGED from prison, Chief Mangosuthu Buthelezi, the head of the Inkatha Freedom Party and the chief minister of KwaZulu, was one of the premier players on the South African political stage. But within ANC circles, he was a far from popular figure. Chief Buthelezi was descended from the great Zulu king Cetywayo, who had defeated the British at the Battle of Isandhlwana in 1879. As a young man, he attended Fort Hare and then joined the ANC Youth League. I saw him as one of the movement's upcoming young leaders. He had become chief minister of the KwaZulu homeland with the tacit support of the ANC, and even his launching of Inkatha as a Zulu cultural organization was unopposed by the organization. But over the years, Chief Buthelezi drifted away from the ANC. Though he resolutely opposed apartheid and refused to allow KwaZulu to become an "independent" homeland as the government wished, he was a thorn in the side of the democratic movement. He opposed the armed struggle. He criticized the 1976 Soweto uprising. He campaigned against international sanctions. He challenged the idea of a unitary state of South Africa. Yet, Chief Buthelezi had consistently called for my release and refused to negotiate with the government until I and other political prisoners were liberated.

Chief Buthelezi was one of the first people I telephoned after my release to thank him for his long-standing support. My inclination was to meet with the chief as soon as possible to try to resolve our differences. During my initial visit to Lusaka, I brought up the idea of such a meeting and it was voted down. While I was at Victor Verster, Walter had been invited by the Zulu king, Goodwill Zwelithini, to visit him in Ulundi, KwaZulu's capital, and I urged him to accept. I thought it was an excellent opportunity to influence the head of one of the most respected and powerful royal families in the country. The visit was tentatively approved by the NEC provided Walter went to the king's palace in Nongoma; it was thought that going to Ulundi would suggest recognition of the authority of the homeland.

When I returned from Lusaka I telephoned both Chief Buthelezi and the king, and explained that Walter would be coming to see the king, not in Ulundi but at Nongoma. The king said he would not accept Walter coming to see him anywhere else but in the capital. "I am the king," he said. "I have invited him to see me in Ulundi, and he has no right to say I will see you elsewhere." "Your Majesty," I said, "we are facing a wall of opposition from our membership who did not want Mr. Sisulu to go to

KwaZulu at all. We managed to get this compromise approved, surely you can bend as well." But he could not, and he refused to see Walter.

Relations deteriorated after this, and in May, I persuaded the ANC of the need for me to make a visit to the king and Buthelezi. The king approved, but a week or so before the visit I received a letter from him saying I must come alone. This proved to be the last straw, and the NEC would not give in to such a demand. I told the king that I could not come unless I was accompanied by my colleagues; the king regarded this as another slight and canceled the visit.

My goal was to forge an independent relationship with the king, separate from my relationship with Chief Buthelezi. The king was the true hereditary leader of the Zulus, who loved and respected him. Fidelity to the king was far more widespread in KwaZulu than allegiance to Inkatha.

In the meantime, Natal became a killing ground. Heavily armed Inkatha supporters had in effect declared war on ANC strongholds across the Natal Midlands region and around Pietermaritzburg. Entire villages were set alight, dozens of people were killed, hundreds were wounded, and thousands became refugees. In March 1990 alone, 230 people lost their lives in this internecine violence. In Natal, Zulu was murdering Zulu, for Inkatha members and ANC partisans are Zulus. In February, only two weeks after my release, I went to Durban and spoke to a crowd of over 100,000 people at King's Park, almost all of whom were Zulus. I pleaded with them to lay down their arms, to take each others' hands in peace: "Take your guns, your knives, and your pangas, and throw them into the sea! Close down the death factories. End this war now!" But my call fell on deaf ears. The fighting and dying continued.

I was so concerned that I was willing to go to great lengths to meet Chief Buthelezi. In March, after one particularly horrifying spasm of violence, I announced on my own that I would meet Chief Buthelezi at a mountain hamlet outside of Pietermaritzburg. On a personal level, my relations with Chief Buthelezi were close and respectful, and I hoped to capitalize on that. But I found that such a meeting was anathema to ANC leaders in Natal. They considered it dangerous and vetoed my meeting. I did go to Pietermaritzburg, where I saw the burned remains of ANC supporters and tried to comfort their grieving families, but I did not see Chief Buthelezi.

104

IN MARCH, after much negotiation within our respective parties, we scheduled our first face-to-face meeting with Mr. de Klerk and the government. These were to be "talks about talks," and the meetings were to begin in early April. But on March 26, in Sebokeng Township, about thirty miles south of Johannesburg, the police opened fire without warning on a crowd of ANC demonstrators, killing twelve and wounding hundreds more, most of them shot in the back as they were fleeing. Police had used live ammunition in dealing with the demonstrators, which was intolerable. The police claimed that their lives were endangered, but many demonstrators were shot in the back and had no weapons. You cannot be in danger from an unarmed man who is running away from you. The right to assemble and demonstrate in support of our just demands was not a favor to be granted by the government at its discretion. This sort of action angered me like no other, and I told the press that every white policeman in South Africa regarded every black person as a military target. After consultation with the NEC, I announced the suspension of our talks and warned Mr. de Klerk that he could not "talk about negotiations on the one hand and murder our people on the other."

But despite the suspension of our official talks, with the approval of the leadership, I met privately with Mr. de Klerk in Cape Town in order to keep up the momentum for negotiations. Our discussions centered primarily on a new date, and we agreed on early May. I brought up the appalling behavior at Sebokeng and the police's unequal treatment of blacks and whites; police used live ammunition with black demonstrators, while they never unsheathed their guns at white right-wing protests.

The government was in no great rush to begin negotiations; they were counting on the euphoria that greeted my release to die down. They wanted to allow time for me to fall on my face and show that the former prisoner hailed as a savior was a highly fallible man who had lost touch with the present situation.

Despite his seemingly progressive actions, Mr. de Klerk was by no means the great emancipator. He was a gradualist, a careful pragmatist. He did not make any of his reforms with the intention of putting himself out of power. He made them for precisely the opposite reason: to ensure power for the Afrikaner in a new dispensation. He was not yet prepared to negotiate the end of white rule.

His goal was to create a system of power-sharing based on group rights, which would preserve a modified form of minority power in South Africa. He was decidedly opposed to majority rule, or "simple majoritarianism" as he sometimes called it, because that would end white domination in a single stroke. We knew early on that the government was fiercely opposed to a winner-takes-all Westminster parliamentary system, and advocated instead a system of proportional representation with built-in structural guarantees for the white minority. Although he was prepared to allow the black majority to vote and create legislation, he wanted to retain a minority veto. From the start I would have no truck with this plan. I described it to Mr. de Klerk as apartheid in disguise, a "loser-takes-all" system.

The Nationalists' long-term strategy to overcome our strength was to build an anti-ANC alliance with the Inkatha Freedom Party and to lure the Coloured Afrikaans-speaking voters of the Cape to a new National Party. From the moment of my release, they began wooing both Buthelezi and the Coloured voters of the Cape. The government attempted to scare the Coloured population into thinking the ANC was anti-Coloured. They supported Chief Buthelezi's desire to retain Zulu power and identity in a new South Africa by preaching to him the doctrine of group rights and federalism.

The first round of talks with the government was held over three days in early May. Our delegation consisted of Walter Sisulu, Joe Slovo, Alfred Nzo, Thabo Mbeki, Ahmed Kathrada, Joe Modise, Ruth Mompati, Archie Gumede, Reverend Beyers Naude, Cheryl Carolus, and myself. The setting was Groote Schuur, the Cape Dutch-style mansion that was the residence of South Africa's first colonial governors, among them Cecil Rhodes. Some of our delegation joked that we were being led into an ambush on the enemy's ground.

But the talks, contrary to expectation, were conducted with seriousness and good humor. Historic enemies who had been fighting each other for three centuries met and shook hands. Many wondered out loud why such discussions had not taken place long before. The government had granted temporary indemnities to Joe Slovo, the general secretary of the Communist Party, and Joe Modise, the commander of MK, and to see these two men shaking hands with the National Party leaders who had demonized them for decades was extraordinary. As Thabo Mbeki later said to reporters, each side had discovered that the other did not have horns.

The very fact of the talks themselves was a significant milestone in the history of our country; as I pointed out, the meeting represented not only what the ANC had been seeking for so many years, but an end to the master/servant relationship that characterized black and white relations in South Africa. We had not come to the meeting as supplicants or petitioners, but as fellow South Africans who merited an equal place at the table.

The first day was more or less a history lesson. I explained to our counterparts that the ANC from its inception in 1912 had always sought negotiations with the government in power. Mr. de Klerk, for his part, suggested that the system of separate development had been conceived as a benign idea, but had not worked in practice. For that, he said, he was sorry, and hoped the negotiations would make amends. It was not an apology for apartheid, but it went further than any other National Party leader ever had.

The primary issue discussed was the definition of political prisoners and political exiles. The government argued for a narrow definition, wanting to restrict the number of our people who would qualify for an indemnity. We argued for the broadest possible definition and said that any person who was convicted of an offense that was politically motivated should qualify for an indemnity. We could not agree on a mutually satisfactory definition of "politically motivated" crimes, and this would be an issue that would bedevil us for quite a while to come.

At the end of the three-day meeting, we agreed on what became known as the Groote Schuur Minute, pledging both sides to a peaceful process of negotiations and committing the government to lifting the State of Emergency, which they shortly did everywhere except for the violence-ridden province of Natal. We agreed to set up a joint working group to resolve the many obstacles that still stood in our way.

When it came to constitutional issues, we told the government we were demanding an elected constituent assembly to draw up a new constitution; we believed that the men and women creating the constitution should be the choice of the people themselves. But before the election of an assembly, it was necessary to have an interim government that could oversee the transition until a new government was elected. The government could not be both player and referee, as it was now. We advocated the creation of a multiparty negotiating conference to set up the interim government and set out the guiding principles for the functioning of a constituent assembly.

105

ALTHOUGH I HAD WANTED to journey to Qunu immediately after my release from prison, it was not until April that I was able to go. I could not pick up and leave whenever I wanted; security had to be arranged, as well as speeches prepared for local organizations. By April, the ANC and General Bantu Holomisa, the military leader of the Transkei and an ANC loyalist, had arranged for a visit. But what was foremost in my mind and heart was paying my respects to my mother's grave.

I went first to Qunu and the site where my mother was buried. Her grave was simple and unadorned, covered only by a few stones and some upturned bricks, no different from the other graves at Qunu. I find it difficult to describe my feelings: I felt regret that I had been unable to be with her when she died, remorse that I had not been able to look after her properly during her life, and a longing for what might have been had I chosen to live my life differently.

In seeing my village again after so many years, I was greatly struck by what had changed and what had not. When I had been young, the people of Qunu were not political at all; they were unaware of the struggle for African rights. People accepted life as it was and did not dream of changing it. But when I returned I heard the schoolchildren of Qunu singing songs about Oliver Tambo and Umkhonto we Sizwe, and I marveled at how knowledge of the struggle had by then seeped into every corner of African society.

What had endured was the warmth and simplicity of the community, which took me back to my days as a boy. But what disturbed me was that the villagers seemed as poor if not poorer than they had been then. Most people still lived in simple huts with dirt floors, with no electricity and no running water. When I was young, the village was tidy, the water pure, and the grass green and unsullied as far as the eye could see. Kraals were swept, the topsoil was conserved, fields were neatly divided. But now the village was unswept, the water polluted, and the countryside littered with plastic bags and wrappers. We had not known of plastic when I was a boy, and though it surely improved life in some ways, its presence in Qunu appeared to me to be a kind of blight. Pride in the community seemed to have vanished.

That month, I had another homecoming: I returned to Robben Island in order to persuade twenty-five MK political prisoners to accept the government's offer of amnesty and leave the island. Though I had left the island eight years before, my memories of prison were still fresh and untinged by nostalgia. After all the years of being visited by others, it was a curious sensation to be a visitor on Robben Island.

But that day, I did not have much opportunity to sight-see for I met immediately with the men protesting the government offer of amnesty. They maintained that they would leave only after a victory on the battlefield, not the negotiating table. They were fiercely opposed to this particular settlement, in which they had to enumerate their crimes before receiving indemnity. They accused the ANC of retreating from the Harare Declaration demand for an unconditional, blanket amnesty covering political prisoners and exiles. One man said, "Madiba, I have been fighting the government all my life, and now I have to ask for a pardon from them."

I could sympathize with their arguments, but they were being unrealistic. Every soldier would like to defeat his enemy on the field, but in this case, such a victory was out of reach. The struggle was now at the negotiating table. I argued that they were not advancing the cause by remaining in jail. They could be of greater service outside than inside. In the end, they agreed to accept the government's offer.

In early June, I was scheduled to leave on a six-week tour of Europe and North America. Before going, I met privately with Mr. de Klerk, who wanted to discuss the issue of sanctions. Based on the changes he had made in South Africa, he asked me to mute the call for the continuation of international sanctions. While we were mindful of what Mr. de Klerk had done, in our view sanctions remained the best lever to force him to do more. I was aware that the European Community and the States were inclined to relax sanctions based on Mr. de Klerk's reforms. I explained to Mr. de Klerk that we could not tell our supporters to relax sanctions until he had completely dismantled apartheid and a transitional government was in place. While he was disappointed at my response, he was not surprised.

The first leg of the trip took Winnie and me to Paris, where we were treated in very grand style by François Mitterrand and his charming wife, Danielle, a longtime ANC supporter. This was not my first trip to the European mainland, but I was still entranced by the beauties of the Old World. Although I do not want to stint on the loveliness of the City of Light, the most important event that occurred while I was in France was that the government announced the suspension of the State of Emergency. I was pleased, but well aware that they had taken this action while I was in Europe in order to undermine my call for sanctions.

After stops in Switzerland, Italy, and the Netherlands, I went to England, where I spent two days visiting with Oliver and Adelaide. My next stop was the United States, but I would be returning to England on my way back to South Africa, which is when I was scheduled to meet with Mrs. Thatcher. As a courtesy, however, I phoned her before I left, and Mrs. Thatcher proceeded to give me a stern but well-meaning lecture: she said she had been following my travels and noting how many events I attended each day. "Mr. Mandela, before we discuss any issues," she said, "I must warn you that your schedule is too heavy. You must cut it in half. Even a man half your age would have trouble meeting the demands that are being made on you. If you keep this up, you will not come out of America alive. That is my advice to you."

I had read about New York City since I was a young man, and finally to see it from the bottom of its great glass-and-concrete canyons while millions upon millions of pieces of ticker tape came floating down was a breathtaking experience. It was reported that as many as a million people personally witnessed our procession through the city, and to see the support and enthusiasm they gave to the anti-apartheid struggle was truly humbling. I had always read that New York was a hard-hearted place, but I felt the very opposite of that on my first full day in the city.

The following day I went up to Harlem, an area that had assumed legendary proportions in my mind since the 1950s when I watched young men in Soweto emulate the fashions of Harlem dandies. Harlem, as my wife said, was the Soweto of America. I spoke to a great crowd at Yankee Stadium, telling them that an unbreakable umbilical cord connected black South Africans and black Americans, for we were together children of Africa. There was a kinship between the two, I said, that had been inspired by such great Americans as W. E. B. Du Bois, Marcus Garvey, and Martin Luther King Jr. As a young man, I idolized the Brown Bomber, Joe Louis, who took on not only his opponents in the ring but racists outside of it. In prison, I followed the struggle of black Americans against racism, discrimination, and economic inequality. To us, Harlem symbolized the strength of resistance and the beauty of black pride. This was brought home to me by a young man I had seen the previous day who wore a T-shirt that read, "BLACK BY NATURE, PROUD BY CHOICE." We were linked by nature, I said, but we were proud of each other by choice.

After journeying to Memphis and Boston, I went to Washington to address a joint session of Congress and attend a private meeting with President Bush. I thanked the U.S. Congress for its anti-apartheid legislation and said the new South Africa hoped to live up to the values that created the two chambers before which I spoke. I said that as freedom fighters we could not have known of such men as George Washington, Abraham Lincoln, and Thomas Jefferson "and not been moved to act as they were moved to act." I also delivered a strong message on sanctions, for I knew that the Bush administration felt it was time to loosen them. I urged Congress not to do so.

Even before meeting Mr. Bush, I had formed a positive impression of him, for he was the first world leader to telephone me with congratulations after I left prison. From that point on, President Bush included me on his short list of world leaders whom he briefed on important issues. In person, he was just as warm and thoughtful, though we differed markedly on the issues of the armed struggle and sanctions. He was a man with whom one could disagree and then shake hands.

From the United States I proceeded to Canada, where I had a meeting with Prime Minister Mulroney and also addressed their Parliament. We were due to go to Ireland next, and before crossing the Atlantic, our plane, a small jet, stopped for refueling in a remote place above the Arctic Circle called Goose Bay. I felt like having a walk in the brisk air, and as I was strolling on the tarmac, I noticed some people standing by the airport fence. I asked a Canadian official who they were. Eskimos, he said.

In my seventy-two years on earth I had never met an Innuit and never imagined that I would. I headed over to that fence and found a dozen or so young people, in their late teens, who had come out to the airport because they had heard our plane was going to stop there. I had read about the Innuit (the name "Eskimo" was given to them by the colonists) as a boy, and the impression I received from the racist colonialist texts was that they were a backward culture.

But in talking with these bright young people, I learned that they had watched my release on television and were familiar with events in South Africa. "Viva ANC!" one of them said. The Innuit are an aboriginal people historically mistreated by a white settler population; there were parallels between the plights of black South Africans and the Innuit people. What struck me so forcefully was how small the planet had become during my decades in prison; it was amazing to me that a teenaged Innuit living at the roof of the world could watch the release of a political prisoner on the southern tip of Africa. Television had shrunk the world, and had in the process become a great weapon for eradicating ignorance and promoting democracy.

After Dublin, I went to London, where I had a three-hour meeting with Mrs. Thatcher. Standing out in the cold talking with the young Innuits had given me a chill. On the day I was to see Mrs. Thatcher it was wintry and raining, and as we were leaving, Winnie told me I must take a raincoat. We were already in the lobby of the hotel, and if I went back for my coat we would be late. I am a stickler about punctuality, not only because I think it is a sign of respect to the person you are meeting but in order to combat the Western stereotype of Africans as being notoriously tardy. I told Winnie we did not have time, and instead I stood out in the rain signing autographs for some children. By the time I got to Mrs. Thatcher I was feeling poorly, and I was later diagnosed as having a mild case of pneumonia.

But it did not interfere with our meeting, except that she chided me like a schoolmarm for not taking her advice and cutting down on my schedule. Even though Mrs. Thatcher was on the opposite side of the ANC on many issues, such as sanctions, she was always a forthright and solicitous lady. In our meeting that day, though, I could not make the slightest bit of headway with her on the question of sanctions.

106

WHEN I RETURNED to South Africa in July, after brief trips to Uganda, Kenya, and Mozambique, I requested a meeting with Mr. de

Klerk. Violence in the country was worsening; the death toll of 1990 was already over fifteen hundred, more than all the political deaths of the previous year. After conferring with my colleagues, I felt it necessary to speed up the process of normalization. Our country was bleeding to death, and we had to move ahead faster.

Mr. de Klerk's lifting the State of Emergency in June seemed to set the stage for a resumption of talks, but in July, government security forces arrested about forty members of the ANC, including Mac Maharaj, Pravin Gordhan, Siphiwe Nyanda, and Billy Nair, claiming that they were part of a Communist Party plot called Operation Vula to overthrow the government. De Klerk called for an urgent meeting with me and read to me from documents he claimed had been confiscated in the raid. I was taken aback because I knew nothing about it.

After the meeting I wanted an explanation and called Joe Slovo. Joe explained that the passages read by Mr. de Klerk had been taken out of context and that Vula was a moribund operation. But the government was intent on using this discovery to try to pry the ANC from the SACP and keep Joe Slovo out of the negotiations. I went back to Mr. de Klerk and told him that he had been misled by his own police and that we had no intention of parting ways with the SACP or dropping Joe Slovo from our negotiating team.

In the middle of July, shortly before a scheduled meeting of the National Executive Committee, Joe Slovo came to me privately with a proposition. He suggested we voluntarily suspend the armed struggle in order to create the right climate to move the negotiation process forward. Mr. de Klerk, he said, needed to show his supporters that his policy had brought benefits to the country. My first reaction was negative; I did not think the time was ripe.

But the more I thought about it, the more I realized that we had to take the initiative and this was the best way to do it. I also recognized that Joe, whose credentials as a radical were above dispute, was precisely the right person to make the proposal. He could not be accused of being a dupe of the government or of having gone soft. The following day I told Joe that if he brought up the idea in the NEC, I would support him.

When Joe raised the idea in the NEC the next day there were some who firmly objected, claiming that we were giving de Klerk's supporters a reward but not our own people. But I defended the proposal, saying the purpose of the armed struggle was always to bring the government to the negotiating table, and now we had done so. I argued that the suspension could always be withdrawn, but it was necessary to show our good faith. After several hours, our view prevailed.

This was a controversial move within the ANC. Although MK was not active, the aura of the armed struggle had great meaning for many people. Even when cited merely as a rhetorical device, the armed struggle was a sign that we were actively fighting the enemy. As a result, it had a popularity out of proportion to what it had achieved on the ground.

On August 6, in Pretoria, the ANC and the government signed what became known as the Pretoria Minute, in which we agreed to suspend the armed struggle. As I was to say over and over to our followers: we suspended armed action, we did not terminate the armed struggle. The agreement also set forth target dates for the release of political prisoners and the granting of certain types of indemnity. The process of indemnity was scheduled to be completed by May 1991, and the government also agreed to review the Internal Security Act.

Of all the issues that hindered the peace process, none was more devastating and frustrating than the escalation of violence in the country. We had all hoped that as negotiations got under way, violence would decrease. But in fact the opposite happened. The police and security forces were making very few arrests. People in the townships were accusing them of aiding and abetting the violence. It was becoming more and more clear to me that there was connivance on the part of the security forces. Many of the incidents indicated to me that the police, rather than quelling violence, were fomenting it.

Over the next few months, I visited townships all across the violence-racked Vaal Triangle south of Johannesburg, comforting wounded people and grieving families. Over and over again, I heard the same story: the police and the defense force were destabilizing the area. I was told of the police confiscating weapons one day in one area, and then Inkatha forces attacking our people with those stolen weapons the next day. We heard stories of the police escorting Inkatha members to meetings and on their attacks.

In September, I gave a speech in which I said there was a hidden hand behind the violence and suggested that there was a mysterious "Third Force," which consisted of renegade men from the security forces who were attempting to disrupt the negotiations. I could not say who the members of the Third Force were, for I did not know them myself, but I was certain that they existed and that they were murderously effective in their targeting of the ANC and the liberation struggle.

I came to this conclusion after becoming personally involved in two specific incidents. In July of 1990, the ANC received information that hostel dwellers belonging to the Inkatha Freedom Party were planning a major attack on ANC members in Sebokeng Township in the Vaal Triangle on July 22. Through our attorneys, we notified the minister of law and order, the commissioner of police, and the regional commissioner, warning them of the impending attacks and urging them to take the proper action. We asked the police to prevent armed Inkatha members from entering the township to attend an Inkatha rally.

On July 22, busloads of armed Inkatha members, escorted by police vehicles, entered Sebokeng in broad daylight. A rally was held, after which the armed men went on a rampage, murdering approximately thirty people in a dreadful and grisly attack. I visited the area the next day and witnessed scenes I have never before seen and never hope to see again. At the morgue were bodies of people who had been hacked to death; a woman had both her breasts cut off with a machete. Whoever these killers were, they were animals.

I requested a meeting with Mr. de Klerk the following day. When I saw him, I angrily demanded an explanation. "You were warned in advance," I told him, "and yet did nothing. Why is that? Why is it that there have been no arrests? Why have the police sat on their hands?" I then told him that in any other nation where there was a tragedy of this magnitude, when more than thirty people were slain, the head of state would make some statement of condolence, yet he had not uttered a word. He had no reply to what I said. I asked de Klerk to furnish me with an explanation, and he never did.

The second incident occurred in November, when a group of Inkatha members entered a squatter camp known as Zonkizizwe (Zulu for "the place where all nations are welcome") outside the city of Germiston, east of Johannesburg, and drove ANC people out, killing a number of them in the process. Inkatha members then proceeded to occupy the abandoned shacks and confiscate all the property. Residents of the area said that the Inkatha members were accompanied by the police. Once again, in the wake of this tragedy, the police and the government took no action. Black life in South Africa had never been so cheap.

Again, I met with Mr. de Klerk and his minister of law and order, Adriaan Vlok. Again, I asked Mr. de Klerk why no action by the police had been taken in the aftermath of these crimes. I said the attackers could easily be found because they were now occupying the shacks of the people they had killed. Mr. de Klerk asked Mr. Vlok for an explanation and then Vlok, in a rather rude tone, asked me on whose property the shacks were located, the implication being that these people were squatters and therefore had no rights. In fact, I told him, the land had been made available to these people by the local authorities. His attitude was like that of many Afrikaners who simply believed that black tribes had been killing each other since time immemorial. Mr. de Klerk again told me he would investigate and respond, but never did.

* * *

During this time, the government took another action that added fuel to the flames. It introduced a regulation permitting Zulus to carry so-called traditional weapons to political rallies and meetings in Natal and elsewhere. These weapons, assegais, which are spears, and knobkerries, wooden sticks with a heavy wooden head, are actual weapons with which Inkatha members killed ANC members. This gave me grave doubts about Mr. de Klerk's peaceful intentions.

Those opposed to negotiations benefited from the violence, which always seemed to flare up when the government and the ANC were moving toward an agreement. These forces sought to ignite a war between the ANC and Inkatha, and I believe many members of Inkatha connived at this as well. Many in the government, including Mr. de Klerk, chose to look the other way or ignore what they knew was going on under their noses. We had no doubts that men at the highest levels of the police and the security forces were aiding the Third Force. These suspicions were later confirmed by newspaper reports disclosing that the South African police had secretly funded Inkatha.

As the violence continued to spiral, I began to have second thoughts about the suspension of the armed struggle. Many of the people in the ANC were restive, and in September, at a press conference, I said that the continuing violence might necessitate taking up arms once more. The situation looked very grim, and any understanding that had been achieved with the government seemed lost.

107

IN DECEMBER OF 1990 Oliver returned to South Africa after being in exile from his native land for three decades. It was wonderful to have him near. He returned for an ANC consultative conference in Johannesburg, which was attended by over fifteen hundred delegates from forty-five different regions, home and abroad.

At the meeting, I spoke in tribute to Oliver as the man who had led the ANC during its darkest hours and never let the flame go out. Now, he had ushered us to the brink of a future that looked bright and hopeful. During the twenty-seven years that I was in prison, it was Oliver who saved the ANC, and then built it into an international organization with power and influence. He took up the reins when most of its leaders were either in prison or in exile. He was a soldier, a diplomat, a statesman.

Although I criticized the government for its orchestrated campaign of counterrevolutionary activities, it was Oliver's address that created a storm.

He opened the meeting with a controversial speech in which he called for our sanctions policy to be reevaluated. The ANC, he maintained, faced "international marginalization" unless it took the initiative to deescalate sanctions. The European Community had already begun to scale back sanctions. The countries in the West, particularly the United Kingdom and the United States, wanted to reward Mr. de Klerk for his reforms, believing that this would encourage him to go further. We felt this was the wrong strategy, but we had to recognize international realities.

Although Oliver's speech had been discussed and approved by the NEC, his proposal was met with indignation by ANC militants, who insisted that sanctions must be maintained unchanged. The conference decided to retain the sanctions policy as it was.

I myself was the target of complaints by those who charged that the negotiators were out of touch with the grass roots and that we spent more time with National Party leaders than our own people. I was also criticized at the conference for engaging in "personal diplomacy" and not keeping the rank-and-file of the organization informed. As a leader of a mass organization, one must listen to the people, and I agreed that we had been remiss in keeping the entire organization informed about the course of the negotiations. But I also knew the delicacy of our talks with the government; any agreements that we arrived at depended in part on their confidentiality. Although I accepted the criticism, I believed we had no alternative but to proceed on the same course. I knew that I had to be more inclusive, brief more people as to our progress, and I proceeded with that in mind.

Each day, each weekend, the newspapers were filled with fresh reports of new and bloody violence in our communities and townships. It was clear that violence was the number one issue in the country. In many communities in Natal and on the Reef around Johannesburg, a poisonous mixture of crime, political rivalries, police brutality, and shadowy death squads made life brutish and untenable. As long as the violence was not dealt with, the progress to a new dispensation would remain uneven and uncertain.

To try to arrest the spiral of violence, I contacted Chief Buthelezi to arrange a meeting. We met at Durban's Royal Hotel in January. Chief Buthelezi spoke first to assembled delegates and media and in the process opened old wounds rather than healing them. He catalogued the verbal attacks the ANC had made on him and criticized the ANC's negotiating demands. When it was my turn to speak, I chose not to respond to his remarks but to thank him for his efforts over many years to secure my release from prison. I cited our long relationship and underlined the many matters that united our two organizations rather than divided us.

Progress was made during our private talks, and Chief Buthelezi and I signed an agreement that contained a code of conduct covering the behavior of our two organizations. It was a fair accord, and I suspect that if it had been implemented it would indeed have helped to staunch the bloodletting. But as far as I could tell, Inkatha never made any effort to implement the accord, and there were violations as well on our own side.

The violence continued between our two organizations. Each month people were dying by the hundreds. In March, Inkatha members launched an attack in Alexandra Township north of Johannesburg in which forty-five people were killed over three days of fighting. Again, no one was arrested.

I could not sit idly by as the violence continued, and I sought another meeting with Chief Buthelezi. In April I went down to Durban and we again made strong statements and signed another agreement. But again, the ink was no sooner dry than it was drenched in blood. I was more convinced than ever that the government was behind much of the violence and the violence was impeding the negotiations. Mr. de Klerk's failure to respond put our own relationship in jeopardy.

In April, at a two-day meeting of the National Executive Committee, I discussed my doubts about Mr. de Klerk. The NEC believed that the government was behind the violence and that the violence was upsetting the climate for negotiations. In an open letter to the government, we called for the dismissal of Magnus Malan, the minister of defense, and Adriaan Vlok, the minister of law and order; the banning of the carrying of traditional weapons in public; the phasing out of the migrant-worker hostels, where so many Inkatha members lived in the townships around Johannesburg; the dismantling of secret government counterinsurgency units; and the appointment of an independent commission to probe complaints of misconduct on the part of the security forces.

We gave the government until May to meet our demands. Mr. de Klerk responded by calling for a multiparty conference on violence to be held in May, but I replied that this was pointless since the government knew precisely what it had to do to end the violence. In May, we announced the suspension of talks with the government.

In July 1991, the ANC held its first annual conference inside South Africa in thirty years. The conference was attended by 2,244 voting delegates who were democratically elected at ANC branches at home and abroad. At the conference I was elected president of the ANC without opposition. Cyril Ramaphosa was elected secretary-general, evidence that the torch was being passed from an older generation of leadership to a younger one. Cyril, whom I met only upon my release from prison, was a worthy successor to a long line of notable ANC leaders. He was probably the most accomplished negotiator in the ranks of the ANC, a skill he honed as secretary-general of the National Union of Mine Workers.

In my speech I expressed my appreciation for the great honor that had been bestowed on me, and spoke of how difficult it would be to follow in the large footsteps of my predecessor, Oliver Tambo. Though we were then at loggerheads with the government, negotiations in and of themselves, I said, constituted a victory. The mere fact that the government was engaged in negotiations at all was a sign that they did not have the strength to sustain apartheid. I reiterated that the process would not be smooth, as we were dealing with politicians who do not want to negotiate themselves out of power. "The point which must be clearly understood is that the struggle is not over, and negotiations themselves are a theater of struggle, subject to advances and reverses as any other form of struggle."

But negotiations could not wait. It was never in our interest to prolong the agony of apartheid for any reason. It was necessary, I said, to create a transitional government as soon as possible.

The conference underlined one of the most important and demanding tasks before the ANC: to transform an illegal underground liberation movement to a legal mass political party. For thirty years, the ANC had functioned clandestinely in South Africa; those habits and techniques were deeply ingrained. We had to reconstruct an entire organization, from the smallest local branch to the national executive. And we had to do so in a matter of months during a period of extraordinary change.

A large part of the ANC and Communist Party leadership had been in exile. Most of them had returned for the conference in July. They were unfamiliar with present-day South Africa; it was a newfound land for them as well as me. There was, however, an extraordinary crop of young leaders of the United Democratic Front and COSATU who had remained in the country, who knew the political situation in a way that we did not. These organizations had in some measure been surrogates for the ANC inside South Africa during the 1980s. The ANC had to integrate these men and women into the organization as well.

We faced not only logistical problems but philosophical ones. It is a relatively simple proposition to keep a movement together when you are fighting against a common enemy. But creating a policy when that enemy is across the negotiating table is another matter altogether. In the new ANC, we had to integrate not only many different groups, but many different points of view. We needed to unite the organization around the idea of the negotiations.

In the first seventeen months of legal activity, the ANC had recruited

700,000 members. This was an impressive number, but there was no room for complacency. A proportionately low number of these members were from the rural areas, the regions where the ANC had historically been weakest. At the same time, the National Party was throwing open its doors to nonwhites and was busily recruiting disaffected Coloureds and Indians.

Ever since my release from prison, the state had continued its campaign to discredit my wife. After the alleged kidnapping of four youths who were staying in the Diepkloof house and the death of one of them, Winnie had first been vilified by a whispering campaign and was then charged with four counts of kidnapping and one of assault. The continuing aspersions cast on her character were such that both Winnie and I were eager for her to have her day in court and prove her innocence of the charges.

My wife's formal trial began in February in the Rand Supreme Court in Johannesburg. I attended the trial on the first day, as did many senior figures in the ANC, and I continued to attend as often as I could. I did this both to support my wife and to show my belief in her innocence. She was ably defended by George Bizos, who attempted to demonstrate that Winnie had no involvement with either the kidnappings or the beatings.

After three and a half months, the court found her guilty of kidnapping charges and being an accessory to assault. The judge, however, acknowledged that she had not taken part in any assault herself. She was sentenced to six years in prison, but was released on bail pending her appeal. As far as I was concerned, verdict or no verdict, her innocence was not in doubt.

108

ON DECEMBER 20, 1991, after more than a year and a half of talks about talks, the real talks began: CODESA — the Convention for a Democratic South Africa — represented the first formal negotiations forum between the government, the ANC, and other South African parties. All of our previous bilateral discussions had been laying the groundwork for these talks, which took place at the World Trade Centre, a modern exhibition center near Jan Smuts Airport in Johannesburg. CODESA comprised eighteen delegations covering the gamut of South African politics, plus observers from the United Nations, the Commonwealth, the European Community, and the Organization of African Unity. It was the widest cross section of political groups ever gathered in one place in South Africa.

The opening of such talks was an historic occasion, certainly the most important constitutional convention since that of 1909 when the former British colonies of the Cape and Natal and the Boer republics of the Transvaal and the Orange Free State agreed to form a single union. Of course, that convention was not a tribute to democracy but a betrayal of it, for none of the representatives there that day were black. In 1991, the majority of them were.

Our planning delegation, led by Cyril Ramaphosa, and including Joe Slovo and Valli Moosa, had been engaged in weekly discussions with the government on the issues of elections, the constitution, a constituent assembly, and a transitional government. Delegates from twenty different parties including the homeland governments had already agreed on the ground rules for the convention.

The optimism at the opening of the talks could not be dampened even by a few spoilers. The PAC decided to boycott the talks, accusing the ANC and the National Party of conspiring together to set up a multiracial government. This occurred despite the formation, a month before, of the Patriotic Front, an alliance of the ANC, the PAC, and the Azanian People's Organization around a declaration of common goals. The PAC feared democratic elections because they knew such a vote would expose their meager popular support. Chief Buthelezi also boycotted the talks on the grounds that he was not permitted three delegations: for Inkatha, the KwaZulu government, and King Zwelithini. We argued that the king should be above politics, and that if he were included then every tribe in South Africa should be able to send their paramount chief.

There was not only a sense of history at the World Trade Centre, but of self-reliance. Unlike the negotiations preceding new dispensations in African states like Zimbabwe and Angola, which required outside mediators, we in South Africa were settling our differences among ourselves. Mr. de Klerk talked about the need for a transitional, "power-sharing" government on a democratic basis. The National Party's chief delegate to the talks, Dawie de Villiers, even offered an apology for apartheid.

In my own opening remarks, I said that with the dawn of CODESA, progress in South Africa had at last become irreversible. Governments, I said, derive their authority and legitimacy from the consent of the governed, and we had assembled to create such a legitimate authority. I said that CODESA marked the beginning of the road to an elected assembly that would write a new constitution, and I did not see any reason why an election for such a constituent assembly could not occur in 1992. I called on the government to usher in an interim government of national unity to supervise such an election, control the state media and the military, and generally oversee the transition to a new, nonracial, democratic South Africa.

On the convention's first day, the lion's share of the participating parties, including the National Party and the ANC, endorsed a Declaration of Intent, which committed all parties to support an undivided South Africa whose supreme law would be a constitution safeguarded by an independent judiciary. The country's legal system would guarantee equality before the law, and a bill of rights would be drawn up to protect civil liberties. In short, there would be a multiparty democracy based on universal adult suffrage on a common voters' roll. As far as we were concerned, this was the minimum acceptable constitutional threshold for a new South Africa. Inkatha refused to sign on the grounds that the phrase an "undivided" South Africa implied that a federal system was off-limits.

The convention created five working groups that would meet in early 1992 to prepare the way for the second round of CODESA scheduled for May 1992. The groups would explore the question of creating a free political climate, the future of the homelands, the restructuring of the South African Broadcasting Corporation, the examination of various constitutional principles such as federalism, and the creation and installation of an interim government. The parties agreed that decisions would be taken by "sufficient consensus," which was never defined, but in practice meant an agreement between the government and the ANC and a majority of the other parties.

The first day of CODESA 1 was uneventful, until it came to a close. The night before the convention I had been negotiating with Mr. de Klerk on the telephone until after eight in the evening. Mr. de Klerk asked me whether I would agree to permit him to be the final speaker the next day. Though I was scheduled to give the concluding remarks, I told him that I would take up the matter with our National Executive Committee. I did so that evening, and despite their misgivings, I persuaded them to permit Mr. de Klerk to have the last word. I did not see the issue as a vital one, and I was prepared to do Mr. de Klerk the favor.

At the end of the session, all seemed well; I spoke about the importance of the talks and I was followed by Mr. de Klerk. He proceeded to underline the historic significance of the occasion and discuss the need for overcoming mutual distrust. But then Mr. de Klerk did a curious thing. He began to attack the ANC for not adhering to the agreements that we had made with the government. He began to speak to us like a schoolmaster admonishing a naughty child. He berated the ANC for failing to disclose the location of arms caches and then rebuked us for maintaining a "private army," Umkhonto we Sizwe, in violation of the National Peace Accord of September 1991. In intemperate language, he questioned whether the ANC was honorable enough to abide by any agreements it signed.

This was more than I could tolerate and I would now be damned if I would permit Mr. de Klerk to have the last word. When he finished, the meeting was meant to be over. But the room had grown very quiet; instead of allowing the session to end, I walked to the podium. I could not let his remarks go unchallenged. My voice betrayed my anger.

I am gravely concerned about the behavior of Mr. de Klerk today. He has launched an attack on the ANC and in doing so he has been less than frank. Even the head of an illegitimate, discredited minority regime, as his is, has certain moral standards to uphold. He has no excuse just because he is the head of such a discredited regime not to uphold moral standards. . . . If a man can come to a conference of this nature and play the type of politics he has played — very few people would like to deal with such a man.

The members of the government persuaded us to allow them to speak last. They were very keen to say the last word here. It is now clear why they did so. He has abused his position, because he hoped that I would not respond. He was completely mistaken. I respond now.

I said it was unacceptable for Mr. de Klerk to speak to us in such language. I reiterated that it was the ANC, not the government, that started the initiative of peace discussions, and it was the government, not the ANC, that time and again failed to live up to its agreements. I had told Mr. de Klerk before that it served no useful purpose to attack the ANC publicly, yet he continued to do so. I noted that we had suspended our armed struggle to show our commitment to peace, yet the government was still colluding with those waging war. We told him that we would turn in our weapons only when we were a part of the government collecting those weapons.

I added that it was apparent the government had a double agenda. They were using the negotiations not to achieve peace, but to score their own petty political gains. Even while negotiating, they were secretly funding covert organizations that committed violence against us. I mentioned the recent revelations about million-rand payoffs to Inkatha that Mr. de Klerk claimed not to have known about. I stated that if a man in his position "doesn't know about such things, then he is not fit to be the head of government."

I knew I had been harsh, but I did not want to capsize the whole ship of negotiations, and I ended on a more conciliatory note.

I ask him to place his cards on the table face upwards. Let us work together openly. Let there be no secret agendas. Let him not persuade us that he would be the last speaker because he wants to abuse that privilege and attack us in the hope that we won't respond. I am prepared to work with him in spite of all his mistakes.

CODESA convened the following day for its final session, and both Mr. de Klerk and I took pains to show that no irreparable harm had been done. At the beginning of the session, he and I publicly shook hands and said we would work together. But much trust had been lost, and the negotiations were now in a state of disarray.

Six weeks after the opening of CODESA 1, the National Party contested an important by-election in Potchefstroom, a conservative university town in the Transvaal, traditionally the party's stronghold. In a stunning upset, the Nationalists were defeated by the candidate of the right-wing Conservative Party. The Conservatives resolutely opposed the government's policy of negotiations with the ANC, and were composed mainly of Afrikaners who felt that Mr. de Klerk was giving away the store. The election result seemed to cast doubt on Mr. de Klerk's policy of reform and negotiations. The National Party was alarmed; these were their own voters in their own heartland rejecting their policies.

Mr. de Klerk decided to gamble. He announced that as a result of the by-election in Potchefstroom he would call a nationwide all-white referendum for March 17 so that the people of South Africa could vote on his reform policy and on negotiations with the ANC. He stated that if the referendum was defeated, he would resign from office. The referendum asked a plain and direct question of all white voters over the age of eighteen: "Do you support the continuation of the reform process which the state president began on 2 February 1990 which is aimed at a new constitution through negotiation?"

The ANC opposed the referendum on the principle that it was a vote that excluded all nonwhites. At the same time, we were realistic: we certainly did not want white voters to rebuff Mr. de Klerk's efforts to pursue negotiations. Though we disdained the election on principle, we urged whites to vote yes. We saw such a vote as a signal of support for negotiations, not necessarily for de Klerk.

We watched Mr. de Klerk's campaign with interest and some consternation. He and the National Party conducted a sophisticated, expensive, American-style political campaign accompanied by extensive newspaper and television advertisements, bumper stickers, and colorful rallies. We saw this as a dress rehearsal for the campaign Mr. de Klerk would wage against us.

In the end, 69 percent of the white voters supported negotiations, giving de Klerk a great victory. He felt vindicated; I think the margin even swelled his head a bit. His hand was strengthened, and as a result, the Nationalists toughened their negotiating positions. This was a dangerous strategy.

109

ON APRIL 13, 1992, at a press conference in Johannesburg, flanked by my two oldest friends and comrades, Walter and Oliver, I announced my separation from my wife. The situation had grown so difficult that I felt that it was in the best interests of all concerned — the ANC, the family, and Winnie — that we part. Although I discussed the matter with the ANC, the separation itself was made for personal reasons.

I read the following statement.

> The relationship between myself and my wife, Comrade Nomzamo Winnie Mandela, has become the subject of much media speculation. I am issuing this statement to clarify the position and in the hope that it will bring an end to further conjecture.
>
> Comrade Nomzamo and myself contracted our marriage at a critical time in the struggle for liberation in our country. Owing to the pressures of our shared commitment to the ANC and the struggle to end apartheid, we were unable to enjoy a normal family life. Despite these pressures our love for each other and our devotion to our marriage grew and intensified. . . .
>
> During the two decades I spent on Robben Island she was an indispensable pillar of support and comfort to myself personally. . . . Comrade Nomzamo accepted the onerous burden of raising our children on her own. . . . She endured the persecutions heaped upon her by the Government with exemplary fortitude and never wavered from her commitment to the freedom struggle. Her tenacity reinforced my personal respect, love and growing affection. It also attracted the admiration of the world at large. My love for her remains undiminished.
>
> However, in view of the tensions that have arisen owing to differences between ourselves on a number of issues in recent months, we have mutually agreed that a separation would be best for each of us. My action was not prompted by the current allegations being made against her in the media. . . . Comrade Nomzamo has and can continue to rely on my unstinting support during these trying moments in her life.
>
> I shall personally never regret the life Comrade Nomzamo and I tried to share together. Circumstances beyond our control however dictated it should be otherwise. I part from my wife with no recrimi-

nations. I embrace her with all the love and affection I have nursed for her inside and outside prison from the moment I first met her. Ladies and gentlemen, I hope you will appreciate the pain I have gone through.

Perhaps I was blinded to certain things because of the pain I felt for not being able to fulfill my role as a husband to my wife and a father to my children. But just as I am convinced that my wife's life while I was in prison was more difficult than mine, my own return was also more difficult for her than it was for me. She married a man who soon left her; that man became a myth; and then that myth returned home and proved to be just a man after all.

As I later said at my daughter Zindzi's wedding, it seems to be the destiny of freedom fighters to have unstable personal lives. When your life is the struggle, as mine was, there is little room left for family. That has always been my greatest regret, and the most painful aspect of the choice I made.

"We watched our children growing without our guidance," I said at the wedding, "and when we did come out [of prison], my children said, 'We thought we had a father and one day he'd come back. But to our dismay, our father came back and he left us alone because he has now become the father of the nation.' " To be the father of a nation is a great honor, but to be the father of a family is a greater joy. But it was a joy I had far too little of.

110

IN MAY OF 1992, after a four-month interruption, the multiparty conference held its second plenary session at the World Trade Centre. Known as CODESA 2, the talks had been prepared by secret meetings between negotiators from both the ANC and the government as well as talks between the ANC and other parties. These meetings culminated in a final session between me and Mr. de Klerk the day before the opening of CODESA 2, the first time the two of us had met since before CODESA 1.

Only days before CODESA 2 was to begin, the government was hit by two scandals. The first involved the revelation of massive corruption and bribery at the Department of Development Aid, which was responsible for improving black life in the homelands, and the second was the implication of high government security officials in the 1985 murder of four UDF activists, the best known of whom was Matthew Goniwe. These revelations were added to the recent evidence implicating the police in murders in Natal and suspicions that the Department of Military Intelligence was conducting covert operations against the ANC. These two scandals coming together undermined the credibility of the government and strengthened our hand.

Over the previous months, the government had made numerous proposals that fell by the wayside. Most of them, like the idea of a rotating presidency, sought to preserve their power. But through negotiations over the past months, the ANC and government teams had put together a tentative agreement involving a two-stage transitional period to a fully democratic South Africa. In the first stage, a multiparty "transitional executive council" would be appointed from the CODESA delegations to function as a temporary government in order to "level the playing field" for all parties and create an interim constitution. In the second stage, general elections would be held for a constituent assembly and legislature in which all political parties winning 5 percent or more of the vote would participate in the cabinet. Half the members of the assembly would be elected on a national basis and half on a regional one, and the assembly would be empowered both to write a new constitution and to pass legislation. An independent commission would preside over the election and make sure it was free and fair.

Yet there were many matters on which the ANC and the government could not reach agreement, such as the percentage of voting necessary in the assembly to decide constitutional issues and to agree on a bill of rights. Only days before CODESA 2, the government proposed a second body, a senate, composed of regional representatives, as a way of insuring a minority veto. They also proposed that before all this, CODESA 2 first agree on an interim constitution, which would take months to draw up.

All of this bargaining was going on behind the scenes and by the time CODESA 2 opened on May 15, 1992, prospects for agreement looked bleak. What we disagreed about was threatening all that we had agreed upon. Mr. de Klerk and I had not managed to find a consensus on most of the outstanding issues. The government seemed prepared to wait indefinitely; their thinking was that the longer we waited, the more support we would lose.

The convention was deadlocked at the end of the first day. At that time, the two judges presiding over the talks told Mr. de Klerk and me to meet that evening to attempt to find a compromise. We did meet that night over coffee, and though we did not find a way out of the impasse, we agreed that the negotiations must not founder. "The whole of South Africa and the world is looking at you and me," I told Mr. de Klerk. "Let us save the peace process. Let us reach some kind of agreement. Let us at least fix a date for the next round of talks." We decided that we would each speak the following day in a spirit of constructive compromise.

The next afternoon we spoke in the reverse order that we had agreed to at CODESA 1: Mr. de Klerk first and I last. In his remarks, Mr. de Klerk insisted that the National Party did not seek a "minority veto," but that he did want a system of "checks and balances" so that the majority would not be able "to misuse its power." Although this certainly sounded to me like outright opposition to the idea of majority rule, when I spoke after Mr. de Klerk, I merely said we needed to work in a constructive manner and dispel the tensions around the negotiations.

Despite our attempts to put a positive face on the matter, the convention ended the second day in a stalemate. The impasse, as I saw it, was caused by the National Party's continuing reluctance to submit their fate to the will of the majority. They simply could not cross that hurdle.

Ultimately, CODESA 2 broke down on four fundamental issues: the government's insistence on an unacceptably high percentage of votes in the assembly to approve the constitution (essentially a backdoor veto); entrenched regional powers that would be binding on a future constitution; an undemocratic and unelected senate that had veto power over legislation from the main chamber; and a determination to make an interim constitution negotiated by the convention into a permanent constitution.

These were all difficult issues, but not insoluble ones, and I was determined not to let the deadlock at CODESA 2 subvert the negotiation process. The government and the ANC agreed to continue bilateral talks to work toward a solution. But, then, other matters intruded to render this impossible.

With negotiations stalled, the ANC and its allies agreed on a policy of "rolling mass action," which would display to the government the extent of our support around the country and show that the people of South Africa were not prepared to wait forever for their freedom. The mass action consisted of strikes, demonstrations, and boycotts. The date chosen for the start of mass action was June 16, 1992, the anniversary of the 1976 Soweto revolt, and the campaign was meant to culminate in a two-day national strike set for August 3 and 4.

But before that happened, another event occurred that drove the ANC and the government even further apart. On the night of June 17, 1992, a heavily armed force of Inkatha members secretly raided the Vaal township of Boipatong and killed forty-six people. Most of the dead were women and children. It was the fourth mass killing of ANC people that week. People across the country were horrified by the violence and charged the government with complicity. The police did nothing to stop the criminals and nothing to find them; no arrests were made, no investigation begun. Mr. de Klerk said nothing. I found this to be the last straw, and my patience snapped. The government was blocking the negotiations and at the same time waging a covert war against our people. Why then were we continuing to talk with them?

Four days after the murders, I addressed a crowd of twenty thousand angry ANC supporters and told them I had instructed ANC secretary-general Cyril Ramaphosa to suspend direct dealings with the government. I also announced an urgent meeting of the National Executive Committee to examine our options. It was as if we had returned to the dark days of Sharpeville. I likened the behavior of the National Party to the Nazis in Germany, and publicly warned de Klerk that if he sought to impose new measures to restrict demonstrations or free expression, the ANC would launch a nationwide defiance campaign with myself as the first volunteer.

At the rally, I saw signs that read, "MANDELA, GIVE US GUNS" and "VICTORY THROUGH BATTLE NOT TALK." I understood such sentiments; the people were frustrated. They saw no positive results of the negotiations. They were beginning to think that the only way to overthrow apartheid was through the barrel of a gun. After Boipatong, there were those in the NEC who said, "Why did we abandon the armed struggle? We should abandon negotiations instead; they will never advance us to our goal." I was initially sympathetic to this group of hardliners, but gradually realized that there was no alternative to the process. It was what I had been urging for so many years, and I would not turn my back on negotiations. But it was time to cool things down. Mass action in this case was a middle course between armed struggle and negotiations. The people must have an outlet for their anger and frustration, and a mass action campaign was the best way to channel those emotions.

When we informed the government that we were suspending talks, we sent Mr. de Klerk a memo outlining the reasons for our withdrawal. In addition to resolving the constitutional deadlocks at CODESA 2, we demanded that the people responsible for the violence be tracked down and brought to justice and that some mechanism be found for fencing in and policing the hostels, the seedbeds of so much violence. Mr. de Klerk sent us back a memo asking for a face-to-face meeting with me, which we rebuffed. I felt such a meeting would suggest that we had something to talk about, and at the time we did not.

*   *   *

The mass action campaign culminated in a general strike on August 3 and 4 in support of the ANC's negotiation demands and in protest against state-supported violence. More than four million workers stayed home in what was the largest political strike in South African history. The centerpiece of the strike was a march of one hundred thousand people to the Union Buildings in Pretoria, the imposing seat of the South African government, where we held an enormous outdoor rally on the great lawn in front of the buildings. I told the crowd that we one day would occupy these buildings as the first democratically elected government of South Africa.

In the face of this mass action, Mr. de Klerk said that if the ANC made the country ungovernable, the government might be forced to consider some unpleasant options. I warned Mr. de Klerk that any antidemocratic actions would have serious repercussions. It was because of such threats, I said, that it was absolutely critical to set up a transitional government.

Inspired by the success of the mass action campaign, a group within the ANC decided to march on Bisho, the capital of the Ciskei homeland in the eastern Cape, a bantustan led by Brigadier General Oupa Gqozo. The Ciskei had a history of repression against the ANC and in 1991 Brigadier Gqozo had declared a State of Emergency in the Ciskei to curtail what he called ANC-sponsored terrorism. On the morning of September 7, 1992, seventy thousand protesters set out on a march to Bisho's main stadium. When a group of marchers attempted to run through an opening in a fence and take a different path to town, the poorly trained homeland troops opened fire on the marchers and killed twenty-nine people, wounding over two hundred. Now Bisho joined Boipatong as a byword for brutality.

Like the old proverb that says that the darkest hour is before the dawn, the tragedy of Bisho led to a new opening in the negotiations. I met with Mr. de Klerk in order to find common ground and avoid a repetition of another tragedy like Bisho. Our respective negotiators began meeting regularly. Both sides were making a good-faith effort to get the negotiations back on track, and on September 26, Mr. de Klerk and I met for an official summit.

On that day, Mr. de Klerk and I signed the Record of Understanding, an agreement which set the mold for all the negotiations that followed. The agreement established an independent body to review police actions, created a mechanism to fence in the hostels, and banned the display of "traditional weapons" at rallies. But the real importance of the Record of

Understanding was that it broke the constitutional deadlock of CODESA 2. The government finally agreed to accept a single, elected constitutional assembly, which would adopt a new constitution and serve as a transitional legislature for the new government. All that was left to negotiate was a date for the election of the assembly and the percentage of majorities necessary for it to reach its decisions. We were now aligned on the basic framework that would take the country into a democratic future.

The Record of Understanding prompted Inkatha to announce its withdrawal from all negotiations involving the government and the ANC. The agreement infuriated Chief Buthelezi, who severed relations with the NP and formed an alliance with a group of discredited homeland leaders and white right-wing parties solely concerned with obtaining an Afrikaner homeland. Chief Buthelezi called for the abolition of the Record of Understanding, the ending of CODESA, and the disbanding of Umkhonto we Sizwe.

Just as Joe Slovo had taken the initiative concerning the suspension of the armed struggle, he again took the lead in making another controversial proposal: a government of national unity. In October, Joe published a paper in which he wrote that negotiations with the government were not armistice talks in which we could dictate terms to a defeated enemy. It would probably take years for the ANC to control the levers of government, even after an election. An ANC government would still require much of the present civil service to run the country. Joe proposed a "sunset clause" providing for a government of national unity that would include power-sharing with the National Party for a fixed period of time, an amnesty for security officers, and the honoring of contracts of civil servants. "Power-sharing" was a debased term within the ANC, considered a code-phrase for the government's quest for a minority veto. But in this context it merely meant that the National Party would be part of any popularly elected government provided it polled enough votes.

After much discussion, I supported Joe's proposal and it was endorsed by the National Executive Committee on November 18. The NEC agreed to support power-sharing, provided the minority parties did not have a veto. In December, we began a new round of secret bilateral talks with the government. These were held over a five-day period at a game lodge in the bush. The talks proved to be critical, for they built on the foundation established in the Record of Understanding. At this bush meeting we agreed in principle on a five-year government of national unity in which all parties polling over 5 percent in a general election would be proportionally represented in the cabinet. After five years, the government of national unity would become a simple majority-rule government. In February, the ANC and the government announced an agreement in principle on the five-year government of national unity, a multiparty cabinet, and the creation of a transitional executive council. Elections would be held as early as the end of 1993.

111

I HAVE ALWAYS BELIEVED that a man should have a home within sight of the house where he was born. After being released from prison, I set about plans to build a country house for myself in Qunu. By the fall of 1993, the house was complete. It was based on the floor plan of the house I lived in at Victor Verster. People often commented on this, but the answer was simple: the Victor Verster house was the first spacious and comfortable home I ever stayed in, and I liked it very much. I was familiar with its dimensions, so at Qunu I would not have to wander in the night looking for the kitchen.

In April, I was at my house in the Transkei on a brief holiday. On the morning of April 10, I had just gone outside to greet some members of the Transkei police rugby team when my housekeeper ran out and informed me of an urgent telephone call. She was weeping. I excused myself from the young men and learned from a colleague that Chris Hani, the secretary-general of the SACP, the former chief of staff of MK, and one of the most popular figures in the ANC, had been shot at point-blank range in front of his home in Boksburg, Johannesburg, a mostly white working-class suburb that Chris was seeking to integrate.

Chris's death was a blow to me personally and to the movement. He was a soldier and patriot, for whom no task was too small. He was a great hero among the youth of South Africa; a man who spoke their language and to whom they listened. If anyone could mobilize the unruly youth behind a negotiated solution, it was Chris. South Africa was now deprived of one of its greatest sons, a man who would have been invaluable in transforming the country into a new nation.

The country was fragile. There were concerns that Hani's death might trigger a racial war, with the youth deciding that their hero should become a martyr for whom they would lay down their own lives. I first flew via helicopter to pay my respects to Chris's eighty-two-year-old father in Sabalele, a tiny, dusty town in the Cofimvaba district in the Transkei, a place well known to me because it was the home region of the Matanzima family. As I arrived in this village with no running water or electricity, I marveled at how this poor and tiny village could produce a man like Chris Hani, a man who stirred the entire nation with his passion and ability. His concern for the rural poor came from his childhood in Sabalele, for his roots were deep and true, and he never lost them. Chris's father spoke eloquently of the pain of losing a son, but with satisfaction that he had died in the struggle.

Upon my return to Johannesburg I learned that the police had arrested a member of the militant right-wing Afrikaner Weerstandsbeweging (AWB), a Polish immigrant to South Africa who had been captured after a courageous Afrikaner woman had phoned the police with the killer's license plate number. The murder was an act of mad desperation, an attempt to derail the negotiations process. I was asked to speak on the SABC that night to address the nation. In this instance, it was the ANC, not the government, that sought to calm the nation.

I said that the process of peace and negotiations could not be halted. With all the authority at my command, I said, "I appeal to all our people to remain calm and to honor the memory of Chris Hani by remaining a disciplined force for peace."

> Tonight I am reaching out to every single South African, black and white, from the very depths of my being. A white man, full of prejudice and hate, came to our country and committed a deed so foul that our whole nation now teeters on the brink of disaster. A white woman, of Afrikaner origin, risked her life so that we may know, and bring to justice this assassin. . . . Now is the time for all South Africans to stand together against those who, from any quarter, wish to destroy what Chris Hani gave his life for — the freedom of all of us.

The assassination of Chris was an attempt by white supremacists to arrest the inevitable. They preferred that the country descend into civil war rather than have majority rule by peaceful means.

We adopted a strategy to deal with our own constituency in the ANC. In order to forestall outbreaks of retaliatory violence, we arranged a week-long series of mass rallies and demonstrations throughout the country. This would give people a means of expressing their frustration without resorting to violence. Mr. de Klerk and I spoke privately and agreed that we would not let Hani's murder derail the negotiations.

We learned within days that a member of the Conservative Party, Clive Derby-Lewis, had been arrested in connection with the murder. More confirmation of a Third Force. It was Chris himself who had criticized a recent theft of weapons from an air force base; preliminary police reports suggested that the gun that killed him had come from that stockpile.

Exactly two weeks later, there was another significant passing. This one did not shake the nation as Chris's had, but it shook me. Oliver had not been well for a long time, but the stroke that killed him occurred suddenly and without warning. His wife Adelaide phoned me early in the morning and I rushed to Oliver's bedside. I did not have a chance to say a proper good-bye, for he was already gone.

In Plato's allegory of the metals, the philosopher classifies men into groups of gold, silver, and lead. Oliver was pure gold; there was gold in his intellectual brilliance, gold in his warmth and humanity, gold in his tolerance and generosity, gold in his unfailing loyalty and self-sacrifice. As much as I respected him as a leader, that is how much I loved him as a man.

Though we had been apart for all the years that I was in prison, Oliver was never far from my thoughts. In many ways, even though we were separated, I kept up a lifelong conversation with him in my head. Perhaps that is why I felt so bereft when he died. I felt, as I told one colleague, like the loneliest man in the world. It was as though he had been snatched away from me just as we had finally been reunited. When I looked at him in his casket, it was as if a part of myself had died.

Though we were not yet in power, I wanted Oliver to have a state funeral, and that is what the ANC gave him. At a mass rally at a stadium in Soweto, hundreds of dignitaries from foreign governments gathered to pay their respects to the man who kept the ANC alive during its years of exile. MK troops marched in his honor and a twenty-one-gun salute was given at his graveside. Oliver had lived to see the prisoners released and the exiles return, but he had not lived to cast his vote in a free and democratic South Africa. That was what remained to be accomplished.

112

ALTHOUGH FEW PEOPLE will remember June 3, 1993, it was a landmark in South African history. On that day, after months of negotiations at the World Trade Centre, the multiparty forum voted to set a date for the country's first national, nonracial, one-person-one-vote election: April 27, 1994. For the first time in South African history, the black majority would go to the polls to elect their own leaders. The agreement was that voters would elect four hundred representatives to a constituent assembly, which would both write a new constitution and serve as a parliament. After convening, the first order of business for the assembly would be to elect a president.

The talks had reconvened in April. This time, the twenty-six parties included Inkatha, the Pan Africanist Congress, and the Conservative Party. We had been pressing the government to establish a date for months, and they had been stalling. But now the date was written in stone.

A month later, in July, the multiparty forum agreed on a first draft of an interim constitution. It provided for a bicameral parliament with a four-hundred-member national assembly elected by proportional representation from national and regional party lists and a senate elected indirectly by regional legislatures. Elections to regional legislatures would take place at the same time as national elections, and the regional bodies could draw up their own constitutions consistent with the national constitution.

Chief Buthelezi wanted a constitution drawn up before the election and walked out in protest against the setting of an election date before a constitution was finalized. A second draft interim constitution in August gave greater powers to the regions, but this did not placate either Chief Buthelezi or the Conservative Party. The Conservative Party described the resolutions as hostile to Afrikaner interests. A group called the Afrikaner Volksfront, led by General Constand Viljoen, a former chief of the South African Defense Force, was formed to unite conservative white organizations around the idea of a *volkstaat,* a white homeland.

Just after midnight on November 18, an interim constitution was approved by a plenary session of the multiparty conference. The government and the ANC had cleared the remaining hurdles. The new cabinet would be composed of those winning more than 5 percent of the vote and would make decisions by consensus, rather than the two-thirds majority proposed by the government; national elections would not take place until 1999, so that the government of national unity would serve for five years; and finally, the government gave way on our insistence on a single ballot paper for the election, rather than separate ballots for national and provincial legislatures. Two ballot papers would only confuse a majority of voters, most of whom would be voting for the first time in their lives. In the period leading up to the election, a Transitional Executive Council with members from each party would ensure the right climate for the elections. In effect, the TEC would be the government between December 22 and the election on April 27. An Independent Electoral Commission with extensive powers would be responsible for the administration of the election. We were truly on the threshold of a new era.

I have never cared very much for personal prizes. A man does not become a freedom fighter in the hope of winning awards, but when I was notified that I had won the 1993 Nobel Peace Prize jointly with Mr. de Klerk, I was deeply moved. The Nobel Peace Prize had a special meaning to me because of its involvement with South African history.

I was the third South African since the end of the Second World War to be so honored by the Nobel committee. Chief Albert Luthuli was awarded the prize in 1960. The second was Archbishop Desmond Tutu, who selflessly fought the evils of racism during the most terrible days of apartheid.

The award was a tribute to all South Africans and especially to those who had fought in the struggle; I would accept the award on their behalf. But the Nobel award was one I never thought about. Even during the bleakest years on Robben Island, Amnesty International would not campaign for us on the grounds that we had pursued an armed struggle, and their organization would not represent anyone who had embraced violence. It was for that reason that I assumed the Nobel committee would never consider the man who had started Umkhonto we Sizwe for the peace prize.

I had tremendous respect for the nations of Norway and Sweden. In the 1950s and 1960s, when we went to Western governments seeking contributions to the ANC, we were turned down flat. But in Norway and Sweden, we were greeted with open arms, and given assistance and scholarships and money for legal defense and humanitarian aid for political prisoners.

I used my speech in Norway not only to thank the Nobel committee and sketch out a vision of a future South Africa that was just and equitable, but to pay tribute to my fellow laureate, Mr. F. W. de Klerk.

> He had the courage to admit that a terrible wrong had been done to our country and people through the imposition of the system of apartheid. He had the foresight to understand and accept that all the people of South Africa must, through negotiations and as equal participants in the process, together determine what they want to make of their future.

I was often asked how could I accept the award jointly with Mr. de Klerk after I had criticized him so severely. Although I would not take back my criticisms, I could say that he had made a genuine and indispensable contribution to the peace process. I never sought to undermine Mr. de Klerk, for the practical reason that the weaker he was, the weaker the negotiations process. To make peace with an enemy one must work with that enemy, and that enemy becomes one's partner.

Although the official campaign for the national assembly was not scheduled to begin until February 1994, we started to campaign in earnest after the new constitution was ratified. That did not give us a head start; the National Party began its campaign the day they released me from prison.

Although the polls showed the ANC with a healthy margin, we never took victory for granted. I counseled everyone against overoptimism. We had all read dozens of accounts of parties favored to win who came in second. We faced an experienced, well-organized, and well-financed rival.

Our campaign was under the capable leadership of Popo Molefe, Terror Lekota, and Ketso Gordhan, all veteran UDF activists adept at mass mobilization. The task was a formidable one. We estimated that there would be over twenty million people going to the polls, most of them voting for the first time. Many of our voters were illiterate, and were likely to be intimidated by the mere idea of voting. According to the Independent Electoral Commission, there would be ten thousand polling stations around the country. We sought to train over one hundred thousand people to assist with voter education.

The first stage of our election effort was what was known as People's Forums. ANC candidates would travel all over the country and hold meetings in towns and villages in order to listen to the hopes and fears, the ideas and complaints, of our people. The People's Forums were similar to the town meetings that candidate Bill Clinton held in America on his way to the presidency. The forums were parliaments of the people, not unlike the meetings of chiefs at the Great Place that I witnessed as a boy.

I reveled in the People's Forums. I began in Natal in November, and then went to the PWV area, the northern Transvaal, and the Orange Free State. I attended as many as three or four forums in a day. The people themselves enjoyed them immensely. No one had ever come to solicit their opinion on what should be done in their own country.

After incorporating the suggestions from the forums, we traveled the country delivering our message to the people. Some in the ANC wanted to make the campaign simply a liberation election, and tell the people: Vote for us because we set you free. We decided instead to offer them a vision of the South Africa we hoped to create. We wanted people to vote for the ANC not just because we had fought apartheid for eighty years, but because we were best qualified to bring about the kind of South Africa they hoped to live in. I felt that our campaign should be about the future, not the past.

The ANC drafted a 150-page document known as the Reconstruction and Development Program, which outlined our plan to create jobs through public works; to build a million new houses with electricity and flush toilets; to extend primary health care and ten years of free education to all South Africans; to redistribute land through a land claims court; and to end the value-added tax on basic foodstuffs. We were also committed to extensive affirmative action measures in both the private and public sectors. This document was translated into a simpler manifesto called "A Better Life for All," which in turn became the ANC's campaign slogan.

Just as we told the people what we would do, I felt we must also tell them what we could not do. Many people felt life would change overnight after a free and democratic election, but that would be far from the case. Often, I said to crowds, "Do not expect to be driving a Mercedes the day after the election or swimming in your own backyard pool." I told our supporters, "Life will not change dramatically, except that you will have increased your self-esteem and become a citizen in your own land. You must have patience. You might have to wait five years for results to show." I challenged them; I did not patronize them: "If you want to continue living in poverty without clothes and food," I told them, "then go and drink in the shebeens. But if you want better things, you must work hard. We cannot do it all for you; you must do it yourselves."

I told white audiences that we needed them and did not want them to leave the country. They were South Africans just like ourselves and this was their land, too. I would not mince words about the horrors of apartheid, but I said, over and over, that we should forget the past and concentrate on building a better future for all.

Each rally was also designed to teach people how to vote. The ballot itself was a long, narrow piece of paper with the parties listed in descending order to the left, and then the symbol of the party and a picture of its leader to the right. Voters were to place an X in the box next to the party of their choice. I would tell audiences, "On election day, look down your ballot and when you see the face of a young and handsome man, mark an X."

113

THE ROAD TO FREEDOM was far from smooth. Although the Transitional Executive Council began functioning in the new year, some parties opted out. Inkatha rejected participation in the election and gave itself over to the politics of resistance. King Zwelithini, supported by Chief Buthelezi, called for an autonomous and sovereign KwaZulu, and discouraged everyone in his province from voting. The white right called the elections a betrayal and clamored for a *volkstaat,* yet they still had not proposed where it would be located or how it would work. There was no magisterial district in all of South Africa where whites constituted a majority of residents.

February 12, 1994, was the deadline for registration of all parties, and on that day, Inkatha, the Conservative Party, and the Afrikaner Volksfront failed to sign. The government of the Bophuthatswana homeland also refused to participate and resisted reincorporation into a united South Africa. I was disturbed that these important groups were choosing not to participate. To bring them on board, we proposed certain significant compromises: we agreed to the use of double ballots for provincial and national legislatures; guarantees of greater provincial powers; the re-naming of Natal province as KwaZulu/Natal; and the affirmation that a principle of "internal" self-determination would be included in the con-stitution for groups sharing a common cultural and language heritage.

I arranged to meet Chief Buthelezi in Durban on March 1. "I will go down on my knees to beg those who want to drag our country into bloodshed," I told a rally before this meeting. Chief Buthelezi agreed to provisionally register for the elections in exchange for a promise to subject our differences over constitutional issues to international medi-ation. To this I gladly assented. Before the final registration deadline, General Viljoen also registered under a new party known as the Freedom Front.

Though Lucas Mangope, the president of Bophuthatswana, had chosen to keep his homeland out of the election, the tide of events soon altered the situation. I spoke to him on a number of occasions urging him to let his people decide, but he would not listen. Those who wanted to partic-ipate launched mass demonstrations and strikes, which soon spread to the Bophuthatswana civil service. The radio and television networks went off the air. On the streets of Mafikeng, battles broke out between the homeland police and striking workers and students. Mangope called in military help from his white right-wing allies. Soon, his own forces de-serted him and he was ousted in a coup in early March. A few weeks later, Brigadier Gqozo in the Ciskei capitulated and asked South Africa to take over the homeland.

Violence in Natal worsened. Inkatha supporters were blocking our efforts to campaign in Natal. Fifteen ANC election workers were shot and hacked to death after putting up ANC posters. In March, Judge Johann Kriegler reported to me and Mr. de Klerk that because of the lack of cooperation from the KwaZulu government, free elections could not be held there without direct political intervention. To demonstrate our strength in Natal, the ANC held a mass march through the center of Durban. Then Inkatha attempted to do the same in Johannesburg, with dire results.

On March 28, thousands of Inkatha members, brandishing spears and knobkerries, marched through Johannesburg to a rally in the center of town. At the same time, an armed Inkatha group attempted to enter Shell House, the ANC headquarters, but were repulsed by armed guards. Shots by unidentified gunmen were also fired in the city center, and altogether fifty-three people died. It was a grisly spectacle that made South Africa appear as if it was on the brink of internal war. Inkatha was attempting to postpone the election, but neither Mr. de Klerk nor I would budge. That day was sacrosanct.

I had agreed to international mediation, and on April 13 a delegation arrived led by Lord Carrington, the former British foreign secretary, and Henry Kissinger, the former American secretary of state. But when Inkatha was informed that the election date was not subject to mediation, they refused to see the mediators, who left without talking to anyone. Now Chief Buthelezi knew the election would take place no matter what. On April 19, barely a week before the election, Chief Buthelezi accepted the offer of a constitutional role for the Zulu monarchy and agreed to participate.

Ten days before the vote, Mr. de Klerk and I held our single television debate. I had been a fair debater at Fort Hare, and in my early years in the organization I had engaged in many impassioned debates on the platform. On Robben Island, we had honed our debating skills while we chipped away at limestone. I was confident, but the day before, we held a mock debate in which the journalist Allister Sparks ably performed as Mr. de Klerk. Too ably, according to my campaign advisers, for they chided me for speaking too slowly and not aggressively enough.

When the time came for the actual debate, however, I attacked the National Party quite firmly. I accused the National Party of fanning race hatred between Coloureds and Africans in the Cape by distributing an inflammatory comic book that said the ANC's slogan was "Kill a Coloured, kill a farmer." "There is no organization in this country as divisive as the new National Party," I declared. When Mr. de Klerk criticized the ANC's plan to spend billions of dollars on housing and social programs, I scolded him, saying he was alarmed that we would have to devote so many of our resources to blacks.

But as the debate was nearing an end, I felt I had been too harsh with the man who would be my partner in a government of national unity. In summation, I said, "The exchanges between Mr. de Klerk and me should not obscure one important fact. I think we are a shining example to the entire world of people drawn from different racial groups who have a common loyalty, a common love, to their common country. . . . In spite of criticism of Mr. de Klerk," I said, and then looked over at him, "sir, you are one of those I rely upon. We are going to face the problem of this country together." At which point I reached over to take his hand and said, "I am proud to hold your hand for us to go forward." Mr. de Klerk seemed surprised, but pleased.

114

I VOTED ON APRIL 27, the second of the four days of voting, and I chose to vote in Natal to show the people in that divided province that there was no danger in going to the polling stations. I voted at Ohlange High School in Inanda, a green and hilly township just north of Durban, for it was there that John Dube, the first president of the ANC, was buried. This African patriot had helped found the organization in 1912, and casting my vote near his grave site brought history full circle, for the mission he began eighty-two years before was about to be achieved.

As I stood over his grave, on a rise above the small school below, I thought not of the present but of the past. When I walked to the voting station, my mind dwelt on the heroes who had fallen so that I might be where I was that day, the men and women who had made the ultimate sacrifice for a cause that was now finally succeeding. I thought of Oliver Tambo, and Chris Hani, and Chief Luthuli, and Bram Fischer. I thought of our great African heroes, who had sacrificed so that millions of South Africans could be voting on that very day; I thought of Josiah Gumede, G. M. Naicker, Dr. Abdullah Abdurahman, Lilian Ngoyi, Helen Joseph, Yusuf Dadoo, Moses Kotane. I did not go into that voting station alone on April 27; I was casting my vote with all of them.

Before I entered the polling station, an irreverent member of the press called out, "Mr. Mandela, who are you voting for?" I laughed. "You know," I said, "I have been agonizing over that choice all morning." I marked an X in the box next to the letters ANC and then slipped my folded ballot paper into a simple wooden box; I had cast the first vote of my life.

The images of South Africans going to the polls that day are burned in my memory. Great lines of patient people snaking through the dirt roads and streets of towns and cities; old women who had waited half a century to cast their first vote saying that they felt like human beings for the first time in their lives; white men and women saying they were proud to live in a free country at last. The mood of the nation during those days of voting was buoyant. The violence and bombings ceased, and it was as if we were a nation reborn. Even the logistical difficulties of the voting, misplaced ballots, pirate voting stations, and rumors of fraud in certain places could not dim the overwhelming victory for democracy and justice.

It took several days for the results to be counted. We polled 62.6 percent of the national vote, slightly short of the two-thirds needed had we wished to push through a final constitution without support from other parties. That percentage qualified us for 252 of 400 seats in the national assembly. The ANC thoroughly dominated the northern and eastern Transvaal, the northwest, the eastern Cape and the Free State. We won 33 percent of the vote in the western Cape, which was won by the National Party, which did extremely well among Coloured voters. We captured 32 percent in KwaZulu/Natal, which was won by Inkatha. In Natal, fear of violence and intimidation kept many of our voters at home. There were charges, as well, of vote fraud and vote rigging. But in the end, that did not matter. We had underestimated Inkatha's strength in KwaZulu, and they had demonstrated it on election day.

Some in the ANC were disappointed that we did not cross the two-thirds threshold, but I was not one of them. In fact I was relieved; had we won two-thirds of the vote and been able to write a constitution unfettered by input from others, people would argue that we had created an ANC constitution, not a South African constitution. I wanted a true government of national unity.

On the evening of May 2, Mr. de Klerk made a gracious concession speech. After more than three centuries of rule, the white minority was conceding defeat and turning over power to the black majority. That evening, the ANC was planning a victory celebration at the ballroom of the Carlton Hotel in downtown Johannesburg. I was suffering from a bad case of the flu and my doctors ordered me to remain at home. But there was nothing that could keep me away from that party. I went onstage at about nine o'clock and faced a crowd of happy, smiling, cheering faces.

I explained to the crowd that my voice was hoarse from a cold and that my physician had advised me not to attend. "I hope that you will not disclose to him that I have violated his instructions," I told them. I congratulated Mr. de Klerk for his strong showing. I thanked all those in the ANC and the democratic movement who had worked so hard for so long. Mrs. Coretta Scott King, the wife of the great freedom fighter Martin Luther King Jr., was on the podium that night, and I looked over to her as I made reference to her husband's immortal words.

This is one of the most important moments in the life of our country. I stand here before you filled with deep pride and joy — pride in the ordinary, humble people of this country. You have shown such a calm, patient determination to reclaim this country as your own, and now the joy that we can loudly proclaim from the rooftops — Free at last! Free at last! I stand before you humbled by your courage, with a heart full of love for all of you. I regard it as the highest honor to lead the ANC at this moment in our history. I am your servant. . . . It is not the individuals that matter, but the collective. . . . This is a time to heal the old wounds and build a new South Africa.

From the moment the results were in and it was apparent that the ANC was to form the government, I saw my mission as one of preaching reconciliation, of binding the wounds of the country, of engendering trust and confidence. I knew that many people, particularly the minorities, whites, Coloureds, and Indians, would be feeling anxious about the future, and I wanted them to feel secure. I reminded people again and again that the liberation struggle was not a battle against any one group or color, but a fight against a system of repression. At every opportunity, I said all South Africans must now unite and join hands and say we are one country, one nation, one people, marching together into the future.

115

MAY 10 DAWNED bright and clear. For the past few days, I had been pleasantly besieged by arriving dignitaries and world leaders who were coming to pay their respects before the inauguration. The inauguration would be the largest gathering ever of international leaders on South African soil.

The ceremonies took place in the lovely sandstone amphitheater formed by the Union Buildings in Pretoria. For decades, this had been the seat of white supremacy, and now it was the site of a rainbow gathering of different colors and nations for the installation of South Africa's first democratic, nonracial government.

On that lovely autumn day I was accompanied by my daughter Zenani. On the podium, Mr. de Klerk was first sworn in as second deputy president. Then Thabo Mbeki was sworn in as first deputy president. When it was my turn, I pledged to obey and uphold the constitution and to devote myself to the well-being of the republic and its people. To the assembled guests and the watching world, I said:

Today, all of us do, by our presence here . . . confer glory and hope to newborn liberty. Out of the experience of an extraordinary human disaster that lasted too long, must be born a society of which all humanity will be proud.

. . . We, who were outlaws not so long ago, have today been given the rare privilege to be host to the nations of the world on our own soil. We thank all of our distinguished international guests for having come to take possession with the people of our country of what is, after all, a common victory for justice, for peace, for human dignity.

We have, at last, achieved our political emancipation. We pledge ourselves to liberate all our people from the continuing bondage of poverty, deprivation, suffering, gender, and other discrimination.

Never, never, and never again shall it be that this beautiful land will again experience the oppression of one by another. . . . The sun shall never set on so glorious a human achievement.

Let freedom reign. God bless Africa!

A few moments later we all lifted our eyes in awe as a spectacular array of South African jets, helicopters, and troop carriers roared in perfect formation over the Union Buildings. It was not only a display of pinpoint precision and military force, but a demonstration of the military's loyalty to democracy, to a new government that had been freely and fairly elected. Only moments before, the highest generals of the South African Defense Force and police, their chests bedecked with ribbons and medals from days gone by, saluted me and pledged their loyalty. I was not unmindful of the fact that not so many years before they would not have saluted but arrested me. Finally a chevron of Impala jets left a smoke trail of the black, red, green, blue, and gold of the new South African flag.

The day was symbolized for me by the playing of our two national anthems, and the vision of whites singing *"Nkosi Sikelel' iAfrika"* and blacks singing *"Die Stem,"* the old anthem of the republic. Although that day, neither group knew the lyrics of the anthem they once despised, they would soon know the words by heart.

On the day of the inauguration, I was overwhelmed with a sense of history. In the first decade of the twentieth century, a few years after the bitter Anglo-Boer War and before my own birth, the white-skinned peoples of South Africa patched up their differences and erected a system of racial domination against the dark-skinned peoples of their own land. The structure they formed the basis of one of the harshest, most inhumane societies the world has ever known. Now, in the last decade of the twentieth century, and my own eighth decade as a man, that system had been overturned forever and replaced by one that recognized the rights and freedoms of all peoples regardless of the color of their skin.

That day had come about through the unimaginable sacrifices of thousands of my people, people whose suffering and courage can never be counted or repaid. I felt that day, as I have on so many other days, that

I was simply the sum of all those African patriots who had gone before me. That long and noble line ended and now began again with me. I was pained that I was not able to thank them and that they were not able to see what their sacrifices had wrought.

The policy of apartheid created a deep and lasting wound in my country and my people. All of us will spend many years, if not generations, recovering from that profound hurt. But the decades of oppression and brutality had another, unintended effect, and that was that it produced the Oliver Tambos, the Walter Sisulus, the Chief Luthulis, the Yusuf Dadoos, the Bram Fischers, the Robert Sobukwes of our time — men of such extraordinary courage, wisdom, and generosity that their like may never be known again. Perhaps it requires such depth of oppression to create such heights of character. My country is rich in the minerals and gems that lie beneath its soil, but I have always known that its greatest wealth is its people, finer and truer than the purest diamonds.

It is from these comrades in the struggle that I learned the meaning of courage. Time and again, I have seen men and women risk and give their lives for an idea. I have seen men stand up to attacks and torture without breaking, showing a strength and resiliency that defies the imagination. I learned that courage was not the absence of fear, but the triumph over it. I felt fear myself more times than I can remember, but I hid it behind a mask of boldness. The brave man is not he who does not feel afraid, but he who conquers that fear.

I never lost hope that this great transformation would occur. Not only because of the great heroes I have already cited, but because of the courage of the ordinary men and women of my country. I always knew that deep down in every human heart, there is mercy and generosity. No one is born hating another person because of the color of his skin, or his background, or his religion. People must learn to hate, and if they can learn to hate, they can be taught to love, for love comes more naturally to the human heart than its opposite. Even in the grimmest times in prison, when my comrades and I were pushed to our limits, I would see a glimmer of humanity in one of the guards, perhaps just for a second, but it was enough to reassure me and keep me going. Man's goodness is a flame that can be hidden but never extinguished.

We took up the struggle with our eyes wide open, under no illusion that the path would be an easy one. As a young man, when I joined the African National Congress, I saw the price my comrades paid for their beliefs, and it was high. For myself, I have never regretted my commitment to the struggle, and I was always prepared to face the hardships that affected me personally. But my family paid a terrible price, perhaps too dear a price for my commitment.

In life, every man has twin obligations — obligations to his family, to his parents, to his wife and children; and he has an obligation to his people, his community, his country. In a civil and humane society, each man is able to fulfill those obligations according to his own inclinations and abilities. But in a country like South Africa, it was almost impossible for a man of my birth and color to fulfill both of those obligations. In South Africa, a man of color who attempted to live as a human being was punished and isolated. In South Africa, a man who tried to fulfill his duty to his people was inevitably ripped from his family and his home and was forced to live a life apart, a twilight existence of secrecy and rebellion. I did not in the beginning choose to place my people above my family, but in attempting to serve my people, I found that I was prevented from fulfilling my obligations as a son, a brother, a father, and a husband.

In that way, my commitment to my people, to the millions of South Africans I would never know or meet, was at the expense of the people I knew best and loved most. It was as simple and yet as incomprehensible as the moment a small child asks her father, "Why can you not be with us?" And the father must utter the terrible words: "There are other children like you, a great many of them . . ." and then one's voice trails off.

I was not born with a hunger to be free. I was born free — free in every way that I could know. Free to run in the fields near my mother's hut, free to swim in the clear stream that ran through my village, free to roast mealies under the stars and ride the broad backs of slow-moving bulls. As long as I obeyed my father and abided by the customs of my tribe, I was not troubled by the laws of man or God.

It was only when I began to learn that my boyhood freedom was an illusion, when I discovered as a young man that my freedom had already been taken from me, that I began to hunger for it. At first, as a student, I wanted freedom only for myself, the transitory freedoms of being able to stay out at night, read what I pleased, and go where I chose. Later, as a young man in Johannesburg, I yearned for the basic and honorable freedoms of achieving my potential, of earning my keep, of marrying and having a family — the freedom not to be obstructed in a lawful life.

But then I slowly saw that not only was I not free, but my brothers and sisters were not free. I saw that it was not just my freedom that was curtailed, but the freedom of everyone who looked like I did. That is when I joined the African National Congress, and that is when the hunger for my own freedom became the greater hunger for the freedom of my people. It was this desire for the freedom of my people to live their lives with dignity and self-respect that animated my life, that transformed a frightened young man into a bold one, that drove a law-abiding attorney to become a criminal, that turned a family-loving husband into a man without a home, that forced a life-loving man to live like a monk. I am no more virtuous or self-sacrificing than the next man, but I found that I could not even enjoy the poor and limited freedoms I was allowed when I knew my people were not free. Freedom is indivisible; the chains on any one of my people were the chains on all of them, the chains on all of my people were the chains on me.

It was during those long and lonely years that my hunger for the freedom of my own people became a hunger for the freedom of all people, white and black. I knew as well as I knew anything that the oppressor must be liberated just as surely as the oppressed. A man who takes away another man's freedom is a prisoner of hatred, he is locked behind the bars of prejudice and narrow-mindedness. I am not truly free if I am taking away someone else's freedom, just as surely as I am not free when my freedom is taken from me. The oppressed and the oppressor alike are robbed of their humanity.

When I walked out of prison, that was my mission, to liberate the oppressed and the oppressor both. Some say that has now been achieved. But I know that that is not the case. The truth is that we are not yet free; we have merely achieved the freedom to be free, the right not to be oppressed. We have not taken the final step of our journey, but the first step on a longer and even more difficult road. For to be free is not merely to cast off one's chains, but to live in a way that respects and enhances the freedom of others. The true test of our devotion to freedom is just beginning.

I have walked that long road to freedom. I have tried not to falter; I have made missteps along the way. But I have discovered the secret that after climbing a great hill, one only finds that there are many more hills to climb. I have taken a moment here to rest, to steal a view of the glorious vista that surrounds me, to look back on the distance I have come. But I can rest only for a moment, for with freedom comes responsibilities, and I dare not linger, for my long walk is not yet ended.

INDEX

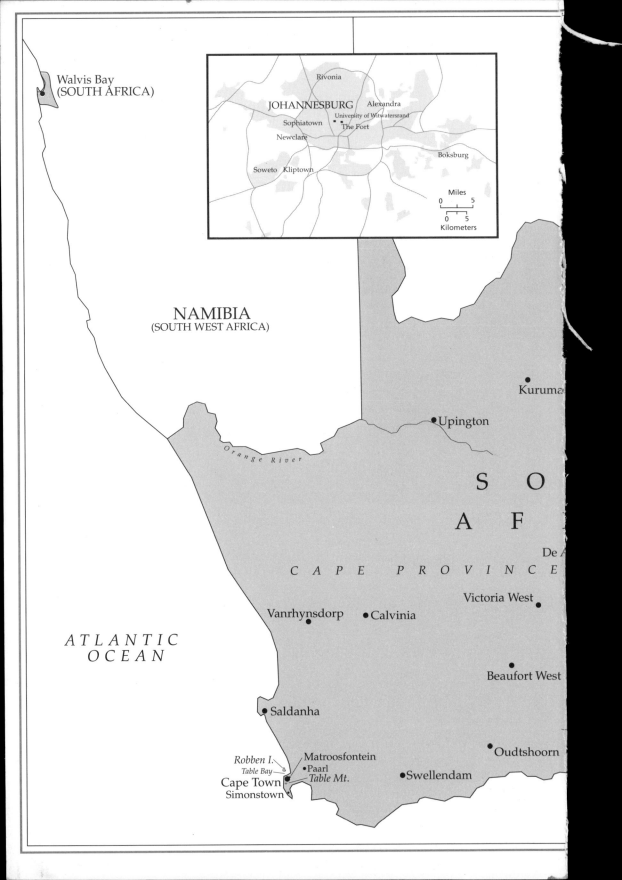

Walvis Bay
(SOUTH AFRICA)

Rivonia

JOHANNESBURG   Alexandra
University of Witwatersrand
Sophiatown   ■ ■
The Fort
Newclare

Boksburg

Soweto Kliptown

Miles
0   5

0   5
Kilometers

NAMIBIA
(SOUTH WEST AFRICA)

Kuruma

●Upington

Orange River

S O

A F

De A

C A P E   P R O V I N C E

Victoria West
●

Vanrhynsdorp   ●Calvinia

●

Beaufort West

ATLANTIC
OCEAN

●Saldanha

Robben I.   Matroosfontein
Table Bay   ●Paarl
Cape Town●   *Table Mt.*
Simonstown   ●Swellendam

●Oudtshoorn